The Ortho Book of

GARDENING
BASICS

The Ortho Book of

GARDENING
BASICS

Project Editor
Norm Rae

Text Writer
Susan Lang

Encyclopedia Writer
Deni Stein

ORTHO BOOKS

Ortho Books

Publisher
Edward A. Evans

Editorial Director
Christine Jordan

Production Director
Ernie S. Tasaki

Managing Editors
Robert J. Beckstrom
Michael D. Smith
Sally W. Smith

System Manager
Linda M. Bouchard

Product Manager
Richard E. Pile, Jr.

Marketing Administrative Assistant
Daniel Stage

Distribution Specialist
Barbara F. Steadham

Operations Assistant
Georgiann Wright

Technical Consultant
J. A. Crozier, Jr., Ph.D.

This book is dedicated
to the memory of
Georgiann Wright

Address all inquiries to:
Ortho Books
Chevron Chemical Company
Consumer Products Division
Box 5047
San Ramon, CA 94583

Copyright © 1983, 1991
Chevron Chemical Company
All rights reserved under international and Pan-American copyright conventions.

Previously published as *Ortho's Complete Guide to Successful Gardening*.

1 2 3 4 5 6 7 8 9
91 92 93 94 95 96

ISBN 0-89721-233-9
Library of Congress Catalog Card
Number 90-86169

Chevron Chemical Company
6001 Bollinger Canyon Road, San Ramon, CA 94583

Consultant
Tom Eltzroth

Cover Designer
Gary Hespenheide

Illustrator
Sally Shimizu

Copy Chief
Melinda E. Levine

Editorial Coordinator
Cass Dempsey

Copyeditor
Barbara Feller-Roth

Proofreader
Deborah Bruner

Indexer
Trisha Feuerstein

Associate Editor
Sara Shopkow

Composition by
Laurie A. Steele

Editorial Assistants
John Parr
Nancy Patton Wilson-McCune

Layout and Production by
Studio 165

Separations by
Color Tech Corp.

Lithographed in the USA by
Ringier America, Inc.

Photo Editor
Sarah Bendersky

Photographers
Names of photographers are followed by the page numbers on which their work appears. R=right, C=center, L=left, T=top, B=bottom.

R. Adleins/Ortho Information Services: 261L
William C. Aplin/Ortho Information Services: 70, 74, 79, 239, 250L, 258, 361, 365, 366
M. Baker/Ortho Information Services: 119, 340L
Liz Ball: 251, 340R, 342T
Liz Ball/PHOTO/NATS: 286B
Laurie A. Black/Ortho Information Services: 38B, 77B, 126, 127T, 127B, 200B, 254, 280TL, 372L
John Blaustein/Ortho Information Services: 110, 113TL, 113BL, 113TR, 114R, 339L
A. Boger/Ortho Information Services: 292
Gay Bumganer/PHOTO/NATS: 274
John Bruneau/VALAN PHOTOS: 51
John Bryan/Ortho Information Services: 8
R. Butler/Ortho Information Services: 302
R. Byther/Ortho Information Services: 59
Kristie L. Callen: 306B
Clyde Childress/Ortho Information Services: 362, 364
R. Christman/Ortho Information Services: 152
Josephine Coatsworth/Ortho Information Services: 40T, 40B, 41T, 88, 100TL, 128, 136, 150, 182T, 193, 215, 237, 278, 279, 354T, 357, 360
Kennon Cooke/VALAN PHOTOS: 21B
S. Cotner/Ortho Information Services: 284
M. Cummings/Ortho Information Services: 293T
Michael Dirr/Ortho Information Services: 52R
Clyde Elmore/Ortho Information Services: 261R, 269T
Thomas E. Eltzroth: 252
B. Emerson: 260
Derek Fell: 32, 225, 227B, 241C
Barbara Ferguson/Ortho Information Services: 335R
J. Feucht/Ortho Information Services: 169
John Fowler/VALAN PHOTOS: 49T, 300
Barry Friesen/Ortho Information Services: 303
Mark E. Gibson: 17T, 17B, 30, 43, 81T, 100BL, 232L
Nelson Groffman/Ortho Information Services: 294
G. Hankes/Ortho Information Services: 168
Saxon Holt: front cover, 14, 16R, 24, 25T, 34, 66, 67, 68, 69, 77T, 81B, 87L, 103, 160, 173, 187, 282, 304

Photographers (continued)
Saxon Holt/Ortho Information Services: 22, 23, 72, 159, 178, 206, 263B, 264B, 265, 266, 273, 277, 312, 315, 317, 319, 321C, 321B, 324
Jeannie R. Kemp/VALAN PHOTOS: 298
M. K. Kennedy/Ortho Information Services: 301
Susan M. Lammers/Ortho Information Services: 102T
Michael LaMotte/Ortho Information Services: 172
Michael Landis/Ortho Information Services: back cover TL and TR, 16L, 31BL, 31BR, 37B, 48L, 55, 56, 62, 84, 92, 99, 122, 123TL, 123BL, 123TR, 123BR, 124TR, 124BR, 125TL, 125BL, 125TC, 125TR, 125BR, 140, 145, 147, 149, 171, 174, 175, 179, 184, 236, 241B, 247L, 247R, 263T, 264T, 280B, 283T, 306T, 322B
Robert E. Lyons: 135, 253
Michael McKinley/Ortho Information Services: back cover BR, 10, 13, 19, 21T, 27T, 27B, 31T, 36, 38T, 41B, 42, 44, 46, 53T, 58, 61B, 63, 64T, 64B, 73, 75T, 78BL, 78R, 82, 108, 142, 164, 280TR, 339R, 346, 353, 354B, 355, 356, 358, 359, 363, 372R, 375
James McNair/Ortho Information Services: 11, 18, 50, 202
Jeff March/PHOTO/NATS: 285, 286T
C. Millard/Ortho Information Services: 100TR, 100BR
R. Moller/VALAN PHOTOS: 52L
Douglas Muir/Ortho Information Services: 78TL
J. R. Natter/Ortho Information Services: 166R
Bernard J. Nist/Ortho Information Services: 61T
Ortho Information Services: 37T, 57T, 57B, 65T, 65B, 75T, 80, 94L, 94R, 102T, 106, 117, 121, 124BL, 130, 144, 154, 157, 181T, 181B, 182B, 191, 205, 214, 216, 222, 223, 224, 226T, 226B, 228, 229, 230, 231, 232R, 233T, 233B, 234T, 234B, 235L, 235R, 238, 240, 241T, 242, 243, 244T, 244B, 246, 248T, 248B, 249, 250R, 255, 256, 257, 269B, 281, 295, 296, 305, 334, 338, 352, 367, 368, 369, 370
J. R. Page/VALAN PHOTOS: 49B
J. Parker/Ortho Information Services: 283B
Pam Peirce: 60, 227C, 262
Pam Peirce/Ortho Information Services: 76
Bill Reason/Ortho Information Services: 209
Ann Reilly/PHOTO/NATS: 162, 227T, 245, 342B
Douglas Ross/Ortho Information Services: 194, 197, 198
Susan Roth: 200T
A. Sabarese/Ortho Information Services: 48R
Charles M. Sacamano/Ortho Information Services: 146
A. Sherf/Ortho Information Services: 299
Michael D. Smith/Ortho Information Services: 167
Arthur Strange/VALAN PHOTOS: back cover BL, 343
Rob Stuart-Vail/PHOTO/NATS: 53B
Judith P. Tankard/PHOTO/NATS: 20
Tom Tracy/Ortho Information Services: 25B, 26, 35, 105TL, 105BL, 105TR, 105BR, 293B
Rod Whitlow: 12, 109L, 109R, 111, 114TL, 114BL, 120, 163, 183, 267, 268, 276, 318, 320, 321T, 322T, 323T, 323B, 335TL, 335BL
Marilyn Wood/PHOTO/NATS: 336

Front Cover
An annual flower bed of zinnia and white sage

Title Page
A harvest of fresh homegrown vegetables

Page 2
A bed of mixed snapdragons and phlox

Page 3
Kaffir-lily (*Clivia miniata*), a bright perennial

Back Cover
Top left: Mixed annual and perennial flower bed
Top right: Sprinkler-coverage test
Bottom left: Gardener planting cuttings
Bottom right: Restored colonial garden

VAPAM is a registered
trademark of ICI Americas, Inc.

Contents

GARDEN STYLE

Many of us garden for the sheer delight of surrounding ourselves with plants. However, our pleasure with plants can be greatly enhanced if we first take the time to consider the kind of style we want our garden to display. Throughout history, each culture and civilization developed its own unique gardening style. Today we can draw from this wealth of techniques and styles, many of which can be adapted to our own gardens, whether large or small. We can design our gardens to be formal or informal, traditional European and English or native and natural. Whatever style we choose, it should be one that suits our needs and reflects our own creativity.

We enjoy plants with all of our senses, but plants do much more than enrich our lives with beauty. They are the mainstay of life on this planet. They replenish the atmosphere with oxygen and provide us with all our food either directly, or indirectly through the food chain. We build many of our shelters and furnishings with wood and other plant products.

The earliest records of plant cultivation date back to 8000 B.C. The first agricultural efforts of early civilizations were of a functional nature only; plants were grown exclusively for food or other utilitarian purposes.

Gardening as the art of plant cultivation developed much later. Gardens designed with decorative plantings first appeared in 1500 B.C. in ancient Egypt, where the civilization had developed beyond the subsistence level. The leisure available to the royalty and privileged members of that society gave them the time to enjoy and admire beautiful plants.

The garden at Versailles, with intricately patterned boxwood hedges, epitomizes formal French-style landscaping. The curving lines of the hedges are symmetrically arranged and repeated throughout the parterres.

This restored colonial garden is very informal. The entire garden is designed asymmetrically and has curving instead of straight lines.

A GARDEN TO SUIT YOUR NEEDS

The enthusiastic and creative gardener can derive as much gratification from a tiny urban rooftop garden as from an extensive garden of several acres. Planning, planting, and caring for a garden can provide as keen a sense of connection with nature to the patio gardener as to the gardener who is tending a 5-acre orchard.

In fact, any size garden can be planned to suit your needs. If you have the time and interest, you can design and plant an exquisite garden filled with greenery, flowers, fruit, and vegetables. If you lead a busy life without much time for garden maintenance, you can make a garden that requires minimal care. In this, as well as many other aspects, gardening is a versatile art. With garden plots becoming increasingly smaller, imaginative gardeners are choosing plants that play more than one role: Potted lemon trees can serve as patio specimens and produce fruit; grape vines can be trained along an arbor to provide shade and yield a luscious crop of grapes.

This is contrary to the often-held belief that the key to a beautiful and productive garden lies in the number and variety of plants it contains. All too often, the intricately designed and newly planted garden resplendent with color and variety soon begins to look shabby and unkempt.

Ultimately, the beauty, productivity, and success of any garden depends upon the health and vigor of the plants, as well as on the gardener's attention to the area. Even the simplest of gardens can be appealing if the plants are well cared for.

This book explains how to create a garden that meets both your needs and those of the plants populating the garden. It also explains how to care for the garden properly—including such aspects as soil management, pruning, and pest and disease control—so that the garden is a continuing source of joy and fulfillment.

CHOOSING THE STYLE

You can buy plants that appeal to you and plant them randomly in your yard, and you will have a garden. However, the results will be much more pleasing if you first choose a style for your garden. Style is the overall character of a garden—how you arrange it and the way it looks. You should begin with a plan, a notion of what the finished garden will look like.

The style you choose for your garden may be borrowed from other gardens or it may be highly individual. A garden with a consistent style has a special harmony. It is not simply a collection of unrelated features and ideas, but a unified whole with parts that work together to achieve an overall effect.

A garden need not be modeled after a particular style in order to be coherent. A garden that suits one region or even one person may not be suited to other regions or other people. The style you choose—traditional, contemporary, or personal—should reflect your personality and fit in with the garden's surroundings.

There are some design concepts, such as formality versus informality, to consider when selecting and implementing a style for your garden.

Topiary is a very specialized pruning that is appropriate in a formal design. Here, poodled shrubs and sculptured animals create whimsy in the garden.

FORMAL VERSUS INFORMAL

When thinking of style in the garden, it may help to think in terms of formality versus informality. One reason for making a garden is to create some degree of organization (or formality) out of the natural (informal) setting. There are degrees of formality and informality. At one extreme, absolute formality reduces all natural elements to geometric shapes. The other extreme is complete naturalness, as is found in the untouched wilderness, where no hand has modified natural forms or imposed any sort of human order.

Most gardeners find it satisfying to create a style that falls somewhere between the two extremes and combines elements of each. There is no right or wrong balance between formality and informality. The successful choice is the one that suits both the setting and your taste.

There's a tendency to think that the choice of plants is largely responsible for making a garden formal or informal, but that's not so. The same plants may appear in both types of gardens, and the formal or informal feeling will remain intact. It's how the plants are used—for example, whether they are sheared into geometric shapes or left to assume their natural form—that makes the difference.

Often, the shape and topography of a yard determine whether a garden should be formal or informal. If your yard is irregular, with slopes, hills, or rock outcroppings, or if there are mature trees that you wish to leave standing, you'll find it difficult to carry out a formal design. Such a site lends itself naturally to an informal garden. On the other hand, if your yard is flat, with no outstanding natural features, you'll be free to choose any style you like.

In this garden informality is characterized by the natural forms of the plants which complement the contours of the terrain.

Formal Design

The earliest recorded garden designs—in Egypt in 2200 B.C.—were laid out along formal lines. The ancient Greeks, and the Romans after them, also created gardens in the formal style. Much later, during the Renaissance, the classical formal garden was revived in Europe; as a type of garden design, the formal garden has been used ever since.

Formal designs have survived for thousands of years because they are simple and pleasing to the eye. The key to a formal garden is symmetry. What appears on the left side of the garden is matched, sometimes nearly perfectly, on the right. The overall shape of the formal garden is frequently rectangular, and this shape is repeated in other elements, such as pools, patios, and flower beds. Often a single object—perhaps a statue or a sundial—serves as the center of interest. For optimum effect, it is usually placed at the rear of the garden, directly in the line of vision from the gardener's favorite viewing spot.

In a formal garden design is obvious. Almost all buildings and other constructed features, such as patios and pathways, impart a strong sense of structure. Even the plants are pruned into highly structured, unnatural forms. The hallmarks of a formal garden are neatly sheared hedges and topiary—a type of pruning in which small-leaved evergreen shrubs are clipped into geometric or animal shapes.

Although a formal garden may be easy to design, it is not always easy to maintain. The precise, tailored look favored in most formal gardens requires frequent pruning. Because order reigns supreme, any untidy growth and clutter will stand out in sharp contrast.

Informal Design

Informality is characterized by a lack of symmetry and by flowing lines, curves, and natural-looking plant forms. Beds, borders, walkways, and lawns are usually curved in gentle, wide arcs that frequently follow the natural terrain. One curve leads into another, creating a feeling of harmony. Wooden structures in the garden are often allowed to weather; the raw wood will then darken or turn gray, taking on a softness that unites it with nature.

Although a well-designed informal garden isn't symmetrical, it is balanced. This type of balance is called asymmetrical balance. It is accomplished by placing comparable visual weight on either side of a major accent or focal point. The two sections on either side of the accent don't have to be the same size or contain the same elements, but they should look comparable. Each part should offer approximately the same amount of visual interest.

When creating an informal garden, don't make the mistake of skipping the design step. Just because a garden looks natural doesn't mean it hasn't been carefully planned. The best informal gardens are laid out every bit as carefully as their formal counterparts.

Both deciduous and evergreen plants combine well in informal settings, with as many different combinations as there are gardens. Because no precise rules govern the informal garden, more design freedom, and consequently more choices, are possible in every step of the way.

With less emphasis on order, maintenance chores are somewhat reduced. Plants will need less pruning, leaves can be left where they fall, and a few scraggly branches won't make the garden look unkempt.

The antebellum style of this home suggests a period and atmosphere that is enhanced by the landscape.

STYLE AND THE ENVIRONMENT

Before determining what kind of garden to create, you should take a long, thoughtful look at the setting. The garden should be compatible with the architectural style of your house and with the topography of your property. It must coexist with other gardens in your neighborhood. It is also part of a geographic region whose climate, topography, native vegetation, and perhaps traditional garden styles you should examine before committing yourself to a particular style.

Architecture of Your House
To be effective, the style of your garden should be in keeping with the architectural style of your house. If the house is designed in a particular period style—colonial American

or English Tudor, for instance—one possibility is to design a landscape that reflects the same period. However, strict adherence to a period style can be limiting or impractical. Materials may be unavailable or too costly, the terrain and space may be unsuitable, or traditional plants may be inappropriate for the region.

A more workable solution is to simply use a style that is compatible with the house. Symmetry and a high degree of structure are fitting if the house is symmetrical and the yard is level or nearly so. An informal style is appropriate for an older house without pronounced symmetry or the strong suggestion of a period. Almost any style can be adapted to a modern house that has simple, clean lines and doesn't evoke a period style.

The best approach is to study the atmosphere that your house creates in its setting. If that atmosphere is appealing, decide how the style of the garden might enhance it. If the atmosphere isn't particularly appealing, consider what style might best neutralize or mask the deficiencies of the house.

Be realistic about the size and topography of your property. Uneven terrain that is too costly or impractical to alter lends itself to a natural, asymmetrical garden design that follows the contours of the land.

Surrounding Gardens

As you walk around your neighborhood, notice whether there is a discernible garden style, or in the absence of a prevalent style whether there is any sort of unity, even if only in plant selection. If the neighborhood is a patchwork of garden styles, think about what you can do with your property to help minimize that effect—or at least to avoid intensifying it.

In some neighborhoods in parts of the southeastern United States, a satisfying style is achieved by eliminating boundary markers, such as fences, walls, and hedges, between front gardens and instead growing the indigenous longleaf pine (*Pinus palustris*). This creates an unbroken sweep of lawn and airy pines that can be underplanted with azaleas (*Rhododendron* species), camellias (*Camellia* species), and dogwoods (*Cornus* species), occasionally punctuated with southern magnolias (*Magnolia grandiflora*). The unity and continuity make the sense of neighborhood more complete.

The gardens adjoining your property may be attractive and appealing enough to act as a catalyst for your design. If so, you can coordinate your garden with those of your neighbors, especially the areas in the front of the house.

Regional Environment

In deciding on a style, you need to consider your garden in the broad context of the region. If the style is to be appropriate and practical, it must take into account the climate, types of plants suitable for the area, and other relevant factors such as water availability. A lush English-style garden will look out of place and languish in the desert. On the other hand, the southeastern garden style based on the longleaf pine, described above, works well in parts of the Southeast, largely because it uses plants that are native to the region.

Many regions of the United States have traditional styles. If you live in an area with a traditional landscaping style, you may decide to adopt it or at least borrow from it. Some styles were established early and have strong

This landscape style maximizes the pleasures of nearly year-round outdoor living in a gentle climate.

ethnic flavor—for example, the Spanish-American courtyard garden in California and the Southwest. Other styles are more recent in origin. The northern California style emerged in the 1930s when landscape architect Thomas Church, largely responsible for the style, began to design gardens that merged house and garden, in effect making the garden an outdoor room.

TRADITIONAL GARDEN STYLES

In determining a style for your garden, it may help to know something about how garden styles developed historically. Although some of these styles in their traditional forms may be inappropriate for your yard, you may be able to adapt or modify one to suit your taste.

Italian

During the Renaissance, the renewed interest in art, literature, business, and philosophy spread to the outdoors. Looking to the past, the Italians were influenced by the Greeks and Romans. The design principles they uncovered in their study of the ancients led directly to the Italian landscape style: the use of classic forms, columns, symmetry, and sculpture.

The classic Italian garden utilizes a single or double axis to divide the entire site. An axis can be thought of as a dividing line creating equal parts on both sides of the garden space. Symmetry and balance are paramount in the Italian style. Plantings, walkways, and other elements are balanced on either side. If six trees are planted on the right side, six are planted on the left. The formality of this type of garden makes it easy to lay out.

Hills and mountainous terrain surround the major centers of culture and commerce in Italy, and it was in these hilly environs that the Italian style developed. Slopes and cascading water play a major part in the style.

Since wood was a rare resource in Italy, most constructed garden elements were made of local rock. Although marble and travertine may not be readily available in the United States, concrete and masonry are easily substituted.

This irregularly shaped patio is like an outdoor room, extending the living space into the garden.

This Italian-style garden features a parterre on the upper terrace of a sloping lot.

Symmetry, balance, and masonry are the hallmarks of Italian-style gardens.

A landscape in the true Italian style fits wonderfully into a sloped or hilly yard—unless the yard is very irregular and can't easily be made symmetrical. Multilevel terraces joined by steps are typical of the Italian villa and garden. Some of the early Italian gardens used ramps instead of stairs to connect one level to another. This made for easy strolling throughout the garden. A masonry or stucco house topped with a clay-tiled roof is compatible with this type of garden.

A wide variety of plant materials suits an Italian-style garden. Typical trees include Italian cypress (*Cupressus sempervirens*), olive (*Olea europaea*), and citrus (*Citrus* species). Shrubs include boxwood (*Buxus sempervirens*), privet (*Ligustrum japonicum*), holly (*Ilex* species), and yew (*Taxus baccata*). Common vines are creeping fig (*Ficus pumila*) and ivy (*Hedera* species). Lantana (*Lantana montevidensis*) and dwarf rosemary (*Rosmarinus officinalis* 'Prostratus') are common ground covers.

Simple parterres—the formal geometric plantings laid out with clipped boxwood

The elaborate patterns of a French garden are recreated in this park in Milwaukee, Wisconsin.

hedges and often containing brightly colored flowers within their borders—are a feature of the classical Italian garden.

French

France was greatly influenced by the Italian Renaissance, and travel and trade between the two countries led to a sharing of ideas and styles. French landscape design thus has much in common with the Italian style. Because the great gardens of France were built in flat areas, the simple geometry and balance of the Italian style did not work well in every situation. Without natural level changes to create interest, the French developed a more complex and elaborate system of landscape geometry.

The gardens at Versailles and Vaux-le-Vicomte were prototypes for the French formal garden. Although the designers adhered to the principles of symmetry and balance on which the Italian landscape is based, they enlarged upon these principles to develop the multiaxis and complex woven patterns. Parterres of intricate design, flowers of many colors, long vistas, and tree-shaded alleys and garden walks became the symbols of traditional French landscapes. As in Italy, water played an important role, not so much for its playfulness but for its use as a design form. Long reflecting pools, moats, and diverted rivers became a major part of the French-style garden.

A large, older home on an expansive, flat site with grand views is well suited to the French landscape style. The intricacy of this style and its emphasis on symmetry, balance, and order make it the perfect setting for long rows of trees, flower beds, clipped hedges, and large expanses of lawn. This type of garden is particularly suitable for strolling around and for displaying perennial and annual collections.

Trees found in the French landscape typically include horsechestnut (*Aesculus* × *carnea*), London plane (*Platanus* × *acerifolia*), and Lombardy poplar (*Populus nigra* 'Italica'). Common shrubs are boxwood (*Buxus sempervirens*), holly (*Ilex* species),

Opposite: The Luxembourg Gardens in Paris are a good example of the French-style landscape, with intricate symmetrical patterns of different colored flowers.

The geometric arrangement of flowers transforms this flat lot into an attractive French-style garden.

and yew (*Taxus baccata*). Coniferous trees such as pine (*Pinus* species), false-cypress (*Chamaecyparis* species), and cypress (*Cupressus* species) are sometimes used. Perennials and annuals contribute a spectrum of seasonal color.

English

Balance and symmetry took on new meaning in the English landscape. Tired of the contrived geometry brought from the European continent, English landscape designers began to experiment with the idea of re-creating nature. Although early attempts at English garden design included formal parterres, evergreen hedge mazes, topiary, and knot gardens, the style most closely associated with the English is informal and natural looking.

Horticultural knowledge and a developing interest in the aesthetic arrangement of plants led to the distinct English style. Plants chosen for their form, color, texture, and size were grouped to imitate the English ideal of nature. Constructed elements such as gazebos and picturesque ponds were included in this ideal. Many different types of trees and shrubs planted along curving lakeshores and pathways characterize the typical English garden.

This style works well with a very large, gently rolling site. A flat site can also be used if you create mounds or build walls. Steep slopes don't work well, since the English style requires an effortless flow of one space into another. Although the early English landscape centered around lakes and ponds, a large, irregularly shaped lawn can be substituted. Not a particularly functional garden, it does offer pleasant viewing points and a wonderful atmosphere for strolling.

A traditional English-style landscape requires careful thought about the placement and juxtaposition of plants. Arranging them according to height requires large, open spaces to achieve the effect of foreground, middle ground, and background. This type of landscape is well suited to the northern regions of the United States. A large lot and mature trees (if you are to enjoy the effect of the landscape in your lifetime) are required. Tudor, chateau, and large masonry homes are compatible with an English-style garden.

A great variety of native and exotic plants are appropriate, as long as the principles of loosely defined space and large lawn areas are considered. Weeping willow (*Salix babylonica*) is often combined with evergreen hedges such as euonymus (*Euonymus* species) and holly (*Ilex* species). Coniferous trees especially suited to the English-style

The effortless flow of one space into another characterizes the English style of landscaping a large tract of land. This style requires careful thought about the placement and juxtaposition of plants.

garden include fir (*Abies* species), cedar (*Cedrus* species), false-cypress (*Chamaecyparis* species), and bald cypress (*Taxodium distichum*). Native flowering shrubs such as redosier dogwood (*Cornus sericea*), vernal witch hazel (*Hamamelis vernalis*), rhododendron (*Rhododendron* species), and shrub roses (*Rosa* species) can also be integrated into this style of garden.

The cottage garden is another kind of English garden style. Humble in its origins, the cottage garden is small, relatively unstructured, crowded, and colorful. It consists of a variety of carefully arranged plants that bloom at different times for an ever-changing show. Unlike the traditional English garden, which developed on large country estates, the cottage garden needs only a tiny bit of land. The cottage garden can be found all over England, especially in rural villages.

This English-style cottage garden has been adapted to a small New England backyard.

A true English cottage garden is a seemingly unstructured jumble of colorful flowering plants. It consists of a variety of plants that bloom at different times of the year.

Weeping forms of Japanese flowering cherry and Japanese maple are positioned in front of a carefully detailed, weathered fence.

Japanese

A traditional Japanese garden can take many forms: a garden for strolling, a tea garden, or a Zen meditation (rock and sand) landscape. Every element in the garden has a meaning or significance. Plants take on special importance as specimens in the landscape, and water or the illusion of water, such as a dry rock stream, is almost always present. A Japanese garden can be a place to sit, think, stroll, or converse with a friend or guest.

The size of the garden is not important; what is important is the careful placement of garden elements. The placement of plants and rocks and the art of wood joinery are all carried out with an eye toward quality and uniqueness. Pruning is treated as a high art form in the Japanese garden.

The Japanese style is adaptable to all climates and locations. A rock and sand garden is perfectly suited to the southwestern desert, whereas a strolling garden works well on steep wooded sites in many parts of the United States. A small courtyard or a secluded corner of the yard may be the perfect place to add a Japanese touch to your landscape.

Trees traditionally used include Japanese maple (*Acer palmatum*), pine (*Pinus* species), maidenhair (*Ginkgo biloba*), and Japanese flowering cherry (*Prunus serrulata*). Some of the most popular shrubs are glossy abelia (*Abelia* × *grandiflora*), camellia (*Camellia* species), Japanese pieris (*Pieris japonica*), and mugo pine (*Pinus mugo*). Suitable ground covers include blue fescue (*Festuca ovina* var. *glauca*), English ivy (*Hedera helix* 'Hahn's Self-branching'), bigleaf lilyturf (*Liriope muscari*), mondograss (*Ophiopogon japonicus*), and low-growing junipers (*Juniperus* species). Flowering vines such as pink jasmine (*Jasminum polyanthum*) and wisteria (*Wisteria* species) are commonly used to cover arbors and trellises.

The old lantern in this Japanese garden is surrounded by low junipers, lilyturf, and a carefully shaped Japanese maple.

The large trees, shrubs, lawn, white picket fence, and straight pathway typify the Early American garden.

Early American

This garden style is the traditional backdrop and framework for both Early American– and colonial-style homes. Usually designed for a lot that slopes gently toward the street, the style is suitable for any site on which a traditional home is built.

The main design elements of an Early American–style garden are an expansive lawn, which serves as a foreground setting for the house; foundation plantings; a few large trees in groupings; and a straightforward walkway to the front entry. Simple geometric shapes and curves are used. Any number of special features, such as flower borders and low clipped hedges, can be added to the basic design. Because of its simplicity, this style gives a garden an established look quickly.

A large shade tree is the hallmark of the Early American–style garden. Among the commonly grown trees are red maple (*Acer rubrum*), silver maple (*Acer saccharinum*), white alder (*Alnus rhombifolia*), and European beech (*Fagus sylvatica*). Popular foundation shrubs include winter daphne (*Daphne odora*), euonymus (*Euonymus* species), holly (*Ilex* species), and rhododendron (*Rhododendron* species).

Many elements of a Moorish-style garden are found in this New Mexico home landscape.

Moorish

Walls and water in a courtyard setting are the main features of the Moorish style. Colored tile, stucco walls, grill work, and fountains are also integral to the Moorish garden. Originating in the Middle East, this style has come to be associated with Spain, Mexico, and the American West.

Designed to provide a shelter from harsh winds, sun, and noise, the Moorish style is well suited to both the southwestern and southeastern United States. It is also adaptable to urban settings in other areas. Contemporary, Spanish, and stucco homes are all compatible with this style.

A fountain or pool is the focal point, and stucco walls and lush plantings serve as a backdrop. Once the main elements are in place, the surrounding areas are relatively easy to design and plant. Drought-tolerant plantings and paved areas keep maintenance to a minimum.

Trees common in the Moorish-style garden are trident maple (*Acer buergeranum*), silk tree (*Albizia julibrissin*), common hackberry (*Celtis occidentalis*), beefwood (*Casuarina cunninghamiana*), citrus (*Citrus* species), mayten (*Maytenus boaria*), and black locust (*Robinia pseudoacacia*). Appropriate shrubs

A backdrop of lush plantings and a colorfully tiled fountain and pool characterize a Moorish-style garden.

that tolerate drought and heat include rock-rose (*Cistus* species), Spanish broom (*Genista hispanica*), oleander (*Nerium oleander*), and pomegranate (*Punica granatum*). Dwarf coyotebush (*Baccharis pilularis*) and pink clover blossom (*Polygonum capitatum*) are excellent ground covers for this style of garden. Bougainvillea (*Bougainvillea* species) and scented vines are used to cover and add texture to the walls.

Native and Natural

Informal, highly naturalistic gardens have existed since the beginning of garden building. For the most part, they were attempts to re-create a natural paradise.

A native garden is a type of natural landscape that uses only indigenous plants and building materials; the garden takes on the quality of the region in which it is located. Other types of natural gardens use plants and building materials that are natural looking but not necessarily indigenous to the region. There may be a mix of native and nonnative plants in a natural garden.

Both native and natural gardens are informal, loosely structured, and they work well in large and small spaces. The house seems built around the garden, rather than vice versa. The style of your home will dictate whether this informal garden style is appropriate for you. Rural and rustic settings are especially suited to a native or natural garden, whereas an urban or a suburban lot may not look natural enough for this style.

When selecting nonnative plants, be especially careful of their growing requirements. It's a good idea to select plants from similar climates. For example, plants from Australia, New Zealand, Chile, South Africa, and the Mediterranean thrive in central and southern coastal California, since all these areas share a temperate climate, with dry summers and rainy winters.

There are no hard-and-fast rules for patios, walkways, and structures in a native or natural garden. However, arranging the plants in this type of garden may require more thought than for other styles. The plants should appear as natural groupings; they should look as if they have evolved into communities such as those seen in fields, woods, prairies, and deserts.

The natural garden on this property extends to the narrow access on the side of the house. Ferns and other shade-loving plants grow among the tree-stump rounds, which are used to define the pathway.

26

This native garden contains wild plants often found in prairies, such as yellow ratibida, liatris, and Queen-Anne's-lace.

This natural garden features a carpet of colorful ground covers spilling down the slope. Native and natural gardens work well in both large and small spaces.

DESIGNING WITH PLANTS

At some point in any successful garden's beginning, a thoughtful plan was devised and carried out. Each element in the garden was considered individually and as part of the whole. Unfortunately, this planning stage is often ignored by beginning gardeners. The majority of gardens grow willy-nilly by bits and pieces, and if some overall design eventually does emerge, it is more by luck than by conscious effort.

Beginning gardeners are usually faced with one of two situations: renovating an existing garden planted by a former owner or creating a new garden from bare earth surrounding a new home. In either case, the temptation is to hurry off to the nursery or garden center to buy whatever plants are available and then put them into the ground for immediate effect. However, you will create a more beautiful garden if you take the extra time to plan the design.

This garden was constructed like an outdoor room: A large tree forms the ceiling, shrubs make up the walls, and a lawn is the floor. A fountain serves as an accent.

PLANNING THE DESIGN

Designing your garden may be easier if you think of it as building an outdoor room. Instead of using construction materials, you use plants to create the framework—the floor, the ceiling, and the walls—of your outdoor room. The floor can consist of a lawn, ground covers, and sprawling vines. High-branching trees and vines trained on overhead structures can serve as the ceiling. Outdoor walls can be formed from shrubs, hedges, trees, and vine-covered fences and trellises.

Once the floor, ceiling, and walls are in place, you use other plantings—such as flower beds and specimen plants—to enhance the basic framework. Plants used as accents should be selected for their fine or unusual features. Often they look best when planted together, either in small groups or in masses. Some accents, especially large ones, are best planted alone; when using an accent alone, place it in a location where it will command center stage, and emphasize it by surrounding it with simpler plants.

CHOOSING PLANTS

The contemporary trend is to limit the number of plant species in the garden. There are sound reasons for this trend. Grouping one plant species makes a stronger design statement than planting individual, unrelated specimens. Spindly plants with an open habit look more substantial when several of them are planted in a group. Also, gardens containing a limited number of species have an organized, purposeful look and are easier to take care of than gardens that are a potpourri of plants.

Granted, a garden with a limited variety of plants may not be your idea of what a garden should look like. If you prefer variety, as in the deliberate and charming confusion of an English cottage garden, don't feel constrained to follow present trends. Your garden should reflect your particular taste and no one else's.

However many plants you choose, remember that your goal is to create a garden that embraces and nurtures the plants within it. Use plants whose characteristics you like,

Newly planted gardens will look sparse at first, but if the plants are properly spaced the bare spots will fill in and the mature plants won't be overcrowded.

Beds and Borders

For as long as there have been gardens, beds and borders have been key elements in garden design. These planting areas may be designed formally or informally: They are usually either square or rectangular in a formal garden and are usually curving in an informal garden.

A bed is a cultivated area surrounded by a lawn or other open expanse; it is accessible from all sides and should be planned accordingly. A border is at the edge of an area, next to a fence or walkway or around the perimeter of a lawn. Most borders are accessible from one side only, and for that reason they should be planted no more than 5 feet deep. If they're any deeper it becomes difficult to tend the plants in the back without walking on the plants in the front.

In most home gardens, borders are more practical than beds. For maximum effect, a bed needs a comparatively large area around it; putting one into an average-sized garden is like placing a large table in the middle of a small room—there's little space left for anything else. Borders not only save space, they also serve a useful function in a garden by softening the edges of buildings, fences, walkways, and lawns.

If the bed or border adjoins a lawn, an edging is useful. A row of bricks laid side by side and set slightly lower than the level of the turf not only defines the planting area but makes an excellent mowing strip. Railroad ties are another material that makes a strong edge, although you have to edge the grass by hand where it meets the wood. For a less formal look, set fieldstones in mortar and allow the plants to trail over the stone edging.

Whatever you choose as edging, remember that unless you provide some kind of underground barrier between the bed or border and the lawn, you'll have extra weeding. Garden centers usually carry inexpensive rolls of metal or plastic strips for use as a barrier.

such as flowers and fall color, but first and foremost make sure that the plants are appropriate for your climate and for the growing conditions in your garden.

From the list of suitable plants, you can make your selections based on other considerations, such as size, form, texture, and color. Don't judge on the basis of any one criterion; rather, consider the total picture.

Size

Be sure to select plants whose mature height and spread will fit the intended space and serve the intended function. For example, plants that are to serve as walls in the garden should grow tall enough to provide privacy while keeping within their allotted space. The size of young shrubs and trees can be deceptive; it is often difficult to image how tall and wide they will grow. Keep in mind that unless a plant climbs or is very columnar, usually it grows wider as it grows taller.

Make a conscious effort to choose plants of varying height, which will make the garden much more interesting than one in which the plants are all approximately the same height. However, avoid extreme changes; try stair-step planting, placing the tallest plants in the rear and the shortest in front. Of course, make sure you don't inadvertently screen off a desired view by choosing plants that will grow too tall.

Newly landscaped gardens, if planted with the correct spacing between plants, naturally look sparse, with more soil showing than plants. In the eagerness for a lush garden, many gardeners space the young plants closer together than recommended. They soon find that they must deal with overcrowded plants that are competing for light, water, and nutrients. Although it may seem a nuisance to look up the mature size of each plant and allow for it in your plan, it is worth the effort.

Form

Most plants fall into five basic categories: rounded, vertical, open, upright and spreading, and prostrate. A pleasing garden should have a mix of forms but not too many, especially in a small space, or the result will be a confusing jumble.

Stair-step planting places the tallest plants in the rear and shorter plants in the front. Stair-step planting also permits easier maintenance.

FORMS OF SHRUBS

Rounded

Gives a casual, natural look in the landscape. Use as a specimen.

Vertical

The branches angle upward sharply, keeping the outline narrow. Use for dramatic emphasis in the landscape.

Open

The shrub can be seen through, making its framework visible. Typical of shrubs grown in the shade. Use as a specimen.

Upright and Spreading

More than 8'. Use as a background for a large garden, as a wind or sound screen, or as a small tree.

Prostrate

The branches either grow horizontally or are weak and lie on the ground. Use as a ground cover.

If fine-textured plants are combined with coarse-textured plants, they can provide dramatic contrasting effects in the garden.

The majority of plants are rounded, and it is this shape that should be dominant in the garden. Many outstanding gardens are made up of complementary forms—for example, a combination of rounded and vertical shapes. A rounded form makes a good background for more unusual forms, such as spiky or weeping shapes, which make good accents.

It is essential to allow ample room for trees and shrubs with a pronounced vertical form, because you won't be able to prune your way out of the problem if they outgrow their space. When you cut off the central leader of a columnar or pyramidal plant, multiple leaders result, destroying the form of the plant.

If you find it hard to consider form in your design, it may help to imagine the garden in silhouette.

Texture

This refers to the appearance of a plant, not to the way it feels to the touch. Plants are described as coarse, medium, or fine in texture. The texture of a plant is determined primarily by the size and shape of the leaves. Fine-textured plants have small leaves that may be delicate or intricately divided. Coarse-textured plants have large, bold leaves. Plants that fall between these two extremes are considered to be medium textured.

Colors, textures, heights, and positioning of plants having different forms create diversity and lushness in this garden.

Judge the texture of a plant close up, then look at it again from a distance. Some fine-textured plants lose their pleasing effect when they are planted too far away. Similarly, the texture of a large-leaved plant may be out of scale if it is planted where it will be viewed up close.

The general rule is to plant fine-textured plants in front of plants with a coarser texture; the combined pattern of textures that are graduated is a pleasing one. In most gardens there should be more fine-textured plants than coarse ones for a balanced effect. However, if a dramatic effect is your goal, lean heavily toward coarse-textured, large-leaved plants. If you favor a tailored, formal garden, look for compact, fine-textured plants with small leaves or slender needles.

You can use texture to create spatial illusions. Coarse-textured plants tend to surge forward; fine-textured plants tend to recede into the background. You can use this characteristic to make your garden seem larger or smaller. Coarse-textured plants at the far end of the garden will make the boundary appear closer than it really is. Fine-textured plants at the end will make a shallow garden seem deeper.

Color

A few gardeners prefer the understatement of a totally green garden, but most want the added variety and interest that color brings. When used properly, color can turn a drab yard into a striking, cheerful landscape. It is usually more satisfactory to plan for some

The shrubs lining this walkway were selected for their color. Ample space was allotted so that they could assume their natural shape and grow into a tall screen.

Flowering fruit trees can bring dramatic color to a home landscape in early spring.

Ripening fruit can provide color in the garden.

color throughout the year rather than concentrating it all in a single season.

Most people think only of annual and perennial flowers when they plan color. Although flowers—including flowering trees, shrubs, ground covers, and vines—may present the most obvious choices, don't overlook other sources of color in the garden.

Many plants bear brilliant berries or other fruit. Some plants contribute color with their bark and twigs. Others have colorful foliage throughout the growing season; the palette of leaf color includes various shades of green, as well as gray, silver, red, purple, bronze, yellow, and variegated colors. The leaves of many deciduous plants turn bright colors in fall. Usually, fall color is more spectacular in cold climates, although some plants are colorful in mild-winter regions. Check with a local nursery for varieties that have fall leaf color in your area.

It is important to know not only what color a plant will contribute to the garden, but also when the plant will be colorful. Knowing when different plants flower or fruit can help you plan for color throughout most of the year. Then you can plot the location of the plants so that the colors are properly distributed in the garden and are pleasing to the eye.

Because color is such a vital element in the appearance of a garden, it's worthwhile to look at some of the basics of using color.

Groupings of warm and cool colors provide eye-catching contrast.

The flaming red of this Japanese maple signals the onset of fall and contributes dramatic color.

USING COLOR

When you walk for the first time into a garden filled with flowering plants and lush foliage, your most enduring memory will likely be of the colors rather than some other feature of the garden. It's true that the success of a garden is based on more than just color, but color is the most impressive and memorable of all garden qualities.

Ideas for color schemes can come from anywhere: a neighbor's garden, the colors found in a single blossom, or from something as practical as the color of the exterior paint on your house.

Understanding the principles of color can help in selecting plants and blending them into the garden. However, although the value of these principles has been proven over time, color is a highly personal subject, and the garden is a forgiving place where even mistakes can have merit. You will find that, even when you follow the principles discussed below, using color is a continual process of discovery. You could be surprised by some color combinations. Colors that you never thought would look well together may turn out to be very pleasing.

If you are reluctant to combine certain flower or leaf colors, one good way to experiment on a small scale is to plant combinations in pots or other containers. Or plant one kind in each pot and move the pots around until you find combinations that please you. This does not require much time or effort, and the results can be surprisingly good. The plantings can then be carried out on a larger scale in the garden.

Vita Sackville-West, the noted English gardener, used to carry a branch of a flowering plant around the garden until she found a place where it was most pleasing. It was then, and only then, that she decided either to leave the plant where it was or move it to a new, more desirable location. You can do the same with several pots of experimental color combinations, trying them in various locations until you find one where they look best.

The Color Wheel

A color wheel is the easiest way to explain the interrelationships of colors. Red, yellow, and blue are the primary colors; all other

COLOR WHEEL

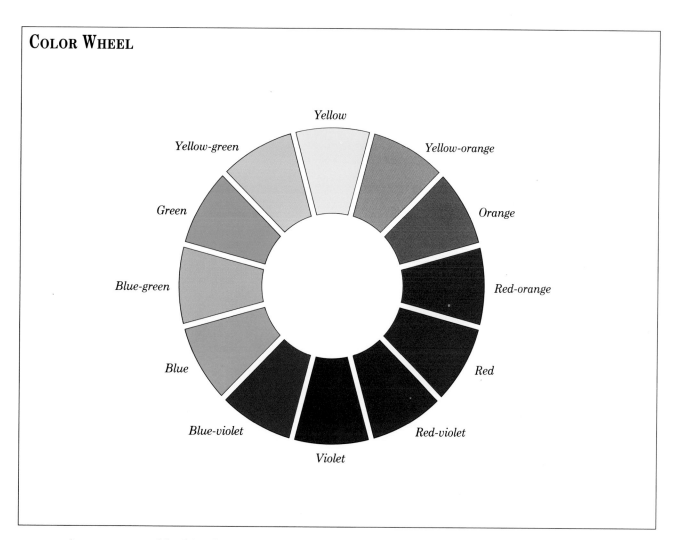

colors are created by blending these three in various proportions. Because you can't blend two colors of flowers or leaves to produce a third, the information is more important to artists than to gardeners. What is important to gardeners is how colors relate to each other and the distinction between warm colors and cool colors.

The colors in the wheel can be divided into those that are warm or cool. Of course, colors aren't literally warm or cool, but they can make you feel that way. The colors on the right-hand side of the wheel, yellow through red, are called warm colors. The colors on the left-hand side, green through violet, are the cool colors. Red-violet and yellow-green have both warm and cool properties, one more than the other, depending on what other colors they are combined with.

Generally, cool colors are good for close-up viewing and warm colors for dramatic displays. A garden composed primarily

of cool colors exudes an aura of peace and serenity; one consisting mainly of warm colors seems intense and animated. Be careful how you combine warm and cool colors in the garden. Warm colors can easily overwhelm cool ones; it takes four to five times as much of a cool color to balance a warm one.

To the eye, warm colors seem to jump out and cool colors seem to recede. If planted side by side at a distance, the warm colors appear closer and the cool colors seem farther away. You can use these effects to create spatial illusions. Warm colors at the back of a garden seem to surge forward, making the space appear smaller than it really is. A planting of cool colors at the rear of a shallow garden makes the garden seem longer; however, beware of planting cool colors at the rear of a deep garden, since they may seem to disappear. You can use groupings of warm or cool colors elsewhere in the garden to deepen a part of the yard or to bring it closer.

Very little warm color (red and pink dianthus) balances the cool color (blue delphinium).

This pleasing jumble of flowers provides a warm and cool color mixture that mimics nature.

Color Schemes

There are four types of color schemes: monochromatic, analogous, complementary, and polychromatic. If you are new at designing with color, your chances of success will be greater if you restrict yourself to one of these color schemes.

Monochromatic colors This color scheme consists of the various tints and shades of one—and only one—of the pure colors (often called a hue) on the color wheel. A tint is lighter than the pure color, and a shade is darker. Some of the most impressive flower gardens are planted in a monochromatic color scheme. An example would be red, various tints of pink, and a deep shade of red, or maroon. Visualize a flower border planted with maroon snapdragons (*Antirrhinum majus*), red and rose-colored nicotiana (*Nicotiana* species), and pale pink dianthus (*Dianthus* species), and you can begin to see the possibilities of such a color scheme.

In reality, there are no totally monochromatic gardens: The various shades of

Vita Sackville-West's all-white garden at Sissinghurst, England, blooms today much as when she was alive.

foliage and bark are always part of the combination, although their presence is a pleasant one that usually does not detract from the more predominant flower colors.

Analogous colors   This scheme makes use of neighboring colors on the color wheel. Any three colors used in the same sequence in which they are found on the color wheel are said to have an analogous relationship. An example is blue, blue-violet, and violet.

To expand the possibilities of such a color scheme, you can include the tints and shades of each of the colors. Because you have more colors to choose from, an analogous scheme is easier to work with than a strictly monochromatic one, and the results can be memorable.

The English writer and gardener Gertrude Jekyll developed what she called a tonal garden, based on rules similar to those for an analogous color scheme. In the best of the gardens designed by Jekyll, all the colors,

The pinks, violets, and purples of these potted geraniums and petunias are an example of an analogous color scheme.

including leaf color, are tonally related. One garden (Folly Farm in Berkshire, England, which was planted at the turn of the century) made use of silver-leaved plants and white, pale lavender, and ivory flowers. The colors of the foliage and flowers in turn complemented the colors of the stone walks and walls.

Complementary colors   This scheme consists of two colors that appear directly opposite each other on the color wheel. These are powerful combinations: red and green, orange and blue, yellow and violet, and so on. For the maximum effect, the purest hues (rather than shades or tints) should be combined. If you want to balance complementary colors, you will need four to five times as much of the cool color as the warm color. Some people might say that complementary colors clash; others find them vibrant and vital. Often these combinations are predominantly displayed in parks and other public areas. They are not always the best choices for a small garden. Confining a powerful color scheme in a small space intensifies its effect and can make it overwhelming.

If you want to try to blend strong complementary colors, place the plants so that they intermingle where they meet, rather than clearly defining the juncture. Intermingling colors in this way enhances their vibrancy, and from a distance they will appear to blend somewhat at the edges. You can always tone down the colors with silver-leaved or white-flowered plants.

This combination of blue forget-me-nots and orange tulips shows how vibrant a complementary color scheme can be.

The color scheme of this border is an example of plants with opposite colors on the color wheel.

Polychromatic colors   This color scheme, which combines any and all colors, can produce a carnival-like effect in the garden. An English cottage garden, with its riot of color, is an example of a polychromatic scheme. In most cases, however, this type of color scheme is the result of the gardener's inexperience rather than a conscious design.

There is nothing wrong with a polychromatic color scheme, and some gardeners prefer it because it mimics nature. One benefit of random planting is the possibility of happy accidents—color combinations that you would never think of but that work well.

Succession of Color

Since flowers provide the bulk of the color in a garden, one of the most important aspects of planning for color is the timing of bloom.

When designing, you must know when each plant will bloom and for how long. Different plants bloom at different times throughout the season and for different periods of time. The bloom times of some plants coincide and others overlap. Timing must be coordinated to produce the effect you want. The object is to have new flowers appearing as others fade. For many gardeners this is the most challenging, most interesting, and most exciting feature of flower gardening.

Many flowering shrubs, trees, and other woody plants bloom for short periods in the spring or summer, although some flower for months. Most perennials usually bloom for two to four weeks, whereas annuals generally bloom throughout the growing season.

In general, even when you plant for a succession of bloom, there will be three or four peak periods of bloom during the season, interspersed with periods of quiet.

UNDERSTANDING PLANTS

Successful gardening begins with a basic understanding of plants and their growth processes. It isn't necessary to study botany in order to be a good gardener, but it is helpful to know something about the way plants grow and reproduce. This will be invaluable in identifying problems that are sure to develop at one time or another in your garden.

Knowing how plants grow and reproduce is essential because of the very nature of a garden—an artificial environment in which a collection of plants with diverse needs are grown. These plants are well equipped to survive and thrive on their own—in their native habitats, where their temperature, light, soil, moisture, and other requirements are met. In a garden, you as the gardener must take an active role in nurturing your plants and monitoring their growth. This requires at least some basic understanding of how they function. This chapter also focuses on other scientific aspects of gardening, including the way garden plants are categorized and named, which makes the process of buying, propagating, and growing plants easier to understand.

In natural habitats where temperature, light, soil, moisture, and other requirements are met, plants thrive without help from the gardener.

PHOTOSYNTHESIS

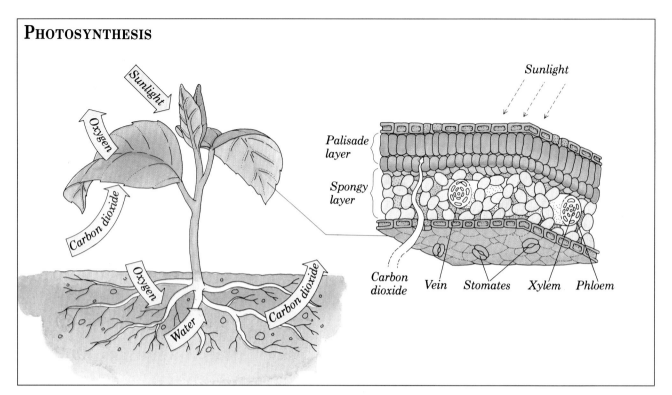

HOW A PLANT WORKS

Every good gardener has a healthy respect for plants. These amazing green life forms developed and refined their methods of growth and reproduction over the billions of years they have inhabited the earth. Green plants are unique in their ability to feed themselves, harnessing the power of the sun to synthesize their own food.

Photosynthesis

The process by which green plants make their own food—photosynthesis—is often described as the most important life process on earth. It is a complicated chemical reaction occurring only in green plants. Sunlight reacts with chlorophyll, the green pigment in plants, to convert water and carbon dioxide into sugars. Oxygen is released into the air as a by-product of the reaction. The plant stores some of the sugars as carbohydrates and uses others in the production of proteins. Since humans and animals cannot survive without the sugars and oxygen produced by plants, it can be said that all life on earth depends on photosynthesis.

The reaction takes place in the leaves in a group of cells called the palisade layer. Carbon dioxide from the air enters the leaves

All plants need sunlight. Some will flourish in direct sunlight, others in reflected sunlight or shade.

46

TRANSPORT SYSTEM

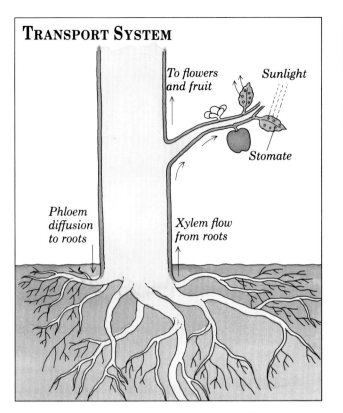

To flowers and fruit

Sunlight

Stomate

Phloem diffusion to roots

Xylem flow from roots

TOP GROWTH

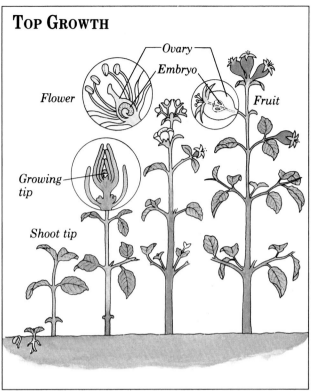

Ovary

Embryo

Flower

Fruit

Growing tip

Shoot tip

through stomates, or tiny pores. There the carbon dioxide combines with water, which has been absorbed from the soil and transported up into the leaves. The sugars formed as a result of the reaction are transported to all parts of the plant, where they are used for various plant functions. Through this process plants are able to fuel their own growth.

Many gardeners think that plants depend on fertilizer for nutrition and that they cannot survive without regular feedings, just as animals cannot survive without eating. In fact, plants manufacture their own food. They do require mineral nutrients as raw materials for growth processes, and it is only when any of the minerals are in short supply in the soil that fertilizers are needed as a supplementary source. This misunderstanding about the role of fertilizers may be the reason some gardeners overfertilize.

Sunlight The energy source in photosynthesis is sunlight. The more light a plant receives, the more sugar it makes, the faster it grows, and the more flowers and fruit it produces. In dim light, most plants make barely enough sugar to maintain life, but in bright light they make a surplus of sugar that they use for growth and reproduction.

Since photosynthesis occurs only in the presence of light, all plants need some light in order to grow. Not all plants need direct sunlight, however; many plants can exist on relatively small amounts of reflected light. These shade-loving plants usually have more chlorophyll than plants adapted to the sun. Their leaves are more sensitive to light and better able to make use of a small amount of it. The price they pay for this sensitivity is that they are not tough enough to tolerate direct sun for long. The brightness of direct sunlight bleaches their leaves to yellow or gray by destroying the chlorophyll.

Water stress If a plant doesn't have enough moisture to supply its needs, it closes its stomates, or tiny pores in the leaf surface, to avoid losing water. Since carbon dioxide can't enter the leaves when the stomates are closed, photosynthesis comes to a halt.

Movement of Water and Sugars

The transport system of a plant is somewhat similar to the circulatory system in a human, but it doesn't move in a circle, as the bloodstream does. Plants have two transport systems: One carries water and dissolved minerals upward from the roots to the top of

These impatiens prefer growing in shady areas of the garden where sunlight is filtered by other plants.

Lack of water turns the soil dry, depriving the roots of enough moisture to keep the plant from wilting.

the plant, and the other carries sugars and other materials manufactured by the leaves downward to all parts of the plant.

Xylem flow   Water and dissolved minerals travel upward from the roots through a system of microscopic tubes called the xylem (pronounced *zye*-lem). In woody plants the xylem consists of the outermost layer of wood; in herbaceous (nonwoody) plants it is found in patches inside the stem. The xylem extends up the trunk or stem and through the leaf veins into every part of the leaf. Water moves from the xylem by evaporating through the stomates, or tiny pores, in the leaf surface.

Three main factors reduce the upward flow of water and dissolved minerals in a plant: dry soil, a sick root system, or a plugged or severed xylem system. Any of several diseases or injuries can cause these problems. If the xylem flow is reduced below a certain point, the leaves receive fewer mineral nutrients than they need to maintain good health. They begin to show symptoms of nutrient deficiencies, usually by turning pale green or yellow (see page 170). If the xylem flow diminishes when the water demand is high—during hot weather, for example—the leaves may wilt or become scorched. This happens because the leaves lose water faster than it can be replaced.

Transpiration   The evaporation of water through the stomates is called transpiration. This process of losing water cools the plant. It also provides the power that moves water to the top of the plant. Although the principles are different, transpiration pulls water or moisture up through the plant just as sucking on a drinking straw moves liquid up through the straw.

Stomate control   Plants control transpiration, or the loss of water from their leaves, by opening and closing their stomates, the tiny pores in the leaf surface. The stomates normally close at night and open in the morning. To conserve moisture they shut down if a leaf runs out of water, usually before any sign of wilting is visible. If this happens to a leaf in the sun when the weather is hot, the leaf may overheat and burn. The result is called sunburn or scorch, depending on the pattern of the burning. Plants that tolerate sun won't burn even in hot sun as long as they have enough water.

Phloem flow   The part of the transport system that carries sugars and other manufactured material from the leaves to other parts of the plant is called the phloem (pronounced *flo*-em). This system of tubes lies within the bark of woody plants. If you peel off some bark in the spring, the phloem is visible as

The growing point of a shoot is a dormant bud. In spring, buds develop into leaves or flowers or both.

The end of the dormant stage occurs when a new leaf begins to unfurl from the bud.

the white part of the bark. In herbaceous plants the phloem is located with the xylem in patches inside the stem. Sugars diffuse through the phloem to the growing shoots, flowers, fruit, and roots.

If the phloem is cut partially, the flow of sugars is interrupted and the growth is slowed. If the phloem is cut all the way around, the plant will eventually starve to death (see Girdling on page 52). Often a

great bulge, consisting of sugar that cannot travel downward, occurs just above the place where the phloem was severed.

Top Growth

Unlike human growth, which takes place in all parts of the body, plant growth occurs in only a few places, called the growing points. These are located in the tips of the roots and shoots. They are also found just under the bark in woody plants.

Tip growth   The growing points in the tips of the roots and shoots consist of tiny bunches of cells that divide repeatedly, building the specialized organs of the plant but always remaining at the tip of the new growth. The new plant parts are tiny while they are in the growing point, but they contain all the cells they will ever have. As the growing point moves beyond them, the new parts fill with water and swell until they reach their full size.

Buds   When the growing point of a shoot is dormant, it is a bud. When the growing point of a shoot moves ahead, it leaves a bud at the base of every leaf. Buds can develop into leaves or flowers or both. On some plants, such as tomatoes, these axillary buds begin growing as soon as they are formed. On other plants, such as apple trees, the buds remain dormant until the following spring and then they all begin growing at once. Some of the buds never open by themselves, although they can be forced to open and begin growing if the growing point at the end of the branch they are on is pinched off.

Stem growth   The other place a woody plant grows is under the bark. A thin sheet of cells, called the cambium, lies between the wood and the bark. These cells divide repeatedly, just as cells in the shoot and root tips do. As the cells divide they produce xylem cells toward the center of the stem and phloem cells toward the outside. When growth is fastest, in the spring, large xylem cells are formed; as growth slows in the summer, smaller cells are formed. The difference in the size of these cells creates the annual rings visible in most wood. Each ring represents one year's growth.

Just as it produces leaves, the growing point of a plant also produces flowers that come into bloom in late spring or early summer.

All plants are anchored to the soil by roots, which absorb water and dissolved minerals.

Flowers The growing point produces flowers just as it produces leaves and stems. Flowers begin as buds. On some plants the flower buds open in late spring or summer right after being formed. These plants are said to bloom on new wood. Plants whose buds open the following spring are said to bloom on old wood. Knowing whether a plant blooms on new or old wood is important in determining when to prune it. If you prune at the wrong time of the year, you may remove all the flower buds (see page 186).

Fruit Only on plants whose flowers contain pistils, or female organs, will fruit develop. The base of a pistil consists of an ovary, the part of the flower that grows into the fruit. Many plants have male and female parts in the same flower, whereas others have separate male and female flowers on the same plant. Some plants, such as holly (*Ilex* species), have male and female flowers on separate plants. If you want fruit on these plants, you must plant the female. In some cases, it is preferable to plant the male and forego the fruit. Most gardeners plant a male ginkgo tree (*Ginkgo biloba*), since the female's fruit is notorious for its foul odor.

Root Growth

Roots anchor a plant in the soil. They also absorb water and dissolved minerals, the raw materials used by the plant. These raw materials are transported up the plant to the leaves, where they are combined with carbon dioxide to make sugars and complex chemicals (see Photosynthesis on page 46). Sugars and processed chemicals are then transported back to the roots, where they are used for growth.

Roots grow only where oxygen is available in the soil. Oxygen from the air diffuses through the spaces between soil particles, and it is this soil air that roots absorb. If the soil is too wet or the spaces between soil particles are too small, not enough oxygen is able to enter the soil and the roots may suffocate. (See Soil Components on page 85.)

Root tips The tip of each root contains a growing point that divides repeatedly. It produces a region of cells that elongate and push the root farther into the soil. The root tip also produces downy root hairs, which absorb most of the water and dissolved minerals used by the plant. As the root ages it turns yellow and then brown, and the root hairs disintegrate. By the time the root turns brown, it no longer absorbs very much water.

Just under the bark of trees and the stems of woody plants is a layer of dividing cells called the cambium.

Serious bark wounds will interrupt the flow of water and sugars through the tree and stunt its growth.

The root system Although the root mass of a plant is often visualized as extending about the same distance through the soil as the top growth extends above the ground, this is not always the case. Some trees have roots that descend dozens of feet beyond their top growth, especially in arid areas where the roots must search for water. The roots of most trees in cultivation (those not growing in the wild) spread outward rather than downward. Approximately 80 percent of tree roots are found in the upper 2 feet of soil and approximately 95 percent in the upper 3 feet. A root system may not be symmetrical; it may be denser on the side that is fertilized or watered more often.

Garden plants receive most of their mineral nutrients from the top foot of soil so they are sensitive to the condition of the surface. If it is compacted or paved over, the roots near the surface receive less oxygen and water, and they may die.

Trunk Growth

The growth in diameter of a woody stem or tree trunk takes place in the cambium, a thin layer of dividing cells just under the bark. As each cell in the cambium divides, one of the two resulting cells becomes either a xylem cell or a phloem cell. The other cell remains a cambium cell and divides again.

Wood As the newest xylem cells expand, they push the cambium layer a little farther away from the center of the tree. The new cells live for only a year or two; then they die and only their woody cell wall remains. The cell continues to transport water and nutrients for another year or two, and then it becomes plugged and stops working. By then the cell is deep in the wood of the tree, and it is heavily packed with a rigid material called lignin. This is the substance that gives stiffness and rigidity to wood.

Bark The phloem cells formed by the cambium are pushed to the outside of the tree. Like the xylem cells, phloem cells are able to transport sugars only for a couple of years. As they die and dry out, they become the bark of the tree.

Girdling If the phloem and xylem are cut all the way around a tree trunk, the tree will probably die. The flow of water and sugars stops, the leaves wilt, and the top dies. The

HOW PLANTS SPREAD

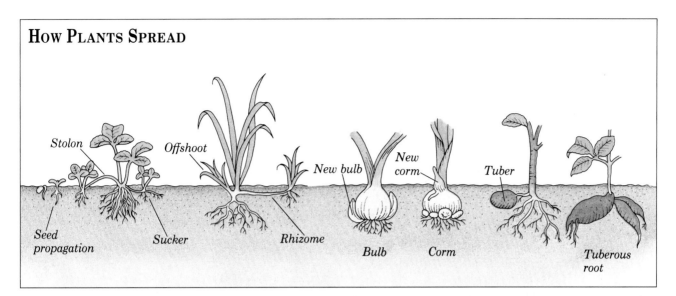

Stolon

Offshoot

New bulb

New corm

Tuber

Seed propagation

Sucker

Rhizome

Bulb

Corm

Tuberous root

Top: Control annual weeds by killing the seeds.
Bottom: Suckers from tree trunks should be removed.

roots may die, or they may resprout and grow a new top. If only the bark is cut, the phloem will be severed but the xylem will be intact. The tree won't wilt, since water can still travel upward. However, the flow of sugars from the leaves to the roots will be severed, and the roots will slowly starve. As the roots stop working, the top of the tree will also starve and eventually the entire plant will die.

Bark wounds Any wound in a tree trunk interrupts the flow of water and sugars through the tree. If a spot is repeatedly wounded, as happens when a tree is bumped continually by a lawn mower, the growth of the plant will slow and become stunted.

Reproduction

Plants have two ways of reproducing themselves: by seed and by growing new plants from parts of the old one.

Seeds   Most plants form seeds. Annual plants (see Annuals on page 56) depend on seeds to continue their species. They often direct all their energy into ripening a crop of seeds. Annual weeds, such as crab grass, usually produce thousands of seeds per plant. It is important to kill these weeds before they form seeds, or you will have many more weeds to contend with the following year.

Offshoots   New plants that arise from the base of the old plant are called offshoots. As more offshoots grow, a dense clump of plants is formed. Offshoots can usually be broken off or cut off and planted elsewhere.

Rhizomes and stolons   These are horizontal stems that form new plants at a distance from the mother plant. Rhizomes travel underground, sending up new growth every so often. Stolons grow above ground, making new plants where they come in contact with the soil.

Suckers   The word *sucker* has two different meanings. It refers to a stem that arises from the base of a trunk. It also refers to a plant that arises from the roots of the parent plant, often at some distance from that plant. This type of sucker is an entire plant that can be severed and planted elsewhere. If left to their own devices, plants that sucker freely will form a thicket in a couple of years.

Bulbs   Plants form many different kinds of underground food-storage organs (see Bulbs on page 59). Most of these organs remain dormant, or inactive, for the majority of the year. Because of the large amount of food stored in them, they burst into vigorous growth for a limited period.

UNDERSTANDING SOME BASIC TERMS

Hardy, Half-hardy, and Tender
Hardiness refers to a plant's ability to withstand cold, not to its general strength or vigor. There are many degrees of hardiness.

Hardy plants are the most cold tolerant. They can withstand prolonged exposure to freezing temperatures without being killed or badly damaged. Some plants can withstand a few degrees of frost, whereas others can survive subzero temperatures. To clarify the degree of hardiness, plants are sometimes described as being hardy to a specific temperature (for example, "hardy to -5° F").

Half-hardy plants can tolerate long periods of damp or cold weather, but they may be damaged or killed by frost. Sometimes they die to the ground in a freeze but grow back.

Tender plants, which are native to countries with mild climates, die when the temperature drops below freezing.

Herbaceous and Woody
Herbaceous plants are mainly soft and succulent, without a woody stem. They are sometimes described as soft stemmed. In cold climates herbaceous perennials die back to the ground every winter and regrow from the roots in the spring.

Woody plants have hard stems and branches that survive cold weather and do not die back.

Deciduous and Evergreen
Deciduous plants lose all their leaves at once, usually in fall, and grow new leaves in spring. Deciduous plants are usually quite hardy; in fact, some deciduous plants require cold in order to flower or fruit properly.

Evergreen plants keep their foliage the year around. They drop their older leaves each year, but this is not always noticeable. There are two major categories of evergreens: broadleaf evergreens and coniferous (cone-bearing) evergreens. Broadleaf evergreens are usually less hardy than deciduous plants, and they grow best in mild-winter areas.

The term *broadleaf* distinguishes plants with wide, flat leaves from conifers and grasses, which have narrow leaves. The term is most often used in referring to broadleaf evergreen trees and in differentiating them from coniferous evergreens.

Coniferous evergreens do well in most climates. A coniferous plant, or conifer, is a woody tree or shrub that produces cones. Almost all conifers are evergreen plants, and they have needlelike or scalelike leaves. Coniferous plants include pine (*Pinus* species), fir (*Abies* species), spruce, (*Picea* species) juniper (*Juniperus* species), redwood (*Sequoia* species), and hemlock (*Tsuga* species).

Daffodils, yellow and purple violas, and white candytuft are annuals that make an attractive mixed border. Annuals are herbaceous plants that complete their life cycle in a year or less.

Zinnias are annuals that are inexpensive, easy to grow, and provide color in the garden over a long season.

CATEGORIES OF GARDEN PLANTS

Plants are categorized by their life cycle—annual, biennial, or perennial—meaning that they complete their life cycle in one year, two years, or longer. They are further categorized by growth habit; for example, plants with a low, spreading habit are called ground covers and plants that climb are called vines.

Annuals

Herbaceous, or soft-stemmed, plants that complete their life cycle in one year or less are called annuals. They germinate, grow, bloom, produce seeds, and die within the same year. Generally, they are planted in spring, bloom during summer and fall, and die with the first frost. In mild climates some annuals, such as pot marigold (*Calendula officinalis*), thrive in winter gardens. Annuals are temporary plants, as opposed to permanent woody plants such as trees and shrubs. Some annuals reseed themselves, but most must be replanted each year.

Many vegetables, such as peas and corn, are annual. However, most gardeners associate the term *annual* with ornamental plants grown for their flowers—for example, zinnia (*Zinnia elegans*) and marigold (*Tagetes* species). Some tender perennials (see Perennials on page 57) are treated as annuals and replaced yearly. Annuals generally are inexpensive and easy to grow.

Biennials

Although biennials complete their life cycle in two years instead of one, these herbaceous plants are often grouped with annuals in garden centers and mail-order nursery catalogs. Biennials grow from seed into a leafy plant the first year; then they bloom, set seed, and die the second year. In warm-winter climates some biennials may grow from seed to flowering plant in a single growing season.

Many biennials, such as foxglove (*Digitalis purpurea*) and sweet william (*Dianthus barbatus*), are usually purchased as started plants in the nursery. Thus, the grower has taken care of the first phase of the plant's life. The gardener sees only the second phase, during which the plant flowers and dies, along with the annuals in the garden, at the end of the growing season. There are some vegetables, such as brussels sprouts and celery, that are biennial.

Perennials

Plants that live from year to year are perennials. Many plants are perennial, but the category generally refers to flowering plants that are herbaceous, meaning that their stems are soft and fleshy, not woody like those of shrubs and trees. Generally, perennials have a shorter bloom period— from one week to one month—than annuals. (Although bulbs are perennials, they are dealt with separately because of their method of storing food.)

Shrubs and trees survive winters because their woody stems and trunks resist extreme cold. Herbaceous perennials survive varying degrees of winter cold because their roots are stronger and more vigorous than those of annuals and biennials. With the onset of cold, the tops of perennials may die to the ground, but the roots remain alive in a dormant state, producing new foliage and flowers each year when the weather warms. In warm-winter areas some perennials are evergreen (they retain their foliage throughout the year). Others may die to the ground yearly in response to an environmental factor such as drought or heat.

Popular perennials include yarrow (*Achillea* species), chrysanthemum (*Chrysanthemum* hybrids), delphinium (*Delphinium*

Not all annuals are ornamentals; some vegetables, such as corn and peas, are also annuals.

The term perennial *generally refers to an herbaceous plant that has soft, fleshy stems, such as this chrysanthemum.*

Perennials, such as these Shasta daisies, yellow lilies, red gerberas, and white dianthus, make a colorful bed. Perennials have a short blooming period, but live from year to year.

elatum), primrose (*Primula* species), and plantain lily (*Hosta* species). Some vegetables, such as asparagus and artichokes, along with many herbs, are also perennials.

Bulbs

Any plant that grows from an underground food storage organ is called a bulb. Only a portion of plants in this category are true bulbs. Although the various kinds of bulbous plants have their distinct differences, they share the ability to store food to carry them through a dormant period. Dormancy is one of nature's many solutions for getting through a time of adverse weather conditions. Dormancy is brought on naturally by winter or drought. In mild climates it may be necessary to force the bulb into dormancy by withholding water or digging it up and keeping it in cold storage. (See page 120 for information on dividing and planting bulbs and bulblike plants.)

True bulbs A package of fleshy leaves or scales containing a shoot and held together at the bottom by a small plate from which roots grow is called a true bulb. New bulbs (called bulblets or offsets) are formed on this basal plate. Many bulbs have a paper-thin covering called a tunic. Daffodils (*Narcissus* species), tulips (*Tulipa* species), and lilies (*Lilium* species) are examples of true bulbs.

Corms A storage organ formed from a vertical stem is called a corm. Solid inside, it is covered by dry leaf bases similar to the tunic covering a bulb. The top of a corm has one or more growing points, or eyes. Roots grow from a basal plate on the underside. As the plant grows, the original corm shrivels away

BULBOUS PLANTS BY TYPE

True Bulbs	Corms
Allium	*Brodiaea*
Amaryllis	*Bulbocodium*
Camassia	*Colchicum*
Chionodoxa	*Crocus*
Clivia	*Erythronium*
Eucharis	*Freesia*
Fritillaria	*Gladiolus*
Galanthus	*Ixia*
Hippeastrum	*Moraea*
Hyacinthus	*Sparaxis*
Hymenocallis	*Tigridia*
Iris reticulata	*Tritonia*
Ixiolirion	*Watsonia*
Leucojum	
Lilium	**Tubers**
Lycoris	*Anemone*
Muscari	*Caladium*
Narcissus	*Cyclamen*
Nerine	*Eranthis*
Ornithogalum	*Gloriosa*
Oxalis	*Polianthes*
Scilla	*Ranunculus*
Sprekelia	*Sinningia*
Tulipa	
Zephyranthes	**Rhizomes**
	Achimenes
Tuberous Roots	*Agapanthus*
Alstroemeria	*Canna*
Begonia	*Convallaria*
Dahlia	*Iris* (rhizomatous)
Eremurus	*Zantedeschia*

A bulb is a plant that stores food and continues to live when dug up and stored during its period of dormancy.

and new corms form on top of or beside the old one. These large corms bloom the following year. Some plants also form tiny corms, or cormels, around the basal plate or roots. These must develop for two to three years before they will bloom. Gladiolus (*Gladiolus* species) and crocus (*Crocus* species) are examples of plants that grow from corms.

Tubers A storage organ formed from an underground stem is called a tuber. It consists of a solid mass like a corm, but it lacks a basal plate and the corm's tuniclike covering. Roots and shoots grow from buds, or eyes, scattered over the surface. During growth the tubers of some plants, such as potatoes, shrink and form new tubers, whereas those of other plants, such as Persian buttercup (*Ranunculus asiaticus*), grow bigger and develop new eyes for the following year.

Tuberous roots Although they resemble tubers, tuberous roots are actually swollen roots rather than stems. During growth they produce fibrous roots, which absorb water and nutrients. New growth buds appear on the base of the old stem, where it joins the tuberous roots. Dahlias (*Dahlia* species) and sweet potatoes are examples of tuberous-rooted plants.

Rhizomes Sometimes called a rootstock, a rhizome is actually a thickened, branching storage stem that grows horizontally just below the ground. Roots grow from the bottom of the rhizome and buds grow along the top. These buds produce the new plants during the growing season. Calla lily (*Zantedeschia* species) and lily-of-the-Nile (*Agapanthus africanus*) are good examples of rhizomatous plants.

A tuber is a storage organ formed from an underground stem. Potatoes are perhaps the most familiar of all plants that grow from tubers.

Shrubs are woody plants that survive from year to year without dying back.

Shrubs

A shrub is generally considered to be a woody plant that is less than 15 feet tall when mature and has multiple stems or trunks, although it can be trained to have only a single trunk. Low-growing shrubs are often referred to as subshrubs. Since shrubs are woody, they survive from one year to the next without dying back to the ground after each growing season. They can be deciduous (lose all their leaves at one time) or evergreen (retain their foliage throughout the year).

Some shrubs, such as roses (*Rosa* species) and azaleas (*Rhododendron* species), are grown for their flowers; other shrubs, such as cotoneaster (*Cotoneaster* species) and Oregon grape (*Mahonia aquifolium*), are grown for their fruit display; and yet other shrubs, such as mirror plant (*Coprosma repens*) and juniper (*Juniperus* species), are valued for their foliage.

Hedges are often used to form garden backdrops and mark property boundaries.

Hedges   Shrubs that have been planted close together so that they form an unbroken line are called a hedge. It can be low (a foot or less) for bordering flower beds and walks; medium (up to 6 feet) for marking property boundaries and for using as a backdrop behind other plants; or tall (more than 6 feet) for screens and windbreaks.

A hedge in which the natural form of the shrub is retained is said to be informal. A formal hedge is sheared and has a solid, even appearance. Some shrubs—such as boxwood (*Buxus* species), yew (*Taxus* species), and privet (*Ligustrum* species)—are suited to formal hedging because they grow uniformly and adapt well to trimming.

Trees

A tree is a woody plant, usually with a single trunk, that is taller than 15 feet when mature. Some trees, the coast redwood (*Sequoia*

sempervirens), for example, can reach several hundred feet in height in the wild and live for thousands of years. Other trees, such as acacia (*Acacia* species), generally grow less than 40 feet tall and live for only 20 to 30 years. Trees may be deciduous or evergreen. They come in various shapes: pyramidal, columnar, roundheaded, arching, and weeping. Some trees have foliage all the way to the ground; others develop a canopy that you can walk under. Certain trees, such as eastern hemlock (*Tsuga canadensis*) and western red cedar (*Thuja plicata*), can be sheared into a formal hedge. To maintain health and looks, most trees require pruning and trimming.

A tree is a woody plant, usually with a single trunk, that may be deciduous or evergreen and will be at least 15 feet tall when mature.

Flowering shrubs, such as azaleas, should not be forced into a formal shape but should be allowed to retain their natural form when planted as a hedge.

There are many kinds of plants that can be used as ground covers. False-Solomon's-seal and violets combine to make an attractive ground cover in a shady area.

When violets are used as a ground cover, they should be planted in partial shade. When the flowers bloom the effect can be striking.

A lawn is the most common ground cover and is available in many varieties.

Ground covers can make attractive borders around hard surfaces.

Ground Covers

A ground cover is any low-growing plant that blankets the ground and binds the soil. A ground cover may consist of herbaceous perennials or subshrubs planted in masses, or a sprawling vine used to cover the ground. In mild-winter climates ground covers are usually limited to evergreen plants that look attractive throughout the year.

Lawns   The most commonly used ground cover is a lawn, consisting of a single variety of grass or a mixture of several different varieties. Grasses are categorized by the time of year in which they grow best. Warm-season grasses, such as Bermuda grass, grow vigorously in the warm summer months and then become dormant, often turning brown in cool weather. They are adapted to the southern half of the United States. Cool-season grasses, such as blue grass, grow actively in the cool weather of spring and fall.

This plant is called Aquilegia formosa. *Its common name is columbine.*

They slow down during the hot summer but remain green if given ample water. They are grown primarily in the North.

Vines
Climbing plants that may or may not need support are called vines. Vines that climb by twining or by thorns may need to be tied to structures. Some vines support themselves with suction disks (called holdfasts) or aerial rootlets. Other vines grow upward by mounding. Certain plants, such as ivy (*Hedera* species), can be grown as a vine or can be allowed to sprawl as a ground cover.

UNDERSTANDING PLANT NAMES

Two types of names are used to refer to plants: common names and botanical names. Although common names may be easier to remember, they can be confusing. A plant may be known by different common names in different regions, or several plants may share the same common name.

Since anyone can make up new common names for plants on a whim, standardization of names is needed to avoid confusion. Every plant has a two-part scientific Latin name, the genus and the species, that identifies it anywhere in the world. Garden centers and mail-order nursery catalogs generally list plants by their scientific names, so that you know precisely what you are getting.

Genus and Species
The genus (plural is genera) is the first word in the two-part scientific name that every plant is given. It is italicized and begins with a capital letter. The genus identifies the plant as belonging to a general grouping of

This plant is a hybrid of columbine. Hybridized plants are usually bred to produce specimens that have the best qualities of each parent.

plants based on flower parts. Some plants in this grouping may bear little resemblance to each other, especially when they are out of bloom. For example, *Cornus florida*, flowering dogwood, is a 20- to 30-foot tree; *Cornus canadensis*, commonly known as bunchberry, is a ground cover growing less than a foot high.

The species (singular and plural are the same) is the plant's second name. It is always italicized and lowercased. The species is a more specific, or narrower, grouping. Plants in the same species not only resemble each other, they are also closely related and can interbreed. You can refer to an individual species or to all species in the genus—for example, *Erica carnea* is a specific reference to spring heath; *Erica* species refers to heaths in general. Some plants have a large number of species; for instance, *Aquilegia* (columbine) has over seventy variable species.

Hybrids

Sometimes there is a multiplication sign ($\times$) between the genus and species names. This signifies a hybrid plant, the result of crossbreeding two or more different species or varieties. Border forsythia (*Forsythia $\times$ intermedia*) is an example of a hybrid.

The purpose of hybridizing is usually to produce plants that have the best qualities of each parent. Seeds saved from your garden plants, if they are hybrids, may revert unpredictably to a parent and may not develop the form you expect. However, seeds sold commercially have a predictable form when grown. Hybrid plants can also be reproduced by cuttings or another vegetative method.

There are more than two hundred species of iris. Most are grown as ornamentals, but some are used in perfumes. This is a variety of Iris douglasiana.

Varieties

After the species there may be another name identifying a variety. A variety may differ from the straight species in size, form, leaf color, flower color or size, or tolerance to environmental extremes such as heat and cold. There are two kinds of varieties: Those occurring in the wild are called botanical or natural varieties; those produced under controlled conditions by plant breeders are called cultivated varieties, or cultivars. Some cultivars are propagated by seed and others by vegetative means such as cuttings or grafting. Depending on the cultivar, it may or may not grow as expected when you use seed saved from the plant. A botanical variety will reproduce itself true to seed, whether purchased commercially or saved from a plant in your garden.

Natural varieties always appear in lowercased italics and are preceded by the abbreviation "var."—for example, *Gleditsia triacanthos* var. *inermis*, the thornless honeylocust (it is also acceptable to omit the "var.").

Cultivar names are enclosed in single quotation marks and appear in roman letters. They can consist of more than one word, each of which begins with a capital letter. An example of a cultivar is the green hawthorn *Crataegus viridis* 'Winter King'.

Named varieties of plants—whether naturally occurring or cultivated—often outperform the straight species. The fact that breeders are constantly at work developing superior garden plants is evident in the number of plants in nurseries and catalogs that bear variety names. Most vegetables and all modern roses are sold only by named varieties—for example, 'Early Girl' tomato and 'Peace' rose.

The named varieties in your local garden center may not be the same ones that are available in other regions. Many plants are bred to be tolerant of heat, cold, and other environmental conditions, and the nurseries in each area stock those varieties that grow best locally. Consult the staff of a local nursery or garden center to find out which cultivars are desirable in your area.

This is a Pacific Coast iris, a hybrid of I. douglasiana. *It has been developed as a hardier version of several Pacific Coast native irises.*

UNDERSTANDING THE GARDEN ENVIRONMENT

After gaining a basic understanding of plants, the next step is to learn a little about the environment in which they will live. The two most important environmental factors affecting plant growth are climate and soil. Some plants are quite adaptable and tolerate a wide variety of growing conditions, such as sun or shade, or wet or dry soil. However, many plants have very specific needs and will struggle along or die if their needs are not met. Fussy or not, all plants grow better in the right environment.

Climate defines the limits of gardening, unless you garden in the controlled environment of a greenhouse. Every plant has a minimum and a maximum temperature range beyond which it will die. Wind and rain can devastate plants by knocking them over, breaking branches, and washing away soil. Wind also dries out plants and increases their need for water. Lack of rain places a burden on the gardener to provide the amount of water that a plant requires. Plants that aren't adapted to the climatic conditions will be weakened and unable to defend themselves against insects and diseases.

Not only should a plant be suited to the general climate of your area, it should also be adapted to the particular part of the garden in which you place it. Learning to recognize microclimates—the sunny locations, cool spots, moist areas, and so on—will make it easier to select plants that will thrive in your garden.

All gardens have microclimates. Learn where the sunny locations, cool spots, and moist areas are in your garden and select appropriate plants for those microclimates.

71

This garden, with its shade trees, open areas, and low shrubs, contains both cool and hot microclimates.

CLIMATE

Such factors as temperature range, rainfall, and wind conditions that typify a region characterize its climate. Climate is largely determined by latitude, topography, and distance from a large body of water. If you've ever moved from one part of the country to another, you may have been surprised at the differences in gardening in the two regions. These differences play an important role in the location of plants in the garden. For instance, the azalea that can take almost full sun in Oyster Bay, Long Island, needs plenty of protection in Louisville, Kentucky.

One reason for the difference is latitude: The intensity of the sun increases the closer you are to the equator. Another factor is proximity to water. Coastal areas are warmer in winter and cooler in summer than inland areas. Add to that the multitude of other climatic influences, such as fog and clouds, and you quickly realize that blanket statements about the type of exposure and care to give a plant are difficult to make.

Experience and common sense are the best guides in interpreting a plant's needs. For example, a plant listed as requiring light shade will tolerate more sun in a mild, foggy, coastal environment than it will in a hot, sunny, inland area.

Once you get to know your climate and the many little climates around your house, the process of providing the right conditions for each plant becomes easier. It also helps to know where a plant comes from; that will tell you a lot about the plant's temperature, light, moisture, and other requirements. In fact, more and more gardeners are realizing it makes sense for them to grow plants that have come from a climate similar to their own. For example, plants from Chile, Australia, and other Mediterranean climates are becoming increasingly popular in parts of California that share the same climate.

This natural garden, with tall trees that provide a good deal of shade throughout the day, is predominantly a cool and moist microclimate.

Climate Zones

A slightly modified version of the USDA Plant Hardiness Zone Map is illustrated on pages 350 to 351. Locate your zone on it and use it as a reference when you consult this book. Be aware that the map is meant to be a general guide and that the zones are approximate, based on average data. The climate often varies within zones. Your local climate can be warmer or colder than the average for the zone, especially in mountainous regions. The conditions in your garden may differ even further.

MICROCLIMATES

The many climatic variations in your garden are called microclimates. Structures, existing plants, exposure to the sun, and elevation differences combine to create these small climates. For example, a cool, shady microclimate may be found on the north side of a house, a hot one in an unprotected south-western corner, a cold one in a hollow at the bottom of a hill, a humid one near a dense planting of shrubs, and so on. Differences in microclimates affect many aspects of gardening. For instance, you may find that your daffodils bloom several weeks earlier than those in a neighboring garden, and your maples may not change color as quickly in the fall.

Microclimates change with time. On a new home site, the only shade may be beneath overhangs, under the patio roof, and in the northern exposure. As plants grow, so does the amount of shade. Plant growth also affects the temperature, wind pattern, humidity, and other elements that make up microclimates.

The most successful gardeners are acquainted with all the different climates in their gardens. Before you buy any new plants, take an inventory of your microclimates. You will be able to choose plants best

The red-flowering gum (Eucalyptus ficifolia) *from West Australia does very well in the similar coastal climate of the western United States.*

adapted to the general climate. For example, you may be able to stretch a plant's adaptation by a zone or even two zones if you place the plant in a warm, protected spot. There is a limit to the protection a microclimate can offer, however. You won't be able to provide a safe location for a tropical plant in a New England, midwestern, or western climate where subfreezing temperatures prevail and snow blankets the garden throughout the winter months.

Sun

Tolerance to sun dictates the placement of most plants. Some plants require full sun, whereas others perform best in varying amounts of shade. Become familiar with the light patterns in your garden. Notice that the south side of your house and the south-facing slopes and other surfaces receive the most direct sunlight throughout the day and are the hottest spots in the garden. Observe that the west side receives morning shade and hot afternoon sun, whereas the east side receives mild morning sun and afternoon shade. Notice that planting areas in front of north-facing walls are never exposed to direct sunlight and are predominately shady, cool, and moist as a result.

This hybrid shrub rose creates a microclimate that allows plants liking partial shade to grow around its base.

These treasureflowers (Gazania rigens) are native to South Africa. They prefer light, sandy, well-drained soil in full sun, and mild winters.

Citrus trees, such as lemon, orange, and grapefruit, do well in subtropical and semitropical areas because they can tolerate hot summer sun.

Be aware that in midsummer the sun rises in the northeast and sets in the northwest. Delicate shade-loving plants growing in either northwestern or northeastern exposures won't receive direct sunlight during the cooler months, but they may be damaged in midsummer.

If a plant that cannot tolerate hot sun is placed in a sunny southwestern exposure, it will do poorly and perhaps even die. When the temperature climbs above 90° F, an unadapted plant will be unable to transpire (use water evaporation to cool its tissues) quickly enough. Mature leaves will dry out and turn brown around the edges, and leaf tips and new growth will wilt.

Even when temperatures are moderate, intense sunlight can burn plants that prefer a shadier site or that haven't been adequately watered. Yellowish white damage on older leaves is a sign of sunlight injury. The greatest damage occurs on bright, clear summer days. Reflected sunlight from light-colored walls and other surfaces increases the intensity. Plant growth slows or comes to a stop.

Intense sunlight can also burn the bark of young trees. Protect a young tree by loosely wrapping the trunk with a tree wrap material or by painting it with white water-soluble paint. Once the tree has developed a thicker bark, it will no longer need protection from the sun.

Other plants adapted to full sun may be damaged if exposed to intense light before their roots are established in the soil. Rather than plant in very sunny exposures in summer, wait until fall or early spring.

Shade

One of the most important elements in the garden environment is shade. Unlike some of the other components, shade occurs to some extent in every garden. It dramatically alters the air and soil temperature, especially in arid regions, and it often raises the humidity.

When selecting plants for a shady area, keep these important points in mind: Most sun-loving plants will accept some amount of shade during part of the day as long as they

The bark of young trees can be protected from intense sunlight with water-soluble white paint.

A patio shade structure can create dappled shade in which both shade- and sun-loving plants can grow.

also receive the amount of direct sun they need. Shade-loving plants, on the other hand, will wilt, sunburn, or develop other signs of distress from too much direct sun (especially the hot late-afternoon sun) even if they receive adequate shade for the rest of the day.

When a sun-loving plant is placed in too much shade, it produces long, weak stems and fewer leaves than normal. The plant stretches toward the light it needs, a phenomenon called etiolation. The process of etiolation often weakens the plant. It may appear healthy for a while, but it is using stored energy. If left in this declining state for too long, the plant may not regain its vigor even if it is transplanted to a sunny spot in the garden.

There are four distinct categories of shade, and the plant lists on pages 370 to 375 carry recommendations keyed to each of these categories.

Dappled shade   Shade produced by open trees—such as birch (*Betula* species), which create a moving pattern of sunlight and shade across the ground—is called dappled.

Buildings can create an open shade area penetrated by bright light but not direct sunlight.

Medium shade is that which occurs in north-facing locations further darkened by structures or trees.

Tall walls, fences, and buildings can create deep shade in north-facing locations.

Lath houses also provide dappled shade. This is the lightest shade category, although direct sun is minimal. A great many shade-loving as well as sun-loving plants grow well in dappled shade.

Open shade Shade cast by a north-facing wall, fence, or building is open shade. The distance the shade is cast varies with the season. Open shade provides bright light but not direct sunlight. Fiberglass-roofed patios and whitewashed greenhouses under direct sun also provide open shade.

Medium shade Shade occurring in north-facing locations further darkened by a structure or by trees—in other words, open-shade in which light is further obscured—is called medium shade. This situation also occurs under decks and stairwells.

Dense shade The deepest shade is dense shade. It is found in north-facing side yards in which tall walls or fences block all but the narrowest strips of light. There is some reflected light. Plant selection is severely limited in these areas.

Tall shrubs and trees can create deep shade. There is some reflected light but plant selection can be limited for such areas.

Moisture

Air moisture and soil moisture, both of which affect plant growth, can vary dramatically within a garden. Rainfall is not consistent among microclimates. The ground beneath thick-canopied trees and beneath eaves is usually dry. If the wind blows rain over the top of the house or trees, the ground on the leeward side may be dry.

The humidity may be high in a deeply shaded, north-facing, enclosed section of the garden where the air remains still. Plant diseases that thrive in wet conditions will be more of a problem in these moist spots. On the south side of the house, the situation may be the complete reverse. Plants may be exposed to intense afternoon sun and drying breezes, and temperatures may fluctuate significantly from day to night.

Whether your soil retains moisture depends on the type of soil you have and how well it drains (see pages 90 to 91 and 101 to 102). Water evaporates more rapidly from soil in a sunny exposure than a shady one.

Wind

Even moderate wind can do physical damage to plants, cause excess water loss, dry out soil quickly, and blow disease-causing spores to new host plants. Certain geographical areas are especially subject to winds. A home located in a canyon, at the base of a bluff, or along a shoreline may be buffeted almost constantly by winds.

If you live in a windy area, be aware of the locations in your garden that are particularly exposed. Use tough, deep-rooted plants in these areas, or construct a windbreak,

In dry, windy areas a windbreak formed by a row of deep-rooted shrubs will help to slow and dissipate the flow of air. However, some wind should be allowed to pass through to avoid strong downdrafts behind the barrier.

which is any barrier—a row of trees or shrubs or a structure such as a fence—that slows or dissipates the flow of air. It should allow some wind to pass through; otherwise, when the wind passes over the windbreak it will come down with greater force directly behind the barrier.

Cold

Every plant has a minimum temperature beyond which it will be harmed or die. Avoid cold damage by choosing plants that will survive normal low temperatures in your area.

Since cold air sinks, low spots in the garden are the most susceptible to frost. Low spots in which cold air is trapped are called frost pockets. In most gardens frost pockets are suitable only for hardy plants. However, in a mild-winter climate, a frost pocket may

Peaches cannot tolerate extreme winter cold or late frosts.

A line of olive trees that are planted along a wall or fence makes an especially good windbreak in a windy and dry climate.

be the only spot in the garden providing consistently low temperatures for plants that require a winter chill. Some deciduous plants, such as lilacs (*Syringa* species), need winter cold for optimum flowering. Most fruit trees must be exposed to temperatures below 45° F for four to eight weeks if they are to fruit properly. Many spring-blooming bulbs require cold in order to naturalize (grow and bloom year after year without special care).

Protect tender plants by locating them in a warm microclimate, such as under eaves. In areas where winter nights are often clear and dry, plants located under trees or beneath eaves or other overhangs are not as likely to suffer from cold damage as plants located in the open. Ordinarily, heat collected during the day is lost at night in the form of heat waves radiating from the earth's surface. When these heat waves encounter a tree, an overhang, or other overhead object, they are reradiated back to earth. Therefore, soil and plants that have something above them do not lose as much overall heat as plants in the open. This same principle explains why plants in the open are much less susceptible to frost during cloudy or foggy nights: The heat waves do not penetrate the cloud or fog layer effectively and are reradiated back to the ground.

Covering plants helps protect them from frost. If a plant has adequate soil moisture to replace water transpired through its leaves, the plant is less likely to suffer damage. In a hard-freeze region, water the garden until the ground freezes. Then mulch the plants so that frost will not penetrate deep into the ground (see Applying Mulch on page 103). Periodic thawing and freezing of the soil can heave small plants out of the ground. Once frozen in the ground, a plant is better left until spring. Alternate freezing and thawing of water-filled plant cells causes the cells to burst.

Exposing plants to coolness, even temperatures well above freezing, can damage some plants. Gradually acclimatize seedlings and plants raised indoors to cool outdoor conditions.

The snow is not as heavy on the shrub next to the house because the eaves trap heat and melt the snow.

Apples need some cool winter weather, but there is an enormous range in this requirement.

SOIL

The soil is the weathered surface of the earth's crust. The development of soil is the end result of plant life moving from the ocean to the land. As the first primitive plants gradually inhabited the earth's surface, they began to change the nature of the rocky terrain on which they grew. The result was soil.

The depth of soil is variable: It can range from a few inches deep in some locations to hundreds of feet deep in others. Soil provides plants with a reservoir of water, air, and mineral nutrients as well as a means of anchoring their roots. Understanding and managing soil is one of the most important aspects of growing plants.

Soil Profile

If you could dig deep enough into your soil, you would see several distinct layers. This layering is known as the soil profile. It can tell you much about the soil's potential for gardening success.

The soil profile consists of several major layers in varying stages of development: topsoil, subsoil, and often a layer of fragmented rock. These sit on bedrock, or the solid rock base from which soil slowly forms.

The topsoil, which can range from a fraction of an inch to several feet deep, is the most valuable layer for gardening. In most gardens it is a few inches deep. Since the topsoil contains most of the organic matter found in the soil, it is darker and looser than the other layers. It takes about a thousand years for one inch of topsoil to form.

The subsoil is lighter in color and the only organic matter and nutrients it contains are those that filter down from the topsoil. The subsoil may contain one or more impenetrable layers, or soil pans, that impede drainage and root growth. There are different kinds of soil pans, including claypan and hardpan. Caliche, a chalklike layer of concentrated minerals, is a kind of hardpan common in the desert areas of the Southwest. If there is a soil pan where you want to grow deep-rooted plants, you must break through it (see page 101). If the problem is severe, you may choose to garden in raised beds (see page 102). That's also a good solution if your soil is very shallow and you can dig down to a rocky base.

Soil Components
Typical garden soil contains 50 percent solid material, 25 percent water, and 25 percent air. The solid material consists of about 45 percent minerals and 5 percent organic matter.

Minerals Sand, silt, and clay particles are the mineral portion of soil. The particles range from large (sand), to intermediate (silt), to extremely small (clay). The proportions of the different particle types determine the texture of the soil. (See Soil Texture at right below.)

Organic matter Living and dead plant and animal matter in various stages of growth and decay constitute the organic part of the soil. Most native, or unamended, soils contain from less than 1 percent to 5 percent organic matter, whereas a well-amended garden soil may contain 30 percent or more. Adding organic matter is one of the best things you can do to your soil. In addition to being a reservoir of nutrients, organic matter helps structure the soil (see Soil Structure on page 86).

Live organic matter includes creatures such as earthworms and insects. Earthworms perform a valuable service by creating tunnels for air and water to flow through the soil. An invisible world of soil bacteria, fungi, and algae is even more crucial. These microorganisms decompose organic matter and contribute to the chemical reactions that allow plants to absorb nutrients.

Water Soil water enables plants to absorb minerals by first dissolving them. Water is also needed for the physiological and chemical processes of plant growth.

Water is so strongly attracted to small spaces, or pores, in the soil that it actually moves from large spaces to smaller ones, even if the movement is upward or sideways. That is why a soil with mostly small pores, such as clay, holds water so well. If the pores remain saturated for too long, plant roots will be deprived of oxygen and they may die. An ideal soil has a mix of large and small spaces, so that it holds both water and air. (See Soil Texture below.)

Air Soil with a loose surface and large pores permits air to diffuse easily into it. Entry is limited if the soil is crusted over or compacted. Soil air is more humid than the air that humans breathe, and it has a higher carbon dioxide content. The oxygen it contains is vital to the root growth of plants. In fact, roots grow only where oxygen is present in the soil.

Soil Texture
Soils are classified by texture, which is determined by the proportion of sand, silt, and clay particles the soils contain. There are twelve textural classes, or types, of soils. (See page 90 for information on determining soil texture.) Texture has a profound effect on the physical properties of the soil. Sandy soils are one extreme of soil texture; clay soils are the other extreme.

SOIL PROFILE

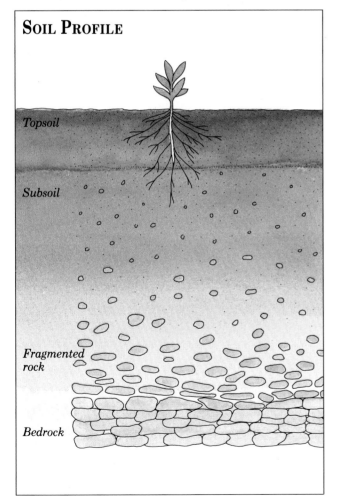

Topsoil

Subsoil

Fragmented rock

Bedrock

SOIL TEXTURE

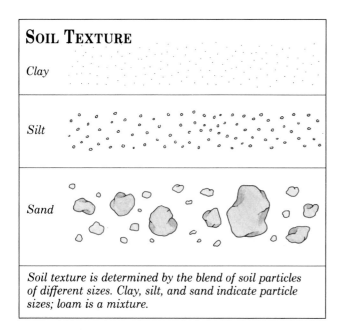

Clay

Silt

Sand

Soil texture is determined by the blend of soil particles of different sizes. Clay, silt, and sand indicate particle sizes; loam is a mixture.

Sandy soils are made up mostly of large particles with large spaces, or pores, between them. Since air is attracted to large pores, it moves into and out of sandy soils easily. Water soaks into sandy soil immediately, but the soil drains rapidly as air rushes in to fill the large spaces. Since water is held in small pores, and sandy soils are deficient in these, very little moisture is retained. Sandy soils are less fertile than finer-textured soils because nutrients are not held as tightly to the large particles and are easily washed away.

Clay soils consist mostly of tiny particles with very small spaces between them. Since the particles are so closely arranged, water doesn't infiltrate easily. Once water does enter clay soil, it is strongly attracted to the tiny pores. Clay soils hold water extremely well, but if they're not carefully managed, they may become waterlogged. Because clay soils are deficient in large pores, they hold little air. This limits drainage and root growth. Clay soils should never be cultivated when wet because the tiny particles will compress to an adobelike consistency, further reducing water and oxygen flow through the soil. Clay soils are naturally more fertile than sandy soils, and fertilizers do not wash away as quickly. Because clay soils consist of such small, tightly packed particles, they are difficult to work.

The intermediate soil textures, such as loam, have desirable properties of both sandy and clay soils. Loam is an ideal soil texture, consisting of about 40 percent sand, 40 percent silt, and 20 percent clay.

Soil Structure

The term *soil structure* refers to the arrangement of sand, silt, and clay particles in the soil. Although it is difficult to alter the texture of soil (the proportions of each particle type), you can more easily change your soil structure by adding organic matter.

As dead organic matter gradually decomposes in the soil, it forms humus. Humus helps the sand, silt, and clay particles stick together in larger groups, or aggregates. These aggregates give the soil a granulated, crumbly property often described as friable. Aggregation, or structure, increases the capacity of soil to hold air and water, improves drainage, and makes the soil easy to work. The soil aggregates are easily destroyed by tilling and compaction from foot traffic and heavy rains. You must add organic matter every year if you are to maintain good soil structure. (See Soil Amendments on page 92.)

Soil pH

The acidity or alkalinity of a soil—the soil pH—is measured on a scale from 0 (totally acid) to 14 (totally alkaline), with 7 being the neutral point. Only the middle range of the scale, from 4 to 8, is of interest to gardeners. Most plants grow best in the slightly acid to neutral range (pH 6.0 to 7.0). Some plants, such as rhododendrons and blueberries, thrive only in strongly acid soil, with a pH range of 4.0 to 5.5.

Although soil pH influences a number of processes in the soil, it affects plants mainly by decreasing or increasing their ability to absorb nutrients from the soil. If the pH is too high or too low, plants may suffer nutrient deficiencies, even if sufficient quantities of the nutrients are present in the soil.

Whether your soil is acid, alkaline, or neutral may depend on where you live. If you live in a high-rainfall region, your soil is probably acid—below pH 7.0. Soils high in organic matter—for example, areas with primarily deciduous plants, whose leaves work their way into the soil year after year—also tend to be acid. If a soil test shows that your soil has become too acidic, you can correct it by adding lime (see the chart on page 96).

Alkaline soils—those above pH 7.0—are found in areas with low rainfall or where the soil contains large amounts of lime or sodium. Soils in much of the arid western United States are alkaline. Soils irrigated by softened water are likely to be alkaline. The most effective way to lower the pH is to add soil sulfur (see the chart on page 96).

Salty Soils

There are two kinds of salty soils: saline soils and alkali, or sodic, soils. These conditions are most common in low-rainfall areas. Salt in the soil can prevent seed germination, retard plant growth, and burn leaves.

Saline soils Salinity is an accumulation of soluble salts. It is particularly troublesome in valleys; the salts collect in low-lying areas and there isn't enough rain to wash them down into the soil. Sometimes white salt deposits can be seen on the soil surface. A high salt content in the local water supply can create or add to a problem of soil salinity. Salts can also build up in a garden from repeated use of fertilizers and manure. You can eliminate soluble salts by leaching the soil: Once or twice a year, apply water slowly

THE pH SCALE

Some Common Substances	Acid	Soils
Grapefruit	3	Peat moss
Grapes	4	
Bread	5	Best for rhododendrons, azaleas, and other acid-loving plants
Milk	6	
Pure water Neutral	7	Average eastern soils
Baking soda	8	Average western soils
Soap	9	
Milk of magnesia	10	Alkali soils
	11	

Alkaline

for several hours until the salts are washed down past the plant's root zone.

Alkali, or sodic, soils Low rainfall and poor drainage can cause alkali soils. These are high-pH clay soils that have enough sodium bonded to the clay particles to interfere with growth. If the soil is well drained and salts don't accumulate, the soil may be alkali without being saline. If so, salt won't be in evidence on the surface. To correct an alkali soil, add gypsum (calcium sulfate); the calcium in the gypsum will chemically displace the sodium in the soil. Then apply water to leach the dislodged sodium.

Soil Temperature

Most plants, even those that can withstand severe cold, stop growing when the soil temperature is lower than 50° F. If the soil temperature drops below the plant's minimum tolerance, the plant may die.

Soil temperature also affects the speed of chemical reactions in the soil. For example, some organic fertilizers release nutrients only when the soil is warm, and the beneficial effects of soil organisms occur only when the soil is warm.

A hand-held pH meter will help you determine the types of soil in your garden.

TAKING CARE OF THE SOIL

Probably the single most important factor in a successful garden is good, workable soil. Most experienced gardeners come to regard their soil as their most valued asset. You can create a beautiful planting design and buy the highest quality plants, but without adequate soil, your efforts will be in vain.

Some gardeners are blessed with rich, loamy soil, but most aren't. If you're among the majority, you will have to pay more attention to your soil and work a little harder at improving it, tending it, and protecting it. Equipped with a basic understanding of soil gained from the last chapter, you are now ready to test and evaluate your soil. Once you know your soil type and discover any deficiencies that need correcting, you can transform a less-than-perfect soil into a valuable commodity.

For any garden to flourish, the soil must be in good condition. Testing and improving your soil are the first steps toward creating a productive garden.

EVALUATING YOUR SOIL

Without even touching your soil, you can get an approximate idea of its general condition simply by looking at the plants growing in it. If the soil is supporting garden plants or even weeds that are growing well and look healthy, and if water does not puddle up, then the soil is probably in reasonably good condition—although it might still benefit from improvement. If the plants are stunted or if water collects on the surface, then the soil is probably in poor shape and likely needs correction.

You can perform some simple tests, described below, that will give you more detailed information about your soil and pinpoint any problems. More sophisticated tests are available through a laboratory.

The Touch Test

Here's a quick way to determine your soil type, or texture. Wet a small handful of soil try to roll it into a cigar shape. Clay feels smooth; it forms and holds a pencil-thin shape and stains your hands a dark color. If the soil feels gritty and immediately crumbles when you try to roll it, it's sandy. If it crumbles before you can form it into a thin roll, it's loamy—a desirable mixture of sand, silt, and clay.

You can't easily change the texture of your soil, but you can improve the structure of a clay or sandy soil by adding organic matter (see Soil Amendments on page 92).

The Settling-Out Test

This test will help you determine your soil texture more scientifically. A soil is classified by the proportions of sand, silt, and clay particles in it. You can use the fact that larger particles sink in water faster than smaller particles to calculate the percentage of each type of particle in your soil. Since sand particles are the largest, they sink first, followed by silt and then clay.

Fill two thirds of a quart jar with water. Add a teaspoon of a water softener, such as Calgon brand, to separate the soil particles. Then fill the jar almost to the top with dry, pulverized soil. Screw on the lid and shake the jar vigorously. Then set the jar down and wait for the materials to settle.

Measure the depth of the soil that has settled to the bottom after 20 seconds. This is sand. Then measure the depth of material that settles out between 20 seconds and 2 minutes after shaking. This is silt. The clay will settle out over the next 2 weeks.

When the water is clear or almost clear, measure the total depth of soil and divide to find the percentages of sand, silt, and clay in the soil. An ideal soil, loam, will have about equal amounts of sand and silt and a smaller amount of clay. If your soil contains a preponderance of one type of particle, you can improve the soil by adding organic matter (see Soil Amendments on page 92).

DETERMINING SOIL TEXTURE

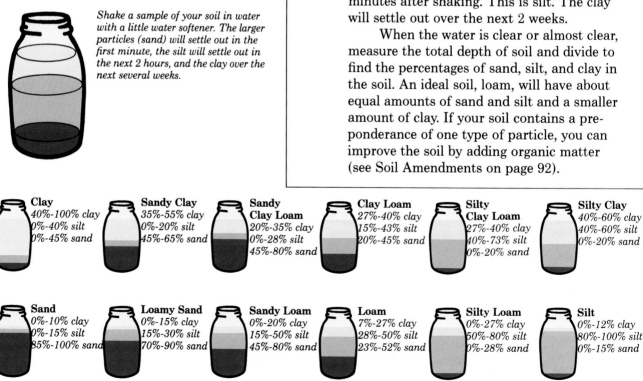

Shake a sample of your soil in water with a little water softener. The larger particles (sand) will settle out in the first minute, the silt will settle out in the next 2 hours, and the clay over the next several weeks.

Clay
40%-100% clay
0%-40% silt
0%-45% sand

Sandy Clay
35%-55% clay
0%-20% silt
45%-65% sand

Sandy Clay Loam
20%-35% clay
0%-28% silt
45%-80% sand

Clay Loam
27%-40% clay
15%-43% silt
20%-45% sand

Silty Clay Loam
27%-40% clay
40%-73% silt
0%-20% sand

Silty Clay
40%-60% clay
40%-60% silt
0%-20% sand

Sand
0%-10% clay
0%-15% silt
85%-100% sand

Loamy Sand
0%-15% clay
15%-30% silt
70%-90% sand

Sandy Loam
0%-20% clay
15%-50% silt
45%-80% sand

Loam
7%-27% clay
28%-50% silt
23%-52% sand

Silty Loam
0%-27% clay
50%-80% silt
0%-28% sand

Silt
0%-12% clay
80%-100% silt
0%-15% sand

Evaluating Drainage

First, look for obvious signs of poor drainage, such as standing water, areas that remain wet or muddy, or a white crust on the soil in low spots. A white crust is caused by water evaporating from the surface of the soil instead of moving down through the soil. You may detect some of these signs, or you may find no obvious evidence of poor drainage.

In either case, looking at your soil profile will be helpful. It can provide you with clues to existing drainage problems, and it can tell you if you're likely to have problems in the future. Dig a hole 3 feet deep, or as deep as you can, and look at the layers of soil (see Soil Profile on page 84).

A soil profile can point to several possible causes of poor drainage. If the subsoil is a tight-textured clay, you can expect poor drainage. Another cause of poor drainage is a soil pan—a hard or impervious layer in the subsoil. Poor drainage can also be caused by strongly contrasting layers of soil, such as a layer of fine-textured clay on top of a layer of gravelly soil. Water must saturate one texture before it can move into the next. Water drains faster through a soil profile when the layers are of a uniform texture, preferably loose and porous.

Test your drainage by filling the hole with water. (You can perform this test in a hole 2 feet deep by any width, even one made by a posthole digger.) Allow the water to drain completely so that the surrounding soil is saturated. Fill the hole again and note the rate of drop in the water level. The level should drop at least 6 inches in a 24-hour period (that equals ¼ inch per hour). This is adequate drainage, because more than 6 inches of rainfall or irrigation is unlikely to occur in a single day. If the level drops less than 6 inches, the soil drains too slowly.

See page 101 for ways to improve drainage and to deal with soil pans.

Testing for pH

Home soil-test kits give approximate, but useful, pH readings—that is, the relative acidity or alkalinity of the soil. (See Soil pH on page 86.) Some kits provide strips of paper that can be pressed against wet soil. Others provide a special liquid into which a sample of soil is placed. In most cases pH is

TAKING A SOIL SAMPLE

Whether you're using a home soil-test kit or sending the sample to a laboratory, it's important that the sample be truly representative of your soil. Here's a good method for collecting soil for your sample.

1. Determine which areas you want to test. Make separate tests for lawns, vegetable gardens, flower beds, and any other special-use areas in your landscape.

2. With a clean shovel dig a hole about 12 inches deep.

3. From the side of the hole, take a ½-inch slice of soil along the full 12 inches. Discard the top ½ inch of the slice. (A coring tool is a handy device that allows you to take a soil sample without all the digging. You simply plunge the hollow cylinder into the ground and extract a core of soil.)

4. Place this soil slice into a clean bucket and remove any obvious rocks or litter.

5. Take at least five such samples from each test area.

6. Thoroughly mix all five samples together in the bucket. This makes a sample that is average for the test area.

If a laboratory is conducting the test, send a pint of soil mixture from each test area in separate unbreakable containers, along with any information you know about the history of your soil. Note whether it has been limed, fertilized, or amended in the past five years and also indicate what you want to plant there.

Many states perform soil tests for home gardeners free or for a nominal charge. Contact a state university or cooperative extension office for information. Inquire about commercial soil-testing laboratories through a local nursery or check the telephone book.

TAKING SOIL SAMPLES

Take a soil sample by scraping the side of a hole you dig with a shovel.

With this hollow rod, you can extract a soil sample without digging.

read by comparing a color change with a chart. A soil-testing laboratory can perform a more accurate test. If your pH is too acid or too alkaline, you can alter it (see page 97).

Testing for Salts and Nutrients

An electrical conductivity test will determine whether your soil has excess salt. This situation is common in low-rainfall areas of the arid western United States (see Salty Soils on page 87). This test is simple, but it requires special equipment, so it should be done by a soil laboratory.

The levels of nutrients in the soil can be measured, but taking accurate measurements is tricky. It is usually simpler and cheaper for the home gardener to add fertilizers routinely than to add them according to the needs of the soil, as farmers do.

IMPROVING THE SOIL

There is no reason to garden in a difficult soil, if the soil can be improved. Some problems are easily remedied, often simply by adding organic matter on a regular basis or by altering the pH. The joy of digging in rich, workable soil and tending healthy, flourishing plants more than compensates for the effort that must be expended to improve your soil.

Soil Amendments

Organic materials that are dug into the soil to improve drainage, aeration, structure, microbial activity, and other soil properties are called soil amendments. By contrast, mulches are materials placed on top of the soil for purposes such as reducing erosion, preventing soil crusting, slowing evaporation, and minimizing weeding. Many of the same materials are used for mulching as for amending. In fact, mulches are often dug into the soil at the end of the gardening season to become amendments.

The most common soil amendments are described on pages 94 to 96. There may be other good amendments available locally in your area.

Organic materials can be composted inexpensively in the backyard, but composting does require time and labor for the gardener.

Compost can be made from decomposed organic matter, such as dried leaves and lawn clippings.

Simple backyard compost bins can be constructed with such inexpensive materials as wire mesh and stakes.

Wood by-products Ground bark and sawdust are widely sold as soil amendments. Any wood by-product used as an amendment should be either well composted or fortified with nitrogen. Soil bacteria need nitrogen to fuel their decomposition of the wood. Because there isn't enough nitrogen in fresh wood, the bacteria will take it from the soil, leaving little or none for plants. Ground bark, especially from redwood and fir trees, is usually sold partly decomposed. It requires

less added nitrogen than sawdust products, which are often sold fresher. Both provide good soil aeration, and they are long lasting and available inexpensively in most areas.

Manure Animal manure of all types has long been used as a soil amendment. The nutrient value depends on the animal source and the feed that the animal received. All manures work better if they are composted first. If you obtain manure from a feedlot or farm, don't use it until it has aged at least six months, or until it loses its strong odor. Since manure is high in salts, add only a small amount each year. Leach water through the manure to dissolve the salt and carry it into the subsoil before planting. Chicken manure is particularly salty. Manures often carry weed seeds, depending on where the animals were grazing.

Peat moss The longest lasting of the organic amendments, peat is derived from moss from ancient swamps. Although peat moss is difficult to wet thoroughly, it retains moisture well and drains superbly. It has an acidic effect (its pH is 3.5 to 4.5) that may be desirable for acid-loving plants. You can neutralize this

40% AMENDMENT

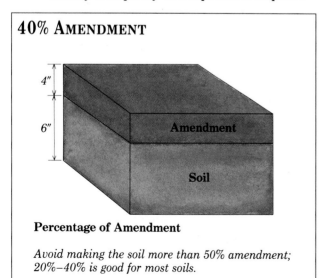

Percentage of Amendment

Avoid making the soil more than 50% amendment; 20%–40% is good for most soils.

acidity by adding 5 pounds of lime per 100 square feet of 4-inch-deep peat moss.

In some areas other types of peat, such as sedge peat, are available, but these are inferior to peat moss as a soil amendment. Sphagnum moss is sometimes confused with peat moss; this is moss that is dried but not decomposed. Sphagnum moss is fine when used as a packing material, in making hanging baskets, and for covering the surfaces of pots, but it should not be used as a soil amendment.

Crop by-products   These include a wide variety of materials. Peanut hulls, cottonseed meal, and bagasse (a sugarcane by-product) are often sold as soil amendments in the South. Ground corncobs are available in the Midwest. Rice hulls and cocoa-bean hulls are frequently sold in the West. Straw, a

MAKING COMPOST

A properly made compost pile heats up enough (about 160° F) to kill weed seeds, insect eggs, and most disease-causing organisms. If the pile is to attain this temperature, there must be a balance between nitrogen and carbon as well as adequate moisture, oxygen, and mass. A pile measuring 3 feet by 3 feet by 3 feet is about the minimum size for effective composting.

Begin by gathering garden refuse, dried leaves, lawn clippings, and organic kitchen scraps, such as fruit and vegetable wastes, coffee grounds, and eggshells. Do not add meat, bones, or fat, since they take too long to decompose and may attract flies and rodents. Cut the materials as finely as possible. Small particles have a greater surface area exposed to moisture, air, and soil bacteria.

In building the pile, remember to balance high-nitrogen green matter (green plant refuse, kitchen scraps, manure, and nitrogen fertilizers) with material high in carbon (yellow or dried plant matter, such as dead leaves, sawdust, and straw). Be sure to moisten all dried materials when adding them.

Dried materials alone, such as all dead leaves, will not heat up because there is not enough nitrogen. If the pile doesn't have enough green matter, add a few handfuls of a nitrogen-rich fertilizer to maintain the balance.

If you don't have manure to add to the pile, sprinkle some garden soil or aged compost on each layer to provide the microorganisms necessary for the composting.

If you turn the pile every day, the compost will be ready in as little as two weeks. Or you can use a slower method that requires less turning. Place an iron pipe or a crowbar in the pile to serve as a thermometer. After a week, the pipe will be too hot to hold. It will begin to cool down after a few weeks. Turn the compost pile as soon as you notice that the temperature is dropping. The pile has cooled down because it is no longer receiving enough oxygen. Turning it allows air to reach all parts of the pile, which will cause it to heat up again. The pile will probably need to be watered as you turn it.

You will know the compost is ready when it has decomposed into a uniform, dark, crumbly material.

COMPOSTING PROBLEMS

Here are some common composting problems and their solutions.

The Pile Doesn't Heat Up
• The pile may be too small. Rebuild it, adding material to make it larger.
• The pile may be too dry. Rebuild it, watering it as you go. Because it's difficult to wet the pile uniformly by top watering, it is important to moisten dry materials when you add them.
• The pile may have too much dried material and too little nitrogen. Turn it and add some high-nitrogen fertilizer or leafy green organic matter.

The Pile Smells Bad
• If it smells like ammonia, it contains too much nitrogen. Layer in some straw, leaves, or sawdust.
• If it smells like rotten eggs, it is too wet. Turn it and add some dry material.

The Pile Attracts Pests
• If the pile attracts insects, rodents, or dogs, there may be some meat or manure from a meat-eating animal in the pile. Remove the material or bury it deep within the pile. If the pile attracts insects, take measures to warm it up, such as shredding the material as finely as possible, adding sufficient nitrogen, and turning the pile often. Insects cannot tolerate the heat of a working compost pile, and after it cools, it is too decomposed to be of interest to them.

traditional mulch, especially in the East, must be supplemented with nitrogen when it is dug into the ground. It often carries weed seeds. In addition to the products listed here, there may be others available in your area.

Compost   You can make your own compost, or decomposed organic matter, from garden refuse, dried leaves, lawn clippings, and organic kitchen waste. (See page 95 for details on making compost.) When the process is properly managed, the high heat (160° F) of decomposition kills most weed seeds, insect eggs, and disease organisms. Compost makes an excellent, nutrient-rich amendment that is not only free but saves on dump costs.

Lawn clippings   If you have a lawn, clippings are plentiful and free. Moderate amounts of lawn clippings can be worked directly into the soil without composting. If your grass has gone to seed or if it is a variety that grows from its stems, such as Bermuda grass, be sure to compost it first. Otherwise, you will have to weed lawn grass out of your planting beds.

Leaf mold   Decomposed leaf material, or leaf mold, is sometimes sold commercially. If you have a lot of deciduous trees, you can gather leaves and compost them yourself. The leaf mold may be acidic, depending on the leaves used, making it a favored amendment for acid-loving plants, such as azaleas and rhododendrons.

Fertilizers as Soil Amendments
If a laboratory test has indicated specific nutrient deficiencies in your soil, you can add the missing nutrients before planting. They are usually added in the form of commercial fertilizers, which clearly state their nutrient content on the label. Although organic soil amendments release nutrients as they break down in the soil, the content and amount of nutrients is extremely variable. Not all organic matter contributes the same nutrients or has the same effect in soil.

Most commercial fertilizers contain three primary nutrients: nitrogen, phosphorus, and potassium. Many fertilizers supply additional elements, such as iron and zinc, that may be lacking in the soil. If you don't know exactly which nutrients are missing from your soil, an all-purpose fertilizer will satisfy the requirements of most plants. See pages 165 to 183 for more information on fertilizers.

GROUND LIMESTONE: AMOUNTS TO RAISE SOIL pH

(Pounds of Ground Limestone per 1,000 Square Feet**)

Change in pH Desired	Sandy	Sandy Loam	Loam	Silt Loam	Clay Loam
4.0–6.5	60	115	161	193	230
4.5–6.5	51	96	133	161	193
5.0–6.5	41	78	106	129	152
5.5–6.5	28	60	78	92	106
6.0–6.5	14	32	41	51	55

SOIL SULFUR: AMOUNTS TO LOWER SOIL pH

(Pounds of Soil Sulfur per 1,000 Square Feet)

Change in pH Desired	Sandy	Loam	Clay
8.5–6.5	46	57	69
8.0–6.5	28	34	46
7.5–6.5	11	18	23
7.0–6.5	2	4	7

** In the southern and coastal states, reduce the application by approximately one half.

Correcting Soil pH

Soil that is too acidic or too alkaline (see Testing for pH on page 91) can be corrected fairly easily.

If the soil is too acid, a common condition in the eastern United States, add ground limestone. One type, called dolomitic lime, supplies calcium and magnesium, nutrients in short supply in acid soils. Nitrogen fertilizers containing nitrate (rather than ammonium or urea) will also raise the pH.

The clay soils of the western United States are often too alkaline, particularly for acid-loving plants. To acidify these soils apply soil sulfur. You can also apply aluminum sulfate or ferrous sulfate, but they aren't as effective as soil sulfur since they contain less sulfur, the acidifying agent. Regular use of acidifying mulches, such as conifer needles, also helps. Maintain the acidity by fertilizing with nitrogen fertilizers containing urea or ammonium. These are often labeled for use on acid-loving plants.

The amount of sulfur or lime you'll need to add depends on the type of soil you have and how much you want to change the pH. If you have your soil tested professionally, the report will indicate how much to add. Otherwise, consult the chart on page 96 and add the amount of lime or sulfur recommended for your soil type. (See page 85 for information about your soil texture.)

After adding the recommended amount of lime or sulfur, till it in well. The lime reacts quickly; you can retest the pH soon after adding it. Repeat the application if necessary. Sulfur reacts more slowly; wait a month before retesting the pH.

Preparing the Soil for Planting

Before planting, the soil should be cultivated. This process of loosening the soil and turning over amendments increases aeration, which improves drainage and root growth. Do not try to cultivate soil that is too wet or too dry. The moisture content is an important consideration in all but the sandiest soils, but it is especially important in clay soils.

When clay soils are too wet, cultivating can compact the particles and destroy the structure of the soil. To test the soil, turn over a shovelful and try to break a clod. If it breaks easily, it is ready to be worked. If it is

too sticky to break, wait a few more days. If the clods are too hard to break, they have dried too long. Soak the soil thoroughly and let it drain for a day or two. When the soil clods break easily, you're ready to prepare the planting area.

First, remove any debris that you don't want to incorporate into the soil. Then spread soil amendments (see page 92) and fertilizer (see page 96), and mix them into the soil. Till by hand or, if the planting area is large, use a rotary tiller.

Tilling by hand Divide the soil into rows and dig one row at a time with a shovel, spade, or fork. Turn the soil on its side, not upside down, so that any weeds are buried but do not make a layer in the soil. Forks are more effective in sandy and loamy soils. Spades work best in clay soil and soil that has not been cultivated before. Shovels are general-purpose tools that can be used in any situation. Shovels and forks turn over about 6 inches of soil. It is possible, although difficult, to turn over about 8 inches with a spade.

Using a rotary tiller If the soil is heavy and hard to dig, it may be necessary to make several passes across the garden with a rotary tiller, with each pass tilling a couple of inches deeper than the one before. Make these successive passes at right angles to one another. Tillers do not reach into corners well, so plan to do the corners by hand. Unless the tiller is especially large, it will till about 6 inches deep.

Smoothing the bed After tilling, use a cultivator to smooth the surface. For a seedbed in which more finely textured soil is desired, use a garden rake. A quick way to dispose of hard clods and rocks that you rake up is to dig a deep hole at the end of the planting bed and bury them. Make sure that they're buried below tilling depth or you'll have to deal with the rocks again next year.

Preparing for a Lawn

Properly preparing the soil for a lawn is as crucial to the success of the lawn as the choice of grass and the later care you give the area. Regardless of the planting technique, the soil preparation is the same, except that

DOUBLE-DIGGING

This method of soil cultivation incorporates air and organic material deep into the root zone of the plants. Double-digging is especially beneficial for vegetable gardens. Most ornamental plants don't need double-dug beds.

1. Spread a layer of compost or another organic soil amendment over the entire planting area.

2. With a spade dig a trench 1' wide and one spade deep. Place the soil in a pile at the end of the planting bed.

3. Loosen the soil in the bottom of the trench.

4. Dig a second trench adjacent to the first and throw the soil forward into the first trench. Mix the soil and amendment together with the spade.

5. Loosen the soil in the bottom of the second trench.

6. Continue this procedure for the remaining trenches. Fill the last trench with the soil you removed from the first.

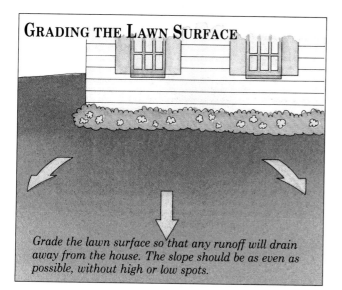

GRADING THE LAWN SURFACE

Grade the lawn surface so that any runoff will drain away from the house. The slope should be as even as possible, without high or low spots.

Soil tests will indicate the kinds of amendments that should be added to your soil before cultivating it.

the grade level should be ¾ inch lower for a sod lawn, to allow for the thickness of the sod pieces. After completing the following steps, refer to pages 122 to 127 for instructions on planting the lawn.

Clearing the soil   Remove rocks and other debris. If there are any desirable plants growing on the site, dig them up and transplant them. If you are replacing an old lawn, remove the grass with a sod cutter. Kill any existing weeds with an herbicide and remove the weeds after they are dead. (See Using Herbicides on page 266.) Dig out any roots that will interfere with a tiller.

Rough-grading the area   Create a slight slope away from the house so that rainwater will drain away from the foundation. In high-rainfall areas make a slope of at least 1 to 2 percent (a drop of 1 to 2 feet per 100 feet). When grading around trees, don't change the soil level around the trunk, and avoid exposing tree roots.

Killing weed seeds   You can kill weed seeds by watering the soil daily for a month and killing newly sprouted weeds with an herbicide or shallow tilling (see Killing Weeds on page 264).

An alternative is to sterilize the soil with vapam, a fumigant available to the homeowner. It kills everything in the soil, including weed seeds. Allow six weeks for the gas to escape from the soil before planting. Follow label instructions carefully.

Adding soil amendments   Add amendments as indicated by your soil tests (see pages 90 to 97). These may include organic matter to improve soil structure, additional topsoil if your soil has a thin top layer, or lime or sulfur to correct the pH. Apply a high-phosphorus starter fertilizer now. (A complete fertilizer should be applied after the lawn is planted.) Cultivate thoroughly with a tiller.

Installing an irrigation system   If you want an underground sprinkler system it should be installed before the final grading. The tilled soil will be easy to dig in for placing underground pipes and sprinkler heads. See pages 150 to 154 for details on installing one.

Finishing the final grading   Rake and smooth the area thoroughly. If the soil is not level, water will collect in low spots, and the mower will scalp high spots.

An underground sprinkler system should be installed after the soil has been cultivated.

Once the amendments have been spread, turn them evenly into the soil with a spade.

After the soil has been cultivated, add the amendments and spread evenly with a rake.

Mowing strips help to prevent grass from creeping beyond the lawn area.

Installing boundaries   Header boards or mowing strips make the lawn look neater and help prevent the grass from creeping out beyond the lawn area.

Rolling   Use a roller half-filled with water. Rake the ground level again, water to settle it, and roll once more. If the roller causes spots to settle, repeat the cycle several times until the ground is level after rolling. Three or four rollings and rakings may be necessary.

IMPROVING DRAINAGE

Most plants demand good drainage. If the soil doesn't drain well, the root zone becomes saturated with water, leaving no room for air and causing plants to suffocate. Fortunately, the most common drainage problems are fairly easy to identify and correct. The easiest and least expensive ways to correct poor drainage are to add organic matter to the soil, to garden in raised beds, and to construct a simple dry well—a deep hole filled with porous gravel or rock. Wait to make any decisions about drainage until you have observed the drainage patterns in your garden over the course of a year.

Correcting Slow Drainage

As explained on page 84, your soil profile can point to three major causes of slow or obstructed drainage: a very tight-textured soil, a soil pan (a hard or impervious layer in the soil), and abrupt changes in soil texture.

You can improve a slow-draining, tightly textured clay soil by adding organic matter. Organic matter helps structure soil so that it drains well while holding moisture. (See Soil Structure on page 86.) So much organic matter is required to significantly change the structure of an adobe or heavy clay soil that gardeners often give up in frustration. There are alternatives: You can either garden in raised beds (see page 102) filled with improved soil or you can grow plants that thrive in the native soil.

Beware of adding sand to heavy clay soil to improve drainage. Unless the resulting blend is more than 80 percent sand, the amended soil will have worse drainage than clay alone. The clay will fill in the spaces between the sand particles, acting like cement. If you hit a soil pan, the simplest way to provide drainage is to break up the pan with a pick or crowbar. In severe cases you may need a jackhammer or a well auger to break through. You do not have to remove the soil pan completely, just provide a way for the water to pass through it under each plant. Again, if the problem is very severe, you may decide to plant in raised beds.

If you determine that abrupt changes in soil texture are the cause of poor drainage, you can improve the situation by making the soil more homogeneous.

LAYING A DRAIN LINE

If you have drainage problems caused by a high water table or if your property is graded so that water collects in the yard or around structures, then you may want to install a drain line. A system of drain lines under the garden or along retaining walls will carry water away safely.

1. A slight slope (at least 1 foot drop for each 100 lateral feet) is necessary for water to drain. First, locate the outfall, or the place where water will leave the drain line. Plan backward toward the area that needs draining to see how deep you can install the drain line. The elevation of the outfall often limits the depth of the drain line. Because the water table cannot rise higher than the drain line (the water drains away as it reaches the level of the pipe), install the drain line as deep as you want the water table to be. Most trees need at least 4 feet of drained soil, but a lawn needs only about 2 feet.

2. Dig a trench from the outfall to the area you wish to drain. The steeper the pitch, the less likely it will be to fill with silt and plug up later. Line the bottom of the trench with a couple of inches of sand, and lay the drain line in it. Flexible, corrugated drain line is easiest to work with. The holes in the pipe should be facedown.

3. Cover the line with 4 inches of drain rock, then backfill the ditch with soil. To drain a large area, run several parallel lines about 6 feet apart.

Till through the layers to break them up and then mix the different soils together.

Raised beds are useful for separating flower and vegetable beds and make it easier to work around them.

Raised beds can be placed in a sloping landscape to achieve a level garden area.

GARDENING IN RAISED BEDS

The raised bed is one of the oldest concepts in gardening history. Wherever soil conditions and drainage problems have made good gardens difficult, the solution has been to plant above the ground level. The raised soil can stand alone—for example, a mound—or it can be framed with such materials as wood, stone, brick, and concrete. Above are two examples of raised beds that are easy to build and maintain.

Correcting Fast-Draining Sandy Soil

When performing the drainage test (see Evaluating Drainage on page 91), you may find that your soil drains very quickly. For fast-draining soils, the length of time it takes the water to drain is not as important as its water-holding capacity. Some loamy soils may drain fast but still hold water in the spaces between soil particles. On the other hand, very sandy soils drain quite quickly—sometimes in a matter of minutes—but without retaining much water.

A fast-draining loamy soil doesn't need any correction. Improve the water-holding capacity of sandy soil by adding organic matter. (If you don't know your soil type, see page 90 to find out how to identify it.)

MULCHING

A mulch is a protective layer of material spread on the surface of the soil. Mulching is one of the simplest but most effective measures you can take to protect your soil and make it a more hospitable environment for your plants.

Mulch conserves soil moisture so that plants can go longer between waterings. Mulch also insulates the soil: In summer it keeps the soil cool and prevents crusting; in winter it shields plants from the cold and helps prevent the cycle of freezing and thawing that kills many plants.

Mulching helps protect the soil from erosion and keeps it from being compacted by foot traffic and heavy rains. A thick layer of mulch reduces runoff by slowing the flow of rain and irrigation water and letting it trickle into the soil. Mulching is invaluable for weed control: It keeps most weeds from sprouting, and those that do grow are easier to pull.

A mulch can be either organic, such as bark, or inorganic, such as stone chips. Generally, organic mulches are used in planting beds. As they break down, they improve the fertility and structure of the soil.

If you have experienced problems with a fungus disease, you may want to remove all the old mulch yearly and replace it with clean, fresh material. Doing this in early fall prevents disease organisms from wintering over in the soil.

Mulching Materials

Almost any organic material can be used as mulch. Your choice will depend primarily on what's available in your area. Other considerations may include cost, appearance, longevity, and ease of application. Some mulches to avoid are rice hulls, which are so light and fluffy that they are carried away by the wind, and peat moss, which mats together and repels water—if it doesn't blow away first. Avoid mulches that may contain weed seeds and other weed parts. If you select an inorganic mulch, keep in mind that it will do nothing to improve soil tilth (suitability to grow plants) or quality.

Bark   Both shredded and chunk bark from fir, pine, cedar, or redwood trees make an attractive, long-lasting mulch. They break down over time and improve the soil. Medium and coarse grades make longer-lasting mulch; a fine grade breaks down faster and is more suitable for amending the soil.

Wood chips   Tree trimmings that have been put through a chipper are often available free of charge from tree trimming companies. The chipped material is not as uniform or as attractive as shredded or chunk bark, but the chips make a satisfactory mulch. The chips are often mixed with green leaves and twigs. During the first year, this green matter decomposes and disappears, and the thickness of the mulch shrinks by as much as 50 percent. It isn't necessary to fortify wood chips with nitrogen unless you dig them into the soil as an amendment (see Wood By-products on page 94).

Pine needles   An attractive and fairly long-lasting mulch, pine needles can often be gathered for free. The needles are acidic and provide good aeration for surface roots, making them ideal for acid-loving plants such as azaleas, camellias, and rhododendrons.

Crop by-products   These include such materials as ground corncobs, sugarcane bagasse, and the hulls of cocoa beans, buckwheat, peanuts, and other seeds. All of these are long lasting and usually inexpensive in areas where they are produced. Straw is a traditional mulch in rural areas. Although it

A bark mulch can look attractive in the garden as well as help improve the soil over time.

breaks down quickly, it can be tilled in to improve the soil. Straw frequently carries grain and weed seeds, and it should not be used where it could be ignited.

Lawn clippings and raked leaves   Leaves and lawn clippings make satisfactory mulches, provided that they are either composted first or spread in a thin layer—no more than 2 inches deep. If applied thick, when fresh, these materials may form an impermeable mat on the surface of the soil. Do not use clippings from a weedy lawn or one that has been sprayed recently with an herbicide.

Gravel and crushed rock   These inorganic materials make attractive ornamental mulches. They do not have the soil-building properties of organic mulches, but they discourage weeds, control soil temperature, curtail evaporation, and help stop erosion. They don't reduce in volume over time, as the organic mulches do. Gravel and crushed rock are used primarily on pathways and other unplanted areas.

Applying Mulch

Mulch in spring after the soil has warmed up and after any early weeds have been removed. If you mulch too early, you will insulate the soil and it will not warm up as quickly as it would otherwise. Spread the mulch 2 to 4 inches thick, tapering off toward the base of the plants. (A thick layer of mulch around the base of a plant encourages pests and diseases.)

Mulches can also be used to insulate the soil to prevent frost heaving, the forcing of a plant from the ground when the soil alternately freezes and thaws. In late fall, after the ground freezes, spread a thick layer of a fluffy material, such as pine boughs or straw, over the entire bed. The mulch will shade and insulate the soil, keeping it frozen until the following spring.

Estimating the Amount of Mulch

Most mulches are applied 2 to 4 inches thick. A coarse mulch, such as chunk bark, or a mulch that decomposes rapidly, such as fresh wood chips, can be applied as thick as 6 inches. Use one of the following formulas to calculate the amount of mulch you need.

Cubic feet of mulch = area to be covered (in square feet) × depth of mulch (in inches) ÷ 12

Cubic yards of mulch = area to be covered (in square feet) × depth of mulch (in inches) ÷ 324

For example, if your garden is 20 by 20 feet (400 square feet) and you want to apply a 3-inch-thick layer of mulch, you can calculate the amount like this.

400 × 3 ÷ 12 = 100 cubic feet, or
400 × 3 ÷ 324 = 3.7 cubic yards

POTTING MIXES

A good container mix drains quickly while holding water, and it is free of insects, disease organisms, and weed seeds. Garden soil, even good loam, usually doesn't have all those characteristics. Any problems you've had growing plants in your garden soil will only intensify in the confined environment of a container. Potted plants have a better chance of thriving in a mix formulated especially for containers.

Ready-made bagged potting mixes are available in nurseries and garden centers.

Common ingredients in these mixes include peat moss, ground wood, sand, perlite, and vermiculite. Some manufacturers add ground corncobs and other crop by-products available locally. Most container mixes also have small quantities of nutrients for plant growth.

Because the quality of these mixes varies, usually the only way to judge a mix is to try it. If your plants thrive in it, if you don't have to water too often, and if no problems develop in a few months, it is a good mix.

Making Your Own Potting Mix

All the recipes given here make about 1 cubic yard of potting mix. The components add up to more than 27 cubic feet (1 cubic yard), but because the particles fit into one another the mix takes up less space than its separate ingredients. For making smaller amounts, substitute half gallons for cubic feet and ounces for pounds.

The mixes call for readily available sterile ingredients. You can substitute locally available materials that may be less expensive. It's a good idea to experiment with small batches and grow plants in the mix for several months before drawing a conclusion about it.

Heavy mix   This is a basic potting mix based on sand, sawdust, and peat moss. It is lighter than garden soil but heavy enough to keep most containers from blowing over in a breeze. It is also relatively inexpensive. This mix can be made lighter by substituting perlite for any part of the sand.

11 cubic feet peat moss
11 cubic feet sand
11 cubic feet sawdust
5 pounds 5-10-10 fertilizer
5 pounds ground limestone

Light mix   Based on peat, perlite, and vermiculite, this lightweight mix is good for rooftop containers and large pots that must be moved. It does not contain any sand.

21 cubic feet peat moss
6 cubic feet vermiculite
6 cubic feet perlite
5 pounds 5-10-10 fertilizer
8 pounds ground limestone

Add vermiculite to potting soil to ensure that there will be fast drainage.

Hold the plant securely and tap the roots out of the container.

Position the plant in a new pot containing the soil with vermiculite.

Firm the soil around the plant's roots and water the soil well.

Special mixes For acid-loving plants, such as azaleas (*Rhododendron* species) and camellias (*Camellia* species), you can use either of the mixes above but leave out the limestone and add 1 pound iron sulfate. Azaleas are often grown commercially in straight peat moss or a combination of peat moss and ground bark.

For plants that need quick drainage, such as cactus, increase the proportion of sand or perlite in one of the above mixes to 75 percent of the mix.

For shade-loving plants, such as begonias (*Begonia* species) and piggyback plant (*Tolmiea menziesii*), substitute ground bark or leaf mold for the sawdust in the heavy mix, reduce the limestone to 2 pounds, and add 1 pound iron sulfate.

For starting seeds, use an unmixed horticultural-grade vermiculite. Don't add nutrients until the first true leaves open.

For rooting cuttings, mix 5 parts perlite to 1 part peat moss. Don't add nutrients until you transplant the young rooted plants to a potting mix.

Using garden soil Soilless potting mixes use sterile ingredients. They have better drainage and better water-retaining properties than soil-based mixes. However, if you want to use garden soil in a potting mix, this combination works well.

1 part good garden soil
1 part sand
1 part peat moss or leaf mold

PLANTING

Like most gardeners you are probably filled with great expectations when you buy a packet of seeds or a healthy plant from a nursery. You envision the plant growing surely and swiftly into a mature specimen that adds beauty to your garden or abounds with flowers or fruit—and you are disappointed when the plant doesn't perform as expected. Growth may be negligible, or the plant may decline and even die.

Disappointing performance often is directly attributable to poor handling and inappropriate planting. Plants come in many forms—seeds, flats, cell packs, small pots, large cans, bare root, balled and burlapped, and sod—and each requires a different planting technique. By following the correct technique, you will increase your chances of success. When a plant is properly set in the ground, it is better able to spread its roots into neighboring soil and obtain the nutrients it requires to grow.

Many crops in a vegetable garden are direct seeded either because they germinate and grow so easily (beans, corn, squash) or because they don't transplant well (carrots and other root crops). Other plants, such as tomatoes and eggplant, should be set out as transplants if they are to bear fruit early enough in the season.

Seeds can be started in flats and pots from the nursery, but any small disposable container will work just as well.

WHEN TO PLANT

In cold climates spring is the favored planting time, although hardy plants can often be planted in fall. In mild-winter areas fall is the best time to set out most plants. The soil is still warm enough to foster root growth, there is ample time for plants to become established before the stress of hot weather, and watering is less critical. Winter rains in many areas help in this task. In all climates bare-root plants must be planted during the dormant season.

Some wilting is natural immediately after planting, but you can minimize the problem by planting during the relatively cool weather of the morning and evening or by planting on overcast or misty days. However, never plant if the soil is very wet. Working wet soil compresses it, driving out the air and suffocating the roots. Try not to plant when it is windy or extremely hot and sunny, but if it can't be avoided, protect the plants with a screen and be sure to provide ample moisture.

PLANTING SEEDS OUTDOORS

The seeds of many plants can be sown directly in the ground where you want the plants to grow. Direct seeding is simpler than starting seeds indoors and transplanting them outside, and it requires no special equipment. However, the germination rate outdoors is lower than indoors; about 60 percent of the seeds will sprout outdoors. You can expect to lose some seedlings to the weather and to animals and insects. You'll have the additional task of distinguishing seedlings from weeds. When planting seeds outdoors, it is wise to sow twice as many seeds as you need.

The seeds of some plants should not be sown directly in the ground. The seeds of beans, peas, corn, and squash germinate and grow so easily that there is no need to start them indoors. Other plants—such as California poppy (*Eschscholzia californica*) and vegetable root crops, such as carrots and beets—don't transplant well and should be seeded in place.

Pot marigold (*Calendula officinalis*), sweet pea (*Lathyrus odoratus*), and other hardy annuals can be sown directly in the ground in very early spring. In mild-winter areas they can be planted in fall. Some half-hardy annuals, such as cosmos (*Cosmos* species) and nasturtium (*Tropaeolum majus*), can be sown directly in the ground in spring after all danger of frost has passed. Tender annuals, such as cockscomb (*Celosia cristata*) and eggplant, should not be set out or sown outdoors until the soil is thoroughly warm. It is better to start them indoors to get a jump on the season; otherwise, these tender plants won't start blooming and won't be ready for harvest until late in the season.

Before planting seeds outdoors, you should determine the right number of plants for your needs, the amount of space the mature plants will need, and the times at which the particular varieties you've chosen should be planted. Seed catalogs and packets provide useful information. Make sure that the season is right for planting the varieties you've chosen. Soil temperature is an important factor in seed germination: Seeds of warm-weather plants, for example, rot in cold, wet soil.

Planting the Seeds

Properly prepared soil increases your chances of success (see Preparing the Soil for Planting on page 97). If necessary, water the ground the day before planting so that the soil will be moist but not wet. You can improve germination by filling each planting furrow or hole with a small amount of packaged soil mix. This will give you a finer growing medium that holds moisture well, usually contains some nutrients, and won't form a crust over the seeds.

Make furrows or dig holes for the seeds. The planting method you use will depend on the plant. Seed packets usually provide important planting information: the best planting method to use; any treatment, such as soaking, that the seeds may need; and how deep to plant the seeds. Seeds that are planted too deep or too shallow may not germinate. A rule of thumb is to plant seeds to a depth of approximately three to four times their diameter. Weigh this rule against your own judgment. If the weather is wet or the soil is heavy, plant shallower. If dry weather is expected and the soil is light and sandy, plant deeper.

Large seeds are easy to plant, but small seeds are difficult to sow evenly. There are several methods you can use to distribute them more uniformly. One method is to mix the seeds with an equal amount of sand, flour, or cornmeal and distribute the mixture in the planting area. Another method is to take a pinch of seeds between your thumb and forefinger and rub your fingers together, letting the seeds fall over the planting area. A third method is to place pieces of tissue paper in a shallow furrow and mist them to keep them from blowing away. Shake the seeds onto the tissue, enabling you to see them, then distribute them evenly. Some vegetable and flower seeds are available on seed tapes. The seeds are properly spaced on the tape, which disintegrates from moisture in the soil.

Seeds should be pressed into the soil with your hand, the flat side of a small board, or the back of a hoe. Seed packets specify whether the seeds should be covered. Some seeds need light to stimulate germination, but most prefer darkness and need to be covered. When you cover seeds press the soil

down if it is dry or sandy, and leave it loose if it is wet or heavy. Seeds sprout better and faster if covered with sand rather than a garden soil containing clay. Seedlings can push through sand more easily.

Caring for the Seedbed

Since seeds need moisture for germination, keep the soil evenly moist. Use a fine spray or mist attachment on your garden hose. A strong spray may wash away the seeds or developing seedlings.

A light mulch of peat moss, ground fir bark, or compost over the seeds will help keep the seedbed moist during hot, dry

A fine spray or mist attachment on your garden hose will keep seeds and developing seedlings from washing away.

A flat can be enclosed in a clear plastic bag held up with a wire hoop.

weather. Shade the seedbed if sunlight is intense and drying, but remove the shade cloth or other covering as soon as the seeds begin to germinate. If the seedlings develop in the dark, they will grow long, weak stems and stretch toward the light.

Once the seedlings have developed true leaves (the first set of leaves are cotyledons, or seed leaves), be sure to thin the plants to the spacing that is recommended on the seed packet. It is best to be ruthless at this stage to prevent an overcrowded planting. Use a pair of scissors to snip off the unwanted plants rather than trying to pull them out. The roots of several plants may be intertwined, and pulling one plant may result in removing several.

STARTING SEEDS INDOORS

You can get a head start on the growing season by starting plants indoors. Many vegetables and flowers can be started in a sunny window four to six weeks before they could normally be set out in the garden. Plants begun as transplants also avoid some of the hazards common to seedlings—damage from birds, insects, and heavy rain and competition from weeds.

You can use almost any kind of container for starting seeds as long as it has drainage holes in the bottom and holds at least 3 tablespoons of soil. Some gardeners purchase commercial seed-starting kits. Others buy containers that are sold especially for starting seeds. These may be reusable (flats, trays, and pots) or suitable for only a single planting (peat pots and pellets). Paper cups, milk cartons, margarine tubs, and other containers found in the kitchen work just as well. The depressions in egg cartons are too small.

If the containers have been previously used for growing plants, sterilize them before reuse: Clean them thoroughly with hot water and soap, soak them for 30 minutes in a solution of 1 part household bleach to 9 parts water, rinse well, and let them dry.

You can use a commercial potting mix or make your own (see Potting Mixes on page 104). Fill the containers to within ½ inch of the top and water thoroughly. Let the containers drain before planting the seeds. Make shallow indentations in the potting mix and distribute the seeds in these furrows. Press the seeds onto the soil and sprinkle them lightly with ground sphagnum moss. Large seeds should be planted to a depth twice their thickness.

The edge of a ruler pressed into the soil makes a neat, straight furrow in which to sow seeds. Once the seedlings have developed a set of true leaves, they can be moved into small containers.

Transplant seedlings into individual pots by lifting them gently by their leaves while supporting their roots.

If you are using peat pellets as containers, soak the pellets until they swell with moisture. Insert two seeds into the top of each pellet. If both germinate snip out the weaker one.

Label the seed containers and place them in bright but indirect light. Fluorescent lights can help if your seed-raising environment has poor light or if the natural light is dim. Use a 40-watt bulb placed 6 inches from the seedbed and leave it on 24 hours a day until the seeds germinate.

Until germination, keep the seeds warm and moist by covering the container with plastic, glass, or moist paper towels. Moisture is especially crucial for small seeds, which can dry out easily. Maintain a temperature of 70° to 75° F for the germinating seeds, unless the seed packet specifies otherwise. If the indoor temperature is lower than the desired range, you can try placing the seed containers on top of a refrigerator, water heater, or television set. If that doesn't produce sufficient heat, you can purchase heating cables or a heating mat at a nursery.

When the seedlings germinate, place the container in bright light. Seedlings of sun-loving plants need full sunlight for at least four hours a day. Bright light and cool temperatures (65° to 70° F) are best for healthy growth. Too much warmth and low light produce leggy plants.

Water the seedlings every few days to keep the soil moist but not saturated. Use a fine spray or mist so that you won't wash out the seedlings as you water. If the seeds were sown in a flat or tray, move the seedlings to 2-inch pots after the first set of true leaves appears. To move the seedlings, lift them out by their leaves rather than by their stems or roots, supporting the roots, along with some soil, with a fork or spoon in your other hand.

Begin feeding the young seedlings after the first true leaves have opened fully, a few days after germination. Feed weekly with a half-strength solution of a complete fertilizer high in phosphorus. Apply a fungicide at the same time you fertilize.

Harden off seedlings (gradually acclimate them to the outdoors) when they are 2 to 4 inches high. Place them outside for gradually longer periods over a week. Cold frames help in acclimating seedlings to the outdoors. Eventually the mature seedlings will be ready for transplanting outside in the garden.

Cold Frames and Hotbeds

Some protection for seedlings outdoors can be provided by cold frames and hotbeds. These devices also take the whole process outdoors, leaving the house free of gardening clutter.

A cold frame is basically a bottomless wooden box placed on the ground (or sunk into the ground a foot or so) and filled with a good quality soil mix. The size of the box is up to you; the sides don't have to be taller than 8 to 10 inches. The essential part of a cold frame is some type of transparent or semitransparent cover. In the past the most common covers were sash windows; more often than not the size of the cold frame was dictated by whatever extra windows were available. Windows are still perfectly acceptable covers; some gardeners prefer rigid plastic or film plastic, which are unbreakable.

A cold frame resembles a small greenhouse. The best placement for it is close to the house in a location that receives plenty of sun. The cover should be adjustable to admit varying degrees of fresh air. Seeds can be started in a cold frame in the same way that they are started indoors, but it takes a little experimentation to keep the temperature within a desirable range.

In cold-winter areas cold frames work best for the early starting of hardy and half-hardy annuals. The temperature inside a cold frame is usually insufficient to germinate and protect seedlings of tender annuals.

A hotbed is a variation of a cold frame but one in which the temperature is easier to control. The structure of the unit is the same, but before the frame is filled with soil, electric heating cables are installed. Hotbeds are particularly useful in very cold weather and during long periods when there is insufficient warmth from the sun.

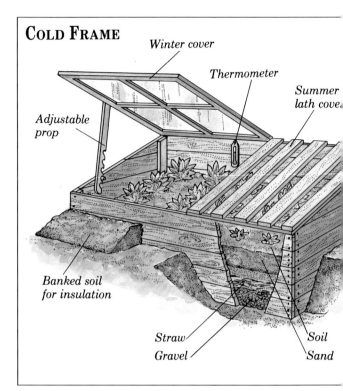

COLD FRAME

Winter cover

Thermometer

Summer lath cover

Adjustable prop

Banked soil for insulation

Straw
Gravel

Soil
Sand

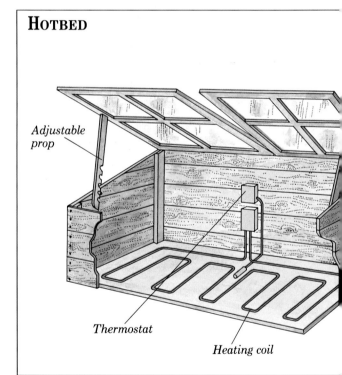

HOTBED

Adjustable prop

Thermostat

Heating coil

Both cold frames and hotbeds can be fitted with an electrical heat-sensitive mechanism that opens and closes the cover when the temperature reaches preset highs and lows. Available from greenhouse equipment suppliers, this device greatly increases the effectiveness of the cold frame and hotbed.

Peat planters come in a variety of shapes and sizes. Soak them in water a few minutes so they will swell and soften.

Put two seeds in each planter. Place the planters in a tray with water so that the planters will soak it up.

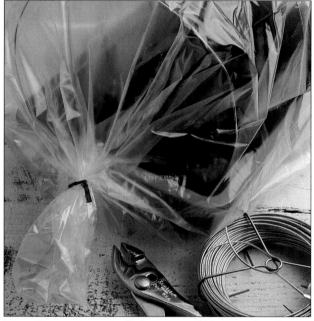

Place the tray in a plastic bag to retain heat and moisture. Put it in a warm spot out of direct sunlight.

As soon as the seedlings are big enough to handle, snip off the weaker seedling in each planter.

TRANSPLANTING SEEDLINGS

Seedlings may be plants you've purchased at the nursery in flats, cell packs, or other small containers, or they may be plants you've started indoors from seeds or cuttings (see page 343).

Don't transplant a dry plant. Seedlings in pots or other containers should be thoroughly watered and allowed to drain for 5 to 10 minutes before being removed from their containers. A damp rootball will not fall apart or stick to the edge of the container.

To remove a plant from a pot without damaging its roots, turn the pot upside down, tap the rim on a hard surface, and catch the soil ball in your hand. For plants in plastic cell packs, push up on the bottom of each cell to loosen the seedling. Pinch off any long, coiled bottom roots. If you are planting from a flat, gently pull apart the seedlings by hand; don't try to cut apart the intermingled roots. Always remove one plant at a time. The rootballs may dry out if you remove the seedlings from their containers before you're ready to plant them.

Remove plants from cell packs by pushing up each seedling from the bottom.

Tear the rim from peat pots and other fibrous containers before planting, since any exposed rim will wick water from the rootball.

With a trowel dig a planting hole roughly the same depth as the rootball and about twice as wide. If the plant was growing in a light potting mix, don't set it in a small hole in heavy clay soil. Instead, dig a larger planting hole and blend organic matter into it. This will prevent an abrupt change in soil texture. Place the seedling in the hole, firm the soil with your hands, and water thoroughly with a gentle spray.

Set a seedling in a hole the same depth and approximately twice as wide as the rootball.

Seedlings grown in peat pellets and fibrous pots should not be removed from their containers. Plant the entire container in the ground, being sure to place the pot below soil level, since any aboveground pieces of fiber will draw water like a wick.

Newly transplanted seedlings need extra water and protection for the first several days. Water them daily if the weather is dry, but don't let the soil become soggy. Protect the seedlings from the sun, the wind, and slugs and snails by setting a pot or other covering over them for a couple of days.

SETTING OUT NURSERY PLANTS

Nursery plants come in a variety of containers and forms. Medium-sized shrubs and trees usually come in plastic or metal cans. During the dormant season roses, fruit trees, and deciduous ornamental trees are sold bare root. Large trees and evergreen shrubs, particularly those sold in severe-winter climates, may come balled and burlapped. Each form of nursery plant requires a slightly different method of handling and planting.

Container Plants

Most container plants purchased from a nursery or garden center come in 1-gallon and 5-gallon sizes. Plants in larger containers are usually quite expensive and are used as specimens in the garden.

Dig a hole no deeper than the rootball and approximately twice as wide. Plants have a tendency to sink after they have been planted, so it is better to plant a little high. The rootball should be sitting on firm, undisturbed soil. Roughing up the sides of the hole makes it easier for the roots to move into the native soil.

Amending the backfill soil (the soil used to fill the planting hole) actually retards a plant in becoming established rather than helping it. Unless the soil is rocky or a heavy clay, it is best to leave it alone and plant directly in it. This way the roots will become established in the native soil from the beginning, rather than having to adjust to the amended soil, only to have to readjust months later when they grow into the native soil.

If you are planting in early spring or when you expect leaf growth to begin, add a complete fertilizer to the backfill soil according to the manufacturer's recommended rate. Stir the dry fertilizer into the soil so that the fertilizer does not come into direct contact with the rootball.

Remove the plant from the container only after you've prepared the planting hole. Water the plant thoroughly; as long as the rootball is moist, you can remove it from a plastic or tapered metal container by placing your hand across the top of the can, turning the can upside down, and shaking it slightly. Straight-sided metal cans must be cut with a pair of tin snips. (If you intend to plant right away, you can ask the nursery to cut the metal can. If you plan to hold the plant awhile, leave the can intact and cut it yourself when you're ready to plant.)

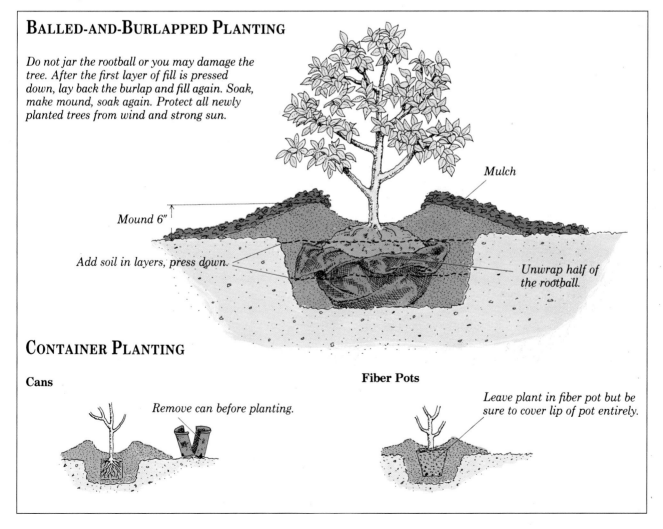

BALLED-AND-BURLAPPED PLANTING

Do not jar the rootball or you may damage the tree. After the first layer of fill is pressed down, lay back the burlap and fill again. Soak, make mound, soak again. Protect all newly planted trees from wind and strong sun.

Mulch

Mound 6"

Add soil in layers, press down.

Unwrap half of the rootball.

CONTAINER PLANTING

Cans

Remove can before planting.

Fiber Pots

Leave plant in fiber pot but be sure to cover lip of pot entirely.

TEMPORARY PLANTING

If you can't plant a bare-root tree immediately, heel in the tree by digging a shallow hole and planting it temporarily. Keep the roots moist at all times.

Examine the roots of any plant that appears root-bound. Loosen any large roots circling the rootball and spread them before planting, so that they will grow outward. If left uncorrected, circling roots will stunt the plant's growth. If the roots form a solid mass around the inside of the container, trim off the outer 2 inches of the rootball. Otherwise, make four vertical slashes an inch or so deep down the sides of the rootball and cut an *X* on the bottom. New growth will emerge from the cuts. These new roots will grow more readily into the surrounding soil than the undisturbed roots would have.

Place the plant in the hole and adjust the depth of the hole if necessary. The plant should sit slightly above the soil line. Fill the hole with backfill soil to the level of the surrounding soil.

Build a shallow basin around the plant so that irrigation water will be concentrated in the area where it is needed most. Be sure to build the basin so that water drains away from the plant stem or trunk. Fill the basin with water until the soil is loose and muddy. Gently jiggle the plant until it is positioned exactly as you want it. This action will eliminate any remaining air pockets. Check again to be sure that the water drains away from the stem.

Mulch around the plant, taking care not to let the mulch build up around the stem or trunk. Provide support for the plant if necessary (see "Supporting Plants" beginning on page 129).

Balled-and-Burlapped Plants

Trees and shrubs that have been raised in a field are marketed as balled-and-burlapped (B and B) plants. When they are ready to be sold, they are dug up and the rootball is wrapped in burlap. Since field-grown plants are better able to survive winter freezing than those grown in containers, B and B plants are commonly sold in cold-winter climates. They are less frequently available in warm-winter areas.

The dormant season—fall and early winter—is the usual time for planting B and B plants. They can also be planted during the growing season because of the protection provided by the soil around the rootball.

Keep the burlap on B and B plants until you are ready to set them in the ground. Sprinkle the rootball and the foliage to keep them moist. Store the plant in a shady location, covering the burlapped rootball with a plastic sheet or moist organic material, such as sawdust, leaves, or straw.

To plant a balled-and-burlapped tree or shrub, dig a hole no deeper than the rootball and twice as wide. The plant should be at the same depth as it grew in the field or slightly higher. It is better to plant too high than too low; many plants die from crown rot caused by the plant sinking so that some of the trunk is below grade. Rough up the sides of the hole to encourage root penetration into the native soil. Add some fertilizer to the backfill soil. There should be a gradual transition from the soil around the rootball to the native soil, or else the roots may remain in the amended soil. Determine how the tree or shrub will be oriented. If it is not perfectly symmetrical but has a dominant side branch, orient the plant so that the branch will grow in the direction you wish.

Handling the rootball carefully, slide the plant into the hole with the burlap still on. You can leave natural burlap on the

Transplants tend to sink, so plant container or balled-and-burlapped plants a little high. The rootball should sit on firm, undisturbed soil. Rough up the sides of the hole so that the roots can establish themselves more easily.

rootball after planting, because it will disintegrate, although you should untie the burlap from the trunk and pull it away from the top of the rootball. Some so-called burlap is actually a synthetic plastic and should be removed at planting, because it will not disintegrate. Inquire at the nursery about the type of burlap on the plant.

A newly planted balled-and-burlapped tree may require staking to anchor the roots and prevent the tree from leaning or falling in the wind. If the tree is fairly large, stakes may not support it and it may need guy wires. (See Supporting Trees on page 130.)

Fill the space around the rootball with the soil you took from the hole. Form a watering basin twice as wide as the rootball and a few inches high. Fill it with enough water to soak through the rootball.

Water frequently for the first few weeks if the weather is warm and dry. The plant is very susceptible to drying out until its roots have grown into the native soil. During the first few months, water regularly but don't overwater. Check whether the plant needs water by feeling the rootball soil, not the backfill soil. Water by filling the basin whenever the rootball soil is only slightly moist.

If you live in a region that has a rainy season, break a hole in the lip of the basin during this period so the plant isn't overwatered.

The roots should grow into the native soil in a few months, and within a year the plant should be well rooted. If you are still able to jiggle it in the soil after a year, something is wrong. Dig up the plant and examine the rootball. If the roots are still tightly packed, it might be best to discard the plant and make a fresh start.

Bare-Root Plants

Some deciduous plants, such as fruit trees and roses, are grown commercially in fields. When they are ready to be sold, they are dug up during the dormant season and all the soil is removed from the roots. They are sold in this bare-root form.

Bare-root plants must be set in the ground before they begin spring growth. It is best to set out these plants as soon as you bring them home. If a bare-root plant breaks out of dormancy and begins growing before you're ready to plant it in the garden, pot it up in a container of soil and let it grow for a few months. Then transplant it into the ground in the summer.

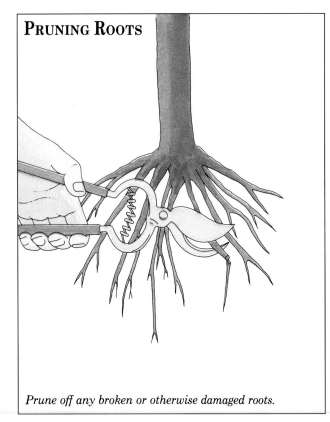

PRUNING ROOTS

Prune off any broken or otherwise damaged roots.

LEVELING THE TREE

Use a board to set the tree at the correct level.

Spread the roots of a bare-root plant over the soil mound in the hole. A shovel handle can aid in placing the bud union at the appropriate level.

When you bring home a bare-root plant, check the roots carefully. With sharp, clean pruning shears, remove any broken and damaged roots. Soak the roots for a couple of hours in a bucket of water. If you can't plant at once because the soil is too wet, plant as soon as the soil can be worked. Meanwhile, store the bare-root plant in a cool, shady spot with its roots and some stem in moist sawdust, bark, or soil. The process of storing a bare-root plant in a trench of loose soil is called heeling in (see page 116).

To plant a bare-root plant, dig a hole large enough to accommodate the roots without bending them. If the roots radiate in a circle, form a cone-shaped mound in the bottom of the hole, then spread out the roots on the mound. The plant should be at the same depth at which it was originally grown. A change of color on the bark just above the roots should show where the soil line was. If you can't find the original soil line, position the plant so that the top root is 1 inch below the surface. Plant slightly high to allow for some settling.

Some fruit trees have a thickened central taproot with a few smaller radiating roots. A cone-shaped mound is not practical for these trees. Look for the soil line on the bark and plant the tree at the same depth at which it was grown in the nursery.

If the plant is grafted or budded, as many fruit trees are, the union (the knobby protuberance at the base of the trunk) should be at least 2 inches above the soil line. The union must remain dry and must not be allowed to send roots down into the soil. When planting, lay a board or a rake handle over the hole and hold the bud union in place against it as you fill the hole with soil.

Work the soil between the roots with your hands to fill any air pockets. Build an irrigation basin and fill it with water. While the soil is still soupy, wiggle the plant to help eliminate air pockets. A bare-root plant usually does not need staking unless the site is especially windy.

Do not fertilize a bare-root plant when you set it out. A dormant plant does not require much nutrition, and much of the fertilizer will leach away and be wasted before the plant needs it. Instead, fertilize when the first leaves appear on the plant in spring. The plant probably won't need another watering until the leaves appear.

Prune the tree after planting (see Pruning Young Trees on page 195).

Bare-root roses While you're clipping off any dried or broken roots, trim all the roots back by about one sixth. Dig a hole wide and deep enough to fit the roots without bending them, and make a cone-shaped mound of soil in the center of the hole. Spread the roots over the mound of soil.

It is important to protect the bud union on a rose plant from freezing. How deep you plant the rose will depend on your average low temperature in winter. Place the bud union 2 inches below the soil level if the temperature drops below −10° F, slightly above the soil level if the low is between 10° and −10° F, and 2 inches above the soil level if the temperature remains above 10° F. More canes will develop from an exposed bud union than from one that is below ground.

In cold climates keep loose soil or moist organic matter around the canes until the rose breaks dormancy. The soil will protect the canes against drying winds and will keep them moist.

After planting, examine the branches of the rose plant. Although roses are top-pruned when they arrive at the nursery, trim the branches further if necessary to make sure that the top bud on each branch points in the direction you wish it to grow. Also eliminate all crossing stems so that the center of the plant is open. See the sidebar on Pruning Roses, page 212.

PLANTING BULBS

To prevent bulbs and bulblike plants (see page 59) from drying out, plant them as soon as possible after bringing them home. Lilies are especially delicate and should go into the ground immediately. If fall weather is warm in your area, delay planting early-spring bulbs by keeping them refrigerated or storing them in a cool place until the warm weather is over.

Most bulbs should be planted at a depth equal to three times their diameter. Many bulbs look better when planted in clusters rather than straight lines, and odd-numbered groupings tend to look more attractive. When you plant several bulbs close together, it is easier to dig up the entire area to the proper depth, set the bulbs in the hole, and cover them. When planting smaller numbers, and especially in crowded areas among other plants, dig individual holes with a bulb planter or a trowel. Place a bulb in each hole, cover it with soil, and firm the soil slightly with your hands.

Some bulbs, such as corn-lily (*Ixia* species) and tuberous begonia (*Begonia* × *tuberhybrida*), should not be left in the ground during their dormant period. In fall, after the foliage has yellowed or been killed by frost, dig up the bulbs and dry them for a few days in a shady spot. Then brush off the dirt and store them at 35° to 45° F in a shallow pan of dry sand, peat moss, or perlite until the next planting season.

Some bulbs can be left in the soil and will flower from year to year without further attention. Only certain bulbs naturalize well; these include daffodil (*Narcissus* species), crocus (*Crocus* species), ornamental onion

Most bulbs look better when planted in odd-numbered clusters (three, five, seven, etc.). Plant bulbs at a depth equal to three times their diameter.

For a better appearance, plant bulbs closer together in containers than would be appropriate in the ground.

(*Allium* species), brodiaea (*Brodiaea* species), snowdrop (*Galanthus* species), and squill (*Scilla* species).

Whether you are leaving the bulb in the ground or digging it up, you must give the plant time to store energy for the next year. After the flowers die, the leaves continue to manufacture food for next year's flowers; since bulb size determines the size of the flowers, the leaves should be allowed to remain on the plants until they turn yellow.

You can get more bulbous plants from the ones you already have by dividing or separating them and planting the pieces. For more information on propagating bulbs, see page 347.

Planting Bulbs in Containers

Good drainage is even more important for bulbs planted in containers than it is for those that are planted in the ground. Plant your bulbs in a commercial potting mix or make your own potting mix (see Potting Mixes on page 104).

Shallow clay pots known as bulb pans, which are 4 to 5 inches deep, are attractive, useful containers for many bulbs. However, amaryllis (*Hippeastrum* species), lily (*Lilium* species), and other large bulbs, and even some smaller, deep-growing ones, such as crown-imperial (*Fritillaria imperialis*), need deeper pots.

Cover the drainage holes with pieces of window screen, add soil, and position the bulbs, setting them closer together than you would in the ground. Most pots of flowers look better if the bulbs are almost touching. Plant each tulip bulb with the flat side facing the edge of the pot. Large bulbs, such as amaryllis and lily, should be planted individually in 6- to 8-inch pots.

If the containers won't be subject to frost, set the bulbs with their tips just under the soil surface instead of at the depth suggested for garden planting. Fill the pot to the rim with loose soil. The first watering will settle the soil enough to make room for future waterings. Soak the soil thoroughly after planting and place the pots in a cool area until the bulbs root.

Keep container-planted bulbs evenly moist throughout their growing and blooming period. Then reduce watering as the bulbs begin their rest period, signaled by yellowing leaves. Most bulbs grown in containers should be repotted annually. Each year knock out some of the soil and add a fresh mixture.

1. Prepare the Site. After preparing the soil (see page 97), make any last-minute changes to ensure an even grade with no dips or bulges. Water well the day before seeding.

PLANTING A LAWN

Before installing a new lawn, you must first decide on the kind of grass to plant and the method of installation.

Grasses are categorized by the time of year during which they grow best. Warm-season grasses (Bermuda grass, bahia grass, centipede grass, St. Augustine grass, and zoysia grass) grow actively during the warm summer months and then become dormant, sometimes turning brown in cool weather. Adapted to the southern half of the United States, warm-season lawns should be started in late spring or early summer. Depending on the grass species, a warm-season lawn can be planted from seed, sod, sprigs, or plugs (see the chart on page 127).

Cool-season grasses (bent grass, fescue, blue grass, and rye grass) grow actively in the cool weather of spring and fall. They slow down during the hot summer months but remain green if given sufficient water. Grown primarily in the North, cool-season lawns are

most often started in spring or fall. They are usually planted from seed or sod.

Select a grass that is adapted to your climate and to your site. New cultivars that are tolerant of drought, shade, heat, cold, and other conditions come on the market each year. Check with the staff of a local nursery or with a cooperative extension office for a suitable variety for your area.

Seeding
The most common and least expensive method of installing a lawn is seeding. More grasses are available as seed than as sod, so you have a greater choice when you select your grass. Some packages of lawn seed consist of one type of grass, whereas others are mixtures or blends. A mixture contains seed from two or more grass species; a blend is a combination of cultivars from one species of grass. A good mixture or blend most often produces a better quality, more disease-resistant lawn.

Grass seed takes an average of 14 to 21 days to germinate, followed by a 6- to 10-week establishment period. This may vary, depending on the grass type and the weather. Be sure to plant your lawn at the recommended time, when temperatures are ideal for seed germination.

2. Sow the Seeds. Use a hand-held or wheeled spreader to sow the grass seeds at the rate recommended on the seed box. Divide the seeds into two lots and sow the lots at right angles to each other. When using a wheeled spreader, touch up the edges by hand.

3. Rake in the Seeds and Roll. Lightly rake the entire area to ensure good contact between the seeds and the soil. Don't rake too hard or you'll bury the seeds and ruin the final grade. Seeding at a depth of ⅛ to ¼ inch is usually sufficient. To establish this depth and to firm the seeds in the soil, go over the entire area with a water-filled roller.

4. Add Mulch. Apply a thin (⅛-inch) layer of mulch, making sure the seeds aren't buried too deep. You can spread the mulch by hand, or you can rent a special roller that automatically dispenses mulch in a thin layer. The mulch will help the soil retain moisture, hastening seed germination. In rainy or windy areas a heavy mulch is advisable.

5. Water Thoroughly. For seeds to germinate evenly, the top layer of soil must remain moist. After sowing, thoroughly soak the soil to a depth of 6 inches. Then lightly sprinkle by hand as often as three to four times a day until the young grass is established. Water more often if it is hot or windy. Use a fine spray or mist nozzle on your garden hose so that the seeds won't wash away. Don't use a sprinkler system until all the seeds have germinated.

Starting a Sod Lawn

Sod is turf that is grown commercially, cut into strips from 6 to 9 feet long and 2 feet wide, and lifted intact along with a thin layer of soil held together by runners, roots, or netting. Installing a sod lawn is similar to laying a carpet, and it yields quick results: A sod lawn can be functional in two weeks, although it shouldn't be walked on until the roots have knitted properly with the soil.

Sod can be installed in places where a seed lawn may be difficult to establish, such as a heavily trafficked area or a slope that erodes easily. You can plant a sod lawn any time the weather permits and irrigation is available, although it is best to install a cool-season lawn in spring or fall and a warm-season one in late spring or early summer.

The only drawbacks of a sod lawn are the initial cost and the labor involved, which should be weighed against the advantages a sod lawn offers.

2. Prepare the Soil. Before the sod is delivered, prepare the soil thoroughly according to the instructions on page 97. Do not be fooled into thinking that this step is unnecessary since the sod already has soil attached. When you are preparing the soil, remember that the final grade should be ¾ to 1 inch lower than you want the lawn to be. This allows for the thickness of the sod to fit flush against sprinklers, sidewalks, and driveways.

1. Select High-Quality Sod. You can avoid many problems by buying high-quality, healthy sod that is adapted to your climate and site. Most states have sod-inspection programs to ensure that sod is free of weeds, diseases, and insects, and that it is the cultivar or species it is advertised to be. A cooperative extension office or local nursery should be helpful in providing information. Many nurseries also sell and install sod.

3. Be Ready to Start. Be prepared to install the sod when it's delivered. In hot weather sod should not remain rolled or stacked for more than a day. In cool weather it can remain healthy for two or three days if the soil on the outer pieces is kept moist. Thoroughly water the soil a day or two before the delivery date. Also plan to have two or three people help unload the rolls and stack them in a convenient spot. The rolls of sod are heavy—each strip can weigh as much as 40 pounds.

4. Begin With a Straight Edge. The easiest way to begin laying sod is to start with a straight edge, such as a sidewalk or driveway. If you have an irregularly shaped lawn, draw a straight line through it or string a line across it, and start laying sod on either side of it.

Handle the sod strips carefully to avoid tearing or stretching them. Place the loose end of the rolled sod tightly against the previously laid strip and carefully unroll it. Stagger the ends of sod pieces much like a brick layer staggers the ends of the bricks. On a hot day it is a good idea to lightly sprinkle the strips as soon as they are laid.

When laying sod on a slope, start from the lowest point and move uphill. Always lay the sod so that it runs perpendicular to the slope.

6. Cut Pieces to Fit. Use a sharp knife or garden spade to cut the sod to fit along curved edges or in odd-shaped areas. A knife with a serrated edge, such as an old bread knife, works best. You should begin laying sod in a straight line and work toward irregular areas.

7. Place Edges Tightly Together. To keep the edges from drying out, place the sod strips as close together without overlapping them. If gaps cannot be avoided, fill them with good soil or organic matter and pay close attention to them when watering; they will be the first areas to dry out. Do not attempt to fill small gaps with sod. Small pieces of grass usually dry out and die.

5. Roll to Ensure Contact. After all the sod has been laid, go over it with a water-filled roller to ensure good contact between sod roots and underlying soil. Roll perpendicular to the length of the strips. If the weather is warm, you may have to roll the sod in sections as it is laid. Rolling will have a leveling effect, but it is better to start with a level sod bed. If you try to correct the grade by repeatedly rolling, you will only compact the soil.

8. Water Thoroughly. Improper watering after installation is probably the most common cause of failure in sod lawns. Once the sod has been rolled, water it thoroughly. After watering, lift a corner of a sod strip to be sure the soil underneath is wet. Watch the lawn closely until the roots have knit. The edges along sidewalks and driveways are the first to dry out and the last to knit with the soil. They may require spot watering every day, perhaps even more often in hot weather. Make sure the underlying soil is always moist.

Plugs are sections of sod that have been cut into small circles or squares.

Sprigging and Plugging

In areas of the United States where warm-season grasses predominate, sprigging and plugging are common methods of starting a lawn. Sprigs are pieces of torn-up sod; planting them is similar to seeding. Plugs are small squares or circles of sod; planting them is similar to sodding.

Sprigging and plugging work only with grasses whose stems grow horizontally and produce new plants. The sprigs and plugs root and spread, eventually filling in and forming a lawn. Some grasses, such as improved or hybrid Bermuda grass, which do not produce viable seed, can be planted only from sprigs, plugs, or sod. Both sprigging and plugging are economical ways of using sod.

Sprigging This technique consists of planting individual sprigs, or stems, at spaced intervals. A suitable sprig should have at least one node or joint from which it can spread. Bent grass, Bermuda grass, and zoysia grass are commonly planted by the sprigging method.

You can buy sprigs by the bushel, or you can buy sod and pull it apart or shred it into separate sprigs. Sprigs bought by the bushel by mail order are shipped in bags or boxes, usually within 24 hours after mechanical shredding.

The soil should be ready to plant when the sprigs arrive. (Instructions for preparing soil are on page 97.) Keep the sprigs cool and moist until they're planted. It takes only five minutes of sunlight to damage sprigs enclosed in plastic bags. Even when stored properly, sprigs decay rapidly.

Any of several planting techniques can be used for sprigging. Whichever method you use, space the sprigs according to the grower's recommendation and water them once or twice a day for the first week.

Long stems can be planted in 2- to 3-inch-deep furrows, spaced 4 to 12 inches apart, depending on the coverage desired. Place the stems against one side of the furrow so that any foliage is above ground. Firm the soil around each stem and level the site as well as possible. Rolling with a half-filled roller helps to firm the soil around the sprigs and aids in the leveling.

A faster technique is called broadcast sprigging, stolonizing, or shredding. Sprigs are shredded into short stems and spread by hand like a mulch over the planting area. They should be covered with soil and rolled lightly with a water-filled roller.

A third method of planting sprigs is to place the stems at desired intervals and lightly press them into the soil with a stick.

Plugging This technique is exactly what it sounds like: Small squares or circles of sod are inserted into holes made at regular intervals with a steel plugger. You can buy sod and cut the plugs yourself, but it is easier to order precut plugs by mail. The holes should be spaced 6 to 12 inches apart, depending on the type of grass you choose. Insert the plugs, roll the site with a water-filled roller, and water the plugs. Although plugs do not dry out as fast as sprigs, keeping the surrounding soil moist is still important. Water daily for the first week.

Centipede grass and St. Augustine grass are usually cut into plugs 3 to 4 inches in diameter and planted 1 foot apart. Bermuda grass and zoysia grass are usually cut into plugs 2 inches in diameter and planted 6 to 12 inches apart. The spacing between plugs determines the time it takes to achieve complete coverage.

After a plugged lawn is established, it is usually necessary to add soil to level the lawn. Irrigation and rain may cause the soil to wash out between the plugs, creating an uneven, bumpy lawn.

Plugging is simple. Just use a steel plugger to remove cores of soil at regular intervals (6 to 12 inches apart).

PLANTING METHODS FOR WARM-SEASON GRASSES

Grass	Method
Bahia grass	Seed
Bermuda grass	
Common	Sprigs, plugs, sod, seed
All others	Sprigs, plugs, seed
Carpet grass seed	Sprigs, plugs, sod,
Centipede grass	Sprigs, plugs, sod, seed
St. Augustine grass	Sprigs, plugs, sod
Zoysia grass	Sprigs, plugs, sod

A square yard of sod provides 2,000 to 3,000 Bermuda grass or zoysia grass sprigs, 500 to 1,000 St. Augustine grass or centipede grass sprigs, 324 two-inch plugs, 84 four-inch plugs, or 1 bushel of sprigs. Row planting requires 2 to 6 bushels per 1,000 square feet. Broadcast sprigging requires from 5 to 10 bushels.

Insert the plugs into the holes, then roll the site with a water-filled roller. Water the plugs daily the first week.

SUPPORTING PLANTS

Many plants look more attractive and grow better if they are supported. Some trees need temporary support until their trunks strengthen or their root systems grow large enough to support them. Shrubs seldom require this sort of temporary assistance. Other plants needing support are those annuals and perennials that produce such large flowers that their stems can't hold them up without some help.

Additional plants benefiting from support are vines that sprawl or climb trees in nature but look more pleasing and bear better if supported on a trellis or an arbor. In nature vines are adapted to using other plants for support. Instead of their energy being spent on forming wood for support, it is used to produce more leaves, flowers, and fruit. Although some vines are annual, most are woody perennials that grow to the size of a small tree if given proper support.

Arbors, pergolas, and other structures supporting woody vines should be constructed sturdily.

Trained into a stylized tree form, this top-heavy camellia will require staking for many years to prevent the slender trunk from snapping.

SUPPORTING TREES

Newly planted trees may need to be staked for three reasons: to support or straighten the trunk, to protect the trunk, or to anchor the roots. Unless a tree requires support for one of these reasons, it shouldn't be staked.

Always think of staking as a temporary measure. A year after planting a tree, inspect it for strength. If supporting the trunk was the reason for staking, undo the ties to see if it can stand upright; if it can, remove the stakes. If anchoring the roots was the reason for staking, rock the tree in the ground to see if it is firmly rooted; if so, remove the stakes. If the trunk or root system is gaining in strength but cannot yet support the tree, encourage the strengthening process by lowering the stakes and ties.

Check staked trees periodically to be sure the ties are not too tight, causing damage to the bark and cutting off the flow of nutrients. Loosen or replace ties as necessary.

A tree that still needs staking after two years should be dug out and replaced. Its roots are probably circling and kinked and not spreading into the native soil. Such a tree will never be strong and stable.

Supporting the Trunk

Trees that are allowed to grow in one spot from seedlings seldom need support at any point in their lives. Nursery-grown trees—except for conifers—often require support. Most nursery trees are pruned to look like miniature versions of mature trees, with all the branches coming from the top third of the trunk, leaving the bottom two thirds bare. The lack of branches on the lower portion keeps the trunk from expanding as it should. (The fact that conifers are generally allowed to retain their lower branches explains why those trees rarely need support.) To make a weak-trunked nursery tree look straight, the trunk is lashed tightly to a stake. To make matters worse, the trees are often grown tightly together, partly to save space in the nursery but also to make the trees grow taller than they would if the sun could reach all their leaves.

All these practices lead to a slender, weak trunk that cannot support the weight of the top of the tree. When a newly purchased

SUPPORTING TREES WITH TWO STAKES

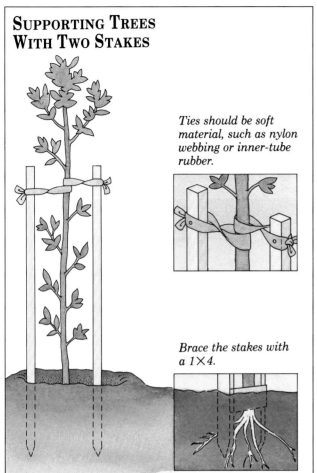

Ties should be soft material, such as nylon webbing or inner-tube rubber.

Brace the stakes with a 1×4.

Tie the tree in only one spot, as low on the trunk as possible. Ties should be looped in a figure 8. Cut off the stakes just above the tie.

SUPPORTING TREES WITH THREE STAKES

Three stakes provide trunk protection as well as support.

tree is cut from its stake, it often flops to one side, sometimes far enough to touch the ground.

If the tree flops only slightly, you may be able to avoid staking it. Sometimes thinning the branches will be enough to reduce the weight and wind resistance of the top. Occasionally, tilting the rootball slightly will be enough to straighten the tree. Try these methods before making the decision to stake a tree.

Often, you will have no choice but to stake. This support should be viewed as a temporary crutch until the trunk grows strong enough to hold itself upright. There are two things you can do to help strengthen the trunk during this period. One is to allow temporary branches to grow from the trunk. These branches can be headed back to keep them small until they are no longer needed. They encourage the trunk to grow in girth, thicker at the base and tapering toward the top. This taper makes the trunk strongest where it needs strength. The temporary branches also help to protect the developing trunk by keeping animals and people away from it.

The other way to encourage the trunk to grow stronger is to allow it to move in the wind. Tie the tree to the stake at only one point, as low as possible, so that the trunk flexes and bends in the wind. This bending stresses the trunk, causing it to grow thicker and stronger where it is stressed, in the same way that exercising your muscles makes them larger and stronger.

How to stake for support Two stakes provide better support for the trunk than a single stake. Two stakes also reduce the likelihood of a rubbing injury and uneven trunk development that may occur with one stake. Position the stakes so that a line between them is perpendicular to the prevailing wind.

The tree should be tied at only one point on the trunk. Run your hand slowly up the trunk to find the lowest point at which the tree remains vertical when you hold it. This is where the tree should be staked. If the trunk is so weak that it does not remain upright when tied at only one point, tie it at several points to a flexible pole, such as a

⅛-inch iron rod, and tie this pole to the stake at one point. The pole will support the trunk while allowing it to bend.

When buying or cutting stakes, keep in mind that they should be driven 18 inches into the ground and should be cut off just above the ties. Insert the stakes on either side of the rootball. They should press tightly against but not penetrate the rootball.

Tie the tree at the point you found when running your hand up the trunk. Loop the ties around the tree in a figure-eight pattern. Place the ties as close as possible to the tops of the stakes. The ties can be made of rubber, nylon webbing, polyethylene tape, tire cording, or other soft material. Wire, even when covered with garden hose, harms the trunk if it is left on too long. Use rustproof tacks or staples to hold the tie firmly onto the stake.

In very windy locations a cross brace made of a 1 by 4 board at the bottom of the stakes, at or just below ground level, will help keep the stakes upright.

Anchoring the Roots

Sometimes the trunk is strong enough to support the tree but the root system is too small to hold it upright. This is often the case in a windy location. Heavy rains or frequent irrigation, particularly in loose soil, may also make a young tree vulnerable to toppling by the wind. A few short, stout stakes will brace the tree until the roots grow into the native soil and anchor it. If the wind is not too strong, thinning out the top of the tree so that the wind doesn't have so much to push on will substitute for staking. A large tree being transplanted into the garden will need stronger support than stakes can provide. You must stake it with guy wires (see How to Stake for Anchorage on page 133).

There are three things you can do to foster a strong root system. One is to allow the tree to bend a little in the wind. Bending stresses not only the trunk but also the roots, causing them to grow thicker and stronger. To allow the roots to be stressed, tie the tree to the stake with flexible ties. These can be nylon rope or wire rope with compression springs in them. Compression springs are available from hardware stores; they allow the wire to stretch a little, then become firm.

The second thing you can do to encourage a strong root system is to backfill the planting hole with unamended soil. Research

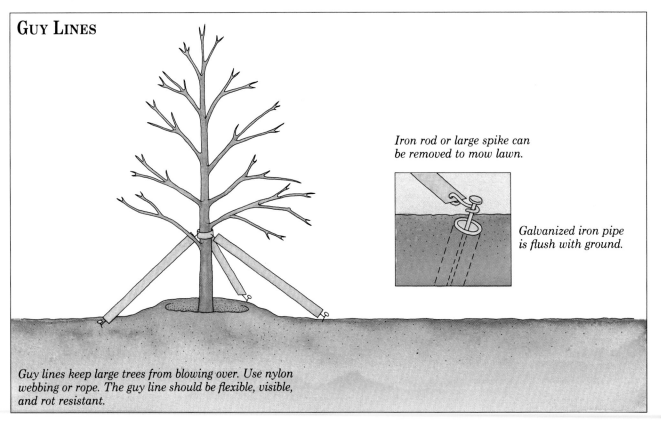

GUY LINES

Iron rod or large spike can be removed to mow lawn.

Galvanized iron pipe is flush with ground.

Guy lines keep large trees from blowing over. Use nylon webbing or rope. The guy line should be flexible, visible, and rot resistant.

has shown that trees and shrubs become established faster if the backfill soil (the soil used to fill the planting hole) is not improved by added organic matter. Roots grow well in improved backfill soil, but they do not move out from it easily to grow into the native soil—and a tree is not firmly established in a location until its roots have grown well into the native soil.

The third thing you can do to help the roots grow strong is to feed and water the tree correctly. If you live in a dry climate, check the rootball regularly after it has been planted, and water whenever the rootball is only slightly moist. You will find that the tree requires frequent watering for a few weeks after planting, but then the need for water diminishes. This happens when the roots begin to spread through the soil, so that they are receiving water from a larger soil volume. At this point, gradually change your watering practices so that you water deeply but infrequently. Allowing the soil to dry out somewhat between waterings encourages the roots to explore more widely and deeply for a source of water.

How to stake for anchorage If you are staking the tree to support the trunk, the same stakes will also anchor the roots. If you are using three stakes to protect the tree (see below), you can also anchor it simply by using stronger and longer stakes and tying the tree to them about one third of the distance up the trunk. This works well with smaller trees.

Large trees transplanted into the garden may need a type of support that is stronger than stakes for the first year. This is particularly important because the tree must be kept from blowing over. Use three guy wires, spaced equidistant from each other and 5 to 10 feet from the trunk of the tree. Nylon webbing or nylon rope makes excellent guy lines. Attach the lines to a collar, made of a soft material, such as 3-inch nylon webbing, around the tree trunk. You can fasten the wires to pins inserted into pipes sunk in the ground. You can easily remove the pins when mowing the grass or when performing other maintenance tasks. Alternatively, you can attach the guy lines to stakes or pins buried in the ground.

Mower Protection

Protect trees with 3 or 4 stakes. Paint stakes white for visibility, or tie rope between them.

Protecting the Trunk

Even a sturdy young tree needs protection if it is located where it may be damaged by lawn mowing and other garden activities. Mechanical damage can have a severe dwarfing effect on trees. Until the bark grows thick and tough, it is susceptible to tearing. Since sugars flow through the thin tissue between the bark and the wood, a tear in the bark reduces the flow, stunting the top of the tree.

Several stakes around the trunk, but not attached to it, generally offer adequate protection. Drive three or four short (1 to 1½ feet long) stakes 6 inches into the ground. Space the stakes a foot away from the trunk and equidistant from one another. If the staking is to offer protection, the aboveground part of the stakes should be clearly visible. Join the stakes with nylon rope, or use twine with pieces of cloth tied to it to make it visible. Another approach for maximum visibility is to run a wire through a plastic pipe between the stakes.

LADDER TRELLIS

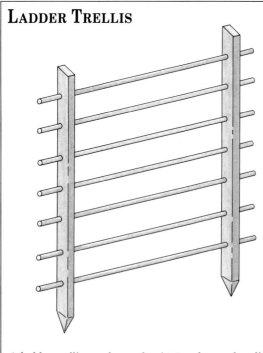

A ladder trellis can be made of ¾" or larger doweling. Drill holes in 2×4 or 4×4 posts to receive dowels.

BASKET-WEAVE TRELLIS

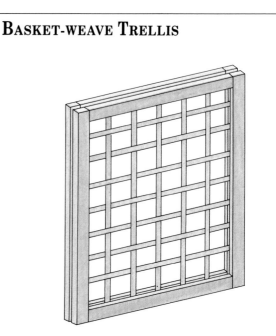

A basket-weave trellis of lath is sandwiched between 1×2 or 1×4 boards. This lightweight trellis can be mounted anywhere.

SUPPORTING VINES

Vines can be trained onto supports to perform various functions in the garden. They can be grown on structures to hide ugly views, create shade, and provide color. Although allowing a vigorous vine to climb a garden tree can damage or even kill the tree, training a vine onto a dead tree is often a way to extend the tree's usefulness for several years. If a favorite tree is weakening and you are afraid you may lose it, plant a wisteria or a grapevine at its base. In about three years, the vine will be well into the tree. If the tree lives, remove the vine or restrict its growth.

Annual vines, such as sweet pea (*Lathyrus odoratus*) and morning glory (*Ipomoea tricolor*), grow extremely fast: In one season they can cover a wall 8 feet tall. Although new plants must be set out each year, annual vines are useful for hiding a structure or an undesirable view quickly. They are lightweight and can be supported by tall stakes or by vertical strings along the side of a building. Tie the top of the strings to nails or dowels in the eaves, loop the bottom of the strings around nails in a board, then tie a slipknot in each string. Later, as the string stretches, you can take up the slack

by sliding the slipknot up the string. Train one or two vines on each string. To keep the trellis neat, don't let the vines cross from one string to another.

Woody vines, such as wisteria (*Wisteria* species) and grape (*Vitis* species), grow slowly, at least for the first few years. Eventually, they can cover the side of a large building and weigh hundreds of pounds. Arbors, pergolas, and other structures built to support woody vines must be very sturdy. Since the supports are exposed to the weather and are difficult to repaint when covered with vines, they should be made from rot-resistant wood, such as redwood or cedar, or from pressure-treated wood. To keep the vine from becoming too massive and putting stress on the support, prune the vine back to a basic scaffold each year (see Pruning Ornamental Vines on page 201).

When growing a vine against a wall, it is advisable to use a trellis or other spacer to allow for some air circulation in back of the vine; this helps prevent plant diseases. Maintaining a space between the vine and the wall also helps prevent damage to the surface of the wall as well as moisture from being trapped and dry rot from forming. You can make a hinged lath frame that can be lowered from the wall so you can clean or paint the wall without damaging the vine.

Lightweight vines should be tied to their supports with twine, polyethylene tape, or twist ties. Heavier vines require sturdier ties, such as those made from insulated wire or strips of rubber.

How Vines Cling

Climbing vines cling to supports in three ways: They twine around a support, wrap tendrils around a support, or cling with hold-fasts. Some vines don't cling at all and must be tied to supports.

The stem of a twining vine may twist or spiral around a support, around itself, and around other stems of the vine. Twining vines, which include moonflower (*Ipomoea alba*) and clematis (*Clematis* species), climb well on thin, vertical supports. They are particularly attractive climbing up a string or pole.

Some vines, such as passionflower (*Passiflora* species), grape (*Vitis* species), and sweet pea (*Lathyrus odoratus*), wrap tendrils around a support. Tendrils are modified leaves along the stem that reach out and

Twining vines especially like vertical supports, such as poles, wires, or securely fastened strings.

How Vines Cling

Vine	How It Clings	Leaves
Bittersweet (*Celastrus* species)	Twining	Deciduous perennial
Boston ivy (*Parthenocissus tricuspidata*)	Holdfasts	Deciduous perennial
Bougainvillea (*Bougainvillea* species)	Must be tied	Evergreen perennial
Carolina jasmine (*Gelsemium sempervirens*)	Twining	Evergreen perennial
Clematis (*Clematis* species)	Twining	Deciduous perennial
Climbing hydrangea (*Hydrangea anomala*)	Holdfasts	Deciduous perennial
Climbing rose (*Rosa* species)	Must be tied	Deciduous perennial
Creeping fig (*Ficus pumila*)	Holdfasts	Evergreen perennial
English ivy (*Hedera helix*)	Holdfasts	Evergreen perennial
Grape (*Vitis* species)	Tendrils	Deciduous perennial
Japanese honeysuckle (*Lonicera japonica*)	Twining	Evergreen perennial
Moonflower (*Ipomoea alba*)	Twining	Perennial grown as annual
Morning glory (*Ipomoea tricolor*)	Twining	Annual
Nasturtium (*Tropaeolum majus*)	Twining	Annual
Passionflower (*Passiflora* species)	Tendrils	Evergreen perennial
Potato vine (*Solanum jasminoides*)	Twining	Evergreen perennial
Scarlet runner bean (*Phaseolus coccineus*)	Twining	Annual
Starjasmine (*Trachelospermum jasminoides*)	Twining	Evergreen perennial
Sweet pea (*Lathyrus odoratus*)	Tendrils	Annual
Trumpetcreeper (*Campsis radicans*)	Holdfasts	Deciduous perennial
Trumpet vine (*Distictis* species)	Tendrils	Evergreen perennial
Virginia creeper (*Parthenocissus quinquefolia*)	Holdfasts	Deciduous perennial
Wisteria (*Wisteria* species)	Twining	Deciduous perennial

wrap around string, wire, stakes, the plant itself, and other plants. These vines need slender supports, such as wire or lath, to cling to, since their tendrils usually can't encircle objects larger than a couple of inches in diameter.

Certain vines cling with holdfasts. These can be disk-shaped suckers, hooking claws, or aerial rootlets, all of which attach themselves to the support. Boston ivy (*Parthenocissus tricuspidata*) and English ivy (*Hedera helix*) are common examples. These vines climb almost anything, including smooth walls. The holdfasts mar the surface of the support; over time they can even cause bricks to crumble.

Nonclinging vines, such as primrose jasmine (*Jasminum mesnyi*) and climbing roses (*Rosa* species), must be given support by the gardener. They must be tied to a trellis, fence, or other structure with string or wire in a manner that won't impede growth.

SUPPORTING FLOWERS

Many flowering plants need support, especially when they are in full bloom. These include tall plants, plants with floppy stems, plants that produce heavy blossoms, and sprawling plants.

Tall plants that produce flowers on a single stalk, such as delphinium (*Delphinium* species), hollyhock (*Alcea rosea*), and gladiolus (*Gladiolus* species), usually need to be staked. When setting out the plant, place the stake an inch from the stalk or bulb. Drive the stake as far into the ground as necessary for stability. Tie the flower stem to the stake as soon as it begins to form. If you wait too long, the stem can develop a bend that will never straighten out. Tie the stem to the stake in a loose figure-eight pattern. As the flower stalk grows, add higher ties.

You can avoid staking gladiolus flowers by planting each corm at the normal depth

A framework of woody prunings, well anchored in the soil, will provide ample support for these perennial sunflowers.

but covering it with less soil than usual. As the stalk develops, gradually cover it with more soil until the level is even with the surrounding soil. The continual addition of soil in this way anchors the developing flower stalk.

Plants with many floppy stems, including aster (*Aster* species), coreopsis (*Coreopsis* species), and carnation (*Dianthus caryophyllus*), may need support. These bushy plants can often be staked with prunings from woody plants; simply place a circle of branches around the plant when it is 8 to 10 inches high.

Plants with heavy blossoms, such as chrysanthemum (*Chrysanthemum* species), may also need to be staked. Insert a single stake at planting time; then gather the developing stems and loop them around the stake. Or you can place additional stakes in a circle around the plant and enclose the stems within the circle with twine. For dahlias (*Dahlia* species), insert a stake 2 inches from the tuberous root at planting time. If many stems emerge, insert three more stakes around the first stake, about a foot away, and tie twine around the stakes at intervals to support the stems.

Sprawling plants can be supported with stakes and wire or twine, or they can be confined in mesh cages. A wire hoop taped or tied to two or three stakes is also effective in supporting flowering plants that have a great many stems.

Flower Staking Systems

A multitude of staking systems are available that are suited to various plant configurations. A plant with one flowering stalk, such as delphinium (*Delphinium* species), is best supported by being tied to a single stake. But to use an individual stake for every bloom on a large chrysanthemum plant would require a forest of stakes.

If your flowers are in a cutting garden that is out of sight, the appearance of the stakes is unimportant. However, the most beautiful flowers are usually in conspicuous locations, where they can be admired, and their beauty should not be marred by mechanical supports. The easiest way to make a staking system inconspicuous is to hide it in the flower foliage.

SUPPORTING A SINGLE FLOWER STALK

Position support stake when you set plant in the ground or as soon as it begins to grow in spring. As the plant grows, add more ties to support it. When the plant is ready to bloom, cut off the top of the stake to below bloom level.

You can purchase staking devices from many nurseries and garden supply catalogs; some of these devices are made of thin, green parts that blend in with foliage. You can also make your own supports from a variety of materials. The following ideas for staking systems work well and are easy to make.

Stakes and ties The stakes can be bamboo cane, lengths of 1 by 1 wood, or stiff wire pushed into the ground. Attach the stem to the stake with a plant tie, looping the tie in a figure-eight pattern around the stake and the stem. You can use polyethylene plastic tape, cloth strips, insulated wire, or any other material that won't damage the stem. To keep the tie from sliding down the stake, tap small nails into the stake on each side of the tie, or staple the tie to the wood. As the plant grows, you may have to add additional ties.

There is a danger that a person bending over to smell a flower can be poked in the eye

Supporting Multiple Flower Stalks

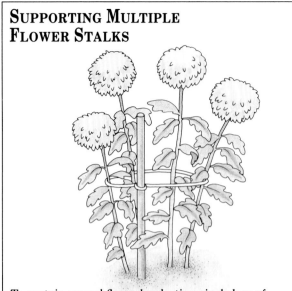

To contain several flower heads, tie a single loop of twine around all of them and around a stake. Add more loops as the plants grow.

Wire Cage

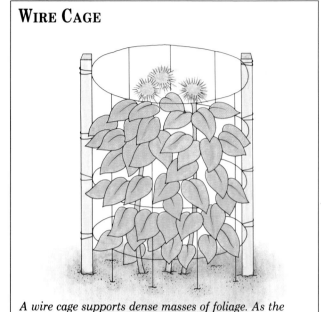

A wire cage supports dense masses of foliage. As the plant grows, the foliage hides the cage.

by the end of a stake, which may be difficult to see from above. As a plant begins to bloom, cut off the top of the stake so that it is below the level of the flower.

Woody prunings Bushy or climbing flowers can be trained to grow on prunings from trees and shrubs. This woody framework for flowers is often called pea brush, because it was used traditionally to support climbing flowers, such as sweet pea (*Lathyrus odoratus*). Cut the woody prunings into 16- to 20-inch pieces and insert them around the plant when it is 8 to 10 inches high. The developing foliage will hide the supports.

Wire cages Galvanized wire mesh with 4- or 6-inch openings can be formed into cages to support short, multistemmed plants. Use wire or twine to tie the ends of the cage together in a circle. For a sturdier cage attach the mesh to 1 by 1 pieces of wood. As the plant grows, the foliage grows through and hides the cage.

Wire hoops Tie a ring of heavy wire to two or three stakes, and place the support around the young plant. As the plant grows, slide the hoop up the stakes. If the plant has many flower stalks, crisscross the hoop with a few pieces of string or lighter wire to keep the flowers from leaning on one edge.

Supporting Vegetables

Support systems for vegetables are usually more functional than those for flowers, although more and more vegetable gardens are being designed for appearance. Support systems save space in the vegetable garden, and they make harvesting easier. The supports also increase yield: Vining plants, such as cucumbers and melons, produce more fruit per square foot when grown on a trellis than if they were sprawling on the ground.

Many vegetable plants are large and heavy, thus support systems tend to be bulky and rigid and aren't usually discarded at the end of the season. If your storage space is limited, you must consider how you will store the supports before you purchase or construct them. If a trellis can be taken apart for storage, or if it is weatherproof, storage won't be a problem.

Tomatoes

Both bush and vining tomatoes benefit from support. A good tomato support performs several functions: It allows the foliage to shield the fruit from sunscald and cracking, it keeps the fruit away from slugs and snails, and it permits good air circulation. It should also be sturdy if it is to support one of the large tomato varieties; these plants can weigh more than 50 pounds.

Vining tomatoes are generally staked or caged; if left alone they sprawl over a large area and much fruit is lost to insects and slugs. Staked tomato plants take up little space, because only one or two vines are allowed to develop. Tall stakes measuring at least 2 by 2 inches should be driven well into the ground. Place one plant at the base of each stake and tie the stem loosely to the stake. Limit the growth to one or two vines by pinching off the sprouts that grow at the base of each leaf. As each vine grows, tie it to the stake every foot or so. About four weeks before the first fall frost, begin pinching off newly formed blossoms, since fruit set from these blossoms won't have time to ripen. This method of supporting tomatoes takes regular attention but produces a high yield of large fruit per square foot.

It won't be necessary to pinch off the side growth if you cage the tomato plants. Tomato cages are wire cylinders used to support the plants. Several commercial models are available, but you can make your own from welded wire fencing or concrete reinforcing wire that has at least 4-inch-square holes, which allows for easy harvesting. The wire is usually available in 50-foot rolls,

4 to 6 feet high. Concrete reinforcing wire is thicker than wire fencing, but it is not galvanized and will rust; however, a cage made from concrete reinforcing wire will last for several years before needing to be replaced.

Although a cage may be sturdy enough to stand on its own, a 2 by 4 stake driven 2 feet into the ground and extending 4 feet up the cage gives needed stability in the wind. For vining tomatoes make the cage 2 feet in diameter and 5 feet high.

Short cages work well for bush tomatoes. For small bush tomatoes, wire tomato hoops are available inexpensively at most nurseries and garden centers.

Beans

Pole beans are twining plants, and as the name implies, their most common support is a pole. (Bush beans don't need support.) Most beans can grow to cover a 7-foot pole, so be sure to use one that is long enough. Because the bean vines may slide to the bottom of a smooth pole when shaken by the wind, either use a rough pole, wrap the pole loosely with jute twine, or drive small nails into the pole to keep the vines from sliding.

TOMATO CAGE

A tomato cage must be made of wire mesh large enough to reach through.

TOMATO STAKES

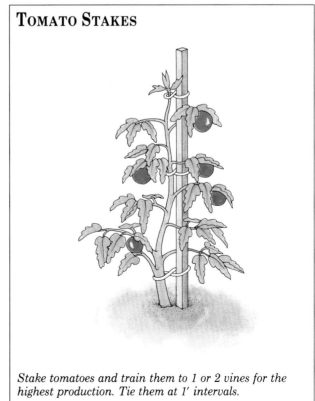

Stake tomatoes and train them to 1 or 2 vines for the highest production. Tie them at 1' intervals.

An A-frame trellis is designed for growing vine crops vertically. This trellis supports lemon cucumbers on one side and beans on the other.

Poke a hole in the ground with a crowbar or pick, then force the pole into the hole. Plant 10 beans around each pole; thin to 4 to 6 after they germinate. For greater strength tie three or more poles together at the top to make a tepee.

Peas

Peas cling to their support with tendrils—modified leaves that wrap tightly around small objects. The two most common supports for peas are brush (dead branches driven into the ground) and fencing. A pea fence is supported by fence posts; it can consist of woven wire fencing, chicken wire, or smooth wire strung between the posts.

Tall peas need supports about 5 feet high. Low peas grow well without supports, but harvesting is easier if the plants are trained on a fence about 2 feet high. Build the fence or secure the brush support in place first, then plant the peas in rows on each side of it. You may have to place the young vines on their support at first, but from then on they will climb without help.

Melons, Squash, and Cucumbers

Although melons and squash are usually grown sprawling on the ground, their vines can also be tied to wood or wire supports. If well supported, the neck of the vine next to the fruit can withstand a surprising amount of weight. Fruit that might tear a stem can be supported with slings made of rags.

Vining cucumbers will climb on strings and on wood or wire racks. Bush cucumbers hug the ground; their fruit can be kept off the ground with lattice supports. Cucumber varieties that are curved when grown on the ground often grow almost straight when trained on a trellis.

POLE BEAN STAKES

Rough poles are easy for pole beans to climb. Tie the poles together at the top for strength.

PEA FENCING

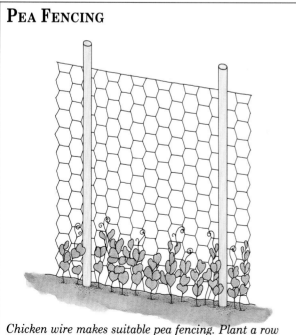

Chicken wire makes suitable pea fencing. Plant a row of peas on each side and help them get started on the wire.

CUCUMBER TRELLIS

This cucumber trellis is self-supporting. It can be hinged at the top for easy storage. Make the openings large enough to reach into easily, since the cucumbers hang down inside.

WATERING

Proper watering is among the most important gardening techniques to learn—and probably the most difficult to master, because there are so many variables. Watering practices depend on the moisture needs of individual plants, the soil type, the planting location, and all the continually changing components of the weather, including temperature, humidity, and wind. Other considerations, such as whether the soil is covered by a mulch, may come into play as well. The watering method you use—hand watering, portable sprinklers, an underground sprinkler system, or a drip irrigation system—will also influence the way you water.

Because so many variables are involved, it is easy to overwater or underwater a plant. In fact, improper watering is the single greatest factor responsible for the decline or death of plants. Too much water is a more common cause of death than not enough water. Overwatered plants are susceptible to root rot and other diseases, and they may even suffocate and die in a soil that stays wet for too long. Too little water will stress and may kill plants that require moisture.

Once you understand the basics of watering, you will find that proper watering is simply a matter of experience. The more time you spend tending the garden, the more opportunity you will have to refine and perfect your watering technique.

As water is added to the soil, the first inch of soil must become very wet before the water can move to the second inch. A quick watering wets the top inch but doesn't even moisten the soil below it.

Watering can refresh more than just the lawn on a hot summer day.

THE BASICS OF WATERING

Proper watering begins with an understanding of the major factors influencing the water needs of the garden. You will be better able to provide your garden with the water it needs once you learn how water behaves in the soil, how to recognize when a plant needs water, and how to modify your watering practices to keep pace with changes in the weather.

Water and Soil Type

Soil type is one of the most important factors influencing watering practices. If you've improved your soil to the point that it is loose and friable, more than half the watering battle has been won. (See "Taking Care of the Soil," starting on page 89.) A friable soil containing lots of organic matter will absorb nearly all the water that falls on it. It will

drain efficiently while still holding ample water on which plants can draw. Most plants grown in this type of improved soil are far more tolerant of a range of watering practices, good and bad, than if they were grown in either clay or sandy soils.

Because sandy soils contain mostly large pores, they hold very little water—most of it drains away—and thus must be watered frequently. At the other extreme, clay soils have tiny pores that hold a great deal of water. However, drainage is so poor that it is easy to overwater clay soils. The gardener who manages a clay soil must learn to provide alternate wetting and partial drying of the soil. The drying allows air into the soil so that plant roots won't suffocate.

Water Movement in the Soil

Water enters the soil by moving into the pores between the soil particles. The soil becomes saturated as water fills all the pores and drives out the air. Each layer of soil must become very wet before the wetting front is able to move deeper into the soil. The rate at which the wetting front moves depends on the soil type. It moves quickly through sandy soils, which have large pores, and much more slowly through compacted soils and clay soils, which have small pores.

After the wetting front stops moving downward, the soil below it remains dry and the soil above it starts to dry out. That's why there is no such thing as keeping the soil slightly moist. Soil moisture is in a constant state of flux. At each rainfall or irrigation, the soil is soaked and then dries slowly until the next watering.

The way the soil dries out can be compared to what happens to a sponge when it is lifted from a tub of water. Drawn by gravity, water runs freely from the sponge. When gravity has pulled out all the water it can, the sponge stops dripping. The water remaining in the small pores of the sponge is held there by a force called capillary action. Water behaves similarly in soil. After water saturates the soil, gravity pulls out all the water it can. Even after the soil has finished draining, capillary action keeps the small spaces between the soil particles filled with water. This is the water available for use by the plants in your garden.

The depletion of capillary water in the soil can be compared to squeezing a sponge and then allowing it to air-dry. When you first squeeze the sponge, water drips readily from it. As you continue to squeeze, more and more effort is required to make the sponge drip, until you can't squeeze out any more water even though the sponge is still damp. Gradually the sponge dries out completely as the remaining moisture evaporates. In the same way, a plant can draw water easily from very moist soil—when the small pores are filled with capillary water. Gradually the soil dries out as the plant depletes the water supply and as water evaporates from the surface of the ground. Water moves less and less freely into the plant, until finally the plant can't extract any more. When the plant can't absorb enough water for its needs, it wilts. Even at this point, the soil still contains some water, but it isn't available to the plant. If you let the plant

It is important to understand the major factors influencing the water needs of your garden.

remain too long in this condition, it will not recover even if you saturate the soil.

Healthy plant growth requires free movement of water into the plant. The best time to irrigate is when the plant has used about half the water available to it, before the plant is under any stress.

Knowing When to Water
There are many methods, some of them very sophisticated, for figuring out when to water a plant. A very simple but reliable method is to feel the soil in the root zone of the plant. Don't just feel the surface, since it dries out

first and is not a true indicator of soil moisture. Use a probe or dig down to the root zone with a trowel. Depending on the plant, you should irrigate when the soil in the root zone reaches a certain level of dryness.

Plants can be divided into three broad groups based on moisture requirements. The first group of plants can't tolerate drought. They thrive in soil that is moist but not wet. Water these plants when the soil is damp. When you touch damp soil, it feels cool and wets your finger but does not muddy it. If you squeeze a ball of damp soil, water will not run out.

The second group of plants is made up of those that require an average amount of water. The soil in the root zone should be just barely moist before watering. Barely moist soil feels cool and moist but doesn't dampen your finger. The soil is crumbly but it is not dry and dusty.

The third group of plants can't tolerate wet soil. Although these plants can usually withstand long periods of drought, they grow better when watered periodically. Water these plants as soon as the soil in the root zone feels completely dry and no longer cool to the touch. Keep in mind that these plants are drought tolerant only after they are well rooted. When they are put into the ground, they should be treated as needing average water until they are established. This usually takes one to two full seasons.

In the Encyclopedia of Plants beginning on page 377, watering instructions include one of three recommendations: "Wet; don't let dry out," for plants that can't tolerate drought; "Medium water," for average plants; and "Let dry out between waterings," for plants that can't tolerate wet soil.

In addition, it is always a good idea to observe plants for signs of water need. Curling leaves are the first indication of stress. The surface area of the plant is being reduced to cut down on transpiration (loss of water from the leaves). Normally shiny leaves grow dull. Bright green leaves take on a blue or gray-green appearance. New growth wilts or droops and older leaves turn brown, dry up, and fall off. Flowers fade quickly and drop prematurely. In most cases, these symptoms signal a lack of water, and the plant will recover if watered soon enough.

If footprints remain on a dry lawn, it's time to water.

Weather and Other Factors

When you irrigate, basically what you are doing is replacing the water that has evaporated from the soil surface and the water that the plant has transpired (water extracted from the soil moves up the plant and is lost as vapor through the leaves). Together these two processes are known as evapotranspiration. The evapotranspiration rate is influenced dramatically by such factors as temperature, humidity, wind, light, day length, and whether or not the soil is mulched. The faster the rate of water loss, the sooner you will need to add water.

During hot, dry, or windy weather, plants transpire at a faster rate and more water evaporates from the soil surface than during cool or humid weather. Plants in full sun transpire more rapidly than plants in shady locations; in addition, more water evaporates from soil in a sunny site than in a shady one.

Day length is an important factor because plants transpire only during daylight. June is usually the month with the greatest water demand, because it has the longest days, even though it may not be the hottest month of the summer.

Mulching also affects the evapotranspiration rate. A thick layer of mulch keeps the soil cool and cuts down on the amount of water that evaporates from the surface. Additionally, when a plant's roots are covered by mulch, the plant doesn't need to transpire as much to cool itself. Thus, mulching reduces the amount of water that must be added to your garden.

How Much Water to Apply

Shallow, frequent irrigation promotes rooting near the soil surface. Deep, infrequent watering encourages roots to grow down where water is available. Deep roots are better insulated against temperature extremes. They are anchored better against winds, and have a greater reservoir of water from which to draw.

Each time you irrigate, apply enough water to wet the soil to the bottom of the root zone. Rooting depth depends on the type of plant. Most lawn grasses root within the top 6 inches of soil, annuals and some perennials within the top 1 to 1½ feet, and shrubs within

Test the evenness of a conventional sprinkler system's coverage by placing flat-bottomed containers on the lawn and comparing the amount collected in each.

the top 3 feet. Although most trees have some deep roots, the majority of their roots are in the top 3 feet of soil.

Since water penetrates deeper in sandy soils than it does in clay soils, it takes less water to wet a sandy soil to the same depth. Generally, 1 inch of water in a sandy soil will penetrate about 15 inches deep. In clay soils 1 inch of water will penetrate only 4 to 5 inches deep. Loamy soils fall between the two extremes.

To see how much water your soil needs to wet it to the bottom of the root zone of a plant, measure the amount of water you apply at an irrigation. It is easy to measure water in gallons if you use a watering can, or if you use drip emitters, which dispense water in a certain number of gallons per hour. You can also measure water in inches. For example, if you fill a 3-inch-deep watering basin to the top, you are applying 3 inches of water to the soil. If a flat-bottomed container is placed on the lawn when the sprinklers are turned on, you will know you have applied an inch of water when the water in the container is an inch deep.

The next day, after the wetting front has moved down into the soil as far as it will go (clay soils may take two to three days), dig a hole to see how deep the water penetrated. You will be able to calculate from this how much water you need to apply to wet the soil to the bottom of the root zone. By measuring the time it takes your watering system to apply an inch of water, you can also calculate how long you need to water.

Some watering methods, including hand watering and many sprinkler systems, apply water faster than the soil can absorb it. When this happens the soil surface becomes soggy and the water puddles up or runs off. Many gardeners stop watering at this point, even though only the top few inches of the soil are wet. If your irrigation system cannot be adjusted to apply water more slowly, either switch to another method, such as a drip system, or punctuate your irrigation. Punctuating, or cycling, means watering in short on-off cycles, such as 10 minutes on and 20 minutes off, to let the water soak in. Keep cycling until the soil has been watered as deeply as required.

DRIP LINE

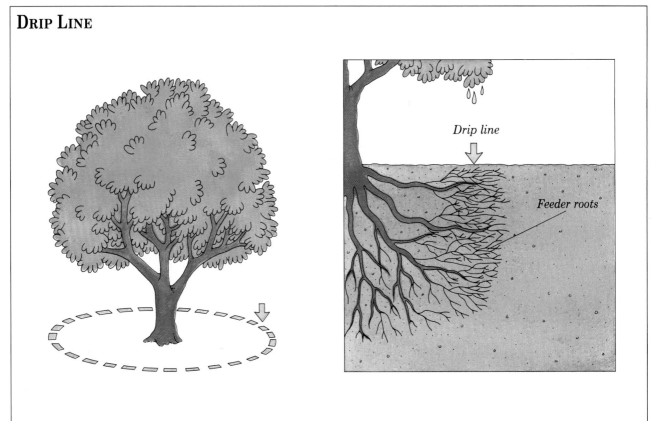

Most of a plant's feeder roots are concentrated near the drip line—the line beneath the outer edge of the plant's foliage.

The most often neglected step after planting a new tree is frequent watering. Create a soil basin to make watering easier in the first few weeks.

Applying Water

The best time to water plants is during the relative cool and calm of the early morning or evening. High temperatures and wind increase the evapotranspiration rate (see Weather and Other Factors on page 146). Wind also blows water away from plants. If you use overhead sprinklers, it is better to water early in the day so that leaves have a chance to dry before nightfall.

Where to apply water is as important as when to apply it. As a plant grows, its root zone also grows and extends out and down. The roots that absorb water—the feeder roots—are concentrated at the outside edges of the plant's drip line (where rainwater drips off leaves to the ground). This is the area that should receive water.

The method you use to apply water is also critical, since proper watering depends on controlling the amount and direction of flow. Hand watering is the least efficient method, partly because it is difficult to regulate the amount of water being delivered to plants—and partly because many gardeners forget to do it. Portable sprinklers are also difficult to control. Water is usually applied to a larger area than necessary and at a faster rate than the soil can accept. An underground sprinkler system is the best way to water a lawn, and a drip system is the most efficient way to water all other plantings.

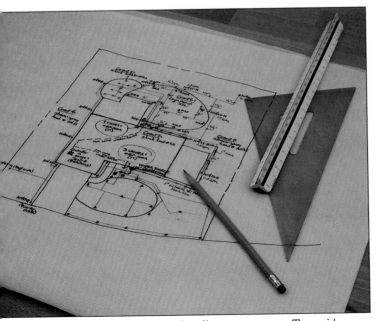

A plan can help you visualize your system. To avoid problems, have it reviewed by a specialist.

UNDERGROUND SPRINKLER SYSTEM

A conventional underground sprinkler system is often referred to as a lawn sprinkler system—and for good reason, since this type of system is the most efficient way to water a lawn. Sprinkler heads, which are connected to a system of underground pipes, are positioned for uniform distribution of water over the entire planting surface of the lawn. The water application is expressed in gallons per minute (gpm).

Lawn sprinklers can also be used to deliver water to other types of plantings, although there are drawbacks. The system is wasteful if used on a lightly planted area, and water delivery is uneven on windy days. Because sprinklers wet leaves, plants with foliage susceptible to diseases may suffer. The lack of flexibility of an underground sprinkler system is another disadvantage; this type of system is not easily expanded or rerouted.

Planning the Sprinkler System

On a piece of graph paper, make a scale drawing of the area you want to water. If you are going to automate the system with a timer, select a location for it. It should be in the house, garage, or other protected location that you can reach conveniently in rainy weather and in the dark.

Next, decide where to locate the sprinkler valves. Each group of valves, called a manifold, should be easily accessible in an area that isn't covered by spray. The front and backyards are usually controlled by separate manifolds.

Then decide where to make the connection to the house water supply. The easiest spot is usually at an outdoor faucet. On your plan draw a line showing where the pipe will be laid from the connection point to the valve manifold.

Before going any further determine the flow rate, in gallons per minute (gpm), available to run the sprinklers. Measure how many seconds it takes your outdoor water tap, turned wide open, to fill a 1-gallon container; then divide the number of seconds into 60 to determine your flow rate in gpm. If a gallon bucket fills in 5 seconds, the flow rate is $60 \div 5$, or 12 gallons per minute. You

SPRINKLER SYSTEM

A sprinkler system is composed of circuits. Each circuit is a group of sprinkler heads controlled by a single valve. This lawn is watered with 2 circuits; only 1 will be operated at a time. The size of the circuits depends on the flow rate.

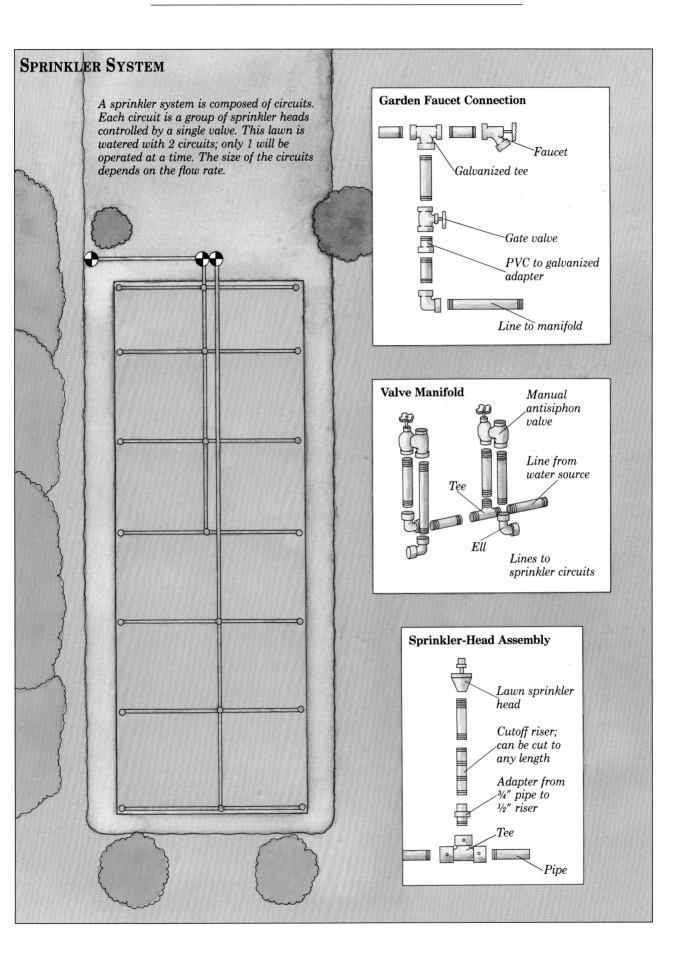

Garden Faucet Connection

Faucet

Galvanized tee

Gate valve

PVC to galvanized adapter

Line to manifold

Valve Manifold

Manual antisiphon valve

Line from water source

Tee

Ell

Lines to sprinkler circuits

Sprinkler-Head Assembly

Lawn sprinkler head

Cutoff riser; can be cut to any length

Adapter from ¾" pipe to ½" riser

Tee

Pipe

Hand watering is the least efficient method of watering. The best way to water thickly planted areas, such as this hillside, is to install an automatic sprinkler or drip system.

will need to know this figure before you can lay out the sprinkler heads.

Using a sprinkler parts catalog available from an irrigation system supplier, check the specifications for different sprinkler heads, including how many gallons per minute a head emits and the radius of coverage. Plan where to place sprinkler heads, spacing them so that the water from each head almost touches each adjacent head. It is better to have the sprinkler heads too close than too far apart. Now, group the heads together into circuits. All the plants covered by a single circuit should have the same watering needs. Each sprinkler circuit is composed of several heads that are connected by pipe and operated by a single valve. All the heads in a circuit turn on together. Only one circuit is on at a time. The combined flow rate (sometimes called precipitation rate in catalogs) of all the heads on each circuit should not exceed 75 percent of the available flow rate. (The flow rate is the figure you arrived at by filling the 1-gallon container.)

On your scale drawing, indicate pipe to connect all of the sprinkler heads on each circuit; the pipe should end at the valve operating that circuit. Since the polyvinyl chloride (PVC) pipe you will use is not very flexible, plan to lay it in straight lines, with 45-degree or 90-degree bends. Run pipes in shared ditches whenever you can, and try to avoid placing them close to trees and under walks and driveways.

Make a list of parts and check local plumbing requirements before making any purchases. You will need sprinkler heads, antisiphon valves, and enough PVC pipe and fittings to tie the system together. Use ¾-inch Schedule 40 pipe between the house water supply and the valves and ¾-inch Class 200 pipe between the valves and heads. Buy the right kind of tee to connect the sprinkler system with the house water line, and buy a gate valve to shut off water to the system. If you intend to automate your sprinkler system, buy electric (instead of manual) valves, a controller (the time clock), and enough direct-burial electrical wire to connect each valve to the controller.

Always keep a copy of your plan, noting any changes during installation, so that you will be able to locate underground parts.

Installing the Sprinkler System

Begin by driving stakes into the ground to mark the location of each sprinkler head. Then draw lines on the ground with gypsum or agricultural lime to indicate where the pipes will go.

Turn off the main water valve to your house, and cut the water line at the point you intend to tie in the sprinkler system. A riser to an outdoor faucet is usually the most convenient spot. If you live in an area where the ground freezes during the winter, make the connection in the basement or near the water meter. Install a gate valve at the connection point so that you will be able to work on or repair the sprinkler system without having to turn off the water to the house. After making the connection, dig a ditch about 8 inches deep to the valve manifold and lay pipe in it.

Assemble the valve manifold, consisting of the valves, the risers (the instructions that come with the valves will tell you how high they must be, or ask the dealer), and the pipe leading from each valve to its circuit. Attach the manifold to the pipe and then connect it with the main water supply. Turn off the manifold valves, and open the gate valve to test for leaks.

Dig the rest of the pipe trenches, about 8 inches deep, and lay the pipe in them. Fit the sections of pipe together and install the heads. Use a hacksaw or PVC cutter to cut the pipe as needed. If you use a hacksaw, remove the burrs left on the pipe by scraping with a knife or sandpaper. Apply PVC cement (actually a solvent that welds the connections) to the outside of the pipe and the inside of the fitting. Fit the parts together, seating the pipe all the way into the fitting and turning the pipe a quarter of the way in the fitting to spread the solvent. Wipe off the excess solvent. Don't handle the joint for a couple of minutes as it sets up.

Leave the trenches open until you've run a test for leaks. Wait 24 hours for the glue to harden before running this test. In addition to looking for leaks, make sure that the spray from the sprinkler heads covers the lawn or planting area adequately. Fill in the trenches only after you have fixed all leaks and added, eliminated, or moved sprinkler heads as needed.

Checking an Existing System

If you already have an automatic sprinkler system, check it periodically to see if it is operating efficiently. If you rarely see it in operation because it runs early in the morning, turn it on every so often. Make sure that all heads are working properly and that coverage is even. Fix leaks immediately.

If the system is old, the heads may emit water faster than the soil can absorb it, resulting in runoff. Low-gallonage spray heads, which emit water at a slower rate, can be substituted. Heads with a lower trajectory for less wind disruption are also available, as are more efficient nozzle patterns. Older heads may not have matched precipitation rates and may apply the same amount of water regardless of the spray pattern. Newer heads apply water proportionately; a half-circle head, for example, applies half the water of a full-circle head.

DRIP IRRIGATION

The term *drip irrigation* is used to describe any low-pressure system that applies water slowly in a small, confined area. It is also called low-volume irrigation or micro-irrigation. Water application is expressed in gallons per hour (gph) rather than gallons per minute (gpm), as it is for conventional sprinklers. A system can combine drip emitters, minisprays, minisprinklers, and misters to irrigate all plantings except lawns.

Economical and easy to install, a drip system is the most water-conserving method of irrigation. A key feature of the system is that it applies water very slowly, so that the soil is able to absorb it without sealing up or crusting over. Slow, direct application of water to the root zone also promotes deep rooting and healthy plant growth. This method of watering eliminates runoff and cuts down on the amount of water lost through evaporation and overspray.

Because drip emitters dispense water so slowly, the same water source can supply a much larger area than can be watered with a conventional sprinkler system. Since the system operates on low pressure, leaks are less critical. A major advantage over conventional systems is flexibility. It is easy to add on to and reroute a drip system.

To effectively irrigate a plant's root zone, set a coffee can without a bottom next to it and fill it with water.

Although a drip system clearly has many benefits, it does have disadvantages— but nothing that can't be overcome with some care and vigilance. A drip system is subject to clogs and leaks and should be checked regularly. Because not enough water is applied to wash down salts that accumulate in saline soils and that build up from fertilizer and manure use, it is usually necessary to leach the soil periodically.

Planning a Drip System

Begin by sketching on graph paper the areas you want to irrigate. Indicate the water source, the different kinds of plantings, any elevation changes, and pathways and other obstacles that drip tubing will have to circumvent. Accurate measurements will help determine the length of tubing and the number of emitters and fittings needed. Many irrigation supply stores will help you select the components that work best for your situation.

The system will be easier to set up if plants are grouped by water need (see Knowing When to Water on page 145). A very small system can be attached to an outdoor faucet and automated with a battery-operated timer. A larger system can have several lines or circuits, as long as there is a separate valve for each. For example, you could have four circuits to serve a vegetable garden, several flower beds, a mixed planting of ground covers and shrubs, and a grouping of containers. It is difficult to water small containers on the same circuit as other plants, since the containers need to be watered daily and water runs out the bottom quickly.

Minisprays and minisprinklers must be positioned according to their radius of throw. Most have a radius of a few feet, although some throw water as much as 12 feet. Position each of the heads so that the sprays overlap and each spray almost touches the next spray head.

The placement of drip emitters depends on the size of the plant and what its water needs may be. Plan to use more emitters, or emitters that dispense more water, for larger plants.

Since drip systems use such little water, it's not usually necessary to worry about exact water consumption on each valve. If you have a very large garden or plan to exceed 200 gph on a single circuit, discuss your plans with the irrigation equipment supplier to make sure that enough water is available.

Installing a Drip System

Drip system installation begins at the water source and works out to the emitters. The head assembly—the components that attach to the water source—consists of a valve, a backflow preventer, a filter, a pressure regulator, and an optional fertilizer injector. A simple system can be attached to a garden faucet. A Y-connector allows you to run two circuits on a single faucet. A battery-operated timer that attaches directly to the faucet or to the Y-connector is available.

The ½-inch main line leading from this assembly can branch into several ⅜-inch lateral lines to carry water to different groups of plants. You can bury the lines in the soil (if burrowing animals are not a problem in your area) or hide them beneath mulch or behind plants. Lay the tubing throughout the garden so that it passes by the plants you want to water. Be careful not to get any dirt in the tubing, and leave the end of each line open for now.

You can punch holes in the main and lateral lines with a special tool and insert emitters directly into the lines. You can also attach emitters to microtubing leading from the lines; a barbed connector joins the microtubing to the line. A drip system is extremely flexible because emitters can be removed at any time and goof plugs (stoppers) inserted to seal the holes. In that way one or more plants in a grouping can be taken off the drip system without affecting the rest of the line. The plugs can easily be removed and emitters snapped in again.

Flush the system by turning it on and letting it run for a few minutes to wash any dirt from the lines. Then turn it off and cap the ends of the lines. Turn the system back on and check each emitter to make sure it is working.

Monitor your plants to make sure that you are providing them with the right amount of water. If one plant wilts on a hot afternoon, add another emitter or change to a larger emitter. If several plants wilt, adjust the timer so that the system runs longer at each irrigation. If it appears that some plants are receiving too much water, remove one of the emitters or use some emitters that deliver less water.

Clean the filter periodically, and each month check for clogged emitters. Once a year, or more often if your water contains sediment, open the ends of the lines and flush them out. The illustration below shows how a typical drip system is put together. The components are described below.

Emitters

Many more types of emitters are available today than when drip systems first came on the market. The plants and terrain generally determine the type of emitter used.

Drip emitters Usually available with flow rates of ½ to 4 gph, these emitters drip water at the base of individual plants, such as trees, shrubs, and container plants. Emitters with different flow rates can be used on the same line. Most emitters have barbed ends that snap into punched holes in ½- or ⅜-inch tubing or that may be pushed into ¼-inch microtubing. Pressure-compensating emitters provide a steady flow rate; use them if there is an elevation change of more than 10 feet, if lateral lines exceed 200 feet, or if emitters on a line total more than 100 gph.

Misters These spray water at 2 to 5 gph. Use their fine spray on ferns and other plants that require frequent, light irrigation or high humidity. Even slight breezes can carry away water, so locate misters in protected areas and operate them in the early morning. Misters are useful in a propagation area, if you grow your own plants from seeds and cuttings.

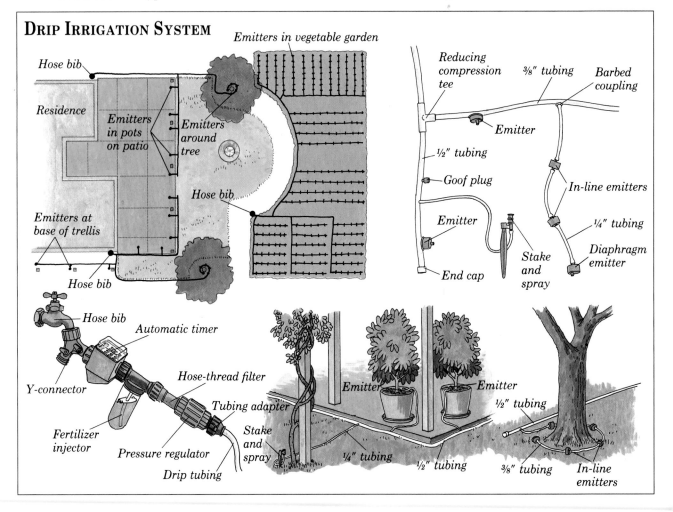

DRIP IRRIGATION SYSTEM

Emitters in vegetable garden

Hose bib

Residence

Emitters in pots on patio

Emitters around tree

Hose bib

Emitters at base of trellis

Hose bib

Reducing compression tee

⅜" tubing

Barbed coupling

Emitter

½" tubing

Goof plug

In-line emitters

Emitter

¼" tubing

Stake and spray

Diaphragm emitter

End cap

Hose bib

Automatic timer

Y-connector

Fertilizer injector

Pressure regulator

Hose-thread filter

Tubing adapter

Stake and spray

Drip tubing

Emitter

Emitter

¼" tubing

½" tubing

½" tubing

⅜" tubing

In-line emitters

Minisprays These come in several spray patterns—90, 180, 300, and 360 degrees, as well as patterns for watering narrow strips—and throw water from 4 to 10 feet. Flow rates vary between 3 and 30 gph. Minisprays are usually positioned 10 to 15 inches above the soil and are held by an anchor or stake. They are used for irrigating ground covers, flower beds, and vegetables.

Minisprinklers These emit larger droplets than minisprays. They distribute 4 to 45 gph in a full circle from 10 to 30 feet in diameter. Minisprinklers are useful in large beds and ground-cover areas.

Microspray nozzles These nozzles use conventional sprinkler system components, such as underground PVC pipe and pop-up spray sprinklers. The microspray nozzle replaces the standard nozzle on a pop-up sprinkler and applies one tenth of the water over the same area.

Other Components

Most of the components listed below are required in a drip system; the fertilizer injector, soil moisture sensor, and rain sensor are all optional.

Gate valve This system shutoff valve controls the water to the entire drip system. It allows you to add on to the system or make needed repairs without having to turn off the water to the house.

Controller A multiprogram automatic controller allows you to operate each valve independently. Since drip systems apply water slowly, it is advisable to have a clock that can be programmed in hours as well as minutes.

Circuit valve Manual, low-flow electric, or battery-operated valves can be used. Electric and manual valves are usually combined with an antisiphon backflow preventer—a device required by most water districts. A battery-operated electronic timer combines the functions of a valve and a controller. It requires a separate backflow preventer. Although not as reliable or long lasting as an electric or manual valve, it is automatic and needs no electrical wiring.

Drip irrigation promotes healthy vegetables by delivering water slowly and consistently to root zones.

Fertilizer injector This device provides a convenient way to feed plants. Frequent dilute feedings are better than several larger feedings. However, fertilizer salts can clog emitters and build up on the surface of the soil.

Filter Even where water is generally free of sediment, the occasional particle flushed loose is enough to clog an emitter. Use a filter with a 150- to 200-mesh stainless steel or fiberglass screen. A Y-filter is better than an in-line filter, because you don't have to take the system apart to clean it.

Pressure regulator Drip systems operate at a water pressure of 20 to 30 pounds per square inch (psi). Since house water pressure ranges from 50 to 100 psi or even higher in some areas, this device is needed to reduce and regulate the pressure.

Tubing Polyethylene tubing in ½-inch and ⅜-inch diameters is used to distribute water throughout the system. The tubing is flexible; sold in coils, it is easy to cut and connect without glue or clamps. Polyvinyl chloride (PVC) pipe is sometimes used for main lines, especially under walkways, and polyethylene tubing for lateral lines. The PVC pipe is a better choice for buried lines; polyethylene tubing can be easily damaged by burrowing animals.

Microtubing This ¼-inch-diameter tubing delivers water from the main tubing to the plants. Because it's easier to conceal than the larger tubing, it's often used to distribute water to containers and hanging baskets. Microtubing with perforations in it is sold as soaker or laser tubing; it is commonly used to water rows of vegetables and flowers.

Fittings Compression tees, elbows, and connectors are used to join two pieces of tubing, to split off into different lines, and to make turns. Barbed fittings are used to join microtubing to the main tubing.

Soil moisture sensor When the sensor detects that the soil moisture is adequate, it will override the controller and turn off the irrigation cycle.

Rain sensor This device should be mounted on the eave of the house or somewhere else in the open. After it has accumulated about ⅛ inch of rain, it overrides the drip system.

WATERING A LAWN

A lawn should be watered when the soil begins to dry out but before the grass wilts. You can often tell when a lawn is thirsty by walking on it or simply by looking at it. If footprints remain after a few minutes, the lawn needs water. A green lawn that takes on a bluish cast is also showing water stress. However, if a lawn that is not dormant looks brown but the blades bounce back, it may need fertilizer instead.

You can determine more precisely when to water by feeling the soil. Lawns should be treated as average plants requiring medium water (see Knowing When to Water on page 145). Water whenever the soil in the root zone is just barely moist; it should feel cool and moist without dampening your finger. If the soil in the root zone is hard and dry, you have waited too long. If it makes your finger wet or muddy, it's too soon to water.

Rarely should a lawn be watered more than twice a week, even in very hot climates. It is better to water longer than more often. More frequent watering encourages shallow rooting and greater dependence on water. The amount applied each time depends on climate, grass variety, and soil type.

When watering, always wet the soil thoroughly to the depth of the root zone. Water areas exposed to full sun more frequently than shady sections of the lawn. If trees or shrubs are competing with the grass roots, water sufficiently for all the root systems. Otherwise, the trees or shrubs will rob the lawn of available water. After irrigating,

WATERING YOUR LAWN ACCORDING TO ET

In arid regions of the West, where lawns won't survive without regular irrigation, many water companies use a system based on the local evapotranspiration (ET) rate to help customers figure out how much to water. The ET refers to the amount of water that evaporates from the soil plus the amount that is transpired by the lawn. By knowing roughly how much water is lost, you know how much to replace. Any water applied beyond this is not used by the lawn and is wasted.

First, measure the output from your lawn sprinklers. Distribute several flat-bottomed containers of the same size on the lawn. Run the sprinklers for 15 minutes, then measure to the nearest ¹/₁₆ inch the average depth of water in the containers. (If there is more than a ¼-inch difference among containers, your sprinkler system will need some adjustment.)

Taking into account the amount of water in the containers and the grass variety, many water companies and cooperative extension offices are able to provide local residents with a watering schedule specifying the number and length of weekly irrigations. The schedule will vary seasonally to accommodate temperature, humidity, and other changes.

Drip irrigation systems are a flexible and efficient way to water all plants except lawns. Some of the many available system components are shown here.

dig into the lawn with a screwdriver in order to see whether the water is penetrating to the root zone.

Adjust the watering pattern from season to season. In spring and fall, lengthen the intervals between watering, but apply the same amount of water each time. Some climates require winter irrigation. In Colorado, for example, where winters are often windy and dry with little snow cover and above-freezing temperatures, lawns suffer stress unless given a good midwinter soak.

Water Evenly

Patchy areas of brown grass in a lawn may indicate uneven water distribution. Test the coverage of your sprinkler system by comparing the depth of water that accumulates in flat-bottomed containers placed on the lawn when the sprinklers are on. Replace sprinkler heads or alter their placement as needed to ensure uniform watering.

Most portable sprinklers wet a large circle or rectangle of lawn, but they don't always distribute the water evenly within that area. Usually the sprinkler applies lots of water close in and only a small amount at the edge of the pattern, even though the surface of the entire area looks evenly moist. To avoid repeated underwatering of some parts of the lawn and overwatering of others, change the location of portable sprinklers with each watering.

Avoid Runoff

You may find that much of the water you're applying to the lawn is running off onto sidewalks or the driveway instead of being absorbed by the lawn. Runoff may result if the lawn is on a slope, if the soil drains poorly or is overly compacted, or if the lawn has built-up thatch (dead grass roots and stems that accumulate between the leaf blades and soil surface). There are several measures you can take to avoid runoff.

If runoff occurs because the lawn is on a slope or the soil drains poorly, punctuate the irrigation. Water in short on-off cycles, such as 10 minutes on and 20 minutes off, to let the water soak in.

Water can't easily penetrate tight or compacted soils. Make holes in the lawn with an aerator, a special tool available at most

Soaker hoses are a simple way to water flower gardens. These soaker hoses have small holes to allow water to drip slowly and evenly into the soil.

equipment rental shops. Use the type that removes a core of soil rather than one that just punches a hole. The holes should be at least ¾ inch in diameter, 3 inches deep, and no more than 3 inches apart. If necessary, make several passes to get the holes close enough together. Water the lawn well before aerating.

Excess thatch keeps water from penetrating evenly and should be removed. A small amount (less than ½ inch) of thatch is normal and is no cause for worry. Cut a plug from the lawn to see if the lawn tends to build up excess thatch. If so, remove it periodically. Rent a powered dethatching rake, or buy a hand-operated rake. These rakes tear

up the grass as well as thatch, so carry out the operation at a time when the lawn is growing vigorously: in the spring or fall for cool-season grasses (bent grass, fescue, blue grass, rye grass), and in late spring or early summer for warm-season grasses (Bermuda grass, bahia grass, centipede grass, St. Augustine grass, zoysia grass).

VEGETABLES AND FLOWERS

Vegetable and flower gardens are most commonly watered by sprinklers or drip irrigation. Row crops are also watered by furrow irrigation (filling the furrows between the rows with water).

Most plants in a vegetable or flower garden grow best when watered consistently and evenly. Many problems—including root rot of many plants, bud drop of many flowers, blossom-end rot of tomatoes, and cracking of cabbage heads—are a result of inconsistent watering.

Plants adapt to a certain level of available water. Plants that are watered frequently are succulent and soft and will be damaged by even a short period of drought. Plants that are watered sparingly become accustomed to a smaller amount of water; their tissues toughen so that the plant is able to withstand dry periods. Some plants, such as herbs, improve in flavor when grown under dry conditions. However, drought-resistant tissue is undesirable in other plants, particularly many vegetables. Ample water produces sweet lettuce, celery, and cabbage. Without a steady supply of water, these plants are tough and bitter. Many flowering

*Container plants can be watered by drip irrigation.
Use the smallest drip emitters available.*

plants look their best and bloom prolifically
when given ample water.

Watering Vegetables
All the major watering methods can be used
for vegetables. If you use overhead sprinklers, water in the morning so that the leaves
will dry quickly. Wet leaves are often susceptible to plant diseases. Other methods of
watering can be used at any time of day.
Vegetables respond particularly well to drip
irrigation systems.

Provide enough water to wet the root
zone. Although some vegetables are rooted
deeper than others, all vegetables draw most
of their water from the upper levels of their
root zones. Thus, it is most important to wet
the top foot of soil.

Vegetables need a steady supply of water, especially when they are flowering or
fruiting. At these times they are very sensitive to fluctuations in soil moisture. Conserve
soil moisture with a thick layer of mulch.
Some vegetables need less water as they
mature. Onions keep better if they are allowed to go dry in the last month. Winter
squash and melons have an improved flavor
and keep better if left somewhat dry during
the last few weeks.

Watering Flowers
Both sprinklers and drip irrigation are commonly used to water flower gardens. If you
are using overhead sprinklers, water early in
the day so that the plants dry quickly. Wet
foliage makes the plants more susceptible to
diseases. The spray from overhead sprinkling
can also weigh down and damage large flower
heads. Stake flowers to keep them from
breaking (for information about Supporting
Flowers, see page 136).

Annuals need a steady supply of water
if they are to produce abundant flowers during their short life cycle. Irregular watering
can cause flowers of their buds to drop
prematurely.

Perennials usually have more established root systems and can be watered less
often than annuals. If you are growing
perennials in a climate that is too warm for
them to become dormant, you can sometimes
force them into dormancy by withholding
water from them.

Continue to water bulb and bulblike
plants after the flowers have dropped. Keep
providing moisture until the leaves have
turned yellow—the yellowing signifies that
the bulb has rebuilt its food supply for next
year's flower production. At this point, with-
draw water so that the bulb will dry out and
store well.

WATERING PLANTS IN CONTAINERS

Container plants should be treated as plants requiring average amounts of water (see Knowing When to Water beginning on page 145). Water whenever the soil in the root zone is just barely moist. When it's time to water, the soil just under the surface will feel cool to the touch but not wet or muddy. If you are having problems with root rot (whole plants dying suddenly), be sure to wash your hands before handling other pots to avoid spreading the problem.

As you become familiar with your container plants, you will be able to tell by their weight whether they need water. As the soil dries out, the container feels much lighter. Another way to tell when a container plant needs water is by the sound the pot makes when tapped with a knuckle. A hollow sound indicates that it's time to water.

A container plant needs enough water to wet the bottom layer of soil. Water draining from the bottom of the container not only tells you that you have wet all the soil in the container, it also flushes out soluble salts. Fertilizer salts and any salts that are dissolved in the irrigation water will accumulate in the potting mix if it is not flushed regularly. Concentrations of these salts are toxic to plants, causing the tips of the leaves to turn black and die.

Always give the plant the same amount of water. You should vary only the frequency of watering, not the amount. If the container is in a saucer, empty the saucer after the pot has finished draining, usually after 10 minutes. If the container is too big to lift, use a turkey baster to remove the water.

A common problem with containers is that the rootball shrinks if the soil becomes overly dry. Water runs around the rootball, down the inside of the container, and out the drain hole without wetting the roots. You can poke holes in the rootball to get better drainage, or try adding a tablespoon of liquid detergent to a gallon of water to break the surface tension. An alternative is to totally immerse the container in a tub of water to rewet the rootball. Leave it in the water for about 15 minutes or until no more air bubbles rise to the surface of the water. Then remove the container and allow it to drain.

Watering Houseplants

Houseplants generally need less warmth but more humidity than most gardeners realize. Thin, papery leaves need more humidity than thick, leathery ones. The low humidity in most houses can be a problem, especially during winter. You can increase the humidity around your houseplants by setting the containers on pebbles or gravel in a pan partially filled with water.

When the air is too dry, the leaf tips may turn brown and the leaves and buds or flowers may shrivel and drop. Too much humidity may cause botrytis blight, also known as gray mold, on leaves or flowers (see page 308). Patches of rot may appear on leaves and stems, especially on succulents that can't tolerate too much moisture.

If your indoor water is softened, water your houseplants with rainwater or use water from an outdoor faucet. The high sodium levels in softened water cause a toxic buildup of salts in plants. If your plants have been damaged by sodium buildup, flush them with unsoftened water.

Water houseplants less often during their dormancy period, usually in winter.

A watering wand makes the process of watering hanging containers simpler and easier.

FEEDING

Plants don't rely on fertilizers for sustenance in the same way that animals rely on food. Green plants make their own food through photosynthesis, a process in which they use sunlight and the green pigment chlorophyll to convert air and water into sugars (see Photosynthesis on page 46). However, plants do need mineral nutrients as raw materials for many functions.

Most of the mineral nutrients required by plants are found naturally in the soil. Unfortunately, much of that mineral reserve is in a form that plants can't use or that isn't supplied fast enough to produce satisfactory plant growth. Gardeners usually have to add fertilizers—materials that contain one or more plant nutrients—to make up for this deficiency. Thus, fertilizers play an important role in keeping plants at the peak of their performance.

Lawns and other plants need more than watering, mowing, and pruning to look good and remain healthy. Mineral nutrients usually have to be added periodically.

NUTRIENTS IN THE SOIL

Of the more than 100 chemical elements that have been isolated, 16 are known to be essential to plant growth. Three of the elements (carbon, hydrogen, and oxygen) are provided primarily by air and water. The remaining elements are usually absorbed from the soil by plant roots. These nutrients are divided into three groups according to the relative amounts needed: the three primary nutrients (nitrogen, phosphorus, and potassium); the three secondary nutrients (calcium, magnesium, and sulfur); and the seven micronutrients, or trace elements (chlorine, iron, manganese, boron, zinc, copper, and molybdenum). Although some nutrients are needed in larger quantities than others, all are equally essential to plants.

Even when these elements occur naturally in the soil, they are not always readily available to plants. Soil chemistry is complex and dynamic. Dozens of elements—including those essential to plant growth—are present in the soil in thousands of combinations. They keep recombining as the soil temperature changes, as the pH is altered, as water moves through the soil, and as plants and

This Swedish ivy is deficient in nitrogen. The older leaves are turning yellow and will eventually drop off.

animals inhabit the soil. Sometimes the elements combine into forms that can be absorbed by plants, and sometimes they combine into unavailable forms. With only a few exceptions, mineral nutrients must be dissolved before plants can absorb them. If an element is in a form that is insoluble, it is not available to the plants.

Nitrogen

The one plant nutrient that is in chronic short supply and must be added routinely, regardless of your location and your soil type, is nitrogen. Most of the nitrogen in the soil is tied up in organic matter, which must break down before nutrients are released. Once nitrogen is in its available form, it easily washes out of the soil. What isn't washed away is rapidly depleted. All plants and microorganisms compete for nitrogen because it is a constituent of protein, the basic substance of all living matter.

Most plants are capable of absorbing nitrogen as either nitrate or ammonium. Most of the nitrogen is taken up in the highly soluble nitrate form. Eventually, all forms of nitrogen fertilizer are converted to nitrate by soil organisms. In nature, nitrogen is recycled

---

SIXTEEN ESSENTIAL PLANT NUTRIENTS

Carbon (C)
Hydrogen (H)
Oxygen (O)

Primary nutrients: *
  Nitrogen (N)
  Phosphorus (P)
  Potassium (K)

Secondary nutrients: *
  Calcium (Ca)
  Magnesium (Mg)
  Sulfur (S)

Micronutrients: *
  Chlorine (Cl)
  Iron (Fe)
  Manganese (Mn)
  Boron (B)
  Zinc (Zn)
  Copper (Cu)
  Molybdenum (Mo)

* Nutrients absorbed from the soil

---

endlessly through plant and animal tissues. Free nitrate is absorbed and becomes part of living matter, which dies, decomposes, and becomes nitrate again.

Nitrogen is often used to regulate plant growth in addition to maintaining plant health. Nitrogen stimulates shoot growth in plants. A high level of nitrogen in the soil results in vigorous shoot growth at the expense of other types of growth, such as flower, fruit, and root growth. If you are raising lettuce, this is highly desirable; lettuce that grows rapidly is succulent and sweet. It is undesirable in fruiting plants such as tomatoes. The plants might go on making vigorous leafy growth well into the summer and not begin to make blossoms and fruit until cool weather approaches.

Fertilizers without nitrogen or with only a little nitrogen are sold to promote flowering and fruiting. It isn't the presence of other minerals that encourages plants to bloom or to fruit, but rather the absence or slight presence of nitrogen.

Since available nitrogen either washes away easily or is absorbed by plants within weeks of application, it must be reapplied regularly. Unless you are using a slow-release form of nitrogen (see Fertilizers on page 170), you must add nitrogen to the soil every three to four weeks during the growing season.

Phosphorus

The second primary plant nutrient—phosphorus—is essential in all phases of plant growth. It is particularly associated with early maturity of crops, fruit and seed formation, and root growth.

Phosphorus must be added to the soil in most parts of the United States. Phosphorus deficiency is common, especially in clay soils and often in red soils. Phosphorus is highly reactive, bonding quickly with a wide variety of elements in the soil. It usually combines with oxygen to form phosphate; then the phosphate combines with calcium and other minerals to form almost insoluble compounds. Because phosphorus compounds are not easily dissolved, they are very stable in the soil. Unlike nitrogen, phosphorus can be replenished every few years, since it does not move in the soil or wash out of the root zone.

Dissolved phosphates are present in the soil in extremely low concentrations. Their presence is constant, however. As soon as the dissolved phosphates are absorbed by plants,

Dull and droopy leaves indicate that these tomato plants are suffering from a phosphorus deficiency.

A potassium deficiency is causing these walnut leaves to yellow, scorch, crinkle, and turn upward.

Potassium

The third primary plant nutrient—potassium—is essential in several plant growth processes, such as the movement of sugars and starch formation. Potassium also encourages root growth, improves the size and quality of fruit, and increases disease resistance. Potassium is said to contribute to the general vigor of plants.

Like phosphorus, it must be added in most parts of the United States, although not usually in the West. Potassium is highly soluble in water, but since it clings tightly to clay particles in the soil, it is not easily leached. A single application of potassium usually lasts an entire growing season.

You will often see potassium referred to as potash. The word *potash* goes back to colonial days when wood and other organic materials were burned in pots for the manufacture of soap. The ashes were rinsed with water; the rinse water was collected and allowed to evaporate, leaving a residue of potassium salts. These salts were used as fertilizer. Today, potassium is mined. Although potassium can be bought in a mined form and added separately to the soil, it is most commonly purchased as part of a complete fertilizer (one containing nitrogen, phosphorus, and potassium).

Secondary Nutrients

Calcium, magnesium, and sulfur are the secondary nutrients. They are classified this way not because their importance is secondary, but because they are found in most soils and seldom need to be added as fertilizer. These nutrients not only are essential to plant functions, they also affect the acidity or alkalinity of soils (see Soil pH on page 86).

Calcium and magnesium are the elements largely responsible for the pH of a soil. They are moderately soluble, so in regions of high rainfall they are washed from the soil. As a result, soils in these regions are usually acidic, and lime (calcium carbonate) is customarily added every year to make the soil less acid. Dolomitic limestone adds both calcium and magnesium to the soil. In low-rainfall areas as well as areas where the soil is derived from limestone, the soil is high in calcium and magnesium and is usually alkaline.

more phosphate is dissolved to replace them. Plants with large root systems, such as trees, are able to absorb sufficient phosphorus for their needs, but plants with small root systems, especially seedlings, don't have enough root area to absorb a sufficient quantity of the dilute chemical. Mature trees, even those growing in phosphorus-deficient soils, seldom need added phosphorus. However, seedlings almost always benefit from extra phosphorus. Since phosphorus does not move in the soil, it should be placed in the root zone of the plants.

Without sufficient phosphorus, top growth slows until the root system has grown large enough to absorb the needed amounts. Since absorption by roots slows in cold soils, plants set out in winter and early spring grow better with added phosphorus. Gardeners often add phosphorus in the form of bonemeal or superphosphate. Bonemeal is almost insoluble and only slightly available to plants. Superphosphate is phosphate rock that has been treated with acid to make it soluble; it remains soluble in the soil for between a few weeks and a few months.

The sulfur that is found naturally in the soil does not influence pH; it is tied up in organic matter. The sulfur is released slowly as the organic matter decomposes. However, when sulfur is added in its elemental form, it makes an alkaline soil more acid (see Correcting Soil pH on page 97). Sulfur is present in many commercial fertilizers, although you may not realize it unless you read the label very carefully.

Micronutrients

Although micronutrients—chlorine, iron, manganese, boron, zinc, copper, and molybdenum—are essential for plant growth, they are needed in tiny quantities and are usually added only when a deficiency is noted. When an element is deficient, plants exhibit characteristic symptoms of the deficiency (see the chart on page 170). Micronutrients are seldom truly deficient, but they sometimes form insoluble compounds, especially in alkaline soils. Iron, zinc, and manganese deficiencies are seen almost as commonly in the West as is nitrogen deficiency. Adding elemental iron, zinc, or manganese seldom helps, since the added mineral is immediately bound into an insoluble form in the soil.

Plants are able to absorb iron, zinc, and manganese if they are added as chelates. Derived from the Greek word for claws, chelates are specialized organic compounds that combine with and protect a nutrient, making it difficult for the nutrient to react chemically with soil particles. Instead of becoming insoluble, chelated nutrients will remain available to plants and are easily absorbed by them.

Since chelates are expensive and must be added at regular intervals, many gardeners look for a more permanent solution. The answer is to make the soil more acid, thus freeing the micronutrients already present in the soil. Adding soil sulfur is the most effective way to acidify the soil (see Correcting Soil pH on page 97). Some fertilizers are blended especially for plants that need acid conditions. These fertilizers contain chelated minerals in addition to having an acidifying effect on the soil.

The iron deficiency in this oak is causing the younger leaves to turn yellow between the veins. In western gardens iron, zinc, and manganese deficiencies are commonly seen.

Symptoms of Nutrient Deficiencies

Nutrient deficiencies show up in characteristic ways on plants; these symptoms are clues that the experienced gardener learns to recognize and to associate with a particular nutrient. Once the problem is identified, the deficient nutrient can be added. The symptom that gardeners encounter most often is chlorosis, or yellowing of the leaves, and it is usually due to a nitrogen shortage. Symptoms of the most common nutrient deficiencies are described below.

Nitrogen
The older leaves turn yellow, die, and drop. Growth is slow, and new leaves are smaller than normal. A plant may have a heavy bloom but not much fruit develops. The fruit that does develop is smaller than usual and highly colored, and it matures early.

Phosphorus
The leaves turn abnormally dull gray-green to dark green, and they are set close together on shorter stems. Veins, petioles (leafstalks), and lower leaf surfaces may be reddish purple. A light flower bloom is followed by fewer and smaller fruit.

Potassium
The older leaves turn yellow and then scorch, beginning at the edges and progressing toward the center. The leaves become crinkled and curl upward. Shoots die back late in the season. Lateral buds grow in a zigzag pattern and produce short, brushy growth.

Iron
The young leaves turn yellow between the veins, although the veins stay green. The older leaves remain green.

Manganese
The young leaves turn yellow between the veins. The veins remain green but there is a gradual fading of the green color from the veins outward. There is no sharp distinction between veins and interveinal areas as with an iron deficiency.

Zinc
The leaves are yellow and small. (This deficiency is sometimes called little leaf.) Leaves may be deformed and mottled. Shoots may be dwarfed, and twigs may die back. Fewer flowers than normal produce fruit; the fruit is small, pointed, and highly colored.

Fertilizers

A fertilizer is any natural or manufactured material that supplies one or more plant nutrients. Legally, the nutrients must amount to at least 5 percent of the fertilizer.

Fertilizers differ not only in their nutrient content but also in the form in which they are applied and in the speed with which their nutrients are released to plants. Some fertilizers contain a full spectrum of plant nutrients, whereas others contain only a single nutrient. Fertilizers can be made from natural organic materials or from synthetic substances, and they are available both in liquid and dry forms. Most fertilizers are very soluble; they are taken up quickly by the plant and bring about an almost immediate response. Their effects are short-lived, however, so they must be replenished regularly.

The most familiar, and usually the most economical, fertilizers are dry chemical fertilizers sold as granules, crystals, powders, and pellets. These are scattered on the soil and watered in. Most dry fertilizers are soluble in water and become instantly available to plants. They usually leach from the soil in a few weeks and must be reapplied every three to four weeks.

Other dry fertilizers are insoluble in water but become available to plants over a period of time. These are known as slow-release fertilizers. Urea formaldehyde is a commonly used form of slow-release nitrogen. The action of soil bacteria slowly releases the nitrogen so that plants can use it. Some slow-release fertilizers are applied as solid chunks, such as spikes or pellets, that are hammered into or buried in the soil in the root zone of the plant. Depending on the fertilizer used, the effect in the soil can last from six weeks to two years. Slow-release fertilizers are applied less frequently but are more expensive than the soluble forms.

Natural organic fertilizers, such as manures, fish emulsion, seaweed extract, and blood meal, also release nutrients slowly as they decompose in the soil. The effects last a long time, and it is difficult to overfertilize. The rate at which these fertilizers release nutrients is unpredictable, however. Natural organic fertilizers are often bulky and heavy to handle. Since the percentage of nitrogen is usually lower than in synthetic fertilizers,

A drop spreader is the easiest and most precise tool for applying dry fertilizer to a small- or average-sized lawn. After the dry fertilizer is spread it should be watered in.

you must add more to provide plants with the same amount of nutrients.

Other commonly used forms of fertilizers are liquids or soluble powders that are dissolved in water before application. They can be applied by hand with a watering can or a hose-end sprayer, or they can be applied automatically through a fertilizer injector attached to a watering system. Their effects are immediate although short-lived.

Liquid fertilizers and soluble powders are also used for foliar feeding. In this case, a dilute fertilizer solution is sprayed directly onto the leaves. Foliar feeding is useful when a soil problem restricts the uptake of nutrients by the roots. Any excess fertilizer falling to the soil is available for absorption by the plant's roots.

How to Read a Fertilizer Label

Every package of commercial fertilizer must, by law, clearly state the contents. The percentages by weight of the three major nutrients—nitrogen, phosphorus (phosphate), and potassium (potash)—appear on the front of the package. These three elements are always listed in that order; sometimes they are abbreviated NPK (the chemical symbols for the nutrients). Other nutrients in the fertilizer are listed elsewhere on the package.

A fertilizer with the label 12-8-16 contains 12 percent nitrogen, 8 percent phosphorus, and 16 percent potassium by weight. The remainder of the fertilizer is filler material; some of this material is inert, and the rest consists of elements such as oxygen, sulfur, and calcium that are used by plants. Fertilizers with different concentrations of nutrients but the same ratio are equivalent. For example, 1 pound of 10-20-20 has the same amount of nutrients as 2 pounds of 5-10-10.

Fertilizers that contain all three primary nutrients are called complete fertilizers. If a fertilizer lacks any primary nutrient, an *0* appears in that place in the NPK sequence. Ammonium sulfate (21-0-0), for instance, contains nitrogen but no phosphorus or potassium.

Nutrient Ratio

The most important factor in selecting a fertilizer is the ratio between nitrogen and the other two major nutrients. The ratio determines the kind of growth that will be produced. Since the same kind of growth isn't desirable on all plants, no single fertilizer is suitable for all garden plantings.

A high-nitrogen fertilizer—one with a ratio of 2:1:1 or greater (for example, 12-6-6 or 32-10-10)—stimulates foliage growth. This is desirable in lawns, leafy vegetables, such as lettuce, and most young plants, but it can be detrimental in other plants. For instance, too much leafy growth in a tomato plant will delay its fruiting. Using a high-nitrogen fertilizer in a bed of annuals and perennials will result in a lot of foliage and fewer flowers. On plants susceptible to insect damage, a high-nitrogen fertilizer may cause succulent growth that attracts aphids and mites. You may want to withhold nitrogen intentionally so that a planting—a hedge, for example—will grow more slowly and require less pruning. As a basic rule, you should use a high-nitrogen fertilizer only when you want a lot of leafy growth.

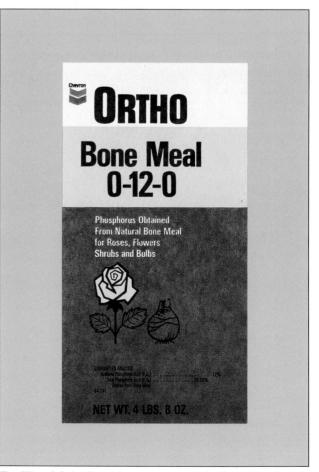

Fertilizer labels show the percentages of mineral nutrients.

For general growth use a balanced, all-purpose fertilizer. This type of fertilizer will usually have a ratio of 1:1:1 (for example, 10-10-10). Many fertilizers sold for flowering and fruiting have a 1:2:2 ratio (for example, 5-10-10) or a 1:2:1 ratio (for example, 5-10-5). These are low-nitrogen fertilizers.

Nitrogen Persistence

Several forms of nitrogen may be found in a fertilizer—for example, a fertilizer label may list varying amounts of nitrate nitrogen (NO_3), ammoniacal nitrogen (NH_4), and water-insoluble nitrogen. These different forms tell you how soon the nitrogen will be available to plants and approximately how long it will last in the soil. A combination of quick-release and slow-release forms of nitrogen in a single fertilizer tells you that the fertilizer will have an immediate effect as well as a long-term one.

Nitrate nitrogen is water-soluble and easily absorbed by plants, but it does not remain in the soil for long. Heavy rain or irrigation will leach it out of the soil in a couple of weeks.

Ammoniacal nitrogen is also water soluble, but many plants cannot absorb it. Ammonium attaches to soil particles and does not leach from the soil. Bacteria in the soil slowly convert it into nitrate, which either is absorbed by plants or leaches from the soil.

Water-insoluble, or slow-release, nitrogen is available in synthetic or natural organic forms. Most of these fertilizers are expensive, but they last for a long time in the soil. In making synthetic water-insoluble nitrogen, manufacturers slow the release of nitrogen in several ways. One way is to change the fertilizer chemically to make a portion of it insoluble. Another way is to coat the fertilizer in a material that dissolves slowly in the soil. Resin and sulfur are two commonly used coating materials.

Soil Reaction

When used over a period of time, fertilizers can make the soil more acid or more alkaline, depending on the kind of ingredients used. Nitrogen fertilizers can be used to change the pH of the soil. Ammonium-containing fertilizers, such as ammonium sulfate and ammonium phosphate, have an acidifying effect.

Slow-release fertilizers should be placed in the root zone of a plant.

Calcium nitrate is an example of a nitrogen fertilizer that makes the soil more alkaline.

Fertilizers that have strong acid reactions are best used in alkaline soils or to feed acid-loving plants. Fertilizers with weak acid reactions are best used in naturally acid or neutral soils.

The degree to which a fertilizer makes a soil more acid can be determined by checking the calcium carbonate equivalent listed on the product label. This number refers to the pounds of calcium carbonate (lime) required to neutralize the acid produced by a ton of the fertilizer. The higher the number, the more acid the fertilizer. For example, an equivalent of 200 pounds indicates that the fertilizer has a moderate acid reaction; an equivalent of 1,200 pounds indicates a strong acid reaction.

A deep root feeder delivers nutrients directly to the root zones of plants. It is handy for feeding deep-rooted plants, such as trees.

APPLYING FERTILIZERS

Every package of fertilizer sold for use in home gardens lists recommendations for the amount and frequency of application. Either follow these directions, or feed half as much as directed but twice as often. Don't try to outguess the manufacturer by adding more than the recommended amount. After adding any fertilizer to the soil, be sure to water thoroughly to dissolve and dilute the nutrients and to keep the salts in the fertilizer from burning your plants. Packaged fertilizers are often high in salts; always follow the package directions to avoid fertilizer burn.

When to Fertilize

The general rule to remember about timing fertilizer applications is that they are necessary when a plant is growing. They shouldn't be added to make a plant grow. Upsetting the natural rhythm of growth can result in injury to the plant.

Nitrogen is the nutrient most responsible for stimulating vegetative growth. Applying a nitrogen fertilizer to a dormant plant can cause it to leaf out before the time is right. New leaf tissue is particularly sensitive to cold, so an untimely feeding could result in a frost- or cold-damaged plant.

Plants need nitrogen when they are growing rapidly. For this reason, the heaviest application should be made just before or during rapid spring growth. Heavy applications of nitrogen should not be made in late summer, because they will encourage new top growth that will not have time to harden off before winter.

Since nitrogen stimulates leaf growth, it should be used in moderation on any tree or shrub that you must prune regularly. Nitrogen should also be used sparingly on flowers and vegetables that seem to be producing more leaves than flowers or fruit.

Plants need phosphorus and potassium all the time they are growing, but the nutrients don't have to be added often since they persist in the soil for long periods.

How to Apply Fertilizer

There are several effective ways to apply both dry and liquid fertilizers. In unplanted areas, dry fertilizer is generally mixed into

A hose-end sprayer can be used for applying liquid fertilizer to lawns and gardens, and for foliar feeding.

the soil before planting. The following methods are used for applying fertilizer in existing plantings.

Broadcasting Dry fertilizers, including bulk organic materials, can be broadcast—that is, spread by hand or with a device such as a wheeled push spreader or a crank-type hand-held spreader. Broadcasting is a good way to spread fertilizer over large areas.

Banding This method is often used to fertilize newly planted rows of vegetables or flowers. Placement of the band of dry fertilizer depends on your irrigation system. With overhead sprinkling, place the fertilizer in bands on both sides of the seed furrow or row of seedlings. The bands should be about 2 inches away from the seeds or plants and about 2 inches deeper. For furrow irrigation, place the bands between the seeds and the watering furrow so that the water will dissolve the fertilizer and carry it to the plants.

Side-dressing This application method consists of placing dry fertilizer alongside a plant or a row of plants, usually midway through the growing season. Side-dressing usually supplements the fertilizer applied at the time of planting.

Watering with fertilizer solution Fertilizers that are completely water soluble (this will be clearly marked on the package) are ideal for applying as part of your watering regimen. The fertilizer is mixed with water and is either applied by hand from a watering can or injected into the irrigation system. In the latter case, dissolve a small sample of the fertilizer to see if it leaves any residue that could plug up the system. If it does, you should strain the solution first.

Deep root feeders are also used to apply fertilizer solution. They provide a quick, efficient way to deliver nutrients directly to the root zone of trees and other deep-rooted plants. The feeder is a long, thin tube that is attached to a hose and inserted into the soil. Fertilizer pellets are placed in a receptacle in the top of the feeder; water pressure dissolves the pellets and forces the fertilizer solution down through the feeder tube.

Foliar feeding This method consists of spraying plant leaves with a fertilizer solution. Plants suffering from micronutrient deficiencies are often fed this way. The fertilizer is readily absorbed by the leaves, causing a rapid change in the plant's condition. Foliar feeding is common in many areas of the West, where alkaline soils restrict the uptake of iron, zinc, and manganese by plant roots.

Using slow-release fertilizers Slow-release fertilizers last from several months to a couple of years in the soil. They are more expensive than water-soluble fertilizers but are valuable where low maintenance is a goal. The application method depends on the form of the fertilizer; for example, granules are usually broadcast and fertilizer spikes are hammered into the root zone.

Fertilizing Trees and Shrubs

Young trees and shrubs that are establishing their roots in the soil benefit from a complete fertilizer (one containing nitrogen, phosphorus, and potassium). They will grow more rapidly and reach their mature size faster. Once mature, these plants do not need a complete fertilizer as long as they have good leaf color and are growing reasonably well. Nitrogen is the only added nutrient they require at this stage. (The method for determining the appropriate amount of actual nitrogen to use when you are fertilizing mature ornamentals is shown in the chart on page 178.)

All fruit trees, whether young or fully grown, benefit from a complete fertilizer. You are removing substantial amounts of nutrients when you harvest fruit trees. Pruning also causes nutrient loss, and fruit trees are pruned more often than ornamental trees. You must replace these nutrients through the soil in order to maintain the health of the plant.

Proper fertilizing will usually invigorate a tree or shrub threatened by insects or diseases. It may also reverse the decline of unhealthy trees and shrubs. However, overfertilization can provoke too much growth and make the plant vulnerable to cold and to certain diseases. When a tree grows too vigorously, much of the growth is vertical (rapidly growing vertical shoots are called water sprouts), which spoils the shape of the tree.

A tree or shrub suffering from a micronutrient deficiency may be fed with a foliar spray, but in most cases fertilizer is applied to the soil. To be effective, the fertilizer must penetrate into the root zone of the plant. Although some trees may have roots dozens of feet deep, most of the nutrients and water that a tree receives are absorbed in the top 3 feet of soil. Tree roots may extend hundreds of feet from the trunk, particularly if the tree is growing in dry or infertile soil, but the feeder roots are concentrated at the outside edges of the drip line. Apply fertilizer from a point midway between the trunk and the drip line to a point 2 feet beyond the drip line. For shrubs and small trees, apply the fertilizer to an area starting a foot from the

FERTILIZING TREES

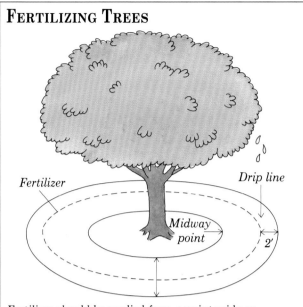

Fertilizer should be applied from a point midway between the trunk and the drip line to a point 2' beyond the drip line.

FERTILIZING SHRUBS AND SMALL TREES

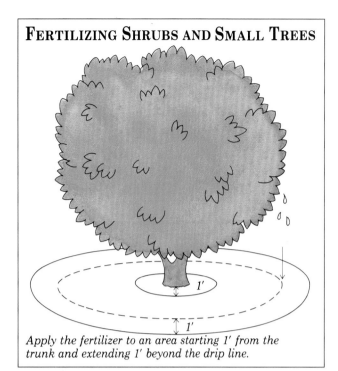

Apply the fertilizer to an area starting 1' from the trunk and extending 1' beyond the drip line.

trunk and extending a foot beyond the drip line. Be careful not to spread the fertilizer too close to the trunk.

Timing Fertilizer Applications

Fertilize deciduous trees and shrubs in spring as soon as the leaves appear. Evergreen plants should also be fed just before or during spring growth. In areas where the ground freezes in winter, nitrogen is some-times applied to trees and shrubs in fall as well, after top growth has stopped. Root growth, which continues into early winter and resumes in early spring, is stimulated by this practice. Don't fertilize too early in fall, or the plant may develop new top growth that will be susceptible to frost damage.

Fertilize fruit trees twice: Apply two thirds of the recommended yearly application in early spring and one third in June. In cold-winter areas, make an application in late fall instead of early spring. Fruit trees in contain-ers benefit from monthly feedings during the growing period.

Citrus trees flourish when given three feedings: in late winter, midsummer, and late summer. Use a fertilizer with the full spec-trum of micronutrients, especially zinc.

Study your plants to see how they re-spond to feeding. If growth is excessive on young trees, apply less fertilizer the next time or skip a year. If shoot growth is shorter than desired and leaf color is pale, apply more fertilizer. As trees mature, fertilize them only if growth or leaf color is not up to expectations.

Feeding Trees in Lawns

Trees growing in lawns are often underfed, even when the lawn receives more fertilizer than the rest of the garden. This occurs partly because lawn grasses are voracious feeders and partly because grass roots form a dense network in the upper foot of soil. Use one of the following methods to fertilize a tree in your lawn.

For quick greening, use a nitrate-based nitrogen source (rather than an ammonium or urea fertilizer). Spread it across the entire lawn, but use twice the recommended quan-tity around the drip line of the tree. Water in the fertilizer as usual, but water even longer around the tree. Apply a total of 2 to 3 inches of water around the drip line of the tree. (Place a flat-bottomed container on the lawn when the sprinklers are on; when the water in the container measures 2 to 3 inches, you know you've applied the right amount of water.) This heavy watering carries the nitro-gen below the reach of the grass roots. Apply-ing twice as much nitrate-based nitrogen fertilizer as recommended ordinarily would

Estimating the Nitrogen Need of Trees

You can determine a tree's yearly requirement of actual nitrogen based on the diameter of the trunk at a point 4 feet above the soil level. To figure out the diameter of the trunk, divide the circumference, or distance around the tree trunk, by 3.14. For example, a tree with a circumference of 12 inches has a diameter of 3.82 inches (*12 ÷ 3.14 = 3.82*).

Trunk Diameter (inches)	Actual Nitrogen (pounds)
1	0.15–0.30
2	0.30–0.60
3	0.45–0.90
4	0.60–1.20
5	0.75–1.50
6	0.90–1.80
7	2.10–4.20
8	2.40–4.80
9	2.70–5.40
10	3.00–6.00

burn the lawn, but watering heavily counteracts this.

Another method to feed a lawn tree is to use a deep root feeder to bypass the lawn grass and deliver water-soluble fertilizer directly to the root zone of the tree.

A third method consists of digging holes around the drip line of the tree with a soil auger. This tool is available at most equipment rental shops. Dig holes 2 to 3 inches in diameter and 2 feet deep every couple of feet around the drip line. Pour dry fertilizer or slow-release pellets into the holes and fill with soil. Fertilizer will be carried to the tree roots every time you water the lawn.

Feeding Lawns

Unlike many other plants, lawn grasses need frequent applications of fertilizer for healthy, attractive growth. Lawn grasses are dependent on fertilizer because they live in an unnatural environment. The grass plants are crowded together and compete with one another, along with neighboring trees and shrubs, for water and nutrients. They are mowed regularly and their clippings, a source of nutrients, are often removed.

A properly fertilized lawn has good color and is thick and lush. Fertilizer also gives vigor to a lawn, so that it will not easily succumb to insects, weeds, or diseases. In fact, some lawn fertilizers are multipurpose; in addition to nutrients, they may contain an herbicide for weed control, an insecticide for insect control, and a fungicide for disease control.

Nutrients That Lawns Need
A fertilizer with a ratio of 3:1:2 or 6:1:2 should be used for feeding lawns. A typical lawn fertilizer may have a 24-8-16 or 24-4-8 formula. It's not critical to use either exact formula, but something close to it is best.

Most lawns require an annual application of 4 to 6 pounds of actual nitrogen per 1,000 square feet (see Calculating Actual Nitrogen on page 180). Lawn clippings are a natural source of nitrogen. If you leave them on the lawn each time you mow, you won't need to apply as much chemical nitrogen. If the soil is waterlogged or compacted, the

A hand-held broadcast spreader operates by turning a crank. The fertilizer flies out from a whirling wheel.

A wheeled, push-type broadcast spreader is ideal for fertilizing large lawns.

nitrogen you add won't be available to the grass. Cut down on watering and aerate the lawn (punch holes in the lawn with an aerating tool) whenever necessary.

Lawns also require an annual application of 1 to 2 pounds of actual phosphorus and 1 pound of actual potassium per 1,000 square feet. In many parts of the West, phosphorus and potassium are plentiful in the soil and don't need to be added. It doesn't hurt to add these elements if you don't know the nutrient content of your soil. Phosphorus and potassium should be added in much of the East, where they are deficient. If you are using a complete fertilizer (one containing nitrogen, phosphorus, and potassium), you need to calculate only how much nitrogen to add. Most lawn fertilizers are formulated so that you will be adding the proper amounts of phosphorus and potassium if you calculate the nitrogen correctly.

If you are using a fertilizer containing only nitrogen, you can add phosphorus and potassium separately. Cool-season grasses benefit from a phosphorus application in fall and a second one in spring; add phosphorus to warm-season grasses in spring. It is best to apply potassium all at once just before a period of stress for the lawn—before hot summer weather for cool-season lawns and before fall for warm-season lawns.

Of the micronutrients—the nutrients needed in tiny amounts—iron is the one most often added to lawn fertilizers. If your lawn does not green up with an application of nitrogen, the problem is most likely a shortage of iron. This is particularly likely if your lawn is growing in an alkaline soil. Soils that are alkaline tend to make iron unavailable to plants.

The fertilizing schedules recommended for warm-season and cool-season grasses (see below) are based on using soluble synthetic fertilizers, the most common type of fertilizer used on lawns. Relatively inexpensive and predictable, these fertilizers are quick release—that is, they go to work immediately. Since their effects are short-lived, they must be replenished regularly.

Feeding Cool-Season Grasses

Cool-season grasses require a total of 4 to 6 pounds of actual nitrogen divided into four applications yearly.

In cold areas, where cool-season lawns turn brown in winter, feed one quarter of the yearly total of actual nitrogen in fall as soon as top growth is stopped by cold weather but the grass is still green. Feed one quarter of the nitrogen in spring as soon as the grass begins growing vigorously. About six weeks later, or when the grass begins to lose its bright green color, feed one eighth of the yearly total. At this feeding, use a fertilizer high in potassium as well as nitrogen. As soon as the weather cools in fall, feed the remaining three eighths of the total amount of nitrogen.

In mild areas where cool-season grasses remain green in winter, you can make four applications as follows: one quarter of the yearly total of actual nitrogen at the beginning of March, one quarter in mid-April, one quarter in early September, and one quarter in mid-October.

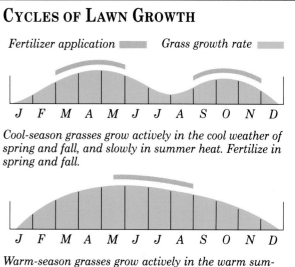

CYCLES OF LAWN GROWTH

Fertilizer application ▬▬▬   Grass growth rate ▬▬▬

J F M A M J J A S O N D

Cool-season grasses grow actively in the cool weather of spring and fall, and slowly in summer heat. Fertilize in spring and fall.

J F M A M J J A S O N D

Warm-season grasses grow actively in the warm summer months, then become dormant in cold weather. Fertilize throughout the growing season.

COOL- AND WARM-SEASON GRASSES

Cool-Season Grasses
Blue grass
Bent grass
Fescue
Rye grass

Warm-Season Grasses
Bahia grass
Bermuda grass
Carpet grass
Centipede grass
St. Augustine grass
Zoysia grass

CALCULATING ACTUAL NITROGEN

You must be able to calculate the amount of actual nitrogen in a package of fertilizer in order to know how much fertilizer to add. Multiply the percentage of nitrogen by the total weight of the fertilizer. For example, a 20-pound bag of 21-0-0 fertilizer contains 4.2 pounds of actual nitrogen ($.21 \times 20 = 4.2$). Then divide the amount of actual nitrogen your tree requires by the amount of actual nitrogen in the package of fertilizer. For example, you would use half the bag if you wanted to lightly fertilize a tree with a 7-inch diameter ($2.10 \div 4.2 = 0.50$). You would add the entire bag if you wanted to fertilize more heavily.

In both cold and mild areas, if the grass appears underfed or turns yellow in summer, apply an additional ⅛ pound of actual nitrogen.

Feeding Warm-Season Grasses
Warm-season grasses should be fertilized monthly as long as the grass is growing. The fact that a lawn is green doesn't mean it is growing; you will know the grass is growing if mowing produces clippings. In the warmest climates lawns may grow the year around; if so, they should be fertilized each month. In the northern range of warm-season grasses, lawns may go dormant and turn brown in October; these lawns should be fed monthly from the time they begin active growth in spring until they turn brown.

Apply ½ pound of actual nitrogen at each feeding. If you apply more nitrogen, you will only increase the rate of growth and the amount of mowing you'll have to do. Some warm-season grasses, such as hybrid Bermuda grass, can take as much as 1 pound of actual nitrogen at each feeding, but it is not necessary to apply that much if the lawn is performing well.

Applying Lawn Fertilizers
The three basic methods of applying lawn fertilizers are spraying, broadcast spreading, and drop spreading. A hose-end sprayer is generally used to apply liquid fertilizer. A broadcast spreader or drop spreader is the

best way to apply dry fertilizer; spreading the fertilizer by hand usually results in an uneven application.

The easiest way to apply dry fertilizer is with a broadcast spreader—either a crank-type hand-held spreader or a wheeled push spreader. Both throw dry fertilizer over a wide area, usually in an 8- to 12-foot arc. For even coverage, apply half of the fertilizer while moving in one direction, and apply the balance while moving in the opposite direction. Walk at a normal pace and keep the spreader level. Overlap the adjacent passes by about one third, since more material tends to fall in the middle of the arc than at the edge. A wheeled spreader works well on large lawns, but it may throw granules in too wide a pattern for small areas. A hand-held spreader is suitable for small areas; you can even reduce the throw by rotating the crank in the reverse direction.

A drop spreader is useful on small- and medium-sized lawns. It is more precise, but slower, than a broadcast spreader. Rather than throw the fertilizer, it drops it through a bottom slot. Adjustments on the bottom of the hopper calibrate the amount of fertilizer that falls to the lawn as you walk at a steady pace. Overlap the wheels enough so that no strips are left underfertilized, but also be careful not to double-feed any sections.

VEGETABLES AND FLOWERS

Both vegetables and flowering plants perform better when they are fertilized regularly. Here are some general guidelines for achieving the best results with fertilizers.

Vegetables
Most vegetables are heavy feeders and require a steady, reliable supply of fertilizer for optimum growth. Lettuce and other leafy vegetables require large amounts of nitrogen; use a high-nitrogen fertilizer on these crops. Tomatoes and other fruiting crops should be given an all-purpose fertilizer or a low-nitrogen fertilizer formulated for flowering and fruiting. (See Nutrient Ratio on page 172.)

Culinary herbs generally require less fertilizer than vegetables. Minimal fertilizing stresses culinary herbs, forcing a concentration of oils that enhances their taste.

The flavor of culinary herbs is enhanced when the plants are fertilized minimally.

Acid soil causes hydrangeas to grow blue flowers; alkaline soil will produce pink flowers.

An all-purpose or low-nitrogen fertilizer formulated for flowering and fruiting will work best with most flowers.

A complete fertilizer, applied in spring and every three to four weeks throughout the growing season, is required for roses.

FEEDING A FLOWER BED

Each of the following dry fertilizers, added in the amount listed, will feed a 100-square-foot flower bed. Each fertilizer will add about 0.2 pound (3.2 ounces) of actual nitrogen. Work about one third of the fertilizer into the soil in spring and use the remainder for monthly feedings throughout the growing season.

Fertilizer	Pounds
5-10-10	4
6-20-10	3¼
8-24-8	2½
10-10-8	2
16-16-16	1¼

If you use a packaged fertilizer, follow all label directions. Many gardeners use manure or homemade compost to fertilize vegetable gardens. If you do, before planting the bed in early spring, spread a layer ½ to 1 inch deep and till it in well. Use only aged manure and, if possible, work it into the ground a month or two before planting, then water well to leach out salts. If you're using poultry manure, apply only half as much, since it contains a very high level of salts.

For more information on fertilizing various vegetables, see "Growing Vegetables," starting on page 217.

Flowers

Most flowers benefit from an all-purpose fertilizer or a low-nitrogen fertilizer formulated for flowering and fruiting (see Nutrient Ratio on page 172). Refer to the chart on this page for general guidelines on feeding flower beds. The following are special instructions for different types of flowers.

Bulbs At planting time apply phosphorus. Use 1 teaspoon of bonemeal per bulb or 3 pounds of superphosphate (0-20-0) per 100 square feet of planted area. When the bulbs emerge, apply a complete fertilizer (one containing nitrogen, phosphorus, and potassium) following label directions.

Roses Because roses are high-powered flower producers, they need abundant, attentive feeding. Apply a complete fertilizer in early spring, just after pruning and before the leaves are fully open. Repeat every three to four weeks. Stop fertilizing six weeks before the first anticipated frost.

Azaleas, camellias, and rhododendrons These plants should be fed lightly once a month from the time they finish blooming through August. Use a complete fertilizer formulated for acid-loving plants.

Hydrangeas Whether the soil is acid or alkaline determines the color of hydrangea flowers. The flowers are blue when the plant is grown in acid soil and pink when grown in alkaline soil. The plant grows best in acid soil. Add aluminum sulfate to an alkaline soil to make it more acidic and to turn the

To fertilize container plants, use a siphon injector, which draws a liquid concentrate from a bucket and injects it into the irrigation water.

flowers blue. If you want pink flowers and your soil is acid, add lime (calcium carbonate) or superphosphate to make the soil alkaline. Since the foliage will turn yellow above pH 6.0, apply chelated iron to keep the leaves green.

FEEDING CONTAINER PLANTS

Container plants can be fed with liquid fertilizers, granular fertilizers, or slow-release fertilizer capsules or pellets. Because of the small amount of soil, plants in containers are more dependent on the gardener for feeding than are plants in the ground. Always moisten the soil before adding fertilizer and pay careful attention to concentrations. Too much fertilizer can easily damage or kill container plants.

Many gardeners prefer liquid feedings twice a month. Follow package directions for strength and frequency of use, or feed at half strength but twice as often. Never feed more than is recommended.

Ferns are especially susceptible to damage from too much fertilizer. Use a low-analysis fertilizer diluted to half strength. Fish emulsion is safe for ferns.

Since many container plants are indoor houseplants, be aware of their seasonal growing cycles. In response to the low light of winter, many indoor plants may become dormant. Don't feed them during this period, but resume when they begin to grow again in spring.

Foliage plants in containers, such as philodendron, respond best to a high-nitrogen fertilizer (for example, 12-6-6), since nitrogen stimulates leaf growth. Flowering plants, such as impatiens, respond best to a low-nitrogen fertilizer (for example, 5-10-5).

A newly potted plant in a rich potting soil will need feeding in three weeks to two months, depending on the amount of watering and its leaching effect on nutrients in the potting soil. Fertilizer generally leaches more quickly from perlite than from vermiculite.

PRUNING

Correct pruning is part science and part art. The science is in understanding how plants grow and respond to different pruning cuts. You should develop a good sense about how, where, and when to make a pruning cut. The art is in creating a shape—deciding which branches to remove and which to leave intact, which to shorten, and which to allow to grow. The result is a plant that grows into the shape envisioned in the mind's eye—a shape that suits the plant and looks appropriate in the garden.

In the same way that the artistic side of pruning changes as preferences and garden styles change, so does the scientific side of pruning evolve with new discoveries. Pruning techniques used today are different from—and better than—those used 10 years ago because of recent discoveries about how woody plants respond to pruning wounds. These important changes in technique mean healthier, longer-lived trees and shrubs.

You may be able to do much of the pruning yourself, but there may be times when hiring a professional is advisable. You may lack the skill or equipment for major pruning jobs. Tree pruning can be dangerous and often should be left to a professional, especially if the branches to be removed are heavy or high up. It is safer in many cases to call a professional arborist or tree-care company with the proper expertise, equipment, and insurance coverage.

Pruning keeps this garden tidy and gives it a formal, manicured look.

REASONS FOR PRUNING

There are several main reasons for pruning a plant: to control size, direct growth, improve health, and increase flower or fruit production.

Most home gardeners prune to control the size of plants. They commonly plant trees and shrubs too close to each other, too near the house, or in a location where the plant's ultimate size is unacceptable. In many cases, the plant is allowed to grow unrestricted until it is too large, and then it must be drastically pruned. Pruning and training trees and shrubs early in their growth can prevent the need for major pruning later.

Directing growth is another important function of pruning. Often, newly purchased trees have a poor branching structure. By beginning to prune right after planting, you can reshape the structure of the tree.

Plants are also pruned to improve their health and vigor. Skillful pruning can do much to prevent plant diseases by bringing sunlight and air circulation into the middle of the plant. With less plant material competing for water and nutrients, the remaining plant parts grow stronger. Pruning can often help a plant that is already diseased or infested; by pruning off the affected parts, you may be able to remove the problem and restore the plant to good health.

When a plant has been damaged, such as a tree with branches shorn off in a windstorm, proper pruning can eliminate the jagged stub that would allow rot to enter the tree. Anticipated wind or snow load damage can be reduced by pruning vulnerable branches.

Pruning is also used to increase flower, fruit, and leaf production. Removing some of the flower buds will force the plant's energy into the remaining flowers, making them larger. Pruning back part of the wood on a fruit tree each winter forces plant energy into setting bigger fruit on the remaining branches. Thinning some fruit, such as peaches, is a form of pruning that results in fewer but larger fruit.

In addition, pruning expresses the artistry and style of the gardener. The plants become an artistic medium. Depending on how they're pruned, hedges can have an informal, natural appearance or a formal, manicured look. You can prune plants so that their texture, color, and flowering lend interest to the garden.

PRUNING AND PLANT GROWTH

Some fundamental knowledge about how plants grow explains a great deal about the way they respond to pruning cuts. By understanding the basics of plant growth, you will be able to prune more intuitively—and more successfully.

The Role of the Bud

Almost all new growth on trees and shrubs develops from buds on the branches. There are three types of buds: dormant, latent, and adventitious. Dormant buds form during one growing season and remain dormant until the next growth period, when, depending on the type of bud, they grow into stems, leaves, or flowers. New stems arise from dormant buds at the branch tip (called terminal buds). Side branches develop from the dormant buds on the side of a branch (called lateral buds). When lateral buds are located at the base of a leaf, they are called axillary buds. Some axillary buds produce leaves or flowers.

Not every bud grows into a branch, leaf, or flower. Some buds on young twigs remain inactive for many seasons. When dormant buds persist on older stems, they are known as latent buds; they remain at or near the surface of the bark as the branch grows larger. Both dormant buds and latent buds are strongly linked to the stem's pipeline of water and nutrients by a connection called a bud trace. These latent buds are the plant's insurance. Should a branch be cut or broken above a dormant or a latent bud, a new shoot can quickly grow from the bud.

Adventitious buds develop where no buds previously existed. These sometimes grow after a branch has been wounded or cut back to mature tissue. These buds differ from latent buds because they develop close to the branch surface from deeper mature tissue and are not connected by a bud trace; as a result, the branches that develop from adventitious buds are not strongly connected to the trunk or main branches and can be easily broken during a storm.

Pruning controls the size of this deciduous azalea, emphasizes its graceful shape, and promotes larger flowers by forcing the plant's energy into the remaining flowers.

Types of Buds

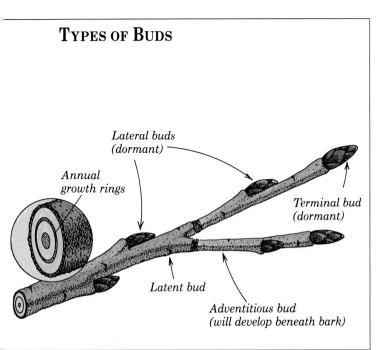

Annual growth rings

Lateral buds (dormant)

Terminal bud (dormant)

Latent bud

Adventitious bud (will develop beneath bark)

Natural Target Pruning

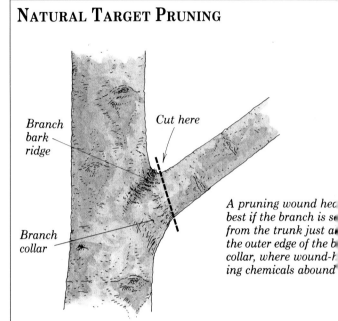

Branch bark ridge

Cut here

Branch collar

A pruning wound hea best if the branch is se from the trunk just ar the outer edge of the b collar, where wound-h ing chemicals abound

Improper pruning techniques, such as cutting branches back to stubs, may cause adventitious buds to form behind the stub. The young shoots that arise from these buds are weakly attached and easily broken. Not until new layers of wood form annual growth rings are the branches strongly anchored.

Apical Dominance
By looking at the current season's growth on a woody plant, you can see that few, if any, lateral buds close to the tip of the branch have grown into side branches. Not until a lateral bud is far enough from the terminal bud—usually after two to three years—does it begin to grow. This phenomenon, known as apical dominance, is controlled by a hormone called auxin produced in the terminal bud. Auxin suppresses the growth of the other buds, signaling them to remain dormant. Buds farther and farther away receive weaker and weaker signals, until they are released from dormancy and begin growing.

This hormonal effect determines a plant's branching pattern and its response to pruning. As long as the terminal bud remains alive, it will be the first to grow in the spring. This natural system results in an orderly, controlled growth rate and gives a characteristic shape to all plants; prune off the terminal bud and the growth pattern changes drastically.

The science of pruning lies in understanding and manipulating bud growth. Removing a terminal bud releases dormant, latent, or adventitious buds from the growth inhibition caused by apical dominance. Removing the terminal bud alters the orderly, natural growth patterns. Many of the buds behind the cut sprout into branches; where one stem once grew, now a cluster of many stems emerges. This growth pattern is nowhere more apparent than on a sheared hedge or a tree whose crown has been cut horizontally below a utility wire. Not only does the plant lose its natural shape, but exceptionally fast growth creates a branch structure resembling a candelabra.

On the other hand, the growth pattern of a plant is preserved by pruning back a stem or side branch to where buds have already broken dormancy and formed a side shoot. The terminal bud on the lateral branch may then assume apical dominance.

Wound Healing
Research carried out by the U.S. Forest Service has shown that many old pruning ideas and practices are no longer valid. Botanists now know that healthy trees have the intrinsic ability to resist the invasion of wood-decaying organisms. Trees can close off pockets of decay and prevent its spread into neighboring wood by a process called compartmentalization.

The structure of the branch connection to the trunk plays an important role in decay resistance. A swollen branch collar is usually visible at the point where a side branch connects to the woody parent stem or trunk. This collar results from the meeting of two patterns of growth: the branch and the trunk. Over the years the branch collar continues to grow around the base of the branch, strengthening the attachment. As the collar grows, it may compress the bark, causing a visible ridge, called the branch bark ridge, to form where the branch tissue and trunk tissue meet.

The branch collar has special significance for woody plants. It is a storehouse for chemicals known as phenolic compounds, which are highly toxic to fungi that may attack the tree. The phenols help prevent decay-causing organisms from moving from injured or dying branches into healthy tissue.

If a branch is cut off flush with the parent branch or trunk—and the collar is removed, as was once advised—the tree loses its natural protective barrier and decay organisms can readily enter the wound. A better method of removing a branch is called natural target pruning. The branch is severed from the trunk at the edge of the branch collar, where the concentration of phenolic compounds is high. A wound at the edge of the collar heals quickly and is most effective in repelling decay organisms.

Trees are able to shed dead branches, closing over their wounds with callus tissue to help prevent decay. Callus also forms over the surface of wood exposed by a pruning cut. Cuts made on the outside edge of the collar appear first as a circle and later, when callus forms, as a doughnut. Each subsequent year the hole in the doughnut grows smaller, until the wound is completely closed. An improper flush cut not only leaves an oval wound or larger area for callus to close, it also removes the protective branch collar.

PRUNING CUTS

Different pruning cuts result in different growth patterns. The cuts are determined by where they are made on the stem in relation to dormant buds and side branches.

Thinning
Proper thinning entails cutting off a branch at its point of origin on the parent branch.

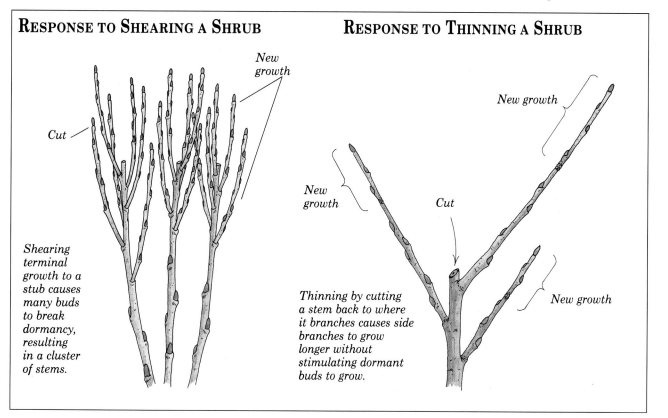

RESPONSE TO SHEARING A SHRUB

New growth

Cut

Shearing terminal growth to a stub causes many buds to break dormancy, resulting in a cluster of stems.

RESPONSE TO THINNING A SHRUB

New growth

New growth

Cut

New growth

Thinning by cutting a stem back to where it branches causes side branches to grow longer without stimulating dormant buds to grow.

189

Thinning cuts are often used to shorten a branch by cutting it back to a crotch (where the branch forms a Y). The terminal bud of the remaining branch becomes dominant and prevents other buds from breaking dormancy and growing into unwanted and possible disfiguring branches.

Pruning by using thinning cuts reduces the size of a plant without stimulating much unnecessary new growth. Thinning results in the most natural appearance and in strong growth that is resistant to storm damage. For these reasons, horticulture departments of major universities recommend thinning as the best pruning method for most shrubs and trees. Plants that are thinned grow at a healthy pace, but they remain neater and require less frequent pruning than plants that are headed or sheared.

Heading

When a branch is headed, it is cut to a stub, a lateral bud, or a small-diameter branch. Since heading removes the terminal bud, apical dominance is lost and many vigorous new shoots develop from buds directly below the cut; buds lower on the branch remain inhibited. Fruit trees, which produce few side branches, are often headed to encourage branching.

Sometimes street trees under utility wires are headed to remove interfering branches. Not only does the resulting flush of new growth soon become a problem, but the tree also loses its natural shape. It is better to thin the branches.

Shearing

Similar in principle to heading, shearing is a pruning cut that removes short lengths of top growth. The cut may fall above or below a bud, often leaving a stub. Because shearing removes the terminal buds on all the stem tips, a flush of new growth directly behind the cuts results in a dense canopy of exterior foliage.

The shearing cut is best reserved for hedges or topiary in formal gardens. Some shrubs—such as yew (*Taxus baccata*) and boxwood (*Buxus sempervirens*)—adapt better to being sheared than others; many otherwise beautiful plants can be ruined by shearing.

Heading a Tree

Pruning a tree by heading the branc and leaving a stub sults in a dense ou shell of weakly attached shoots.

Thinning a Tree

Pruning a tree by t ning branches bac side branches and leaving no stubs pr duces a more open stronger branching pattern.

Pinching

When the top of a succulent stem is pinched off, a growth response is produced that is similar to heading cuts made on woody stems. Pinching young annual and perennial flowering plants encourages bushy growth behind the pinch. When some of the flower buds on a plant are pinched off, energy is diverted to the remaining buds, which produce larger flowers.

Cut a tree branch carefully so as to leave the branch collar intact. Leaving the collar intact promotes better healing.

You can induce the leader (the terminal shoot) of a young tree to branch by pinching 1 to 2 inches off its tip. The resulting new growth must be thinned as the branches begin to grow or else these branches will compete with the main leader.

WHEN TO PRUNE

In general, the best time to prune a woody plant is in late winter or early spring, just before new growth starts. Pruning at this time won't adversely affect a plant's vigor; pruning at other times can rob the plant of stored food energy or open it to infection.

Photosynthesis (see page 46) is most active during summer, when plants produce abundant food and new growth. As the days shorten in late summer, growth slows and sugars accumulate in the leaves. In fall the food moves from the leaves into the woody branches. Pruning in fall or early winter depletes the stored food reserves needed to initiate spring growth. Since many decay fungi produce spores in fall, that is also the time when open wounds are most likely to become infected with decay rot. Later in the dormant season, sugars move farther down the plant and are less likely to be disturbed. Pruning at that time doesn't waste stored energy, and cuts heal more quickly as well.

Although dormant season pruning is recommended for most plants, there are cases in which pruning should be done during the growing season. If spring-flowering trees or shrubs are pruned in winter, the flower buds will be removed and the plants won't blossom that spring. Early spring bloomers, which produce their flowers on the previous season's growth, should be pruned immediately after flowering but before the leaves fully expand. Summer bloomers, which usually flower on the current season's growth, can be pruned in winter without danger of removing flower buds. In fact, dormant season pruning stimulates more flowers.

Midsummer pruning has a dwarfing effect on plants. Removing summer foliage reduces photosynthesis, resulting in lower food reserves for the following spring's growth. Summer pruning is appropriate for slowing the vigorous growth of an immature fruit tree so that it will begin bearing.

Summer pruning prevents an extremely vigorous tree from producing a burst of water sprouts and suckers—its normal response to heavy spring pruning. Summer pruning is also recommended for restricting the growth of a tree or shrub that has reached a desired height and spread. However, because wounds do not callus over as quickly as during the late dormant season, it's best to keep summer pruning cuts small and save heavy shaping for winter.

The worst time to prune is right after the leaves emerge in spring. Stored energy has powered a burst of growth, but the new leaves have not yet begun to accumulate food to replenish the supply. Bud break in spring is also the time of greatest root growth, another heavy drain on stored reserves. At this time the plant cannot afford to lose leaves and the soft tissue beneath the bark tears easily.

HOW TO HOLD HAND-HELD PRUNING SHEAR

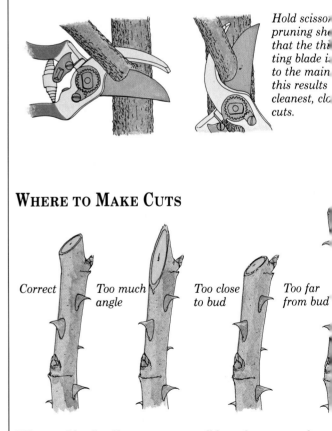

Hold scisso pruning she that the thi ting blade i to the main this results cleanest, cla cuts.

WHERE TO MAKE CUTS

Correct | Too much angle | Too close to bud | Too far from bud

When making heading cuts on a small branch, cut on a slant about ¼" above a bud. If the cut is too close, the bud may die; if is too far away, the resulting stub will die.

BRANCH SPACING

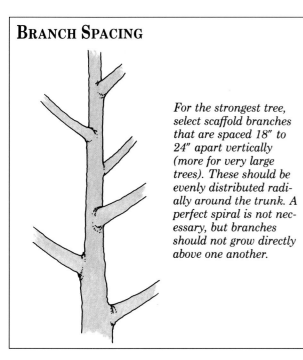

For the strongest tree, select scaffold branches that are spaced 18" to 24" apart vertically (more for very large trees). These should be evenly distributed radially around the trunk. A perfect spiral is not necessary, but branches should not grow directly above one another.

SCAFFOLD BRANCH ANGLES

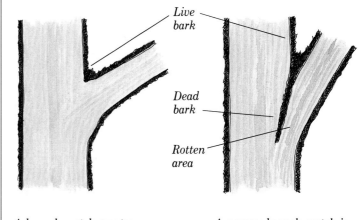

Live bark

Dead bark

Rotten area

A branch crotch greater than 45° forms a strong attachment that can withstand adverse weather conditions.

A narrow branch crotch is weakly attached because bark becomes compressed and dies. As the branch grows larger, it may break.

With judgment and moderation, some pruning can be done at any time. Dead and dying branches, suckers, and water sprouts should be removed whenever you see them.

PRUNING TOOLS

The only pruning tool that many home gardeners own is a pair of hedge shears. These are fine for shearing formal hedges into geometric shapes, but they shouldn't be used for other pruning tasks. For small pruning jobs you are properly outfitted if you have three basic pruning tools: a pair of hand-held pruners, a pair of lopping shears, and a small curved saw. You need these tools to make thinning cuts, which are the most common type of pruning cut. (These and other specialized pruning tools are illustrated and described on pages 330 to 332.)

PRUNING ORNAMENTAL TREES

The ideal ornamental tree has a straight, tapered trunk and a balanced shape, with scaffold branches, or major side branches, emerging from the trunk at an angle greater than 45 degrees. Generally, a branch that angles up too close to the tree trunk produces a weak crotch that will become weaker each year. The wider the angle of a scaffold branch, the stronger the branch becomes.

Regular pruning keeps plants healthy and vigorous. It also helps them blend into a group.

193

Crossed branches, water sprouts, and stubs need to be removed from this flowering cherry tree, which has been pruned incorrectly and then neglected.

The object of pruning a tree is to encourage it to grow in its ideal form. The pruning begun at planting time and continued during the next several years determines the shape and strength of the branch structure. As the tree grows older, it is often necessary to prune off branches that are too low, growing in the wrong direction, or damaged by storms. It is also important to learn how to properly reduce the size of a tree that has grown too large for its place in the landscape.

Pruning Young Trees

It is advantageous to prune a tree when it is newly planted and during its first years in the landscape, not only to ensure its development into a desirable shape, but also to prevent more drastic corrective pruning in later years. Removing poorly positioned branches inflicts a much smaller wound on a young tree than on a mature tree. Removing the same branches after they have been allowed to grow large means more expense, greater disfigurement, a longer time for the wound to close over, and a greater chance of infection by wood decay fungi.

Some corrective pruning is required on newly planted trees to develop a good branching structure. Experts once recommended trimming branches to one quarter to one third of their total length to compensate for roots lost when the tree was dug from the nursery field. Research has shown that this type of severe pruning hinders the tree rather than helps it.

This doesn't mean that trees shouldn't be pruned at planting time; they should, but not severely. The most important reason for pruning a young tree is to encourage its natural shape. At planting time and during the first several years, remove only undesirable and broken branches. If you live in a windy area, thin the top to reduce the force of the wind on the tree. Retain enough foliage so that the tree can produce food to fuel its growth. This is also the time to select some of the primary scaffold branches (see below), if such selection was not done in the nursery.

Follow a light, corrective training program to develop a strong central leader and a good branching structure. If several branches

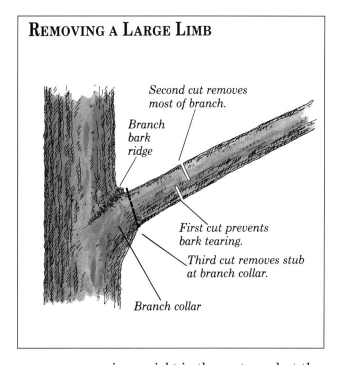

REMOVING A LARGE LIMB

Second cut removes most of branch.

Branch bark ridge

First cut prevents bark tearing.

Third cut removes stub at branch collar.

Branch collar

are growing upright in the center, select the most vigorous or most central as the leader. Remove or shorten the competing branches to prevent the formation of a split leader, which is inherently weak and susceptible to breaking during storms. The greatest mistake in pruning a young tree is to lop off the leader. The principal branches of the tree should arise from the leader. Encouraging a strong central leader when the tree is young results in a sturdier branch structure later.

The best branches to select for main scaffolds emerge from the trunk at an angle greater than 45 degrees. These branches are strongly attached to the trunk. Strive to keep the vertical distance between scaffolds from 10 to 24 inches apart in young trees. Scaffolds of large trees may be several feet apart. Select branches that radiate in alternating positions to avoid shading those positioned below. Do not remove all the branches below any permanent scaffolds. Temporarily leaving them helps the trunk grow stronger. Prune them off when they are about ½ inch in diameter.

As the tree matures and begins to exhibit its characteristic branching pattern, it takes on one of two basic forms: a central leader with a pyramidal or columnar shape and one main trunk, or multiple leaders with trunks or branches the same size or larger than the main leader.

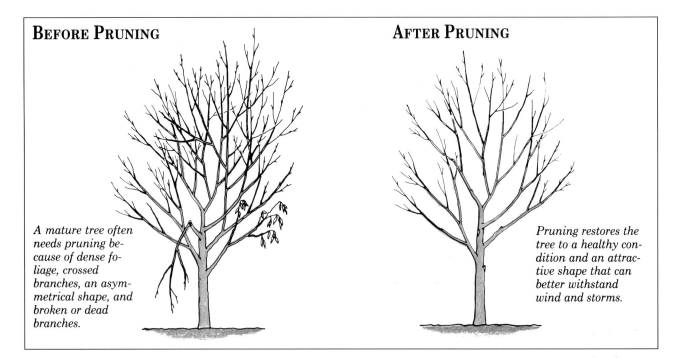

BEFORE PRUNING

A mature tree often needs pruning because of dense foliage, crossed branches, an asymmetrical shape, and broken or dead branches.

AFTER PRUNING

Pruning restores the tree to a healthy condition and an attractive shape that can better withstand wind and storms.

Pruning Mature Trees

If correctly pruned when young, large trees generally require less pruning than most other woody plants. However, they may need occasional removal of dead or dying branches. As a tree grows in height and spread, it may also be necessary to control its size, open it up to allow sunlight through, or prevent branches from rubbing against each other, wires, buildings, or vehicles.

Avoid cutting off, or heading, the central leader or any of the multiple leaders of a mature tree. This only eliminates apical dominance and produces a cluster of weakly attached shoots just behind the cut (see Apical Dominance on page 188). If it is necessary to prune a leader, cut back to a lateral branch with the same or one-third smaller diameter. The side branch then assumes apical dominance. At first, the new leader bends to assume the position of the original leader, but in a few years this bend is no longer noticeable.

Thin or entirely remove branches that are rubbing against the house or are otherwise in the way. A branch that is too large to hold in one hand should be removed with three separate cuts; otherwise the weight of the cut branch will tear a strip of bark from the tree. (See illustration, page 195.)

There are several pruning techniques used on large trees. In most cases, it is preferable to leave this type of work to a qualified arborist or tree pruning service.

Crown lifting   Lifting the crown, or canopy, of a tree involves removing lower branches that create an obstruction or hazard. The result is a tree with high scaffold branches. The crown of a tall shade tree may be lifted if the branches overhang a roof or driveway. Other reasons to lift a crown are to provide more light below, to open up a view, or to accommodate small flowering trees beneath the boughs. Rather than remove all lower branches at once, it is better to do it gradually over several years.

Crown thinning and reduction   When a mature tree becomes densely branched, it may cast too much shade and be susceptible to wind damage. Crown thinning—removing selected branches throughout the canopy—allows more light to filter to the ground, lets wind pass through the foliage, and emphasizes an unusual or picturesque branching pattern. Usually, branches about 1 inch in diameter are thinned back to larger lateral branches.

Crown reduction or size control is necessary when a tree grows beyond the space allotted for it, reaches into utility wires, or hangs over buildings. Begin to control the size before the tree reaches its mature height

Overhead branches can be sawn off easily with a pole pruner.

and spread. Gradually thin the tallest branches over a period of several years, and continue to thin periodically to maintain the tree at a smaller than normal size.

Drop crotching This is another technique used to reduce the overall size of a tree. Thin the main trunk, scaffold branches, and lateral branches, cutting each back to the next lower crotch. The size of the remaining branch should be at least two thirds the diameter of the branch removed, so that it can take over apical dominance. If the drop crotch is made to a branch that is too small, the cut will react like a heading cut which will then result in a cluster of weakly attached shoots.

PRUNING SHRUBS AND HEDGES

Most shrubs are best left to assume their natural form; avoid shearing them into geometric shapes unless they are used as formal hedges. Correctly pruned shrubs appear as if they have not been pruned at all. If a shrub looks as if it obviously has been pruned, probably too much has been done to it. If there is no reason for a pruning cut, don't make it. Slow-growing or well-proportioned shrubs may not need any pruning.

Like ornamental trees, shrubs are pruned to control their size and maintain their shape. However, the key word regarding the pruning of shrubs is *renewal*. If not periodically thinned by cutting the oldest wood to the ground, most flowering shrubs decline into a sparse flowering thicket.

Spring-flowering shrubs, whose buds are formed the previous summer, should be pruned immediately after they bloom. They can also be pruned while they are in bloom, if you want flowers for the house. Summer- and fall-flowering shrubs, which bloom on the current season's wood, should be pruned during the late dormant season after the danger of frost passes and before spring growth begins.

Deciduous shrubs—those that lose their leaves in winter—have a strong ability to renew themselves. Each spring these shrubs send up many new shoots, and pruning off the old wood is essential to keep the shrubs from becoming overgrown. If you want these shrubs to grow vigorously, prune them while they are dormant; early spring is usually the best time. If they are large enough and you would like to restrict their growth, prune them after the spring flush of growth is over.

Remove any shoots that are dead, diseased, misshapen, or crossing other branches. Then thin the shrub by cutting older branches to the ground. You can follow a three- or five-year pruning cycle with deciduous shrubs. Removing one fifth to one third of the mature wood each year keeps the plant open and allows new shoots to become major branches. The three-year cycle of pruning old wood produces more new shoots; the five-year cycle is best for some slow-growing shrubs such as lilac (*Syringa* species) and spirea (*Spiraea* species).

Broadleaf evergreens often grow slowly, developing compact forms that need little pruning. The best time to prune these shrubs is just before a period of fast growth, usually

Pruning small-leaved broadleaf evergreens with hand shears helps to maintain a neat, soft-edged appearance.

STARTING A HEDGE

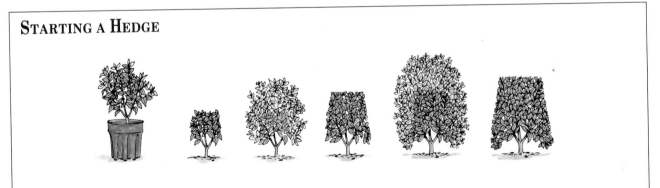

Begin with plants in gallon containers spaced 18"–24" apart.

The first year shear off ⅓ or more of the height and width to stimulate thick, twiggy growth.

Before new growth begins the second year, shear the plants, keeping the base wider than the top.

PRUNING CONIFERS

Coniferous trees and shrubs usually need little pruning. When you do prune, you should know whether the conifer is determinate or indeterminate and prune accordingly.

Determinate conifers—including fir (*Abies* species), spruce (*Picea* species), and most pines (*Pinus* species)—have branches radiating from the trunk in whorls. They don't have latent buds in older wood behind the foliage area. If you prune to behind the foliage, the branch will die. Determinate conifers should be pruned by heading back new growth to a bud. For pines, prune by pinching the candles. If you pinch off half the candle as it is expanding, the branch will grow only half the size. For spruce and fir, prune back the new growth halfway to increase density. Don't prune the leader of most determinate conifers or you'll destroy the natural shape of the tree. New terminal buds develop on some determinate conifers (see the illustration of a pine) when one- and two-year-old leaders are cut.

Indeterminate conifers—including arborvitae (*Thuja* and *Platycladus* species), hemlock (*Tsuga* species), juniper (*Juniperus* species), and yew (*Taxus* species)—have branches radiating in a random fashion. Since indeterminate conifers have many latent buds all along the branches, you can cut back to old wood—or even shear the plants into hedges—without disastrous consequences.

Prune most conifers after the new growth is completed in late spring or early summer. Juniper and cypress can be pruned safely at any time, although early spring to late July is best. Regardless of when and how much you prune, be sure to give conifers ample water at pruning time.

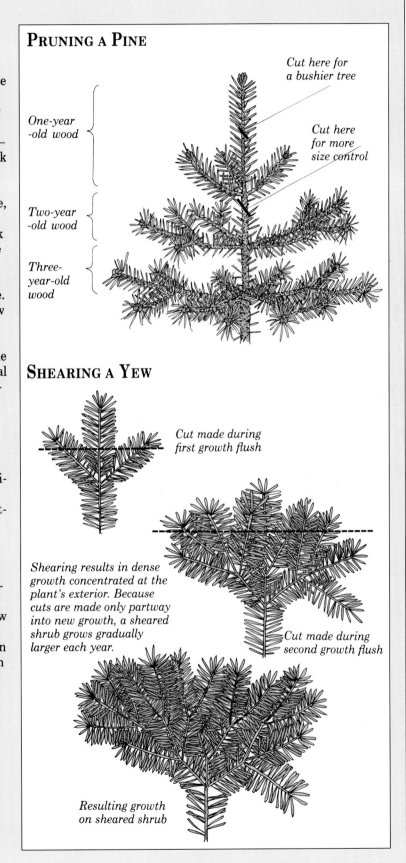

PRUNING A PINE

Cut here for a bushier tree

Cut here for more size control

One-year-old wood

Two-year-old wood

Three-year-old wood

SHEARING A YEW

Cut made during first growth flush

Shearing results in dense growth concentrated at the plant's exterior. Because cuts are made only partway into new growth, a sheared shrub grows gradually larger each year.

Cut made during second growth flush

Resulting growth on sheared shrub

An informal hedge retains the natural shape of the plant. This row of hemlock is pruned with thinning cuts made with hand-held pruners.

A formal hedge is sheared into a living wall of foliage. This boxwood hedge is trimmed with hand-held or electric hedge shears.

in early spring. The removal of dead, broken, and diseased branches is usually the main task if pruning broadleaf evergreen shrubs is necessary.

Pruning Hedges

Formal hedges are sheared into flat-sided shapes to form low or tall walls; they look neat if kept trimmed. Informal hedges, maintained with hand-held pruners or loppers (see photograph on page 198), have a looser, more natural shape than formal hedges. It may seem like more work to prune an informal hedge, but it really isn't because the hedge needs to be pruned less often.

Since formal hedges are trimmed to smooth geometric shapes, they require small-leaved plants. Boxwood (*Buxus* species), lavender (*Lavandula* species), and rosemary (*Rosmarinus* species) are examples of plants that respond well to repeated shearing. Large-leaved, open shrubs—such as English laurel (*Prunus laurocerasus*), cotoneaster (*Cotoneaster* species), and lilac (*Syringa*

species)—are more suited to informal hedging; they should be thinned, not sheared.

At planting time, decide whether you want a formal or an informal hedge. A formal hedge must be pruned to a definite size and shaped at least once, and usually two or more times, each growing season. Shrubs making up an informal hedge are allowed to grow naturally and are thinned yearly to limit height and spread and to maintain a uniform rate of growth. An informal hedge requires more space to accommodate the natural branching pattern of the shrubs.

PRUNING ORNAMENTAL VINES

Unless most vines are kept under control with training and pruning from the time they are planted, they can easily become unmanageable—almost beyond the help of pruning.

Vines do best when planted at least a foot away from a wall or fence, so that the roots have room to fan out. After planting, select three to five of the strongest shoots

PRUNING VINES

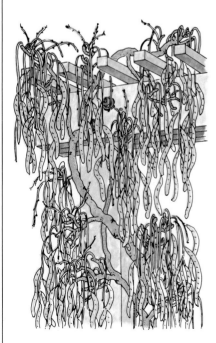

Chinese wisteria (Wisteria sinensis) needs pruning in late winter before new growth begins. Remove the tangle of flower stems and pods and any crowded or crossed side branches.

Leave only the flowering spurs and the permanent framework of the vine—the desirable main stems and smaller branches.

Shorten the flowering spurs to 6 or more buds to encourage larger flowers and separate, free-hanging clusters.

The bougainvillea is a vigorous tropical evergreen vine that requires regular pruning to keep it in bounds; otherwise it can become unmanageable.

and trim them to half their original length. This will encourage new growth to develop at the bottom of the vine and increase the vigor of the shoots that remain.

Annual thinning encourages new growth and continual rejuvenation. When pruning a vine, always cut back to a lateral branch, twig, or bud and do not leave a stub. Cut dead and weak branches back to healthy, vigorous stems. When stems become too crowded, cut some of them to the ground.

Most vines respond best to pruning in the late dormant season, before spring growth begins. Very vigorous growers should be cut severely at this time to induce new growth close to the ground. This practice is not harmful as long as it is done before spring growth begins. The late dormant season is also the time to prune flowering vines that bloom on new growth; cut them back to a basic framework or to the ground.

The late dormant season is not the time to prune flowering vines that bloom on the previous season's growth; if you prune at this time, you will remove the flower buds. Prune these vines after they flower. Either remove shoots that have bloomed, or cut back to where new growth is emerging.

When a vine becomes unmanageable from lack of yearly pruning, cut it to the ground and let it start over. When the new stems appear, select the most desirable and remove the rest. Pinch the tops of climbing stems to slow their upward growth temporarily.

PRUNING FRUIT TREES

In order to grow good quality fruit, you must prune. No other plants in the garden are as dependent on pruning as fruit trees. Unfortunately, no other group of plants varies so widely in the type of pruning required; there are no rules that apply to all fruit trees.

During the first three years of cultivation, most fruit trees are pruned similarly to establish the basic framework. When they begin to bear fruit, however, each species requires different pruning. (See Pruning Mature Fruit Trees on page 204.)

Three pruning systems are commonly used for fruit trees. The central-leader system emphasizes one tall main trunk with

FRUIT TREE PRUNING SHAPES

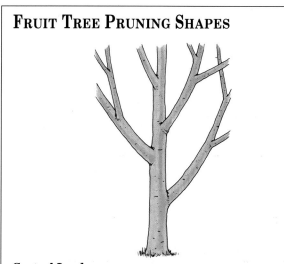

Central Leader
With 1 main trunk this shape can hold a heavy crop of fruit and resist storm damage.

Vase
The vase, or open-center, shape allows plenty of light and air into the tree's interior, encouraging fruit production on lower branches.

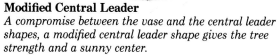

Modified Central Leader
A compromise between the vase and the central leader shapes, a modified central leader shape gives the tree strength and a sunny center.

tiers of branches arising from it; the vase, or open-center, system features a short trunk about 3 feet tall and an open center with three or four main branches; the modified central-leader system features a short trunk and several tiers of branches. Although any type of fruit tree can be pruned according to any of these systems, most types respond best to a particular system.

Fruit trees, like ornamental plants, generally benefit from pruning during the late dormant season before the start of new growth. Pruning can be delayed, however, as much as a week after flowering with little harm to the plant.

Under certain conditions, fruit trees can be pruned lightly during the summer. Thinning the tree in early summer promotes fruit set in addition to removing unwanted growth. Pruning from early to mid-August dwarfs an overly vigorous tree; restrict this practice to fruit trees that are at least three years old.

Thinning cuts are the primary pruning technique used on fruit trees. Every thinning cut increases sunlight to the tree's interior and promotes greater flowering and better-quality fruit. Any part of a fruit tree that receives less than 30 percent full sun will bear a reduced crop of smaller fruit of poor quality and color.

Heading cuts, which encourage new growth directly behind the cut, are sometimes used to advantage on fruit trees. For example, heading cuts are used to induce side branches on apple varieties that don't branch adequately, such as spur-type 'Delicious', 'Rome Beauty', and 'Tydeman's Red'.

Pruning Young Fruit Trees

When training a fruit tree to a central leader or modified central leader, prune only enough to develop a desirable scaffold branch system, since needless pruning delays fruit production. The process of selecting scaffolds for a fruit tree is the same as for an ornamental tree; see Pruning Young Trees on page 195.

To develop a vase shape, cut off the central stem 2 to 3 feet above the ground, and prune back any side branches to two buds. During the first dormant season (one year after planting the tree), remove the

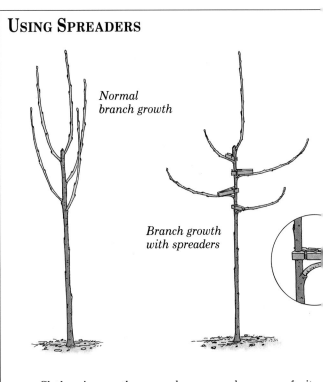

USING SPREADERS

Normal branch growth

Branch growth with spreaders

Clothespins or other spreaders are used on young fruit trees to force the scaffolds to grow at a more desirable angle.

leader and direct growth to three or four strong scaffolds. Choose branches that radiate evenly around the trunk. Maintain about 6 vertical inches between the branches, and keep the lowest scaffold at least 18 inches off the ground. Prune back scaffolds to one third their length.

Apple and pear trees, in particular, tend to produce water sprouts—vertical branches that grow vigorously upward—at the expense of fruit-bearing wood. By using wooden or metal spreaders between the trunk and scaffold branches on young trees, it is possible to change the position of unfruitful upright branches and make them more productive (see illustration above).

Pruning Mature Fruit Trees

Once the basic shape of a fruit tree has been developed, make pruning decisions according to which branches produce fruit. Most fruit trees bear fruit on short branches, or spurs, which are productive for several years. Each year, prune to remove excessive growth and crossing branches, and cut out a portion of the older fruiting wood. Developing fruit should be thinned on some types of fruit trees; this should be done before the fruit is half-grown.

Here are guidelines for pruning specific fruit trees.

Apple   Train to any of the three basic forms. The modified central-leader method is used most often for dwarf and semidwarf trees. Fruit is borne on knobby spurs that remain productive for up to 20 years. Each year, remove about one twentieth of the older wood; prune to save the spurs. Thin apples so that they are 8 inches apart, or one fruit per spur.

Apricot   Prune to a vase shape. Fruit is produced on the previous year's stems and on long spurs that last three to four years. Prune moderately, removing about one quarter of the spur-bearing branches yearly. Thin the apricots so that they are 2 to 3 inches apart.

Cherry   Train cherries to the modified central-leader shape. Fruit is produced in clusters on long spurs that last 10 to 12 years. Prune lightly, removing about one tenth of the old wood yearly. The fruit doesn't require thinning.

Citrus   Mature citrus should not be pruned except if there is a need to remove broken, twisted, or diseased branches. These plants produce a great many shoots at pruning cuts, which results in a broom effect. Fruit is borne on one- or two-year-old wood. There is no need to thin the fruit.

Dwarf fruit trees, such as this apple tree, are especially effective in small home gardens. They are decorative, bear good fruit, and take up less space than full-sized trees.

PRUNING CITRUS

Prune citrus if the fruit crop is so heavy it may break a branch.

Pinch

Cut

To correct, cut side branches back by half and then pinch new growth several times during summer.

Cutting flowers is a form of pruning. Be sure to cut rhododendron stems just above a set of leaves.

Fig The best form for a fig tree depends on the variety; some naturally have an open center and others grow like spreading shrubs. Fruit is produced on spurs that last only one to two years. The tree bears twice a year, at the end of spring and in late summer or fall. Prune in winter if you want two crops. The first crop is produced on last year's growth, and the second crop is produced on wood formed after the first harvest. There is no need to thin the fruit.

Peach and nectarine Train to a vase shape. Fruit is borne only once on the previous year's wood. If the tree is to produce again next year, you must remove about half of the growth yearly. Annual pruning is more critical for peaches and nectarines than for any other type of fruit tree. When thinning the fruit be sure that each is spaced between 4 to 6 inches apart.

Pear Train to a central leader with five or six scaffold branches. Fruit is produced on spurs that last as long as 15 years. Prune lightly, removing about one twentieth of the old wood yearly. Pear trees are notorious for producing water sprouts, or unproductive vertical growth; remove these each year. No fruit thinning is needed.

Plum There are two types of plums: Japanese (dessert plums, such as 'Santa Rosa') and European (prune plums). They are distinguished by the length of their fruiting spurs. Japanese spurs are 3 inches long and European spurs are up to 3 feet long. Both types of spurs bear fruit for six to eight years; some fruit is also produced on one-year-old wood. Remove one third of the growth yearly. Thin the fruit so that it is 2 to 3 inches apart.

PRUNING RHODODENDRONS AND THEIR RELATIVES

Rhododendrons, azaleas (*Rhododendron* species), Japanese pieris (*Pieris japonica*), and mountain laurel (*Kalmia latifolia*) are closely related plants belonging to the family *Ericaceae*. These ericaceous plants, as they are called, are primarily broadleaf evergreens noted for their exquisite flowers.

When planted very close together or too near a building, these popular landscape plants often outgrow their space allotment. To produce compact plants with more flowers, pinch the tips of the new growth. To increase the number of trusses, or flower clusters, for the next year, pinch off about 1 inch of the new growth when it reaches 4 inches long and before the leaves expand fully. Two or three new shoots will sprout from each shoot pinched. Pinch again right after the new shoots emerge but before the next season's flower buds are formed.

Even with pinching, these plants can become too tall and leggy. Shorten long branches by thinning to a fork, a side branch, or a dormant or latent bud. Although difficult to see, growth buds appear all along the stems of ericaceous plants; cutting just above a bud causes a new shoot to emerge.

To renew an ericaceous plant, gradually thin it at the base over several years. The entire plant can also be cut off at ground level and allowed to resprout; it will take several years for the plant to reach an attractive size and shape. This drastic, sometimes risky, measure works only for vigorous shrubs; very weak plants may not resprout. Don't cut a grafted specimen to the ground; you will remove the desirable top cultivar and leave the rootstock.

Ericaceous shrubs grow more vigorously and flower better the following year if the old flowers are removed just after they fade and before they set seed. This practice is known as deadheading.

DEADHEADING A RHODODENDRON

Remove faded flower trusses by bending them over and gently snapping them off between thumb and forefinger.

PINCHING A RHODODENDRON

When new growth is about 4" long and the leaves are still immature, pinch off about 1" of the stem just above a set of leaves.

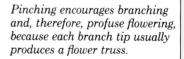

Pinching encourages branching and, therefore, profuse flowering, because each branch tip usually produces a flower truss.

PRUNING CANE BERRIES

After harvest remove the canes that bore fruit and tie 5 new canes to the wire. Head them back to about 3' high.

That winter prune the lateral branches back to 12"–18".

PRUNING BERRIES AND GRAPES

To establish the framework of berry and grape plants, pruning is essential. Pruning also encourages these plants to produce large quantities of fruit.

Cane Berries

The most commonly planted cane berries are blackberries and raspberries. New branches, called canes, sprout from the root system; they grow the first year and produce fruit the next year. A cane that has fruited once will not fruit again. Pruning cane berries is mainly a matter of removing canes that have already fruited and then training the canes that will fruit next.

After a cane has fruited, cut it off at ground level. Some gardeners paint identifying marks on the base of each new cane as it appears in spring to make sure it isn't accidentally pruned off that same year.

Cane berries produce many new canes each year, but if all these are allowed to mature and produce fruit, the crop and the individual fruit will be small. In spring, select the five largest canes from last year's growth and remove the others. Cut back the five canes you've selected to about 3 feet. Also cut back the side branches, or laterals, on each cane to 12 to 18 inches.

Some types of raspberries are called everbearing. This type produces a small crop at the tips of the new canes in fall. After the fall harvest cut off the part of the cane that bore fruit. The rest of the cane will bear fruit the following spring, after which it can be cut to the ground. Prune the lateral branches of everbearing raspberries back to 6 to 8 inches during early summer to encourage bushiness, larger crops, and larger fruit.

Bush Berries

Blueberries, currants, and gooseberries are three of the most commonly grown types of bush berries. All bear heavily with little pruning.

Blueberries need cross-pollination, so plant more than one variety that blooms at the same time. Each winter remove branches that are more than three years old.

Currants produce best on a plant with six to eight stems. Don't prune for the first few years except to shape the plant, remove damaged branches, and eliminate suckers (straight, vigorous shoots that come from near the base of the plant). Wood that is two and three years old produces the most fruit. Remove four-year-old or any older branches each spring.

Gooseberries bear on one-year-old wood and on short side branches on older wood. Any branches that are three years or older will not bear fruit and should be removed. Thin the bush when planting and every year afterward to encourage an open shape that will make harvesting easier among the thorny branches.

PRUNING EVERBEARING RASPBERRIES

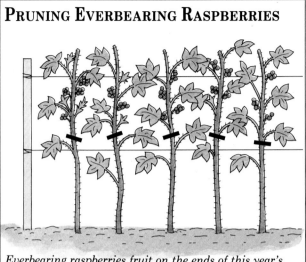

Everbearing raspberries fruit on the ends of this year's canes. Cut off the portion that has fruited. The bottom of the cane will fruit in spring.

Grapes

During the first few years after planting grapevines, they should be pruned to encourage the formation of a strong trunk. Before planting, cut the roots back to 6 inches and the stem to three buds. The first dormant season after planting, cut off all new growth except the strongest branch. Cut that branch back to three buds and tie it to a vertical support. Later that growing season, when sprouting shoots from the three buds are 12 to 14 inches long, tie the strongest shoot to the vertical support. Tie the two other shoots to a wire about 30 inches off the ground or to another type of horizontal support. Train one shoot in each direction.

Grapes are produced each year on new growth, but only on new growth that sprouts from a stem that is one year old (last year's new growth). The new shoots that come directly from the trunk or other old branches do not produce fruit. A simplified view of grape pruning is that half the previous year's growth should be cut off and the other half cut back to a few buds.

There are two basic types of grapes, and they need to be pruned differently. Most wine grapes (except for Thompson seedless) and muscadines should be spur-pruned. Spur-pruning cuts back the stems to two buds every year. Thompson seedless and many American varieties, such as Concord, should be cane-pruned. Cane-pruning leaves several long stems on the plant each year.

To spur-prune, look for the branches that fruited last year. If you pruned back to two buds per stub last year, there will be two branches coming off each stub or spur. Pick the stronger of these two branches and cut it back to two buds; remove the other branch. Train the main branches that come off the trunk so that the fruiting spurs are about a foot apart along the stem.

If you cut back the stems to two buds each year on grapes that must be cane pruned, you will not get any fruit. When the young vine has a large enough trunk (usually after the second year), cut back the side branches to two or three buds. These buds will produce two or three long canes. Every year from then on, cut back one cane to two or three buds, cut the other cane back to ten buds, and remove the third cane. Tie the cane with ten buds to the wire; this cane will bear fruit. After a cane has borne fruit, cut it off. From the branch where you left two or three buds, new canes will grow, one of which should be cut back to two or three buds, one cut back to ten buds and allowed to fruit, and one removed.

Depending on the type of grape you grow, you will either cane-prune or spur-prune them.

TRAINING SPUR AND CANE GRAPES FOR THE FIRST THREE SEASONS

When Planting
Plant a rooted cutting with 2 or 3 buds left above the soil, then bury in light mulch.

First Growing Season
The plant will grow a number of shoots; leave these alone.

First Dormant Season
Choose the best shoot and cut all the others to their bases. Head the remaining shoot to 3 or 4 strong buds.

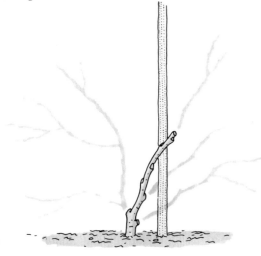

Second Growing Season
When new shoots reach about 12" long, select the most vigorous and pinch others off at the trunk. Tie the remaining shoot to a support (arbor or trellis post). When the shoot reaches the arbor top or trellis wire, pinch it to force branching. Let 2 strong branches grow. Pinch any others at 8"–10" long.

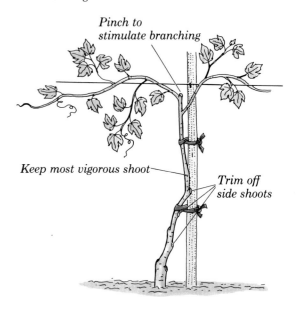

Pinch to stimulate branching

Keep most vigorous shoot

Trim off side shoots

Second Dormant Season
Cut away side shoots, leaving only the trunk and 2 major branches. Tie these to the arbor top or the trellis wire.

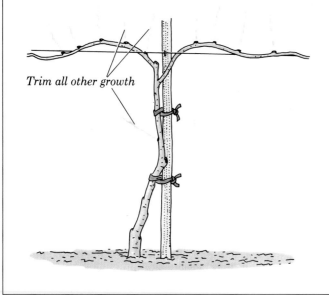

Trim all other growth

Third Growing Season
Let the vine grow. Pinch tips off sprouts on trunk. After this, spur and cane pruning differ.

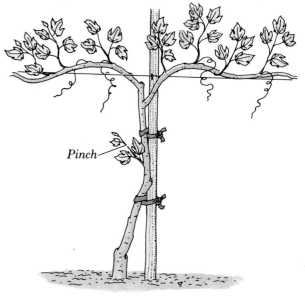

Pinch

SPUR TRAINING OF GRAPES AFTER THIRD GROWING SEASON

Third Dormant Season
Remove the weakest shoots along the horizontal branches at their bases, choosing the strongest side shoots spaced 6"–10" apart. Cut these to 2 buds. Remove all shoots from the vertical trunk.

Annually
Every dormant season after this, each spur will have 2 shoots that fruited during the summer. Cut the strongest spurs to 2 or 3 buds; these will produce fruit-bearing shoots in summer. Remove any weak spurs. Keep the trunk free of growth. Repeat pruning procedure each year.

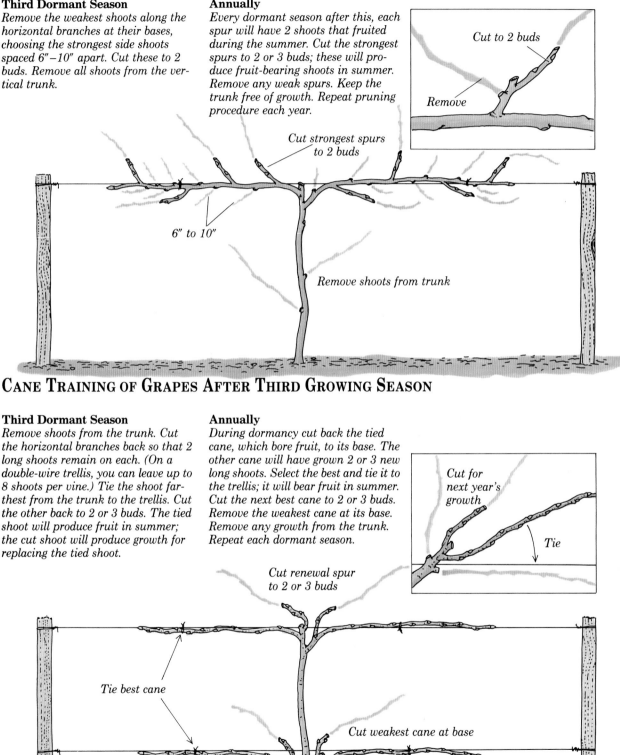

Cut to 2 buds

Remove

Cut strongest spurs to 2 buds

6" to 10"

Remove shoots from trunk

CANE TRAINING OF GRAPES AFTER THIRD GROWING SEASON

Third Dormant Season
Remove shoots from the trunk. Cut the horizontal branches back so that 2 long shoots remain on each. (On a double-wire trellis, you can leave up to 8 shoots per vine.) Tie the shoot farthest from the trunk to the trellis. Cut the other back to 2 or 3 buds. The tied shoot will produce fruit in summer; the cut shoot will produce growth for replacing the tied shoot.

Annually
During dormancy cut back the tied cane, which bore fruit, to its base. The other cane will have grown 2 or 3 new long shoots. Select the best and tie it to the trellis; it will bear fruit in summer. Cut the next best cane to 2 or 3 buds. Remove the weakest cane at its base. Remove any growth from the trunk. Repeat each dormant season.

Cut for next year's growth

Tie

Cut renewal spur to 2 or 3 buds

Tie best cane

Cut weakest cane at base

Cut off old cane

Pruning Roses

Before pruning a rose, you should know whether it blooms on wood produced during the current year or the previous year. Most modern roses bloom on the current season's growth, but many species roses and old garden roses bloom on the previous year's wood.

Roses that bloom on old wood should be pruned after flowering, before new shoots emerge. Most of these roses bloom once in spring and are not repeat bloomers.

Most modern roses—including hybrid teas, floribundas, and grandifloras—bloom on wood produced during the current year. These roses bloom in cycles throughout the growing season. They should be pruned during the dormant season when the buds have begun to swell. This is usually January in the mildest climates and after the last frost in severe climates.

About all that gardeners in severe climates need to do is cut back wood that has been killed during the winter. For those in more moderate or warm climates, there are three basic types of pruning. All three methods are used by different gardeners within the same climatic zone.

Severe, or heavy, pruning consists of cutting back the plant to three or four canes, 6 to 10 inches high. This method is used to produce fewer but showier blooms for cut roses. It is also used to stimulate vigorous growth on weak plants.

Moderate pruning develops a much larger bush than severe pruning and is a better choice for most roses. Five to twelve canes, 18 to 24 inches high, are left. Smaller but numerous flowers are produced this way.

Light pruning, in which less than one third of the plant is cut back, results in an abundance of short-stemmed flowers on a larger bush. This method is practiced mainly with floribundas, grandifloras, first-year hybrid teas, shrubs, and species roses.

Don't prune any climbing roses, except to cut out deadwood, for the first two to three years. Ramblers and once-blooming climbers should be pruned after they have bloomed; climbing hybrid teas and other repeat bloomers should be pruned in early spring while they are dormant. Most climber canes are productive for only two to three years; spare several green, healthy canes and eliminate all others. Cut back the laterals, on which the flowers appear. For ramblers and other once-blooming climbers, cut back to four or five sets of leaves. For climbing hybrid teas and other repeat bloomers, cut back to two leaf buds.

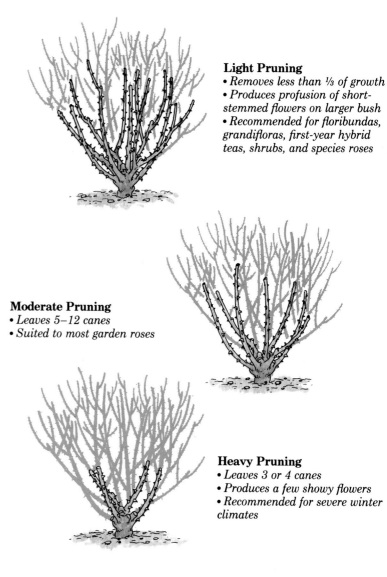

Light Pruning
- *Removes less than ⅓ of growth*
- *Produces profusion of short-stemmed flowers on larger bush*
- *Recommended for floribundas, grandifloras, first-year hybrid teas, shrubs, and species roses*

Moderate Pruning
- *Leaves 5–12 canes*
- *Suited to most garden roses*

Heavy Pruning
- *Leaves 3 or 4 canes*
- *Produces a few showy flowers*
- *Recommended for severe winter climates*

Three Places to Cut

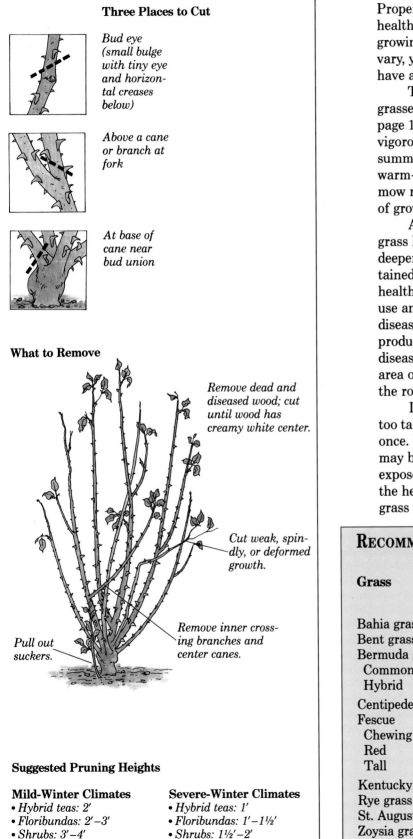

Bud eye (small bulge with tiny eye and horizontal creases below)

Above a cane or branch at fork

At base of cane near bud union

What to Remove

Remove dead and diseased wood; cut until wood has creamy white center.

Cut weak, spindly, or deformed growth.

Remove inner crossing branches and center canes.

Pull out suckers.

Suggested Pruning Heights

Mild-Winter Climates
• *Hybrid teas: 2'*
• *Floribundas: 2'–3'*
• *Shrubs: 3'–4'*

Severe-Winter Climates
• *Hybrid teas: 1'*
• *Floribundas: 1'–1½'*
• *Shrubs: 1½'–2'*

MOWING LAWNS

Proper mowing is essential to a thick, healthy, well-maintained lawn. Because the growing habits of different types of grasses vary, you must know what kind of lawn you have and mow it accordingly.

There are two basic types of lawn grasses: cool season and warm season (see page 122). Cool-season grasses grow most vigorously in spring and fall; the heat of summer is the time of greatest growth for warm-season grasses. It is important to mow regularly during your lawn's period of growth.

A direct relationship exists between grass height and root depth. Roots grow deeper if the proper grass height is maintained. Deep roots promote the growth of a healthy, dense lawn that withstands heavy use and discourages the spread of weeds and disease. Grasses that are mowed too low will produce a shallow-rooted lawn susceptible to disease and weed infestation; the leaf surface area of such a lawn is not sufficient to feed the roots.

If the grass has been allowed to grow too tall, don't mow to the correct height all at once. Weak stems that have been shaded may burn and turn brown when suddenly exposed to bright sunlight. Gradually lower the height over several mowings to give the grass time to adjust to the change.

RECOMMENDED MOWING HEIGHTS

Grass	Mowing Height (inches)
Bahia grass	1½–3
Bent grass	¼–½
Bermuda grass	
Common	½–1½
Hybrid	½–1
Centipede grass	1–2
Fescue	
Chewing	1–2
Red	1–2
Tall	2–3
Kentucky blue grass	1½–2
Rye grass	1–2½
St. Augustine grass	1–2½
Zoysia grass	½–1

It is not necessary to remove grass clippings when you mow the lawn; if you leave them on the lawn, you won't need to apply as much chemical nitrogen. Generally, the more chemical fertilizer you apply, the more frequently you have to mow. Heavy nitrogen feeding in the spring, in particular, increases the need for mowing. Feed only enough to keep the grass a healthy green color. See fertilizer recommendations for cool-season and warm-season grasses on page 180. The accompanying chart recommends the best height for the most commonly planted lawn grasses. After determining the correct height for your grass, mow when the grass is about one-third higher. To adjust the cutting height on reel and rotary mowers, see the illustrations on page 333.

A properly mowed lawn is more luxuriant and better able to resist weeds and diseases than an unmowed lawn.

ESPALIERING

Training plants in a fixed pattern, usually symmetrical, flat against a vertical surface is called espaliering. The plants can be trained on wire, a wooden trellis, or directly on a wall or fence. Every part of the plant receives maximum sunlight, which encourages ample flowering and heavy fruiting.

Almost any deciduous or evergreen tree or large shrub with flexible branches—for example, forsythia (*Forsythia* species), cotoneaster (*Cotoneaster* species), viburnum (*Viburnum* species), firethorn (*Pyracantha* species), and apple trees—can be espaliered. Slow-growing rather than vigorous plants are the best candidates. Avoid woody plants with a stiff, rigid, upright growth habit.

In northern climates gardeners often espalier fruit trees against a sunny, south-facing wall to lengthen the growing season. Use caution in climates where summer temperatures commonly exceed 90° F, since heat from the wall may burn the fruit. In this situation, espalier the plant on a freestanding wire trellis a foot or so from the wall.

The first step in espaliering is to establish a framework of lattice, wires, hooks, or other supports on which to tie the plant. Use rust-resistant nails or special hooks for brick or masonry walls. On wood surfaces leave about 6 inches between the plant and wall for air movement.

Apple and crab apple trees are especially good candidates for espaliering. Stretch wire horizontally at intervals of 18 inches across a wall. Plant a bare-root, one-year-old whip and head it just below the bottom wire. From the emerging shoots select one to grow up to the next wire, and tie two side shoots to grow horizontally along the bottom wire in each direction. Rub off all other growth on the trunk and pinch shoots on

the branches to keep them short.

The following dormant season, cut off the main stem just below the second wire from the bottom. This will initiate another set of buds, two of which should be kept for side branches and one for the trunk extension. Train these as you did the first set. To make fruiting spurs on apples, cut back the lateral branches on the horizontal limbs to three buds.

Continue training until three wires, or more if desired, are covered with branches. When the plant reaches the top wire, eliminate the trunk extension by heading it, and retain the two side branches.

Regular pruning is necessary during the growing season to restrict the plant to a single flat plane. Be sure to use thinning cuts rather than heading cuts.

GROWING VEGETABLES

Almost all gardeners have grown vegetables at one time or another. Whether planting only a child's simple patch of radishes or carrots, or enough vegetables to feed an entire neighborhood, most gardeners can't resist the challenge—and the rewards—of raising vegetables.

One of the attractions of vegetable gardening is being able to eat tender, delectable vegetables within minutes of harvesting them. It's often said that fresh homegrown vegetables are superior to store-bought produce—but it's true only if you choose suitable varieties, plant properly, provide the correct growing conditions, and harvest at the right time.

The range of vegetables appropriate for any given garden expands yearly. Vegetable gardening is not as limited by climate as it once was. More than any other type of plant, vegetables have been bred for specific climatic conditions. You can buy tomato varieties for foggy areas, lettuce varieties that tolerate hot weather, melon varieties for short, cool summers—the list is endless. The breeders haven't forgotten the small-space gardener, either; more and more miniature and bush varieties of favorite vegetables become available every year.

With so many possibilities, the choice of what to plant is a highly personal one, reflecting the interests, knowledge, and imagination of the gardener. Some gardeners plant only the most reliable performers, carefully laying out their plots in neat rows to maximize production. Others remember the unstructured beauty of their grandmother's garden and base their plans on that recollection. Some gardeners are full of surprises, changing their gardens at a whim.

Whatever type of garden you choose, growing vegetables is more rewarding when you plan carefully: map out the space, choose suitable varieties, figure the planting dates, and prepare for harvests.

To be rewarded with fresh, homegrown vegetables, you must plan carefully.

A Continual Harvest

The most common frustration in raising your own vegetables occurs when everything ripens at once. You can solve that problem by planning for a continual harvest. This may pose a challenge for the novice and for the limited-space gardener, but careful planning has its rewards: a plentiful supply of fresh vegetables throughout the growing season.

If you're fortunate enough to have lots of room, you can block out space for the spring garden, to grow cool-season vegetables, and leave some space empty for the summer garden, to grow crops requiring hot weather. By allocating space to each, you can organize and plant the summer garden without interference from the spring garden, which you may not have completely

harvested. If you have only a small patch of land, you must plan both the spring and summer gardens (and the fall-winter garden in warm climates) at the same time and apportion space carefully.

Overplanting, in either a large or a small space, detracts from the enjoyment of vegetable gardening. Although it may seem as if 20 to 30 heads of lettuce couldn't possibly produce enough salads for the whole family, when the 30 heads all mature within a two-week period, you'll know you planted too many. A dozen cabbage plants don't seem excessive in their little nursery trays, but they'll make 30 to 40 pounds of cabbage when mature. To avoid these excesses, take into account the food needs of your family and the length of the harvest period. It is much better to make successive plantings

Planting Schemes

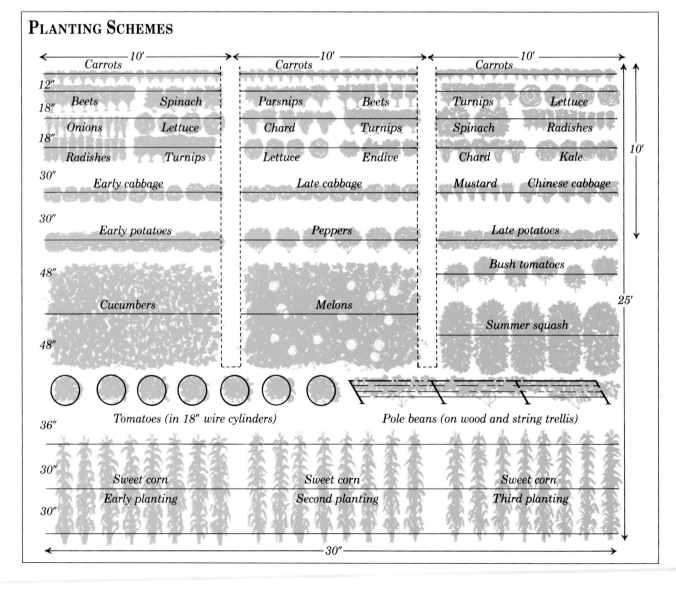

A TYPICAL VEGETABLE GARDEN CALENDAR

You can plan the succession planting and harvest in your garden by making a calendar like this one. This particular calendar is for the Delaware area.

Mar	Apr	May	June	July	Aug	Sept	Oct	Nov
		Snap beans			Snap beans			
		Lima beans			Lima beans			
Cabbage			Cabbage					
				Cabbage		Cabbage		
		Cucumbers			Cucumbers			
Carrots			Carrots					
				Carrots		Carrots		
Beets			Beets					
				Beets		Beets		
				Broccoli		Broccoli		
			Cauliflower			Cauliflower		
		Cantaloupe			Cantaloupe			
Lettuce		Lettuce				Lettuce	Lettuce	
Onions		Green onions			Onions			
Peas			Peas					
		Peppers			Peppers			
Radishes	Radishes					Radishes	Radishes	
Spinach	Spinach					Spinach	Spinach	Spinach
		Sweet corn			Sweet corn			
		Squash	Squash					
		Winter squash				Winter squash		
		Tomatoes		Tomatoes				
	Turnips		Turnips		Turnips		Turnips	
		Watermelon			Watermelon			

Key: Plant   Harvest

PLANTING AND HARVESTING TABLE

	Depth to plant seed (inches)	Distance between plants (inches)	Distance between rows (inches)	Number of days to germination	Needs cool soil	Tolerates cool soil	Needs warm soil	Weeks needed to grow to transplant size	Days to maturity	Comments
Artichoke	½	48–72	72	7–14		•		4–6	1 year	Start with divisions preferred
Asparagus	1½	48–60	36	7–21		•		1 year	3 years	Usually started with 1-year-old crowns
Bean										
Fava	2½	3–4	18–24	7–14		•			120–150	Harvest early for fresh shell beans
Garbanzo	1½–2	3–4	24–30	6–12			•		100	Harvest early for fresh shell beans
Lima bush	1½–2	3–6	24–30	7–12			•		65–75	Needs warmer soil than snap beans
Lima pole	1½–2	6–10	30–36	7–12			•		75–95	Long harvest if kept picked
Scarlet runner	1½–2	4–6	36–48	6–14			•		70–115	Harvest early for tender pods and later for shell beans
Snap bush	1½–2	2–3	18–30	6–14			•		50–65	Make sequence plantings
Snap pole	1½–2	4–6	36–48	6–14			•		60–70	Long harvest if kept picked
Soybean	1½–2	2–3	24–36	6–14			•		55–100	Choose a variety suited to your climate; see pages 227–228
Beet	½	2	12–18	7–10		•			45–70	Use thinnings in salads
Cabbage family										
Broccoli	½	14–18	24–36	3–10		•		5–7*	50–100T	70–120 days direct seeded
Brussels sprout	½	14–18	24–36	3–10		•		4–6*	80–95T	100–115 days direct seeded
Cabbage	½	14–18	24–36	4–10		•		5–7*	50–100T	75–155 days direct seeded
Cauliflower	½	14–18	24–36	4–10		•		5–7*	48–65T	65–120 days direct seeded
Chinese cabbage	½	14–18	18–24	4–10		•		4–6	75–85	Best as seeded crop in fall
Collard	½	10–15	24–30	4–10		•		4–6*	65–85T	Can be direct seeded for a fall crop
Kale	½	12–18	18–24	3–10		•		4–6	55–80	Direct seed for fall crop; use thinnings in salads
Kohlrabi	½	4–6	12–24	3–10		•		4–6	45–60	Harvest when plant is 2"–3" in diameter
Carrots	½	2–4	14–24	10–17		•			50–85	Begin using when ½" in diameter to thin stand
Celery	⅛	6–10	24–30	9–21	•			8–16*	105–130T	Needs lots of water
Corn	2	10–14	30–36	6–10			•		60–90	Make successive plantings; days to maturity depend on heat
Cucumber	1	12	48–72	6–10			•	4–6	50–70	Thin to 2–5 plants if growing in hills
Eggplant	¼–½	18	36	7–14			•	6–9*	60–95T	Best with minimum night temperature of 65° F

* Transplants preferred over seeds
T Number of days from setting out transplants; all others are from seeding

PLANTING AND HARVESTING TABLE

	Depth to plant seed (inches)	Distance between plants (inches)	Distance between rows (inches)	Number of days to germination	Needs warm soil	Needs cool soil	Tolerates cool soil	Weeks needed to grow to transplant size	Days to maturity	Comments
Lettuce										
Butterhead	¼	6–8	18–24	4–10	•			3–5	65–80	
Celtuce	¼	8–12	18–24	4–10	•			3–5	90	
Crisphead	¼–½	12–14	10–24	4–10	•			3–5	80–90	Proper thinning is essential
Leaf	¼	6–10	18–24	4–10	•			3–5	40–50	Proper thinning is important
Romaine	¼	6–8	18–24	4–10	•			3–5	70–85	
Melon										
Cantaloupe	1	12–16	48–72	4–8			•	3–4	60–100	Use transplants in cool-summer or short-season areas
Watermelon	1	12–16	60–84	3–12			•		80–100	Harvest icebox size earlier
Winter melon	1	12–16	48–72	4–8			•	3–4	90–120	Best in hot, dry climates
Onion										
Plants	2–3	2–3	12–24		•			12	65–150	
Seeds	½	2–3	12–24	7–12	•				120–165	
Sets	1–2	2–3	12–24		•				95–150	Harvest green onions in 50–60 days
Parsnip	½	3	16–24	14–24		•			100–120	Needs winter cold to change starch into sugar
Peas	1–2	2–3	18–36	6–14	•				55–75	
Pepper	¼	24	24–36	10–20			•	7–10*	60–80T 70–120T	Maturity for sweet peppers Maturity for chiles
Potato	4	12	24–36	8–16		•			90–120	Use certified seed potatoes
Pumpkin	1–1½	30	72–120	6–10			•		90–120	Needs lots of room
Radish	½	1–2	6–12	3–10	•				20–50	Best planted during early spring or late fall
Spinach	½	3–4	12–14	6–14	•				40–50	Best grown during cool weather
Squash										
Summer	1	16–24	36–60	3–12			•		50–65	
Winter	1	24–48	72–120	6–10			•		60–110	
Sweet potato	2–3	9–12	36–54				•		120	Use certified sprouts or slips; require prolonged heat
Swiss chard	½	4–8	18–24	7–10		•			50–60	Use thinnings in salads
Tomato	½	12–48	36–60	6–14			•	5–7*	55–90T	Leave 1–2 feet between plants when staked, 2–4 feet when unstaked
Turnip	½	1–3	14–18	3–10	•				30–60	Thin early for salad greens

* Transplants preferred over seeds
T Number of days from setting out transplants; all others are from seeding

Successive plantings throughout the growing season can provide you with a continual harvest of a variety of vegetables.

throughout the season than all at once and watch your crops spoil.

There are several ways to arrange for a continual harvest. One way is to make successive plantings of crops that must be harvested within a short period of time—for example, corn, radishes, and lettuce. Plant every week to 10 days and you can harvest over an extended period, rather than having to pick the entire crop at once. The shorter the harvest period, the more important small, successive plantings are.

Certain vegetables, such as cabbage, have early, mid, and late varieties. You can harvest over a longer period by planting varieties that mature over different lengths of time.

Another way to extend the harvest is to plant vegetables with a long harvest period—for example, snap beans, eggplant, peppers, zucchini, and tomatoes. In most cases, these crops are ready for harvest a couple of months after they are planted and they keep producing until frost. Generally, the more you pick, the more the plant produces.

Some root crops, such as carrots and beets, can be harvested over a long period, because they store well in the soil. Begin harvesting when they are baby sized and continue until maturity. They will last in the soil for weeks or months, depending on the climate and the time of year.

The best way to plan for a continual harvest is to chart the plantings on paper. You will be working within the confines of your growing season, which consists of the number of days from the last frost in spring to the first frost in fall. The local cooperative extension office can provide you with these dates if you don't know them. Don't rush the season when mapping out the first plantings in spring. It's critical to the success of your vegetable garden that you let the soil warm up enough before planting. Seeds sown in soil too cold for germination decay rather than sprout, or if they do sprout, their overall vigor is reduced.

Check the listings of vegetables in this chapter for the crops you want to plant. Note on pages 220 to 221 when they should be planted and the average number of days to harvest. References to specific varieties include the approximate time to harvest.

Seed catalogs also give the number of days to harvest for every variety listed; seed packets contain this information, too. Using these figures within the bounds of your growing season, you'll know when to plant certain vegetables, when to harvest, and when to replant for a steady harvest. Once you've charted your plantings in this way, you can easily make adjustments that will lengthen the harvest season.

ARTICHOKE

The artichoke is a perennial plant that produces edible flower buds. Often spreading 6 feet, it is a massive plant unsuitable for small-space vegetable gardens. Hardy to 30° F, the plant grows best in cool, moist summers and mild winters, although it has also been produced by determined gardeners in northern states. In cold-winter climates the plant is usually cut to the ground in fall. In these areas it is important to mulch the crown (where the stem meets the roots) for protection, but not so heavily that it is smothered. In areas with warm, arid summers, the plant tends to die back during summer but sprouts again in fall.

Artichoke

Generally, artichokes do not produce true from seed—you may or may not get good artichokes. Most are planted from root divisions, available at garden centers and mail-order nurseries. Plant the divisions 6 to 8 inches deep and 4 to 6 feet apart. Locate artichoke plants in a sunny place to the side of a vegetable garden, where they won't be in the way of the more frequent planting and cultivating of annual vegetables. If you're in a hot-summer area, choose a spot with some afternoon shade.

Artichokes can also be grown from seeds, available from seed companies. After the last frost in spring, direct sow the seeds, or set out transplants started indoors four to six weeks previously.

The plant grows best in rich, moist, well-drained soil with a pH between 6.0 and 6.5. Artichokes benefit from extra nitrogen partway through the growing season and after harvest. Slugs and snails are common pests (see control measures on page 291). In areas where the artichoke plume moth is troublesome, a regular insecticide program may be needed to control the pest.

If you cut the artichokes when they are young and tightly formed, you can eat the entire head instead of just the heart. Harvest in spring the first year after planting and in fall to spring in subsequent years. To harvest, cut the stem 1 inch below the head.

'Green Globe Improved', the most common variety of artichoke, is readily available.

ASPARAGUS

This extremely hardy perennial should grow in your garden for two years before it is harvested, but then it keeps providing for 10 to 15 more years. What you harvest yearly in spring are the tender young shoots.

Asparagus is the earliest vegetable that can be harvested from the garden, and it thrives in most areas of the United States. It grows best in areas where the soil freezes a few inches deep in winter. Asparagus does poorly in Hawaii and the Deep South, where the warm, humid climate keeps the plants from going dormant.

Asparagus grows best in deep, fertile, well-drained soil with a pH between 6.0 and 7.0. Before planting work in plenty of organic

Asparagus

matter and a balanced, low-nitrogen fertilizer, such as 5-10-10. If the soil pH is below 6.0, add lime (see page 96).

Although you can start asparagus from seed, it is usually started with one-year-old crowns, available from nurseries, garden centers, and mail-order seed companies. Look for large, well-formed crowns with many roots; thinly rooted crowns are a common cause of weak plants. Do not allow the roots to wither or dry out before planting them. Plant the crowns in spring.

In a sunny spot dig trenches 8 inches deep and 4 to 5 feet apart to accommodate the wide-spreading roots. Spread some compost or manure in the bottom of each trench and cover it with an inch of garden soil. Set the crowns 18 inches apart in the bottom of the trench and cover the plants with 2 inches of soil. As the new shoots come up, gradually fill in the trench; never cover the tops of the emerging shoots. Asparagus requires only moderate water, but do not stint when the tops are developing.

For high production and thick spears, follow a twice-a-year feeding program. Apply a balanced, all-purpose fertilizer, such as 10-10-10, once before growth starts in spring and again right after the plant is harvested.

224

No harvesting should be done the first year and very little the second year. The plant needs this time to build up a large reserve of root power; even if you plant two-year-old crowns, they still need this establishment period. During the third year in the garden, your asparagus plant should give you four full weeks of harvesting.

To harvest asparagus, cut or snap off the spears when they are 6 to 8 inches long. Snapping—bending a spear over sharply until it breaks—avoids injury to other shoots below ground. Asparagus can also be cut; an asparagus knife is available for this purpose. Whether snapping or cutting, be sure to leave a white stub. Let very thin spears, less than ¼ inch wide, remain on the plant and turn into foliage. In fall when the foliage turns brown, cut the plant to within 3 inches of the ground.

'Mary Washington' and 'Martha Washington' are the two most commonly available varieties of asparagus.

BEANS

Snap beans—also known as garden beans, green beans, and string beans—are grown for their immature, edible green pod. (The wax bean has a yellowish, waxy pod.) Other beans are raised for the green seeds growing inside the pod. Shell beans are grown for their immature seeds; other varieties are cultivated for mature seeds, which are then dried.

Beans are further classified as bush or pole, depending on their growth habit. Bush beans grow 1 to 2 feet high and are usually planted in rows. Pole beans require the support of a trellis or stake (see Supporting Vegetables on page 138). They grow more slowly than the bush types but produce more beans per plant.

The many types of beans vary in their heat requirements and length of time needed to make a crop. All except the fava require warm soil to germinate and should be planted after the last frost in spring.

Garbanzo beans

Fava beans

Beans require rich, well-drained soil with a pH between 6.0 and 6.8. Mix a low-nitrogen fertilizer, such as 5-10-10, into the soil before planting. Although beans get by on less water than many vegetables, don't let the plants go dry when they are forming flowers and pods. Lack of moisture will cause the plants to produce "pollywogs"—only the first few seeds develop and the rest of the pod shrivels to a tail.

To avoid the spread of disease from plant to plant, cultivate shallowly and only when the leaves are dry. Beans should be harvested also only when the leaves are dry. Since beans are subject to diseases that survive in the soil, growing sites should be rotated each season.

Fava Beans

Favas—also called broad beans, horse beans, or windsors—are not true beans at all but are related to another legume, vetch. They grow in cool weather unsuitable for snap beans, and they will not produce in summer heat. In mild-winter areas plant them in fall for a spring crop. Wait until early spring in cold-weather climates. The plants grow 3 to 4½ feet high, and the beans mature in 120 to 150 days. You can harvest the pods a little earlier for fresh shell beans.

Although most people can safely eat fava beans, some people are violently allergic to them.

Garbanzo Beans

Botanically, the garbanzo is neither a bean nor a true pea but rather the chick pea, or gram. This bush-type plant is similar to the snap bean in culture but requires a longer growing season, about 100 days. Garbanzos produce one or two seeds in each puffy little pod. Harvest during the green-shell stage or let them mature for dry beans.

Lima Beans

Needing a warmer soil than snap beans to germinate properly, limas also need higher temperatures (although pods may fail to set if days are extremely hot) and a longer season to produce a crop. Bush limas need 65 to 75 days to mature, and pole limas 75 to 95 days. If the soil temperature is below 65° F at planting time, pretreating the seeds with both an insecticide and a fungicide is good insurance. Harvest lima beans as soon as the pods are well filled but still bright and fresh in appearance. To hull limas, press firmly on

Lima beans

the pod seam with your thumb; the beans should pop out.

'Henderson's Bush', 'Jackson Wonder', and 'Fordhook 242' are popular bush lima varieties; 'Prizetaker' and 'Sieva' are readily available pole lima varieties.

Scarlet Runner Beans

These beans are closely related to snap beans, but they are more vigorous and have larger seeds, pods, and flowers. The plant grows rapidly to 10 and even 20 feet, forming a dense yet delicate vine with pods 6 to 12 inches long. Because of its large clusters of bright red (sometimes white) flowers, it is often grown as an ornamental plant. Only pole varieties are commonly available. Culture is similar to the other beans, but these need more space. Harvest after about 70 days for tender pods, and 115 days for shell beans.

Snap Beans

These beans are said to be the foolproof vegetable for the beginning gardener. They require only about 60 days of moderate temperatures to produce a crop of tender green pods. With such a short growth period, they can be grown throughout the United States. Plant every few weeks for a continual harvest throughout the summer. In mild-winter climates, snap beans may be grown virtually all year, but pods do not form when the weather is too hot or too cold.

Bush snap beans are slightly hardier than pole varieties, and generally they can be planted as much as two weeks earlier. They are also somewhat less susceptible to heat and drought. Pole snap beans produce over a longer period. Poles or other supports for the beans should be about 8 feet tall.

To harvest a full crop of snap beans, pick them before large seeds develop. A few old pods left on a plant will greatly reduce the set of new ones. Keep them picked in the young, succulent stage.

There are dozens of snap bean varieties available. Two of the most popular, 'Kentucky Wonder' and 'Blue Lake', are readily available in both bush and pole forms.

Soybeans

An exceptionally rich source of protein and a staple of diets throughout the world, soybeans

'Blue Lake' snap beans

Scarlet runner beans

Soybeans

are now being recognized as a superior home garden vegetable. Most varieties have a narrow latitude range in which they mature properly and produce a satisfactory crop. Varieties chosen for your latitude range will mature at the same date regardless of when you plant them. Early-maturing varieties can be planted as close as 2 feet between rows; late-maturing varieties require 3 feet.

Avoid cultivating around or harvesting wet plants, which are easily bruised and broken. Wet leaves also facilitate the spread of disease. Most home gardeners harvest soybeans in the green stage. Pick the pods when they are plump and the seeds are nearly full sized but still green. All the beans on the plant ripen at about the same time, so you might as well pull the plant, then find a shady spot to pick the pods.

The pods are easily shelled if plunged into boiling, salted water for five minutes, allowed to cool, then gently squeezed.

BEETS

Since they don't transplant well, root crops such as beets are seeded in place outdoors. In cold-winter climates seeds are usually sown as soon as the soil is workable in spring, but additional plantings can be made every three weeks until summer. In mild-winter areas beets can be planted from fall to early spring.

Although beets are grown primarily for their edible roots, which are ready for harvest 45 to 70 days after seeding, the tops of young plants are also edible.

Like other root crops, beets grow best in a loose, deep soil without any clumps or stones. The soil should be fertile and have a pH between 6.0 and 6.8. Sow the seeds about ½ inch deep in rows a foot or more apart. Keep the seedbed moist. When the seedlings are a few inches high, thin to 2 inches apart and use the thinned greens in salads. Unless you use a monogerm (single-seeded) variety,

Beets

each beet seed will produce three to five seedlings in a tight clump. Each clump should be thinned to a single plant.

Stringy and tough beets are the result of a lack of moisture, which may be caused by improper watering or by overplanting beets and then not thinning them adequately.

Although the most familiar beets are round and red, there are white and yellow varieties as well as elongated beets. Commonly available varieties include the deep red, globular 'Red Ace', 53 days; the sweet, yellow 'Burpee's Goldenbeet', 55 days; and the red, 'Lutz Green Leaf', 70 days.

BROCCOLI

See Cabbage Family.

BRUSSELS SPROUTS

See Cabbage Family.

CABBAGE FAMILY

Many members of the cabbage, or cole, family—broccoli, brussels sprouts, cabbage, cauliflower, Chinese cabbage, collards, kale, and kohlrabi—are excellent vegetable garden crops. Planted annually, these cole crops are grown in every climate of the United States.

The cole vegetables are adapted to cool weather, growing best when temperatures are between 65° and 80° F. Cole crops are hardy, most tolerating temperatures into the low 20° F range. In cold-winter areas plant for a late summer or early fall harvest. In mild climates plant for late spring or fall harvest. If your winters are warm, you can plan for a harvest in late fall or winter.

Cole crops grow well in reasonably fertile, well-drained soil with a pH range of 6.0 to 6.8, although brussels sprouts, kohlrabi, and kale grow well even when the pH is as low as 5.5. Before planting, work a balanced,

Assorted cabbage

Broccoli

all-purpose fertilizer, such as 10-10-10, into the soil. Nitrogen is quickly leached in sandy soils and in high-rainfall areas. In these cases, a side-dressing of fertilizer halfway through the growing season will benefit the plants.

All of the coles can be either direct seeded or sown indoors and later transplanted into the garden. Direct seeding is usually recommended for the more sensitive Chinese cabbage and kohlrabi. If you must transplant these, use peat pots.

Plant seeds about ½ inch deep and 1 inch apart. Thin the seedlings to approximately 18 inches apart. Seeds should be sown about two weeks before you plan to set out transplants, if they are to mature at the same time. Transplants should be set into the ground when they are one to one-and-a-half months old and have four or five true leaves. Transplants frequently have crooked stems; these should be planted as deep as up to the first leaves, which will strengthen the plant and keep it from flopping over as it grows.

Bolting—the rapid formation of a seed stalk before the plant is ready for harvest—is common to cabbage, brussels sprouts, and kohlrabi. Young plants may bolt if exposed to temperatures below 50° F for two to three weeks. Bolting will be less of a problem if transplants with stems the thickness of a lead pencil are used.

Broccoli

Probably the most popular cole crop among home gardeners, broccoli is easy to grow and highly productive. Unless a considerable amount is to be preserved, six to twelve plants are adequate for most families.

Broccoli needs 50 to 100 days to mature from transplants to harvest; direct-seeded plants need another two weeks. Late spring or early summer is the best time to plant in most of the United States. In mild-winter areas plantings are frequently made in fall for a winter harvest.

Harvest the center green bud cluster while the buds are still tight and before there is any yellow color. Broccoli will continue producing bonus side shoots as long as the harvested shoots are not cut back to the main stem. If you leave the base of the shoots and a couple of leaves, new shoots will then grow, and the harvest season should last a month or more. (Some varieties do not form side shoots after the main harvest.)

Common problems encountered in growing broccoli are small plants that flower early or form heads poorly. Bolting may also occur during hot weather—a problem exacerbated by planting late in spring. Premature flowering may also be caused by any of several factors: prolonged chilling of young plants, extremely early planting, transplants that are too old or too dry, or severe drought conditions.

Two of the best early-maturing varieties are 'Green Comet', 55 days, and 'Premium Crop', 58 days. 'Romanesco', 75 days, is a variety that is grown for its chartreuse heads and sweet flavor.

Brussels Sprouts

This plant produces as many as a hundred sprouts, which resemble tiny cabbages, clustered around its main stem. The most cold tolerant of the cole family, brussels sprouts is a relatively long-season plant. In most areas set out transplants in May, June, or July for fall harvest. In mild-winter areas plant in fall for winter and spring harvest.

The sprouts mature in sequence from the bottom of the stem up. Pinch out the growing tip when the plants are 15 to 20 inches tall to promote uniform development and maturity of the sprouts. This technique

Growing vegetables does not necessarily mean straight rows of crops. You can plant vegetables and flowers together to bring color and variety to the garden.

Brussels sprouts

Cabbage

is particularly helpful where winter sets in early, although it may somewhat reduce the harvest.

You can harvest brussels sprouts individually while they are growing on the plant, or you can pull the entire stalk and hang it in a cool, dry place. To harvest sprouts on the plant, snap off firm, young, green sprouts from the bottom of the stalk first and work your way upward. Picked when small, they are sweet—unlike the large, strong-flavored sprouts usually sold in grocery stores. If you pull the entire stalk, remove the brussels sprouts as you need them throughout winter.

Two popular early varieties of brussels sprouts are 'Jade Cross E', 95 days, and 'Green Marvel', 80 days.

Cabbage

Plant so that you can harvest a succession of a few heads of cabbage at a time. Buy transplants for the earliest planting, then sow seed directly in the garden for succeeding crops. Plants can be spaced as close as 12 inches apart.

Cabbage needs 50 to 100 days to mature. In cold-winter climates plant in spring for a summer harvest or in summer for a fall harvest. In mild-winter climates plant in late winter and early spring for a late spring and summer harvest, or in late summer and fall for a winter and spring harvest.

Like other cole crops, cabbage is a heavy user of nitrogen and potassium. In addition to applying a balanced, all-purpose fertilizer, such as 10-10-10, before planting, follow up in three to four weeks with a side-dressing of a high-nitrogen fertilizer.

Cabbage responds very favorably to cool, moist soil and a mulch of hay or straw. A mulch also helps control weed growth without deep hoeing. This can be important because cabbage has a shallow root system that can be damaged during cultivation.

Begin harvesting when the cabbage heads are firm and about the size of a softball. Cut just beneath the head, leaving some bottom leaves to support new growth.

In warm weather the heads of early varieties tend to split soon after they mature. You can solve the problem by either holding off on water or partially root-pruning the plant when the heads are formed. (Some gardeners root-prune by simply twisting the plant to break some of the roots.) Splitting is seldom a problem with later varieties maturing during cool weather.

Cabbages come in different sizes, shapes, colors, and leaf textures. There are midget varieties such as 'Baby Head', 72 days, and red varieties such as 'Red Acre', 76 days. The crinkly-leaved savoy varieties include 'Savoy Ace', 85 days. 'Earliana', 60 days, is a small, round, green variety.

Cauliflower

Cauliflower

More restricted by climate than either cabbage or broccoli, cauliflower is not as tolerant of cold weather and does not form a head properly in hot weather. It needs approximately two months of cool weather to mature. This means planting for spring and fall crops in most cases, although winter crops are possible in mild climates, as are summer crops in some gardens at high elevations. For a spring crop set out transplants a week or two before the average date of the last frost.

For the most vigorous seedling growth, cauliflower is nearly always grown as a transplant. Transplants must grow rapidly; if old or stunted they will produce "buttons"—very small heads on immature plants.

Start seeds one to two months before the outdoor planting date. Cauliflower plants are not tolerant of poor soil conditions: They need rich, firm, moist soil. When the head begins to develop, gather the leaves over it and tie them together with soft twine or plastic tape. This is called blanching, because with light excluded the head remains white and tender. The leaves of the variety 'Self-Blanche' curl naturally over the head when grown in cool weather. There is no need to blanch purple varieties such as 'Purple Head', which have a mild broccoli flavor and hold longer in the garden than white cauliflower.

If the weather turns hot, mist or sprinkle the plants to maintain humidity and to keep the plants cool. Unwrap the heads occasionally to check for hiding pests.

Some of the most popular varieties include 'Early Snowball', 60 days; 'Snow Crown', 48 days; and 'Snow King', 50 days.

Chinese Cabbage

The name *Chinese cabbage,* or celery cabbage, covers a number of greens quite different in character. All are cool-weather crops that bolt—or go to seed prematurely—during the long days of late spring and summer. Grow as a fall and early winter crop.

Sow seeds thinly and later thin the seedlings to 18 inches apart. If you must transplant, start the seeds in peat pots.

Plant from early August into September. Chinese cabbage requires 75 to 85 days from seed to harvest. Keep the plants well watered and mulch to conserve moisture. If frost hits before the heads form, you will still be able to harvest a good crop of greens.

One of the best varieties is 'Michihili', 75 days. Others include the loose-leaved variety 'Crispy Choy', 45 days, and the slow-bolting 'Early Hybrid G', 50 to 60 days.

Chinese cabbage

Collards

Kale

Collards

These greens have been a southern favorite for generations. Often described as headless cabbage plants, they tolerate cold better than cabbage. A light freeze only sweetens collards. Unlike their close relative kale, collards also withstand considerable heat.

Set out plants or sow seed in spring and fall. Successive plantings are not necessary for a continual supply, since you can gradually pick leaves from the bottom up after the plants are about 1 foot high. Collards are one of the most productive of all vegetables, particularly in southern gardens. They need plenty of fertilizer and water to produce tender, succulent leaves.

Two of the best varieties are 'Georgia', 70 to 80 days, and 'Vates', 75 days.

Kale

Grown for its delectable leaves, kale has been raised as long as vegetables have been cultivated. Kale is the closest relative of the wild cabbage plant, from which all of the cole crops are derived.

No other vegetable is as well adapted to fall sowing in areas of moderately severe winters. Kale does not tolerate heat as well as collards, but it is extremely hardy and grows best in the cool of fall. In fact, the flavor is improved by frost. Transplants may be used for early spring planting, but direct seeding is best in fall. Scatter seeds in a 4-inch band and thin gradually to 12 to 18 inches apart, using the thinnings in salads. Supply the plant with plenty of fertilizer and water for tender, sweet leaves.

'Dwarf Blue Curled Scotch Vates', 55 days, is the most widely planted variety of kale.

Kohlrabi

This unusual, little-known vegetable deserves to be grown and appreciated more. It looks like a turnip that is growing above ground and sprouting long leafstalks and leaves like those of a cabbage. The flavor is similar to both turnip and cabbage but milder and sweeter than either.

Kohlrabi is more tolerant of heat and drying winds than other cole crops. Similar to cabbage in culture, it has a shorter season, requiring only 45 to 60 days to mature. It should be started in early spring so that most growth is complete before the full heat of summer. Start in midsummer to harvest in fall. In mild-winter areas plant for a winter and spring harvest.

Kohlrabi is usually direct seeded. Thin to approximately 4 to 6 inches apart, leaving

Kohlrabi

Carrots

1 to 2 feet between rows. Harvest when the head is 2 to 3 inches in diameter; it gets increasingly tough as the size increases.

Recommended varieties: 'Early Purple Vienna', 60 days; 'Early White Vienna', 55 days; and 'Grand Duke', 45 to 50 days.

CANTALOUPE AND MUSKMELON

See Melons.

CARROTS

A cool-season crop, carrots are adaptable, tolerant of neglect, and unequaled for supplying food over a long period, using nothing more complicated for storage than the soil in which they are grown.

Since they do not transplant well, root crops such as carrots should be seeded in place outdoors. The most important planting times are early spring and early summer. Each sowing matures in 50 to 85 days and can be harvested over a two- to four-month period. Small plantings every three weeks ensure a continual harvest.

For straight-shafted carrots, make sure that the soil is deep, loose, and free of lumps and stones. Any obstructions in the soil will cause carrots to bend, fork, or become otherwise misshapen. The soil pH should be between 5.5 and 6.8. If you add manure, be sure that it is well aged. Manure that hasn't rotted sufficiently will produce rough, branching carrots. After preparing the soil, sow seeds ½ inch apart, cover lightly with soil, and keep the seedbed moist. Thin seedlings to 2 inches.

Carrots differ mainly in their size and shape. Among the most commonly planted long varieties is 'Imperator', 75 days. 'Nantes' and 'Red-Cored Chantenay', both 70 days, are popular medium-length varieties. 'Short 'n' Sweet', 68 days, is an excellent short carrot. The short to medium or very short types are better adapted to heavy or rough soils than the long kinds. They are also easier to dig. The tiny finger carrots, such as 'Little Finger' and 'Lady Finger', both about 65 days, are often the sweetest.

CASABA

See Winter Melons, under Melons.

CAULIFLOWER

See Cabbage Family.

CELERY

More time and attention are demanded for celery than for most garden vegetables. Celery needs 105 to 130 days of cool weather. If you don't start from transplants, sow seed two to four months before it is time to plant outdoors. The very small seeds should be sown ⅛ inch deep and kept moist; they will germinate in two to three weeks. In most areas celery is planted outdoors in early spring. In warm-winter climates you can also plant in fall and winter for a spring crop; a light frost improves the flavor of celery.

Transplant carefully to a shady spot, spacing the plants 6 to 10 inches apart. Celery grows naturally in wet, almost boggy locations, so the water supply must be plentiful and continual. The plant grows best in rich, well-drained soil with a pH between 6.0 and 6.8. Since celery is a heavy feeder, use ample quantities of a low-nitrogen fertilizer, such as 5-10-10.

Although blanching usually is not necessary with modern varieties, it may make the stalks more tender. White stalks are less common in markets now, so you may want to grow your own. Wrapping the plants with paper or shading with boards will blanch the stalks.

For early spring planting use slow-bolting varieties such as 'Summer Pascal' or 'Golden Self-Blanching', both 115 days. 'Tall Utah 52-70R Improved', 105 days, is a good disease-resistant variety.

CHINESE CABBAGE

See Cabbage Family.

COLLARDS

See Cabbage Family.

CORN

Easily grown from seed, corn can be harvested continually through the summer and into the fall by planting early, midseason, and late varieties, or making successive plantings every two to three weeks.

Keep in mind that the number of days to maturity is a relative figure, depending on

Celery

the total amount of heat the corn receives. Corn does not really start growing until the weather turns warm. Varieties listed as taking 65 days to mature may take 80 to 90 days when planted early, but they may come close to the 65 days if planted a month later.

When planting for a succession of harvests, the effect of a cool spring should be considered. Rather than plant every two weeks, make the second planting when the first planting is knee-high.

Since corn is wind-pollinated, plant in short blocks of three or four rows rather than a single long row of plants. Don't interplant different types of corn at the same time, since they may cross-pollinate. If you want to plant different kinds, such as a standard sweet and an extrasweet, wait about four weeks between plantings to ensure that the plants will not pollinate simultaneously.

Corn needs rich, well-drained soil with a pH between 6.0 and 6.8. Sow seeds 2 inches deep and 2 to 3 inches apart, leaving 30 to

Corn

36 inches between rows in the block. Thin to 10 to 14 inches between plants. If you plant any closer, you risk a crop of nubbins.

At planting time, fertilize in bands on both sides of each seed row (see Banding on page 175). Use a low-nitrogen fertilizer, such as 5-10-10. Side-dress when the corn reaches 8 inches high, and repeat when the corn is knee-high (approximately 18 inches high). Don't pull off any suckers. They don't take any strength from the main stalk, and removing them may actually reduce the yield.

Corn requires a steady supply of water. Its moisture need is greatest from the time the plants form tassels until the ears are harvested. If the edges of the leaves turn downward, check the soil to be sure of adequate moisture.

Watch for the corn earworm. The eggs hatch on the silk of the developing ear and the larvae burrow into and feed on the kernels. Ears with tight husks and good tip covers are somewhat resistant to corn earworm damage.

As a general guide, corn is ready to harvest three weeks after the silk first appears, although this depends on the weather. The silk becomes dry and brown when the ears are near perfect ripeness. Probably the only sure way to tell when corn is ripe is to open the husk of a likely ear and press a kernel. If it spurts milky juice, it is ripe.

Varieties differ, but most produce two ears per plant, the top ear ripening a day or two ahead of the lower one. Harvest by breaking the ear from the stalk: Hold the ear at its base and bend downward, twisting at the same time. The idea is to break the ear off close to its base without damaging either it or the main stalk.

There are many excellent corn varieties available. Some of the best include the sweet white corn 'How Sweet It Is', 80 days; the bicolor 'Honey 'n' Pearl', 78 days; and the early-maturing 'Early Xtra-Sweet', 71 days.

Cucumbers can be trained on a trellis. There will be fewer culls, and even those varieties that curve when grown on the ground will grow straight on a trellis.

COWPEAS

See Peas.

CRENSHAW

See Winter Melons, under Melons.

CUCUMBERS

Because of their short growing season, 50 to 70 days from seed to harvest, cucumbers can usually find a warm enough spot in almost every garden. They should be seeded in place after the soil has warmed in spring and the air temperature is between 65° and 70° F. If your growing season is very short, start seeds indoors four to six weeks before it is time to set out transplants. When setting out the plants, cover them with hot caps or plastic to create a warmer environment and protect the plants from frost.

Cucumbers respond to generous amounts of organic matter in the soil. Dig the planting furrow 2 feet deep and fill the first foot with manure mixed with peat moss, compost, sawdust, or other organic material. Fill the rest of the furrow with soil, peat moss, and a low-nitrogen fertilizer, such as 5-10-10.

Sow seed 1 inch deep. If growing cucumbers in rows, sow 3 to 5 seeds per foot of row and thin the seedlings to about 12 inches apart, leaving 4 to 6 feet between rows. To grow cucumbers in hills, sow 9 to 12 seeds in a cluster and thin to 4 or 5 and finally to only 2 or 3 plants per hill. Space the hills 2 to 3 feet apart. There is no specific advantage to hill planting; this practice probably became popular for ease of watering young plants.

Since cucumber roots grow down 3 feet, watering should be slow and deep. If the plant is under stress from lack of moisture at any time, it simply stops growing. It will pick up again when moisture is supplied. It is normal for leaves to wilt in the middle of the day during hot spells, but check the soil to make sure that there is ample moisture below the surface.

If the first early flowers fail to set fruit, don't worry. The male flowers open first, then about a week later you'll see the female

Cucumber

flowers with baby cucumbers at their bases. (Gynoecious hybrids—varieties that have almost all female flowers—set fruit with the first blossoms.) Keep all fruit picked from the vines as they reach usable size. The importance of this can't be overstressed, because even a few fruit left to mature on the plant will completely stop the set of new fruit from maturing.

Cucumbers are classified by their growth form—bush or vining. They are also divided into slicing and pickling varieties. Most slicing cucumbers should be harvested when they are 6 to 8 inches long. Harvest small pickling cucumbers for sweet pickles and larger ones for dills.

Greenhouse cucumbers—the long, plastic-wrapped cucumbers sold as English cucumbers or burpless cucumbers in grocery stores—should not be grown outdoors, since they are seedless and self-pollinating. (Insect pollination would form seedpods, making the fruit gourdlike.) The culture of these is demanding and not for the casual grower.

Training cucumbers on a trellis saves ground space and results in more attractive fruit and fewer culls. Varieties that are curved when grown on the ground grow almost straight on a trellis. (See Supporting

Vegetables on page 138.) Also consider the midget varieties when space is limited. They can be grown in the ground, in tubs, or in hanging baskets.

Cucumbers are susceptible to many diseases, including anthracnose, particularly a problem in the Southeast; downy mildew, worst in the Atlantic and Gulf states; and powdery mildew, mosaic virus, and scab, most serious in northern states. Look for cucumber varieties that are resistant to the diseases prevalent in your area.

EGGPLANT

Because this tomato relative can take 150 days to mature from seed, most gardeners grow transplants started six to nine weeks before the last frost in spring. Wait until daily temperatures are in the 70° F range before setting out the plants, since eggplant is very susceptible to low-temperature injury, especially on cold nights. A minimum night temperature of 65° F is ideal for a good eggplant crop. Once the plant's growth is stunted by cool weather, it seldom recovers

enough to produce quality fruit. If frost dates are unpredictable in your area or if very late frosts are common, protect plants with hot caps or plastic covers.

Set the transplants about 18 inches apart, leaving 36 inches between rows. Eggplant grows best in deep, fertile, well-drained soil with a pH around 6.0. Fertilize about three times during the growing season. Don't allow the soil to dry out.

Harvest eggplant 60 to 95 days after setting out the transplants. Cut the woody stem with pruning shears, leaving some of the stem on the fruit. Pick the fruit when it is young, at about one third to two thirds its normal mature size. Good fruit has a high gloss. One test for ripeness is to push on the side of the fruit with the ball of your thumb; the fruit is ready to be harvested if the indentation does not spring back. If the seeds are brown when you open the fruit, you will know that the best eating stage is past.

Eggplant grows well in containers. Use at least a 5-gallon container and a synthetic soil mix as insurance against the diseases that plague eggplant in some areas. Where

Eggplant

summers are cool, place the containers in the hot spots around the house—in the reflected heat from a south wall, for example.

Although the most common eggplant varieties sold in grocery stores are large fruited, the home garden trend is toward the smaller varieties. These include 'Black Beauty', 70 to 80 days (from transplant to harvest); 'Dusky', 56 days; 'Black Bell', 68 days; and 'Ichiban', 61 days.

HONEYDEW

See Winter Melons, under Melons.

KALE

See Cabbage Family.

KOHLRABI

See Cabbage Family.

LETTUCE

This cool-season vegetable is usually sown directly in the ground, although transplants are also used. In cold-winter climates sow seed or set out plants as soon as the soil is workable in spring and make successive sowings or plantings while the weather remains cool. Resume growing lettuce again when the weather cools in fall. In winter climates that are mild sow seed or set out plants from fall through spring. Heat causes lettuce to become bitter and to bolt (go to seed prematurely).

Lettuce grows best in rich, well-drained soil with a pH between 6.0 and 6.8. A light feeding and regular moisture are essential for tender, sweet leaves. Young lettuce plants never fully recover if their growth is stunted by a lack of nutrients. Keep the soil moist, since a lack of water makes the leaves tough and bitter.

There are five types of lettuce: butterhead lettuce, celtuce, crisphead lettuce, leaf lettuce, and romaine.

Butterhead Lettuce

This is a head-forming type of lettuce in which the leaves are loosely folded. The outer leaves may be green or brownish and the

Bibb lettuce

Iceberg lettuce

Ruby lettuce

241

inner leaves cream or butter colored. Butterhead lettuce matures in 65 to 80 days. The most familiar variety is 'Bibb'. Other good varieties include 'Big Boston', 'Buttercrunch', and 'Dark Green Boston'. Butterhead types are not favored commercially because they bruise and tear easily, but they're no problem in the home garden.

Sow seeds ¼ inch deep and 1 to 2 inches apart, leaving 18 to 24 inches between rows. Thin seedlings to 6 to 8 inches apart. Harvest butterhead lettuce when a loose head is formed. Cut just below the base of the head.

Celtuce

Resembling a cross between celery and lettuce, celtuce looks and tastes like leaf lettuce when picked young. If given a full 90 days to mature and pinched to encourage multiple shoots, it develops celerylike stalks. If not pinched, the plant produces only one stalk.

Sow seeds ¼ inch deep and 2 inches apart, leaving 18 to 24 inches between rows. Thin seedlings to 8 to 12 inches apart. Use the thinnings in salads.

Crisphead Lettuce

Also known as head lettuce, the most familiar variety of this lettuce type is 'Iceberg', which matures in 80 to 90 days. Crisphead lettuce tolerates more heat than butterhead types.

Sow seeds ¼ to ½ inch deep and 1 to 2 inches apart, leaving 18 to 24 inches between rows. Thin to 12 to 14 inches between plants. Thinning is extremely important for crisphead lettuce. If you leave two plants where only one should grow, you'll probably harvest two poor heads or none. Harvest crisphead lettuce when the heads are firm and the tops start to turn yellowish green. Cut the heads off the plants.

Leaf Lettuce

The many different varieties of leaf lettuce, which produce loose bunches of leaves, vary in color (green, red, or bronze) and texture (lobed, frilled, or crinkled). Since all varieties mature quickly, in 40 to 50 days, it is easy to plant for a succession of crops. Among the many varieties easily available are 'Black-Seeded Simpson' (light green, frilled leaves); 'Red Sails' (red-bronze, ruffled leaves); and 'Green Ice' (dark green, wavy leaves).

Sow seeds ¼ to ½ inch deep and 1 to 2 inches apart, leaving 18 to 24 inches between rows. Thin to 4 to 6 inches between plants in the first thinning and later to 6 to 10 inches. The final spacing depends on the mature size of the variety you are growing. It is important to thin the plants properly. The best part of leaf lettuce is the light green leaves in the center of a nearly mature plant. These develop only if there is adequate spacing.

Harvest leaf lettuce by pulling off individual leaves as needed and allowing the plant to continue growing. You can also harvest by removing the entire plant.

Romaine

Also known as cos, this type of lettuce grows upright to 8 to 9 inches high. The tightly folded, crisp leaves are medium green on the outside and greenish white inside. Romaine needs 70 to 85 days to mature. Sow seeds ¼ inch deep and 1 to 2 inches apart, leaving 18 to 24 inches between rows. Thin seedlings to 6 to 8 inches apart. As with leaf lettuce, harvest romaine by pulling off individual leaves or by removing the entire plant.

'Dark Green Cos' and 'Parris Island Cos' are widely grown. 'Valmaine Cos' is similar to 'Parris Island Cos' but is tolerant of mildew.

Romaine lettuce

242

Cantaloupe

MELONS

These warm-season annual plants include cantaloupe, muskmelons, winter melons, and watermelon. Most varieties need plenty of space and are not at all suitable for small vegetable gardens. Save space by training melons on trellises (see Supporting Vegetables on page 138) or by growing miniature and bush melons.

All melons grow best in rich, well-drained, highly organic soil with a pH between 6.0 and 6.8. Before planting, work in generous amounts of organic matter and a low-nitrogen fertilizer, such as 5-10-10. When the plants are established and the runners are 12 to 18 inches long, fertilize them again. Make a third application after the first melons are set.

Most melons need about three months of warm weather. Wait until daytime temperatures are consistently above 60° F before direct seeding or setting out transplants in the spring.

Melons can be planted in rows or in hills. When planting in rows provide at least 12 inches between plants. (Some bush varieties can be spaced much closer.) When planting in hills sow four or five seeds per hill and thin to two plants. Keep rows and hills 4 to 6 feet apart. Expect to harvest two or three melons per vine.

Even though melons need plenty of heat, you can grow them in short-season or cool-summer areas if you help speed the maturing process and raise the temperature around the plants. Grow extra-early varieties, either buying transplants or starting seed indoors three to four weeks before the outdoor planting date. Use black plastic mulch to raise the soil temperature, and protect new plants with hot caps or row covers.

Melon vines require ample moisture until the fruit is fully grown. To make the melons sweeter, hold back on water during the ripening period.

Cantaloupe

The true cantaloupe is not grown in North America, but the term is used generally to describe the early shipping types of muskmelon. Cantaloupe needs 60 to 100 days from seed to harvest. In short-season or cool-summer areas, start transplants three to four weeks before it is time to plant outdoors. Also, look for early-maturing varieties, such as 'Sweet 'n' Early', which is ready for harvest in 75 days. 'Minnesota Midget' bears 4-inch fruit and matures in 60 days.

Harvest cantaloupe when the stem breaks cleanly when you lift the melon.

Watermelon

Casaba

Watermelon

The watermelon requires more summer heat than muskmelons. In areas too cool for the standard 25- to 30-pound watermelon but where muskmelons can be grown, the icebox-sized varieties of watermelon are the best bet.

'Sugar Baby', which produces 7- to 8-inch fruit weighing about 8 pounds, matures in only 80 days.

Picking a watermelon when it's neither too green nor too ripe is not easy. Some gardeners claim that the sign of ripeness is when the little pig's-tail curl at the point of attachment to the vine turns brown and dries up; but in some varieties it dries up 7 to 10 days before the fruit is really ripe. The differing sounds of a thump—a ringing sound if the fruit is green, or a dull or dead one when the fruit is ripe—are unreliable, because the dull sound is also the sign of overripeness.

The surest sign of ripeness in most varieties is the color of the bottom surface. As the melon matures, the area that is in contact with the ground turns from a light straw color to a rich yellow. In addition, most watermelons lose the powdery or slick appearance on the top surface, becoming dull when ripe.

Winter Melons

Winter melons—casaba, crenshaw, honeydew, and Persian—are late-maturing varieties of muskmelon. Long, hot summer melons would more aptly describe them. Their best growing conditions are in the hot, dry interior valleys of California, Arizona, and other areas of the Southwest. A good indicator of ripeness is a strong, fruity aroma at the blossom end (the end opposite the stem).

The casaba is wrinkled and golden when ripe, with very sweet, juicy white flesh. It takes as long as 120 days to mature. A good keeper, casaba appears in grocery stores for months after being harvested.

The crenshaw has dark green skin, salmon pink flesh, and a distinctive flavor. The melon matures in about 110 days. 'Burpee Early Hybrid' is ready for harvest in only 90 days.

The skin of most honeydew varieties is creamy white, smooth, and hard. The flesh is usually lime green, with a slight golden tinge at maturity, which takes about 112 days. 'Earli-dew', which bears 5-inch fruit, matures in only 95 days.

The Persian melon is large, round, and heavily netted and has thick orange flesh. It needs about 95 days in a hot, dry climate.

ONIONS

The nature of the onion is to grow a top in cool weather and form a bulb in warm weather. Bulbing is controlled by both temperature and day length. Onions are so sensitive to day length that they are divided into short-day and long-day varieties. It is very important to plant varieties designated for your area.

Short-day varieties are planted in the southern half of the United States as a winter crop started in fall. They form bulbs as the days lengthen to about 12 hours in early summer. Long-day onions are grown in the northern latitudes. Most require 14 to 16 hours of daylight to form bulbs. Planted in spring as early as the soil can be worked, they form bulbs when the days are longest in the summer.

'Yellow Bermuda' is a standard short-day variety for southern climates. Because of early bulbing, it makes only a small bulb in northern gardens. (However, a good-sized transplant planted early will make a larger bulb.) To harvest very small pearl or pickling onions in the North, plant the short-day variety 'Eclipse' thickly in late April to May. When grown in winter in southern gardens, it develops normal-sized bulbs.

Any variety of onion can be used as a green onion, or scallion, if it is harvested when the bulb is small. In addition to the bulbing type of green onions, there are several perennial bunching types—those that do not produce bulbs but continue to divide at the base to form new shoots throughout the growing season. Shoots are crisp and mild early in the season; they are more pungent later on.

Onions

Onions are heavy feeders, so before planting work into the soil generous amounts of organic matter and a low-nitrogen fertilizer, such as 5-10-10. The soil should be loose and well drained, with a pH between 6.0 and 6.8. A steady moisture supply is essential, particularly during bulb formation.

Start onions from seeds, transplants, or sets (the small dry onions available in late winter and early spring). Seeds are generally used for starting transplants; sow indoors 12 weeks before the outdoor planting date. If direct seeding outdoors, thin seedlings to 2 to 3 inches apart.

Transplants are popular because of the large bulb size produced over a short time (65 days or less). Obtain plants from a garden center or mail-order seed company. Plant 1 to 2 inches deep and 3 to 4 inches apart.

Sets are usually the most reliable, although the choice is more limited. Sets are available in three colors: white, red, and brown. Generally, sets smaller in diameter than a dime should be used for bulbing. Larger sets should be used for green onions, since they may bolt and not produce a good bulb. Plant sets 1 to 2 inches deep and 2 to 4 inches apart.

To harvest large, mature onions, simply pull the plants from the ground at the time half of the tops have broken over naturally. When the tops have fully wilted, cut them off 1½ inches above the bulb. Prepare the onions for storage by curing them in an open crate or mesh bag for two weeks or longer. Remove any dirt and loose outer skins, and store the onions in a dry, cool spot where the temperature is between 35° and 50° F.

Among the best onions for the West are 'California Early Red' and 'Walla Walla Sweet'. Good varieties for the South include 'Red Granex' and 'Crystal White Wax'. 'Danvers Yellow Globe' and 'Yellow Sweet Spanish' do well in all parts of the United States.

PARSNIPS

Like other root crops, parsnips should be direct seeded, since they don't transplant well. These carrot relatives are generally sown in spring after the soil has warmed, and they are harvested in fall and winter. They form 1- to 1½-foot-long white roots in 100 to 120 days.

Parsnips need deep, loose soil to grow undistorted roots that can be harvested intact. Ideally, the soil pH should be between 6.0 and 6.8. Parsnips are more tolerant than carrots of poor, dry soil, but work in organic matter and keep the soil moist for a tender crop. Sow seeds 1 inch apart and thin to 3 inches between plants.

Parsnips can be left in the ground all winter (they should be mulched in very cold winter climates). In fact, they need winter cold near the freezing point to change their starch to sugar and develop their characteristic sweet, nutlike flavor. They may also be dug in late fall and stored in moist sand. Although they can stand alternate freezing and thawing in the ground, freezing after harvest will damage them.

One of the most commonly available varieties is 'Hollow Crown', 100 to 105 days.

Parsnips

'Sugar Snap' peas

Garden peas

PEAS

The most common peas grown in home gardens are garden peas, also called English peas in the South to avoid confusing them with cowpeas (see below). Requiring 55 to 75 days from seed to harvest, garden peas include shelling varieties and edible-pod varieties that are also known as sugar peas, snow peas, or sugar snap peas.

A cool-season crop, garden peas are grown mainly in early spring to midsummer in cold-winter climates. They are generally grown in fall, winter, and very early spring in mild-winter areas.

Garden peas thrive in well-drained soil with a pH between 5.5 and 6.8. Use nitrogen fertilizer sparingly. After the plants are up and growing, a side-dressing containing a low-nitrogen fertilizer, such as 5-10-10, is usually adequate. Keep the soil moist.

Since garden peas grow so easily, they are usually direct seeded. Sow them 1 to 2 inches deep and 1 inch apart. The low-growing varieties that do not require staking are the easiest to grow. They need only 18 to 24 inches between rows. Climbing varieties trained on chicken wire or a trellis need 3 feet between rows, but you can plant in double rows 6 inches apart on each side of the support. (See Supporting Vegetables on page 138.)

Pick edible-pod peas when they are very young, just as the peas are starting to form. If you miss that stage, the pods will be too tough for eating, although you can still shell them and eat the peas.

The all-time All-America Selection (AAS) vegetable winner is 'Sugar Snap', which in 70 days bears a heavy crop of edible pods on 6-foot vines. Other outstanding edible-pod varieties include 'Sugar Bon', 57 days, and 'Oregon Sugar Pod', 68 days. An exceptionally sweet shelling variety is 'Maestro', 60 days, and 'Green Arrow', 70 days.

Cowpeas

Also called black-eyed peas, field peas, or southern peas, cowpeas have a more distinctive flavor than garden peas. They are a warm-season crop requiring warm days and warm nights, and they are damaged by even the slightest frost. Cowpeas require soil conditions similar to those needed by garden peas. After the soil has thoroughly warmed in spring, sow five to eight seeds per foot of row, leaving 2 to 3 feet between rows. Thin to 3 to 4 inches between plants. Pick cowpeas in the green-shell stage, when the seeds are fully developed but not yet hard. You can also let them ripen and store them as dried peas.

Among the most popular varieties of cowpeas are 'California Blackeye', 75 days, and 'Purple Hull', 78 days.

PEPPERS

Although peppers are warm-weather vegetables, their heat requirements are not as high as generally supposed. Both sweet peppers and hot peppers (or chilies) set fruit when night temperatures are between 60° and 75° F. Sweet peppers grow best when daytime temperatures are between 70° and 75° F; hot peppers do well when daytime temperatures are between 70° and 85° F. Extreme heat (above 90° F) causes blossoms to drop, but fruit setting resumes with the return of cooler weather. Small-fruited varieties are more tolerant of high temperatures than the larger-fruited ones.

Peppers seem to protect themselves from overloading the plant. When a full quota of fruit is ripening, new blossoms drop. When some of the peppers are harvested, the plant again sets fruit—if the weather is right.

The easiest way to start peppers is to buy transplants from a nursery or garden center. Varieties of sweet peppers adapted to your area are generally available. Growing your own transplants from seed is not difficult, however. Allow 7 to 10 weeks for germination and enough growth to make good-sized transplants. Peppers also can be direct seeded in areas with a long growing season. The shorter the season, the more reason to use transplants and to select early-maturing varieties.

Don't set out transplants until the soil has thoroughly warmed in spring. When night temperatures fall below 55° F, small plants just sit, turn yellow, and become stunted. If there is any chance of a late frost, use hot caps or other protection.

Peppers grow best in a sunny spot in rich, well-drained soil, with a pH between 5.5 and 6.8. Give the plants plenty of room to grow. Set them 24 inches apart, leaving 2 to 3 feet between rows. Some gardeners set out more plants than are needed and pull out the weaklings after a few weeks of growth.

When the first blossoms open, fertilize lightly with a low-nitrogen fertilizer such as 5-10-10. Water regularly, since any stress from lack of moisture at flowering time may cause blossoms to drop. Harvest peppers by cutting them off with pruning shears or a sharp knife.

Assorted peppers

Chile peppers

Sweet Peppers

Bell peppers are probably the most familiar kind of sweet peppers in the United States. There are hot bells but most are sweet. A green bell pepper is simply one that has been harvested before it has matured and developed its full sweetness; left on the plant, the pepper becomes sweeter and turns red, yellow, or orange, depending on the variety.

Other kinds of sweet peppers include pimientos, sweet Hungarian yellow peppers, and cherry peppers. Many of these peppers are used for pickling and in cooking.

Most sweet peppers are ready to harvest 60 to 80 days after transplants are set out. Among the most widely planted sweet bells are 'Bell Boy', 72 days; 'California Wonder', 75 days; and 'Yolo Wonder', 73 days. Other outstanding sweet peppers include the elongated 'Gypsy', 65 days; the long, pointed 'Sweet Banana', 65 to 72 days; and the small, round 'Sweet Cherry', 78 days.

Hot Peppers, or Chilies

This is perhaps the most intensely flavored and most confusing group of vegetables. Part of the problem is the many varieties: More than one hundred have been counted and they all cross-pollinate with great ease. If that were not enough, a variety that is mild when grown in the temperate conditions of a California coastal valley becomes hot when grown in the more stressful conditions of New Mexico. Hot peppers require more time to mature than sweet peppers.

In Mexico all peppers are called chiles and are commonly named by their use, such as *chile para relleno* (for stuffing) and *huachinango* (to be cooked with red snapper). Some are named for a region, such as Tabasco. Other names are derived from shape (*ancho* is broad) and color (*guero* is blond). Usually, the name changes again when the chile is dried.

Among the varieties commonly available in the United States, 'Chile Jalapeno', 72 days, is widely adapted; 'Serrano Chile', 75 days, is highly recommended for the Southwest; and 'Greenleaf Tabasco', 120 days, was bred for southern gardens.

POTATOES

The potato is a cool-season vegetable requiring a frost-free growing season of 90 to 120 days. The ideal climate is one with a cool summer. Plant early potatoes just before the last frost. Sprouts will develop at low temperatures but may be injured if exposed to frost above ground. Usually, it is safe to plant when the soil is warm enough to be worked.

In warm-winter climates potatoes are also planted in late summer or early fall for a winter or an early spring crop. In short-season areas plant late-maturing varieties in late spring for a fall crop.

Potatoes

Potatoes need rich, loose, acid soil with a pH between 4.8 and 5.4. Although potatoes will grow in a higher-pH soil, they may develop scab disease, which shows up as brown corky tissue on the outer surface of the potato. If necessary, add lime or soil sulfur to adjust the pH of the soil (for information about adjusting soil pH see page 96). Work in plenty of organic matter and add a low-nitrogen fertilizer, such as 5-10-10.

Buy certified disease-free seed potatoes from a local garden center or mail-order nursery. Don't start a crop with potatoes from a grocery store; the store-bought potatoes may carry plant viruses, and they may have been treated to prevent sprouting.

Cut the seed potatoes into 1½-inch-square pieces, making sure that each piece has at least one eye. Expose the pieces to the air for a week before planting them. Some gardeners dip the cut pieces into a dilute bleach solution or a fungicide to prevent rot. You can also plant small potatoes whole and avoid the risk of rot altogether.

Set the pieces, with the eye facing up, about 4 inches deep and 12 inches apart; leave 2 to 3 feet between rows. To fertilize when planting, place seed pieces in the center of a 6-inch-wide trench and work in a balanced, all-purpose fertilizer, such as 10-10-10, at the edges, being careful not to let the fertilizer touch the seed pieces. Too much nitrogen promotes foliage at the expense of the tubers.

Tubers form not on the roots but on the stems rising from the seed potato. Sprouts usually appear in two to three weeks. If the seed potatoes are spaced correctly, the foliage will shade and cool the soil as the tubers mature, preventing damage from high temperatures. To further cool the soil, mulch with 6 inches of a loose organic material. When the plants are 5 to 6 inches high, hill up the mulch and soil around the growing stems. Potatoes exposed to light will turn green, an effect associated with the naturally occurring poison solanine. (Small amounts of green tissue can be scraped away, but excessively green potatoes should be discarded.)

Potatoes need a steady moisture supply. Growth will stop if the soil dries out after the tubers begin to form. The potatoes will resume growth when the soil is watered. The result of this stop-and-start growth is misshapen, knobby, split, or hollow potatoes. Try to keep the soil moist to a 1-foot depth throughout the growing season. In dry-climate regions, that usually means one heavy watering weekly.

Harvest new potatoes as soon as the plants flower. New potatoes are not a variety but simply any potato harvested before full maturity. They are smaller and more tender, but they do not store well. If the soil is loose, simply reach in and pick the potatoes; otherwise, gently uproot the plants to check on their progress.

Potatoes intended for winter storage need to mature fully in the soil. For full-sized tubers, wait until the plants turn yellow or die back. Harvest the potatoes by digging them up, being careful not to puncture any. Keep the potatoes in the dark for a week or so at 70° F to condition them and heal any bruises. Then store them in a humid place where the temperature is between 35° and 40° F.

There are many varieties of potatoes but only four basic types: russet, round red, round white, and long white. Although most potatoes have white flesh, there are some with yellow, purple, and even bluish flesh. Among the commonly grown varieties are 'Kennebec', 'Norland', 'Russet Burbank', and 'Red Pontiac'.

PUMPKINS

See Squash and Pumpkins.

RADISHES

Give a youngster a package of radish seeds and say "go plant" and you'll have radishes. But to grow crisp, mild, nonpithy radishes, you must meet the fundamentals of fertilizing and watering. Spring radishes mature in three to four weeks after sowing seeds, so there's little time to correct mistakes.

Work a balanced, all-purpose fertilizer, such as 10-10-10, into the soil before planting so that nutrients are quickly available to the young seedlings. Sow seeds ½ inch apart and cover lightly with soil. Keep the soil evenly moist. After the seedlings emerge, thin to 1 to 2 inches apart to reduce competition. It is important to do this quickly, since the roots begin to expand when the plant is only two weeks old.

Radishes

There are two kinds of radishes: spring and winter. Spring radishes can be raised throughout the growing season in cooler areas and in all but the hottest months in warmer climates. For a continual supply of crisp radishes, start early with small plantings and repeat every 10 days. There are many varieties of spring radishes available. Among the most popular are 'Cherry Belle', 22 days; 'Champion', 28 days; and 'Scarlet Globe', 24 days.

Winter radishes—including the Asian, or daikon, types—grow more slowly, are larger, and keep longer than spring radishes. They grow best in the cool temperatures and shortening day length of fall. If planted too early in spring, they tend to flower before sizable roots can develop. Most varieties should be planted in late spring or in mid-summer. 'Summer Cross Hybrid', a daikon type, matures in 45 days.

The most common problem for home gardeners growing radishes is the cabbage maggot. Everything looks fine from the top, but at harvest, wormy radishes are discovered. For control see page 290.

SOYBEANS

See Beans.

Spinach

SPINACH

Growing this cool-season vegetable successfully is a problem in many home gardens. The biggest obstacle is its tendency to bolt (go to seed prematurely), which stops the production of leaves.

Bolting in spinach is controlled by day length and is further influenced by temperature. Long days hasten flowering; low temperatures during early growth and high temperatures in the later stage speed the bolting process. In addition, certain spinach varieties are more susceptible to premature flowering.

These circumstances make spring planting of a susceptible variety almost certain to fail. If you plant in spring, select a bolt-resistant, or long-standing, variety. Some quick-bolting varieties can be grown successfully in fall and winter in mild areas.

In northern climates plant spinach as early as possible in spring and about a month before the first frost in fall. In mild-winter areas plant anytime from October 1 to March 1. Plant every few weeks to have a continual harvest.

Spinach grows best in a sunny location and a fertile, well-drained soil with a pH between 6.0 and 6.5. In a higher-pH soil, spinach shows evidence of manganese deficiency, or yellowing between the veins (see page 170). Sow seeds 1 inch apart and thin to 3 to 4 inches between plants. Keep the soil moist. After 40 to 50 days they will be ready to harvest, either by removing individual leaves or cutting the entire plant at the base.

In selecting a spinach variety, you may also need to consider resistance to two important diseases: downy mildew, or blue mold; and spinach blight, or yellows. Varieties also differ by having either savoyed (heavily crinkled) or smooth leaves. Savoy types are harder to clean but are dark green, thick, and usually preferred. Good bolt-resistant varieties include the savoy 'America', 50 days; the savoy 'Bloomsdale Long-Standing', 48 days; the semicrinkled 'Avon', 44 days; and the semicrinkled and downy mildew–resistant 'Melody', 42 days. Varieties suitable for fall and winter planting include the blight- and downy mildew–resistant 'Hybrid No. 7', 42 days, and 'Virginia Savoy', 42 days.

Squash

Pumpkin

SQUASH AND PUMPKINS

Most squash and pumpkins, with the exception of the bush varieties, are space users. They are not suitable for small-space gardeners lacking ways to use vertical space, such as training up a fence or trellis. On the ground, vining types need 10 feet or more between rows, although they can be grown in less space by vertical training or pruning. Long runners may be cut off after some fruit sets if a good supply of leaves still remain to feed the fruit.

Squash and pumpkins are warm-season crops. Plant them when the soil has thoroughly warmed in spring. Direct seeding is best, but if your growing season is very short, use transplants from nurseries or start your own in individual pots four to five weeks before it is time to plant outdoors.

Squash and pumpkins can be planted in hills or rows. For vining pumpkins sow about a half dozen seeds in each hill, leaving about 7 feet between hills, and thin to two plants per hill. For vining squash sow four or five seeds in each hill, leaving 8 to 12 feet between hills, and thin to two plants per hill. If planting in rows, sow seeds 12 to 18 inches apart, leaving 7 feet between rows. Depending upon the vigor of the variety, thin seedlings to 2 to 4 feet between plants. Bush varieties can be grown with as little as 16 to 24 inches between plants.

Fertilizing and watering requirements are the same as for cucumbers and melons.

Before planting, work in generous amounts of organic matter and a low-nitrogen fertilizer, such as 5-10-10. Both squash and pumpkins do well in a soil whose pH is between 6.0 and 6.8. Watering should be slow and deep. Avoid overhead watering, which promotes leaf diseases. Leaves may wilt during midday but should pick up again as the day cools.

Some female flowers bloom before there are male flowers to pollinate them; these female flowers dry up or produce small fruits that abort and rot. This is natural behavior, not a disease. The same thing happens when a good load of fruit is set and the plant is using all of its resources to develop them. The aborting of young fruits occurs as a self-pruning process.

Pumpkins are ready for harvest 90 to 120 days after seeding. Two of the best varieties are 'Autumn Gold', 90 days, and 'Big Max', 120 days. 'Jack Be Little', 95 days, is a good miniature variety.

Summer squash comes in many shapes and colors. Begin harvesting it when it is young and tender, usually 50 to 65 days after seeding. Pick continually for a steady supply of young fruit. The seeds should be undeveloped and the rind soft. Zucchini and crookneck types are usually harvested when they are 1½ to 2 inches in diameter. Some outstanding varieties are 'Sunburst', 50 to 53 days, a round, scalloped, yellow squash; the blackish green 'Fordhook Zucchini', 57 days; and 'Pic-N-Pic', a yellow crookneck squash, harvested 50 days after seeding.

252

Winter squash is ready to harvest 60 to 110 days after the seeds are sown. It develops a hard rind when fully mature and thus can be stored. The squash must be thoroughly mature to be good quality. When picked immature it is watery and poor in flavor. The flavor is usually better after some cold weather increases the sugar content. Learn to judge varieties by color. Most green varieties turn partially brown or bronze, and butternut types lose all their green color and turn a distinct tan. Some outstanding varieties include 'Waltham Butternut', 85 days; 'Table King' acorn squash, 75 days; and 'Blue Hubbard', 110 days.

SWEET POTATOES

No vegetable commonly grown in the United States withstands more summer heat than the sweet potato—and very few require as much heat. This tropical plant does not thrive in cool weather; light frost kills the leaves, and soil temperatures below 50° F damage the sweet potatoes.

Commercial crops are feasible where mean (average of day and night) daily temperatures are above 70° F for at least three months. Louisiana, North Carolina, and Georgia all produce large commercial crops. Only the hottest summer areas of Arizona and California support commercial crops.

Sweet potatoes are started from slips, or sprouts, produced by the tuberous roots. It is best to buy disease-free slips from a nursery or mail-order seed company. Supermarket sweet potatoes may carry plant diseases, and they are usually treated to prevent sprouting.

Fertilizing sweet potatoes is tricky. Given too much nitrogen, they develop more vines than roots. However, they are not a poor-soil crop, and a low-nitrogen fertilizer, such as 5-10-10, worked into the soil before planting will improve the yield. In soils that are potassium deficient its addition improves the crop by promoting shorter and chunkier sweet potatoes; a lack of potassium usually means long, stringy potatoes. Prepare the soil two weeks before planting, making sure that the pH is between 5.5 and 6.5.

Since the length of the growing season is often the limiting factor in growing sweet potatoes, plant as soon as the soil is warm in

Sweet potatoes

spring. Where the season is long enough, plant two weeks after the last frost to ensure thoroughly warm soil. If the drainage is poor or plants are overwatered, the roots may be elongated and less blocky. To ensure good drainage, plant sweet potatoes in 6- to 12-inch ridges, located 3 to 4½ feet apart. (Ridge planting offers no advantage in fast-draining sandy soil.) Plant the slips 2 to 3 inches deep, leaving 9 to 12 inches between each plant.

Since sweet potatoes are deep-rooted plants, they are usually able to find enough water to survive, as evidenced by their successful growth in moisture-poor sandy soils. For the best crop, however, provide adequate water. As a general guide, sweet potatoes need about 18 inches of water per season.

Harvest sweet potatoes when they are slightly immature, if the size is adequate. Otherwise, wait until the vines begin to turn yellow. Try to avoid bruising the potatoes when digging, since this invites decay. If the leaves are killed by frost, harvest the sweet potatoes immediately.

The flavor of sweet potatoes improves during storage, because part of their starch content turns to sugar. Cure the sweet potatoes before storing them. Let them lie exposed for two to three hours to dry them thoroughly, then move them to a humid (85 percent relative humidity) and warm (85° F) storage area. After two weeks lower the temperature to 55° F. Under these conditions they should keep for two to six months.

There are two types of sweet potatoes: dry fleshed and moist fleshed. 'Jersey Orange', 'Nugget', and 'Nemagold' are popular varieties with dry, slightly sweet pale yellow flesh. 'Centennial', 'Vineless Puerto Rico', and 'Gold Rush' are the commonly planted varieties with moist, very sweet orange flesh.

Grown in the South, the moist varieties are commonly called yams, although the yam is a different plant. Rarely grown outside the tropics, yams consist almost entirely of starch and are gluey when cooked.

SWISS CHARD

A cool-season crop, Swiss chard is a type of beet that forms edible leaves and stalks instead of edible roots. Swiss chard's greatest virtue is its ability to take high summer temperatures in stride, whereas spinach and lettuce bolt.

Swiss chard grows best in rich, moist, well-drained soil with a pH between 6.0 and

Swiss chard

6.8. It should be planted at the same time as beets: spring to midsummer in cold-winter climates and fall to early spring in mild-climate areas. Sow seeds ½ inch deep and 1 to 2 inches apart, leaving 18 to 24 inches between rows. Thin seedlings to 4 to 8 inches apart; thinnings can be used in salads.

The plant is ready for harvest 50 to 60 days after seeding. The large, crinkly leaves and fleshy stalks can be cut as the plant grows, so that one planting can be harvested over many months. Even if the entire plant is cut off 1 to 2 inches above the soil level, new leaves will emerge.

Some of the best varieties are 'Fordhook Giant', 'Lucullus', and 'Rhubarb Chard', all of which mature in 60 days.

TOMATOES

These warm-season vegetables require a minimum of six hours of direct sunlight daily. They should be planted at least one week after the last frost in spring. Tomatoes are very sensitive to nighttime temperatures, and many varieties will not set fruit when nights are below 55° F, even though the days may be warm. In summer you can expect blossoms to drop when days are above 90° F or nights above 76° F. As a rule, most early-maturing varieties set fruit at lower temperatures than the main-season kinds.

The soil for tomatoes should be well drained and have a pH between 5.5 and 6.8. It should also have a good supply of nutrients, especially phosphorus. About two weeks before planting, work in plenty of organic matter and a low-nitrogen fertilizer, such as 5-10-10. This first fertilizer application will take care of the tomato plants until they set fruit. Afterward, feed the plants once monthly while the fruit is developing and stop when it nears mature size.

Most gardeners start tomatoes from transplants, available at local nurseries and garden centers, usually at the earliest possible planting time. To start your own transplants, sow seeds ½ inch deep in peat or other plantable pots five to seven weeks before the outdoor planting date. The last 10 days before transplanting the seedlings, gradually expose them to sunlight and outdoor temperatures.

Tomatoes are very responsive to training on stakes, a trellis, or a wire cage. These have been trained to grow on stakes set in the ground tepee fashion.

Transplants should be stocky, not leggy, and have four to six true leaves. Avoid plants already in bloom or bearing fruit, especially if they are growing in very small containers. Set the transplants deep, the first leaf just above soil level. Set leggy plants with the rootball positioned horizontally. Roots will form along the buried stem and will improve subsequent growth. Set the plants that are to be staked 1 to 2 feet apart; unstaked plants should be spaced 2 to 4 feet apart. If cold or wind threatens, cover the seedlings with hot caps or other protection.

No vegetable responds better to training than the tomato, and few plants are trained as easily. Tomato plants can be grown against stakes, on trellises, and in wire cages. (See Supporting Vegetables on page 138.) These supports keep the fruit off the soil and reduce damage from slugs, cracking, sunscald, and decay.

Wilting during a hot spell at midday is normal. Once watered, the plants recover quickly. Tomatoes require uniform moisture after the fruit has set: Alternating wet and dry spells can stunt the tomatoes and cause blossom-end rot. Symptoms of this disease appear as a leathery scar or rot on the fruit's blossom end (opposite the stem end). Staked and heavily pruned tomatoes seem to be more susceptible to the disease.

Some kinds of leaf curl are normal on tomato plants. The curling is more pronounced in some varieties, and you can expect it during hot, dry spells and during and after a long wet period. Heavy pruning also seems to encourage leaf curl.

In hot-summer areas high temperatures when the fruit is maturing can prevent the normal development of fruit color. The plant's red pigment does not form in temperatures above 86° F. Both high temperatures and

Tomatoes trained in a wire cage

TRANSPLANTING

Leggy transplant

Good transplant

Both should be planted deep. R will develop along the leggy stem

DETERMINATE/INDETERMINATE

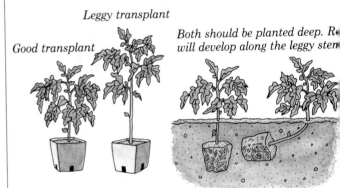

Determinate
These are commonly called bush or self-topping tomatoes. The terminal buds set fruit and stop the growth of the main stems.

Indeterminate
Terminal buds do not set fr just more leaves and stem. vine will grow indefinitely i killed by frost.

high light intensities stop the color from forming in fruit exposed to the direct sun, and the fruit may sunscald. Where high temperatures are the rule, choose varieties with dense foliage so that the fruit is protected.

Tomatoes are ready to harvest 55 to 90 days after seedlings are planted. There are more than a hundred varieties—including beefsteak types, paste tomatoes, and cherry tomatoes—available to home gardeners. The shorter the growing season, the more you should limit your choices to the early and early-to-midseason varieties. Select varieties that are adapted to your area. Also look for varieties that are resistant to soilborne pests, including verticillium wilt, fusarium wilt, and nematodes. It may be that your soil is not infested with these pests and you can successfully grow any variety, but if you've had trouble with tomatoes in the past, favor the resistant varieties.

Whether you plan to stake each tomato or grow it as a freestanding bush, be sure to pick the right type. There are two types of tomato plants: determinate and indeterminate. The determinate are the bush types, generally growing to 3 feet or less. The indeterminate are tall-growing, vining types that can be trained with stakes, a trellis, or on a wire cage.

Turnip

TURNIPS

Both the tender young leaves and the mature root of the turnip are edible. A cool-weather crop that can withstand frost, turnips are best planted in early spring in northern climates. In milder climates, fall and winter are preferred times to plant, because the roots are tastier when they mature during cool weather. For successive harvests, make two or three sowings at two-week intervals.

Turnips aren't exacting about the care they receive, but like other root crops they grow best in loose, deep soil without any clumps or stones. The ideal pH is between 6.0 and 6.8. After preparing the soil, direct seed about ½ inch deep and 1 inch apart, leaving 15 to 18 inches between rows. Thin the seedlings to 2 to 6 inches apart. If you plan to harvest the young greens, you can leave plants as close as 1 inch apart. Harvest the roots 30 to 60 days after seeding. The

roots store well in the ground in fall, but be sure to dig them up before the ground freezes solid in winter.

Turnips are often confused with rutabagas—a cross between a turnip and a cabbage. Turnips have rough, hairy leaves, are fast growing, and turn pithy in a short time. Rutabagas have smooth, waxy leaves, emerge and develop more slowly, are more solid, and have a longer storage life. Although there are white and yellow forms of each vegetable, most turnips are white fleshed and most rutabagas are yellow fleshed.

Among the best turnip varieties are 'Tokyo Cross', 35 days, and 'Purple-Top White Globe', 56 days.

WATERMELON

See Melons.

ZUCCHINI

See Squash and Pumpkins.

CONTROLLING WEEDS

A weed is any plant that is thought to be undesirable or out of place. Blue grass is regarded as desirable when it forms a lush green lawn but out of place when it is growing in a flower bed. Dandelions are considered worthy when raised as greens in a gourmet vegetable bed but weedy anywhere else in the garden. When its growth is kept in check, Japanese honeysuckle (Lonicera japonica) is valued for its fragrance and flowers; but it is labeled a weed when it grows rampantly through other plantings, covering shrubs and strangling young trees.

Sometimes perceptions about plants change over time. Before the tomato became a favorite garden vegetable, it was thought to be a poisonous weed. Attitudes about other plants depend on the gardener. Some gardeners appreciate a dotting of English daisies (*Bellis perennis*) in their lawns, but the plant is a weed to gardeners who prefer an uninterrupted green carpet of grass.

Although weeds can be messy, that is not the main reason to control them. Weeds should be suppressed because they compete with desirable plants for space, water, nutrients, and light. Weeds reduce the yield in a vegetable garden and the number and size of blooms in a flower bed. Trees and many other plants will be stunted if their early growth includes competition from weeds. Another reason to control weeds is that they often serve as hosts for insects and diseases that damage garden plants.

Fortunately, among the many thousands of plant species, only a couple of hundred are undesirable enough to be considered important weeds. All these weeds won't be found in a single garden, but every garden has its share of weeds to plague the gardener.

Dandelions belong in a gourmet vegetable bed, not on the front lawn.

Japanese honeysuckle, a perennial woody weed vine, will strangle more valuable plants.

WEED LIFE CYCLES

Weeds are categorized by their life cycle. Most weeds reproduce by seeds only and live out their lives in either one or two years. These are annual and biennial weeds. Perennial weeds—those that live a minimum of three years—often reproduce by seeds as well as from pieces of root or stem. Understanding a weed's life cycle helps you figure out the best way to control the weed.

Annual weeds germinate, flower, form seeds, and complete their lives within a single year. Most of these weeds are summer annuals, meaning that they live out their lives between spring and fall. They include crab grass, knotweed, and prostrate spurge. Winter annuals prefer cool weather, germinating in fall and growing until the following spring, when they set seed and die. They include annual blue grass, common chickweed, and henbit. Annual weeds should be controlled as early in their life cycle as possible. Preventing annual weeds from forming seeds is an important factor in controlling them. Some weeds, such as purslane and spurge, flower and produce large numbers of seeds only a few weeks after germinating; the new seedlings sprout, flower, and set seed all season.

Biennial weeds are similar to annual weeds except that they need two years to complete their lives. (In warm climates some biennials live accelerated lives, going to seed and dying the first year.) Most biennial weeds spend the first year as a rosette of leaves close to the ground; the second year they send up a shoot that produces flowers and seeds. Bullthistle and wild carrot are common biennial weeds. It is easier to interrupt their growth by eliminating the less conspicuous rosettes their first year.

Perennial weeds, which may be herbaceous or woody, live at least three years. Roots or bulbs of herbaceous perennials, such as oxalis, Bermuda grass, and nutsedge, remain alive even though the tops may die to the ground in winter. After a dormant period new growth emerges from the roots. Woody perennials, such as poison ivy and kudzu, develop woody tissue that persists year after year. Perennial weeds often spread and form colonies by sending up new plants from rhizomes or stolons. They can also increase by seeds. The time that perennials flower and form seeds, however, is restricted to one relatively short period of the year.

PREVENTING WEEDS

The first—and most important—step in preventing weeds is to remove them before they make seeds. There are many steps you can take to keep weeds from reaching maturity. Certain gardening techniques, such as deep mulching and regular hand pulling, can stop weeds dead in their tracks. Thickly planted garden beds discourage the appearance of weeds, and a well-grown lawn shades them out. Herbicides (weed killers) play a role in weed prevention as well. Preemergence herbicides can kill weed seeds as they sprout, and a careful application of a soil sterilant can prevent growth in patios, parking lots, and unplanted areas for more than a year.

Remove Existing Weeds

Weeds should be removed early in their lives before they produce seeds. The saying "seeds one year mean weeds seven years" captures the wisdom of keeping weeds from going to seed in your garden. The average weed produces 25,000 seeds during its lifetime. Some of these germinate right away, but others may lie in the soil for years, germinating only when the soil around them is disturbed.

If you can keep weeds that are now growing in your garden from going to seed, next year's weeding chores will be minimal. Begin by weeding your yard carefully, removing every weed you find (see Killing Weeds on page 264). Then use the preventive measures described below. After that, go through the garden once a week, eliminating every weed you find. With most of the weeds controlled, this weeding tour will become quicker each week. In the next season, you should find only a few weeds each week.

Prevent Weed Seed Germination

Apply a thick layer of mulch to deprive weed seeds of the light they need to sprout. Be sure to remove any existing weeds before applying a mulch. The layer of mulch must be thick enough to prevent light from reaching the seeds. Organic mulches should be at least 2 inches thick to control annual weeds and preferably 4 to 6 inches thick, especially where perennial weeds are a problem. Be sure that the mulch itself is free of weed seeds. (See below for information on mulching materials.)

Landscape fabric is a newcomer to the arsenal of weed controls. It is a thick, feltlike

Eliminate wild carrot, a biennial weed, by removing the rosette it produces the first year.

Oxalis, a perennial weed, will live at least three years even though the tops may die to the ground in winter.

material with pores that allow water and air to enter the soil while blocking weed growth. Landscape fabric is expensive, but it smothers weeds, often very persistent perennial weeds, and doesn't rob desirable plants of moisture. Vigorous perennial weeds cannot push through landscape fabric as easily as they can through black plastic.

Black plastic (polyethylene) film is an inexpensive material that has long been used in controlling weeds. It provides satisfactory control in a vegetable garden but is not a good choice around woody plants. The nonporous plastic encourages rooting nearer the surface than usual, subjecting large shrubs and trees to drought or toppling in high winds. Black plastic is often laid under bark or gravel paths to block weed growth. Since the plastic must be punctured every few feet for drainage, water funneling into those spots encourages weed growth. Landscape fabric doesn't present that problem, since it does not have to be punctured. Landscape fabric, though it costs more, is worth the expense.

Cover the Soil With Plants

A thick covering of desirable plants discourages weeds by shading them out. Space the plants so that their foliage, when mature, will overlap slightly. Weeds may be a problem when the planting is young, but a little hoeing will deter them until the garden plants take over. Such closely spaced plants may need extra water and fertilizer.

A thick, healthy lawn prevents weed seeds from germinating and crowds out those that do germinate. Thin or bare spots in grass invite weeds.

Ground covers are particularly effective at stopping weed growth. Plant low-growing ground covers, such as creeping thyme (*Thymus serpyllum*) or Corsican mint (*Mentha requienii*), in flower beds and between shrubs. Use taller ground covers to blanket large areas of soil and keep it free of weeds.

Keep Unplanted Soil Dry

If you live in a region where it rains every week during the summer, it won't be possible

Turning the soil brings dormant weed seeds to the surface, where they can germinate. The first to appear are mainly annual weeds.

to keep your ground dry. But if you live in a dry-summer region, you have some control over how water is applied to your garden. Most weed seeds won't germinate in dry soil. You will have fewer weed problems if you water only the garden plants and not the ground between plants.

The easiest way to accomplish this is to use a watering technique that doesn't wet all the ground. Since drip emitters wet just a small area under each emitter, a drip system for all areas except lawn will reduce weed germination. If you water your trees and shrubs by hand, build a watering basin around each plant so that you wet only the soil in the basins.

Use Preemergence Herbicides

Preemergence herbicides are weed killers that kill seedlings as they sprout. Since they do not kill plants that are already growing, these herbicides can be used to prevent the growth of weeds in existing plantings.

Preemergence herbicides are usually sprayed or spread on weed-free soil and watered in well. The herbicide moves only an inch or less into the soil, then attaches to soil particles and goes no deeper, no matter how much water is applied. The herbicide remains in the upper soil surface for several weeks, killing all seeds that sprout.

If the soil is cultivated during this period, the effect is diluted or lost. Before applying a preemergence herbicide, remove existing weeds and till the soil. Time your application of the herbicide to coincide with weed germination. Many spring weeds germinate as the soil reaches a temperature of about 50° F. For the best results apply the herbicide at that temperature. (Take the temperature of your soil every week until that reading appears.)

Spread a preemergence herbicide on the lawn in early spring to kill crab grass and other weeds as the seeds sprout. If you live in a mild-winter region, reapply the herbicide in fall to kill winter weeds.

Apply a preemergence herbicide in flower beds and shrub areas in fall and spring to control both warm- and cool-season weeds. Do the same in recently cultivated areas, where new seeds have been brought to the surface.

Space plants so that their mature foliage overlaps; the resulting shade will discourage weed growth.

Drip emitters wet only small areas near desirable plants. This helps prevent weed seed germination.

If this dandelion had been eliminated before flowering, its fluffy seeds wouldn't be blown throughout the garden.

Landscape fabric mulch lets air and water through while blocking weed growth. Cover with bark or pebbles.

Consider Soil Sterilants

Soil sterilants are weed killers that have a residual effect that can last for several years after a single application. They prevent all plant growth in the treated area. Soil sterilants are useful in preventing weed growth in patios, driveways, and sidewalks and along fence lines. Apply the chemical very carefully, and avoid adjacent plantings. Don't apply it on soil that contains roots of trees or other garden plants. Also be careful not to use it where runoff or erosion might carry it onto garden plants.

If you are unsure of the effect of a soil sterilant in your garden, don't use it. Control weeds only after they sprout (see Killing Weeds below.)

Keep Weed Seeds Out of the Garden

There are steps you can take to reduce the number of weed seeds that make their way into your garden.

Don't use mulching materials or imported topsoil that is likely to contain weed seeds. Avoid mulching with lawn clippings containing either weed seeds or stems that could resprout—for example, stems from Bermuda grass and other running grasses. Crop by-products such as hay are often full of weed seeds, and the nutritional value of manures may be offset by the nuisance of weed seeds. Imported materials may carry types of weeds that would not otherwise find their way into your garden.

If you decide to use manures or other weedy materials, compost them first. The heat generated by the decomposing materials will kill most of the weed seeds. For directions on making compost, see page 95.

Many weed seeds will blow into your garden, especially if there are weedy areas adjacent to it. Spray these areas with weed killers, or cut down the weeds before midsummer when most seeds begin to form. Plant hedges to filter wind from areas that cannot be mowed or sprayed.

KILLING WEEDS

There are two approaches to getting rid of existing weeds. You can kill them with herbicides or you can remove them physically. The approach you take will usually depend on

LIFE CYCLES OF WEEDS

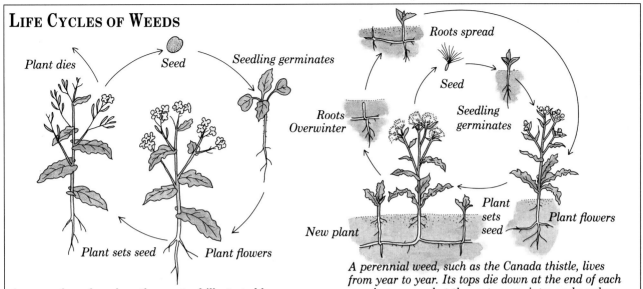

Plant dies

Seed

Seedling germinates

Plant sets seed

Plant flowers

An annual weed, such as the mustard illustrated here, completes its entire life cycle in a single growing season.

Roots spread

Seed

Seedling germinates

Roots Overwinter

New plant

Plant sets seed

Plant flowers

A perennial weed, such as the Canada thistle, lives from year to year. Its tops die down at the end of each growing season, but the roots overwinter and send up shoots the next year.

Preemergence herbicides prevent weed seeds from germinating and kill very young weed seedlings.

whether the weeds are annuals, biennials, or perennials and whether or not you wish to use chemicals. Annual and biennial weeds are easily controlled by pulling, cultivating under, or hoeing out. Removing the crown (where the top and roots meet) usually kills these weeds.

Perennial weeds, such as Bermuda grass, plantain, and dandelion, require more effort. Because they can resprout from pieces of roots or stems left in the ground, these weeds are difficult to remove by hand. Systemic herbicides (see Using Herbicides on page 266) are often used because they kill roots and the aboveground portion of the weed.

Cutting and Cultivating

You can kill annual and biennial weed seedlings simply by cultivating the soil. When the weeds are larger, you can cut them off at ground level and rake them up. Never do this to established perennial weeds unless you have killed them first with a systemic herbicide; the weeds will resprout from roots or other underground parts left in the soil. It is possible to dig out perennial weeds, although the extensive root system of some weeds such as quack grass makes this task unfeasible. The best time to dig out perennial weeds is early spring, when the soil is moist and the weeds don't have much top growth.

A hoe is the tool usually used for removing weeds, although other specialized tools can also be used. When a hoe is used for weeding, it is a cutting tool and should be kept sharp. To sharpen a hoe, file the blade at a 45-degree angle, then run the file flat across the back of the blade to remove the burrs. If a hoe is to be effective in weed

Hoeing Weeds

When hoeing weeds, slice or scrape the weed just below ground level.

Hand pulling is an effective method of weed control in very small areas. It is easier when the soil is moist.

control, it should be sharpened after every couple of hours of weeding, or even more often in rocky soil. To cut a weed, pull the hoe toward you, holding it almost parallel to the ground. Cut off the weed just under the soil surface.

If you hoe properly, you will dig up very little soil. Weeding with any type of cutting or pulling tool is easier if the soil is moist. During dry weather, water the ground before weeding. In dry weather you can leave small weeds on the surface to die, but during wet spells rake up the weeds to keep them from rerooting.

Using Herbicides

There are two types of weed-killing chemicals: contact herbicides, which kill only the plant tissue they touch, and systemic herbicides, which are absorbed by weeds and move throughout the plant. Both are postemergence herbicides—that is, they kill weeds that are already growing.

A contact herbicide kills only the aboveground part of the plant that it touches. One drop of a contact herbicide on a leaf creates a dead spot the size and shape of the drop. It is important to cover the entire weed with the herbicide; otherwise, untreated sections of the weed will continue to grow. Contact herbicides are effective against annual weeds, acting quickly and killing the weeds in a day or so. Contact sprays control perennial weeds only temporarily; although the top dies, the weed most likely will resprout from its uninjured roots.

Systemic herbicides are absorbed by the foliage or bark and move throughout the plant, including the roots. The chemical disrupts normal plant growth processes. The result is evident in swollen stems, twisted and deformed leaves, and eventual death. It may take a week or even a month for the effects to become apparent. Systemics are used as a control for perennial weeds, since they kill the roots as well as the aboveground portion of the plant.

Within each category are selective and nonselective herbicides. A nonselective herbicide does not distinguish between types of plants; it kills plants indiscriminately. A selective herbicide is more specific and kills only certain kinds of plants. Some selective herbicides kill broadleaf weeds in a lawn but don't harm the grass. Other selective herbicides kill grassy weeds growing among ground covers, shrubs, or other broadleaf plants. (Grassy weeds have relatively narrow, parallel-veined leaves, whereas broadleaf weeds usually have broad, flat leaves with a lacy network of veins.)

Before using a selective herbicide, check the label for a list of weeds that the product controls as well as the desirable plants on which it can be safely sprayed.

Spraying herbicides Avoid spraying whole areas just to get rid of a few weeds. Occasional or scattered weeds can be controlled with spot treatments. Premixed herbicides in aerosol cans or finger-pump sprayers are useful for this purpose. Never leave a sprayer filled and ready for occasional use.

It is particularly important to spray only in calm weather to avoid spreading the herbicide to desirable plants. Use a tank sprayer or hand-held trigger sprayer so that you can carefully control the application. (See Choosing the Right Equipment on page 319.) Use a shield of cardboard, plywood, or sheet metal to protect garden plants when you spray near them.

Sprayers should be thoroughly cleaned before you use them to apply fungicides or insecticides. Even a small amount of herbicide residue in a sprayer may harm or kill desirable plants. Some gardeners avoid the problem by keeping separate sprayers.

WEEDS AROUND TREES

The shade cast by large plants usually weakens the ability of weeds to survive, but don't wait for weeds to languish on their own. You still need to take steps to keep weedy growth from becoming established around your trees and shrubs.

Broadleaf weeds in the lawn can be killed with some selective herbicides without harming the grass. Be sure to read the label carefully.

You can suppress weeds under a tree or shrub with a thick layer of mulch.

Apply preemergence herbicides in early spring to prevent weed seeds from germinating. Pull any weeds that emerge as soon as you see them. In addition, you can use a nonselective herbicide to spot-treat stubborn weeds. Take care not to spray the foliage and stems of shrubs and trees. Mature corky bark may not absorb the chemical, but plants with thin green bark may be seriously damaged. Some shrubs and trees, such as yews (*Taxus* species), are so sensitive to herbicides that it is best to avoid using weed killers around them. Always check the herbicide label first.

Suppress weeds around trees and shrubs with a thick layer of mulch, keeping it away from the trunk to prevent rot. If pesky perennial weeds push through, discourage their growth with landscape fabric (see Prevent Weed Seed Germination on page 261). Fit the fabric around trunks and stems, and cover it with wood chips or other kinds of organic mulch.

Weed whips—power tools with a spinning filament or blade—are commonly used to cut back weeds growing around or right next to tree trunks. If you use one, be very careful not to cut the bark. A girdled or injured stem can kill a tree or shrub.

Bermuda grass is a stubborn, hard-to-control perennial that can cause vexing problems in ground covers.

A thick layer of straw is an effective organic mulch to keep vegetable gardens weed free.

CONTROLLING BRUSH

Invasive woody plants can be removed by hand, but generally the entire root system must be dug out if the removal is to be permanent. Hand removal is not always feasible if the plants are dangerously thorny, such as berry brambles, or toxic, such as poison oak and poison ivy. Some herbicides are especially formulated for killing brush. Apply them while the leaves are actively growing; usually late spring or early summer is the best time.

If brambles or weedy vines are growing close to or among desirable plants, do not spray with herbicides. Instead, cut the vines to the ground and paint the undiluted chemical on the stubs of the stems. Make sure that the chemical soaks into the cambium, the thin ring of creamy white tissue just inside the bark.

Mature trees that have thick bark can withstand spraying, which may be necessary if vines are growing up the tree, but do not spray if there is a chance that some of the spray will reach the tree foliage. If possible, try to physically remove vines close to tree foliage.

WEEDS IN THE GROUND

Invasive weeds can be a vexing problem in ground covers, especially if the weed is a stubborn, hard-to-control perennial, such as quack grass or Bermuda grass.

Weeds often take over newly planted ground-cover areas when some of the soil is still bare. If possible, postpone planting a ground cover until you have weed growth under control. If the ground is very weedy, it may be advisable to fumigate the soil or to kill all vegetation with a systemic herbicide. A nonchemical alternative is soil solarization (see page 273). When the soil is clear of weeds and the ground cover is in place, mulch with an organic material, such as bark or wood chips, or use landscape fabric until the ground cover becomes vigorous enough to crowd out and shade the weeds.

Prevent further germination of weed seeds in a ground cover with applications of a preemergence herbicide. Avoid further cultivation of the soil, because each soil disturbance will bring more weed seeds to the surface to germinate.

WEEDS IN FLOWER BEDS

Eliminate weeds before planting a flower or vegetable bed. If the area is very weedy, you may want to begin a weed control program several months in advance. Use a contact weed killer to kill annual weeds. The chemical may have some residual effect, so check the label to see how long to wait before planting. If the weeds are small, you can leave them to be tilled in. If they are large, remove them from the soil after they have been killed.

Take more time to prepare the bed if the weeds are perennial. These weeds are more difficult to eradicate, and small roots left in the soil can resprout and take over the bed in one season. Apply a systemic herbicide before removing any of the top growth. Spray and remove weeds within 5 feet of the planting area to discourage a reinfestation. Again, check the herbicide label to see how long you should wait before planting.

Space young plants so that their leaves will barely overlap when the plants are mature. The canopy creates shade that discourages weed seed germination. Plant the bare space between slow-growing plants. For example, plant lettuce between early pepper plants set out in spring, and then harvest the lettuce as the weather warms up and the pepper plants increase in size.

A layer of mulch also suppresses weeds. Many organic mulches, such as ground bark and compost, are suitable for flower and vegetable beds. Straw is a favorite mulch in the vegetable garden; it is usually dug into the soil after the crop is harvested.

When hand weeding, be careful not to disturb the roots of adjacent plants. Pinch or cut the tops of weeds rather than pull up the entire weed since its roots may be intertwined with those of desirable plants. Cut off weeds at the soil level instead of digging deep to get them out. Digging will only bring more weed seeds to the surface that will start the germinating process all over again.

WEEDS IN LAWNS

Weed control begins before you plant the lawn. Remove weeds that are growing and eliminate as many of the weed seeds in the soil as possible. Water the soil to promote germination of weed seeds, and use herbicides or shallow cultivation to kill the weeds as they sprout. After a few cycles of this treatment, a substantial portion of the weed seeds in your soil will have germinated and died. If you are laying sod rather than seeding a new lawn, the sod will smother most of the annual weeds that sprout. The more tenacious perennial weeds will come right through the sod, however.

The best way to control weeds in an established lawn is to take good care of the lawn. Proper watering, feeding, and mowing produce a thick, vigorous lawn that discourages weed seeds from germinating and crowds out the weeds that do germinate.

Controls for Major Lawn Weeds

If you are not sure which of the following lawn weeds you have, take samples to a local nursery or cooperative extension office for positive identification.

Annual blue grass (Poa annua) This annual grass grows quickly during the cool weather of spring and fall; it dies in summer. The key to control is preventing reseeding. Apply a preemergence herbicide in late summer or early fall.

Bermuda grass (Cynodon dactylon) This extremely persistent perennial grass has vigorous, deep roots and underground stems that spread horizontally. It grows most actively during warm weather and dies back to the dormant underground stems in freezing temperatures. Bermuda grass has a number of hybrid varieties and is quite often used as a lawn grass.

Hand digging does not control Bermuda grass. Use a selective contact grass killer on infestations that have spread into desirable broadleaf plantings. There is no way to save a lawn that has been heavily infested with Bermuda grass. Use a systemic herbicide to kill all growth and then reseed or resod the entire area.

LAWN WEEDS

Annual bluegrass

Oxalis

Curly dock

Wild onion

Purslane

Plantain

Mouse-ear chickweed

Bermuda grass

English daisy

White clover

Crab grass

Spotted spurge

Dallis grass

Dandelion

Crab grass (Digitaria species*)*   This annual grass grows from seeds that germinate in early spring. It matures during summer, then produces seeds in the late summer and fall. Control crab grass with a preemergence herbicide in early spring. In warm climates make two applications: in late winter to prevent spring-germinating seeds and in early fall just before the rainy season to prevent fall-germinating seeds. Spot-treat individual clumps with a selective herbicide during the summer. Keep the lawn thick and lush, and set the lawn mower high so crab grass seedlings are shaded out.

Curly dock (Rumex crispus)   This broadleaf perennial grows most actively during spring and fall, although its long, thick taproot allows it to compete successfully against lawn grasses during hot, dry weather. Control curly dock by spraying with a selective herbicide or by spot-treating.

Dandelion (Taraxacum officinale)   This broadleaf perennial appears mainly in spring and fall. Control the weed by applying a selective herbicide during spring or fall to prevent it from setting seed. Spot-treat any new plants that appear during the summer. Hand weeding is difficult because the long taproot tends to break off; the piece remaining in the soil gives rise to new plants.

Dallis grass (Paspalum dilatatum)   This grassy weed is a serious pest in the South. Spot-treat with a grass killer to control it.

English daisy (Bellis perennis)   A broadleaf perennial, English daisy grows the year around in a moist, cool location. It is very difficult to control and should be sprayed with a selective herbicide or spot-treated in late spring.

Mouse-ear chickweed (Cerastium species*)*   A broadleaf perennial weed that grows in full sun, mouse-ear chickweed is most likely to be a problem in thin areas of the lawn where the soil is wet. The stems root where they touch the soil, forming a thick mat that crowds out lawn grass. Apply a selective herbicide in spring or fall while the weed is growing actively.

Oxalis (Oxalis corniculata)   This broadleaf perennial grows most actively during spring and late summer. Selective herbicides suppress but not eradicate it. Spray several times in spring or fall when air temperatures are 60° to 80° F. A thick, vigorous lawn smothers oxalis.

Plantain (Plantago species*)*   Both buckhorn plantain (*P. lanceolata*) and broadleaf plantain (*P. major*) are perennial weeds that resprout from the roots each year. Control them with a selective herbicide in spring or fall. These weeds are difficult to control and may need more than one application.

Purslane (Portulaca oleracea)   A broadleaf annual that thrives during hot weather, purslane grows mainly in sparse lawns. It can be controlled by applying a preemergence herbicide in spring or by treating with a selective contact herbicide during the summer.

Spotted spurge (Euphorbia supina)   This weed is a broadleaf annual that grows most aggressively from late spring through early fall. Apply a preemergence herbicide in spring for partial control. For best results spray with a contact herbicide several times in summer.

White clover (Trifolium repens)   This broadleaf perennial grows best during the cool weather of spring and fall but is most noticeable when the white to pale pink flowers appear in early summer. Clover in a lawn is a sign of nitrogen deficiency. Control the clover by applying a nitrogen fertilizer to the lawn. Clover can also be controlled with a preemergence herbicide in spring and a selective contact weed killer in spring or fall.

Wild onion (Allium canadense)   A perennial weed that resprouts from underground bulbs each year, wild onion looks like a coarse grass but has a distinct onion or garlic scent when crushed. Use a selective herbicide, or spot-treat with a systemic herbicide. Treat again whenever new plants appear. It may take two to three years of repeated applications to entirely eliminate this weed from a lawn.

SOLARIZING THE SOIL

Soil solarization—also known as soil tarping and soil pasteurization—is the technique of trapping the sun's heat under clear plastic to kill weeds and other garden pests. The technique was developed in Israel, where drip irrigation also originated.

You can solarize small beds or large garden areas—as much ground as you have clear plastic to cover. Remove all rocks and brush from the area to be treated, and moisten the soil before tarping it. Cover the area with clear plastic at least 1.5 mils thick; anything thinner will puncture easily, which will minimize the effect. You can lay the plastic around and up to each tree trunk in the area. Seal the edges all around to keep heat from escaping. Drip systems can continue to work under the plastic during the treatment.

It is crucial that you use clear plastic, not black plastic. Black plastic absorbs heat without baking the soil beneath it. The sun's rays are able to penetrate clear plastic, but they cannot escape back through it. As long as the plastic is thick enough and the edges are sealed, the heat will be trapped.

Soil solarization is most effective during hot, sunny weather. Cloud cover, fog, and wind are detrimental to the heat-capturing process. The soil must be covered for a minimum of four to six weeks to allow the soil temperature to build up high enough.

The heat that collects under the clear plastic penetrates 6 to 7 inches into the soil, killing weeds and weed seeds. Some weeds are more easily killed than others. Certain perennial weeds, such as field bindweed, whose roots go down as deep as 4 feet, will resprout. In addition to eradicating many weeds, soil solarization also kills insects and numerous disease-causing organisms. Earthworms won't be harmed, because they move downward to cooler parts of the soil.

CONTROLLING INSECT AND ANIMAL PESTS

Insects and animals are a natural part of every garden. Most of these creatures are harmless, and some are even beneficial. Many insects help gardeners by pollinating flowers, cleaning up decaying organic matter, or eating harmful insects. Earthworms help gardeners by aerating the soil as they move through it, and humming-birds pollinate flowers as well as add beauty to a garden.

Although some insects and animals damage plants, usually the damage is tolerable. It is generally when their populations reach high levels that they become serious pests. Most of the time, natural forces such as predators and weather keep pests under control. When pests are out of balance, they can overwhelm plants and cause severe damage. Some insects and animals harm plants by eating them, whereas others cause indirect damage—for example, moles uproot plants as they tunnel.

Rather than waiting for pests to cause damage and then eradicating them, increasing numbers of gardeners are taking a relatively new approach to controlling pests called integrated pest management (IPM). The object of IPM is to keep the pest population below the level that causes injury. This approach combines preventive measures such as sanitation, traps and other physical controls, use of natural enemies, and chemical controls.

Many insects are not only harmless but some are beneficial. These butterflies help pollinate the garden.

PREVENTING PEST PROBLEMS

You can prevent many pest problems through cultural controls—that is, using gardening practices that make your garden an unfavorable environment for pests. Any one of the following practices by itself isn't enough, but using all of them will help discourage pests—particularly harmful insects—from taking hold in your garden.

Keep Your Garden Clean

Many pests find nesting and hiding places in refuse piles and then leave at night in search of live plants to eat. Discourage these pests by keeping leaves, pruning clippings, and other trash cleared out of the garden.

Often insect eggs and larvae are deposited on flowers, fruit, and other plant parts that fall to the ground. The insects mature as the plant parts lie rotting on the ground. To keep these pests from spreading, clean up and dispose of plant debris on a regular basis.

Many insects feed on weeds, increasing their populations on the host plants before invading your garden plants. Keeping the garden and nearby areas free of weeds is an important way to control insect pests.

Inspect Plants

Carefully examine new plants before bringing them into your garden. Check for any signs of pests or diseases. If you suspect that a plant may be diseased or infested with an

Clean up around fruit trees to prevent insect eggs and larvae from being deposited in fallen, rotting fruit.

insect (eggs and larvae as well as adults), do not bring it into the garden until you have treated it and are sure that it is completely free of pests.

Once a plant is in your garden, inspect it regularly. Check often for signs of chewed leaves, yellowing or distorted foliage, and other damage. Take notice of any insects, even if you see only one or two. Check carefully for more of the same pest. Look under leaves and in other areas that you may have overlooked in your first inspection. A few individuals may be just passing through your garden, or they may be the vanguard of an impending infestation.

Early diagnosis allows you to treat problems more effectively. If you see unfamiliar insects in your garden, find out what they are and whether they are harmless, potentially harmful, or, in fact, may be beneficial to your plants. A local nursery or cooperative extension office should be able to advise you.

Maintain Vigorous Plants

A healthy, vigorous plant produces its own repellents and is less likely to be seriously attacked by insects. If it is chewed or otherwise damaged by insects or animals, growth momentum usually allows the plant to outgrow the damage.

An adequate supply of water and nutrients is important in maintaining plant vigor. Plants should be watered according to their individual needs (see Knowing When to Water on page 145). Use an all-purpose fertilizer, such as 10-10-10, on plants susceptible to insect damage. A high-nitrogen fertilizer may increase succulent growth that attracts aphids and mites.

Plant Resistant Varieties

No single insect pest attacks every species or variety of plant. If you live in an area where a particular pest problem is likely to occur, try to select plants that are least susceptible to the pest. In recent years plant breeders have stepped up their development of resistant varieties, many of which are now on the market. Check with a knowledgeable local nursery or with a cooperative extension office about resistant varieties suited to your garden and your needs.

Regular inspection of plants is the gardener's first line of defense against insect pests.

Some plants should not be used in areas where known pests are particularly destructive. For example, oaks (*Quercus* species) are the preferred food for gypsy moths and thus should not be planted where gypsy moths are prevalent. The Monterey pine (*Pinus radiata*) is more pest prone in hot, dry climates where it receives little water than it is in climates similar to its native environment—the cool, moist, coastal climate of Monterey, California.

Keeping plants vigorous and healthy and the garden well kept can deter insect infestation.

Rotate Crops

Just as farmers rotate crops, you can do the same on a smaller scale in your vegetable garden and annual flower beds. This means not planting the same plants in the same place each season. Crop rotation discourages harmful insects that feed on specific plant species, making the insects travel a longer distance for food, thereby starving them out or reducing their numbers. Changing plant sites can be hard in a small garden, but it is worth trying if you have had a severe infestation in previous years. For example, if cabbage root maggots have infested your cauliflower or other cruciferous crops, or if tomato hornworms have attacked your tomato plants, relocate them the following year.

If you don't have alternate planting sites, vary your crops each year so that pests that feed on specific crops will not have an ongoing food supply.

Change Your Planting Schedule

You can foil some insect pests by changing the time you sow seeds or set out plants. For example, maggots that feed on vegetable seeds are most active in the cool, wet soils of early spring. If you delay planting corn, bean, pea, and melon seeds until the soil warms up thoroughly, the seed maggots will do less damage to your plantings.

Another way you may be able to deter insect pests is to plant varieties that mature earlier or later than the time the pests do their greatest damage. For instance, early-maturing summer squash is ready for harvest before squash vine borers reach peak populations. In areas infested by codling moths, plant fruit and nut trees that bloom after the codling moths lay their eggs in early spring.

Plant varieties that are appropriate to your climate and resistant to insects. Juniperus chinensis (juniper), for example, is resistant to cypress tip miner.

PHYSICAL CONTROLS

You can control some insect and animal pests by physical means, such as trapping them or using barriers. In the case of insects, you may be able to pick or hose pests off plants.

Barriers can prevent certain pests from reaching plants. For instance, if cutworms are a problem in your garden, place a stiff paper collar around each transplant to prevent the pests from gaining access to the seedlings. The best way to deal with certain animal pests such as rabbits and deer is to fence them out.

Traps can be effective against certain pests. Boards or rolled-up newspapers placed in the garden lure earwigs, which like to hide in dark places. Other insect traps include

yellow sticky traps, effective in killing adult whiteflies. Trapping is the best way to get rid of a pesky gopher. Other animals may be protected; consult the local and state departments of fish and game for guidance.

Hand picking is the simplest way to deal with a few large, slow-moving insect pests crawling around on a plant. Just pick them off by hand and dispose of them in plastic bags in the garbage.

Aphid populations tend to build up rapidly; keep aphids in check by knocking them off with a strong stream of water when you see them on a plant. Be careful to wash them off both the upper and lower surfaces of the leaves. Once they are knocked off, most of them die or are unable to find their way back to the plant.

You can also wash mites off leaves. Washing also eliminates the dry, dusty conditions in which mites flourish. Spray the plants regularly with water to discourage reinfestation. Be sure to direct the spray up from below, since mites live mainly on the undersides of leaves.

BIOLOGICAL CONTROLS

Every pest has natural enemies that prey on it. The natural enemies of insect pests include other insects, birds, frogs, and lizards. Beneficial insects that prey on harmful insects may be predators or parasites. Predators kill harmful insects by eating them; parasites kill them by laying eggs in them. Some of these beneficial insects occur naturally in the garden. If you decide to use an insecticide to control harmful insects, be aware that you may be killing beneficial insects at the same time.

Some garden supply stores sell beneficial insects, such as green lacewing larvae, ladybird beetles, praying mantids, and trichogramma wasps. Since each of these insects preys only on certain other insects at specific times of the year, you must use the right beneficial insect for the job and release it at the right time.

Birds and toads in the garden help keep insect pests under control. Encourage birds to visit your garden by providing birdbaths and feeders that are safe from cats. Put out suet or peanut butter to attract birds that

Rotating crops in the vegetable garden and annual flower beds will discourage harmful insects.

One way to foil insects is to relocate plants to different beds from year to year.

By planting varieties that mature either earlier or later than the time that insects do their worst damage is another way to deter them.

Try to plant newly emerged seedlings at a time when the likelihood of insect damage is minimal.

feed mainly on insects. Toads are very effective pest predators and can beneficially assist the gardener. They eat nocturnal bugs and worms and can control these pests in a large garden area. If you have toads in your area, encourage them to stay in your garden by providing them with an appealing environment of half-buried flower pots in moist, shady spots.

Although it may not be obvious, natural enemies also keep animal pests under control. This often happens outside the garden, since many pests stage raids on the garden from the outside and then return to their home base. Introducing natural enemies of animal pests into the garden is risky, since you may be creating an even bigger problem. For example, cats are often used to keep mice under control and to frighten away birds, but the cats themselves may dig up the garden or kill birds.

CHEMICAL CONTROLS

Chemicals are an important component of integrated pest management, but they should be used only when a problem warrants action and the pest can't be controlled just as well by other means. Instead of applying pesticides immediately upon spotting an insect or evidence of an animal in the garden, find out first whether the insect or animal is destructive, neutral, or beneficial, and, if it is a pest, whether it has collected in large enough numbers to do harm. The exception to this rule is preventive spraying of fruit trees and certain vegetables, such as corn and squash, on which certain insect pests cannot be controlled once they begin their damage.

Chemical controls are used more often on insect pests. You will find that poisons are available as controls for very few animal pests and that fencing them out or trapping them, if legally permitted, is usually more effective.

Beneficial insects can be harmed by chemical controls, so it is important to read pesticide directions carefully before applying them.

The chemical you use must be effective against the insect you are trying to control, and it must be applied at the right stage in the insect's life cycle. Life cycles vary greatly. Some insects produce only one generation a year, whereas others may produce as many as nine; depending on the insect, each generation progresses through three or more different stages of life. Some insect pests are more vulnerable at certain times in their development. The most effective chemical at that stage may be different from one that would work at another stage. Always read pesticide labels carefully to make sure that you are applying the right chemical at the right time.

Apply pesticides only during calm weather. Wind blows sprays and dusts, making thorough and accurate coverage impossible. Rain washes off most insecticides, so applications may have to be repeated after heavy rainstorms. Sprays applied during hot weather (over 85° F) can burn plants; apply them during the cooler morning or evening

Knock aphids off a plant with a spray of water. Most will die or be unable to find their way back to the plant.

Examine your tomato plants frequently and pick off tomato hornworms as soon as you see them. One this size can strip a plant of its leaves in a week.

hours to avoid foliage damage. Treat only targeted plants so that you spare the beneficial insects on other plants.

Most insecticides work as a contact poison, a stomach poison, or both. Some work by physical rather than chemical action.

Contact Insecticides

These make up the largest category of insecticides. Insects that come in contact with them are killed either by being sprayed or dusted, by eating the poison, or just by walking across a leaf that has been treated. Contact insecticides are effective against most insects that feed on the outside of plants. When applying the insecticide you must cover all parts of the plant, including the undersides of the leaves. Plant protection lasts for weeks or only a few days, depending on the chemical used.

Systemic Insecticides

A systemic is absorbed through the leaves or roots and is circulated to all parts of the plant, where it acts as a stomach poison to feeding pests. Systemic insecticides are especially effective against small sucking insects, such as aphids (see page 285). In addition to being a stomach poison, most systemics are also contact killers.

Once absorbed, a systemic is not washed off by rain or irrigation water. Plant protection lasts six weeks or longer, depending on the chemical used. Because systemics are so long lasting and cannot be washed off, care must be taken in using them on food crops. Follow label directions carefully.

Biorational Insecticides

This is a relatively new category of insecticides that kill by physical or biological means rather than chemical action. They include horticultural oils, insecticidal soaps, and microbials.

Horticultural oils, applied as a dormant oil or summer oil spray, work by smothering the eggs or larvae of insects and mites. Insecticidal soaps kill mites and soft-bodied insects such as aphids, greenhouse thrips, and whiteflies on contact by disrupting their cell membranes. The pests must be hit directly with the soap spray if they are to be killed; the soapy solution is ineffective once it dries.

Aphid populations build up rapidly. To keep them in check, spray or wash upper and lower surfaces of leaves.

The leaves of some plants will be damaged or killed if they are sprayed with oils or soaps, so always check the label first.

Microbials, another kind of insecticide, include strains of bacteria, fungi, and viruses that attack certain insect pests. *Bacillus thuringiensis* (BT), a bacterium, is available to home gardeners. It is sprayed on certain kinds of destructive caterpillars, such as those of the gypsy moth and the California oakworm. The caterpillars are killed when they ingest the material. BT doesn't harm anything else it comes into contact with.

CONTROLLING GARDEN PESTS

Many different kinds of pests cause damage in gardens. The control measures depend on the pest. In most cases, a combination of controls keeps pests in check. Some are most easily controlled by physical means, whereas others are most vulnerable to biological or chemical controls. The secret of a healthy garden is knowing which controls or combination of controls to use against which garden pests.

The following are the best measures for controlling the insects and animals that most commonly cause damage in gardens. Sucking insects and chewing insects are grouped together because they share many characteristics and cause similar damage.

Sucking Insects

Many insect pests damage plants by piercing leaves, stems, or other plant parts and sucking vital liquids. Some sucking insects cause more damage than others, but generally a large population of the insect is needed to seriously harm a plant.

Aphids are the most common sucking insect found in gardens, but other sucking insects can cause just as much or more damage. Aphids and their relatives—which include whiteflies, scales, mealybugs, and leafhoppers—reproduce prolifically. The key to their evolutionary survival seems to be producing offspring faster than other insects can eat them. They are often relatively defenseless as individuals but spectacularly successful as a species.

The damage caused by all sucking insects is similar: The affected foliage turns pale green or yellow, often in a blotchy pattern; the injured leaves are small and sometimes distorted; and plant growth slows. In a severe case the leaves drop and the whole plant may die.

Many sucking insects excrete excess plant sap as a sweet, sticky substance called honeydew. This excretion drops onto leaves, cars, and patio furniture below the plants and often attracts ants. A black fungus called sooty mold grows on the honeydew, making leaves look dirty and black. Sooty mold is not

Ladybird beetles are sold in garden-supply stores as a natural predator of certain harmful insects. They are carnivorous and do not harm plants.

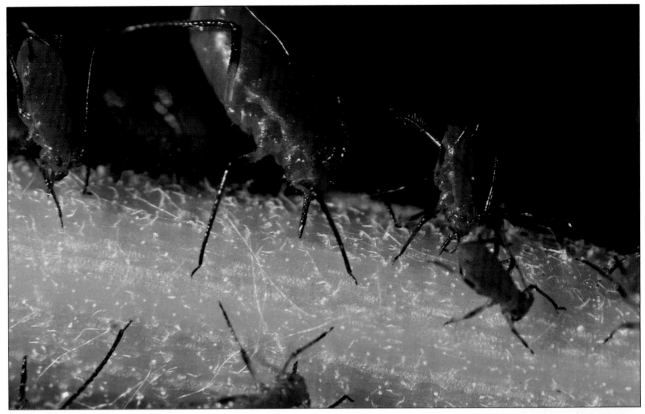

Systemic insecticides sprayed on plants are especially effective in killing sucking insects, such as these aphids.

a plant disease and does not directly harm the plants, but it is unsightly and can block out much of the sunlight that plants need for photosynthesis (see page 46). The sooty mold can be wiped off, or it will eventually be washed off by rain.

Aphids Also known as plant lice, aphids are usually gray, green, or black. They infest a wide range of plants and can accumulate in large numbers on buds, the undersides of leaves, and on the bark and stems.

You may have to take action if natural predators, such as ladybird beetles, don't keep the aphid population in check. You may be able to deter aphids by knocking them off plants with a strong stream of water. If this doesn't work you may want to use an insecticide. Insecticidal soaps as well as contact and systemic insecticides kill aphids. The best choice depends on the plant you are treating.

Horticultural oils sprayed on plants during the dormant season will smother eggs and larvae of insects and mites.

286

Mealybugs These pests are a common problem on outdoor plants in warm climates. They are ⅛ inch long and resemble flecks of white or gray cotton. Older mealybugs are

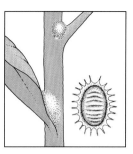

sluggish, but the young move actively. They cluster in crevices and at branching joints and are protected by a waxy covering. Threads and flakes of wax litter the leaves, making them look messy.

For minor infestations, you can try spraying plants with a strong stream of water to dislodge and wash away the mealybugs. Natural predators, such as ladybird beetles and green lacewing larvae, help control mealybugs. A major infestation requires an insecticide. Because of their waxy covering, mealybugs are more easily controlled with a systemic chemical than a contact insecticide. You can use a dormant oil spray to smother overwintering mealybugs on deciduous ornamentals and fruit trees.

Scales These insects attach themselves to branches and leaf stems, and large colonies often develop before they are noticed. Different types of scales have waxy, cottony, hard, or soft shells.

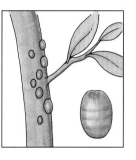

A young scale, called a crawler, looks like a tiny aphid. Crawlers are active and move around before choosing a place to insert their mouthparts. Then they become immobile and develop a shell. At this point they look like small bumps on the wood.

Natural enemies help keep scale populations under control. If the infestation is minor, you can pick or rub the adult scales off the plant. Use insecticides for major infestations. Because of their protective shells, adults are difficult to control chemically. The best time to apply an insecticide is when vulnerable crawlers are moving around the infested plants. Although the exact timing varies with each species of scale, most

scales have a crawler stage in early summer; others have a second generation of crawlers in late summer or early fall. If plants have been infested with scales in previous years, you can apply a dormant oil spray during the winter as a preventive measure. Oil sprays applied in summer control soft scales.

Whiteflies These tiny, white, winged insects explode into the air in large numbers when a plant that is infested is disturbed. Their populations build to enormous numbers

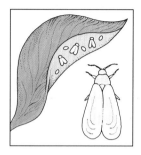

in warm weather; in cold-winter areas whiteflies are primarily greenhouse pests. Eggs, larvae, and adults are usually present on the same plant. The immobile larvae suck more sap and do greater damage than the mobile adults.

Regular washing down of infested plants with a strong stream of water may destroy young whiteflies in the crawling phase. Encarsia wasps, which feed on young whiteflies, are sold as predators, but they are most successful in temperatures of approximately 80° F. Insecticides easily control adults and crawlers, but repetitive spraying is necessary to control newly hatched whiteflies. Sticky yellow traps positioned at the same height as infested plants are an easy way to control adults. The whiteflies are attracted to the yellow color; they fly into it and are trapped on the sticky surface.

Leafhoppers These insects resemble tiny (¹⁄₁₆- to ¼-inch long) green or yellow grasshoppers. They suck juices from the undersides of leaves and prefer to feed

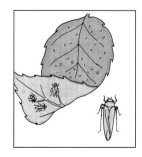

on fruit trees, lawns, and vegetables. White dots appear on the leaves of affected plants, and damaged lawns look wilted. It is important to keep leafhopper populations under control because these insects transmit a great many plant diseases.

Control of leafhoppers is difficult because adults move rapidly from garden to garden. You may have to apply contact or systemic insecticides on a regular basis if leafhoppers are a constant problem. Be sure that the plants you intend to treat are listed on the label. Some plant varieties are more resistant to leafhopper damage than other plant varieties. For example, vegetable varieties with thick, tough leaves rather than thin, fragile ones are more able to withstand leafhopper damage.

Mites These tiny, active spider relatives live mainly on the undersides of leaves. If you suspect that a plant has mites, hold a piece of white paper under the plant and tap 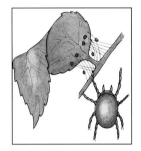 the leaves sharply. The mites will fall to the paper and appear as reddish brown specks on the white background.

Mites seem to cause damage that is out of proportion to their numbers, although it is not clear how they are able to accomplish that. One theory is that they inject a toxin into the plant when they feed. Only a few mites on a leaf can cause it to become spotted and dry. Many mites leave a trail of webbing as they move around the plant. This trail builds up to become a network of fine filaments that catches dirt and makes the plant even more unsightly.

Mite damage is most severe on plants suffering from water stress; you may be able to prevent problems by keeping your garden well watered and mulched. Natural enemies, including green lacewing larvae and predatory mites, are available commercially. Reduce initial mite populations as soon as you see them by hosing down infested plants with a strong stream of water. The mites will be killed, although the water won't destroy the eggs. During the winter use a dormant oil spray on deciduous trees to kill mite eggs. During the growing season a summer oil spray will destroy mites at several stages of life. Most insecticides that are effective against mites work only if repeated for several weeks. Since mites often develop a

resistance to pesticides, it is best to alternate chemicals.

Thrips Rapidly multiplying pests, thrips look like tiny slivers of wood. They rasp leaves and flowers and suck juices from the tissue. Foliage that has been damaged 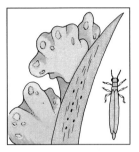 by thrips often appears silvery or has silvery streaks. Flower thrips feed on undeveloped blossoms, causing petals to become distorted and spotted.

Pick off and destroy infested leaves and flowers, and eliminate weeds near the garden where thrips can establish colonies. Natural enemies, including ladybird beetles and green lacewing larvae, help control thrips. For severe infestations of thrips spray the affected plants with contact killers or systemic insecticides.

Chewing Insects

Many of the insect pests in gardens cause damage by chewing leaves and other plant parts. They have mouthparts with jaws that work sideways instead of up and down. Some of these insects live on the outside of leaves and chew holes in them; some live in the soil and chew on roots. Others (called leaf miners) live inside leaves and tunnel through the leaf tissue, and still others (called borers) live inside stems and trunks and tunnel through the wood. Most chewing insects are either beetles or caterpillars.

Beetles About 40 percent of all insects are beetles. Immature beetles, usually called grubs, are legless or nearly so. They often live in the soil or inside a part of the plant.  Adult beetles have a pair of hard, often shiny, wing coverings that meet in a straight line down their back. Both the grubs and the adults chew on plant parts—often the grub eats the roots of a plant, matures into an adult, and continues to feed on the leaves of the same plant. Not all beetles feed on plants; some, such as the ladybird beetle, are carnivorous and feed on harmful insects.

The large scarab beetle family, which includes the Japanese beetle, June beetle, and rose chafer, are among the most destructive garden pests. The adults chew holes in the foliage, fruit, and flowers of plants, and the grubs devour grass roots. The grubs spend the winter in plants or in the soil. Japanese beetles are a major pest in the eastern United States. Arid summers in the West help prevent infestations of this beetle, which prefers a warm, humid, rainy summer.

Similar control methods work for all kinds of scarab beetles. Control must be aimed at both grubs and adults. Kill grubs, which feed on grass roots, by treating lawns with insecticides. The younger the grubs, the easier they are to eliminate. Check with a cooperative extension office to find out when eggs hatch in your area. Spading garden beds in summer and fall also kills some grubs. When using insecticides to control adults, make sure that the plants you intend to treat are listed on the label. Japanese beetle traps are effective; however, they lure beetles from as far as 500 feet away, so you may lure your neighbors' beetles to your garden.

Borers The larvae of beetles or moths, borers hatch from eggs laid under bark and then chew tunnels into the trunks, branches, and stems of trees and shrubs. They disrupt the 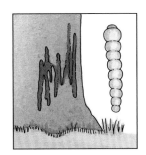 flow of sap through the plant, causing roots and branches to slowly starve.

The first signs of borer infestation are small holes in the bark; sawdust, frass (insect excrement), sap, or pitch are usually conspicuous as well. Vigorous plants are usually able to resist borers, whereas plants that are injured or weakened from drought, overwatering, improper planting, or other problems are more susceptible to borer attacks. Borer damage restricts the flow of nutrients and water in plants and weakens the structure of small plants.

Once borers are established, they are extremely difficult to eliminate. It is far easier to prevent attacks by planting vigorous trees and shrubs suited to your area and giving them the right light and soil conditions. Maintain their vigor by fertilizing yearly and watering deeply during droughts. Prune in late fall or early winter when borers are inactive; the pruning wounds will have time to form a callus before borers become active. If borer damage is limited, cut out and destroy the affected plant parts. In the case of small plants, you may have to remove and destroy the entire plant. Chemical treatment of a serious borer problem depends on the type of borer, the plant, and your area. Consult a cooperative extension office for advice on the most effective treatment.

Caterpillars These smooth, hairy, or spiny pests are the larval form of butterflies and moths. The adults have mouthparts that work like drinking straws; they sip nec- 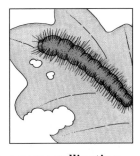 tar from flowers, in the process pollinating the flowers. However, the eggs they lay hatch into caterpillars, which have chewing mouthparts. Caterpillars are among the most common garden pests; they have voracious appetites and can defoliate entire plants.

The gypsy moth caterpillar is in a class by itself because of its destructiveness. It is now the most serious pest of shade trees in the eastern United States. The larvae hatch in early spring and may completely cover and defoliate a tree. The caterpillars attack hundreds of kinds of trees and shrubs but prefer oak. Hardwood trees can grow new leaves after defoliation, but conifers suffer more permanent damage.

To control the gypsy moth caterpillar, spray the entire tree weekly as needed during the larval period. Several contact and systemic sprays as well as *Bacillus thuringiensis* (BT) are effective against the caterpillars; spray before the larvae are 1 inch long. Destroy egg sacs where visible. Keep trees well watered and fertilized to resist further infestations of this caterpillar.

Among other notable caterpillar pests is the California oakworm. Maintain the tree's health, since vigorous oaks are less likely to be attacked. For severe infestations spray the entire tree with an insecticide. BT is effective only on young larvae; the older the caterpillars, the harder they are to kill. The tomato hornworm and green cabbage caterpillar are common in vegetable gardens. Pick off the worms or spray the vegetables with a contact insecticide safe for use on food crops

Cutworms Fleshy, hairless caterpillars, up to 2 inches long, cutworms curl up when disturbed. They feed at night, and are active below ground, at the surface, and among branches.  Surface cutworms damage early-season vegetables and flowers by feeding on seedlings and transplants. One cutworm can destroy an entire row of plants by chewing the stems at the soil surface.

Cutworms can be controlled with baits or with insecticides that are worked into or watered into the soil. For additional protection, place a collar made from stiff paper, a milk carton, a tin can, or aluminum foil around each seedling. Cultivate the soil in late summer and fall to expose and destroy cutworms. At the same time eliminate weeds so that cutworms will have fewer places to hide during the winter.

Earwigs Although many gardeners, especially those in the West, complain about earwigs, these reddish brown insects are not serious pests. Earwigs hide in humid, dark  places during the day and forage for food at night. They feed mainly on decaying vegetable matter but also eat live plant tissue. Their feeding damages leaves and can girdle seedlings.

Earwigs are fairly large, up to 1 inch long, with fierce-looking pincers extending from their back end. These clawlike appendages are used as offensive and defensive weapons and sometimes to catch insects, on which they feed in addition to plant material.

The main control for earwigs is sanitation; eliminate hiding places and reduce their food source by cleaning up plant debris. You can trap earwigs by leaving boards or rolled-up newspapers in the garden. Destroy the earwigs you find hiding there each day. You can also use earwig bait, although the chemical might attract and harm pets.

Leaf miners These pests are insect larvae that feed inside leaves between the upper and lower surfaces. They may be the larvae of flies, moths, or beetles. After the larvae 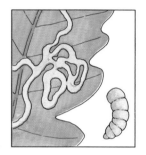 hatch, they tunnel into the leaf. Some leaf miners make straight lines, whereas others create snakelike tunnels. The outline of the tunnel is visible on the leaf surface. The leaves may be rolled, wrinkled, or skeletonized, or they may appear scorched or drop prematurely. Leaf-miner damage is often only cosmetic, but trees may die from repeated attacks, and infested vegetable and fruit plants are often less productive.

On small plants that are lightly infested, pick off and destroy damaged leaves as soon as you see the outline of the tunnels on the leaf surface. For severe infestations on ornamentals, spray with a systemic insecticide. Contact sprays are not effective once the insect is inside the leaf. The systemic you choose depends on the plant being treated. Rake up fallen leaves from infested plants and dispose of them.

Maggots These are small, white, legless larvae of flies. They tunnel through seeds, seedlings, and fleshy plant roots, destroying them entirely or, in the case of vegetables, mak-  ing them inedible. The maggots that most often plague gardeners are the cabbage maggot, onion maggot, pepper maggot, and seedcorn maggot.

Both the cabbage maggot and onion maggot tend to be pests in the North, where cool, wet weather favors their development. Cabbage maggots affect more than just cabbage plants; they tunnel and chew holes in the roots of other cruciferous plants, such as broccoli, cauliflower, radishes, and turnips. Dispose of infested plants and treat the soil with a contact insecticide. Crop rotation helps control maggots.

Roses in eastern and northern gardens are often attacked by rose midge maggots. These maggots, which cluster in the flower buds, can be very destructive and tenacious. The rose midge has a short life cycle and can produce five or six generations per growing season. If adult flies are visible, spray them with a contact insecticide to break the breeding cycle. The most important control measure is to destroy affected plant parts.

Slugs and snails

Although these are mollusks rather than insects, slugs and snails are often grouped with insects in discussions of garden pests. A slug is a snail without a shell. Both slugs and snails eat a wide variety of green plants and usually leave a slime trail that shines when dry. They can cause great damage to seedlings and to leaves of tender vegetables, such as lettuce.

A clean garden, with few places for slugs and snails to hide, is essential for long-term control. You can also protect plants with barriers. Slugs and snails find copper a particularly abrasive material. You can protect raised beds by covering them with a small-mesh screen. Bait—available as pellets, granules, or a thick liquid squeezed out in gooey drops—is commonly used, although you may not want to use it if you have pets. Since these materials are broken down by rain, the bait must be reapplied every two weeks during rainy weather. Begin applying the bait in early spring to keep large populations from developing.

Animal Pests

Garden damage by birds, rabbits, and squirrels, and even, at times, rambunctious pets, is common. Some gardeners have to contend with deer, gophers, woodchucks, and raccoons. These animals can quickly cause extensive damage, and once accustomed to the offerings of your garden, they will probably return for more meals. Dealing with these pests can be frustrating, especially when you see only the results of their handiwork. Scarecrows, windmills, and the like act as deterrents for only a short period of time. Some animals can be excluded with barriers or fences; for others, such as gophers, trapping is the only effective control. Before trapping or using chemicals on any animal, make sure that you use traps and chemicals that are in compliance with local and state fish and game regulations.

Birds Although birds perform a valuable service in the garden by controlling the insect population, they can damage plants. Birds often eat freshly planted seeds and destroy young plants while scratching in the soil for insects. They also eat fruit and are particularly attracted to berries, figs, cherries, strawberries, apples, and grapes.

Barriers are the most effective protection against birds. Mesh screens over seeded areas prevent birds from digging in soft soil, and cages made from chicken wire stretched over frames keep birds away from seedlings. Plastic, nylon, or cheesecloth nets over berry bushes and fruit trees prevent birds from stealing fruit. For grapes, tie a paper bag around each cluster; cut a few small holes in the end for air circulation. Cats may be useful in intimidating nuisance birds.

Cats Besides frightening away birds, cats also keep down populations of mice and other rodents in the garden. However, most cats like to dig in soft garden soil, disturbing seeds and uprooting seedlings.

Commercial odor repellents may be effective in keeping cats away from specific areas. Renew the spray according to label directions. A mesh screen over seedlings or a newly seeded area will also deter cats. You can remove the barrier when the plant foliage covers the ground.

Dogs Damage can result when dogs romp through a cultivated area, trampling plants, digging up soil, and depositing urine or droppings.

Commercial odor repellents may make an area unappealing to dogs. Renew the spray periodically. Sturdy gates and fences keep most dogs out. If barriers are not possible, plant in raised beds with paths for the dog to run along. Arrange alternative play areas for pets so that the garden will be less attractive to them.

Ground squirrels These squirrels live below ground but feed above ground during the day. Emerging from winter hibernation and finding forage scarce, they devour tender greens in the garden in spring. Later in the season ground squirrels feed on seeds, grains, fruits, nuts, and vegetables. They live in large colonies underground, and often the only way to control them is to eliminate the colony. This is a job for a licensed pest-control professional.

Barriers and fences are not effective because these agile climbers easily circumvent

them. Trapping is the most effective control. Set the traps near burrow entrances or along pathways used by the animals. Use baits such as peanut butter, nuts, raisins, or cereals. Always wear gloves and protective clothing when removing ground squirrels from traps, because they and their fleas may carry disease, including plague. Don't handle live or injured squirrels, since they bite, especially when they feel threatened.

Tree squirrels These squirrels damage gardens by digging up newly planted seeds, bulbs, and sometimes entire plants. Omnivorous creatures, tree squirrels survive on seeds, nuts, insects, and bark. They are agile climbers and able to jump 6 feet.

Chicken-wire barriers are the best protection against squirrels in the garden. Place the chicken wire over newly seeded areas or over seedlings and bulbs; remove it when the plants are large enough to withstand damage. If you want to keep the squirrels out of trees, wrap a band of metal 18 inches wide around the trunk and 4 feet above the ground. Prune back any branches within 6 lateral feet and 2 vertical feet of any other tree, fence, roof, or other perch from which the squirrel could jump into and out of the tree.

Deer These animals often damage gardens in rural and suburban areas by eating vegetables and flowers and by stripping the new growth off trees and shrubs. If food is scarce in winter, deer will eat the bark of young trees, causing severe damage.

The best way to discourage deer is to fence them out with a barrier at least 8 feet high. It must be that high because deer are agile jumpers. Electrified wire works but is more of an undertaking than most gardeners care to deal with. There are such things as deer-resistant plants, although their effectiveness is unpredictable. Very hungry deer will nibble at plants they usually forgo, and the tastes of deer often differ from region to region. It is best to check with a local nursery or the cooperative extension office in your county for recommendations of plants that are considered deer resistant in your locale. Deer repellents may be effective but only for a short time. Almost any unfamiliar odor will repel deer for a few days.

Unlike wildlife, the family dog can be trained to stay away from planted areas.

Deer can be very destructive. A well-constructed fence at least 8 feet high may be the only effective barrier to keep them out of the garden.

Rabbits Because they eat herbaceous plants, especially garden vegetables, and gnaw at the bark of young trees and shrubs, rabbits can be a problem.

Keep rabbits from damaging plants by fencing them out with a mesh fence 2 feet high and buried 6 inches underground. Build a simple wooden frame around the garden and attach the mesh to it, or protect individual plants by encircling them with chicken wire or mesh. If the damage occurs during winter in a snowy climate, the barrier should be 2 feet taller than the snow line.

Pocket gophers These animals, named for the cheek pouches they use to carry food, are native to California and are found throughout the western United States. In some areas pests referred to as gophers are really other animals; for example, "gophers" in the Midwest are actually ground squirrels.

Gophers dig tunnels that run a foot or more below the soil surface; they leave distinctive crescent-shaped mounds of dirt on the surface as they make new runs. They live and feed almost entirely underground,

living alone except during brief mating periods. Gophers feed on plant tops and roots. They can kill shrubs and trees by eating the roots or girdling the underground part of the trunk or stems. Their tunnels can drain irrigated areas and keep water from getting to plant roots.

Trapping is the best method of eradication. Search with a long metal probe to locate the main run. Dig down to expose the run

Sometimes the only effective barrier against small animals is a wire-mesh screen that can be fashioned to enclose valued plants.

293

and insert two scissors-type or box traps, one facing in each direction. Tie the traps with wire to a stake above the ground. To keep soil from falling on the traps, cover the hole with sod or with a board; sprinkle with soil to block out all light. Check the traps daily. Look for new mounds, indicating recent gopher activity, and set more traps when mounds appear. Catching one gopher may or may not solve the problem. If there are many gophers in the area, one will probably take over the vacated tunnel.

Poison bait is also effective. With a probe locate the tunnel, dig down, and insert the bait. Be sure that pets can't reach the bait. Fumigation is not considered very effective. You can keep gophers out of a raised bed by tacking ¼-inch hardware cloth to the bottom of the wooden frame.

Raccoons Whether they are fed deliberately or inadvertently, raccoons are a nuisance in many rural and suburban settings. Pet food and unharvested fruit and corn may attract raccoons. These omnivorous animals forage at night. Agile climbers, they are intelligent and inquisitive but can be vicious if cornered.

A fence around a vegetable garden is an effective deterrent. Use 5-foot-high chicken wire that extends a couple of feet above 3-foot-high posts. As the raccoon climbs the unsupported part of the wire, its weight will pull the wire out and down toward the ground so that the animal won't be able to climb over. Low-voltage electric fences are also effective; use two strands, one 6 inches and the other 12 inches from the ground. To keep raccoons out of trees, tie a metal wrap around the trunk. The wrap must be at least 2 feet off the ground and 18 inches wide to prevent the raccoons from crawling over it. Prevent foraging in garbage cans by fastening the lids securely and tieing the cans to a fence or other structure to prevent tipping over. The presence of a large, active dog may also keep raccoons away.

Moles These are small gray or black animals with smooth, velvety fur. Their eyesight is poor, but their senses of smell, touch, and hearing are well developed. Their large front feet have long trowellike claws, which they use for tunneling.

Foraging at night, raccoons are attracted to vegetable gardens, fruit trees, and garbage cans.

Moles seldom feed on plants, but they damage plants indirectly by tunneling. While searching for grubs, slugs, and earthworms, they dig tunnels, uprooting and pushing up lawn grasses or loosening the soil around roots so that the roots dry out and die. Their interconnected tunnels are 6 to 8 inches below ground level. They leave volcano-shaped mounds of soil on the surface.

The best way to control moles in the lawn is to reduce their food supply by controlling insect grubs with an insecticide. You can also eradicate moles by trapping them in their tunnels. In the East, you can buy spear-type traps made specifically for moles. In the West, where the dominant mole species digs a deeper tunnel, scissors-type traps are more effective. For deep runways, explore with a probe and trap as you would for pocket gophers (see page 293). Poison baits, repellents, and fumigants are generally ineffective against moles.

Mice Several kinds of mice, or voles, invade gardens throughout the United States. Mice live in grassy or brushy areas, nesting below ground in shallow burrows or above ground in densely vegetated, protected spots. They may also establish nests in thick hay or leaf mulches. They usually move along narrow runways from their nesting areas to their food source. Mice are active throughout the year, digging up and feeding on seeds and nuts. They also eat bulbs and tender vegetables and flowers and may severely damage young trees by gnawing on the bark and roots. Mice are nocturnal and do most of their damage at night.

You may be able to keep mice out of the garden by enclosing it with a fence of fine-mesh (no larger than ¼-inch) wire or hardware cloth extending a foot above and a foot below ground level. Protect young trees and other valuable plants by encircling them with mesh cylinders a foot high and extending several inches into the ground. Wrap tree trunks with a tough plastic, sold as tree wrap at some nurseries, to protect them. Keep your garden free of grassy areas and piles of leaves and debris where mice can live. Set out traps or poison bait along mouse runways.

Woodchucks These animals, also known as groundhogs, are a problem in many rural and suburban areas in the Northeast. The woodchuck feeds above ground on tender vegetables, flowers, and succulent green leaves. Woodchucks occasionally have diseases that can be transmitted to humans, so always wear gloves and protective clothing when handling these animals.

Fencing can keep woodchucks out of the garden. Surround the area with a wire-mesh fence held in place with 3-foot-high stakes. To prevent woodchucks from burrowing underneath the fence, bend the bottom foot of wire mesh outward and bury it a few inches. To keep woodchucks from climbing over the fence, extend the wire mesh 18 inches above the top of the stakes. The weight of the climbing woodchuck will bend the mesh out and down toward the ground so that the animal won't be able to climb over. Any trapping or shooting of woodchucks must comply with local and state game regulations.

Wire fencing wrapped around plants can protect them from small animals and birds. Scarecrows, windmills, and the like act as a deterrent for only a short time.

CONTROLLING PLANT DISEASES

Any condition that interferes with normal plant development is considered a disease. This definition encompasses a wide range of problems—everything from wounds inflicted by lawn mowers to frost damage to virus infections. Although disease-causing organisms such as fungi and bacteria are responsible for many plant diseases, the majority of plant disorders in a garden are due to unfavorable growing conditions; these are called environmental diseases and their causes include improper watering, nutrient deficiencies or toxicities, temperature extremes, and air pollution. The diseases induced by pathogens, or disease-causing organisms, are referred to as infectious diseases.

When plants show evidence of a problem, it is often difficult to trace the cause of the disorder. Gardeners quickly learn to recognize powdery mildew and other diseases whose signs are obvious, but often the answer is not clear-cut. It may be difficult to tell whether an environmental factor or a microscopic organism is at fault.

Luckily, the ability to accurately diagnose a disease on your own is not the key to disease control for home gardeners. It is far more important to learn how diseases occur, how to prevent them, and if one occurs how to assess the problem and narrow the possible causes. If you can't identify and cure the disease yourself, at least you will be able to discuss the problem intelligently with a professional.

You can disrupt many fungus and bacterial infections by keeping leaves dry when you irrigate. If you must water by overhead sprinkler, schedule it for early morning so that the leaves have a chance to dry.

CONDITIONS CAUSING DISEASE

The presence of a fungus or other pathogen in the garden does not necessarily mean that disease will occur. For infection to take place, there must also be a susceptible plant and an environment favoring development of the disease. Without splashing water, for example, certain waterborne fungi won't spread to plants. Even when the fungi are splashed on plants, disease won't develop unless the plants are vulnerable to infection.

Environmental diseases, which don't involve pathogens, require the presence of both a susceptible plant and an unfavorable growing condition. For example, frost won't damage a very hardy plant but it will harm, or kill, a tender plant.

Since plant diseases won't develop unless a combination of elements is present, the way to control a disease is to eliminate at least one of the required elements. For diseases that flourish only on certain plants, you can disrupt the conditions necessary for disease by not growing those particular plants. For example, by not growing elms, you are eliminating one of the required elements for Dutch elm disease. It will not develop even if the disease organism is present and conditions favor its spread.

For diseases that affect a wide range of plants, it is often easier to disrupt the growing conditions that favor the disease. Since most fungi and bacteria need moisture, you can reduce the chances of infection by keeping the leaves of susceptible plants dry. There's not much you can do to keep leaves dry in an area with frequent summer rainfall, but in a drier climate you can use an irrigation method that avoids wetting leaves. If you use overhead sprinklers, water early in the morning so that the leaves dry quickly.

Disrupting an infectious disease by eliminating the disease-causing organism is not always easy. The following are descriptions of different types of pathogens along with methods of controlling them.

Fungi

The majority of plant diseases are caused by fungi. Since fungi cannot manufacture their own food, they depend entirely on living and dead plant or animal tissue for nourishment.

Dutch elm disease is spread by the elm bark beetle. Keep a healthy elm vigorous so that it will be less susceptible to insect attack.

Some 8,000 species of fungi are pathogens, producing structures that penetrate cells and cause disease in the process. They do not need a natural opening or wound in the plant, as bacteria do. Most fungi aren't active at temperatures below 25° F or above 110° F. Fungus diseases cause a wide range of symptoms in plants. Fungi reproduce primarily by spores, and sometimes mushrooms and other fruiting bodies that form the spores are noticeable. Spores are usually carried to new plants by wind or water. Most spores must remain in a drop of water for six to eight

Fungi, which depend entirely on plant or animal tissue for nourishment, cause the majority of plant diseases.

hours before they germinate and infect plant tissue. Powdery mildew is an exception; it does not need water to germinate.

You can control fungus diseases by keeping plant leaves dry, choosing disease-resistant plants, and applying fungicides. Be sure that the fungicide label indicates it is effective against the fungus you are dealing with and that it is safe for your plant.

Bacteria

Approximately two hundred species of bacteria cause plant diseases. Some of these bacteria secrete poisons that kill the cells of the host plant. Other bacteria manufacture enzymes that break down resistant plant material. A few bacteria exude growth-stimulating substances that result in cancerlike cell growth. Since bacteria need high temperatures and moisture to grow, bacterial diseases are more commonly found in the tropics than in North America. Major symptoms of bacterial diseases are soft rot of tissue, leaf spots that don't cross the veins, and wilt (although most wilts are fungal), blight, and swelling.

Bacteria spread through infected seeds; they are also splashed on plants by rain and irrigation water, and they are transported on cultivating tools, pruning shears, and diseased plants brought into your garden. Bacteria require a natural opening, such as nectar holes in flowers, or a wound in order to enter a plant. Bacteria often live within a protective ooze that they create in the infected plant.

The main controls against bacteria are preventive measures, such as sanitation and using resistant plants. There are very few chemicals, with the exception of copper-containing materials and antibiotics such as streptomycin, effective in combating bacterial diseases.

Viruses

The few viruses that seriously damage or kill plants usually are spread to the plant through hand and tool contact or are carried by insects. Infected cuttings and grafts are a common source of viruses (see page 345). Most viruses only slightly impair plant growth, and symptoms often are evident only under certain conditions. A rapidly spreading

Bacteria can enter plants only through natural openings or wounds. Bees may spread some kinds of bacteria through nectar holes in the blossoms.

virus infection can decrease a plant's ability to manufacture and store food by reducing the supply of chlorophyll, the green plant pigment needed for photosynthesis (see page 46). Different viruses cause different symptoms. Mosaic viruses mottle or streak leaves; ring-spot viruses form pale rings on leaves; and stunt viruses cause stunting of foliage. In some plants viruses thicken, curl, or distort leaves. They may also reduce production of flowers and fruit.

Since viruses live inside plant cells, they can't be controlled chemically without also harming the plants. Severely infected plants should be removed and destroyed to keep the virus from spreading. You can restrict virus diseases by controlling the insects that transmit the viruses; aphids and leafhoppers are the major carriers of viruses and viruslike organisms. (See methods of controlling aphids and leafhoppers on pages 286 and 287.) Eliminate weeds that may be hosts to viruses or to the insects that carry viruses. Buy seeds, bulbs, cuttings, and young plants only from certified nurseries and seed companies that guarantee disease-free stock.

Nematodes

These earthworm relatives are also known as eelworms and roundworms. Some are beneficial, but many are parasitic and cause plant diseases. Practically all of the harmful nematodes are microscopic. Most of them live in the soil and feed on root hairs and root tips, or they live within the roots themselves. A few are foliar nematodes, feeding on leaves and stems. Nematodes are a major problem in some soils in the South, especially moist, sandy soils. Nematodes can move only a short distance each year under their own power, but they are transported by irrigation water, on tools, and in soil. Quarantine restrictions on plants from Hawaii are strict because Hawaiian soil contains parasitic nematodes and other diseases.

Root nematodes, attracted to sap in plant roots, either feed on the outside of the root or they burrow inside. The main damage is from nematode saliva, which causes cells to collapse and disintegrate, resulting in dark lesions and dead areas along the roots. In some cases, toxins from the nematode may cause knots or nodules to form on the roots.

Streaking on gladiolus petals is caused by a virus passed from one generation to the next in the corm.

Nematode damage limits the ability of the roots to supply aboveground parts of the plant with water and nutrients; the results are wilting, discoloration, stunting, and sometimes death. Foliar nematodes feed on plant stems and leaves, swimming on wet plant surfaces. They can cause stunting, distortion, and blotches on foliage.

Don't try to implement control measures for nematodes unless a soil-testing laboratory has positively identified the problem. There are no chemicals available to home gardeners that kill nematodes without also killing plants. In unplanted areas, you can kill nematodes by fumigating the soil before planting. Solarizing the soil reduces nematode populations (see page 273). Remove infected plants and replace them with nematode-resistant varieties. A cooperative

Attracted to sap in plant roots, nematodes feed on the outside or burrow inside.

extension office can supply you with a list for your region.

Preventing Plant Diseases

The most effective way of controlling plant diseases is to prevent them from taking hold in your garden. Every plant disease has a set of conditions that must be met in order for the disease to develop and then flourish. The following are strategies for breaking the cycle and disrupting the disease.

Exclude the Disease
Buy only certified disease-free plants, bulbs, and seeds from reliable nurseries and garden centers. Before bringing a plant into your garden, inspect it carefully. If you suspect that the plant has a disease, treat the problem before bringing it into your yard. Many careful gardeners insist on treating all plants introduced into their gardens with an all-purpose fungicide and insecticide.

Lessen your chances of bringing disease-contaminated soil or mulches into your garden by purchasing them from a reliable soil yard, nursery, or garden center.

Keep Your Garden Clean
Sanitation is an important factor in disease control. Remove fallen fruit, dead flowers, and debris throughout the year. Be particularly thorough in fall, since disease-causing organisms often overwinter on neglected vegetation. Prune off diseased plant parts; remove severely diseased plants, and destroy them by burning them or placing them in the garbage. Don't compost diseased plants.

Control weeds that may be hosts for diseases. Disease organisms often infect weeds and then spread to garden plants. Ask a cooperative extension office or nursery staff which weeds may harbor diseases that affect your garden. Sometimes disease organisms survive only because of elaborate dependencies between garden plants and weeds.

Reduce the Rate of Infection
A regular program of dormant spraying with lime-sulfur and copper-containing materials will help discourage disease organisms on fruit trees and deciduous ornamentals such as roses. These winter sprays are valuable in reducing the incidence of many diseases, including fire blight and stone fruit diseases.

Avoid planting during unfavorable weather. For example, peas planted during cold, rainy weather will be susceptible to powdery mildew and damping-off diseases. Peas planted after the weather turns warm and sunny will be less subject to attack.

Use sterilized potting soil for starting seeds (see Potting Mixes on page 104), and sterilize the flat or container as well. If you use ordinary garden soil to start seeds, damping-off disease may be a problem.

You can reduce the spread of some diseases by controlling the insects that transmit the diseases—in particular, aphids and leafhoppers, which transmit viruses and viruslike organisms from one plant to another. (See pages 286 and 287 for methods of controlling these insects.)

When pruning diseased plants, disinfect your pruning shears after each cut by dipping them in rubbing alcohol.

Use Good Growing Practices

Good growing practices will make your garden an unfavorable place for both environmental and infectious diseases.

Choose plants that are suited to your climate and to the soil and light conditions they will be given. Plants stressed by inappropriate growing conditions are easy prey for disease. Maintain the vigor of your plants so that they can withstand disease and outgrow any damage that does occur.

If you use sprinklers, water early in the morning so that the plants dry quickly. Eliminate overhead watering of plants whose leaves mildew rapidly or are susceptible to leaf spot. Water deeply but infrequently. Let the soil dry out periodically to reduce root-rot organisms; constantly soaked soil invites disease. Do not handle plants when they are wet, since many disease organisms travel in drops of water.

If a disease that attacks only certain plants is a problem in your area, eliminate or rotate those plants (don't plant the same vegetables or flowers in the same place every year). Most disease-causing organisms die if they cannot find a suitable host to infect.

Space plants for good aeration. Plants that are susceptible to powdery mildew, for example, are better able to resist the disease if there is adequate air circulation. Crowded plants succumb more easily to powdery mildew, and the fungus will spread rapidly through the entire planting. Mildew-prone

To help prevent diseases from attacking the garden, practice good sanitation; remove fallen fruit, dead flowers, and debris throughout the year.

plants, such as roses (*Rosa* species) and lilacs (*Syringa* species), should be pruned so that air and sunlight can reach all parts of the plant. A thick mat of foliage encourages the growth of powdery mildew fungus in the center of the plant.

Select Disease-Resistant Plants

If a disease that affects only certain plants is common in your area, avoid those plants and grow resistant varieties instead. Plants vary in their susceptibility and resistance to specific diseases. Some plants are naturally more able to resist diseases than other plants. More and more plants are being bred for disease resistance. For example, a tomato cultivar labeled VFNT has been bred for resistance to verticillium wilt, fusarium wilt, nematodes, and tobacco mosaic virus.

A good local nursery or a cooperative extension office will be able to alert you to plants that resist the diseases most common in your area.

Use Chemical Controls

Nearly all the chemical controls for plant diseases are fungicides (chemicals that kill or inhibit the growth of fungi). There are very few chemical controls for bacteria and none for viruses.

Some fungicides are safe for use on food plants; others should be used only on ornamentals. Several products combine fungicides with insecticides. As with all garden chemicals, read and follow the label directions carefully.

Fungicides act in various ways. Most are protectants; they work by protecting healthy plant parts from infection. These fungicides form a chemical barrier between the fungus and the plant tissue, killing the spores and fungal strands that try to penetrate the plant. Protectants cannot cure fungus infections that are already established. A few fungicides are eradicants; they are capable of killing fungi growing on and sometimes inside plant tissue.

Roses are susceptible to powdery mildew, but adequate air circulation will help control the spread of the disease. Prune roses to allow sunlight and air to reach all parts of the plant.

Some plants, such as strawberries, are being bred for disease resistance. Find out from a nursery what plants are resistant to diseases in your area.

Some fungicides travel systemically through the plant with the sap after the plant absorbs the chemical, but most fungicides are nonsystemic and remain on the surface of the plant. Nonsystemic fungicides should be applied so that they cover the plant thoroughly; areas that are missed and new growth that is not treated are susceptible to infection. The effectiveness of these fungicides diminishes as they are washed off by rain and irrigation water and are broken down by sunlight. An additive called a spreader-sticker helps a fungicide spread evenly over plant surfaces, stick to the surfaces, and resist degradation. Some fungicides already contain a spreader-sticker, so check the label before adding one.

Fungicides are much more useful as preventives than they are as curatives. If you have plants that are likely to develop fungus diseases, apply the fungicide ahead of time. Copper-containing and lime-sulfur sprays applied during winter are effective in reducing the incidence of certain fungus and bacterial diseases, particularly on fruit trees, berry bushes, and roses.

DIAGNOSING PLANT PROBLEMS

Some plant problems are fairly simple to diagnose—for example, the bands or rings on rose leaves are easy to recognize as a virus infection, and the blackened, wilted shoots on a pear tree proclaim fire blight. But determining what is wrong with a plant is not always that straightforward. The same symptom—for example, yellowing leaves—could be due to many different causes, including a nutrient deficiency, improper watering, an infectious disease, an insect attack, or even old age.

Before assuming that a plant is diseased, you should know what the plant is supposed to look like and how it's supposed to grow. For example, if you recently moved into a house and didn't know that the dawn redwood (*Metasequoia glyptostroboides*) in your front yard was deciduous, you might think that the tree was shedding its leaves because it was sick. Before concluding that your holly (*Ilex* species) is diseased because it isn't fruiting, find out whether or not you have a female plant.

If something is actually wrong, be as specific as you can about the problem. Unless it is apparent that the problem is elsewhere, begin by examining the leaves, flowers, and fruit, and work your way down the stem to the roots. Make note of any wounds, cracks, or malformed tissue. Any tissue that feels slimy is a good indication of disease. Check the moisture level to make sure that the plant is being adequately watered. (See Knowing When to Water on page 145.) Dig down and examine a root. A diseased root is brown instead of white, and it may smell. If the roots aren't working properly, the aboveground parts of the plant will be affected sooner or later. Branch dieback, for example, may be due to a malfunctioning root system.

Since most plant problems result from environmental factors, eliminate those before concluding that your plant has an infectious disease. To prevent or control environmental disorders, you must alter the plant's environment and the care you give it.

You may not be able to diagnose a plant disorder by yourself, but you can assess the problem and narrow the possibilities by carefully examining the affected plant and its

*The female of the holly (*Ilex *species) bears the fruit; the male does not.*

This dahlia is infected with powdery mildew, which thrives in both humid and dry weather.

environment. The checklist on page 310 will help you in this process. If you decide to consult a local nursery or a cooperative extension office, you will be better able to describe the problem and provide the necessary information for an accurate diagnosis.

TYPES OF DISEASES

Plant diseases are classified in many different ways. Some plant scientists classify them by type of disease-causing organisms, such as fungus, bacterium, or virus, or by the kinds of environmental factors causing them. Others categorize plant diseases by symptoms, such as wilting, regardless of the cause. Still others classify them by the type of plant affected, such as diseases of camellias. Sometimes diseases are categorized by the part of the plant affected, such as petal, stem, or root diseases. They can also be classified by the way they spread—for example, wind-, water-, and soilborne diseases.

For the purposes of this book, diseases have been divided into two groups: soilborne diseases that attack plant roots and diseases affecting aboveground parts of plants. All the diseases described here are infectious diseases—they are caused by a pathogen.

Soilborne Diseases

The following are some of the most troublesome soilborne diseases found in gardens. The symptoms of each disease are described along with suggested methods of control. Damage from root nematodes is common in certain areas, particularly the South; see page 301 for a description of injuries and control methods.

Damping-off This disease kills seedlings, either before they break through the surface of the soil or shortly afterward. Developing seedlings suddenly fall over and die.  Dark lesions may appear on the roots and at the base of the stem.

The problem is caused by one of several soilborne fungi (*Pythium*, *Phytophthora*, and *Rhizoctonia*). They can attack seeds at any stage of germination and seedlings at any time before the plant matures.

Start seeds in a sterilized potting soil, and sterilize flats and pots before reusing them. When sowing seeds outdoors, avoid conditions that encourage succulent plant growth. Wait to add fertilizer until the seedlings develop at least one pair of true leaves. Let the soil surface dry slightly between waterings. Encourage rapid development of seedlings by planting when the soil temperature is optimum for germination.

Coat the seeds with a fungicide before you plant them.

Oak root fungus

This fungus, which is also known as armillaria root rot, shoestring root rot, and mushroom root rot, attacks oaks and many other woody plants. It kills by gradually decaying the roots and moving into the main stem, where it girdles the plant. There is often a general withering and yellowing of leaves. The disease can be identified by white striated fans of fungus under the bark and between grooves on the bark. Mushrooms often grow around the plant in fall or winter.

The fungus is encouraged by moist conditions during summer in areas that do not normally receive summer rain—the disease is widespread in California. To discourage the oak root fungus, don't irrigate oaks and other susceptible plants during summer. Try to save a partially infected plant by moving soil away from the base of the plant, cutting out diseased tissue, and exposing the fungus to air. When removing a badly infected or dead plant, be sure to eliminate all the infected roots or the fungus will remain in the soil. When replanting, use immune or resistant species; ask a cooperative extension office for a list.

Sclerotium root rot

Also known as southern wilt, southern blight, and crown rot, this fungus is most active in warm, moist soils. It attacks vegetables, flowers, and some woody shrubs. Infection occurs at or below the soil level. White fungal threads surround and cover the infected plant, secreting an acid that kills healthy plant cells and allows the fungus to enter. It causes the roots and crown of plants to rot, the stems to develop cankers, and bulbs or tubers to rot. Infected plants wilt, turn yellow, and decay.

Remove and dispose of the infected or dead plant plus 6 inches of surrounding soil to eliminate fungal pellets. Fungal spores survive as pellets in the soil and on plant debris. The spores remain most active in sandy soils that are low in nitrogen, so improve the soil by adding organic matter and a balanced fertilizer.

Verticillium and fusarium wilts

Both of these fungus wilt diseases attack annual vegetables, flowers, and herbaceous perennials. Verticillium wilt also attacks many woody shrubs and trees. Any soil in which potatoes, tomatoes, strawberries, or cotton have been grown probably contains the verticillium wilt fungus. Both diseases cause wilted growth, discolored leaves and stems, and eventual death. Fungal strands penetrate the roots of a plant and expand into the stem, plugging the water-conducting vessels. Both of these fungi are long-lived, remaining in the soil for years after the host plant has died. Fusarium is favored by warm soil and is a major problem in the South. Verticillium is more prominent in cooler soils.

If either disease is present in your soil, plant resistant varieties of seeds (look for seed packets labeled VF resistant), or use soil solarization (see page 273) or fumigation to kill the fungi.

Water molds

These are a class of fungi that thrive in wet, poorly drained soils, particularly in constantly watered lawns and flower beds. The fungi are most active in warm (55° to 80° F) soils. They cause plant leaves to become dull and individual branches or entire plants to wilt, turn yellow, and die. Gardeners often mistake these symptoms for drought damage and apply even more water in an attempt to correct the problem. This only worsens the situation.

Remove badly infected plants, but try to save partially infected plants by drying out the soil. While the soil is drying out, reduce the water needs of the plants by shading them or applying an antitranspirant, available at nurseries and garden centers. Afterward, discourage the fungi by watering plants thoroughly but infrequently. Improve poor drainage (see page 101), or plant in raised beds.

Leaf, Stem, and Flower Diseases

These make up the majority of plant diseases. In many cases, plants are attacked by fungal spores, bacteria, or viruses carried by wind, insects, or splashing water. Several of the most common infectious diseases along with methods of control are described here.

Botrytis blight
This fungus disease is also known as gray mold, blossom blight, flower blight, and bud blight. Brown spots and blotches grow on plant leaves, flow-

ers, or fruit. Brown or gray mold often appears on affected tissue. The disease thrives in high humidity and cool temperatures. It infects a wide range of plants, especially soft fruits such as strawberries and grapes. Botrytis spores are present in most soils.

Prevent the spread of infection by discarding dead leaves and flowers. Improve air circulation around plants and keep the leaves dry. When irrigating, apply water at the soil level rather than by overhead spraying. Fungicides may be helpful in controlling the disease; make sure that your plant is listed on the label.

Fire blight   A bacterial disease that attacks plants in the rose family, fire blight can be recognized by a sudden wilting and blackening of stems, flowers, and fruit. The

damaged parts look as though they were scorched by fire. The bacterial infection may move down a shoot and into the bark of larger branches, where dark cankers are formed. Pear and quince are particularly susceptible to fire blight. Apple and crab apple (*Malus* species), and firethorn (*Pyracantha* species) are frequently affected as well.

The bacteria thrive in warm, wet weather. In regions with dry summers, the disease occurs during spring. In regions with humid summers, it is active throughout the growing season. Rainwater and overhead sprinkling splash the bacteria on plant parts, and bees also carry the bacteria as they pollinate plants.

Since blossoms are the most vulnerable part of a plant, protect them from infection by spraying with streptomycin or a copper-containing material weekly as the buds gradually open and bloom. Cut down on nitrogen fertilizer, because succulent growth is also susceptible to infection. As soon as you notice any fire blight, prune off and dispose of the diseased plant parts at least 6 inches below the visible infection. Sterilize the pruning tool in rubbing alcohol after each cut to prevent further infection.

Leaf spot   Most leaf spot diseases are caused by fungi, but a few are caused by bacteria. Generally, bacterial leaf spot is angular and is stopped by veins, whereas fungal leaf

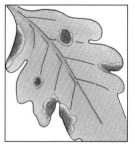

spot is round and crosses veins. The bacteria are carried in drops of water that may be spread from plant to plant in splashing rain or by insects or gardeners working among wet plants. Fungal spores are carried in drops of water or by wind. The bacteria or fungi infect a leaf where they come in contact with it. Each spot or blotch is made by a new infection. All leaves on a plant may be affected. Leaf spot is most commonly seen in regions that receive regular summer rain.

Spray with a fungicide recommended for use on your plant. The fungicide won't cure infected leaves, but it will protect healthy leaves. Reapply the fungicide when new growth appears on the plant or when the previous application is washed off by rain or irrigation. Remove and destroy severely infected leaves. Keep the leaves as dry as possible, and try to avoid misting or watering the plants from overhead.

Mosaic viruses

This group of viruses causes yellow and green mottling, blotching, or streaking on leaves, flowers, or fruit. Plants affected by mosaic viruses grow slowly. Beans, corn, cucumbers, peppers, dahlias, delphiniums, and petunias are particularly susceptible to the disease. Aphids transmit some mosaic viruses from plant to plant, and gardeners handling wet plants can also spread viruses. If you smoke, you may spread tobacco mosaic virus unless you wash your hands thoroughly before handling plants.

There is no cure for mosaic viruses. Prevent infection by controlling aphids (see page 286) and removing weeds that may be hosts to the insect. Many plants can tolerate virus diseases without being severely harmed. Destroy badly damaged plants. Do not compost diseased plants.

Peach leaf curl

This fungus disease causes peach, nectarine, and almond leaves to thicken, curl, and blister. The leaves turn orange or red and fall prematurely. Peach leaf curl occurs in spring as new leaves appear on the tree. The new growth is infected by fungal spores, which overwinter on the bark and buds of the tree.

Once damaged leaves appear in spring, it's too late to do anything about the disease that season. During the next dormant season, spray the trees thoroughly with a copper-containing or lime-sulfur solution as soon as the leaves fall. If leaf curl has been severe in the past, reapply the fungicide just before the buds open in spring.

Powdery mildew

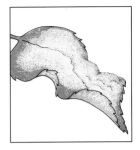

This disease, which can be caused by several different fungi, affects a wide range of plants. The fungal spores are spread throughout the garden on air currents. The mildew appears as a thin layer or irregular patches of a white or grayish powdery material on leaves, stems, or flowers. Infected leaves may turn yellowish or reddish and drop. Powdery mildew is the only leaf disease that is active in dry weather, although it is more severe in damp weather. Plants growing in shady areas may become severely infected.

Use fungicides to control powdery mildew. When the fungus is killed, the mildew disappears. Provide for adequate sunlight and air circulation for particularly susceptible plants, such as lilac (*Syringa* species), rose (*Rosa* species), squash, and cucumber. Since moisture on the leaves encourages mildew, avoid sprinkling the leaves.

Rusts

Rusts There are many different fungi that cause rusts; although collectively they infect a wide range of plants, each fungus usually infects only one or two plant species. Some rusts, such as cedar-apple rust, survive only if they alternate between two specific host plants. In all cases, the fungal spores are spread by wind and splashing water. The rust-colored or brown powdery pustules characteristic of the disease are the actual fungal spores; they live on the underside of leaves or on stems or fruit. The disease may cause premature dropping of leaves or fruit.

Use fungicides to control rusts. Be sure that the label lists your plant. Prune off and dispose of badly damaged plant parts. Keep the leaves dry to reduce the chance of infection. Fertilize to help plants overcome rust damage. An infected lawn grows faster when it is fertilized, and mowing removes the rusted portion of the grass blades.

PLANT PROBLEM CHECKLIST

Use this checklist to develop a case history for each plant problem and to identify symptoms that will lead to an accurate diagnosis. Answer each question that pertains to your plant. When looking for symptoms and answering questions about the plant, begin with the leaves, flowers, or fruit (unless it is apparent that the problem is elsewhere), because they are the easiest to examine. Move down the plant to the stems or branches and trunk. Inspect the roots to see if they are healthy and if they are being adequately watered.

INFORMATION ABOUT THE PLANT

Type of plant
- [ ] What type of plant is it?
- [ ] Does it prefer moist or dry conditions?
- [ ] Can it tolerate cold or does it grow best in a warm climate?
- [ ] Does it grow best in acid or alkaline soil?

Age
- [ ] Is the plant young and tender or old and in a state of decline?

Size
- [ ] Is the plant abnormally small for its age?
- [ ] How much has the plant grown in the last few years?
- [ ] Is the size of the trunk or stem in proportion to the number of branches?

Time in present site
- [ ] Was the plant recently transplanted?
- [ ] Is the plant much older than the housing development or buildings nearby?

Symptom development
- [ ] When were the symptoms first noticed?
- [ ] Have symptoms been developing for a long period of time, or have they appeared suddenly?
- [ ] Have the symptoms appeared in past years?

Condition of plant
- [ ] Is the entire plant affected, is the problem found on only one side of the plant, or are symptoms scattered throughout the plant?
- [ ] What parts of the plant are affected?
- [ ] Are all the leaves affected or only the leaves on a few branches?
- [ ] Are the leaves abnormal in size, color, shape, or texture?
- [ ] Are the flowers and fruit abnormal in any way?
- [ ] Are there any abnormal growths, discolorations, or injuries on the branches, stems, or trunk?
- [ ] Is there anything wrapped tightly around the plant or nailed into the wood?
- [ ] Does the trunk have a normal flare at the base, or does it enter the ground straight like a pole?
- [ ] Are the roots white and healthy, or are they discolored?
- [ ] Have the roots remained in the soil ball, or have they grown into the surrounding soil?
- [ ] Are there insects on the plant, or is there evidence of insects, such as holes, droppings, sap, or sawdust?
- [ ] What other symptoms are visible on the plant?

PLANT ENVIRONMENT

Location
- [ ] Is the property near a large body of fresh or salt water?
- [ ] Is the property downwind from a factory, or is it in a large polluted urban area?
- [ ] Is the property part of a new housing development that was built on landfill?
- [ ] Is the plant growing next to a building? If so, is the location sunny or shady? Is the wall light colored? How intense is the reflected light?

PLANT PROBLEM CHECKLIST

PLANT ENVIRONMENT (*Continued*)

Location
- [ ] Has there been any construction, trenching, or grade change nearby within the past several years?
- [ ] How close is the plant to a road? Is the road de-iced in winter?
- [ ] Is the plant growing over or near a gas, water, or sewer line, or next to power lines?
- [ ] Is the ground sloping or level?

Relationship to other plants
- [ ] Are there large shade trees overhead?
- [ ] Is the plant growing in a lawn or ground cover?
- [ ] Are there plants growing nearby that are also affected? Do the same species show similar symptoms?

Weather
- [ ] Have you had unusual weather (cold, hot, dry, wet, windy, snowy, etc.) recently or in the past few years?

Microclimate
- [ ] What are the weather conditions in the immediate vicinity of the plant?
- [ ] Is the plant growing under something that prevents it from receiving moisture?
- [ ] How windy is the location?
- [ ] How much light does the plant receive? Is it the optimum amount for the type of plant?

Soil
- [ ] What kind of soil is the plant growing in—clay, sand, or loam?
- [ ] How deep is the soil? Is there a layer of rock or a soil pan beneath the topsoil?
- [ ] What is the pH of the soil?
- [ ] Does the soil drain well? Does the soil have a sour smell?
- [ ] Is the soil hard and compacted?
- [ ] Has the soil eroded away from the roots?

Soil coverings
- [ ] Is there asphalt, concrete, or other solid surface covering the soil around the plant? How close is it to the base of the plant?
- [ ] Has the soil surface been mulched? What is the mulch material? Was it obtained from a reputable dealer?
- [ ] Are weeds or grass growing around the base of the plant? How thickly?

Recent care
- [ ] Has the plant or surrounding plants been watered or fertilized recently?
- [ ] If fertilizer was used, was it applied according to label directions?
- [ ] Has the plant been pruned heavily, exposing shaded areas to full sun?
- [ ] Were stumps left after pruning, or was the bark damaged during the pruning process?
- [ ] Has the plant or the area been treated with a fungicide or an insecticide? Which product?
- [ ] Was the treatment for the current problem or another one?
- [ ] Was the plant listed on the pesticide label?
- [ ] Was the pesticide applied according to label directions?
- [ ] Did it rain right after the pesticide was applied?
- [ ] Did you repeat the pesticide application if the label suggested it?
- [ ] Have weed killers or lawn weed and feed products been used in the area in the past year? How close by?
- [ ] Did you spray the weed killer on a windy day?

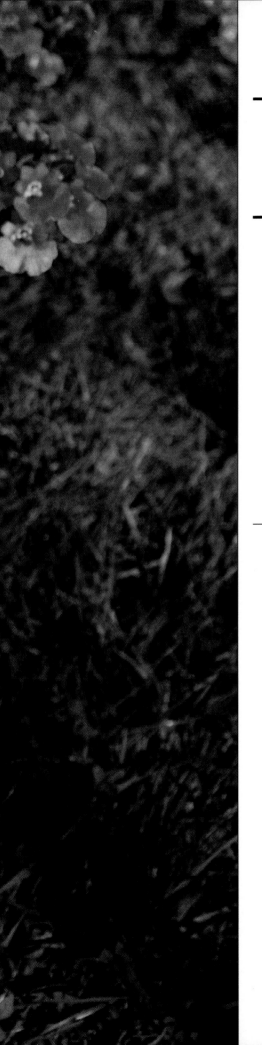

USING PESTICIDES

Keep in mind that pesticides are only one of several controls for garden pests. They are part of an integrated approach that includes such measures as keeping the garden clean, using good growing practices, planting resistant varieties, and excluding pests by physical means. (Refer to the chapters on "Controlling Weeds," "Controlling Insect and Animal Pests," and "Controlling Plant Diseases.") The first step in handling pesticides responsibly is to use them only when the problem warrants action and the pest can't be controlled just as well by other means.

The three most common types of pesticides used by home gardeners are insecticides (for killing insects), herbicides (for killing weeds), and fungicides (for controlling fungus diseases). Within each pesticide group are chemicals that work in different ways and solve different kinds of pest problems. Often there are several pesticides that will solve a particular pest problem. Your choice will usually depend on the plant or part of the garden on which the pesticide will be used, or it may depend on the formulation—whether the chemical is in liquid, dust, or granular form. If you are unsure of the right pesticide for the job, discuss the problem with a professional.

Garden chemicals can solve many pest problems, but they should be used only when necessary and with the understanding that they can be harmful if misused or handled carelessly.

The label on the pesticide container is your best guide to the safe and effective use of the chemical. Always read the label carefully and apply the pesticide exactly as directed. When using pesticides you should apply the right kind of chemical in the right amount with the right equipment.

Dusts often come in ready-to-use squeeze containers. Read the instructions carefully, then squeeze out a fine cloud of dust.

Applying Pesticides Properly

Pesticides must be applied correctly if they are to be effective. Choose a calm day when the temperature is moderate and no rain is expected for 12 hours. Early morning is often the best time. Remove toys, garden furniture, and other objects from the area that you intend to treat, and keep children and pets away. Wear protective clothing when applying pesticides (see Application Precautions on page 317).

Labels on pesticides sold for home garden use include clear instructions on how to apply them. There are also directions for mixing the product if it requires dilution. Because some pests are more difficult to kill than others, the dilution rate will differ depending on the pest you wish to control. Pay close attention to the mixing instructions—too little pesticide may not knock out the pests, but a double dose will not be twice as effective. If you use too strong a mixture, you may injure the plants you are treating.

Thorough coverage is half the battle in applying pesticides. When spraying or dusting plants, be sure to cover all plant surfaces, including the undersides of leaves and all sides of stems and twigs. It is particularly important to cover the lower surfaces of the leaves, because this is where many insects and disease organisms are found. To reach these areas rotate the nozzle of your sprayer or duster upward and hold the wand low while you treat the plant.

With most pesticide sprays, the label instructs you to spray to drip point or to wet thoroughly. This means to spray until the mixture begins dripping off the plant. Unless you let the spray dry and then spray again, you usually won't apply too much. To achieve thorough coverage, spray the foliage from two or three different directions and from below and above. When the excess spray begins dripping off the plant onto the ground, stop spraying.

Never spray a plant that is suffering from a lack of moisture. Water deeply and thoroughly a day before spraying. Avoid spraying altogether if the air temperature is above 85° F. In hot weather some chemical formulations may burn the foliage. Also avoid spraying if it is windy, since it will be difficult to contain the spray and keep it from drifting to areas where it is not wanted. If there is even a slight breeze, stand with the wind at your back to avoid having the mist drift back on you.

Spraying Trees

You need the proper equipment, such as a powerful backpack sprayer, to spray a large tree; otherwise, you won't be able to penetrate the thick foliage or reach the top of the tree. If your water pressure is very high, a hose-end sprayer may do the job. Before you try to spray a tree, test your equipment with plain water to be sure that it's powerful enough to propel the pesticide to the top. If you don't have the right equipment, you may have to call in a licensed pesticide professional to do the job.

If you are able to handle the job yourself, stand far enough away from the tree so that the spray drift settles on the ground, not on you. When you spray trees near a house or wall, anticipate that the spray may bounce back, so aim the stream away from large, solid obstacles. Controlling drift when spraying trees can be especially difficult; do not spray unless the air is completely still.

Adjust the sprayer nozzle so that it tilts upward to reach the undersides of the leaves; the runoff will wet the upper surfaces of the leaves below. Start spraying at the top of the tree and work downward, zigzagging from side to side as you walk in a circle around the tree. Use as much pressure as possible so that the spray hits the trunk and branches.

Pesticide Safety Rules

☐ Keep chemicals locked up, beyond the reach of children.
☐ Keep chemicals in their original bottle or can, never in an old food container.
☐ When finished with a pesticide container, dispose of it according to the instructions on the label and the regulations in your local community.
☐ Mix chemicals outdoors in a well-ventilated area with adequate light.
☐ Wash the applicator thoroughly after use.
☐ Wash your hands after using pesticides, and shower if the spray drifted. Launder sprayed clothes.

When spraying a tree, the equipment you use should propel the spray to the top of the tree. If using a hose-end sprayer, good water pressure is important.

Applying Oil Sprays

Horticultural oils control many insect pests and disease organisms that overwinter on the buds, twigs, and bark of trees and shrubs. Dormant oils, so named because they are meant to be applied during a plant's dormant season, work best when applied in late winter or early spring, just before the buds open. Most labels recommend only one application per season. A few plants are very sensitive to oil sprays, so check the label to make sure that the oil can be applied safely.

On certain plants you can apply a more dilute oil spray during late spring and summer, when the leaves are mature or almost fully grown. If used too early in the season, oil can burn new growth. The label may provide directions for combining the oil with other pesticides for more effective control.

Spray summer oil until the oil completely wets the plant and the spray runs off onto the ground. It is important to cover both the upper and lower surfaces of leaves as well as to reach the trunk and small branches. You cannot overapply oil unless you spray again after the first spray dries. You may injure plants if you apply the oil when the temperature is lower than 40° F or higher than 85° F or if the humidity exceeds 90 percent.

SAFETY MEASURES

Pesticides, like medicines, work safely and effectively when used properly, but they can be dangerous if used without caution or in a way that is not intended. By acting as if the pesticide poses more danger than it does, chances are you will be properly cautious when handling the chemical.

Reading the Label

The first rule in the safe and effective use of pesticides is *read the label*. You should read it five separate times: before purchasing the product, before mixing it, before applying it, before storing it, and finally before disposing of any excess or the empty container.

The product label is the basic source of detailed information about a pesticide. Read carefully to make sure that the product is designed to treat the pests and plants you have in mind. The label directions explain how to use the product so that it performs as the manufacturer intended. The directions may call for restricting the product to certain areas of the garden; for example, the product may be limited to use in a vegetable garden. The label may also include a list of pests the product will control or a list of plants to which the pesticide may be safely applied.

The rest of the label has additional directions for safe and effective use, such as avoiding unfavorable weather conditions or special precautions for very sensitive plants. It also provides the proper application rate for the area to be treated. The best time for treatment and directions for repeat applications are also given.

The Environmental Protection Agency (EPA) requires that the front panel of the pesticide label carry a signal word in large letters to alert the user to any potential hazard. The signal words are *caution*, meaning that the product is slightly toxic; *warning*, meaning that it is moderately toxic; and *danger*, meaning that it is highly toxic and extra care should be taken when using it anywhere around the home or garden.

Most pesticides for home use rate a caution or warning. Sometimes the chemical concentration in the product helps determine which signal word appears on the label. For example, a ready-to-use product might be labeled *caution*, whereas a concentrated version of the same product that requires dilution might state *warning*.

Mixing Precautions

Always wear gloves when diluting or mixing chemicals. Unlined rubber gloves work best, as long as you are not tempted to wear them later for other household chores. Never wear leather or cotton gloves when handling pesticides, because they could absorb any harmful chemicals with which they come into contact.

To prevent spills and splashes, handle containers slowly and carefully, placing the container on a solid surface every time you set it down. Measure precisely for the best results. Purchase separate sets of measuring spoons and cups for pesticide use, and mark them *for pesticide use only* in indelible ink. Never use utensils that you intend to use when cooking or that have been previously used for cooking (to avoid someone accidentally reusing them for food after they have been used for pesticides).

Measure all pesticides outdoors on level ground or on a low wall or step, not on your picnic table or other eating surface. Rinse off measuring spoons and utensils with a garden hose in an out-of-the-way place, never in the kitchen sink.

When mixing chemicals, always place the container and sprayer on a solid surface.

Application Precautions

Protect yourself when applying a pesticide spray or dust. Along with unlined rubber gloves, you may want to wear a long-sleeved shirt, long pants, socks, rubber boots, and a brimmed, nonabsorbent hat. Check the product label to see whether these or other protective garments are recommended. Never smoke when handling or applying pesticides.

Be careful that the spray or dust does not drift where it isn't wanted. Never spray or apply a dust when there is a wind blowing. If there is a slight breeze, stand with the wind at your back to avoid spray mist or dust blowing onto your skin.

After you finish applying the pesticide, set aside your work clothes for laundering. (Do not wash them with other garments.) Shower or wash exposed skin with soap and hot water as soon as possible, and certainly before eating or smoking.

Keep everyone, including pets, away from newly sprayed areas until the spray dries. This may take just a few hours or as long as 24 hours, especially if a lawn has been sprayed. After dusting, wait several hours to be certain that airborne dust particles have settled.

Safe Storage

It is best to purchase only the amount of pesticide you will use in one season. Store all pesticide containers, sprayers, and measuring equipment out of direct sunlight in a dry, well-ventilated place. A locked cabinet is ideal if you have young children. Keep all pesticide containers well away from pilot lights and other open flames or sparks, because the fumes can be flammable. Never store food, beverage, or eating utensils with pesticides. Check pesticide containers regularly for corrosion and leaks.

Never store an undiluted pesticide in a container other than the one it came in, with the original label intact. A pesticide stored in a food container, especially a soft drink bottle, is an accident waiting to happen. When storing pesticides on a shelf, keep the labels plainly visible, and make certain that the container caps are tight.

Safe Disposal

Try to mix only the amount of pesticide you need for each application. If you mix too much spray solution, do not try to save it. During storage the diluted pesticide breaks down into an ineffective product, or it evaporates

and becomes more concentrated. A pesticide stored in a metal sprayer may corrode it. The safest way to use extra solution is to apply it to other affected plants listed on the label. Never pour diluted or undiluted pesticides down the drain or sewer.

When you have used up a container of pesticide, check the label for disposal instructions. In general, it is acceptable to wrap the container in paper and place it in the garbage can after making sure that the container is empty and rinsed it out thoroughly with water. If there are any special rules for pesticide disposal in your area, abide by them.

In Case of Accident

Pesticide poisoning can result from skin exposure, inhalation, or ingestion. If you become ill soon after handling a pesticide, don't take any chances; seek medical attention immediately.

Safe storage of pesticides and other garden chemicals is extremely important.

If any pesticide accidentally splashes on your skin, wash it off right away with detergent and water. If a pesticide splashes into your eyes, flush them immediately with running water while someone calls your doctor or the hospital emergency room. Continue cleansing your eyes for 15 minutes, then seek medical treatment if you are advised to do so. Should you spill any pesticide on your clothing, change as soon as possible and wash the clothing before wearing it again. Do not keep or wash contaminated clothing with any other garments.

If you spill a liquid pesticide indoors or on a deck, ventilate the area with an exhaust fan. Then, wearing protective clothing, absorb the spill with cat litter or old rags, discard the material in a sealed bag, and place it in the garbage. Scrub the floor or deck with strong detergent. Never smoke or strike a match around spills, because the fumes may catch fire.

Most accidents and poisonings occur when pesticides are handled carelessly. Avoid problems by following all the safety measures discussed above.

A hose-end sprayer is an easy way to apply insecticides and fungicides.

CHOOSING THE RIGHT EQUIPMENT

The job of controlling pests is easier when you have the right equipment. This doesn't mean that the equipment has to be expensive or elaborate, but it should equal the task. The simplest equipment is the pesticide container itself; you can purchase ready-to-use sprays in aerosol cans or trigger sprayers, and dusts in squeeze canisters. These are useful for small problems; for larger problems or extensive plantings, you should have your own application equipment. Of the following equipment, the types used most commonly by home gardeners are hose-end sprayers, tank-type compression sprayers, and fertilizer spreaders.

Hose-End Sprayers

Many home gardeners rely on a hose-end sprayer for applying insecticides and fungicides. Inexpensive and easy to use, the sprayer consists of a glass or plastic jar with a nozzle that screws onto a garden hose. You place diluted pesticide in the jar, then the nozzle further dilutes the mixture with water

as you spray. Most hose-end sprayers have a fixed mixing ratio built into the nozzle. Some hose-end sprayers come with a dial on top so that you can adjust the ratio. With these, you place undiluted concentrate in the jar, and the nozzle dilutes the pesticide automatically according to the dial adjustment.

When choosing a hose-end sprayer, select one with a versatile nozzle. One that can vary from a fine mist to a strong stream is desirable: That way you can use the same sprayer for different kinds of garden plants. Some special features to look for when buying a hose-end sprayer include a control valve with an instant on-and-off feature and a thumb slide that locks the sprayer in the *on* position. These features allow you to spray continuously while maintaining control over the operation.

It is important that your hose-end connector have an antisiphon device, to prevent any spray material from being sucked back down the hose and into the water line if the water pressure should drop.

For treating individual plants in the garden or houseplants in containers, a trigger sprayer is useful and inexpensive.

Hand-Held Sprayers

A hand-held trigger sprayer—the type often used for misting houseplants—is a useful and inexpensive sprayer for delicate garden plants. A large sprayer holds about a quart of liquid; after diluting the pesticide according to label directions, all you need to do is point the nozzle and squeeze the trigger. Buy a trigger sprayer with an adjustable nozzle so that you can vary the spray from a fine mist to a stream.

Trigger sprayers are best for treating individual plants; if a lot of foliage must be covered, your hand will become fatigued. A trigger sprayer doesn't work well when held upside down, so spraying the undersides of leaves is difficult. Because the spray emitted from a trigger sprayer does not reach very far, you will probably use it only for close-up problems.

Tank-Type Compression Sprayers

Tank sprayers are easy to use and provide much more precise application control than hose-end sprayers. Versatile and portable, these sprayers are often used by professional pesticide applicators. Home versions are usually available in capacities of 1 to 3 gallons. The tanks are made of chemical-resistant plastic or metal, and they have wide mouths for easy and safe filling.

Tank sprayers require little pumping action. You initially pump air into the container to build up the pressure, but then you need only squeeze the trigger to apply the spray. The trigger is attached to a long wand at the end of a flexible hose. You can usually adjust the nozzle at the tip of the wand to deliver a fine mist or a strong stream. Larger tank sprayers used by licensed applicators have 15- to 30-foot streams for reaching treetops. Tank sprayers for home gardens aren't nearly as powerful; fill your tank with water to test how far the stream will travel.

Following the directions on the pesticide label, mix the proper ratio of chemical and water directly in the tank. Secure the top tightly, then pump air into the tank until pressure builds up and pumping becomes difficult. To apply the spray, simply aim the wand and press the trigger. A valve inside

Versatile and portable, tank sprayers are easy to use and provide more precise application control than hose-end sprayers.

the nozzle will open, and compressed air will force the liquid out through the nozzle. You may have to pump air into the tank again halfway through the spraying process to restore the pressure.

Dusters

To apply fungicidal and insecticidal dusts, use a good duster, which emits a fine cloud of dust with each stroke of the pump. A duster with a nozzle that adjusts up and down offers you the most control and the best coverage.

A small plunger duster that holds about a pint of dust works well for small jobs. To dispense the dust, hold the container in one hand and draw the pump back and forth with the other.

Rotary hand dusters, sometimes called crank dusters, provide excellent coverage in large areas and on shrubs and small trees. Rotary dusters produce a steady stream of dust when you turn the crank. They require one hand to hold the container and the other to turn the handle.

This tank-sprayer nozzle is adjusted for a fine mist.

This tank-sprayer nozzle is adjusted for a strong stream.

A plunger duster that emits a fine cloud is used for applying fungicidal and insecticidal dusts.

Spreaders

Dry, granular pesticides for treating lawns can usually be applied with a spreader—the same one you use for fertilizer applications. A drop spreader provides the greatest control, because the granules drop straight down through a slot in the bottom of the spreader. Adjustments on the bottom of the hopper calibrate the amount of pesticide that falls to the lawn while you walk at a steady pace.

A wheeled broadcast spreader has a rotating wheel that throws the hopper contents outward in a wide arc, usually 8 to 12 feet. However, more material falls in the middle of the arc than at the edge. Proper overlapping of arcs is essential for even distribution of the pesticide. A broadcast spreader works well on large lawns; it may throw granules in too wide a pattern for small areas.

A hand-held broadcast spreader is useful in distributing granules over a small lawn or on a ground cover planting or other rough-surface area. You operate the spreader by turning a crank to disperse the contents. Reduce the width of the arc by rotating the crank in the reverse direction.

A handheld broadcast spreader can be used to apply granular pesticides to lawns and ground covers.

MAINTAINING EQUIPMENT

Although your sprayer or duster may be sturdily built, it will perform optimally only when properly maintained. Every piece of pesticide equipment comes with a label or an instruction booklet detailing the equipment's proper use and care. Read the instructions carefully; then hang them on a wall or shelf near where you plan to store the equipment.

Dusters are easy to maintain. While dusting, occasionally tap the deflector at the tube end to prevent dust buildup. Keep the duster clean by tapping out accumulated dust. Lubricate all moving parts with graphite, not oil; graphite provides lubrication without causing dust to adhere.

Spreaders are also fairly simple to maintain. After every use, clean your spreader by hosing the inside of the hopper and leaving it in the sun to dry before putting it away. When exposed to air, fertilizer and insecticide residues can cake, becoming cementlike and difficult to remove. Keep moving parts lubricated with oil.

Maintaining sprayers usually requires a little more vigilance on the part of gardeners. Most sprayer problems begin when foreign material clogs the nozzle. Clean your sprayer—even a new one—before each use. While using the sprayer, check every so often to see whether any dirt, sand, or grass has clogged the nozzle. Never attempt to clean a nozzle by poking in anything other than the cleaning pin that accompanies the sprayer. Otherwise, you may widen the nozzle and alter the spray pattern. If a nozzle seems plugged, back-flush it with air or water. A hot-water soak will dissolve some stubborn deposits. Never insert the nozzle in your mouth and blow through it. Even if it has been cleaned, pesticide residue may still be clinging to it.

Each time you finish applying spray, wash the sprayer inside and out to prevent corrosion and pesticide accumulation. Without thorough washing, some pesticide residue persists for months or even years. The next time you use the sprayer, the residue may damage plants that are sensitive to that particular pesticide.

After you finish cleaning a tank sprayer, hang it upside down or set it upside down on

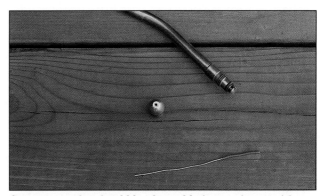

Sprayer nozzles should be cleaned before each use with a cleaning pin.

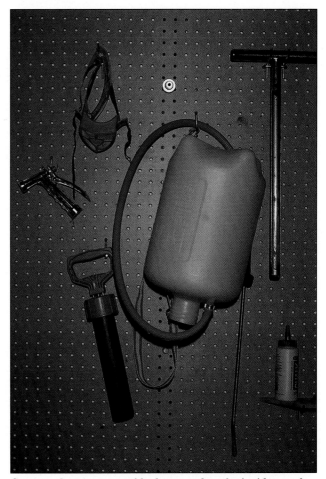

Store tank sprayers upside down so that the inside can dry. Hang the wand on a hook so that it will drain.

a shelf with a wedge beneath the canister so that it can drain and dry completely. Upside-down storage also keeps dust from settling inside the tank.

You may need to lubricate the moving parts of tank sprayers occasionally. Gaskets and pumps made of neoprene rubber or leather also require lubricating.

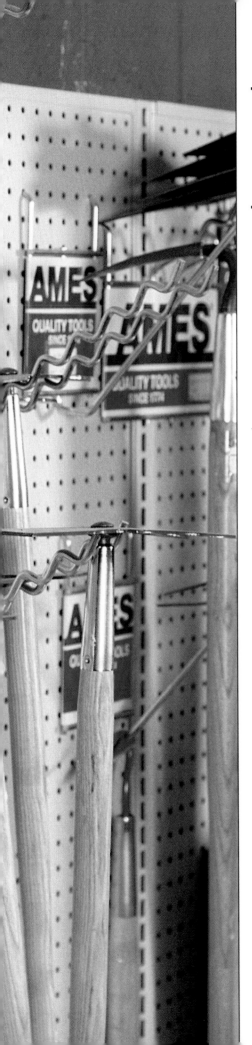

SELECTING GARDEN TOOLS

Planting and properly caring for a garden requires the right tools. They should be appropriate for the task and kept in good condition so that they work efficiently. Well-made tools that do the job they are designed for are a pleasure to use. With good tools, you are more likely to tend to gardening tasks as they come up instead of putting them off.

Before buying a tool, always handle it to make sure that it's the right size and weight for you. If the tool doesn't feel right, don't buy it. In the long run, it's more economical to invest in good-quality, well-constructed tools rather than have to replace cheaper, flimsy tools.

Good-quality tools have steel blades that are treated with heat for extra strength. Look for a die stamp on the tool, which indicates that the steel has been forged, tempered, or heat-treated. The handle may be made of wood, steel, aluminum, or plastic. A good-quality wooden handle is flexible, strong, and durable; beware of painted wood, since paint is often used to hide inferior wood. Look for a strong attachment between the handle and blade. Some tools are constructed entirely of steel, with the blade and handle a single unit. This is not necessarily the strongest tool; a tool that is securely riveted or welded together will also withstand a great deal of stress.

For some gardening jobs, hand tools are all that is available. Other chores can be done with either hand or power tools. Power tools are useful when there is a large area to cover or when the job is particularly arduous or tedious.

Before buying any tool, manual or powered, consider whether your use of it will justify the cost and the space you must allot for storage.

A wide variety of garden tools can be purchased at retail garden centers.

SHOVELS AND SPADES

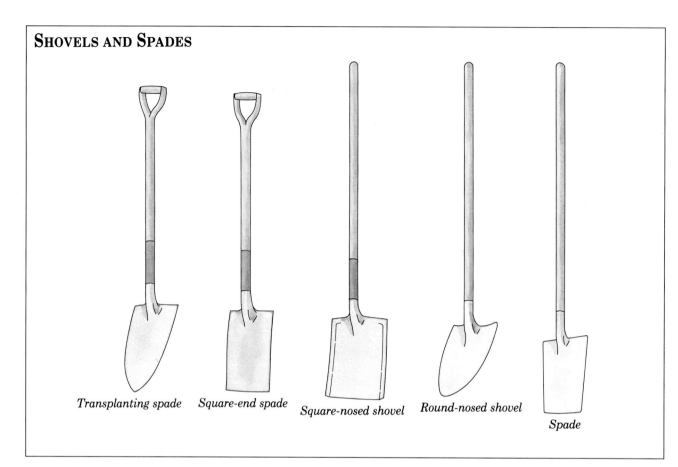

Transplanting spade   *Square-end spade*   *Square-nosed shovel*   *Round-nosed shovel*   *Spade*

BASIC GARDEN TOOLS

If you have a very small, simple garden, you may be able to get by with only a few basic tools for cultivating, planting, and weeding. More extensive yards, formal landscapes, and large areas of lawn may require a shed full of tools.

Shovels and Spades

These digging implements come in many styles, each designed for a different use in the garden. Shovels are available in various sizes, with a round or square blade end and a straight or D-shaped handle. Shovels with a round or a pointed blade are used for digging; those with a square end are used for scooping.

For most gardeners, the first tool to buy is an all-purpose round-nosed shovel. The angle between the wood handle and the blade is important. The more pronounced the angle, the greater the leverage when scooping heavy soil. A straighter angle makes it easier to dig deep into the soil. A long, straight handle allows you to stand more erect, which

lessens back strain. A shorter D-shaped handle is useful when you are working in close quarters.

As you gain experience gardening, you may decide to buy a spade. The most common type is a square-end spade. Unlike the square-nosed shovel, whose function is scooping, the square-end spade is designed for digging. It is useful for turning heavy soil, double-digging (see page 98), and making straight-sided holes. You are unlikely to need a transplanting spade, which has an elongated, pointed blade for reaching under the rootball of a plant.

Some spades are equipped with a tread, a thin metal plate welded to the top of the blade. Treads relieve stress on the bottom of the foot when you step on the spade to force it into the ground. Like shovels, spades come with straight or D-shaped handles.

Garden Forks

A garden fork, or a spading fork, can be handy for digging up plants, cultivating loose soil, and turning a compost pile. If you have a large perennial garden, you may find

Hoes and Rakes

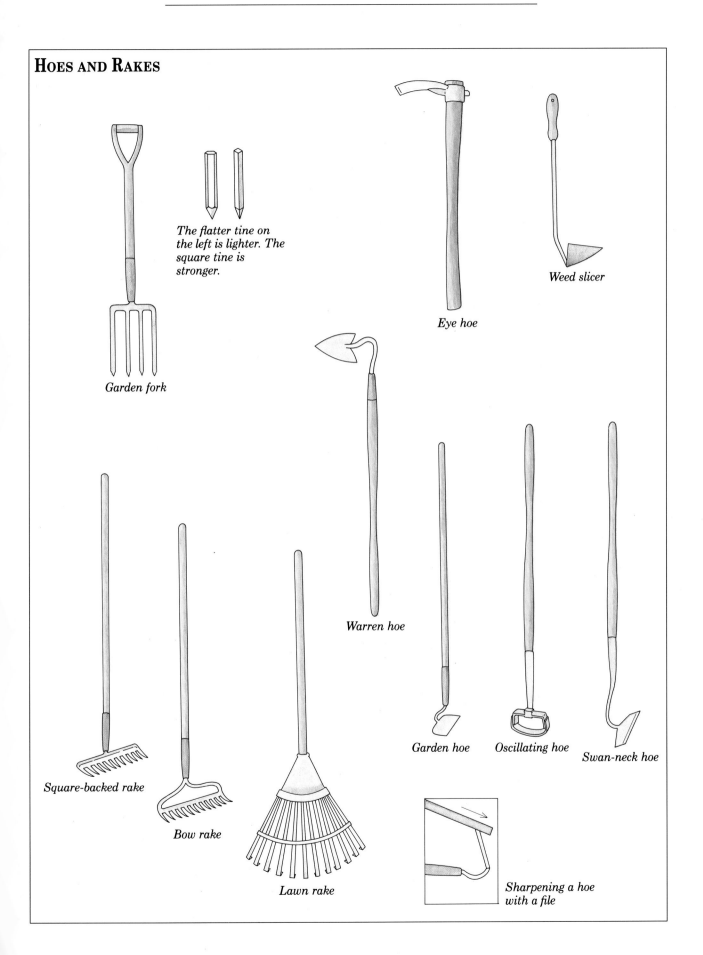

The flatter tine on the left is lighter. The square tine is stronger.

Eye hoe

Weed slicer

Garden fork

Warren hoe

Garden hoe

Oscillating hoe

Swan-neck hoe

Square-backed rake

Bow rake

Lawn rake

Sharpening a hoe with a file

a garden fork—in fact, two garden forks positioned back to back—invaluable in dividing plants (see the illustration on page 344).

The tines and base of the sturdier forks are made as a single cast-iron unit. Square-tined English spading forks are heavier and sturdier than flat-tined forks, which sometimes bend out of shape under the stress of working in heavy soil. Like spades and shovels, garden forks are available with long, straight handles or short, D-shaped handles.

You can also buy a small, hand-held garden fork for cultivating and weeding small areas. The hand fork is especially useful in digging down under the root mass of an established weed.

Hoes

Not only is a hoe effective in breaking up clods of soil, it is one of the best tools for controlling weeds. It enables you to cut weeds off near the surface without going deeper and without cutting the roots of desirable plants. A hoe works most efficiently when you hold it fairly upright and make shallow swipes through the top of the soil. This chops up weed seedlings but does not disturb the soil enough to bring more seeds to the soil surface, where they can germinate.

There are different types of hoes, including the conventional garden hoe, swan-neck hoe, warren hoe, oscillating hoe, and eye hoe. A conventional garden hoe serves the needs of most gardeners nicely. A swan-neck hoe has a curved neck that makes it easier to hold the hoe blade parallel to the ground. A warren hoe has a pointed tip designed for making shallow furrows or cultivating between plants. An oscillating hoe, a variation of the scuffle hoe, has a movable blade that changes to the correct angle as you change direction. An eye hoe, with a wide blade similar to that of a pick mattock, is useful for chopping into hard soil or cutting roots. Some hoes are also available in small, hand-held versions.

Since a hoe is essentially a cutting tool, it works best if kept sharp. Sharpen it as often as after every couple of hours of use, especially in stony soil. To sharpen a hoe, file the blade at a 45-degree angle, then smooth the back by rubbing the file flat across it to take off any burs.

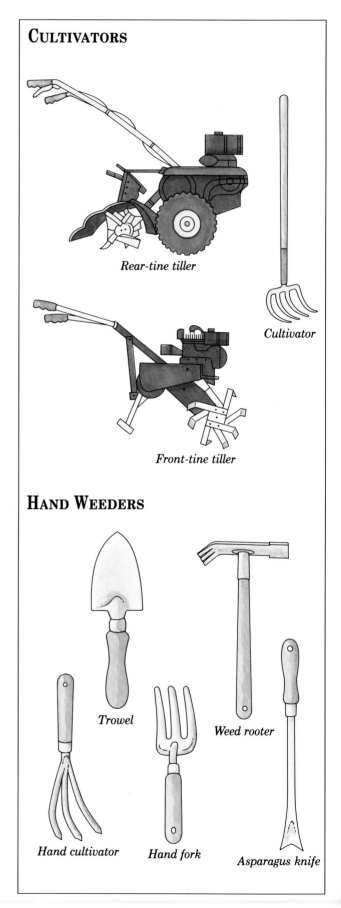

CULTIVATORS

Rear-tine tiller

Cultivator

Front-tine tiller

HAND WEEDERS

Trowel

Weed rooter

Hand cultivator

Hand fork

Asparagus knife

Rakes

There are two basic types of rakes: garden rakes and lawn rakes. Garden rakes have short, rigid tines and are used for leveling and spreading soil and for preparing seedbeds. In the process, they also pull out weeds. Garden rakes may be either square backed or bow. The bow rake is the slightly heavier and sturdier of the two. Turn over either type to use the back for finishing off a seedbed.

Lawn, or leaf, rakes have long, flexible tines of wood or steel and are used for garden cleanup and for raking leaves and lawn clippings.

Cultivators

A cultivator is a pronged tool used for light cultivation in well-tilled soil. It also helps break up clods after you have turned over the soil with a spade or a garden fork. In addition, a cultivator is used in weeding, although it tends to bring up more weed seeds to the soil surface than a hoe does.

Cultivators are available in both a long-handled form, which you can use while standing up, and as a hand cultivator, for fine work in small spaces between plants.

Hand Weeders

These specialized weeding tools include the weed slicer, weed rooter, and asparagus knife, as well as the hand cultivator and hand fork mentioned above. All these are small, hand-held tools that kill weeds by chopping up the seedling, slicing mature weeds off at the soil surface, or digging out the roots.

The type of hand weeder that will be most useful to you will depend on the kinds of weeds in your yard. If most of your weeds are perennials and regenerate from roots left

WEEDING TOOLS

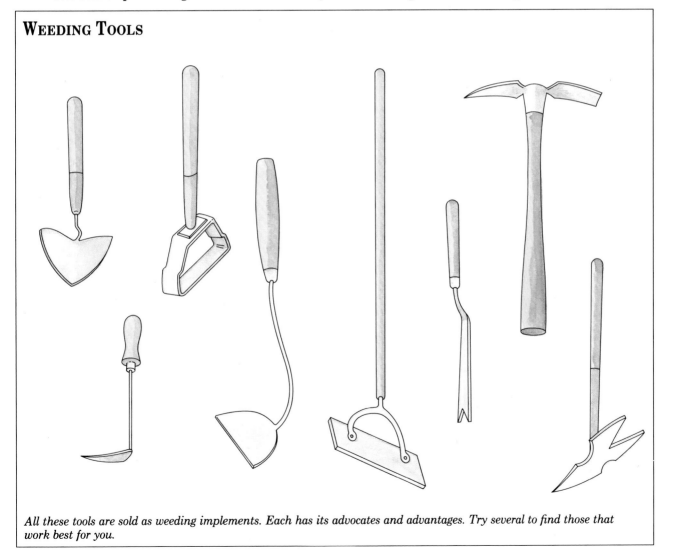

All these tools are sold as weeding implements. Each has its advocates and advantages. Try several to find those that work best for you.

in the soil, your best bet is a tool capable of digging out the entire weed, roots and all. If you have mostly annual weeds, a slicing tool will do the job.

Trowels

A trowel is a general-purpose garden tool used for cultivating, planting, digging, and weeding. For most jobs in the garden, a drop-shank trowel—which has an angle between the handle and blade—is preferred. A straight-shank trowel is not as efficient in digging and scooping; its main use is digging straight-sided planting holes for bulbs.

Both styles of trowels should have a strong handle and a sturdy head of heat-treated steel that will not bend during planting, digging, or weeding.

Rotary Tillers

If you have a large, open garden, you may find a rotary tiller to be invaluable. With this tool it is relatively easy to cultivate extensive areas that would take many tedious hours to spade by hand. Tillers are especially good at mixing soil amendments and fertilizer evenly into the top few inches of soil.

The depth that the tiller will be able to cultivate depends on the length of the tines. Most rotary tillers used in home gardens till only about 6 inches deep. Some tillers have the tines in the front and others have the tines in the back. Front-end models tend to be better for light jobs; rear-end tillers are preferred for heavy-duty tasks.

TOOLS FOR PRUNING

Although the only pruning tool that many home gardeners possess is a pair of hedge clippers, several other tools are more appropriate for pruning plants. Hedge clippers, or hedge shears, are designed to trim the stems of plants into flat wall-like surfaces on the top and sides of a hedge, as the name of the tool implies. These two-handed shears are designed for pruning formal hedges, and for that purpose they are excellent, but don't use them for other pruning chores.

Instead use hand-held pruning shears, long-handled lopping shears, and pruning saws—all of which are used to make thinning cuts, the most common type of pruning cut

you will make. (See the chapter "Pruning," beginning on page 185.) Each type of pruning tool is suitable for cutting to a certain maximum diameter. Always use the right tool for the size of wood you intend to cut. Never force a tool; if you do, you'll probably ruin it.

It is especially important to keep all your pruning tools sharp, because plants callus over more quickly from sharp cuts than from blunt or ragged tears.

Hand-Held Pruners

The first pruning tool to buy is a pair of hand-held shears. Use these for cutting stems up to ½ inch in diameter. Choose from scissor types, with sharpened blades that overlap, or anvil-style pruners, with a sharpened blade that cuts against a stationary metal plate, or anvil. Scissor pruners are preferred by most professionals because they make closer, cleaner cuts than anvil pruners. You sharpen only one side of the beveled blade with a whetstone. Although anvil pruners are lightweight and less expensive, they tend to crush bark against the anvil if the blade is not kept sharp.

Look for sturdily constructed pruners with high-quality steel blades. They should feel comfortable in your hand, particularly if they have a spring mechanism that reopens the pruners after each cut. If the pruners open too far, your hand will tire quickly.

Lopping Shears

These long-handled pruners, also known as loppers, provide extra leverage for cutting branches between ½ and 1½ inches in diameter. They are especially handy for removing stems at the base of deciduous shrubs and for thinning young branches on trees.

Loppers usually have a scissors-type blade design; variations on the basic design include some anvil-style models and some heavy-duty ratchet or gear designs that give you the force to cut branches up to 1¾ inches. If you use loppers on branches larger than they're designed to handle, you may force the blades out of alignment.

Look for loppers that have a rubber cushion to absorb the shock of the cut. If this feature is missing, your arms will absorb the shock and soon tire.

PRUNING TOOLS

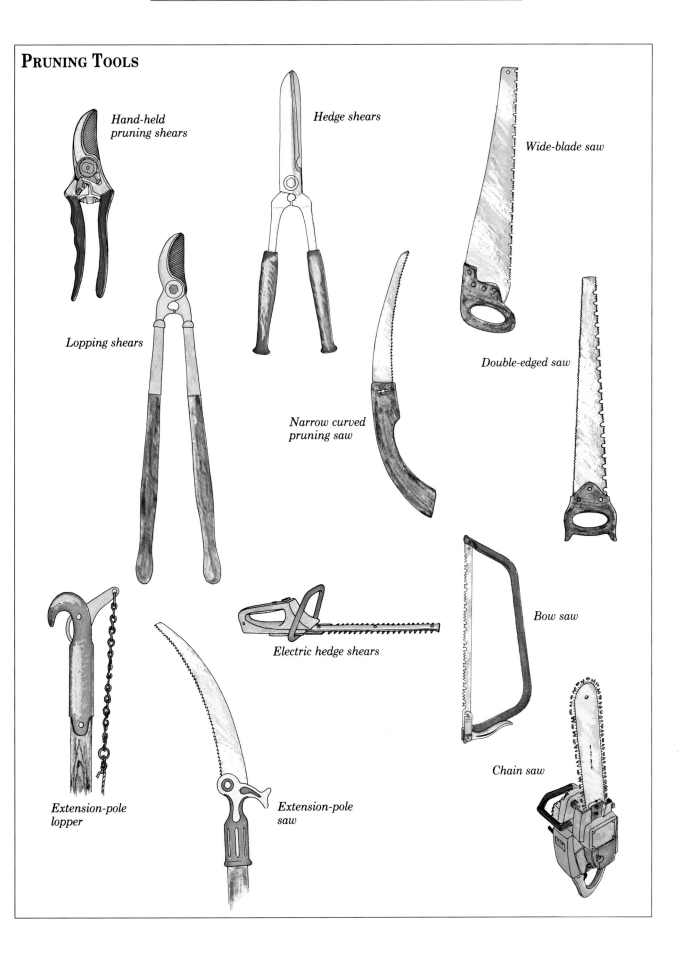

Hand-held
pruning shears

Hedge shears

Wide-blade saw

Lopping shears

Narrow curved
pruning saw

Double-edged saw

Bow saw

Electric hedge shears

Chain saw

Extension-pole
lopper

Extension-pole
saw

Pruning Saws

A pruning saw should be used for cutting branches too large for hand-held pruners and loppers. These are usually any branches greater than 1½ inches in diameter. A saw is also handy in areas where hand pruners or loppers won't fit between the branches for a proper cut.

Most home gardeners find that a small, curved, narrow-blade saw is the only pruning saw they need. Available in rigid and folding models, the saw is useful for cutting in confined spaces. Only if you intend to work on large trees would you need additional saws, such as a bow saw and a wide-blade pruning saw. Designed for heavy pruning, both of these saws require more maneuvering room than the small, curved saw.

Some pruning saws have teeth on both sides—one edge coarse, the other fine. If cutting with a double-edged saw, be sure that the teeth on the back side don't accidentally tear into the bark on another branch.

A chain saw may be necessary to cut through very large branches or tree trunks. Always use extreme caution with chain saws. Climbing into a tree with a chain saw is dangerous and is best left to a professional.

Pole Saws and Pole Pruners

You may find one of these pruning implements useful in cutting relatively small-diameter overhead branches.

Pole saws are small, curved saws mounted on an adjustable extension pole. Be sure that the pole is made of wood or fiberglass if you intend to prune near power lines. A pole saw will cut branches less than 2 inches in diameter up to 15 feet above the ground. A hook on the end of the pole is used to pull down any entangled branches.

Pole pruners are similar to pole saws, except that the end of the pole holds pruning shears, controlled by a pulley and rope. A pole pruner is used to cut small overhead branches, although it is often difficult to maneuver the pruners into position for a clean cut.

Some models feature both a saw and pulley-operated pruning shears. When using the pruning shears, take care not to injure bark with the saw; if necessary, detach the saw temporarily.

LAWN MOWERS

There are two basic types of lawn mowers: reel and rotary. Reel mowers can be manual or powered by engines. All rotary mowers are power mowers, using a gas engine or an electric motor.

Reel mowers shear the grass with a scissorlike action that produces a clean cut. They can cut very low and are preferred for grasses such as hybrid Bermuda grass, bent grass, and zoysia grass, which should be maintained at less than 1 inch high.

Rotary mowers cut with a high-speed rotating blade. The rotary mower is generally more versatile and easier to handle and maintain than the reel type. However, rotary mowers cannot make as sharp or clean a cut as a reel mower.

Both reel and rotary mowers can be adjusted to the mowing height that your grass requires. (See page 213 for the recommended mowing heights of common lawn grasses. See also the illustrations on pages

RENTING TOOLS

Many useful hand and power tools can be rented from hardware stores or equipment rental companies. This list is representative of the tools generally available. Check the local telephone directory for rental companies in your area.

Backpack blowers (for sweeping leaves)
Chain saws
Fertilizer spreaders
Hedge trimmers
Lawn aerators
Lawn dethatchers
Lawn edgers
Lawn mowers
Lawn rollers
Mattocks
Pole pruners
Pole saws
Posthole diggers
Rotary tillers
Seed spreaders
Shovels and spades
Sod cutters
String weed trimmers
Weed mowers
Wheelbarrows
Wood chippers

Lawn Mowers

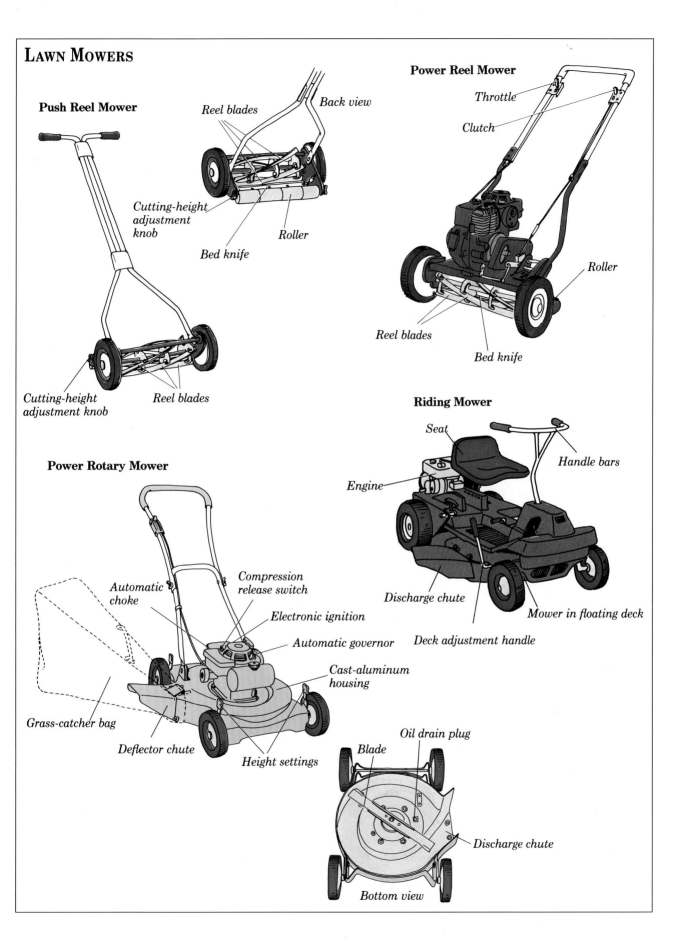

Push Reel Mower

Reel blades
Back view
Cutting-height adjustment knob
Roller
Bed knife
Cutting-height adjustment knob
Reel blades

Power Reel Mower

Throttle
Clutch
Roller
Reel blades
Bed knife

Power Rotary Mower

Automatic choke
Compression release switch
Electronic ignition
Automatic governor
Cast-aluminum housing
Grass-catcher bag
Deflector chute
Height settings

Riding Mower

Seat
Handle bars
Engine
Discharge chute
Mower in floating deck
Deck adjustment handle

Oil drain plug
Blade
Discharge chute
Bottom view

212 and 213.) Place the mower on a level surface. With a reel mower, measure the distance from the surface to the reel bedknife and correct to the desired height with a screw adjustment near the roller. With a rotary mower, measure from the surface to the edge of the skirt; adjust the height by moving the wheels up or down. You can also measure the height of the grass after mowing, and adjust the mower up or down one setting.

HOSES, NOZZLES, AND HEADS

You will probably need a garden hose for small hand-watering chores. If you have ever wrestled with a hose full of kinks, you know the importance of a good-quality, pliable hose. The more reinforcement in the hose, the better it will stand up under pressure. Look for reinforced rubber hoses that will withstand up to 500 pounds of pressure per square inch. Couplings should be heavy-duty octagonal brass that will not crush.

Choose a diameter that best fits your needs. Hoses are usually sold in one of five basic diameters: the ⅜-inch- and ½-inch-diameter sizes are used for watering container plants; the ⅝-inch size is most popular for lawns and gardens; and the ¾-inch and 1-inch sizes are mostly used in commercial applications. The larger the diameter, the more water the hose will deliver in a given period of time.

If your hose is punctured but is in otherwise good condition, try mending it with a hose repair kit instead of buying a new hose. Hose repairers are sold inexpensively in most garden centers and hardware stores.

At these same stores you will also find a variety of nozzles and heads to fit your hose. Nozzles allow you to adjust the flow of water from a fine spray to a hard stream. Different heads—including fan-spray heads, bubblers, and misting heads—offer great flexibility in watering.

MAINTAINING TOOLS

Good garden tools are an investment that will be quickly lost if you don't take care of them properly. Follow a regular program of maintenance and the tools will serve you well for many years.

Cleaning and Lubricating

Clean all tools at the end of the growing season. Use a wire brush to remove caked-on dirt and vegetation. Lubricate all pivot points and springs; then spray all bare metal parts and cutting edges with penetrating oil to prevent rust.

The only hand tools that require lubrication are those with moving parts—for example, pruning tools. Applying a few drops of graphite to the moving parts each time you sharpen the tool will help keep the tool in good working order. Also lubricate the tool if the parts should stick or lack their original smooth action.

A lawn mower should be cleaned after every use. Clean it with water, wipe it dry, then spray lightly with penetrating oil. Use a knife or a screwdriver to remove caked grass from the bottom of a rotary mower. Make sure that any motor oil is at the proper level. Never fill the gas tank or add oil while the mower is on the lawn, because spilled gas or oil will kill the grass it comes in contact with.

One way to keep a garden hose free of kinks is to coil it around a spool. A spool can be made from an old automobile wheel rim.

Whetstones should be used to sharpen hand pruners and other pruning blades.

If a garage or basement is not available to you, a weatherproof toolshed in the garden can be used to store your gardening tools.

Shovels can be sharpened with a metal file or rasp. Don't use a file or rasp on more delicate edges.

Sharpening

A dull tool is always inefficient. A dull lawn mower crushes the blades of grass, causing the tops to wither and turn brown. A dull hoe bends weeds instead of cutting them. A shovel with a dull edge makes digging a chore. Keeping your tools sharpened will make your work much easier and allow you to get the job done quicker and better.

You can easily sharpen the blades of a rotary lawn mower at home. First, disconnect the spark-plug wire, then remove the blades. Use a file or grindstone to sharpen the edge of the blade that comes in contact with the grass; sharpen at a 45-degree angle. Blades on reel mowers should be sharpened at a shop that specializes in lawn mowers.

You can sharpen most garden tools yourself, as long as you have the right sharpener. A metal file or rasp is appropriate for sharpening a shovel, but it shouldn't be used on more delicate edges. Hand pruners and other pruning blades should be sharpened with a whetstone. Specialized tools are available for sharpening teeth on saws.

Storing

Tools should be stored indoors away from sun, rain, and snow. This will protect them from rust, cracked handles, and all the other problems that exposure causes. A garage or a basement is a logical choice for storage space unless it's too far from the garden area.

If you decide to construct a shed or a shelter for your garden equipment and materials, make it weatherproof so that you can safely store tools and materials that would be damaged by moisture.

OBTAINING PLANTS

There are many ways to obtain plants for your garden. You can shop for them in nurseries and garden centers in your area, order them from mail-order suppliers, or buy them at plant sales organized by local botanical gardens or specialty plant societies. When you need a lot of plants, you can save money by starting new plants from seed or from parts of old plants already growing in the garden.

Both methods of obtaining plants—buying them and propagating them—have advantages. When you buy a plant, you can select the size you want, and it's ready for immediate planting. And when you buy in person rather than through the mail, you can see what you're getting. On the other hand, starting new plants is cheaper, especially when you need a large quantity, and it may be the only way to obtain a rare plant. Often, a combination of buying and propagating provides the greatest satisfaction for gardeners.

Shopping in a well-stocked nursery is an excellent way to buy plants. You can choose the kind, size, and shape of plant you want, take it home, and plant it immediately.

337

In a well-run nursery, plant labels and other signs should be informative.

BUYING PLANTS

When you are shopping for plants at a nursery or a garden center, keep your eyes open for clues that tell you something about the establishment and the plants grown there. Are the growing beds and the groupings of plants well ordered and easy to walk through? Do the plants look as if they have been well watered? Are the signs and plant labels informative and do they list both common and botanical names?

Is the sales staff helpful and knowledgeable? A short talk with a good nursery professional can give you information that may be difficult to find otherwise. If a clerk does not know the answer to a specific question, he or she should be able to either find someone who does or refer you to a good source. A highly trained staff is what makes one nursery or garden center better than another. A good staff can be a continuing source of reliable gardening information.

If you are looking for a specific plant that is not in stock at a local nursery, ask the nursery to order it for you. Most good nurseries will be able to find what you need within a few weeks. Certain types of plants are available only during certain seasons (for example, bare-root shrubs and trees are available only during the dormant season), so you may have to delay planting. Place special orders early to be assured of getting the plants when you need them.

For gardeners who don't have access to a local nursery or garden center, mail-order suppliers are a convenient alternative. Their colorful catalogs, sent during the cold days of winter, offer an enticement to garden-hungry readers. Although mail-order nurseries usually have a limited shipping season and limited supplies of certain plants, they are often good sources of rare or unusual plants unavailable at a local garden center.

Many mail-order nurseries have been in business for generations and offer the highest quality plant material. The fact that it may be shipped from some distance away should not deter you; many local nurseries also receive their plants from outside the area. Nonetheless, plants that have been shipped through the mail will have undergone a certain amount of stress and should be pampered upon arrival. Take them out of the shipping container and plant them as soon as you can.

If you are ordering plants from a particular mail-order firm for the first time, it may be a good idea to place a small initial order to find out how you like the company's plants, whether they arrive in good condition, and whether they perform well for you. Most reputable mail-order companies stand behind their stock with a reasonable guarantee.

Plants are sold in many forms: seeds, flats, cell packs, pots, bare root, and balled and burlapped. The form you choose depends on the plant and such factors as the size of your garden and your budget.

Nurseries sell plants in a variety of ways, including seed packets, seedlings, and mature plants.

Buying seedlings in flats is a good value because of the number of plants they contain.

Seeds This is the most economical way to purchase plants, since you will do all the work of growing the plants yourself. When buying seeds, you should consider the time and care required to germinate and grow the seeds to planting size. Specific growing conditions are often necessary for proper seedling development, and these conditions may not be easily achieved. Young seedlings are especially vulnerable to rot and to insect attack, and they require frequent watering to keep them from drying out.

Among the plants commonly started from seed are annual flowers, vegetables, and grasses. Some ground covers and vines are also available as seeds. Many plants can be direct seeded in the garden—that is, the seeds can be sown directly in the ground where the plants will grow. Other plants must be sown indoors in containers and transplanted into the garden later. (See Planting Seeds Outdoors on page 108 and Starting Seeds Indoors on page 110.)

Flats and cell packs A flat is a large, shallow, square or rectangular container with no built-in dividers between plants. Ground covers are commonly sold in flats. Buying flats is a good value when you consider the number of plants each one contains. Flats generally hold four to five dozen plants, which can be separated at planting time. The plants should be well anchored in the flat, but there shouldn't be a visible mass of roots. If the plants seem very young, you may want to leave them in the flat for a week after you bring them home. Set them where they will be protected from the hot sun until you are ready to plant. Since flats dry out very quickly, be sure to water them frequently, perhaps as often as twice daily during hot weather.

A cell pack usually contains either four or six plants in small, individual plastic cells. You remove the plants by pushing up on the bottom of each cell. Bedding plants and some ground covers are sold in cell packs. Avoid cell packs that have masses of roots growing out of the bottom. Because the ball of soil in each cell is so small, it will dry out quickly. Be sure to water frequently if you don't plant immediately.

Containers   Shrubs and trees are commonly sold in containers made of metal, plastic, fiber, or wood. Most shrubs are sold in 1- and 5-gallon containers. Specimen shrubs are often sold in 15-gallon containers. Trees are typically sold in 1-, 5-, 10-, and 15-gallon sizes. Specimen trees are frequently sold in large wooden boxes. Of course, the larger the container, the more expensive it is.

If you need a limited number of plants, you may decide to invest in large sizes. But if you're buying a large quantity of plants, smaller containers are more affordable. When deciding whether to buy plants in 1- or 5-gallon cans, remember that the smaller, younger plants generally transplant better. Although the impact of 5-gallon plants is more immediate, the 1-gallon plants catch up to and often surpass them within a few years.

Make sure that the container is in good shape when you purchase the plant. Rusted metal, split plastic, or disintegrated wood usually means that the roots of the plant grew into the ground soil at the nursery. The plant likely suffered severe shock when its roots were pulled up.

The plant should be well anchored in the container but not to the point of being root-bound. Try gently lifting the plant by the trunk. If the soil moves at all, the plant has not had time to form a well-developed rootball. Too many roots are just as bad; avoid plants with thick masses of roots on the soil surface or around the sides of the soil ball. Root-bound plants have more difficulty establishing a normal root system when transplanted into the garden, and their growth may be stunted. Girdling roots, or roots tightly wrapped around the stem, restrict growth as they slowly choke the plant.

Balled-and-burlapped plants   Referred to as B and B plants, these trees and shrubs are raised in a field and prepared for sale by

If larger-sized plants are your desire, you can buy them in containers made of metal, plastic, fiber, or wood.

In severe winter climates, a shrub or tree is often sold with its rootball wrapped in burlap.

CHOOSING NURSERY STOCK

Pick out plants that look healthy and have good leaf color. The growth of most plants should be compact rather than leggy. Inspect the stems and the upper and lower surfaces of the leaves for pests, and avoid any plants with evidence of problems. Check the root system; it should be well developed but without any large circling roots that may girdle the plant later in life. A mass of roots growing from the bottom of the container is a sign that the plant is root-bound and will have trouble becoming established when transplanted in the ground.

Fresh stock is usually preferable to plants that have been growing in small containers for many months. It's a good idea to find out when the nursery receives shipments from its wholesale growers. If you're there when the truck is unloaded, not only will you get the freshest plants, you'll also be able to pick from the widest selection.

When considering what size plants to buy, you have to decide whether to use seedlings, one-year-old stock, or more expensive larger plants. The extra cost may be worthwhile when you need only a few large plants to make an immediate impact in your garden. Buying young plants makes sense when you're planting in masses and want to economize. Young plants generally transplant better than larger, older plants and in time will catch up, and perhaps even surpass them, in size. For example, shrubs planted from 1-gallon and 5-gallon containers will reach the same size in two and a half to three years.

If you aren't able to put your plants in the ground right away after bringing them home, do not leave them exposed to full sun. Give them shade, and water them regularly until you can place them in their permanent positions.

Flowers and Vegetables

These plants are often available as seeds or in cell packs and small containers. When purchasing seeds, buy from a reliable seed company. The seed packet should be well sealed and the date on the packet should not have expired.

When buying cell packs and small containers, make sure that the plants are well rooted but not root-bound. Select bushy, compact plants rather than sparse, leggy ones. It's tempting to pick out plants that are in full bloom or bearing fruit, but plants without flowers or fruit transplant better and grow more satisfactorily in the long run. Flowering plants that have a mass of buds will bloom longer and more prolifically than those already in bloom.

Trees

Although commonly available in containers, trees are also sold balled and burlapped in cold-winter areas. In addition, fruit trees and many deciduous ornamental trees are sold bare root during the dormant season.

When selecting a tree, look for a straight trunk, a well-balanced branching pattern, and good leaf color. Avoid plants with kinked or large, circling roots. Also refrain from buying trees that have any nicks or cuts in the bark; these can serve as entryways for disease organisms.

Shrubs

Although most commonly sold in containers, shrubs are sometimes available balled and burlapped. Some deciduous shrubs are also sold bare root. Look for a well-balanced shape and good leaf color. If the shrub is in a container, it should not be too large for the pot. Make sure that the shrub isn't root-bound and that there aren't any circling roots.

Vines

These plants are usually sold in flats, cell packs, or 1-gallon containers. A well-grown vine has three or more branches that appear healthy and have good leaf color. Avoid plants that have branches twisted together; they will be more difficult to separate and train after planting.

Ground Covers

Usually sold in flats or cell packs, ground covers are often available in larger containers as well. The plants should have good leaf color and should not appear to have outgrown their container.

Sod

When buying sod, unroll a strip to examine the turf. It should have a healthy green color (or a color typical of the variety). Sod that has been allowed to dry out may have a yellow-green hue and may be more difficult to establish. The soil should be rich, slightly moist, and filled with roots. Blackened, mushy spots in the sod may mean that it has been overwatered or that disease organisms are already present.

Bare-root plants are sold when they are dormant. They are easier to handle and lighter to ship.

When planting a bare-root plant, examine the roots to be sure that they are not shriveled and dry.

digging them up and wrapping the rootball in burlap. In areas where winter freezing is not a problem, only a few plants are commonly sold this way. In mild climates plants most frequently marketed in this form include rhododendrons and conifers sold as living Christmas trees. In severe-winter climates many different types of plants are sold B and B. This is because plants raised in fields are much less susceptible to winter freezing than those grown in containers.

To select a B and B plant, untie the top of the burlap and look carefully at the rootball; it should have a well-developed network of small, fibrous roots. Don't choose a plant with a ball of soil that is loose, cracked, broken, or bone-dry.

In addition, check for roots circling back around the trunk; they can girdle the trunk later in the plant's life. To check for girdling roots, brush away the soil on top of the rootball or insert your finger into the top 2 to 3 inches near the trunk. You can usually see or feel girdling roots.

After you select the plant you want, retie the burlap and carry the plant from the bottom of the rootball; don't use the trunk as a handle. For information on storing and planting B and B plants, see page 116.

Bare-root plants During the winter, roses, fruit trees, berry plants, and many deciduous ornamental trees are sold bare root, meaning that the plants are sold while they are dormant, with no soil around their roots.

A bare-root plant is less expensive than the same kind of plant sold in a container because it is easier to handle and lighter to ship, and requires less attention in the nursery. Bare-root plants are also available in a wider selection.

In the nursery, bare-root plants may be kept in temporary storage in moist sawdust or sand, or the roots may be covered with plastic bags. Even if the plant is packaged, try to examine the roots to be sure that they are moist and plump, not shriveled and dry. Also examine the branches; they should be evenly spaced so that the plant will develop symmetrically.

For information on handling bare-root plants once you have brought them home, see page 118.

One method of propagating plants vegetatively is to take cuttings from a parent plant and root them in 5 parts perlite to 1 part peat moss.

Propagating Plants

Plants can be propagated in two ways: sexually, from seed; and asexually, from a vegetative method such as dividing, taking cuttings, and grafting. The preferred technique usually depends on the kind of plant you want to reproduce. For example, most vegetables and many flowers are started from seed. Most fruit and nut trees and many ornamental shrubs are propagated vegetatively, partly because they often don't grow true (similar in form to their parents) when started from seed. Time is another consideration. Some plants are propagated vegetatively because their seeds may take several years to grow into full-sized plants.

Each seed is the unique genetic product of the parent plants, and the resulting plant can vary slightly or dramatically from its parents. Seeds saved from your garden plants, if they are hybrids, may revert unpredictably to a parent and may not develop into the form you expect. However, seeds sold commercially have a predictable form when grown. (For information on growing plants from seed, see pages 108 to 112.)

Because plants have all their essential genetic information in each cell, vegetative propagation produces genetically identical plants that vary only as a result of environmental factors. Vegetative propagation avoids the time lost in the young period of the plant's life, because you begin with an adult plant. This method of propagation can be used to produce large numbers of new plants quickly and economically.

343

There are four main techniques of vegetative propagation: division, cuttings, layering, and grafting and budding.

Dividing Plants

Division is one of the most common ways to propagate perennials. Plants that can be divided are those that grow new shoots directly from the crown (where the roots and aboveground part of the plant meet) rather than from a trunk. These new shoots often form their own root systems and become individual plants, although they usually remain attached to the parent plant. After several years of growth, the center of the plant may become crowded and die, leaving a ring of new plants around the dying core. To divide the plant, simply dig it up and separate it into two or more parts, making sure that each part has some roots, stem, and foliage.

Divide plants in fall or early spring, when the plant is dormant. Fall is the preferred time to divide spring- and early summer–blooming perennials; early spring is the preferred time to divide late summer- and fall-blooming perennials. In severe-winter climates (-10° to -20° F), it is best to divide only in early spring.

To make digging and dividing easier, water the bed well a few days beforehand. When dividing deciduous perennials, prune back the leaves severely, to about 4 inches above the ground. Don't cut back evergreen perennials. Dig out the entire clump as completely as possible. If the center of the clump has died, divide the living portion into smaller clumps to replant where you like. If the roots are so snarled that you can't simply pull apart the plants, you can cut them apart, although this is likely to cause root damage. The best way to divide a stubborn clump is to insert two spading forks, held back-to-back, into the clump. Press the handles toward each other, using the leverage to pry apart the clump.

Good candidates for division include agapanthus (*Agapanthus* species), astilbe (*Astilbe* species), bellflower (*Campanula* species), bleeding-heart (*Dicentra* species), evergreen candytuft (*Iberis sempervirens*), chives (*Allium* species), chrysanthemum (*Chrysanthemum* species), coralbells (*Heuchera* species), daylily (*Hemerocallis* species), lily-of-the-valley (*Convallaria majalis*), pinks (*Dianthus* species), and violets (*Viola* species).

DIVIDING PLANTS

Divide multistemmed plants by pulling the stems apart. On large clumps a pair of spading forks back-to-back provides leverage. If the stems are too tough to tear apart, use a knife, pruning shears, or even a hatchet to separate them.

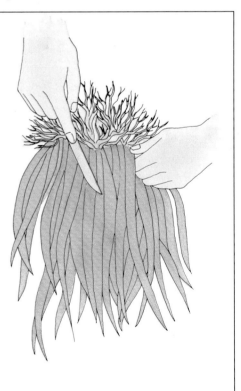

Rooting Cuttings

This is a commonly used form of vegetative propagation, especially for ornamental shrubs. A cutting is an incomplete piece of plant from which a new plant can be grown. Cuttings may be taken from the stem, leaf, or root of the plant.

Cuttings should be rooted as soon as possible after being taken from a plant. A mixture of 5 parts perlite to 1 part peat moss is ideal for rooting most cuttings. Besides keeping the cuttings from falling over, the mixture of perlite and peat moss holds both air and water. To make sure that the cuttings don't dry out, cover the container with a pane of glass or a sheet of plastic film, vented just enough so that condensation doesn't form on the inside.

Place stem and leaf cuttings in bright light but not direct sunlight. The air temperature around the cuttings should be about 70° F and the temperature beneath the container about 85° F. The warm bottom temperature will stimulate root growth, and the cooler air will slow metabolism in the leaves. You can supply bottom heat with heating cables, or you can place the tray of cuttings on top of a refrigerator or water heater.

To help prevent plant disease and insect infestation, keep your work area, containers, tools, and rooting medium as clean as possible. Remove any insects from the cuttings before you plant them, and dust or drench with a fungicide if necessary.

You can increase root formation in many plants by dipping stem and leaf cuttings in a rooting hormone, available at most nurseries and garden centers. Most cuttings will root in about six weeks, although rapid growers might root in as few as three weeks. Hardwood cuttings may take as long as a year. Tug gently at the cutting every couple of weeks to see if roots have begun to form. Transplant the cuttings when the roots begin to branch, or when the rootball is dense and about 2 inches across.

Hardwood stem cuttings   Many deciduous shrubs and trees are propagated this way. Cut 8-inch sections of pencil-thick stems from the previous season's growth. Each cutting should have at least three leaf buds, with the base cut just below a bud. Distinguish

the top from the base by cutting the top straight across and the bottom at a slant.

Take hardwood cuttings early in the dormant season. In mild-winter areas start to root the cuttings in fall. In areas where the

MAKING SOFTWOOD STEM CUTTINGS

Let the top two 5-leaflet leaves remain; pull off lower leaves, being careful not to damage buds. Dip in root hormone stimulant.

Set cuttings into damp soil mix.

Seal in plastic bag until new shoots appear— in 5–8 weeks.

Hybrid roses do not grow well on their own roots, so budding is the best and easiest way to propagate them.

ground freezes, store the cuttings through the winter for spring planting. To store the cuttings, place them either horizontally or vertically in a container of moist sand or wood shavings, with several inches of sand on top. Keep the cuttings between 32° and 40° F.

When you are ready to plant, dip the base (the slanted end) of each cutting in a rooting hormone. To plant the cutting, with a pencil poke a hole in the rooting medium and insert the slanted end of the cutting 3 inches deep. Roots will form under the soil level. Transplant when the roots begin to branch.

Softwood stem cuttings   Both deciduous and evergreen shrubs and trees, as well as many herbaceous perennials, can be propagated by this method. Take these cuttings in spring or summer, and root them as soon as possible after removing them from the plant.

For trees and shrubs, select 8-inch sections of pliable yet mature new growth that bends without snapping; the stem should have leaves attached. For herbaceous plants, cut off the top 5 inches of a stem with the leaves attached.

In both cases, cut just below a leaf node and remove the leaves from the lower third of the cutting. If the leaves are large, cut off half of each remaining leaf to reduce transpiration (loss of water through the leaves). For plants that exude a sticky sap, let the stem base callus over for a few hours before planting. Dip the base in rooting hormone, although this is less important for herbaceous cuttings than for those taken from woody plants. With a pencil poke a hole in the rooting medium. Insert the cutting from a tree or shrub 3 inches deep; herbaceous cuttings should be inserted to half the length of the stem. Transplant when roots have formed.

Leaf cuttings   Some plants, such as begonia and many succulents, root from a leaf or part of a leaf. Choose recently mature leaves for the cuttings. Different methods are used, depending on the kind of plant. In some cases, the main veins on the underside of the leaf should be cut and the leaf laid flat on the rooting medium; in other cases, the leaves should be inserted upright into the rooting medium.

Root cuttings Blackberries, raspberries, and other plants whose roots sprout can be propagated from root cuttings. On roots that are about ¼ inch in diameter, cut 2-inch sections and place them in the rooting medium. They can be laid on their sides ½ inch deep, or they can be inserted upright with their tops at soil level. Moisten the medium thoroughly, then cover the container and place it in the shade. Transplant when sprouts have formed.

Layering
This method fosters the growth of new roots on the stem of a plant while the stem is still attached to the parent plant. After the roots have formed, the stem is detached from the parent plant. There are two main types of layering: ground layering and air layering. In both cases, darkness is a key factor in stimulating the formation of the roots.

PROPAGATING BULBS

Most bulbs and bulblike plants that are commonly found in gardens can be propagated by dividing the underground part of the plant or by separating new, developing bulbs from the original. Nearly all bulbous plants can also be propagated from seed, although bulbs grown from seed may take several years to flower. The following techniques are the most useful for propagating bulbs vegetatively.

Scoring
This propagation method is commonly used on hyacinths (*Hyacinthus orientalis*), but also works on daffodils (*Narcissus* species) and scilla (*Scilla* species). In early summer make three cuts through the basal plate. Store in a dry spot for a few days until the cuts open. Dust each of the cut surfaces with a fungicide, such as captan, then place the bulbs in a warm, dark place with high humidity for a few months. After bulblets have formed in the fall, plant the mother bulb upside down in the garden. The bulblets will sprout in spring.

Bulb Scaling
This method is used to propagate lilies (*Lilium* species) and other scaly bulbs. In fall break or cut the scales close to the basal plate.

You can remove the two outer rows of scales from a large bulb without damaging it. Dust the scales with a fungicide, such as captan, and a rooting powder, then seal them in a plastic bag with damp vermiculite. Keep the bag at room temperature until bulblets form (about two months), then place the bag in the refrigerator for another two months. Plant the new bulblets in spring.

Separating Bulblets
Many true bulbs, such as tulips (*Tulipa* species) and daffodils (*Narcissus* species), form tiny offsets around the parent bulb. Separate these tiny bulbs as soon as they are ripe and plant them 1 to 2 inches deep. They will take a year or two to flower.

Separating Cormels
Gladiolus (*Gladiolus* species), crocus (*Crocus* species), and freesia (*Freesia* species) can be propagated by breaking off the tiny corms that form at the base of the large corm. The shallower a corm is planted, the more cormels it will form. Store cormels in slightly damp peat moss over the winter, and plant them about 2 inches deep in spring. A few might reach flowering size the first year, but most will need a second year of growth before flowering.

Dividing Rhizomes
To divide bearded iris (*Iris* species) and other plants that grow from rhizomes, lift the rhizomes shortly after flowering. Discard old rhizomes (those without shoots) and cut the remainder into sections, leaving one fan of leaves on each section. Trim both the leaves and the roots to about 3 inches. Replant immediately just under the soil surface.

Dividing Tuberous Roots
Dahlias (*Dahlia* species) and other tuberous-rooted plants can be divided in spring after the eyes have begun to swell and are clearly visible. Cut the cluster of roots into segments, each having at least one eye. Dust the cut surface with a fungicide, such as captan, and cure the segments in a dry, warm place for several days. Plant them so that the eyes are about 2 inches deep.

Dividing Tubers
Potatoes and other tubers can be propagated by cutting them into sections, making sure that each piece has one or two eyes. Dust each section with a fungicide, such as captan, and cure it in a warm, dry place for a few days before planting it.

Ground layering Tip layering is a common technique of ground layering that is used on blackberry, loganberry, and raspberry plants. Bend over a flexible stem of the current season's growth in late summer and bury the tip about 4 inches deep. Roots will form and a new shoot will begin to grow in a few weeks. The new plant can be dug up in late fall or early spring and transplanted.

Simple layering is another type of ground layering that is used on such plants as barberry (*Berberis* species), clematis (*Clematis* species), horsechestnut (*Aesculus* species), lilac (*Syringa* species), magnolia (*Magnolia* species), viburnum (*Viburnum* species), and wisteria (*Wisteria* species). In early spring or late fall, select a dormant one-year-old branch and make a cut a few inches from the end. Dig a shallow trench and peg the stem so that the cut is in contact with the soil. Cover the base of the bent stem with soil but leave the tip exposed. The following fall or spring, cut the rooted branch from the parent plant and transplant it.

Air layering This method is used primarily to reroot leggy azaleas (*Rhododendron* species) and magnolias (*Magnolia* species), as well as such houseplants as dumb cane (*Dieffenbachia* species), philodendron (*Philodendron* species), and rubber plant (*Ficus*

elastica). It is best done in spring or summer. In spring select a stem of the previous season's growth; in summer select a stem that has been produced that same season. Take care in choosing the spot where you make your cut; the cut area will be the bottom of the new plant.

Slit the stem at an upward angle and insert a matchstick or pebble to hold the cut open. Apply a rooting hormone to the cut area. Wrap a handful of damp sphagnum moss around the cut and encase it with black plastic, tying both ends securely with rubber bands or tape. Check the wrapping weekly and moisten the moss as needed. Rooting will occur in two to three months, at which time you can cut off the top just below the new roots and transplant.

Grafting and Budding

In grafting and budding, two different plants are joined together to function as one plant. If done properly, almost all grafts within a species and many between different species in a genus are successful; grafts between different genera almost always fail. The two parts that are joined together are called the scion (stem cutting) and the rootstock or understock (root system). For the graft to succeed, the cambium (the thin layer of creamy white tissue just under the bark) of

LAYERING

Select a flexible branch from last year's wood. Make a cut a few inches from the end. Dig a shallow trench and peg or staple the cut to the bottom of it, with the tip of the branch exposed.

AIR LAYERING

Make the cut where you want the roots of the new plant to form.

Tie the bottom of a piece of plastic around the stem and stuff with damp sphagnum moss. Then tie the top.

T-BUDDING

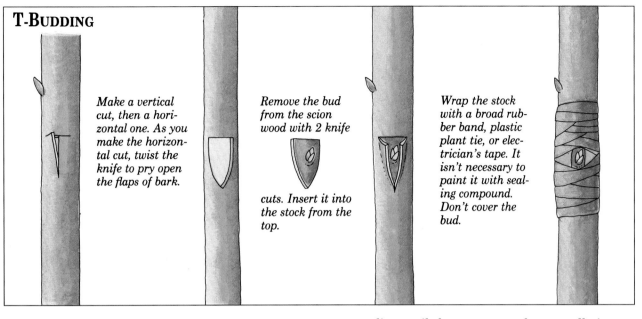

Make a vertical cut, then a horizontal one. As you make the horizontal cut, twist the knife to pry open the flaps of bark.

Remove the bud from the scion wood with 2 knife cuts. Insert it into the stock from the top.

Wrap the stock with a broad rubber band, plastic plant tie, or electrician's tape. It isn't necessary to paint it with sealing compound. Don't cover the bud.

WHIP GRAFT

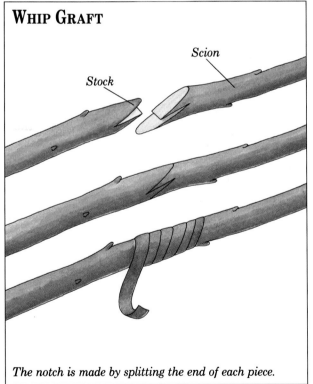

Scion

Stock

The notch is made by splitting the end of each piece.

both parts must line up and grow together to form a continuous path for the flow of water and nutrients.

Budding is a form of grafting in which a small piece of bark with a bud, rather than a whole stem, is used as the scion. Roses and fruit trees are often budded.

The key to success with grafting and budding is to bring the cambium of the scion and rootstock into contact and keep them alive until they grow together, usually in a couple of weeks.

Collect scion wood just before bud break in early spring, or in severe-winter areas you can do it in fall before the wood freezes. Each scion should have two or three leaf buds. Take the scion wood from the middle of the stem, place it in a plastic bag filled with moist sawdust or peat moss, and store it in the refrigerator until the rootstock is ready for grafting. Keep track of which end of the scion is up by making a straight cut at the top and a slanted cut at the bottom. The scion will die if it is inserted upside down into the rootstock.

Grafting can take place whenever the rootstock is in vigorous growth in spring. Most grafting techniques are easier to accomplish when the bark slips, or lifts easily. This occurs during spring growth; after growth slows in summer, the bark usually won't slip.

Work quickly, then protect the graft from air so that the exposed cambium is not killed by drying out. Join the grafted pieces with rubber grafting bands, nursery tape, plastic electrician's tape, or wide rubber bands. The tie material must hold the parts firmly together yet be able to stretch, disintegrate, or be cut as the stem thickens. To prevent drying, apply grafting wax or asphalt emulsion sealing compound to the graft. Also dab some on the cut end of the scion to keep it from drying out. It is not necessary to wax bud grafts; just wrap them tightly.

CLIMATE ZONE MAP

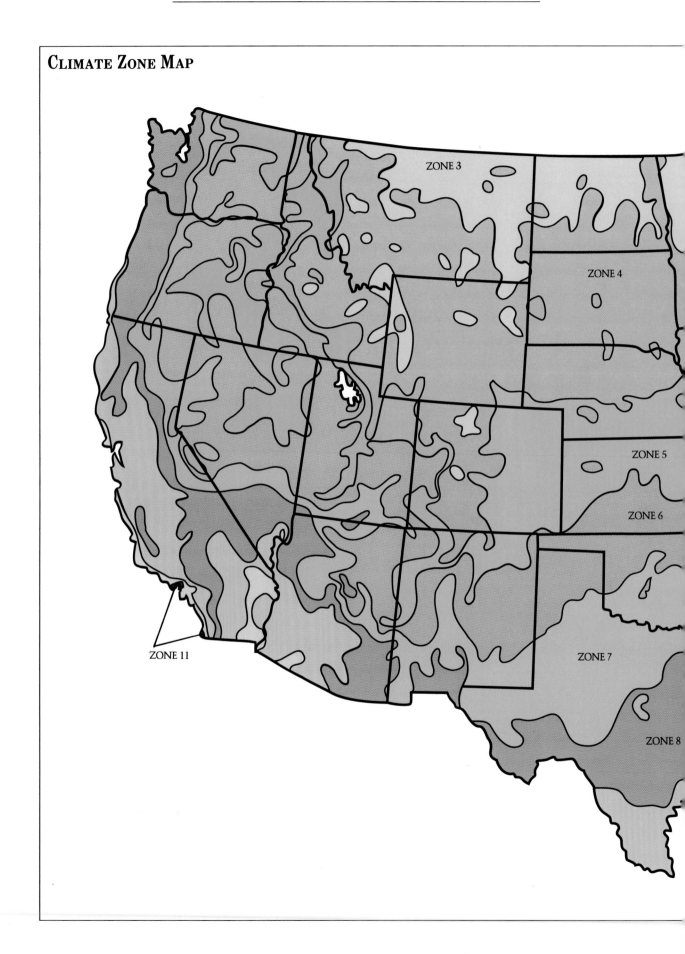

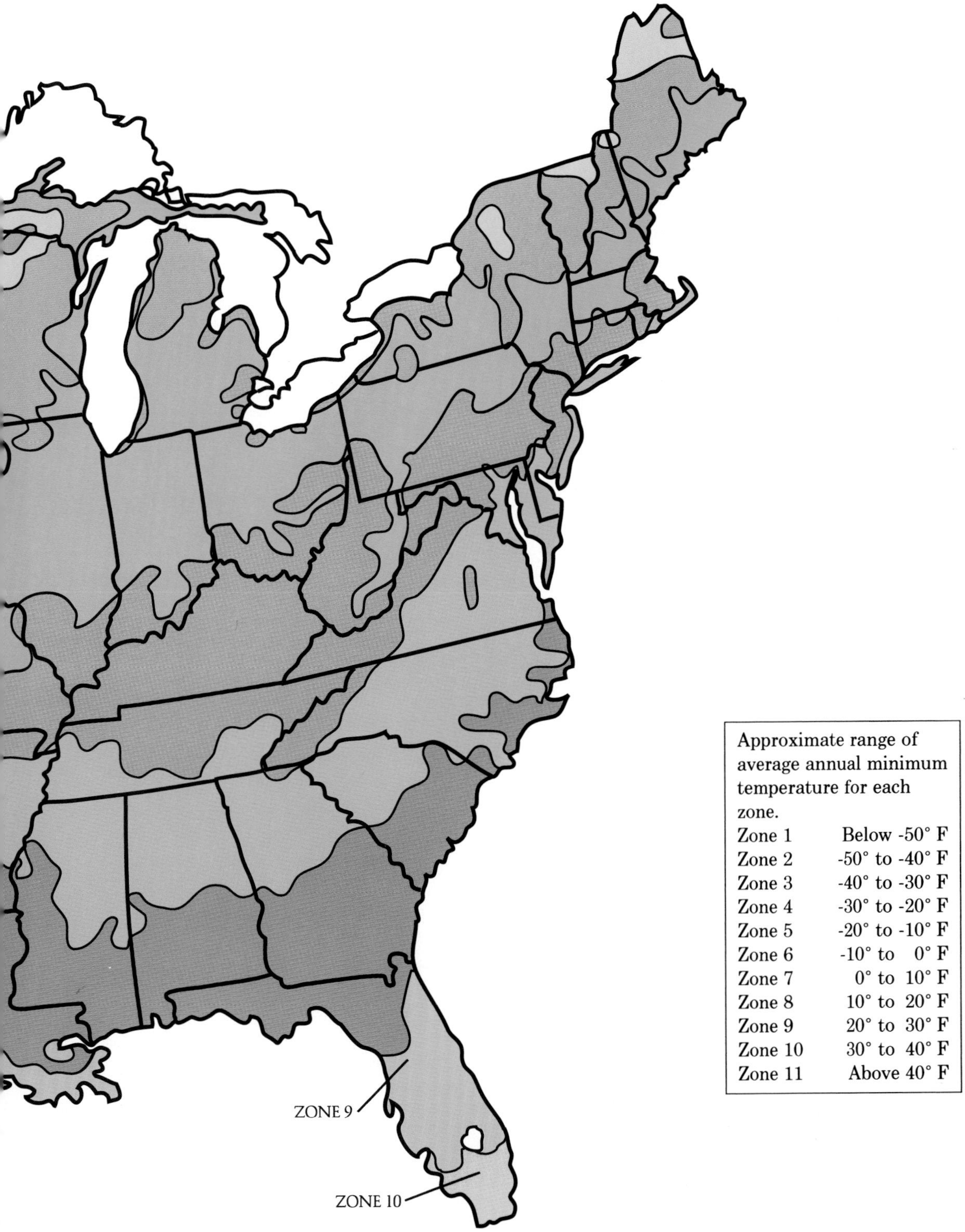

Approximate range of average annual minimum temperature for each zone.

Zone 1	Below -50° F
Zone 2	-50° to -40° F
Zone 3	-40° to -30° F
Zone 4	-30° to -20° F
Zone 5	-20° to -10° F
Zone 6	-10° to 0° F
Zone 7	0° to 10° F
Zone 8	10° to 20° F
Zone 9	20° to 30° F
Zone 10	30° to 40° F
Zone 11	Above 40° F

ZONE 9

ZONE 10

Based on the 1990 USDA Climate Zone map.

Zinnia

PLANT PURCHASING GUIDES

The following pages contain information that you can use to guide you when purchasing plants for your garden. Annuals, perennials, shrubs, trees, ground covers, and herbs are contained in separate plant selection lists that can help you decide, for example, which color, shape, or fragrance will best suit your garden. Following the lists is a special climate, microclimate, and shade chart (page 370) designed to help you with the special shade and climate needs of your garden.

ANNUALS

For that special purpose, problem, or form, the lists that follow will help you identify annuals that will meet your needs. Remember that a plant's appearance on a certain list doesn't mean that all varieties necessarily fit that category. In many cases only selected varieties match the description.

Annuals With Yellow, Orange, and Bronze Flowers

Alcea rosea (hollyhock)
Antirrhinum majus (snapdragon)
Calendula officinalis (pot marigold)
Celosia cristata (cockscomb)
Coreopsis tinctoria (calliopsis)
Cosmos sulphureus (orange cosmos)
Dahlia hybrids (dahlia)
Dimorphotheca sinuata (cape marigold)
Dyssodia tenuiloba (Dahlberg daisy)
Eschscholzia californica (California poppy)
Gaillardia pulchella (blanket-flower)
Gazania rigens (gazania)
Gerbera jamesonii (Transvaal daisy)
Gomphrena globosa (globe amaranth)
Helianthus species (sunflower)
Impatiens balsamina (balsam)
Lathyrus odoratus (sweet pea)
Limonium bonduellii (Algerian sea lavender)
Linaria maroccana (toadflax)
Matthiola incana (stock)
Mimulus × *hybridus* (monkeyflower)
Nemesia strumosa (pouch nemesia)
Papaver species (poppy)
Pelargonium × *hortorum* (geranium)
Portulaca grandiflora (rose moss)
Rudbeckia hirta var. *pulcherrima* (gloriosa daisy)
Sanvitalia procumbens (creeping zinnia)
Tagetes species (marigolds)

Thunbergia alata (black-eyed-susan vine)
Tithonia rotundifolia (Mexican sunflower)
Tropaeolum majus (nasturtium)
Verbena × *hybrida* (garden verbena)
Viola × *wittrockiana* (pansy)
Zinnia species (zinnia)

Annuals With Cream to White Flowers

Ageratum houstonianum (flossflower)
Alcea rosea (hollyhock)
Antirrhinum majus (snapdragon)
Arctotis stoechadifolia var. *grandis* (African daisy)
Begonia × *semperflorens-cultorum* (wax begonia)
Callistephus chinensis (China aster)
Catharanthus roseus (Madagascar periwinkle)
Cleome hasslerana (spiderflower)
Dahlia hybrids (dahlia)
Dianthus species (China pink; sweet william)
Dimorphotheca sinuata (cape marigold)
Eschscholzia californica (California poppy)
Gerbera jamesonii (Transvaal daisy)
Gypsophila elegans (annual baby's breath)
Helichrysum bracteatum (strawflower)
Iberis species (candytuft)
Impatiens balsamina (balsam)
Impatiens wallerana (impatiens; busy-lizzie)

Dahlia hybrid

Impatiens wallerana

Ipomoea alba (moonflower vine)
Lathyrus odoratus (sweet pea)
Lobelia erinus (edging lobelia)
Lobularia maritima (sweet alyssum)
Matthiola incana (stock)
Nicotiana alba (flowering tobacco)
Papaver species (poppy)
Pelargonium × *hortorum* (geranium)
Petunia × *hybrida* (petunia)
Phlox drummondii (annual phlox)
Salvia splendens (scarlet sage)
Scabiosa atropurpurea (pincushion-flower)
Thunbergia alata (black-eyed-susan vine)
Verbena × *hybrida* (garden verbena)
Viola × *wittrockiana* (pansy)

Annuals With Red to Pink Flowers

Alcea rosea (hollyhock)
Amaranthus species (Joseph's-coat; love-lies-
    bleeding)
Antirrhinum majus (snapdragon)
Begonia × *semperflorens-cultorum* (wax begonia)
Callistephus chinensis (China aster)
Capsicum annuum (ornamental pepper)
Catharanthus roseus (Madagascar
    periwinkle)
Celosia cristata (cockscomb)
Clarkia hybrids (godetia; farewell-to-spring)
Cleome hasslerana (spiderflower)
Coleus × *hybridus* (coleus)
Consolida ambigua (rocket larkspur)
Cosmos bipinnatus (Mexican aster)
Cuphea ignea (firecracker plant)
Dahlia hybrids (dahlia)
Dianthus species (China pink; sweet william)

Dimorphotheca sinuata (cape marigold)
Eschscholzia californica (California poppy)
Gaillardia pulchella (blanket-flower)
Gazania rigens (gazania)
Gerbera jamesonii (Transvaal daisy)
Gypsophila elegans (annual baby's breath)
Helichrysum bracteatum (strawflower)
Iberis species (candytuft)
Impatiens species (balsam; impatiens)
Ipomoea × *multifida* (cardinal climber)
Ipomoea quamoclit (cypress vine)
Lathyrus odoratus (sweet pea)
Lavatera hybrids (tree mallow)
Linaria maroccana (toadflax)
Matthiola incana (stock)
Mimulus × *hybridus* (monkeyflower)
Nemesia strumosa (pouch nemesia)
Nicotiana alba (flowering tobacco)
Nigella damascena (love-in-a-mist)
Papaver species (poppy)
Pelargonium × *hortorum* (geranium)
Petunia × *hybrida* (petunia)
Phlox drummondii (annual phlox)
Portulaca grandiflora (rose moss)
Rhynchelytrum roseum (ruby grass)
Salpiglossis sinuata (painted-tongue)
Salvia splendens (scarlet sage)
Scabiosa atropurpurea (pincushion-flower)
Schizanthus × *wisetonensis* (poor-man's-orchid)
Tropaeolum majus (nasturtium)
Verbena × *hybrida* (garden verbena)
Viola × *wittrockiana* (pansy)
Zinnia elegans (zinnia)

Dianthus 'Baby Doll'

Annuals With Blue, Violet, and Purple Flowers

Ageratum houstonianum (flossflower)
Anchusa capensis (cape forget-me-not)
Browallia speciosa (sapphire-flower)
Callistephus chinensis (China aster)
Campanula medium (Canterbury bells)
Centaurea cyanus (bachelor's-button)
Consolida ambigua (rocket larkspur)
Convolvulus tricolor (dwarf morning glory)
Cynoglossum amabile (Chinese forget-me-not)
Gomphrena globosa (globe amaranth)
Heliotropium arborescens (heliotrope)
Ipomoea leptophylla (bush morning glory)
Ipomoea nil; I. purpurea; I. tricolor (morning glory)
Lathyrus odoratus (sweet pea)
Limonium sinuatum (notchleaf sea lavender)
Lobelia erinus (edging lobelia)
Myosotis sylvatica (forget-me-not)
Nemophila menziesii (baby-blue-eyes)
Nierembergia hippomanica (cupflower)
Nigella damascena (love-in-a-mist)
Petunia × *hybrida* (petunia)
Salpiglossis sinuata (painted-tongue)
Salvia farinacea (blue sage)
Salvia splendens (scarlet sage)
Scabiosa atropurpurea (pincushion-flower)
Torenia fournieri (wishbone flower)
Trachymene coerulea (blue lace flower)
Verbena × *hybrida* (garden verbena)
Viola × *wittrockiana* (pansy)

Centaurea cyanus

Lavatera hybrids (tree mallow)
Linaria maroccana (toadflax)
Lobularia maritima (sweet alyssum)
Nemophila menziesii (baby-blue-eyes)
Nigella damascena (love-in-a-mist)
Papaver nudicaule (Iceland poppy)
Papaver rhoeas (field poppy)
Phlox drummondii (annual phlox)
Reseda odorata (mignonette)
Viola × *wittrockiana* (pansy)

Hardy Annuals

These frost-tolerant annuals can be sown outdoors in very early spring.

Arctotis stoechadifolia var. *grandis* (African daisy)
Brassica oleracea (ornamental cabbage and kale; best sown in summer for fall display)
Calendula officinalis (pot marigold)
Centaurea cyanus (bachelor's-button)
Cheiranthus cheiri (wallflower)
Clarkia hybrids (godetia; farewell-to-spring; tolerates light frosts)
Consolida ambigua (rocket larkspur)
Cynoglossum amabile (Chinese forget-me-not)
Eschscholzia californica (California poppy)
Grasses:
   Agrostis nebulosa (cloud grass)
   Avena sterilis (animated oats)
   Briza maxima (quaking grass)
   Lagurus ovatus (hare's tail grass)
Gypsophila elegans (annual baby's breath)
Lathyrus odoratus (sweet pea)

Half-Hardy Annuals (Outdoor Sowing)

These annuals are easy to sow directly into the ground outdoors, but should not be sown until all danger of frost has passed.

Catharanthus roseus (Madagascar periwinkle)
Convolvulus tricolor (dwarf morning glory)
Coreopsis tinctoria (calliopsis)
Cosmos bipinnatus (Mexican aster)
Cosmos sulphureus (orange cosmos)
Dianthus barbatus (sweet william)
Dianthus chinensis (China pink)
Euphorbia marginata (snow-on-the-mountain)
Helianthus species (sunflower)
Iberis species (candytuft)
Ipomoea species (morning glory; cardinal climber; cypress vine; moonflower vine)
Mirabilis jalapa (four-o'clock)
Nicotiana alba (flowering tobacco)
Portulaca grandiflora (rose moss)
Ricinus communis (castor bean)

Sanvitalia procumbens (creeping zinnia)
Scabiosa atropurpurea (pincushion-flower)
Tagetes patula (French marigold)
Trachymene coerulea (blue lace flower)
Tropaeolum majus (nasturtium)
Zea mays var. *japonica* (ornamental corn)
Zinnia species (zinnia)

Half-Hardy Annuals (Indoor Sowing)

These annuals are best when started ahead indoors.

Ageratum houstonianum (flossflower)
Alcea rosea (hollyhock)
Amaranthus caudatus (love-lies-bleeding)
Amaranthus tricolor (Joseph's-coat)
Anchusa capensis (cape forget-me-not)
Antirrhinum majus (snapdragon)
Arctotis stoechadifolia var. *grandis* (African daisy)
Begonia × *semperflorens-cultorum* (wax begonia)
Brachycome iberidifolia (Swan River daisy)
Browallia speciosa (sapphire-flower)
Callistephus chinensis (China aster)
Campanula medium (Canterbury bells)
Capsicum annuum (ornamental pepper)
Catharanthus roseus (Madagascar periwinkle)
Celosia cristata (cockscomb)
Cleome hasslerana (spiderflower)

Tagetes patula

Coleus × *hybridus* (coleus)
Consolida ambigua (rocket larkspur)
Coreopsis tinctoria (calliopsis)
Cosmos bipinnatus (Mexican aster)
Cosmos sulphureus (orange cosmos)
Cuphea ignea (firecracker plant)
Dahlia hybrids (dahlia)
Dianthus barbatus (sweet william)
Dianthus chinensis (China pink)
Dimorphotheca sinuata (cape marigold)
Dyssodia tenuiloba (Dahlberg daisy)
Euphorbia marginata (snow-on-the-mountain)
Gaillardia pulchella (blanket-flower)
Gazania rigens (gazania)
Gerbera jamesonii (Transvaal daisy)
Gomphrena globosa (globe amaranth)
Grasses:
   Coix lacryma-jobi (Job's-tears)
   Pennisetum setaceum (crimson fountain grass)
   Rhynchelytrum roseum (ruby grass)
   Setaria macrostachya (plains bristle grass)
Helichrysum bracteatum (strawflower)
Heliotropium arborescens (heliotrope)
Impatiens balsamina (balsam)
Impatiens wallerana (impatiens; busy-lizzie)
Kochia scoparia (summer cypress; burning bush)
Limonium bonduellii (Algerian sea lavender)
Lobelia erinus (edging lobelia)
Matthiola incana (stock)
Mimulus × *hybridus* (monkeyflower)
Mirabilis jalapa (four-o'clock)
Nemesia strumosa (pouch nemesia)
Nicotiana alba (flowering tobacco)
Nierembergia hippomanica (cupflower)
Pelargonium × *hortorum* (geranium)
Petunia × *hybrida* (petunia)
Rudbeckia hirta var. *pulcherrima* (gloriosa daisy)
Salpiglossis sinuata (painted-tongue)
Salvia farinacea (blue sage)
Salvia splendens (scarlet sage)
Schizanthus × *wisetonensis* (poor-man's-orchid)
Senecio cineraria (dusty-miller)
Tagetes, triploid strains (triploid marigolds)
Tagetes erecta (African marigold)
Thunbergia alata (black-eyed-susan vine)
Tithonia rotundifolia (Mexican sunflower)
Torenia fournieri (wishbone flower)
Verbena × *hybrida* (garden verbena)
Viola × *wittrockiana* (pansy)

Tender Annuals

These annuals should not be set out or sown outdoors until the soil is thoroughly warm.

Amaranthus caudatus (love-lies-bleeding)
Amaranthus tricolor (Joseph's-coat)
Celosia cristata (cockscomb)
Heliotropium arborescens (heliotrope)

Fragrant Annuals

Brachycome iberidifolia (Swan River daisy)
Cheiranthus cheiri (wallflower)
Dianthus barbatus (sweet william)
Heliotropium arborescens (heliotrope)
Lathyrus odoratus (sweet pea)
Lobularia maritima (sweet alyssum)
Matthiola incana (stock)
Mirabilis jalapa (four-o'clock)
Reseda odorata (mignonette)

PERENNIALS

The following lists categorize some common perennials by color and use. Consult these lists to spark your imagination or to solve landscaping problems. Keep in mind that, in many cases, when a name appears on a list, only selected varieties (usually too numerous to mention in the list) may fit the given category. Consult seed catalogs and local experts to help pinpoint the variety best suited to your gardening needs.

Perennials With Yellow, Orange, and Bronze Flowers

Achillea species (yarrow)
Alchemilla species (lady's-mantle)
Anthemis tinctoria species (golden marguerite)
Aquilegia species (columbine)
Asclepias tuberosa (butterfly flower)
Aurinia saxatilis (basket-of-gold)
Caltha palustris (marshmarigold)
Chrysanthemum species (chrysanthemum)
Coreopsis species (calliopsis)
Delphinium species (delphinium)
Digitalis species (foxglove)
Doronicum species (leopard's-bane)
Euphorbia species (spurge)
Gaillardia × *grandiflora* (blanket-flower)
Geum species (avens)
Helenium autumnale (sneezeweed)
Helianthus species (sunflower)
Heliopsis species (heliopsis)

Chrysanthemum 'John Hughes'

Helleborus species (Christmas-rose)
Hemerocallis species (daylily)
Iris species (iris)
Kniphofia species (torch lily)
Ligularia species (groundsel)
Lupinus species (lupine)
Lychnis species (campion)
Lysimachia nummularia (moneywort)
Lysimachia punctata (yellow loosestrife)
Paeonia species (peony)
Papaver species (poppy)
Penstemon species (beardtongue)
Primula species (primrose)
Rudbeckia species (black-eyed-susan)
Solidago species (goldenrod)
Thermopsis caroliniana (false-lupine)
Tradescantia species (spiderwort)
Trollius species (globeflower)

Perennials With Cream to White Flowers

Acanthus mollis (bear's-breeches)
Achillea ptarmica (yarrow)
Aquilegia species (columbine)
Armeria species (sea pink)
Aruncus species (goatsbeard)
Aster species (aster)
Astilbe species (false-spiraea)
Bergenia species (bergenia)
Campanula species (harebell)
Chrysanthemum species (chrysanthemum)
Cimicifuga species (bugbane)
Delphinium species (delphinium)

Dianthus species (pink)
Dicentra species (bleeding-heart)
Dictamnus species (gas plant)
Digitalis species (foxglove)
Echinacea species (coneflower)
Filipendula species (queen-of-the-prairie)
Geranium species (cranesbill)
Gypsophila species (baby's breath)
Hemerocallis species (daylily)
Heuchera species (coralbells)
Hibiscus species (rosemallow)
Hosta species (plantain lily)
Iris species (iris)
Kniphofia species (torch lily)
Liatris species (blazing-star)
Lupinus species (lupine)
Lysimachia clethroides (gooseneck loosestrife)
Monarda species (beebalm)
Paeonia species (peony)
Papaver species (poppy)
Penstemon species (beardtongue)
Phlox species (phlox)
Polygonatum species (Solomon's-seal)
Primula species (primrose)
Stokesia laevis (Stoke's aster)
Thalictrum species (meadowrue)
Tradescantia species (spiderwort)
Veronica species (speedwell)

Perennials With Red to Pink Flowers

Achillea millefolium 'Fire King' (fire king yarrow)
Aquilegia species (columbine)
Armeria species (sea pink)
Aster species (aster)
Astilbe species (false-spiraea)
Bergenia species (bergenia)
Campanula species (harebell)
Chrysanthemum coccineum (painted daisy)
Chrysanthemum hybrids (hardy
   chrysanthemum)
Delphinium species (delphinium)
Dianthus species (pink)
Dicentra species (bleeding-heart)
Dictamnus albus 'Purpureus' (rose gas plant)
Digitalis species (foxglove)
Filipendula species (queen-of-the-prairie)
Gaillardia × *grandiflora* (blanket-flower)
Geranium species (cranesbill)
Geum species (avens)
Grasses:
   Cortaderia species (pampas grass)
   Pennisetum species (fountain grass)

Lychnis chalcedonica

Gypsophila species (baby's breath)
Helleborus species (Christmas-rose)
Hemerocallis species (daylily)
Heuchera species (coralbells)
Hibiscus species (rosemallow)
Iris species (iris)
Kniphofia species (torch lily)
Liatris species (blazing-star)
Lobelia species (cardinal flower)
Lupinus species (lupine)
Lychnis species (campion)
Lythrum species (purple loosestrife)
Monarda species (beebalm)
Paeonia species (peony)
Papaver species (poppy)
Penstemon species (beardtongue)
Phlox species (phlox)
Platycodon species (balloonflower)
Primula species (primrose)
Pulmonaria species (lungwort)
Sedum species (stonecrop)
Thalictrum species (meadowrue)
Tradescantia species (spiderwort)
Veronica species (speedwell)

Perennials With Blue, Violet and Purple Flowers

Amsonia species (bluestar)
Anchusa species (bugloss)
Aster species (aster)
Baptisia australis (false-indigo)
Brunnera macrophylla (Siberian bugloss)
Campanula species (harebell)
Ceratostigma plumbaginoides (blue plumbago)
Delphinium species (delphinium)
Echinacea purpurea (coneflower)
Echinops species (globe thistle)
Geranium species (cranesbill)
Hosta species (plantain lily)
Iris species (iris)
Lupinus species (lupine)
Mertensia species (Virginia bluebells)
Phlox species (phlox)
Platycodon grandiflorus (balloonflower)
Primula species (primrose)
Pulmonaria species (lungwort)
Salvia species (sage)
Scabiosa species (pincushion-flower)
Stachys species (betony)

Stokesia laevis (Stoke's aster)
Tradescantia species (spiderwort)
Veronica species (speedwell)

Cool-Summer Perennials

These perennials are best when grown in climate zones that have cool summers, such as mountainous or coastal regions.

Aquilegia species (columbine)
Astilbe species (false-spiraea)
Delphinium species (delphinium)
Dicentra species (bleeding-heart)
Helleborus species (Christmas-rose)
Ligularia species (groundsel)
Lupinus species (lupine)
Penstemon species (beardtongue)
Primula species (primrose)
Thalictrum species (meadowrue)

Fragrant Perennials

Some of the more fragrant perennials are included in the list below. An asterisk (*) indicates that the plant foliage is fragrant when crushed or bruised.

Achillea species (yarrow)*
Anthemis tinctoria (golden marguerite)*
Artemisia species (wormwood)*
Cimicifuga species (bugbane)
Dianthus species (pink)
Dictamnus species (gas plant)
Filipendula species (queen-of-the-prairie)
Hemerocallis species, selected varieties (daylily)
Hosta plantaginea (fragrant plantain lily)
Iris species, bearded (bearded iris)
Monarda species (beebalm)*
Paeonia species (peony)
Phlox paniculata (garden phlox)
Primula, selected varieties (primrose)
Salvia species (sage)*

Perennials for Cutting

Not all the perennials useful for cut flowers will be found in this list, only some of the best. The flowers of those plants marked with an asterisk (*) are especially suitable for drying and preserving.

Acanthus mollis (bear's-breeches)
Achillea species (yarrow)
Anemone species (anemone)
Anthemis tinctoria (golden marguerite)
Aster species (aster)
Chrysanthemum species (chrysanthemum)

Platycodon

Chrysanthemum

Coreopsis species (calliopsis)
Delphinium species (delphinium)
Dianthus species (pink)
Digitalis species (foxglove)
Echinacea species (coneflower)
Echinops species (globe thistle)*
Gaillardia × *grandiflora* (blanket-flower)
Geum species (avens)
Grasses: All
Gypsophila species (baby's breath)*
Helenium species (sneezeweed)
Helianthus species (sunflower)
Heliopsis species (heliopsis)
Hemerocallis species (daylily)
Heuchera species (coralbells)
Hosta species (plantain lily)
Iris species (iris)
Kniphofia species (torch lily)
Liatris species (blazing-star)
Lupinus species (lupine)
Paeonia species (peony)
Papaver species (poppy)
Rudbeckia species (black-eyed-susan)
Scabiosa species (pincushion-flower)
Solidago species (goldenrod)*
Stokesia laevis (Stokes' aster)
Veronica species (speedwell)

SHRUBS

When searching for the right shrub to solve a particular problem or need, organized lists can be particularly helpful. Use the lists that follow to direct you to the appropriate choice.

Shrubs With Colorful Foliage the Year Around

Bright golds, reds, purples, and blues can be available in your garden all year long if you shop for shrubs with colorful foliage. All should be positioned with care, because brightly colored leaves usually make a very bold statement in the landscape.

Acer palmatum 'Dissectum Atropurpureum' (threadleaf Japanese maple)
Aucuba japonica 'Variegata' (variegated Japanese aucuba)
Berberis thunbergii 'Crimson Pygmy' (crimson pygmy barberry)
Buxus sempervirens 'Aureo-variegata' (variegated common boxwood)
Chamaecyparis obtusa 'Nana Aurea' (dwarf golden hinoki cypress)
Cornus alba 'Argenteo-marginata' (variegated Tartarian dogwood)
Cotinus coggygria 'Royal Purple' (smoke tree)
Elaeagnus pungens 'Maculata' (golden elaeagnus)
Elaeagnus pungens 'Marginata' (silver-edge elaeagnus)
Euonymus fortunei 'Colorata' (purpleleaf wintercreeper)
Dodonaea viscosa 'Purpurea' (purple hop bush)
Hydrangea macrophylla 'Tricolor' (bigleaf hydrangea)
Juniperus horizontalis 'Wiltonii' (blue rug juniper)
Kerria japonica 'Aureo-variegata' (variegated Japanese rose)
Leptospermum scoparium 'Ruby Glow' (New Zealand tea tree)
Leucothoe fontanesiana 'Girards Rainbow' (drooping leucothoe)
Ligustrum × *ibolium* (ibolium privet)
Ligustrum japonicum 'Variegatum' (variegated privet)
Ligustrum ovalifolium 'Albo-marginatum' (white-edge privet)
Myrtus communis 'Variegata' (variegated myrtle)
Osmanthus heterophyllus 'Aureus' (yellow-edge holly olive)
Photinia × *fraseri* (redtip photinia)

Pittosporum tobira 'Variegata'

> *Pieris japonica* 'Variegata' (variegated Japanese pieris)
> *Pittosporum tobira* 'Variegata' (variegated tobira)
> *Platycladus orientalis* 'Aureus' (dwarf golden arborvitae)
> *Prunus* × *cistena* (purpleleaf sand cherry)
> *Santolina chamaecyparissus* (lavender-cotton)
> *Thuja occidentalis* 'Rheingold' (golden American arborvitae)
> *Viburnum tinus* 'Variegatum' (variegated laurustinus)
> *Weigela florida* 'Variegata' (variegated weigela)

Shrubs for Winter Interest

A shrub's structure, bark, stem, twigs, and buds offer a kaleidoscope of winter textures to look at. The effects may be delicate and subtle or bold and dramatic.

> *Acer palmatum* 'Dissectum' (laceleaf Japanese maple)
> *Aronia arbutifolia* (red chokeberry)
> *Cornus alba* (Tartarian dogwood)
> *Cornus sericea* (redosier dogwood)
> *Corylus avellana* 'Contorta' (Harry Lauder's walkingstick)
> *Hamamelis* species (witch hazel)
> *Ilex decidua* (possumhaw holly)
> *Ilex verticillata* (common winterberry)
> *Kerria japonica* (Japanese kerria)
> *Magnolia* species (magnolia)
> *Myrica pensylvanica* (northern bayberry)
> *Rhus copallina* (flameleaf sumac)
> *Rhus typhina* (staghorn sumac)
> *Rosa hugonis* (Father Hugo rose)

Shrubs With Fragrant Flowers

For those who love the beautiful fragrances that only flowers can offer, the following list should prove helpful. Here's a tip: To experience fragrance most intensely in your garden, take a stroll on days that are humid and mild.

> *Buddleia davidii* (butterfly bush)
> *Calycanthus floridus* (carolina allspice)
> *Choisya ternata* (Mexican orange)
> *Clethra alnifolia* (sweet pepperbush)
> *Daphne* species (daphne)
> *Elaeagnus* species (elaeagnus)
> *Escallonia* species (escallonia)
> *Fothergilla major* (large fothergilla)
> *Hamamelis* species (witch hazel)
> *Leucothoe fontanesiana* (drooping leucothoe)
> *Lonicera* species (honeysuckle)
> *Magnolia stellata* (star magnolia)
> *Malus sargentii* (Sargent crab apple)
> *Osmanthus* species (holly olive)
> *Philadelphus* species (mock orange)
> *Pittosporum napaulense* (golden fragrance plant)
> *Pittosporum tobira* (tobira)
> *Prunus tomentosa* (Nanking cherry; Manchu cherry)
> *Rhododendron arborescens* (sweet azalea)
> *Rhododendron* × 'Loderi' (Loderi hybrid rhododendron)
> *Rhododendron nudiflorum* (pinxterbloom)
> *Rhododendron vaseyi* (pinkshell azalea)
> *Rhododendron viscosum* (swamp azalea)
> *Rosa spinosissima* (Scotch rose)
> *Rosa wichuraiana* (memorial rose)
> *Syringa vulgaris* (common lilac)
> *Viburnum* × *burkwoodii* (Burkwood viburnum)
> *Viburnum* × *carlcephalum* (fragrant snowball viburnum)
> *Viburnum carlesii* (Korean-spice viburnum)
> *Viburnum* × *juddii* (Judd viburnum)
> *Viburnum tinus* (laurustinus)

Shrubs With Fall Foliage Color

Many deciduous shrubs are very striking in the fall when their foliage changes to various shades of red, orange, yellow, and bronze. Frequently, their colors are brighter and longer lasting than many flowers.

> *Abelia* × *grandiflora* (glossy abelia)
> *Acer palmatum* 'Dissectum' (laceleaf Japanese maple)
> *Aronia arbutifolia* (red chokeberry)

Berberis thunbergii (Japanese barberry)
Clethra alnifolia (sweet pepperbush)
Cornus alba (Tartarian dogwood)
Cornus sericea (redosier dogwood)
Cotinus coggygria (smoke tree)
Cotoneaster divaricata (spreading cotoneaster)
Cotoneaster horizontalis (rock cotoneaster)
Enkianthus campanulatus (redvein enkianthus)
Euonymus alata (burning bush)
Fothergilla major (large fothergilla)
Hamamelis species (witch hazel)
Hydrangea quercifolia (oakleaf hydrangea)
Mahonia aquifolium (Oregon grape)
Paxistima canbyi (Canby paxistima)
Rhododendron, Knap Hill-Exbury hybrids (Knap Hill-Exbury hybrid azalea)
Rhododendron arborescens (sweet azalea)
Rhododendron kaempferi (torch azalea)
Rhododendron schlippenbachii (royal azalea)
Rhododendron vaseyi (pinkshell azalea)
Rhus species (sumac)
Rosa virginiana (Virginia rose)
Vaccinium corymbosum (highbush blueberry)
Viburnum × *carlcephalum* (fragrant snowball viburnum)
Viburnum dilatatum (linden viburnum)
Viburnum × *juddii* (Judd viburnum)
Viburnum opulus (European cranberry bush)
Viburnum plicatum var. *tomentosum* (doublefile viburnum)
Viburnum trilobum (American cranberrybush viburnum)

Shrubs With Evergreen Foliage

Evergreen shrubs, whether they are broadleafed or coniferous, add their own special warmth to the garden. Their presence is especially appreciated in the winter, when the landscape might otherwise feel bleak and uninviting. In the following list, the abbreviation SE following an entry indicates that a plant is semievergreen—partially or totally dropping its leaves in the northern limits of its hardiness range.

Abelia × *grandiflora* (glossy abelia, SE)
Berberis darwinii (Darwin barberry)
Buxus species (boxwood)
Calluna vulgaris (Scotch heather)
Camellia species (camellia)
Ceanothus, western species (wild lilac)
Chamaecyparis species (false-cypress)
Choisya ternata (Mexican orange)
Cistus species (rockrose)
Coprosma species (coprosma)

Cotoneaster dammeri (bearberry cotoneaster)
Cotoneaster horizontalis (rock cotoneaster, SE)
Cytisus × *praecox* (warminster broom)
Daphne species (daphne)
Elaeagnus pungens (silverberry)
Erica species (heath)
Escallonia species (escallonia)
Euonymus fortunei (winter creeper)
Euonymus japonica (Japanese euonymus)
Euonymus kiautschovicus (spreading euonymus)
Genista species (broom)
Hypericum calycinum (Aaron's-beard; St. John's wort)
Hypericum × *moseranum* (St. John's wort)
Hypericum patulum (goldencup; St. John's wort, SE)
Ilex cornuta (Chinese holly)
Ilex crenata (Japanese holly)
Ilex glabra (inkberry)
Ilex × *meserveae* (Meserve hybrid holly)
Ilex vomitoria (yaupon holly)
Juniperus species (juniper)
Kalmia latifolia (mountain laurel)
Leucothoe fontanesiana (drooping leucothoe)
Ligustrum × *ibolium* (ibolium privet, SE)
Ligustrum japonicum (Japanese privet)
Ligustrum lucidum (glossy privet)
Ligustrum ovalifolium (California privet, SE)

Cornus

Ligustrum 'Suwanee River' (privet)
Lonicera nitida (box honeysuckle)
Mahonia species (oregon grape; holly grape)
Myrtus communis (myrtle)
Osmanthus delavayi (Delavay osmanthus)
Osmanthus fragrans (sweet olive)
Osmanthus heterophyllus (holly olive)
Paxistima canbyi (Canby paxistima)
Photinia × *fraseri* (Fraser photinia)
Photinia serrulata (Chinese photinia)
Picea species (spruce)
Pieris species (pieris)
Pinus species (pine)
Pittosporum species (pittosporum)
Prunus laurocerasus (English laurel)
Pyracantha coccinea (scarlet firethorn, SE)
Raphiolepis indica (India hawthorn)
Rhododendron carolinianum (Carolina
    rhododendron)
Rhododendron catawbiense (Catawba
    rhododendron)
Rhododendron, Gable hybrids (Gable hybrid
    azalea, SE)
Rhododendron impeditum (cloudland
    rhododendron)
Rhododendron, Indica hybrids (Indica hybrid
    azalea)
Rhododendron kaempferi, (torch azalea, SE)
Rhododendron keiskei (Kiesk rhododendron)
Rhododendron lapponicum (Lapland
    rhododendron)
Rhododendron × 'Loderi' (Loderi hybrid
    rhododendron)
Rhododendron maximum (rosebay
    rhododendron)
Rhododendron obtusum (Hiryo azalea)
Rosa wichuraiana (memorial rose, SE)
Rosmarinus officinalis (rosemary)
Taxus species (yew)
Thuja species (arborvitae)
Tsuga canadensis 'Pendula' (Sargent's weeping
    hemlock)
Viburnum × *burkwoodii* (Burkwood viburnum)
Viburnum davidii (David viburnum)
Viburnum tinus (laurustinus)

TREES

From the great world of trees, a few have been chosen to serve as a guide. Some trees are listed by their attributes or characteristics and others, by their functions. Each list covers only a fraction of all the trees that could be included in that category. However, these are the choicest of the lot.

An asterisk (*) indicates that only certain species of the genus listed fall under the category description.

Trees With Attractive Fruit

Bright colors aren't limited to foliage and flowers. Berries and other fruit, both edible and inedible, can be just as attractive—and sometimes they last longer.

Amelanchier canadensis (serviceberry)
Arbutus species (madrone)
Chionanthus species (fringe tree)
Cornus species (dogwood)
Crataegus species (hawthorn*)
Diospyros species (persimmon*)
Elaeagnus angustifolia (Russian olive)
Eriobotrya japonica (loquat)
Ilex species (holly*)
Koelreuteria paniculata (goldenrain tree)
Malus species (crab apple*)
Oxydendrum arboreum (sourwood)
Prunus species (plums, cherries, cherry laurels*)
Sorbus species (mountain ash)

Lagerstroemia indica

Trees With Color in More Than One Season

These trees provide interest over a long period of time with their flowers, fruits, autumn color, or bark.

Acer palmatum (Japanese maple)
Amelanchier canadensis (serviceberry)
Betula species (birch*)
Cercis canadensis (eastern redbud)
Chionanthus virginicus (fringe tree)
Cladrastis lutea (yellowwood)
Cornus species (dogwood)
Crataegus species (hawthorn*)
Diospyros kaki (Kaki persimmon)
Halesia carolina (Carolina silverbell)
Ilex species (holly*)
Koelreuteria paniculata (goldenrain tree)
Lagerstroemia indica (crape myrtle)
Malus species (crab apple*)
Oxydendrum arboreum (sourwood)
Prunus species (plums, cherries, cherry laurels*)
Pyrus calleryana (Callery pear)
Styrax japonicus (Japanese snowbell)

Trees for Fragrance

Although the flowers of some trees are inconspicuous, their presence in the garden is a decided olfactory pleasure.

Acer ginnala (Amur maple)
Cladrastis lutea (yellowwood)
Elaeagnus angustifolia (Russian olive)
Halesia carolina (Carolina silverbell)
Magnolia species (magnolia*)
Malus species (crab apple*)
Oxydendrum arboreum (sourwood)
Prunus species (plums, cherries, cherry laurels*)
Robinia pseudoacacia (black locust)
Sophora japonica (Japanese pagoda tree)
Styrax japonicus (Japanese snowbell)
Syringa reticulata (Japanese tree lilac)
Tilia cordata (littleleaf linden)

Trees With Interesting Bark

Texture, color, and patterns of bark are important considerations when selecting landscape trees.

Acer species (maple*)
Arbutus species (madrone; strawberry tree)
Betula species (birch*)
Calocedrus decurrens (incense cedar)
Cladrastis lutea (yellowwood)
Cryptomeria japonica (Japanese cedar)
Diospyros species (persimmon*)

Liquidambar

Fagus sylvatica (European beech)
Lagerstroemia indica (crape myrtle)
Liquidambar styraciflua (American sweet gum)
Ostrya virginiana (American hophornbeam)
Pinus species (pine*)
Platanus × *acerifolia* (London plane tree)
Prunus species (cherry*)
Salix alba var. *vitellina* (golden willow)
Stewartia species (stewartia*)
Ulmus parvifolia (Chinese elm)

Trees With Excellent Fall Color

In many parts of the country, trees offer a breathtaking kaleidoscope of fall color. Here are trees with reliable fall color.

Acer species (maple*)
Amelanchier canadensis (serviceberry)
Betula species (birch*)
Cercidiphyllum japonicum (katsura)
Cornus species (dogwood*)
Cotinus coggygria (smoke tree)
Diospyros virginiana (American common persimmon)
Franklinia alatamaha (franklinia)
Fraxinus species (ash)
Ginkgo biloba (maidenhair tree)

Lagerstroemia indica (crape myrtle)
Larix leptolepis (Japanese larch)
Liquidambar styraciflua (American sweet gum)
Liriodendron tulipifera (tulip tree)
Nyssa sylvatica (black tupelo)
Oxydendrum arboreum (sourwood)
Pistacia chinensis (Chinese pistache)
Populus species (poplar*)
Pyrus calleryana (Callery pear)
Quercus species (oak*)
Sapium sebiferum (Chinese tallow tree)
Sassafras albidum (sassafras)
Zelkova serrata (Japanese zelkova)

GROUND COVERS

Because ground covers display such a wide range of cultural requirements and growth habits, some are naturally better suited than others to specific landscape situations. The following lists are designed to help you choose plants to meet the particular needs of your home landscape. The lists are not exhaustive but represent the most common ground covers.

Ground Covers for Full Sun

Achillea tomentosa (wooly yarrow)
Arabis species (rockcress)
Arctostaphylos uva-ursi (kinnikinick)
Artemisia schmidtiana (angel's hair)
Baccharis pilularis (dwarf coyotebrush)
Ceanothus species (wild lilac)
Cerastium tomentosum (snow-in-summer)
Cotoneaster species (cotoneaster, low-growing)
Cytisus species (broom)
Helianthemum nummularium (sun-rose)
Juniperus species (juniper)
Lantana species (lantana)
Phlox subulata (moss pink)
Phyla nodiflora (lippia)
Pyracantha koidzumii 'Santa Cruz' (firethorn)
Rosa species (rose)
Rosmarinus officinalis 'Prostratus' (dwarf rosemary)
Santolina chamaecyparissus (lavender-cotton)
Sedum species (stonecrop)

Ground Covers for Sun or Partial Shade

Aegopodium podagraria (goutweed)
Ajuga species (carpet bugle)
Bergenia species (bergenia)

Duchesnea indica

Campanula species (bellflower)
Cyrtomium falcatum (holly fern)
Dichondra micrantha (dichondra)
Epimedium species (barrenwort)
Fragaria chiloensis (wild or sand strawberry)
Hedera helix (English ivy)
Hypericum calycinum (Aaron's-beard)
Liriope spicata (creeping lilyturf)
Mahonia repens (creeping mahonia)
Ophiopogon japonicus (mondo grass)
Paxistima canbyi (Canby pachistima)
Polygonum species (knotweed)
Sagina subulata (Irish moss)
Trachelospermum (jasmine)

Ground Covers That Tolerate Deep Shade

Adiantum pedatum (five-finger fern)
Asarum species (wild ginger)
Athyrium goeringianum (Japanese painted fern)
Convallaria majalis (lily-of-the-valley)
Dryopteris species (wood fern)
Epimedium species (bishop's-hat)
Galium odoratum (sweet woodruff)
Hedera helix (English ivy)
Pachysandra terminalis (Japanese spurge)
Sagina subulata (Irish moss)
Sarcococca hookerana var. *humilis* (small Himalayan sarcococca)
Viola odorata (sweet violet)

Drapers and Trailers

Arctostaphylos uva-ursi (kinnikinick)
Artemisia species (dusty-miller; wormwood)
Asparagus densiflorus 'Sprengeri' (Sprenger asparagus fern)
Campanula species (bellflower)
Cerastium tomentosum (snow-in-summer)
Cotoneaster species (cotoneaster, low-growing)
Euonymus fortunei (euonymus)
Hedera species (ivy)
Juniperus species (juniper, low-growing)
Lotus berthelotii (parrot's-beak)
Rosmarinus officinalis 'Prostratus' (dwarf rosemary)
Trachelospermum jasminoides (starjasmine)
Verbena peruviana (Peruvian verbena)
Vinca minor (periwinkle)

Ground Covers That Tolerate Traffic

Ajuga species (carpet bugle)
Chamaemelum nobile (chamomile)
Dichondra micrantha (dichondra)
Duchesnea indica (mock strawberry)
Juniperus horizontalis 'Blue Rug' (blue rug juniper)
Phyla nodiflora (lippia)
Sagina subulata (Irish moss)
Veronica repens (speedwell)
Zoysia tenuifolia (Korean grass)

Lawn Alternatives (Large Areas)

Aegopodium podagraria (goutweed)
Ajuga reptans (carpet bugle)
Arctostaphylos uva-ursi (kinnikinick)
Baccharis pilularis 'Twin Peaks' (dwarf coyotebush)
Coronilla varia (crown vetch)
Dianthus deltoides (maiden pink)
Dichondra species (dichondra)
Duchesnea indica (mock strawberry)
Euonymus fortunei (wintercreeper euonymus)
Festuca ovina var. *glauca* (blue fescue)
Fragaria chiloensis (wild or sand strawberry)
Hedera species (ivy)
Hypericum calycinum (Aaron's-beard)
Juniperus species (juniper, low-growing)
Lantana species (lantana)
Liriope spicata (creeping lilytruf)
Lonicera japonica (Japanese honeysuckle)
Pachysandra terminalis (Japanese spurge)
Phyla nodiflora (lippia)
Polygonum cuspidatum var. *compactum* (fleece flower)
Potentilla species (cinquefoil)
Sedum species (stonecrop)
Trachelospermum species (jasmine)
Vinca species (periwinkle)
Zoysia tenuifolia (Korean grass)

Pachysandra terminalis

HERB GARDENS

Of the many ways herbs and spices can be grouped, their uses and pleasures for us come first. The accompanying plant lists describe a few theme gardens, along with plants for special purposes.

Shakespeare Garden

Listed below are herbs mentioned in the writings of William Shakespeare. All were popular in Elizabethan England.

Aquilegia species (columbine)
Artemisia absinthium (wormwood)
Brassica juncea (mustard)
Calendula officinalis (pot marigold)
Chamaemelum nobile (chamomile)
Dianthus caryophyllus (carnation)
Dianthus deltoides (maiden pink)
Fragaria chiloensis (wild or sand strawberry)
Hyssopus officinalis (hyssop)
Laurus nobilis (bay)
Lavandula species (lavender)
Melissa officinalis (lemon balm)
Mentha species (mint)
Myrtus species (myrtle)
Origanum majorana (marjoram)
Petroselinum crispum (parsley)
Poterium sanguisorba (burnet)
Rosa species (rose)
Rosmarinus officinalis (rosemary)
Satureja species (savory)
Thymus species (thyme)
Viola tricolor (Johnny-jump-up)

Good Cook's Garden

The plants on this list are indispensable ingredients in the kitchen. You may want to plant them near the kitchen door to save some steps.

Allium ampeloprasum (leek)
Allium cepa (onion)
Allium sativum (garlic)
Allium schoenoprasum (chives)
Anethum graveolens (dill)
Angelica archangelica (angelica)
Anthriscus cerefolium (chervil)
Armoracia rusticana (horseradish)
Artemisia dracunculus (tarragon)
Borago officinalis (borage)
Brassica juncea (mustard)

Mentha species

Carum carvi (caraway)
Chrysanthemum balsamita (costmary)
Coriandrum sativum (coriander)
Cuminum cyminum (cumin)
Eruca sativa (rocket)
Hyssopus officinalis (hyssop)
Laurus nobilis (bay)
Lavandula species (lavender)
Levisticum officinale (lovage)
Marrubium vulgare (horehound)
Mentha species (mint)
Nasturtium officinale (watercress)
Ocimum basilicum (basil)
Origanum majorana (marjoram)
Origanum vulgare (oregano)
Petroselinum crispum (parsley)
Pimpinella anisum (anise)
Poterium sanguisorba (burnet)
Rosa species (rose)
Rosmarinus officinalis (rosemary)
Salvia officinalis (sage)
Satureja species (summer savory)
Sesamum indicum (sesame)
Tropaeolum majus (nasturtium)

Tanacetum vulgare

Tea Garden

Almost every herb and spice can be made into a tea. These are especially good and will make attractive plantings as well.

Aloysia triphylla (lemon verbena)
Anethum graveolens (dill)
Angelica archangelica (angelica)
Borago officinalis (borage)
Chamaemelum nobile (chamomile)
Chrysanthemum balsamita (costmary)
Foeniculum vulgare (fennel)
Galium odoratum (sweet woodruff)
Gaultheria procumbens (wintergreen)
Jasminum species (jasmine)
Levisticum officinale (lovage)
Marrubium vulgare (horehound)
Melissa officinalis (lemon balm)
Mentha species (mint)
Monarda didyma (bergamot)
Myrrhis odorata (sweet cicely)
Nepeta cataria (catnip)
Ocimum basilicum (basil)
Origanum majorana (marjoram)
Petroselinum crispum (parsley)
Rosa species (rose)
Rosmarinus officinalis (rosemary)
Salvia officinalis (sage)
Tanacetum vulgare (tansy)
Thymus species (thyme)

Garden of Fragrances

A walk through a garden designed for fragrances is a delight to all the senses. Not only do these plants smell great but they are also visually pleasing. Some of them taste good, and you can't resist touching the leaves as you listen to the birds and bees enjoying them, too.

Achillea millefolium (yarrow)
Acorus calamus (sweet flag)
Aloysia triphylla (lemon verbena)
Angelica archangelica (angelica)
Artemisia abrotanum (southernwood)
Artemisia dracunculus (tarragon)
Chamaemelum nobile (chamomile)
Chenopodium bonus-henricus (Good-king-henry)
Chrysanthemum balsamita (costmary)
Convallaria majalis (lily-of-the-valley)
Galium odoratum (sweet woodruff)
Heliotropium arborescens (heliotrope)
Hyssopus officinalis (hyssop)
Jasminum species (jasmine)
Lavandula species (lavender)
Melissa officinalis (lemon balm)
Mentha species (mint)
Mentha pulegium (pennyroyal)
Monarda didyma (bergamot)
Myrrhis odorata (sweet cicely)
Nepeta cataria (catnip)
Ocimum basilicum (basil)
Origanum majorana (marjoram)
Origanum vulgare (oregano)
Pelargonium species (scented geraniums)
Rosa species (rose)
Rosmarinus officinalis (rosemary)
Salvia officinalis (sage)
Satureja species (summer savory)
Tanacetum vulgare (tansy)
Thymus species (thyme)
Viola odorata (sweet violet)

The Flowering Garden

A well-planned garden of herbs and spices can provide many flowers for fragrances, cutting, drying, eating, garnishing, or just enjoying. Many other herbs flower, but should be harvested just before flowers open.

Achillea millefolium (yarrow)
Anethum graveolens (dill)
Angelica archangelica (angelica)
Anthriscus cerefolium (chervil)
Borago officinalis (borage)

Brassica juncea (mustard)
Calendula officinalis (pot marigold)
Carthamus tinctorius (safflower)
Chamaemelum nobile (chamomile)
Chrysanthemum balsamita (costmary)
Convallaria majalis (lily-of-the-valley)
Coriandrum sativum (coriander)
Cuminum cyminum (cumin)
Dianthus caryophyllus (carnation)
Dianthus deltoides (maiden pink)
Galium odoratum (sweet woodruff)
Helianthus annuus (sunflower)
Hyssopus officinalis (hyssop)
Inula helenium (elecampane)
Lavandula species (lavender)
Levisticum officinale (lovage)
Monarda didyma (bergamot)
Nigella sativa (fennel flower)
Pimpinella anisum (anise)
Rosa species (rose)
Rosmarinus officinalis (rosemary)
Tanacetum vulgare (tansy)
Taraxacum officinale (dandelion)
Thymus species (thyme)
Viola odorata (violet)
Viola tricolor (Johnny-jump-up)
Zingiber officinale (ginger)

Gray and Silver Garden

A quiet garden of subtle shimmering foliage is a pleasant place to visit, especially on a moonlit evening. Gray foliage highlights the colors of the flowers of these plants and their companions, and provides contrast in vivid flower beds.

Achillea millefolium (yarrow)
Aloe vera (aloe)
Artemisia abrotanum (southernwood)
Artemisia absinthium (wormwood)
Dianthus caryophyllus (carnation)
Lavandula species (lavender)
Marrubium vulgare (horebound)
Mentha × *rotundifolia* (pineapple mint)
Mentha suaveolens (apple mint)
Origanum vulgare (oregano)
Pelargonium × *fragrans* (nutmeg geranium)
Rosmarinus officinalis (rosemary)
Salvia officinalis (sage)
Teucrium chamaedrys (germander)
Thymus nitidus (silver thyme)

Borago officinalis

Indoor Garden

When you plan an indoor herb and spice garden, start with these easy-to-grow plants. If there's insufficient sunlight, group them in an attractive unit under wide-spectrum artificial light.

Allium schoenoprasum (chives)
Aloe vera (aloe)
Aloysia triphylla (lemon verbena)
Anethum graveolens (dill)
Anthriscus cerefolium (chervil)
Artemisia dracunculus (tarragon)
Borago officinalis (borage)
Foeniculum vulgare (fennel)
Hyssopus officinalis (hyssop)
Laurus nobilis (bay)
Lavandula species (lavender)
Levisticum officinale (lovage)
Melissa officinalis (lemon balm)
Mentha species (mint)
Mentha pulegium (pennyroyal)
Ocimum basilicum (basil)
Origanum dictamnus (Dittany of Crete)
Origanum majorana (marjoram)
Origanum vulgare (oregano)
Pelargonium species (scented geraniums)
Petroselinum crispum (parsley)
Poterium sanguisorba (burnet)
Rosmarinus officinalis (rosemary)
Rumex scutatus (sorrel)
Salvia officinalis (sage)
Satureja species (savory)
Thymus species (thyme)
Zingiber officinale (ginger)

Rhododendron

CLIMATE, MICROCLIMATE, AND SHADE

The following lists of shade-tolerant plants are designed to help you select plants to fill special needs in your garden. Is your garden dry and very shady? Is it lightly shaded and moist? Are you looking for a bright-flowering annual to grow in medium shade? Consult these lists and then read about those plants that interest you in the encyclopedia on pages 377 to 499. Each plant on these lists is given a shade tolerance rating between 1 and 4 to indicate the degree of shade the plant can withstand. Ratings of 1 and 2 are dappled and open shade, respectively; both of these fit under the definition of light shade in the encyclopedia. Rating 3 is medium shade, and 4 is dense shade, both of which are described as deep shade in the encyclopedia.

Plants for Very Deep Shade

Botanical Name	Foliage/Flower Color	Type of Plant
Asarum species	Deep green/brown	Ground cover
Aucuba japonica	Variegated/red berries	Shrub
Bergenia cordifolia	Light green/pink	Perennial
Browallia speciosa	Deep green/blue, white	Annual
Clivia miniata	Medium green/orange	Perennial
Digitalis purpurea and hybrids	Medium green/yellow, purple, white, pink	Perennial

Plants for Very Deep Shade (*continued*)

Botanical Name	Foliage/Flower Color	Type of Plant
Epimedium species	Medium green/white, pink, red, violet, yellow	Ground cover
Fatsia japonica	Tropical appearance	Shrub
Gaultheria procumbens	Deep green/white/red berries	Ground cover
Hedera species	Light–deep green	Ground cover
Hosta species	Deep green/blue, white	Perennial
Hydrangea macrophylla	Light green/white, pink, blue	Shrub
Impatiens wallerana	Medium green/mauve, pink, orange, white, red, rose, salmon	Annual
Kerria japonica	Light green/yellow	Shrub
Leucothoe fontanesiana	Bronze new growth/white	Shrub
Mertensia virginica	Deep green/violet, blue	Perennial
Mimulus species	Deep green/yellow, maroon	Annual
Pachysandra terminalis	Light–medium green/white	Ground cover
Pittosporum tobira	Dark green/white	Shrub
Polygonatum species	Medium green/white	Perennial
Polystichum species	Medium green	Fern
Sarcococca hookerana var. *humilis*	Medium green/white/black berries	Ground cover
Soleirolia soleirolii	Light green	Gound cover
Taxus species	Deep blue–green needles/red berries	Shrub or tree
Torenia fournieri	Medium green/blue, violet, yellow	Annual
Tradescantia virginiana	Deep green/white, pink, blue, magenta, purple	Perennial

Flowering Shrubs for Shade

Botanical Name	Flower Color	Shade Tolerance
Abelia × *grandiflora*	Pinkish white	1, 2
Aesculus parviflora	White	1–3
Aesculus pavia	Red (deep rose)	1–3
Camellia japonica	White, pink, red	1, 2
Camellia sasanqua	White, pink, red	1, 2
Fuchsia species and hybrids	Red, pink, white, blue, purple	1, 2
Hydrangea macrophylla	White, pink, blue	1, 2
Kalmia latifolia	Pink, white	1, 2
Kerria japonica	Yellow	1, 2
Mahonia species	Yellow/blue berries	1, 2
Pieris japonica	White, pink/red new growth	1, 2
Rhododendron species and hybrids	All colors	1–3
Sarcococca ruscifolia	White/blue berries	1–4

Bulb and Bulblike Plants for Shade

Botanical Name	Flower Color	Shade Tolerance
Begonia × *tuberhybrida*	White, yellow, bronze, pink, orange	1, 2
Caladium hybrids	Foliage red, pink, white	1, 2
Convallaria majalis	White	1–3
Cyclamen species	White, pink	1, 2
Erythronium species	Yellow, pink, white	1, 2
Fritillaria imperialis	Cream, maroon	1, 2
Leucojum species	White	1
Scilla species	Blue, purple, pink, white	1, 2

Clivia miniata

Impatiens

Perennials for Shade

Botanical Name	Flower Color	Shade Tolerance
Acanthus mollis	White	1, 2
Agapanthus species	White, blue	1, 2
Anemone species	White, pink, red, purple, blue	1, 2
Aquilegia species and hybrids	All colors and combinations	1, 2
Astilbe hybrids	White, pink, red, lavender	1–3
Bergenia cordifolia	Light green/pink	1–4
Brunnera macrophylla	Sky blue	1, 2
Caltha palustris	Yellow	1, 2
Cimicifuga racemosa	White	1
Clivia miniata	Orange	1–4
Dicentra species	Rose pink	1, 2
Digitalis species and hybrids	Yellow, buff, purple, white, pink	1–4
Echinacea purpurea	Purple	1, 2
Helleborus niger	White	1, 2
Hemerocallis species and hybrids	Yellow, orange, red, pink	1, 2
Hosta species	Blue, white	1–4
Hosta species	All shades, variegated/white, blue	1–4
Iris kaempferi	Blue, violet, white	1, 2
Liriope species	Blue, white	1, 2
Lobelia cardinalis	Crimson	1, 2
Mertensia virginica	Violet, blue	3, 4
Ophiopogon japonicus	Purple	1, 2
Polygonatum species	White	1–4
Primula species	All colors, some bicolor	1, 2

Perennials for Shade (*continued*)

Botanical Name	Flower Color	Shade Tolerance
Tradescantia virginiana	White, pink, magenta, purple, blue	1–4
Trollius europaeus	Yellow, orange	1–3

Foliage Shrubs for Shade

Botanical Name	Height/Color	Shade Tolerance
Aucuba japonica	To 10′/brilliant variegation/red berries	1–4
Buxus sempervirens	To 20′/excellent for formal training	1, 2
Calycanthus floridus	To 9′/fragrant maroon flowers	1, 2
Chamaecyparis species	To 5′/most elegant in habit	1, 2
Euonymus fortunei	To 20′/some with variegated foliage	1–3
Fatsia japonica	To 15′/tropical appearance	1–4
Ilex species	To 20′/red berries	1, 2
Leucothoe fontanesiana	To 5′/bronze new growth; variegated	1–4
Ligustrum species	To 25′/white flowers if unpruned	1, 2
Nandina domestica	To 8′/red-bronze foliage	1, 2
Osmanthus species	To 10′/insignificant but fragrant flowers	1–3
Pittosporum tobira	To 10′/white flowers/orange berries	1–4

Understory Trees

Botanical Name	Foliage/Flower Color	Shade Tolerance
Acer palmatum	Green	1, 2
Aesculus species	White, deep rose	1–3
Cercis species	Pink	1, 2
Cornus florida	White, pink	1, 2
Hamamelis × *intermedia*	Yellow	1, 2
Ligustrum species	White	1–3
Tsuga canadensis	Brown cones	1, 2

Annuals and Biennials for Shade

Botanical Name	Flower Color	Shade Tolerance
Begonia × *semperflorens-cultorum*	White, pink, rose, red	1–3
Browallia speciosa	Blue, white	1–3
Campanula medium	Blue, pink, white	1, 2
Clarkia species (godetias)	Pink, salmon, red, white	1, 2
Coleus hybrids	Blue/foliage red, purple, yellow	1–3
Impatiens balsamina	Red, pink, white	1, 2
Impatiens wallerana	Mauve, pink, orange, white, salmon, red, magenta	1–4
Mimulus species	Yellow, maroon	1–4
Myosotis sylvatica	Sky blue	1, 2
Nicotiana alata	White, lime, pink, deep rose	1, 2
Nierembergia hippomanica	Blue	1, 2
Salvia splendens	Red, white	1, 2
Torenia fournieri	Blue, violet, yellow	1–4
Viola hybrids	All colors	1–3

Ground Covers for Shade

Botanical Name	Foliage/Flower Color	Shade Tolerance
Ajuga reptans	Variegated, green, bronze/blue	1, 2
Asarum caudatum	Deep green/brown	1–4
Convallaria majalis	Deep green/white	1–3
Cornus canadensis	Deep green/white/red berries	1, 2
Duchesnea indica	Medium green/yellow/red berries	1, 2
Epimedium species	Medium green/white, pink, yellow	1–4
Euonymus fortunei	Deep green, variegated	1–3
Festuca ovina var. *glauca*	Silvery blue	1, 2
Fragaria chiloensis	Deep green/white	1, 2
Gaultheria procumbens	Deep green/white/red berries	1, 2
Hedera species	Deep–light green, yellow, white	1–4
Liriope species	Yellow or white variegation/blue, white	1, 2
Mahonia repens	Deep green, bronze/yellow	1, 2
Mentha requienii	Light green/pink	1, 2
Ophiopogon japonicus	Deep green/blue	1, 2
Pachysandra terminalis	Medium–light green/white	1–4
Sagina subulata	Light or dark green/white	1, 2
Soleirolia soleirolii	Light green	1–4
Vancouveria hexandra	Medium green/white	1–3
Vinca minor	Deep green/blue	1–3

Shade-Tolerant Plants for Dry Spots

Botanical Name	Type	Shade Tolerance
Acanthus mollis	Perennial	1, 2
Aucuba japonica	Shrub	1–4
Bergenia cordifolia	Perennial	1–4
Cercis canadensis	Tree	1, 2
Cornus canadensis	Ground cover	1, 2
Duchesnea indica	Ground cover	1, 2
Euonymus fortunei	Shrub or ground cover	1–3
Festuca ovina var. *glauca*	Grass	1, 2
Hemerocallis species and hybrids	Herbaceous perennial	1, 2
Kerria japonica	Shrub or vine	1, 2
Ligustrum species	Shrub or tree	1, 2
Mahonia species	Shrub or ground cover	1, 2
Nierembergia hippomanica	Perennial	1, 2
Polygonatum commutatum	Perennial	1–4
Pratia angulata	Ground cover	1–3
Sarcococca hookerana var. *humilis*	Ground cover	1–4
Tradescantia virginiana	Perennial	1–4
Vinca minor	Ground cover	1–3

Shade-Tolerant Plants for Wet Spots

Botanical Name	Type	Shade Tolerance
Aesculus species	Shrub or tree	1–3
Asarum species	Ground cover	1–4
Astilbe species and hybrids	Perennial	1–3
Caltha palustris	Perennial	1, 2
Calycanthus species	Shrub	1, 2
Convallaria majalis	Perennial	1–3
Hemerocallis species and hybrids	Perennial	1, 2
Hosta species	Perennial	1–4
Ilex species	Shrub or tree	1, 2
Iris kaempferi	Perennial	1, 2
Lobelia cardinalis	Perennial	1, 2
Mahonia species	Shrub	1, 2
Mertensia virginica	Perennial	1–4
Mimulus species	Annual	1–4
Myosotis sylvatica	Biennial	1, 2
Soleirolia soleirolii	Ground cover	1–4
Tradescantia virginiana	Perennial	1–4

Hosta

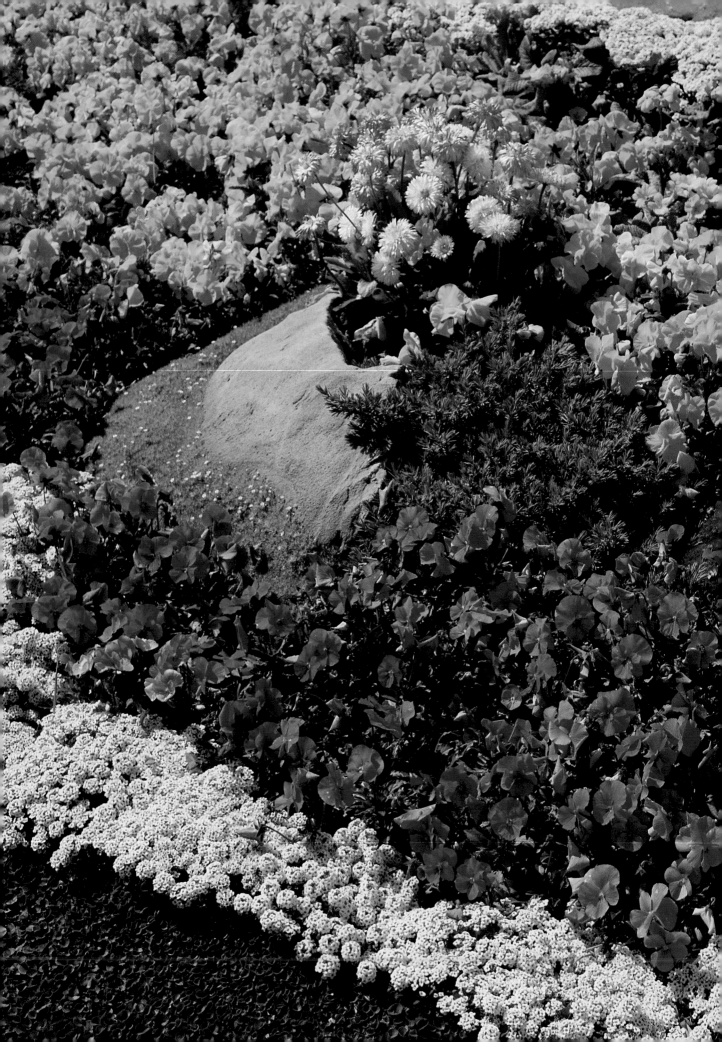

ENCYCLOPEDIA OF PLANTS

The plants in this encyclopedia are listed in alphabetical order. Ornamental plants are listed by their botanical name. This practice is common in horticultural books because many plants have several common names, and different plants are frequently called by the same common name. If you don't know a plant's botanical name, refer to the list of common names on the next page. Food plants—fruits, berries, herbs, nut trees, and vegetables—are entered in the encyclopedia by their common name, so they do not appear in the list of common names.

Zones
The climatic zones listed follow the United States Department of Agriculture system. The zones are based on average winter low temperatures. The zone system is widely used because low winter temperatures limit where many plants can be grown. No zones are given for annuals, biennials, or annual vegetables because they do not usually live through the winter. Find your zone on the map on pages 350 and 351.

Flowers
The two columns showing flower color and bloom time are only filled in if the flowers on that plant are of significant interest. If there are no flowers, or if the flowers are insignificant, the columns are left blank.

Bulbs
In the encyclopedia all bulblike plants are referred to as bulbs even though some grow from tubers, corms, rhizomes, or tuberous roots. To find out which of these bulbous types a plant grows from, see pages 59 and 60.

Shade
Two types of shade are referred to in the encyclopedia: *light shade* and *deep shade*. In the chapter "Understanding the Garden Environment," four types of shade—*dappled shade, open shade, medium shade,* and *dense shade*—are described. The first two are included in *light shade*; the latter two are included in *deep shade*.

Grass Height
The heights given for turfgrasses are the recommended mowing heights.

Sweet alyssum and sweet violet create a a border of striking color contrasts.

COMMON NAMES

Because the common names of plants vary from one part of the country to another, ornamental plants are listed in this encyclopedia by their botanical names. If you don't know the botanical name of a plant, look up the common name you know in the list below. Food plants—vegetables, herbs, and fruit trees—are listed in the encyclopedia by their common names, so they don't appear in this list.

A

Aaron's-beard: *Hypericum calycinum*
Abelia: *Abelia × grandiflora*
Adriatic bellflower: *Campanula elatines* var. *garganica*
African daisy: *Arctotis stoechadifolia, Osteospermum fruiticosum*
African lily: *Agapanthus africanus*
African marigold: *Tagetes erecta*
African sumac: *Rhus lancea*
African violets: *Saintpaulia* species
Airplane plant: *Chlorophytum comosum*
Akebia: *Akebia quinata*
Alaska cedar: *Chamaecyparis nootkatensis*
Alder: *Alnus*
Alder buckthorn: *Rhamnus frangula*
Algerian ivy: *Hedera canariensis*
Alkanet: *Anchusa officinalis*
Almond: *Prunus triloba*
Aloe vera: *Aloe barbadensis*
Alpine cinquefoil: *Potentilla cinerea*
Alstroemeria: *Alstroemeria aurantiaca*
Aluminum-plant: *Pilea cadierei*
Amaryllis: *Hippeastrum* species
Amazon lily: *Eucharis grandiflora*
American arborvitae: *Thuja occidentalis*
American elm: *Ulmus americana*
American filbert: *Corylus americana*
American holly: *Ilex opaca*
American hophornbeam: *Ostrya virginiana*
American hornbeam: *Carpinus caroliniana*
American linden: *Tilia americana*
American olive: *Osmanthus americanus*
American sweet gum: *Liquidambar styraciflua*
Amur corktree: *Phellodendron amurense*
Amur honeysuckle: *Lonicera maackii*
Amur maple: *Acer ginnala*
Amur privet: *Ligustrum amurense*
Anglojap yew: *Taxus × media*
Annual baby's breath: *Gypsophila elegans*
Annual delphinium: *Consolida ambigua*
Annual phlox: *Phlox drummondii*
Annual rye grass: *Lolium multiflorum*
Arabian star-of-Bethlehem: *Ornithogalum arabicum*
Aralia: *Fatsia*
Arborvitae: *Thuja*
Arrowhead vine: *Syngonium podophyllum*

Ash: *Fraxinus*
Asiatic jasmine: *Trachelospermum asiaticum*
Asparagus fern: *Asparagus densiflorus* 'Sprengeri'
Astilbe: *Astilbe* species and hybrids
Atlas cedar: *Cedrus atlantica*
Austrian briar: *Rosa foetida*
Austrian pine: *Pinus nigra*
Autumn-crocus: *Colchicum luteum*
Autumn elaeagnus: *Elaeagnus umbellata*
Autumn zephyr-lily: *Zephyranthes candida*
Avens: *Geum* hybrids
Azalea: *Rhododendron*

B

Baby-blue-eyes: *Nemophila menziesii*
Baby's breath: *Gypsophila*
Baby's tears: *Soleirolia soleirolii*
Bachelor's-button: *Centaurea cyanus*
Bahia grass: *Paspalum notatum*
Bailey acacia: *Acacia baileyana*
Bald cypress: *Taxodium distichum*
Ball fern: *Davallia mariesii*
Balloonflower: *Platycodon grandiflorus*
Balsam: *Impatiens balsamina*
Bamboo palm: *Rhapis excelsa*
Bank's rose: *Rosa banksiae*
Barberry: *Berberis*
Basket-of-gold: *Aurinia saxatilis*
Basswood: *Tilia americana*
Bay: *Laurus*
Bearberry manzanita: *Arctostaphylos uva-ursi*
Bearded iris: *Iris*
Bear's-breeches: *Acanthus mollis*
Beautybush: *Kolkwitzia amabilis*
Beauty-of-the-night: *Mirabilis jalapa*
Beebalm: *Monarda didyma*
Beefsteak-plant: *Iresine herbstii*
Beefwood: *Casuarina cunninghamiana*
Begonia: *Begonia*
Belladonna-lily: *Amaryllis belladonna*
Bellflower: *Campanula*
Bells-of-Ireland: *Moluccella laevis*
Bent grass: *Agrostis palustris*
Bergamot: *Monarda didyma*
Bermuda grass: *Cynodon* species
Bermuda grass: *Cynodon dactylon*
Bigleaf hydrangea: *Hydrangea macrophylla*
Bigleaf lilyturf: *Liriope muscari*
Bigleaf linden: *Tilia platyphyllos*
Big tree: *Sequoiadendron giganteum*
Birch: *Betula*
Bird's-nest fern: *Asplenium nidus*
Biscay heath: *Erica mediterranea*
Bishop's-hat: *Epimedium grandiflorum*
Black alder: *Alnus glutinosa*
Black-eyed-susan: *Rudbeckia fulgida*
Black-eyed-susan vine: *Thunbergia alata*
Blackgum: *Nyssa sylvatica*
Black locust: *Robinia pseudoacacia*
Black snakeroot: *Cimicifuga racemosa*
Black tupelo: *Nyssa sylvatica*
Black walnut: *Juglans nigra*
Blackwood acacia: *Acacia melanoxylon*

Blanket-flower: *Gaillardia*
Bleeding-heart: *Dicentra spectabilis*
Bloodleaf: *Iresine herbstii*
Blood-red geranium: *Geranium sanguineum*
Blue grass: *Poa pratensis*
Blue plumbago: *Ceratostigma plumbaginoides*
Border forsythia: *Forsythia × intermedia*
Boston fern: *Nephrolepis exaltata*
Bottlebrush: *Callistemon*
Bottletree: *Brachychiton populneus*
Boxwood: *Buxus*
Broom: *Cytisus*
Brown-eyed-susan: *Rudbeckia hirta* var.
 pulcherrima
Buckeye: *Aesculus*
Buckthorn: *Rhamnus alaternus*
Bugbane: *Cimicifuga racemosa*
Bugle: *Ajuga*
Bugloss: *Anchusa*
Bunchberry: *Cornus canadensis*
Bunya-bunya: *Araucaria bidwillii*
Burkwood daphne: *Daphne × burkwoodii*
Burkwood viburnum: *Viburnum × burkwoodii*
Burning bush: *Euonymus alata*
Bur oak: *Quercus macrocarpa*
Burro's-tail: *Sedum morganianum*
Bush cinquefoil: *Potentilla fruticosa*
Busy-lizzie: *Impatiens wallerana*
Buttercup: *Ranunculus*
Butterfly-bush: *Buddleia davidii*
Butterfly flower: *Schizanthus × wisetonensis*
Butterfly-iris: *Moraea iridoides*
Button fern: *Pellaea rotundifolia*

C

California poppy: *Eschscholzia californica*
California privet: *Ligustrum ovalifolium*
Calla lily: *Zantedeschia aethiopica*
Callery pear: *Pyrus calleryana*
Calliopsis: *Coreopsis tinctoria*
Camass: *Camassia*
Camellia: *Camellia japonica*
Camphor tree: *Cinnamomum camphora*
Canadian or eastern hemlock: *Tsuga canadensis*
Canary Island pine: *Pinus canariensis*
Candytuft: *Iberis*
Canna: *Canna*
Canoe cedar: *Thuja plicata*
Canterbury bells: *Campanula medium*
Cape forget-me-not: *Anchusa capensis*
Cape marigold: *Dimorphotheca sinuata*
Cape primrose: *Streptocarpus* species
Cardinal flower: *Lobelia cardinalis*
Carnation: *Dianthus caryophyllus*
Carob: *Ceratonia siliqua*
Carolina allspice: *Calycanthus floridus*
Carolina hemlock: *Tsuga caroliniana*
Carolina jasmine: *Gelsemium sempervirens*
Carolina silverbell: *Halesia carolina*
Carpathian harebell: *Campanula carpatica*
Carpet bugle: *Ajuga reptans*
Cast-iron plant: *Aspidistra elatior*
Cedar: *Cedrus*

Cedar-of-Lebanon: *Cedrus libani*
Centipede grass: *Eremochloa ophiuroides*
Century plant: *Agave americana*
Checkerberry: *Gaultheria procumbens*
Cherry-laurel: *Prunus caroliniana*
Cherry plum: *Prunus cerasifera*
China aster: *Callistephus chinensis*
Chinaberry: *Melia azedarach*
China pink: *Dianthus chinensis*
Chinese elm: *Ulmus parvifolia*
Chinese evergreen: *Aglaonema modestum*
Chinese forget-me-not: *Cynoglossum amabile*
Chinese hibiscus: *Hibiscus rosa-sinensis*
Chinese holly: *Ilex cornuta*
Chinese juniper: *Juniperus chinensis*
Chinese-lantern: *Abutilon hybridum*
Chinese lilac: *Syringa × chinensis*
Chinese photinia: *Photinia serrulata*
Chinese pieris: *Pieris forrestii*
Chinese snowball viburnum: *Viburnum
 macrocephalum*
Chinese sweet gum: *Liquidambar formosana*
Chinese witch hazel: *Hamamelis mollis*
Chokecherry: *Prunus virginiana*
Christmas cactus: *Schlumbergera bridgesii*
Christmas-rose: *Helleborus niger*
Cigar tree: *Catalpa bignonioides*
Cinquefoil: *Potentilla*
Climbing lily: *Gloriosa rothschildiana*
Clock vine: *Thunbergia alata*
Coast live oak: *Quercus agrifolia*
Coast redwood: *Sequoia sempervirens*
Cockscomb: *Celosia cristata*
Cockspur thorn: *Crataegus crus-galli*
Coleus: *Coleus × hybridus*
Colorado spruce: *Picea pungens*
Columbine: *Aquilegia*
Columbine meadowrue: *Thalictrum aquilegifolium*
Columnea: *Columnea gloriosa*
Common bald cypress: *Taxodium distichum*
Cootamunda wattle: *Acacia baileyana*
Coralbells: *Heuchera sanguinea*
Coreopsis: *Coreopsis grandiflora*
Corn plant: *Dracaena fragrans*
Cornish heath: *Erica vagans*
Corsican hellebore: *Helleborus lividus* var. *corsicus*
Corsican mint: *Mentha requienii*
Cottage pink: *Dianthus plumarius*
Cottonwood: *Populus deltoides*
Cotoneaster: *Cotoneaster*
Coyotebrush: *Baccharis pilularis*
Crab apple: *Malus* species
Crape myrtle: *Lagerstroemia*
Creeping bent grass: *Agrostis palustris*
Creeping-charlie: *Pilea nummulariifolia*
Creeping fig: *Ficus pumila*
Creeping gardenia: *Gardenia jasminoides*
 'Prostrata'
Creeping juniper: *Juniperus horizontalis*
Creeping lilyturf: *Liriope spicata*
Creeping mahonia: *Mahonia repens*
Creeping thyme: *Thymus praecox* var. *articus*
Crested iris: *Iris cristata*

Crocus: *Crocus* species
Croton: *Codiaeum variegatum*
Crown-imperial: *Fritillaria imperialis*
Crown-of-thorns: *Euphorbia milii*
Crown vetch: *Coronilla varia*
Cucumber tree: *Magnolia acuminata*
Cupflower: *Nierembergia hippomanica*
Cussick camass: *Camassia cusickii*
Cutleaf Japanese maple: *Acer palmatum* 'Dissectum'
Cyclamen: *Cyclamen persicum*
Cypress: *Cupressus*

D
Daffodil: *Narcissus*
Dahlberg daisy: *Dyssodia tenuiloba*
Dahlia: *Dahlia* hybrids
Daisy: *Chrysanthemum*
Danford iris: *Iris danfordiae*
Darwin barberry: *Berberis darwinii*
Dawn redwood: *Metasequoia glyptostroboides*
Daylily: *Hemerocallis* hybrids
Delphinium: *Consolida ambigua; Delphinium elatum*
Deodar cedar: *Cedrus deodara*
Deutzia: *Deutzia*
Devil's ivy: *Epipremnum aureum*
Devilwood osmanthus: *Osmanthus americanus*
Dichondra: *Dichondra micrantha*
Dogwood: *Cornus florida*
Donkey's-tail: *Sedum morganianum*
Douglas fir: *Pseudotsuga menziesii*
Dracaena: *Cordyline stricta; Dracaena*
Drooping leucothoe: *Leucothoe fontanesiana*
Dumb cane: *Dieffenbachia* species
Dusty-miller: *Senecio cineraria*
Dwarf Alberta spruce: *Picea glauca* 'Conica'
Dwarf blue fescue: *Festuca ovina* var. *glauca*
Dwarf flowering almond: *Prunus glandulosa*
Dwarf morning glory: *Convolvulus tricolor*

E
Easter cactus: *Schlumbergera bridgesii*
Eastern poplar: *Populus deltoides*
Eastern redbud: *Cercis canadensis*
Eastern red cedar: *Juniperus virginiana*
Edging lobelia: *Lobelia erinus*
Elephant-foot tree: *Beaucarnia recurvata* var. *intermedia*
Empress tree: *Paulownia tomentosa*
English hawthorn: *Crataegus laevigata*
English holly: *Ilex aquifolium*
English ivy: *Hedera helix*
English laurel: *Prunus laurocerasus*
English lavender: *Lavandula angustifolia*
English oak: *Quercus robur*
English primrose: *Primula vulgaris*
English yew: *Taxus baccata*
Eucalyptus: *Eucalyptus*
European alder: *Alnus glutinosa*
European ash: *Fraxinus excelsior*
European beech: *Fagus sylvatica*
European cranberry bush: *Viburnum opulus*

European hackberry: *Celtis australis*
European hornbeam: *Carpinus betulus*
European linden: *Tilia* × *europaea*
European mountain ash: *Sorbus aucuparia*
European white birch: *Betula pendula*
Evergreen candytuft: *Iberis sempervirens*
Evergreen grape: *Rhoicissus capensis*
Evergreen pear: *Pyrus kawakamii*
Everlasting: *Helichrysum bracteatum*

F
False-aralia: *Dizygotheca elegantissima*
False-spiraea: *Astilbe*
Fancy-leaved caladium: *Caladium* × *hortulanum*
Father Hugo rose: *Rosa hugonis*
Fawn-lily: *Erythronium* species
Fescue: *Festuca*
Feverfew: *Chrysanthemum parthenium*
Fiddleleaf fig: *Ficus lyrata*
Fiddleleaf philodendron: *Philodendron bipinnatifidum*
Field poppy: *Papaver rhoeas*
Fig: *Ficus*
Filbert: *Corylus*
Fir: *Abies*
Firethorn: *Pyracantha*
Five-finger fern: *Adiantum pedatum*
Five-leaf akebia: *Akebia quinata*
Five-stamen tamarisk: *Tamarix ramosissima*
Flameleaf sumac: *Rhus copallina*
Flame violet: *Episcia cupreata*
Flaming-katy: *Kalanchoe blossfeldiana*
Florist's cyclamen: *Cyclamen persicum*
Florist's eucalyptus: *Eucalyptus cinerea*
Flowering almond: *Prunus triloba*
Flowering ash: *Fraxinus ornus*
Flowering cherry: *Prunus serrulata; P. yedoensis*
Flowering crab apple: *Malus floribunda*
Flowering dogwood: *Cornus florida*
Flowering kale: *Brassica oleracea* var. *acephala*
Flowering quince: *Chaenomeles speciosa*
Flowering spurge: *Euphorbia corollata*
Flowering tobacco: *Nicotiana alata*
Forget-me-not: *Myosotis sylvatica*
Fortnight-lily: *Moraea iridoides*
Foster tulip: *Tulipa fosterana*
Fountain grass: *Pennisetum alopecuroides*
Four-o'clock: *Mirabilis jalapa*
Foxglove: *Digitalis purpurea*
Fragrant viburnum: *Viburnum farreri*
Franklinia: *Franklinia alatamaha*
Fraser photinia: *Photinia* × *fraseri*
Freesia: *Freesia refracta*
French marigold: *Tagetes patula*
Friendship plant: *Billbergia nutans*
Fritillary: *Fritillaria*
Fruitless mulberry: *Morus alba*
Fuchsia: *Fuchsia* × *hybrida*

G
Gardenia: *Gardenia jasminoides*
Garlandflower: *Daphne cneorum*
Gas plant: *Dictamnus albus*

Geranium: *Pelargonium*
German iris: *Iris* × *germanica* var. *florentina*
Giant arborvitae: *Thuja plicata*
Giant onion: *Allium giganteum*
Giant redwood: *Sequoiadendron giganteum*
Ginkgo tree: *Ginkgo biloba*
Gladiolus: *Gladiolus hybridus*
Globe amaranth: *Gomphrena globosa*
Globeflower: *Trollius europaeus*
Globe thistle: *Echinops exaltatus*
Gloriosa daisy: *Rudbeckia hirta* var. *pulcherrima*
Glory lily: *Gloriosa rothschildiana*
Glory-of-the-snow: *Chionodoxa luciliae*
Glossy abelia: *Abelia* × *grandiflora*
Glossy privet: *Ligustrum lucidum*
Gloxinia: *Sinningia speciosa*
Godetia: *Clarkia* hybrids
Golden calla: *Zantedeschia elliottiana*
Goldenchain tree: *Laburnum* × *watereri* 'Vossii'
Goldenfleece: *Dyssodia tenuiloba*
Golden garlic: *Allium moly*
Golden marguerite: *Anthemis tinctoria*
Golden polypody fern: *Polypodium aureum*
Goldenrain tree: *Koelreuteria paniculata*
Goldenrod: *Solidago* hybrids
Goldentuft: *Aurinia saxatilis*
Goldflower: *Hypericum* × *moseranum*
Gold-moss stonecrop: *Sedum acre*
Good-king-henry: *Chenopodium bonus-henricus*
Grape hyacinth: *Muscari botryoides*
Grape ivy: *Cissus rhombifolia*
Grecian laurel: *Laurus nobilis*
Green ash: *Fraxinus pennsylvanica*
Greig tulip: *Tulipa greigii*
Gum: *Eucalyptus*

H

Hackberry: *Celtis*
Hardy aster: *Aster* species and hybrids
Hardy chrysanthemum: *Chrysanthemum* hybrids
Hardy fuchsia: *Fuchsia magellanica*
Harvest brodiaea: *Brodiaea coronaria*
Hawthorn: *Crataegus*
Heartleaf bergenia: *Bergenia cordifolia*
Heartleaf philodendron: *Philodendron scandens*
Heath: *Erica*
Heather: *Calluna vulgaris*
Heavenly-bamboo: *Nandina domestica*
Hedge maple: *Acer campestre*
Heliotrope: *Heliotropium arborescens*
Hemlock: *Tsuga canadensis*
Hen-and-chicks: *Sempervivum tectorum*
Herbaceous peony: *Paeonia* hybrids
Hinoki false-cypress: *Chamaecyparis obtusa*
Holly: *Ilex*
Hollyhock: *Alcea rosea*
Hollyleaf cherry: *Prunus ilicifolia*
Holly olive: *Osmanthus heterophyllus*
Honeylocust: *Gleditsia*
Honeysuckle: *Lonicera*
Hong Kong orchid tree: *Bauhinia blakeana*
Hophornbeam: *Ostrya virginiana*
Hornbeam: *Carpinus caroliniana*

Horsechestnut: *Aesculus hippocastanum*
Houseleek: *Sempervivum tectorum*
Hyacinth: *Hyacinthus orientalis*
Hybrid witch hazel: *Hamamelis* × *intermedia*
Hydrangea: *Hydrangea macrophylla*

I, J

Iceland poppy: *Papaver nudicaule*
Impatiens: *Impatiens wallerana*
Incense cedar: *Calocedrus decurrens*
Inch plant: *Tradescantia* species
India hawthorn: *Raphiolepsis indica*
Indian-bean: *Catalpa bignonioides*
Indian-strawberry: *Duchesnea indica*
Inkberry: *Ilex glabra*
Irish moss: *Sagina subulata*
Ironbark: *Eucalyptus*
Iron-cross begonia: *Begonia masoniana*
Italian alder: *Alnus cordata*
Italian alkanet: *Anchusa azurea*
Italian buckthorn: *Rhamnus alaternus*
Italian bugloss: *Anchusa azurea*
Italian cypress: *Cupressus sempervirens* 'Stricta'
Italian grape hyacinth: *Muscari botryoides*
Italian rye grass: *Lolium multiflorum*
Ivy: *Hedera*
Ivy geranium: *Pelargonium peltatum*
Jaburan lilyturf: *Ophiopogon jaburan*
Jade plant: *Crassula argentea*
Jade tree: *Crassula argentea*
Japanese anemone: *Anemone* × *hybrida*
Japanese aralia: *Fatsia japonica*
Japanese aucuba: *Aucuba japonica*
Japanese barberry: *Berberis thunbergii*
Japanese black pine: *Pinus thunbergiana*
Japanese boxwood: *Buxus microphylla* var. *japonica*
Japanese cedar: *Cryptomeria japonica*
Japanese crape myrtle: *Lagerstroemia fauriei*
Japanese dogwood: *Cornus kousa*
Japanese euonymus: *Euonymus japonica*
Japanese flowering cherry: *Prunus serrulata*
Japanese flowering crab apple: *Malus floribunda*
Japanese garden juniper: *Juniperus procumbens*
Japanese holly: *Ilex crenata*
Japanese holly fern: *Cyrtomium falcatum*
Japanese honeysuckle: *Lonicera japonica*
Japanese iris: *Iris kaempferi*
Japanese jasmine: *Jasminum mesnyi*
Japanese kerria: *Kerria japonica*
Japanese larch: *Larix kaempferi*
Japanese maple: *Acer palmatum*
Japanese pagoda tree: *Sophora japonica*
Japanese pieris: *Pieris japonica*
Japanese pittosporum: *Pittosporum tobira*
Japanese primrose: *Primula japonica*
Japanese privet: *Ligustrum japonicum*
Japanese quince: *Chaenomeles japonica*
Japanese red pine: *Pinus densiflora*
Japanese rose: *Rosa multiflora*
Japanese skimmia: *Skimmia japonica*
Japanese snowbell: *Styrax japonicus*
Japanese spirea: *Spiraea japonica*

Japanese spurge: *Pachysandra terminalis*
Japanese tree lilac: *Syringa reticulata*
Japanese white pine: *Pinus parviflora*
Japanese witch hazel: *Hamamelis japonica*
Japanese yew: *Taxus cuspidata*
Japanese zelkova: *Zelkova serrata*
Jasmine: *Jasminum*
Johnny-jump-up: *Viola tricolor*
Jonquil: *Narcissus jonquilla*
Joseph's-coat: *Amaranthus tricolor*
Juneberry: *Amelanchier arborea*
Juniper: *Juniperus*

K, L
Kaffir-lily: *Clivia miniata*
Kale: *Brassica oleracea* var. *acephala*
Kangaroo vine: *Cissus antarctica*
Kashgar tamarisk: *Tamarix hispida*
Katsura tree: *Cercidiphyllum japonicum*
Kentia palm: *Howea forsterana*
Kentucky blue grass: *Poa pratensis*
Kinnikinick: *Arctostaphylos uva-ursi*
Kirk's coprosma: *Coprosma* × *kirkii*
Korean barberry: *Berberis koreana*
Korean grass: *Zoysia tenuifolia*
Korean lilac: *Syringa oblata*
Korean mountain ash: *Sorbus alnifolia*
Korean-spice viburnum: *Viburnum carlesii*
Kousa dogwood: *Cornus kousa*
Kurrajong: *Brachychiton populneus*
Laceleaf Japanese maple: *Acer palmatum* 'Dissectum'
Lady Bank's rose: *Rosa banksiae*
Lamb's-ears: *Stachys byzantina*
Lantana: *Lantana montevidensis*
Larch: *Larix*
Large fothergilla: *Fothergilla major*
Larkspur: *Consolida*
Late lilac: *Syringa villosa*
Laurel bay: *Laurus nobilis*
Lavalle hawthorn: *Crataegus* × *lavallei*
Lawson cypress: *Chamaecyparis lawsoniana*
Leatherleaf mahonia: *Mahonia bealei*
Leichtlin camass: *Camassia leichtlinii*
Lemon bottlebrush: *Callistemon citrinus*
Lemon verbena: *Aloysia triphylla*
Leyland cypress: × *Cupressocyparis leylandii*
Lilac: *Syringa*
Lily: *Lilium*
Lily magnolia: *Magnolia quinquepeta*
Lily-of-the-Nile: *Agapanthus africanus*
Lily-of-the-valley: *Convallaria majalis*
Lilyturf: *Liriope*
Lippia: *Phyla nodiflora*
Lipstick plant: *Aeschynanthus speciosus*
Littleleaf linden: *Tilia cordata*
Live oak: *Quercus virginiana*
Loblolly pine: *Pinus taeda*
Lombardy poplar: *Populus nigra* 'Italica'
London plane tree: *Platanus* × *acerifolia*
Longleaf pine: *Pinus palustris*
Loquat: *Eriobotrya japonica*
Love-in-a-mist: *Nigella damascena*

M
Madagascar periwinkle: *Catharanthus roseus*
Madrona: *Arbutus menziesii*
Madrone: *Arbutus menziesii*
Magicflower: *Achimenes* species
Maidenhair fern: *Adiantum pedatum*
Maidenhair tree: *Ginkgo biloba*
Maiden pink: *Dianthus deltoides*
Maltese-cross: *Lychnis chalcedonica*
Manchu cherry: *Prunus tomentosa*
Manzanita: *Arctostaphylos*
Maple: *Acer*
Marigold: *Tagetes patula*
Marshmarigold: *Caltha palustris*
Martha Washington geranium: *Pelargonium domesticum*
Marvel-of-Peru: *Mirabilis jalapa*
Mascarene grass: *Zoysia tenuifolia*
Mayten tree: *Maytenus boaria*
Mexican aster: *Cosmos bipinnatus*
Mexican orange: *Choisya ternata*
Mexican sunflower: *Tithonia rotundifolia*
Michaelmas daisy: *Aster* species and hybrids
Mimosa: *Albizia julibrissin*
Mirror plant: *Coprosma repens*
Mock orange: *Philadelphus coronarius*
Mock strawberry: *Duchesnea indica*
Modesto ash: *Fraxinus velutina* 'Modesto'
Monarch birch: *Betula maximowicziana*
Mondo grass: *Ophiopogon japonicus*
Moneywort: *Lysimachia nummularia*
Monkeyflower: *Mimulus* × *hybridus* 'Grandiflorus'
Monterey cypress: *Cupressus macrocarpa*
Monterey pine: *Pinus radiata*
Moonflower vine: *Ipomoea alba*
Morning glory vine: *Ipomoea tricolor*
Mosaic plant: *Fittonia verschaffeltii* var. *argyroneura*
Moses-in-the-cradle: *Rhoeo spathacea*
Moss pink: *Phlox subulata*
Moss sandwort: *Arenaria verna*
Mossy stonecrop: *Sedum acre*
Mother-in-law's-tongue: *Sansevieria trifasciata*
Mother-of-thousands: *Tolmiea menziesii*
Mountain laurel: *Kalmia latifolia*
Mugo pine: *Pinus mugo* var. *mugo*
Myrtle: *Myrtus communis*

N
Naked-lady: *Amaryllis belladonna*
Nanking cherry: *Prunus tomentosa*
Naples onion: *Allium neapolitanum*
Nasturtium: *Tropaeolum majus*
Natal plum: *Carissa grandiflora*
Neapolitan cyclamen: *Cyclamen hederifolium*
Nerve plant: *Fittonia verschaffeltii* var. *argyroneura*
Netted iris: *Iris reticulata*
Noble fir: *Abies procera*
Nordmann fir: *Abies nordmanniana*
Norfolk Island pine: *Araucaria heterophylla*
Northern bayberry: *Myrica pensylvanica*

Northern catalpa: *Catalpa speciosa*
Norway maple: *Acer platanoides*
Norway pine: *Pinus resinosa*
Norway spruce: *Picea abies*
Notchleaf sea lavender: *Limonium sinuatum*

O

Oakleaf hydrangea: *Hydrangea quercifolia*
Oakleaf ivy: *Rhoicissus capensis*
Old-fashioned weigela: *Weigela florida*
Oleander: *Nerium oleander*
Olive: *Olea europaea*
Orchid tree: *Bauhinia variegata*
Oregon boxwood: *Paxistima myrsinites*
Oregon grape: *Mahonia aquifolium*
Oriental poppy: *Papaver orientale*
Ornamental cabbage: *Brassica oleracea* var.
  acephala
Ornamental pepper: *Capsicum annuum*
Orris: *Iris* × *germanica* var. *florentina*
Osage orange: *Maclura pomifera*
Oswego tea: *Monarda didyma*
Oxalis: *Oxalis*

P, Q

Pagoda dogwood: *Cornus alternifolia*
Painted daisy: *Chrysanthemum*
  coccineum
Painted-tongue: *Salpiglossis sinuata*
Pampas grass: *Cortaderia selloana*
Pansy: *Viola* × *wittrockiana*
Paper Birch: *Betula papyrifera*
Parlor-maple: *Abutilon pictum*
Parlor palm: *Chamaedorea elegans*
Parrot's-beak: *Lotus berthelotii*
Paulownia: *Paulownia tomentosa*
Peace lily: *Spathiphyllum* species
Pelargonium: *Pelargonium domesticum*
Peperomia: *Peperomia*
Pepperidge: *Nyssa sylvatica*
Perennial rye grass: *Lolium perenne*
Perennial salvia: *Salvia* × *superba*
Periwinkle: *Vinca*
Persian buttercup: *Ranunculus asiaticus*
Persian lilac: *Syringa* × *persica*
Peruvian verbena: *Verbena peruviana*
Petticoat daffodil: *Narcissus bulbocodium*
Petunia: *Petunia* × *hybrida*
Phlox: *Phlox paniculata*
Photinia: *Photinia* × *fraseri*
Piggyback plant: *Tolmiea menziesii*
Pincushion-flower: *Scabiosa caucasica*
Pink: *Dianthus*
Pink clover blossom: *Polygonum capitatum*
Pin oak: *Quercus palustris*
Pistache: *Pistacia chinensis*
Pittosporum: *Pittosporum tobira*
Plane tree: *Platanus* × *acerifolia*
Plantain lily: *Hosta*
Plume celosia: *Celosia cristata*
Poinsettia: *Euphorbia pulcherrima*
Polyantha primrose: *Primula* × *polyantha*
Polyanthus narcissus: *Narcissus tazetta*

Ponytail-palm: *Beaucarnia recurvata* var.
  intermedia
Poor-man's-orchid: *Schizanthus* × *wisetonensis*
Poplar: *Populus*
Poppy: *Papaver*
Poppy anemone: *Anemone coronaria*
Port Orford cedar: *Chamaecyparis lawsoniana*
Possumhaw holly: *Ilex decidua*
Possum oak: *Quercus nigra*
Pothos: *Epipremnum aureum*
Pot marigold: *Calendula officinalis*
Prayer plant: *Maranta leuconeura*
Primrose: *Primula*
Primrose jasmine: *Jasminum mesnyi*
Privet: *Ligustrum*
Purple coneflower: *Echinacea purpurea*
Purple loosestrife: *Lythrum salicaria*
Pussy willow: *Salix discolor*
Pygmy date palm: *Phoenix roebelenii*
Pyrethrum: *Chrysanthemum coccineum*
Queen's-tears: *Billbergia nutans*

R

Rabbit's-foot fern: *Polypodium*
  aureum
Ramanas rose: *Rosa rugosa*
Red alder: *Alnus rubra*
Red ash: *Fraxinus pennsylvanica*
Red buckeye: *Aesculus pavia*
Red cedar: *Thuja plicata*
Red chokeberry: *Aronia arbutifolia*
Red escallonia: *Escallonia rubra*
Red horsechestnut: *Aesculus* × *carnea*
Red-hot-poker: *Kniphofia uvaria*
Red maple: *Acer rubrum*
Red oak: *Quercus rubra*
Redosier dogwood: *Cornus sericea*
Red pine: *Pinus resinosa*
Redwood: *Sequoia sempervirens*
Rhododendron: *Rhododendron*
River birch: *Betula nigra*
River she-oak: *Casuarina cunninghamiana*
Rockcress: *Arabis caucasica*
Rocket candytuft: *Iberis amara*
Rocket larkspur: *Consolida ambigua*
Rock maple: *Acer saccharum*
Rockrose: *Cistus* species
Rocky Mountain juniper: *Juniperus scopulorum*
Rosary vine: *Ceropegia woodii*
Rose: *Rosa*
Rose daphne: *Daphne cneorum*
Rose moss: *Portulaca grandiflora*
Rose-of-Sharon: *Hibiscus syriacus*
Royal paulownia: *Paulownia tomentosa*
Rubber plant: *Ficus elastica*
Russell lupines: *Lupinus*, Russell hybrids
Russian olive: *Elaeagnus angustifolia*
Rye grass: *Lolium multiflorum*

S

St. Augustine grass: *Stenotaphrum secundatum*
St. John's bread: *Ceratonia siliqua*
St. John's wort: *Hypericum*

Sand strawberry: *Fragaria chiloensis*
Sargent cherry: *Prunus sargentii*
Sargent crab apple: *Malus sargentii*
Sargent's weeping hemlock: *Tsuga canadensis* 'Pendula'
Sasanqua camellia: *Camellia sasanqua*
Sassafras: *Sassafras albidum*
Saucer magnolia: *Magnolia* × *soulangiana*
Scarlet oak: *Quercus coccinea*
Scarlet sage: *Salvia splendens*
Scented geraniums: *Pelargonium* species
Schefflera: *Brassaia actinophylla*
Scotch broom: *Cytisus scoparius*
Scotch heather: *Calluna vulgaris*
Scotch pine: *Pinus sylvestris*
Scotch pink: *Dianthus plumarius*
Sea pink: *Armeria maritima*
Sea thrift: *Armeria maritima*
Sea tomato: *Rosa rugosa*
Sea urchin cactus: *Echinopsis*
Serbian bellflower: *Campanula poscharskyana*
Serviceberry: *Amelanchier arborea*
Shadblow: *Amelanchier arborea*
Shadbush: *Amelanchier arborea*
Shasta daisy: *Chrysanthemum* × *superbum*
Shellflower: *Tigridia pavonia*
Shining sumac: *Rhus copallina*
Shiny xylosma: *Xylosma congestum*
Shirley poppy: *Papaver rhoeas*
Shore juniper: *Juniperus conferta*
Showy sedum: *Sedum spectabile*
Showy stonecrop: *Sedum spectabile*
Shrub althea: *Hibiscus syriacus*
Siberian bugloss: *Brunnera macrophylla*
Siberian crab apple: *Malus baccata*
Siberian dogwood: *Cornus alba* 'Sibirica'
Siberian elm: *Ulmus pumila*
Siberian iris: *Iris sibirica*
Siberian squill: *Scilla siberica*
Silk tree: *Albizia julibrissin*
Silverberry: *Elaeagnus pungens*
Silver maple: *Acer saccharinum*
Small Himalayan sarcococca: *Sarcococca hookerana* var. *humilis*
Smoke tree: *Cotinus coggygria*
Smooth Arizona cypress: *Cupressus glabra*
Smooth sumac: *Rhus glabra*
Snake plant: *Sansevieria trifasciata*
Snapdragon: *Antirrhinum majus*
Sneezeweed: *Helenium autumnale*
Snowdrop: *Galanthus*
Snowflake: *Leucojum*
Snow-in-summer: *Cerastium tomentosum*
Snow-on-the-mountain: *Euphorbia marginata*
Soft maple: *Acer saccharinum*
Sourgum: *Nyssa sylvatica*
Solomon's-seal: *Polygonatum commutatum*
Sourwood: *Oxydendrum arboreum*
Southern bush honeysuckle: *Diervilla sessilifolia*
Southern catalpa: *Catalpa bignonioides*
Southern live oak: *Quercus virginiana*
Southern magnolia: *Magnolia grandiflora*
Southernwood: *Artemisia abrotanum*

Spanish broom: *Genista hispanica*
Spanish gorse: *Genista hispanica*
Spatheflower: *Spathiphyllum* species
Speedwell: *Veronica*
Spiderflower: *Cleome hasslerana*
Spider plant: *Chlorophytum comosum*
Spiderwort: *Tradescantia virginiana*
Spike speedwell: *Veronica spicata*
Spike winter hazel: *Corylopsis spicata*
Split-leaf philodendron: *Monstera deliciosa*
Sprenger asparagus: *Asparagus densiflorus* 'Sprengeri'
Spring cinquefoil: *Potentilla tabernaemontanii*
Spring heath: *Erica carnea*
Spring meadow saffron: *Bulbocodium vernum*
Spring snowflake: *Leucojum vernum*
Spruce: *Picea*
Spruce pine: *Pinus glabra*
Spurge: *Euphorbia corollata*
Squill: *Scilla*
Squirrel's-foot fern: *Davallia mariesii*
Staghorn fern: *Platycerium bifurcatum*
Starjasmine: *Trachelospermum jasminoides*
Star magnolia: *Magnolia stellata*
Star-of-Bethlehem: *Ornithogalum*
Statice: *Limonium sinuatum*
Stock: *Matthiola incana*
Stoke's aster: *Stokesia laevis*
Stonecrop: *Sedum*
Strawberry shrub: *Calycanthus floridus*
Strawberry tree: *Arbutus unedo*
Strawflower: *Helichrysum bracteatum*
String-of-beads: *Senecio rowleyanus*
String-of-hearts: *Ceropegia woodii*
Sugar maple: *Acer saccharum*
Sumac: *Rhus*
Summer forget-me-not: *Anchusa capensis*
Summer phlox: *Phlox paniculata*
Summer snowflake: *Leucojum aestivum*
Sunflower: *Helianthus annuus*
Sun-rose: *Helianthemum nummularium*
Swamp maple: *Acer rubrum*
Swamp white oak: *Quercus bicolor*
Swan River daisy: *Brachycome iberidifolia*
Swedish ivy: *Plectranthus australis*
Sweet alyssum: *Lobularia maritima*
Sweet bay: *Laurus nobilis*
Sweet bay magnolia: *Magnolia virginiana*
Sweet gum: *Liquidambar styraciflua*
Sweet mock orange: *Philadelphus coronarius*
Sweet olive: *Osmanthus fragrans*
Sweet pea: *Lathyrus odoratus*
Sweet violet: *Viola odorata*
Sweet william: *Dianthus barbatus*
Sword fern: *Polystichum munitum*

T
Tamarisk: *Tamarix*
Tansy: *Tanacetum vulgare*
Tartarian honeysuckle: *Lonicera tatarica*
Teaberry: *Gaultheria procumbens*
Tea rose: *Rosa odorata*

Tea tree: *Leptospermum laevigatum*
Thornless honeylocust: *Gleditsia triacanthos* var. *inermis*
Tigerflower: *Tigridia pavonia*
Tobacco: *Nicotiana alata*
Tobira: *Pittosporum tobira*
Torch lily: *Kniphofia uvaria*
Trailing African daisy: *Osteospermum fruiticosum*
Trailing lantana: *Lantana montevidensis*
Trailing verbena: *Verbena peruviana*
Transvaal daisy: *Gerbera jamesonii*
Treasureflower: *Gazania rigens*
Tree heath: *Erica arborea*
Tree peony: *Paeonia suffruticosa*
Tuberose: *Polianthes tuberosa*
Tulip: *Tulipa*
Tulip poplar: *Liriodendron tulipifera*
Tulip tree: *Liriodendron tulipifera*
Turban buttercup: *Ranunculus asiaticus*
Turf-type perennial rye grass: *Lolium perenne*
Twice-cut philodendron: *Philodendron bipinnatifidum*

U, V

Umbrella tree: *Brassaia actinophylla*
Vanhoutte spirea: *Spiraea* × *vanhouttei*
Varnish tree: *Koelreuteria paniculata*
Velvet plant: *Gynura aurantiaca*
Verbena: *Verbena* × *hybrida*
Vernal witch hazel: *Hamamelis vernalis*
Victorian box: *Pittosporum undulatum*
Vine hill manzanita: *Arctostaphylos densiflora*
Viola: *Viola* × *wittrockiana*
Violet: *Viola*
Virginia bluebells: *Mertensia virginica*
Virginia creeper: *Parthenocissus quinquefolia*
Virginia rose: *Rosa virginiana*

W

Wallflower: *Cheiranthus cheiri*
Wall rockcress: *Arabis caucasica*
Walnut: *Juglans*
Wandering-Jew: *Tradescantia* species
Washington thorn: *Crataegus phaenopyrum*
Water flag iris: *Iris pseudacorus*
Waterlily tulip: *Tulipa kaufmanniana*
Water oak: *Quercus nigra*
Waxflower: *Hoya bella*
Weeping fig: *Ficus benjamina*
Weeping willow: *Salix babylonica*
Weigela: *Weigela florida*
Western catalpa: *Catalpa speciosa*
Western red cedar: *Thuja plicata*
Western sword fern: *Polystichum munitum*
White alder: *Alnus rhombifolia*
White birch: *Betula pendula*
White cedar: *Thuja occidentalis*
White fir: *Abies concolor*
White lilyturf: *Ophiopogon jaburan*
White mulberry: *Morus alba*
White oak: *Quercus alba*
White pine: *Pinus strobus*
White poplar: *Populus alba*

White spruce: *Picea glauca*
Wild ginger: *Asarum caudatum*
Wild lilac: *Ceanothus* species
Wild strawberry: *Fragaria chiloensis*
Willow oak: *Quercus phellos*
Winged euonymus: *Euonymus alata*
Winter aconite: *Eranthis*
Winterberry: *Ilex verticillata*
Winter-blooming bergenia: *Bergenia crassifolia*
Wintercreeper euonymus: *Euonymus fortunei*
Winter daphne: *Daphne odora*
Wintergreen: *Gaultheria procumbens*
Winter honeysuckle: *Lonicera fragrantissima*
Winter jasmine: *Jasminum nudiflorum*
Wishbone flower: *Torenia fournieri*
Witch hazel: *Hamamelis*
Woadwaxen: *Genista tinctoria*
Woodbine: *Parthenocissus quinquefolia*
Wooly betony: *Stachys byzantina*

Y

Yarrow: *Achillea millefolium*
Yaupon holly: *Ilex vomitoria*
Yellow onion: *Allium flavum*
Yellow poplar: *Liriodendron tulipifera*
Yellow spider: *Lycoris africana*
Yellowwood: *Cladrastis lutea*
Yew: *Taxus*
Yew pine: *Podocarpus macrophyllus*

Z

Zebra plant: *Aphelandra squarrosa*
Zephyr-lily: *Zephyranthes candida*
Zinnia: *Zinnia elegans*
Zoysia grass: *Zoysia* species

NAME	HABIT		FLOWERS		ADAPTATION	
	Type	Height	Color	Time	Zones	Light
Abelia × grandiflora Glossy abelia	Evergreen shrub	4 to 8 ft	White	Early summer to first frost	6 to 10	Full sun to light shade
Abies concolor White fir	Needled evergreen tree	80 to 100 ft			4 to 7	Full sun
Abies nordmanniana Nordmann fir	Needled evergreen tree	55 to 65 ft			5 to 7	Full sun
Abies procera Noble fir	Needled evergreen tree	100 to 150 ft			5 to 7	Full sun
Abutilon hybridum Chinese-lantern	Evergreen viny shrub	to 10 ft	Pink, red, yellow, white	All year	10 or indoors	Half-day sun
Abutilon pictum 'Thompsonii' Parlor-maple	Evergreen viny shrub	to 10 ft	Orange	All year	10 or indoors	Half-day sun
Acacia baileyana Bailey acacia, Cootamundra wattle	Evergreen tree	to 20 ft	Yellow	Winter	8 to 10	Full sun
Acacia melanoxylon Blackwood acacia	Evergreen tree	to 40 ft	White	Spring	9, 10	Full sun
Acanthus mollis Bear's-breeches	Tender perennial	2 to 3 ft	White, lavender, pink	Spring	8 to 10	Light shade
Acer campestre Hedge maple	Deciduous tree	25 to 40 ft			5 to 8	Full sun
Acer ginnala Amur maple	Deciduous tree	to 20 ft	Yellow, cream colored	Spring	4 to 8	Full sun
Acer palmatum Japanese maple	Deciduous tree	15 to 25 ft			6 to 9	Full sun to light shade
Acer palmatum 'Dissectum' Laceleaf Japanese maple, cutleaf Japanese maple	Deciduous shrub	6 to 8 ft			6 to 9	Light shade
Acer platanoides Norway maple	Deciduous tree	40 to 50 ft	Yellow	Spring	4 to 7	Full sun
Acer rubrum Red maple, swamp maple	Deciduous tree	50 to 60 ft	Red	Spring	3 to 9	Full sun
Acer saccharinum Silver maple, soft maple	Deciduous tree	to 70 ft			3 to 8	Full sun

| Soil | CULTURE | | |
	Water	Feeding	Special Characteristics
Good drainage	Medium water	Medium feeder	Effective specimen plant or informal hedge; sometimes deciduous; can be sheared, but doing so reduces flowering; graceful, rounded habit; foliage turns bronze in winter; showy white flowers have pink tinge.
Good drainage	Medium water	Medium feeder	Needles blue-green, 2 in. long; upright cylindrical cones; protect from high winds.
Good drainage	Medium water	Medium feeder	Slow to moderate growing; shiny, dark green needles with silver undersides; dense foliage; can be grown in container for several years.
Good drainage	Medium water	Medium feeder	Fast growing; narrow tree with stiff branching habit; needles blue-green with silver undersides; best in cool climate.
Good drainage	Medium water	Medium feeder	Fast growing; tropical; large, bell-shaped flowers; prune back in winter to 18 to 30 in.
Good drainage	Medium water	Medium feeder	Fast growing; tropical; prune back in winter to 18 to 30 in.; variegated.
Good drainage	Let dry out between waterings	Medium feeder	Blue-gray, ferny foliage; massive spring blooms; fast growing.
Good drainage	Let dry out between waterings	Light feeder	Fast-growing windbreak or screen; root system can break up pavement; not for confined situations.
Good drainage; rich soil	Medium water	Medium feeder	Grown for immense leaves and tall flower stalks; tolerates drought; tolerates full sun in cool climates; invasive roots.
Good drainage	Medium water	Medium feeder	Slow to moderate growing; attractive fall foliage; tolerates dry, poor, or sandy soils; useful as small street tree or trained as hedge.
Good drainage	Medium water	Medium feeder	Fragrant flowers; attractive fall foliage; cold and wind tolerant; unless trained, grows as a multistemmed tree.
Good drainage	Medium water	Medium feeder	Delicate tree; attractive all year long; good fall color; protect from hot, dry winds; attractive patio tree, bonsai, small lawn tree, or in container; prune to accentuate natural growth habit; many different cultivars available.
Good drainage; acid soil; organic matter	Medium water	Medium feeder	Tree used as shrub; open form; slow growing; soft foliage in wide variety of shades and variegations; showy fall color; good as specimen, in containers, or as bonsai subject; protect from cold, drying winds and late spring frosts.
Good drainage	Medium water	Medium feeder	Casts dense shade; attractive fall color; tolerates many soils and climates; vigorous roots can be a problem.
Not particular	Medium water	Medium feeder	Attractive fall foliage; tolerates wet soil; fast growing.
Good drainage	Medium water	Medium feeder	Fast growing; quick shade; tolerates heat and dry winds; limb breakage a problem in storms.

NAME	HABIT		FLOWERS		ADAPTATION	
	Type	Height	Color	Time	Zones	Light
Acer saccharum Sugar maple, rock maple	Deciduous tree	to 80 ft			3 to 7	Full sun
Achillea millefolium Yarrow	Hardy perennial herb	6 to 36 in.	Pink, white, yellow	Late spring to fall	2 to 10	Full sun
Achimenes species Magicflower	Tender bulb	1 to 2 ft	Blue, pink, yellow, purple	Early spring to late fall	10 or indoors	Light shade
Adiantum pedatum Five-finger fern, maidenhair fern	Semievergreen ground cover	to 2 ft			3 to 10	Full sun
Aeschynanthus speciosus Lipstick plant	Houseplant	3 to 4 ft	Orange	All year	10 or indoors	Light shade
Aesculus × carnea Red horsechestnut	Deciduous tree	30 to 50 ft	Pink, red	Spring	4 to 8	Full sun
Aesculus hippocastanum Horsechestnut	Deciduous tree	50 to 75 ft	White	Late spring	3 to 9	Full sun
Aesculus parviflora Bottlebrush buckeye	Deciduous shrub or small tree	8 to 15 ft	White	Summer	5 to 8	Full sun to deep shade
Aesculus pavia Red buckeye	Deciduous shrub or small tree	8 to 15 ft	Red	Spring	5 to 8	Full sun to deep shade
Agapanthus africanus Lily-of-the-Nile, African lily	Tender evergreen bulb	10 to 20 in.	Blue, white, purple	Early spring to late fall	9, 10	Full sun to light shade
Agave americana Century plant	Hardy perennial	to 10 ft	Yellow	Summer to fall	8 to 10	Full sun to half-day sun
Aglaonema modestum Chinese evergreen	Tender perennial, houseplant	to 2 ft	White	Late summer to early fall	10 or indoors	Light shade to deep shade
Agrostis palustris Creeping bent grass	Turfgrass	¼ to ½ in.			3 to 6	Full sun to half-day sun
Ajuga reptans Carpet bugle	Evergreen ground cover	3 to 6 in.	Blue, pink, white	Spring	6 to 10	Half-day sun to light shade
Akebia quinata Five-leaf akebia	Semievergreen vine, ground cover	Twines to 15 to 20 ft	Purple	Spring	4 to 10	Full sun to light shade

| | **CULTURE** | | |
Soil	**Water**	**Feeding**	**Special Characteristics**
Good drainage	Medium water	Medium feeder	Source of maple syrup and lumber for maple furniture; attractive fall foliage; less tolerant of hot, dry conditions and soil compaction than other maples.
Good drainage; grows in poor soil	Let dry out between waterings	Light feeder	Medicinal herb with gray-green, fernlike foliage; flowers in flat-headed umbels; fragrant foliage; tolerates very poor, dry soils; needs yearly division to be kept in place.
Good drainage; organic matter	Medium water	Heavy feeder	Good houseplant, greenhouse plant, or outdoor container plant; prefers partial shade.
Organic matter	Wet; don't let dry out	Medium feeder	Fine-textured fern; dark, wiry stems with 5 frondlets each; spreads by creeping rootstalks; dies back in frosts.
Good drainage	Medium water	Light feeder	Trailing stems; orange blossoms with rust-colored edges; needs warmth, humidity, and bright indirect light.
Good drainage	Medium water	Medium feeder	Slow to moderate growing; striking spring flowers; very manageable; good shade; best in areas of cool, moist summers; protect from winds.
Good drainage	Medium water	Medium feeder	Dense foliage provides heavy shade; palmately divided leaflets; white flowers with pink markings hang in plumes; heavy fruiting may be a nuisance; some mature trees have weak branches.
Good drainage; organic matter	Medium water	Medium feeder	Open, wide-spreading habit; suckers; attractive flowers; good specimen plant.
Good drainage; organic matter	Medium water	Medium feeder	Blooms in early spring; less hardy than *A. parviflora*.
Good drainage; organic matter	Medium water	Heavy feeder	Give shade in hot climates; divide every 5 years or when flowering declines; good container plant.
Good drainage; sandy soil	Let dry out between waterings	Medium feeder	Rosette form; large, triangular leaves with sawtooth edges; blooms once after 15 to 30 years, then dies.
Good drainage	Medium water	Light feeder	Oblong, lance-shaped leaves, 6 to 9 in. long; leaves marked with silver bars between pale lateral veins; yellowish red berries follow flowers; tolerates poor light and dry air; prefers moderate light and humidity.
Good drainage; organic matter	Wet; don't let dry out	Medium to heavy feeder	Favorite grass for golf-course putting greens; mow low; best in full sun; tolerates traffic fairly well.
Good drainage	Medium water	Medium feeder	Fast growing; oval, waxy leaves borne in clusters; forms thick, low mat; spreads by creeping stems; protect from cold winter winds; mow lightly after blooming; a number of cultivars with variation in foliage color are available.
Good drainage	Medium water	Medium feeder	Evergreen in mild climates; deep green leaves divided into 5 leaflets; purple, fleshy pods; very adaptive; plant away from low-growing shrubs—aggressive habit will smother them.

NAME	HABIT		FLOWERS		ADAPTATION	
	Type	Height	Color	Time	Zones	Light
Albizia julibrissin Silk tree, mimosa	Deciduous tree	25 to 40 ft	Pink	Early summer to early fall	7 to 10	Full sun to light shade
Alcea rosea Hollyhock	Tender biennial	2 to 9 ft	Warm colors, pink, white	Early summer to early fall	3 to 10	Full sun
Allium flavum Yellow onion	Hardy bulb	12 to 18 in.	Yellow	Summer	4 to 10	Full sun
Allium giganteum Giant onion	Hardy bulb	to 5 ft	Violet	Summer	5 to 10	Full sun
Allium moly Golden garlic	Hardy bulb	12 to 18 in.	Yellow	Early summer	3 to 10	Full sun
Allium neapolitanum Naples onion	Half-hardy bulb	to 12 in.	White	Early summer	7 to 10	Full sun
Alnus cordata Italian alder	Deciduous tree	40 to 70 ft			5 to 10	Full sun
Alnus glutinosa Common alder, black alder, European alder	Deciduous tree	40 to 60 ft			3 to 10	Full sun
Alnus rhombifolia White alder	Deciduous tree	60 to 70 ft			4 to 10	Full sun
Alnus rubra Red alder	Deciduous tree	40 to 70 ft			4 to 10	Full sun
Aloe barbadensis Aloe vera	Succulent perennial, houseplant	6 to 24 in.	Red, yellow	All year	10 or indoors	Full sun to light shade
Aloysia triphylla Lemon verbena	Shrub	3 to 6 ft	White	Late summer	8 to 10 or indoors	Full sun
Alstroemeria aurantiaca Alstroemeria	Half-hardy bulb	2½ to 4 ft	Orange	Summer	7 to 10	Full sun to light shade
Amaranthus tricolor Joseph's-coat	Tender annual	1 to 5 ft	Red	Summer		Full sun
Amaryllis belladonna Belladonna-lily, naked-lady	Tender bulb	2 to 3 ft	Pink	Late summer	9, 10	Full sun
Amelanchier arborea Serviceberry, shadblow, shadbush, Juneberry	Deciduous tree	20 to 40 ft	White	Early spring	4 to 8	Full sun
Anchusa azurea Italian bugloss, Italian alkanet	Hardy perennial	3 to 5 ft	Blue	Summer	3 to 10	Full sun to light shade

	CULTURE		
Soil	**Water**	**Feeding**	**Special Characteristics**
Good drainage; slightly alkaline soil	Medium water	Medium feeder	Very showy tree; fernlike foliage folds at night; needs plenty of heat and slightly alkaline soil; fast growing; lawn, patio, container tree; prune wide-spreading branches; very susceptible to vascular wilt; some cultivars hardier and wilt resistant.
Good drainage; organic matter	Wet; don't let dry out	Heavy feeder	Prone to rust disease.
Good drainage; rich soil	Medium water	Medium feeder	Bell-shaped flowers in loose umbels; gray-green foliage; may naturalize.
Good drainage; rich soil	Medium water	Heavy feeder	Huge ball-shaped flower clusters; straplike leaves; good for dried arrangements; foliage dies in early summer.
Good drainage; rich soil	Medium water	Medium feeder	Starlike flowers in clusters; gray-green leaves; foliage dies in midsummer.
Good drainage; rich soil	Medium water	Medium feeder	Starlike flowers borne in loose umbels; fragrant; adapted to moist areas; in cold climates dig and store through winter.
Not particular	Medium water	Medium feeder	Fast growing; upright growth; will tolerate wet soil; invasive roots; gray bark; tassellike catkins and small cones in late winter.
Not particular	Medium water	Medium feeder	Fast growing; best as multistemmed tree; tolerates water and does well in poor soils; catkins in late winter.
Not particular	Medium water	Medium feeder	Fast growing; quick screen; valuable in poorly drained soils; catkins in late winter.
Not particular	Wet; don't let dry out	Medium feeder	Fast-growing "weed" tree; thrives in low, damp soil conditions; best as temporary shelter for more permanent trees and shrubs.
Good drainage	Let dry out between waterings	Light feeder	Thick, succulent leaves and spiny edges; older plants produce flower stalks; used in cosmetics and medicinally.
Good drainage	Medium water	Medium feeder	Leggy herb garden shrub with pale green leaves in groups of 3 or 4; usually deciduous; fragrant, lemon-scented foliage.
Good drainage; organic matter	Medium water	Heavy feeder	Difficult to divide; stake in windy areas; shade in hot climates; can be grown in colder climates if dug and protected in winter.
Tolerates clay soil	Let dry out between waterings	Light feeder	Brilliant leaf color; thrives in hot, dry location with poor soil.
Good drainage	Medium water	Heavy feeder	Straplike leaves; fragrant flowers appear later on bare, reddish brown stalks; good container plant; can be grown in colder climates if protected.
Good drainage	Medium water	Medium feeder	Moderate growing; often multistemmed; attractive all year; showy spring flowers; purple fruit in summer; foliage yellow to red in fall; roots noninvasive; casts light shade; good tree to garden under.
Good drainage	Wet; don't let dry out	Light feeder	Striking flower color; cut back after first bloom to encourage second bloom; may need staking.

NAME	HABIT		FLOWERS		ADAPTATION	
	Type	Height	Color	Time	Zones	Light
Anchusa capensis Summer forget-me-not, cape forget-me-not	Half-hardy annual	8 to 18 in.	Blue	Early summer to first frost		Full sun to light shade
Anchusa officinalis Alkanet, bugloss	Hardy biennial herb	to 2 ft	Blue, purple	Late spring to summer	5 to 10	Full sun to light shade
Anemone coronaria Poppy anemone	Half-hardy bulb	6 to 18 in.	Blue, red, violet	Spring	8 to 10	Full sun
Anemone × hybrida Japanese anemone	Half-hardy perennial	2 to 5 ft	White, pink	Spring to fall	6 to 9	Light shade
Angelica *Angelica archangelica*	Hardy biennial herb	4 to 6 ft	White	Summer	3 to 10	Light shade
Anthemis tinctoria Golden marguerite	Hardy perennial	2½ to 3 ft	Yellow	Summer to early fall	3 to 10	Full sun
Antirrhinum majus Snapdragon	Half-hardy annual	½ to 4 ft	Red, pink, white, orange, yellow	Late spring to first frost		Full sun
Aphelandra squarrosa Zebra plant	Houseplant	1½ to 2 ft	Yellow	Fall	10 or indoors	Light shade
Apple *Malus pumila*	Deciduous fruit tree	4 to 30 ft	White	Spring	4 to 9	Full sun
Apricot *Prunus armeniaca*	Deciduous fruit tree	15 to 25 ft	White	Early spring	6 to 9	Full sun
Aquilegia species and hybrids Columbine	Hardy perennial	1½ to 3 ft	Red, white, blue, purple, pink, orange, yellow	Late spring to early summer	3 to 10	Light shade
Arabis caucasica Rockcress	Evergreen ground cover	to 12 in.	White	Spring	6 to 10	Full sun
Araucaria bidwillii Bunya-bunya	Evergreen tree	30 to 50 ft			9, 10 or indoors	Full sun to light shade
Araucaria heterophylla Norfolk Island pine	Evergreen tree	60 to 70 ft			9, 10 or indoors	Full sun to light shade

| | CULTURE | | |
Soil	Water	Feeding	Special Characteristics
Good drainage	Medium water	Light feeder	Easy to grow; tolerates poor soil.
Good drainage; rich soil	Medium water	Heavy feeder	Herb with rough, hairy leaves 3 to 6 in. long; flowers taste like cucumber; root yields red dye.
Good drainage	Medium water	Heavy feeder	Good cut flowers; dig bulbs and store over winter.
Good drainage; organic matter; rich soil	Medium water	Medium feeder	Good fall color; long-lived; fibrous rooted; resents disturbance once established; tolerates full sun in cool climates; avoid wet soil in winter.
Good drainage	Medium water	Medium feeder	Aromatic, celerylike herb with edible leaves; hollow stems; doesn't flower until second or third year.
Good drainage	Medium water	Medium feeder	Fernlike leaves, aromatic when bruised; short-lived flowers; avoid heavy, wet, clay soils.
Good drainage; organic matter	Medium water	Heavy feeder	Good spring color; rust is a serious problem on older cultivars; will bloom through winter in mild climates.
Good drainage	Medium water	Medium feeder	Shiny, nearly black elliptical leaves striped with ivory veins; conelike flowers emerge from golden bracts for 6 weeks in the fall; give indirect light or filtered sun; keep moist and humid; prune back in spring to keep bushy.
Good drainage; organic matter	Medium water	Medium feeder	Requires some cool winter temperatures; partially self-fertile, some require pollinators; pruning method depends on how you want to shape tree; water deeply; thin fruit 4 to 6 weeks after bloom; a wide selection of varieties available; early-, mid-, and late-season cultivars; variation in size, shape, and taste of fruit; choose a cultivar adapted to your climate.
Good drainage; organic matter	Medium water	Medium feeder	Attractive, vigorous tree; early bloom after last frost; thin fruit about 6 weeks after bloom to 3 to 4 in. apart; avoid areas that are hot when fruit ripens (over 90° F) or select heat-tolerant varieties.
Good drainage; organic matter	Wet; don't let dry out	Medium feeder	Usually short-lived; tolerates full sun in cool summer climates; feed regularly with fertilizer applied half strength; flowers are often bicolored.
Good drainage	Let dry out between waterings	Medium feeder	Fine, feltlike, whitish hairs give leaves grayish cast; profuse, fragrant flowers; drought tolerant once established; cut back upright stems after flowering; not a large-scale ground cover.
Good drainage	Medium water	Medium feeder	Moderate growing; overlapping needles are sharp and stiff; unusual branches; can be grown in container as small indoor tree.
Good drainage	Medium water	Medium feeder	Soft, formal character; good near coast; can be container grown for many years; grows indoors to 10 ft; provide very bright, indirect light or a couple of hours of morning sun; watch for spider mites.

NAME	HABIT		FLOWERS		ADAPTATION	
	Type	Height	Color	Time	Zones	Light
Arbutus menziesii Madrone, madrona	Evergreen tree	20 to 40 ft	White, pink	Spring	7 to 9	Full sun
Arbutus unedo Strawberry tree	Evergreen shrub or small tree	10 to 25 ft	White	Fall to winter	7 to 9	Fall sun to light shade
Arctostaphylos densiflora Vine hill manzanita	Evergreen shrub	5 to 6 ft	White, pink	Spring	7 to 10	Full sun to light shade
Arctostaphylos uva-ursi Bearberry manzanita, kinnikinick	Evergreen ground cover	6 to 12 in.	White	Late spring	2 to 8	Full sun to light shade
Arctotis stoechadifolia African daisy	Tender annual	10 to 20 in.	Comes in all colors	Early summer to early fall		Full sun
Arenaria verna (A. caespitosa) Moss sandwort	Evergreen perennial ground cover	to 3 in.	White	Summer	3 to 10	Light shade
Armeria maritima Sea pink, sea thrift	Hardy evergreen perennial ground cover	6 to 10 in.	White, pink	Late spring to early summer	3 to 10	Full sun
Aronia arbutifolia Red chokeberry	Deciduous shrub	6 to 8 ft	White	Spring	5 to 9	Full sun
Artemisia abrotanum Southernwood	Deciduous shrub	3 to 4 ft	Yellowish white	Spring	4 to 10	Full sun
Artichoke Cynara scolymus	Perennial vegetable	2 to 4 ft			8 to 10	Full sun to half-day sun
Asarum caudatum Wild ginger	Evergreen ground cover	7 to 10 in.			5 to 9	Shade
Asparagus Asparagus officinalis	Hardy perennial vegetable	4 to 5 ft			5 to 10	Full sun to half-day sun
Asparagus densiflorus **'Sprengeri'** Sprenger asparagus, asparagus fern	Evergreen ground cover, houseplant	1 to 2 ft	White	Spring to early summer	10 or indoors	Half-day sun to light shade
Aspidistra elatior Cast-iron plant	Evergreen perennial, houseplant	1 to 2½ ft	Purple	Spring	10 or indoors	Light shade to deep shade
Asplenium nidus Bird's-nest fern	Houseplant	1 to 3 ft			10 or indoors	Light shade

	CULTURE		
Soil	**Water**	**Feeding**	**Special Characteristics**
Good drainage	Let dry out between waterings	Medium feeder	Slow to moderate growing; color all year; attractive red bark; leathery, copper to green foliage; red and orange berries in fall; deep, infrequent waterings.
Good drainage	Medium water	Medium feeder	Shrubby plant; slow to moderate growing; attractive red bark; flowers and red fruit appear in fall and winter; tolerates seacoast conditions.
Needs good drainage	Let dry out between waterings	Light feeder	Smooth, red bark; crooked, spreading branches; 'Howard McMinn' is best for dense canopy.
Sandy soil	Let dry out between waterings	Light feeder	Low, mat forming; tiny bell-shaped flowers followed by red berries; relatively slow growing; tolerates poor soil, seacoast conditions.
Sandy soil; organic matter	Let dry out between waterings	Light feeder	Tolerates drought, poor soil; best in mild climates.
Good drainage	Medium water	Medium feeder	Mosslike; small, narrow, dark green leaves; dense, slow-spreading mat tolerates full sun and light foot traffic; give some winter protection in cold, exposed areas.
Good drainage; sandy soil	Let dry out between waterings	Light feeder	Tolerates seacoast conditions; blooms almost all year along coast; grasslike foliage.
Tolerates clay soil	Medium water	Medium feeder	Slow growing; leggy, upright shrub; attractive fall foliage with profuse red berries; tolerates both drought and wet conditions and partial shade; best in masses and large groups; naturalized in wet areas.
Good drainage; sandy soil	Let dry out between waterings	Medium feeder	Lemon-scented herb grown mainly for feathery green foliage; hardy and long-lived; rarely blooms; prune to maintain shape.
Rich soil; organic matter	Wet; don't let dry out	Heavy feeder	Grown for edible flower buds; best in cool, humid, moderate climates; needs protection from frost and summer heat.
High organic matter	Wet; don't let dry out	Medium feeder	Heart-shaped leaves; inconspicuous flowers; gingerlike fragrance; protect from drying winds.
Good drainage; organic matter; sandy soil	Medium water	Medium feeder	Usually grown from 1-year-old crowns; plants produce for 10 to 15 years; thrives in most climates; plant crowns as early in spring as possible; don't harvest first 2 years.
Good drainage	Let dry out between waterings	Light feeder	Arching sprays of light green, needlelike leaves; inconspicuous flowers; small, bright red berries; trailing habit; drought resistant; requires little care; restricted outdoors to warm-winter areas; several other ornamental asparagus available.
Good drainage	Medium water	Light feeder	Leathery, oblong, shiny dark green leaves; bell-shaped flowers; slow growing, long-lived; give indirect sun; tolerant of poor growing conditions.
Good drainage	Medium water	Medium feeder	Wavy, lance-shaped leaves with black rib uncurl from heart of plant; can reach 3 ft long; fronds dislike being touched; can be summered on shady patio; water accumulation in heart may cause crown rot.

NAME	HABIT		FLOWERS		ADAPTATION	
	Type	Height	Color	Time	Zones	Light
Aster species and hybrids Hardy aster, michaelmas daisy	Hardy perennial	½ to 6 ft	Purple, blue, red, pink, white	Late summer to fall	4 to 10	Full sun to light shade
Astilbe species and hybrids False-spiraea, astilbe	Hardy perennial	1 to 3 ft	White, pink, lavender, red	Summer	4 to 8	Light shade to deep shade
Aucuba japonica Japanese aucuba	Evergreen shrub	6 to 10 ft	Purple	Early spring	7 to 10	Light shade to deep shade
Aurinia saxatilis Basket-of-gold, goldentuft	Hardy perennial	9 to 12 in.	Yellow	Spring	3 to 10	Full sun
Baccharis pilularis Dwarf coyotebush	Evergreen ground cover	to 2 ft			7 to 10	Full sun to light shade
Basil Ocimum basilicum	Tender annual herb	to 2 ft				Full sun
Bauhinia blakeana Hong Kong orchid tree	Deciduous tree	to 20 ft	Pink, purple	Fall to winter	9, 10	Full sun
Bauhinia variegata Orchid tree	Deciduous tree	20 to 25 ft	Lavender, pink, white	Winter to spring	7 to 10	Full sun
Beans, lima Phaseolus lunatus	Tender annual vegetable	to 10 ft (climbing)				Full sun
Beans, scarlet runner Phaseolus coccineus	Tender annual vegetable	to 8 ft (climbing)	Red, white	Early summer		Full sun
Beans, snap or string Phaseolus vulgaris	Tender annual vegetable	to 8 ft (climbing)	White	Early summer		Full sun
Beaucarnea recurvata var. intermedia Elephant-foot-tree, ponytail-palm	Evergreen shrub or small tree, houseplant	to 30 ft			10 or indoors	Half-day sun
Beets Beta vulgaris	Hardy annual vegetable	6 to 12 in.				Full sun to light shade
Begonia grandis Evans begonia	Hardy bulb	to 24 in.	Pink	Summer	6 to 10	Light shade
Begonia masoniana Iron-cross begonia	Houseplant	to 18 in.	Pink, not showy		10 or indoors	Half-day sun to light shade

| | CULTURE | | |
Soil	Water	Feeding	Special Characteristics
Good drainage	Medium water	Light feeder	Good, late season color; give light shade in hot summer climates; pinch plants in late spring; stake varieties over 2 ft tall; divide plants every other year.
Rich soil; organic matter; good drainage	Wet; don't let dry out	Heavy feeder	Accepts full sun if watered deeply and often; divide every 3 to 4 years.
Organic matter	Medium water	Medium feeder	Leathery, large leaves; bright red berries in fall and winter; requires both male and female plant to set fruit; tolerates many soils; cultivars with variegated leaves.
Sandy soil	Let dry out between waterings	Light feeder	Attractive gray-green foliage; profuse blooming; dwarf cultivars available.
Not particular	Medium water	Light feeder	Small, lightly toothed, dark green leaves; woody branches; very adaptable; tolerates drought and wet soil; tolerates seacoast conditions; good for erosion control on banks; prune out deep wood and arching branches each spring; several cultivars available.
Good drainage; organic matter	Medium water	Medium feeder	Fragrant, edible herb used medicinally and in cooking; thrives in heat; likes rich soil; dark-leaved cultivar available.
Good drainage	Medium water	Medium feeder	Large, striking flowers; moderate growing; good small shade tree; won't tolerate high heat and drought; umbrellalike canopy.
Good drainage	Medium water	Medium feeder	Moderate growing; umbrellalike forms; tends to get bushy and multitrunked; good street tree in areas of warm spring weather; mild, dry winter produces best bloom.
Good drainage; organic matter	Medium water	Medium feeder	Requires higher temperature than snap beans to germinate well, and longer season to produce crop; pods may fail to set in extremely hot climates; bush types and pole types available.
Good drainage; organic matter	Medium water	Medium feeder	Closely related to common beans; more vigorous; larger seed pods and flowers; flowers are quite attractive.
Good drainage; organic matter	Medium water	Medium feeder	Plant seed when danger of frost is past; requires about 60 days of moderate temperatures to produce crop; beans are grouped as bush beans, bush wax beans, or pole beans; many cultivars are available in each group.
Good drainage; sandy soil	Let dry out between waterings	Medium feeder	Usually grown as a 3 to 5 ft houseplant; base of gray-brown trunk resembles onion when plant is young; long, thin green leaves arch out around apex of stem; likes warm environment; water thoroughly and let dry out between waterings.
Good drainage; organic matter	Medium water	Medium feeder	Prefers cool weather; sow seed as early as ground can be worked; add sand to soil for better root development; plant successively for continual supply; many different cultivars are available.
Good drainage; organic matter	Medium water	Heavy feeder	Good container plant.
Good drainage	Medium water	Medium feeder	Green leaves, puckered surface; brown markings forming cross in center of leaves; give bright, indirect light and 4 hours direct sunlight during fall and winter.

397

NAME	HABIT		FLOWERS		ADAPTATION	
	Type	Height	Color	Time	Zones	Light
Begonia × rex-cultorum Rex begonia	Evergreen perennial, houseplant	to 18 in.			10 or indoors	Half-day sun to light shade
Begonia × semperflorens-cultorum Wax begonia, fibrous-rooted begonia	Half-hardy annual	6 to 12 in.	Pink, red, white	Late spring to first frost		Half-day sun to light shade
Begonia × tuberhybrida Tuberous begonia	Tender bulb	12 to 18 in.	Red, orange, yellow, pink, white	Late spring to fall	10	Light shade
Berberis darwinii Darwin barberry	Evergreen shrub	5 to 10 ft	Yellow	Early spring	8 to 10	Full sun
Berberis koreana Korean barberry	Deciduous shrub	4 to 8 ft	Yellow	Late spring	4 to 7	Full sun
Berberis thunbergii Japanese barberry	Deciduous shrub	3 to 6 ft			5 to 8	Full sun to light shade
Bergenia cordifolia Heartleaf bergenia	Hardy perennial	12 to 15 in.	Pink, white	Spring	4 to 10	Full sun to light shade
Bergenia crassifolia Winter-blooming bergenia	Hardy perennial	to 20 in.	Pink, white, purple	Spring	3 to 10	Light shade
Betula maximowicziana Monarch birch	Deciduous tree	80 to 100 ft			6 to 10	Full sun
Betula nigra River birch	Deciduous tree	50 to 70 ft			5 to 9	Full sun
Betula papyrifera Paper birch	Deciduous tree	40 to 60 ft			3 to 7	Full sun
Betula pendula European white birch	Deciduous tree	to 60 ft			2 to 7	Full sun
Billbergia nutans Queen's-tears, friendship plant	Evergreen perennial, houseplant	1½ to 2 ft	Pink, green	Winter	10 or indoors	Half-day sun
Blackberry *Rubus allegheniensis*	Deciduous berry vine	5 to 8 ft	White	Late spring to summer	3 to 10	Full sun to half-day sun
Black-eyed pea—*See* Cowpea						
Blueberry *Vaccinium corymbosum*	Deciduous berry bush	6 to 12 ft	White	Late spring	3 to 7	Full sun to light shade

	CULTURE		
Soil	**Water**	**Feeding**	**Special Characteristics**
Good drainage	Medium water	Medium feeder	Grown for large, hairy leaves patterned in green, red, silver, and white; give bright, indirect light and 4 hours direct sunlight in fall and winter.
Good drainage; organic matter	Medium water	Heavy feeder	Hard to start from seed; in hot climates keep well watered and avoid full sun; will bloom through winter in mild climates.
Good drainage; organic matter	Medium water	Heavy feeder	Good container plant; dig up in fall and store over winter.
Not particular	Medium water	Medium feeder	Fast growing, loose, open form; profuse bloomer; dark blue berries; tolerates many soils; withstands drought well.
Not particular	Medium water	Medium feeder	Showy flowers and red fruit; dense, oval shape; thorny; suckers heavily; can prune as hedge.
Not particular	Medium water	Medium feeder	Attractive fall foliage; many variegated varieties; moderate growing; tolerates drought; easy to transplant; thorny; best pruned as dense hedge or used as barrier plant.
Good drainage	Medium water	Medium feeder	Evergreen except in coldest climates; cabbagelike leaves turn reddish in winter; tolerates wide range of soils; give shade in areas of hot summers; tolerates deep shade.
Good drainage	Medium water	Medium feeder	Evergreen except in coldest climates; 6 to 8 in. leaves, finely toothed, wavy edges; flowers in winter in mild-climate areas; can take sun in cool, coastal areas; divide clumps when crowded.
Good drainage	Medium water	Medium feeder	Fast growing; largest leaves and catkins of all birches; young bark reddish brown, old bark white; tolerates cold, windy areas and dry sites; provide ample water and regular feedings.
Not particular	Wet; don't let dry out	Medium feeder	Young bark red, turns brown with age and peels off; leaves bright glossy green above, silver below; must have adequate moisture.
Good drainage	Medium water	Medium feeder	Papery, white bark; best grown in clumps; open and erect growth habit.
Good drainage	Medium water	Medium feeder	Attractive white bark with black markings; upright tree with weeping side branches; lends itself to planting in groves or clumps; many cultivars available.
Good drainage	Medium water	Medium feeder	Bromeliad with grasslike, gray-green leaves; rose bracts; blue-edged green arching spray of flowers; keep water in center cup.
Good drainage; organic matter	Medium water	Medium feeder	Stiff-caned, fairly hardy plant; roots are perennial, canes biennial; thorny; trailing.
Good drainage; organic matter; acid soil	Medium water	Medium feeder to heavy feeder	Needs a cool, moist, acid soil and good drainage; edible fruit borne in the summer months; shallow rooted; avoid fertilizing the first year; don't prune for 2 to 3 seasons; choose 2 varieties for cross-pollination; many early, mid-season, and late varieties; some varieties adapted to warmer climates.

NAME	HABIT		FLOWERS		ADAPTATION	
	Type	Height	Color	Time	Zones	Light
Borage *Borago officinalis*	Half-hardy annual herb	1 to 3 ft	Blue	Early summer to early fall		Full sun to light shade
Brachychiton populneus Kurrajong, bottletree	Evergreen tree	25 to 50 ft	White	Late spring to early summer	9, 10	Full sun
Brachycome iberidifolia Swan River daisy	Half-hardy annual	10 to 16 in.	Blue, pink, violet, lavender, white	Summer		Full sun
Brassaia actinophylla Schefflera, umbrella tree	Evergreen shrub, houseplant	to 8 ft			10 or indoors	Light shade
Brassica oleracea* var. *acephala Flowering kale, ornamental cabbage	Hardy annual	10 to 15 in.				Full sun
Broccoli *Brassica oleracea* var. *botrytis*	Hardy annual vegetable	1 to 2 ft				Full sun to half-day sun
Brodiaea coronaria (*B. grandiflora*) Harvest brodiaea	Half-hardy bulb	to 18 in.	Purple, violet	Summer	7 to 10	Full sun
Browallia speciosa Sapphire-flower	Tender annual	10 to 18 in.	Blue, lavender, white	Late spring to first frost		Half-day sun to light shade
Brunnera macrophylla Siberian bugloss	Hardy perennial	to 18 in.	Blue	Spring	3 to 8	Light shade
Brussels sprouts *Brassica oleracea* var. *gemmifera*	Hardy biennial vegetable	to 3 ft				Full sun to half-day sun
Buddleia davidii Butterfly bush	Deciduous shrub	6 to 10 ft	Blue, purple, lavender, white	Summer to first frost	5 to 10	Full sun
Bulbocodium vernum Spring meadow saffron	Hardy bulb	4 to 6 in.	Lavender, pink	Spring	5 to 10	Full sun to light shade
Buxus microphylla* var. *japonica Japanese boxwood	Evergreen shrub	3 to 4 ft			6 to 10	Full sun to light shade
Buxus sempervirens Common boxwood	Evergreen shrub	10 to 20 ft			5 to 10	Full sun to light shade

| | CULTURE | | |
Soil	Water	Feeding	Special Characteristics
Not particular	Medium water	Medium feeder	Herb with gray-green, hairy leaves; star-shaped, showy flowers; needs ample space; foliage and flowers have cucumberlike flavor; self-sows.
Good drainage	Medium water	Medium feeder	Slow to moderate growing; heavy, tapering trunk; dense, conical crown; leaves both lobed and unlobed; drought resistant; effective as screen or windbreak.
Good drainage; organic matter	Medium water	Heavy feeder	Pleasant fragrance; short blooming season; prefers cool summers.
Good drainage	Medium water	Medium feeder	Fast growing; glossy green leaflets spread out like an umbrella; give bright, indirect light.
Good drainage; organic matter	Wet; don't let dry out	Light feeder	Vegetable used as an ornamental; color is best in fall; foliage composed of thick, blue-green outer leaves with white, pink, red, magenta, or purple inner leaves.
Good drainage; organic matter	Medium water	Heavy feeder	Member of cabbage family; cool-weather vegetable; best in temperatures between 65° and 80° F; harvest flower buds while still tight; frost hardy; requires high nitrogen; many cultivars varying in size and maturation time are available.
Good drainage; sandy soil	Medium water	Medium feeder	Needs adequate moisture while blooming, but must dry out following bloom; best in areas with dry summers.
Good drainage; organic matter	Medium water	Medium feeder	Easy to grow from seed; useful in hanging baskets; will bloom through winter in mild climates.
Grows in poor soil	Wet; don't let dry out	Medium feeder	Attractive leaves all season; adapts to full sun in coastal areas of the West; needs little attention.
Good drainage; organic matter	Medium water	Heavy feeder	Cool-weather vegetable, best where temperatures are between 65° and 80° F; most cold tolerant of cabbage family; exposure to frost improves flavor; pinch out growing tips when plants are 15 to 20 in. tall to promote uniform development of sprouts; several cultivars available.
Good drainage	Medium water	Medium feeder	Fragrant flowers; very fast growing; wild, unruly growth habit; large, coarse leaves; best grown as herbaceous perennial in rear of border; prune to within a few inches of the ground after blooming; attracts butterflies.
Good drainage	Medium water	Medium feeder	Good in rock gardens; leaves appear after flowers.
Good drainage; organic matter	Medium water	Medium feeder	Light green leaves; may brown in cold-winter areas; slow growing; compact; flowers are fragrant but not showy; tolerates dry heat and alkaline soil; can be sheared into formal shapes.
Good drainage; organic matter	Medium water	Medium feeder	Does not tolerate extremes of heat and cold; mulch heavily to keep roots cool; protect from drying winds; full sun in mild areas, shade in hotter climates; can be pruned as topiary or sheared into formal hedges.

NAME	HABIT		FLOWERS		ADAPTATION	
	Type	Height	Color	Time	Zones	Light
Cabbage *Brassica oleracea* var. *capitata*	Hardy biennial vegetable	6 to 12 in.				Full sun to light shade
Caladium* × *hortulanum Fancy-leaved caladium	Tender bulb	to 12 in.			10 or indoors	Light shade
Calendula officinalis Pot marigold	Hardy annual	10 to 24 in.	White, orange, yellow	Spring to first frost		Full sun
Callistemon citrinus Lemon bottlebrush	Evergreen shrub or small tree	10 to 25 ft	Red	All year	8 to 10	Full sun
Callistephus chinensis China aster	Tender annual	6 to 36 in.	All colors	Early summer to late summer		Full sun to light shade
Calluna vulgaris Scotch heather	Evergreen shrub, ground cover	4 to 24 in.	Pink, purple, white, red	Summer to early fall	5 to 8	Full sun to half-day sun
Calocedrus decurrens Incense cedar	Needled evergreen tree	70 to 90 ft			5 to 9	Full sun
Caltha palustris Marshmarigold	Hardy perennial	12 to 18 in.	Yellow	Spring	3 to 10	Full sun to light shade
Calycanthus floridus Carolina allspice, strawberry shrub	Deciduous shrub	6 to 9 ft	Bronze	Spring to summer	5 to 9	Light shade
Camassia cusickii Cussick camass	Hardy bulb	3 to 4 ft	Blue	Early summer	3 to 10	Full sun to light shade
Camassia leichtlinii Leichtlin camass	Hardy bulb	2 to 4 ft	Blue, white	Early summer	3 to 10	Full sun to light shade
Camellia japonica Common camellia	Evergreen shrub	6 to 12 ft	White, pink, red	Fall to late spring	8 to 10	Light shade
Camellia sasanqua Sasanqua camellia	Evergreen shrub	6 to 12 in.	Pink, red, white	Early fall to winter	8 to 10	Full sun to light shade
Campanula carpatica Carpathian harebell	Hardy perennial	6 to 12 in.	Blue, white, purple	Early summer to late summer	3 to 10	Full sun to light shade
Campanula elatines* var. *garganica Adriatic bellflower	Ground cover	3 to 6 in.	Blue	Late summer to early fall	3 to 10	Full sun to light shade
Campanula medium Canterbury bells	Hardy annual	12 to 36 in.	Blue, pink, lavender, white	Summer		Full sun to light shade

CULTURE			
Soil	**Water**	**Feeding**	**Special Characteristics**
Good drainage; organic matter	Medium water	Heavy feeder	Cool-weather vegetable; frost hardy; requires high amounts of nitrogen; begin harvest when heads are firm, about the size of a softball; cut just beneath the head; wide choice of cultivars available.
Good drainage; organic matter	Medium water	Heavy feeder	Grown for colorful foliage; best in hot, humid climates; in colder climates plant as annual, and dig up for winter protection.
Good drainage; organic matter	Medium water	Heavy feeder	Successive plantings guarantee color from late spring to fall; long blooming season; best in cool seasons; will bloom through winter in mild climates.
Good drainage	Medium water	Medium feeder	Fast growing; tolerates both heat and cold; tolerates drought; good screen or espalier; can be trained as single-trunked tree; blooms periodically throughout year.
Sandy soil; organic matter	Medium water	Medium feeder	Never plant in same location 2 years in a row; rust is a serious problem, look for disease-resistant varieties; make successive plantings for color all summer.
Good drainage; organic matter	Medium water	Medium feeder	Low, restrained growth; needlelike leaves; needs soil that will retain moisture; tolerates light shade, but flowers less; mulch well and don't cultivate around shallow roots.
Good drainage	Medium water	Medium feeder	Slow growing when young, but becomes fast growing; attractive reddish brown bark; fragrant needles; deep, infrequent watering makes tree very drought tolerant; good screen, windbreak.
Rich soil; organic matter	Wet; don't let dry out	Heavy feeder	Adapted to moist areas; edges of ponds, pools, etc.; will tolerate drier soil if well watered; foliage disappears by midsummer.
Rich soil	Medium water	Medium feeder	Slow growing; neat, rounded shape; fragrant flowers; tolerates many soils; can grow in full sun, but won't grow as tall; prune to shape when flowering is over.
Tolerates clay soil	Wet; don't let dry out	Medium feeder	Delicate flowers, grasslike leaves; prefers heavy soil.
Tolerates clay soil	Wet; don't let dry out	Medium feeder	Delicate flowers, grasslike leaves; prefers heavy soil.
Good drainage; organic matter; acid soil	Medium water	Medium feeder	Dense, polished, dark green foliage; large flowers; bloom time varies according to cultivar; avoid cultivating around shallow roots; if necessary, prune immediately after flowering.
Good drainage; organic matter; acid soil	Medium water	Medium feeder	Blooms earlier than common camellia; range from low-growing, sprawling shrubs to upright forms for hedges or screen; can be pruned as bonsai or espalier.
Good drainage; organic matter	Medium water	Medium feeder	Neat, compact, and long blooming.
Good drainage	Medium water	Light feeder	Loose, mat form; green, heart-shaped leaves; star-shaped flowers; shade in hot-summer areas, give sun elsewhere; divide when crowded, can become invasive.
Good drainage; organic matter	Medium water	Heavy feeder	Stake in windy areas; stems are flexible.

NAME	HABIT		FLOWERS		ADAPTATION	
	Type	Height	Color	Time	Zones	Light
Campanula poscharskyana Serbian bellflower	Ground cover	to 1 ft	Lavender	Late summer to fall	3 to 10	Full sun to light shade
Canna × generalis Old-fashioned canna	Tender bulb	2 to 6 ft	Pink, white, red, orange, yellow	Early summer to first frost	8 to 10	Full sun
Capsicum annuum Ornamental pepper	Tender annual	10 to 12 in.		Summer to first frost		Full sun to half-day sun
Caraway *Carum carvi*	Hardy biennial herb	to 2 ft	White	Late spring to early summer	4 to 10	Full sun
Cardoon *Cynara cardunculus*	Half-hardy perennial vegetable	to 6 ft	Purple	Summer	9, 10	Full sun to half-day sun
Carissa grandiflora Natal plum	Evergreen shrub	to 7 ft	White	All year	9, 10	Full sun
Carpinus betulus European hornbeam	Deciduous tree	30 to 40 ft			4 to 7	Full sun
Carpinus caroliniana American hornbeam	Deciduous tree	20 to 40 ft			2 to 9	Light shade to deep shade
Carrot *Daucus carota* var. *sativa*	Hardy annual vegetable	to 3 ft				Full sun to light shade
Casuarina cunninghamiana Beefwood, river she-oak	Evergreen tree	to 70 ft			6 to 7	Full sun
Catalpa bignonioides Common southern catalpa, Indian-bean, cigar tree	Deciduous tree	30 to 40 ft	White	Late spring to early summer	5 to 9	Full sun
Catalpa speciosa Northern catalpa, western catalpa	Deciduous tree	65 to 75 ft	White	Late spring to early summer	5 to 9	Full sun
Catharanthus roseus (*Vinca rosea*) Madagascar periwinkle	Tender annual	4 to 18 in.	Pink, white, rose	Late spring to first frost		Full sun to half-day sun to light shade
Catnip *Nepeta cataria*	Hardy perennial herb	2 to 3 ft	Lavender, white	Early summer to early fall	4 to 10	Full sun to light shade
Cattleya **orchids**	Houseplant	12 to 20 in.	All colors except blue	Varies	10 or indoors	Light shade

| | CULTURE | | |
Soil	Water	Feeding	Special Characteristics
Good drainage	Medium water	Light feeder	Trailing growth habit; spreads by creeping runners; star-shaped flowers; shade in hot-summer climates, sun elsewhere; can become invasive.
Rich soil; good drainage	Medium water	Heavy feeder	Tropical-looking leaves 6 to 12 in. long; flowers in showy spikes; dig up in fall after frost kills foliage.
Good drainage; organic matter	Medium water	Light feeder	Vegetable used as an ornamental; attractive seedpods are red, yellow, orange, white, purple, or black; very heat resistant.
Good drainage	Medium water	Medium feeder	Herb with carrotlike leaves; develops shoots and flowers during second year; edible foliage and seeds; flowers in umbels.
Rich soil; good drainage	Wet; don't let dry out	Heavy feeder	Cool-season plant; resembles artichoke; grown for young leafstalks; requires 120 to 150 days from seed to harvest; can become a weed where adapted.
Good drainage	Medium water	Light feeder	Shiny, deep green foliage; fragrant flowers bloom throughout the year; small, edible fruit; tolerates shade; many cultivars used as ground covers.
Good drainage	Medium water	Medium feeder	Slow to moderate growing; neat, manageable tree; attractive gray bark; yellow foliage in fall; cultivar 'Fastigiata' best choice for screen or hedge.
Good drainage; rich soil	Medium water	Medium feeder	Moderate growing; hardy; smooth, gray bark; dark green leaves with toothed edges; attractive yellow foliage in fall; good street tree; long-lived and well behaved; thrives in moist conditions.
Deep, loose soil; good drainage	Medium water	Medium feeder	Prolonged heat produces shorter roots; slow to germinate; avoid raw manures and composts, which cause knobby, branching carrots; many cultivars of all different lengths are available.
Sandy soil	Medium water	Medium feeder	Fast growing; pinelike appearance; tolerates dry or wet soil, heat, wind; very useful in desert areas.
Not particular	Medium water	Medium feeder	Fast growing; very adaptive to soils and climates; tolerates city smog; flowers followed by long bean pods that can last into winter; best in large areas; messy.
Not particular	Medium water	Medium feeder	Similar to *C. bigninioides*; leaves larger, fewer flowers, slightly hardier; use only in areas with lots of space.
Good drainage; sandy soil	Medium water	Light feeder	Long blooming season; very heat tolerant; slow growing where summers are cool; will bloom through winter in mild climates.
Organic matter	Wet; don't let dry out	Medium feeder	Medicinal herb with heart-shaped leaves with toothed edges; becomes scraggly when in bloom; cats love this plant.
Good drainage	Medium water	Medium feeder	Vigorous plants; most popular orchids; straplike leaves and pseudobulbs; needs very bright, indirect light, protect from direct sun; ample humidity; avoid getting water on flowers.

NAME	HABIT		FLOWERS		ADAPTATION	
	Type	Height	Color	Time	Zones	Light
Cauliflower *Brassica oleracea* var. *botrytis*	Half-hardy biennial vegetable	to 1 ft				Full sun to half-day sun
***Ceanothus* species** Wild lilac	Evergreen shrubs, ground covers, and small trees	6 in. to 20 ft	Blue, deep violet, white	Spring	8 to 10	Full sun
Cedrus atlantica Atlas cedar	Needled evergreen tree	40 to 60 ft			7 to 9	Full sun
Cedrus deodara Deodar cedar	Needled evergreen tree	40 to 75 ft			7 to 9	Full sun
Cedrus libani Cedar-of-Lebanon	Needled evergreen tree	40 to 70 ft			5 to 9	Full sun
Celeriac *Apium graveolens* var. *rapaceum*	Half-hardy biennial vegetable	to 3 ft				Half-day sun to light shade
Celery *Apium graveolens* var. *dulce*	Half-hardy biennial vegetable	to 3 ft				Half-day sun to light shade
Celery Cabbage—*See* Chinese cabbage						
Celosia cristata (*C. plumosa*) Cockscomb, plume celosia	Tender annual	½ to 3 ft	Red, orange, yellow, pink, purple	Early summer to fall		Full sun
Celtis australis European hackberry	Deciduous tree	40 to 70 ft			7 to 9	Full sun
Celtis occidentalis Common hackberry	Deciduous tree	35 to 45 ft			4 to 9	Full sun
Centaurea cyanus Bachelor's-button	Hardy annual	1 to 3 ft	Blue, red, pink, white	Summer		Full sun
Cerastium tomentosum Snow-in-summer	Hardy evergreen perennial ground cover	4 to 6 in.	White	Spring to summer	3 to 10	Full sun
Ceratonia siliqua Carob, St. John's bread	Evergreen tree	25 to 40 ft			9, 10	Full sun to light shade
Ceratostigma plumbaginoides Blue plumbago	Half-hardy perennial	6 to 10 in.	Blue	Late summer to first frost	6 to 10	Full sun to light shade

| | CULTURE | | |
Soil	Water	Feeding	Special Characteristics
Good drainage	Medium water	Heavy feeder	Member of cabbage family; the edible portion is the flower bud; not cold tolerant; won't grow properly in very hot weather; best in cool, humid climate; self-blanching cultivars are available.
Sandy soil	Let dry out between waterings	Light feeder	Many varieties; attractive flowers and glossy leaves; intolerant of heavy soils; prune only during dry, summer months; best in large masses; most useful in the West; does not grow well in the Southwest.
Good drainage	Medium water	Medium feeder	Slow to moderate growing; wide, pyramid shape when mature; fine-textured, bluish green needles borne in stiff clusters; drought tolerant; fine tree in large area; cultivar 'Glauca' has richest blue foliage.
Good drainage	Medium water	Medium feeder	Fast growing; most refined, graceful cedar; lower branches sweep ground; needles green to bluish green; tree top has nodding tip; good in parks and groves; needs ample space.
Good drainage	Medium water	Medium feeder	Slower growing and hardier than *C. atlantica;* needles bright green; give infrequent, deep watering; good skyline tree.
Rich soil; organic matter	Wet; don't let dry out	Heavy feeder	Grown like celery; harvest when roots reach 2 to 4 in. in diameter.
Rich soil; organic matter	Wet; don't let dry out	Heavy feeder	Demands constant attention; cool-weather plant; seeds small, slow to germinate; requires constant moisture and temperature; blanching not usually necessary with modern varieties; several cultivars available.
Good drainage	Medium water	Light feeder	Will tolerate poor, dry soil.
Not particular	Medium water	Medium feeder	Moderate growing; dark green leaves with toothed edges; deep rooted; once established, tolerates much heat, drought, winds, alkaline soil.
Not particular	Medium water	Medium feeder	Moderate growing; leaves dull green with toothed edges; valuable shade tree in tough conditions; cultivar 'Prairie Pride' resists witch's broom.
Good drainage; rich soil	Medium water	Medium feeder	Good summer color; short blooming season; make successive plantings for prolonged bloom.
Good drainage	Medium water	Medium feeder	Dense, matting growth habit; light gray foliage; profuse blooms; fast spreading; drought tolerant; mow at end of blooming.
Good drainage	Let dry out between waterings	Medium feeder	Moderate growing; dense, dark green foliage; flowers of male tree foul smelling; tolerates heat, drought, city conditions; pods edible, used as chocolate substitute; naturally bushy, prune to tree shape.
Good drainage; organic matter	Medium water	Medium feeder	Tolerates drought; attractive fall foliage; long-lived; vigorous grower.

NAME	HABIT		FLOWERS		ADAPTATION	
	Type	Height	Color	Time	Zones	Light
Cercidiphyllum japonicum Katsura tree	Deciduous tree	40 to 60 ft			4 to 9	Full sun to light shade
Cercis canadensis Eastern redbud	Deciduous tree	20 to 30 ft	Pink	Spring	4 to 9	Full sun to light shade
Ceropegia woodii Rosary vine, string-of-hearts	Houseplant	2 to 4 ft (trailing)			10 or indoors	Light shade
Chaenomeles japonica Japanese quince	Deciduous shrub	3 to 5 ft	Orange, red	Spring	5 to 9	Full sun
Chaenomeles speciosa Common flowering quince	Deciduous shrub	6 to 10 ft	Pink, red, white	Early spring	5 to 9	Full sun
Chamaecyparis lawsoniana Lawson cypress, Port Orford cedar	Needled evergreen tree	60 to 70 ft			6 to 8	Full sun
Chamaecyparis nootkatensis Alaska cedar	Needled evergreen tree	70 to 100 ft			5 to 8	Full sun
Chamaecyparis obtusa Hinoki false-cypress	Evergreen tree	40 to 50 ft			5 to 8	Full sun
Chamaedorea elegans Parlor palm	Houseplant	to 6 ft			10 or indoors	Light shade
Chamomile *Chamaemelum nobile*	Hardy perennial herb	3 to 12 in.	White	Late summer to first frost	4 to 10	Full sun to light shade
Chard, Swiss chard *Beta vulgaris* var. *cicla*	Hardy annual vegetable	to 3 ft				Full sun to light shade
Cheiranthus cheiri Wallflower	Hardy annual	1 to 2½ ft	Red, purple, orange, yellow	Spring to early summer		Full sun to light shade
Chenopodium bonus-henricus Good-king-henry	Hardy perennial	to 2½ ft	Yellow	Summer	4 to 10	Light shade
Cherry, sour or pie *Prunus cerasus*	Deciduous fruit tree	15 to 25 ft	White	Spring	4 to 8	Full sun

	CULTURE		
Soil	**Water**	**Feeding**	**Special Characteristics**
Good drainage	Medium water	Medium feeder	Moderate growing; leaves purple in spring, dark green in summer, gold in fall; becomes vase shaped with age; protect from hot sun and drying winds; some trees single stemmed, others multistemmed.
Not particular	Medium water	Medium feeder	Moderate growing; attractive all year; blossoms appear early in spring; attractive leaves sometimes turn yellow in fall; interesting seedpods; grows in acid or alkaline soil in sun or shade.
Good drainage; sandy soil	Let dry out between waterings	Light feeder	Trailing stems of small, heart-shaped, dark green leaves, marbled with white; tiny flowers; give filtered sunlight; add extra organic matter to sandy potting soil.
Not particular	Medium water	Medium feeder	Lowest growing species of quince; wide-spreading branches; short spines; small fruit; tolerates light to heavy soil; prefers cool-winter climates.
Not particular	Medium water	Medium feeder	Usually rounded, dense shrub; thorns; tolerates drought; flowers best in full sun and when pruned heavily immediately after spring bloom; will not flower as prolifically in warm climates.
Good drainage	Medium water	Medium feeder	Fast growing; pyramid shape with pendulous branches; bright green to blue-green needles; reddish brown, fibrous bark; protect from hot, dry winds; prefers cool, coastal climate; screen, tall hedge, lawn specimen, container plant when young.
Good drainage	Medium water	Medium feeder	Moderate growing; columnar shape; dark green needles fragrant when crushed; tolerates poor soil and low temperatures; thrives in moist, well-drained, acid soil.
Good drainage	Medium water	Medium feeder	Slow growing; pyramid shape; shiny, deep green needles; can prune to shape; good bonsai subject; many dwarf varieties.
Good drainage; organic matter	Medium water	Medium feeder	Often sold as *Neanthe bella*; light green fronds; small yellow fruit near base of trunk; give bright, indirect light; reduce water and fertilizer during winter; protect from dry air.
Good drainage; acid soil	Wet; don't let dry out	Medium feeder	Medicinal herb with soft, spreading, matting appearance; daisylike flowers; fragrant foliage.
Good drainage; organic matter	Medium water	Medium feeder	Both heat and drought resistant; tolerates light frost; grown for edible leaves and stalks; long harvest; several cultivars available.
Good drainage	Medium water	Medium feeder	Fragrant flowers; prefers coastal or mountainous regions with cool summers and high humidity.
Good drainage	Medium water	Medium feeder	Large, arrowhead leaves; edible foliage used as spinach substitute; early shoots eaten as asparagus substitute.
Good drainage	Medium water	Medium feeder	No fruit thinning needed; more tolerant of poor soil and growing conditions than sweet cherry.

NAME	HABIT		FLOWERS		ADAPTATION	
	Type	Height	Color	Time	Zones	Light
Cherry, sweet *Prunus avium*	Deciduous fruit tree	15 to 40 ft	White	Spring	4 to 8	Full sun
Chervil *Anthriscus cerefolium*	Hardy annual herb	1½ to 2 ft				Light shade
Chick pea, garbanzo *Cicer ariethinum*	Tender annual vegetable	to 2 ft				Full sun
Chinese cabbage, celery cabbage *Brassica chinensis*	Hardy annual vegetable	1 to 2 ft				Full sun to half-day sun
Chionodoxa luciliae Glory-of-the-snow	Hardy bulb	to 6 in.	Blue	Spring	5 to 10	Full sun to light shade
Chives *Allium schoenoprasum*	Hardy perennial vegetable	to 2 ft	Lavender	Late summer	3 to 10	Full sun to light shade
Chlorophytum comosum Spider plant, airplane plant	Evergreen perennial, houseplant	to 3 ft			10 or indoors	Light shade
Choisya ternata Mexican orange	Evergreen shrub	4 to 5 ft	White	Spring	8 to 10	Light shade
***Chrysanthemum* hybrids** Hardy chrysanthemum	Hardy perennial	1 to 4 ft	All colors except blue	Summer to late fall	4 to 10	Full sun to light shade
Chrysanthemum coccineum Pyrethrum, painted daisy	Hardy perennial	9 in. to 3 ft	Pink, red, white	Early summer	2 to 10	Full sun to light shade
Chrysanthemum parthenium Feverfew	Hardy perennial	8 to 30 in.	White	Summer	4 to 10	Full sun to light shade
Chrysanthemum × superbum Shasta daisy	Hardy perennial	2 to 4 ft	White	Early summer to first frost	4 to 10	Full sun to light shade
Cilantro—*See* Coriander						
Cimicifuga racemosa Black snakeroot, bugbane	Hardy perennial	2 to 3 ft	White	Early summer	3 to 8	Light shade
Cinnamomum camphora Camphor tree	Evergreen tree	to 50 ft	Yellow	Late spring	6 to 10	Full sun
Cissus antarctica Kangaroo vine	Evergreen vine, houseplant	to 15 ft (trailing)			10 or indoors	Light shade

	CULTURE		
Soil	**Water**	**Feeding**	**Special Characteristics**
Good drainage	Medium water	Medium feeder	Requires winter chilling; damaged by intense cold in the fall and heavy rainfall; bears on long-lived spurs; needs little pruning after first 2 seasons of growth; all sweet cherries except 'Stella' need pollinators; birds are a major pest; many cultivars available; avoid areas of sand where bacterial canker is common; no fruit thinning needed; sweet cherry more upright in growth than sour cherry.
Rich soil	Wet; don't let dry out	Medium feeder	Culinary herb with fernlike green foliage and tiny flowers; self-sows freely.
Good drainage; organic matter	Medium water	Medium feeder	Requires 100 days growing season; produces small pods with 1 or 2 seeds inside; harvested in green-shell stage or as mature beans for drying.
Good drainage; organic matter	Medium water	Medium feeder	Cool-weather crop; bolts to seed in long days of late spring and summer; grow as fall and early winter vegetable; loose-leaf and heading cultivars available.
Good drainage	Medium water	Medium feeder	Star-shaped flowers; grasslike leaves; plant in early fall; blooms best in cold areas.
Good drainage; organic matter; rich soil	Medium water	Medium feeder	Culinary herb with grasslike, hollow leaves; grows in clumps; clip leaves to ground level when harvesting.
Good drainage	Medium water	Medium feeder	Wiry stems up to 5 ft long bear plantlets; grassy green, arching leaves usually striped with yellow or white; best in hanging pot; give bright, indirect light or partial shade; keep in moderate to cool location; water liberally during growing season.
Good drainage; organic matter	Medium water	Medium feeder	Fan-shaped foliage; very fragrant flowers; tolerates full sun on the coast; place where delightful fragrance can be appreciated; very susceptible to spider mites.
Rich soil; good drainage; organic matter	Medium water	Heavy feeder	Tolerates mild drought; mulch in winter; tall varieties may need staking.
Good drainage; organic matter; slightly alkaline soil	Medium water	Medium feeder	Tolerates moderate drought; long-lived; noninvasive.
Good drainage; sandy soil	Medium water	Medium feeder	Profuse bloomer; leaves have strong odor; self-sows freely; sometimes grown as annual.
Good drainage; rich soil	Wet; don't let dry out	Medium feeder	Profuse bloomer; will not tolerate soggy soil in winter; provide good air circulation.
Good drainage; organic matter	Wet; don't let dry out	Medium feeder	Long-lived; excellent rear border; keep soil cool; will not flower well in deep shade.
Good drainage	Medium water	Medium feeder	Moderate growing; foliage aromatic; new growth reddish; small blackish fruit; good street or lawn tree; competitive roots; thrives in summer heat.
Good drainage	Let dry out between waterings	Light feeder	Vigorous, trailing vine; grapelike tendrils; elongated, shiny green leaves; bright indirect light or partial shade; can stand neglect; leach indoor plant frequently.

NAME	HABIT		FLOWERS		ADAPTATION	
	Type	Height	Color	Time	Zones	Light
Cissus rhombifolia Grape ivy	Evergreen vine, houseplant	to 20 ft (trailing)			10 or indoors	Light shade
Cistus species Rockrose	Evergreen shrub	3 to 4 ft	Pink, red, white, bicolored	Late spring to summer	8 to 10	Full sun
Cladrastis lutea Yellowwood	Deciduous tree	30 to 50 ft	White	Early summer	4 to 8	Full sun
Clarkia hybrids Godetia	Hardy annual	1½ to 2 ft	Pink, purple, red, white	Early summer to first frost		Full sun to light shade
Cleome hasslerana Spiderflower	Half-hardy annual	3 to 6 ft	White, pink, lavender	Early summer to early fall		Full sun
Clivia miniata Kaffir-lily	Tender evergreen bulb	to 1 ft	Orange, red	Late spring to summer	8 to 10	Light shade to deep shade
Codiaeum variegatum Croton	Houseplant	to 3 ft			10 or indoors	Half-day sun
Colchicum luteum Autumn-crocus	Half-hardy bulb	4 to 6 in.	Yellow	Early spring	7 to 10	Full sun to light shade
Coleus × hybridus Coleus	Tender annual	1 to 3 ft				Half-day sun to light shade to deep shade
Collards Brassica oleracea var. acephala	Hardy biennial vegetable	1 to 2 ft			3 to 10	Full sun to half-day sun
Columnea gloriosa Columnea	Houseplant	1 to 3 ft (trailing)	Red	Winter to spring	10 or indoors	Light shade
Comfrey Symphytum officinale	Hardy perennial herb	to 3 ft			3 to 10	Full sun to light shade
Consolida ambigua Rocket larkspur, annual delphinium	Hardy annual	2 to 4 ft	White, pink, blue, purple	Early summer to early fall		Full sun to light shade
Convallaria majalis Lily-of-the-valley	Hardy bulb	6 to 8 in.	White	Spring	3 to 7	Light shade
Convolvulus tricolor Dwarf morning glory	Hardy annual	to 1 ft	Blue, pink, white	Early summer to early fall		Full sun

| | CULTURE | | |
Soil	Water	Feeding	Special Characteristics
Good drainage	Let dry out between waterings	Light feeder	Vigorous, trailing vine with grapelike tendrils; dark green leaves consisting of 3 leaflets; give bright, indirect sunlight or partial shade; tolerates neglect; leach indoor plant frequently.
Good drainage	Let dry out between waterings	Light feeder	Bushy, dense, rounded shape; fragrant foliage; tolerates drought, poor soil, seacoast conditions, and desert heat; good as large-scale bank cover and ground cover; doesn't transplant well after established.
Good drainage	Medium water	Medium feeder	Moderate growing; attractive bark and clean foliage that turns yellow in fall; fragrant flowers, profuse in alternate years; may not bloom until 10 years old; brown pods; good lawn, patio, park tree; when mature tolerates drought, heat, cold, alkaline soils.
Good drainage; sandy soil	Let dry out between waterings	Light feeder	Prefers cool nights.
Not particular	Medium water	Light feeder	Tolerates heat and drought; can be grown as temporary shrub if clustered; excellent as rear border; makes a good cut flower.
Rich soil; good drainage	Wet; don't let dry out	Heavy feeder	Green, straplike leaves; fragrant flowers; good in containers; blooms best when crowded.
Good drainage	Medium water	Medium feeder	Lance-shaped, leathery leaves up to 18 in. long; single trunk or stem; foliage color includes pink, red, orange, brown, and white; needs ample sun, warm location, and humidity; avoid dark location.
Good drainage	Medium water	Heavy feeder	Foliage appears after blooming; plant in area where won't be disturbed.
Good drainage; organic matter	Wet; don't let dry out	Heavy feeder	Foliage has solid or multiple colors of pink, red, yellow, bronze, green, and chartreuse; pinch flowers to encourage foliage; makes a good houseplant.
Good drainage; organic matter	Medium water	Heavy feeder	Member of cabbage family; tolerates cold better than cabbage; exposure to frost improves flavor; withstands considerable heat; planting in spring and in fall produces almost year-round crop.
Good drainage	Medium water	Light feeder	Hairy leaves; give bright, indirect light; keep moist; reduce watering in winter; cut back after flowering ceases.
Rich soil; organic matter	Wet; don't let dry out	Medium feeder	Medicinal herb with large, hairy leaves up to 20 in. long; pinch off the star-shaped flowers to encourage leaf growth; foliage and roots edible.
Good drainage; organic matter	Medium water	Heavy feeder	Roots must be kept cool—mulch well; prefers cool climate.
Acid soil; organic matter	Wet; don't let dry out	Medium feeder	Very fragrant flowers; tiny, bell-shaped blossoms; keep moist during growing season, tolerates deeper shade.
Sandy soil; good drainage	Let dry out between waterings	Light feeder	Requires little water and fertilizer; needs summer heat.

NAME	HABIT		FLOWERS		ADAPTATION	
	Type	Height	Color	Time	Zones	Light
Coprosma × *kirkii* Kirk's coprosma	Evergreen ground cover	to 2 ft			9, 10	Full sun to light shade
Coprosma repens Mirror plant	Evergreen shrub	8 to 10 ft			9, 10	Full sun to light shade
Cordyline stricta Dracaena	Houseplant	6 to 12 ft	Lavender	Spring	10 or indoors	Light shade
Coreopsis grandiflora Coreopsis	Hardy perennial	1 to 2 ft	Yellow	Summer	5 to 10	Full sun
Coreopsis tinctoria Calliopsis	Half-hardy annual	1 to 3 ft	Red, orange, yellow, bicolored	Late spring to early fall		Full sun
Coriander, cilantro, chinese parsley *Coriandrum sativum*	Hardy annual herb	1 to 2½ ft				Full sun to light shade
Corn *Zea mays* var. *rugosa*	Tender annual vegetable	5 to 8 ft				Full sun
Cornus alba 'Sibirica' Siberian dogwood	Deciduous shrub	8 to 10 ft	White	Late spring to early summer	2 to 7	Full sun to light shade
Cornus alternifolia Pagoda dogwood	Deciduous tree	15 to 25 ft	White	Late spring to early summer	3 to 7	Full sun to light shade
Cornus canadensis Bunchberry	Deciduous ground cover	to 9 in.	White	Early spring	3 to 10	Half-day sun to light shade
Cornus florida Flowering dogwood	Deciduous tree	20 to 30 ft	White, pink	Late spring	5 to 9	Full sun to light shade
Cornus kousa Kousa dogwood, Japanese dogwood	Deciduous tree	15 to 20 ft	White	Summer	5 to 9	Full sun to light shade
Cornus sericea (*C. stolonifera*) Redosier dogwood	Deciduous shrub	8 to 10 ft	White	Late spring to early summer	2 to 8	Full sun to light shade
Coronilla varia Crown vetch	Ground cover	to 2 ft	Pink	Summer	3 to 10	Full sun to light shade
Cortaderia selloana Pampas grass	Tender evergreen perennial	4 to 20 ft	White, pink	Late summer to winter	8 to 10	Full sun

	CULTURE		
Soil	**Water**	**Feeding**	**Special Characteristics**
Not particular	Let dry out between waterings	Light feeder	Woody, upright, heavily branched stems; yellow-green, oblong leaves; drought tolerant; small-scale ground cover; tolerates seacoast conditions.
Not particular	Let dry out between waterings	Light feeder	Round, very shiny leaves; prone to powdery mildew.
Good drainage	Medium water	Light feeder	Leaves are swordlike, 2 ft long; dark green with a purplish tinge; easy to grow.
Good drainage	Let dry out between waterings	Light feeder	Weedy self-sower; short-lived perennial.
Good drainage; sandy soil	Medium water	Light feeder	Tolerant of poor soils; stems break in strong wind or heavy rain.
Good drainage; rich soil	Medium water	Medium feeder	Fast-growing culinary herb; oval leaves with serrated edges on main stems; fernlike side foliage; flowers in umbels; self-sows freely.
Good drainage; organic matter	Wet; don't let dry out	Heavy feeder	Requires ample heat and water; wind-pollinated, best grown in block plantings; don't interplant different varieties of corn; for continual supply, make successive plantings; wide variety of cultivars available with different maturation dates, cob size, kernel color, taste, and disease resistance.
Not particular	Medium water	Medium feeder	Fast growing; loose, open habit; attractive red stems in winter; best used in shrub border, massed on a large scale; prune hard each spring.
Rich soil	Medium water	Medium feeder	Less showy than other dogwoods, but hardier; red leaves in fall; shade from hot sun; prefers slightly acid soil.
Good drainage; organic matter; acid soil	Medium water	Medium feeder	Spreading habit; bright red fruit turns yellow to red in the fall; needs cool, moist climate.
Rich soil	Medium water	Medium feeder	Moderate growing; showy flowers; attractive red leaves in fall; red fruit; slightly acid soil; shade in hot-summer climates; many cultivars available.
Rich soil	Medium water	Medium feeder	Slow to moderate growing; yellow and scarlet fall color; berries in fall; tends to be multitrunked; can prune to single stem.
Tolerates clay soil	Wet; don't let dry out	Medium feeder	Attractive dark red stems in winter; susceptible to canker.
Not particular	Medium water	Light feeder	Dense growth; deep, soil-building roots; ½ in. leaflets; spreads by underground runners; can become invasive; tolerates drought; good for erosion control; dies back in winter; mass of brown stems may be a fire hazard in some areas.
Rich soil	Medium water	Medium feeder	Tolerates poor, dry soils; tolerates coastal conditions; fast growing; often confused with weedy *C. jubata*.

NAME	HABIT		FLOWERS		ADAPTATION	
	Type	Height	Color	Time	Zones	Light
Corylopsis spicata Spike winter hazel	Deciduous shrub	4 to 5 ft	Yellow	Early spring	6 to 8	Full sun to light shade
Corylus americana American filbert	Deciduous shrub	9 to 10 ft	Brown	Early spring	5 to 9	Full sun to light shade
Corylus avellana '**Contorta**' Harry Lauder's walkingstick	Deciduous shrub	8 to 10 ft	Brown	Spring	5 to 8	Full sun to light shade
Cosmos bipinnatus Mexican aster	Half-hardy annual	3 to 6 ft	Red, white, pink, lavender	Early summer to early fall		Full sun
Cotinus coggygria Common smoke tree	Deciduous shrub or small tree	15 to 25 ft	Lavender, purple	Early summer	5 to 10	Full sun
Cotoneaster apiculatus Cranberry cotoneaster	Deciduous shrub, ground cover	3 to 4 ft	Pink	Late spring	4 to 10	Full sun to light shade
Cotoneaster conspicuus **var. decorus** Necklace cotoneaster	Evergreen ground cover	1 to 1½ ft	White	Early summer	7 to 10	Full sun to half-day sun
Cotoneaster dammeri Bearberry cotoneaster	Evergreen shrub, ground cover	1 to 1½ ft	White	Late spring to early summer	6 to 9	Full sun
Cotoneaster horizontalis Rock cotoneaster	Deciduous shrub, ground cover	2 to 4 ft	Pink	Early summer	5 to 10	Full sun to half-day sun
Cotoneaster lucidus Hedge cotoneaster	Deciduous shrub	10 to 15 ft	Pink	Spring	4 to 7	Full sun
Cotoneaster microphyllus Small-leaved cotoneaster	Evergreen ground cover	2 to 3 ft	White	Early summer	6 to 10	Full sun to half-day sun
Cotoneaster salicifolius Willowleaf cotoneaster	Evergreen shrub	to 15 ft	White	Spring	6 to 10	Full sun
Cowpea, black-eyed pea *Vigna unguiculata*	Tender annual vegetable	to 2 ft			3 to 10	Full sun
Crassula argentea Jade plant, jade tree	Succulent shrub, houseplant	1 to 5 ft	White, pink		10 or indoors	Full sun to half-day sun

| | CULTURE | | |
Soil	Water	Feeding	Special Characteristics
Good drainage; organic matter	Medium water	Medium feeder	Fragrant flowers borne early in season; bright green, roundish leaves; slow growing, open structure; very cold winters or late frosts often kill buds and blossoms; plant in sheltered location.
Not particular	Medium water	Medium feeder	Not as ornamental as *C. avellana*, although widely native on the East Coast; small, rounded nuts; male catkins; may reach 15 ft high; tends to sucker.
Not particular	Medium water	Medium feeder	Unique curled and twisting stems, twigs, and leaves; fast growing; adaptable to many soils and easy to grow; use as accent or focal point; prune out suckers.
Good drainage	Let dry out between waterings	Light feeder	Do not fertilize or flowering will decrease; may need staking.
Good drainage	Let dry out between waterings	Light feeder	Moderate to fast growing; shrubby growth can be pruned to multistemmed tree; faded blooms give smokelike appearance all summer; blue-green leaves; good patio tree or planted in groups; adaptable, drought tolerant, easy to grow.
Good drainage	Medium water	Medium feeder	Similar to *C. horizontalis* in growth habit; roundish leaves bright green above and slightly hairy beneath; pinkish white flowers; bright red fruit; prune out dead wood.
Tolerates clay soil	Medium water	Light feeder	Prostrate; leaves ¼ in. long, dark green on top, paler underneath; fairly large berries; best in containers or rock garden, not dense enough ground cover to shade out weeds.
Good drainage	Medium water	Medium feeder	Fast growing; low, prostrate habit; glossy, dense leaves; red fruit in late summer; good choice for dry, rocky soil in exposed site; used as cover on banks or slopes, massed, or in shrub border.
Good drainage	Medium water	Light feeder	Grows 8 to 10 ft wide; semievergreen in mild climates, deciduous elsewhere; bright red berries; round leaves turn reddish before falling; heavily textured; good on banks and as low dividers; remove any dead wood; susceptible to fire blight.
Good drainage	Medium water	Medium feeder	Very dense growth; lustrous leaves; pinkish white flowers; black fruit; may be pruned as hedge but more susceptible to fire blight and red spider mite in this shape; tolerates wind and poor, dry soils.
Tolerates clay soil	Medium water	Medium feeder	Small leaves, shiny on top, hairy underneath; red berries in the fall; tangled, intermingling stems; well suited for banks or around rocks; benefits from soil amendments before planting; susceptible to fire blight; remove any dead wood.
Good drainage	Medium water	Medium feeder	Semievergreen in colder climates; vigorous, upright growth; arching branches; narrow, willowlike leaves; red fruit; use as screen, background plant, or specimen plant.
Good drainage; organic matter	Medium water	Medium feeder	Requires warm days and warm nights to develop properly; yardlong beans or asparagus beans are a tall-growing variety of cowpea, which are grown as climbers; pods 1 to 2 ft long; very frost tender.
Good drainage; sandy soil	Let dry out between waterings	Light feeder	Compact, treelike form; stout, branching limbs with oblong, fleshy leaves 1 to 2 in. long; in direct sun, leaves become tinged with red; houseplants can be summered outdoors.

NAME	HABIT		FLOWERS		ADAPTATION	
	Type	Height	Color	Time	Zones	Light
Crataegus crus-galli Cockspur thorn	Deciduous tree	20 to 30 ft	White	Late spring	4 to 9	Full sun
Crataegus laevigata English hawthorn	Deciduous tree	15 to 25 ft	White, pink, red	Late spring	5 to 8	Full sun
Crataegus × lavallei Lavalle hawthorn	Deciduous tree	20 to 25 ft	White	Late spring	5 to 9	Full sun
Crataegus phaenopyrum Washington thorn	Deciduous tree	20 to 30 ft	White	Late spring	5 to 8	Full sun
Crataegus viridis 'Winter King' Green hawthorn	Deciduous tree	20 to 35 ft	White	Late spring	5 to 8	Full sun
Crocus species Crocus	Hardy bulb	2 to 6 in.	Lavender, purple, white, yellow	Spring	3 to 10	Full sun to light shade
Cryptomeria japonica Japanese cedar	Needled evergreen tree	70 to 90 ft			6 to 9	Full sun
Cucumber *Cucumis sativus*	Tender annual vegetable	2 to 4 ft (trailing)				Full sun
× *Cupressocyparis leylandii* Leyland cypress	Needled evergreen tree	40 to 50 ft			5 to 10	Full sun
Cupressus glabra Smooth Arizona cypress	Needled evergreen tree	to 35 ft			7 to 10	Full sun
Cupressus macrocarpa Monterey cypress	Needled evergreen tree	40 to 70 ft			8 to 10	Full sun to light shade
Cupressus sempervirens 'Stricta' Italian cypress	Needled evergreen tree	30 to 40 ft			8 to 10	Full sun
Currant *Ribes sativum*	Deciduous berry	3 to 5 ft	Yellow		4 to 9	Full sun to light shade
Cyclamen hederifolium (*C. neapolitanum*) Neapolitan cyclamen	Hardy bulb	4 to 5 in.	Pink, white	Late summer to early fall	5 to 9	Light shade

Soil	CULTURE		
	Water	**Feeding**	**Special Characteristics**
Good drainage; rich soil	Medium water	Medium feeder	Broad-crowned tree; thorny; leathery, toothed leaves; dull red fruit; red and yellow fall color; sunny location; rich, loamy soil.
Not particular	Let dry out between waterings	Medium feeder	Moderate growing, shrublike tree; does poorly in summer heat and humidity; many cultivars available—some with red fruit.
Not particular	Let dry out between waterings	Medium feeder	Moderate growing; abundant flowers; dense foliage turns bronze red in fall; thorns; orange to red fruit in fall and winter; tolerates seacoast conditions, highways, city conditions.
Not particular	Let dry out between waterings	Medium feeder	Broad, columnar tree; attractive fall foliage; red fruit; resistant to fire blight; grows well in city; one of the better hawthorns.
Not particular	Let dry out between waterings	Medium feeder	Glossy green leaves; dense, rounded head; long-lasting red fruits.
Good drainage	Medium water	Medium feeder	Plant in early fall; many varieties.
Good drainage	Medium water	Medium feeder	Moderate growing; light green to bluish green needles; reddish brown bark; graceful appearance; good park tree—needs room to develop; deep soil.
Good drainage; organic matter	Medium water	Medium feeder	Warm-weather plant; water deeply; can be trained on trellis; keep all fruit picked to encourage setting of new fruit; major groups of cucumbers include slicing varieties, pickling varieties, and dwarf plants; many cultivars available within each group.
Adaptive		Medium feeder	Fast growing, columnar shape; good for tall hedges and screens; gray-green needles; tolerates wide range of soils and climates; may reach 100 ft high.
Sandy soil	Let dry out between waterings	Light feeder	Fast growing; compact, narrow pyramid shape; reddish brown bark; silver gray to blue-green, scalelike foliage; good windbreak, screen, hedge; tolerates hot, dry climate, and poor, sandy soils.
Good drainage	Medium water	Medium feeder	Slow to moderate growing; windswept habit develops only in high winds along coast; best on West Coast; windbreak, or clipped hedge; subject to fatal canker disease.
Good drainage	Medium water	Medium feeder	Fast growing; vertical column; scalelike, dark green foliage; tolerates wide range of soils and drought; stiff, formal appearance; needs large garden or driveway setting.
Good drainage; organic matter	Medium water	Medium feeder	Attractive shrub with red or white fruit in summer; productive and easy to care for; good fall color; shade in hot-summer areas; prune to remove weak growth, old canes; maintain balance of 1-, 2-, and 3-year-old wood; currants banned in areas of white pine because they carry diseases to these trees; check with the local cooperative extension office.
Rich soil; organic matter	Medium water	Heavy feeder	Fragrant flowers appear before foliage; marbled leaves.

NAME	HABIT		FLOWERS		ADAPTATION	
	Type	Height	Color	Time	Zones	Light
Cyclamen persicum Florist's cyclamen	Tender bulb	to 10 in.	Lavender, pink, red, white	Late fall to spring	9, 10 or indoors	Light shade
Cynodon **species** Improved Bermuda grass	Turfgrass	½ to 1 in.			7 to 10	Full sun
Cynodon dactylon Bermuda grass	Turfgrass	½ to 1½ in.			7 to 10	Full sun
Cynoglossum amabile Chinese forget-me-not	Hardy biennial	1½ to 2 ft	Blue, pink, white	Late spring to late summer		Full sun to light shade
Cyrtomium falcatum Japanese holly fern	Evergreen ground cover, houseplant	1 to 2 ft			10 or indoors	Half-day sun to light shade
Cytisus × *kewensis* Kew broom	Evergreen ground cover	6 to 10 in.	Yellow	Late spring	6 to 8	Full sun
Cytisus × *praecox* Warminster broom	Deciduous shrub	4 to 6 ft	Yellow	Late spring	6 to 9	Full sun
Cytisus scoparius Scotch broom	Evergreen shrub	to 6 ft	Yellow	Late spring to early summer	5 to 9	Full sun
Dahlia **hybrids** Dahlia	Tender perennial	1 to 5 ft	All colors except blue	Summer to first frost	8 to 10	Full sun to light shade
Daphne × *burkwoodii* Burkwood daphne	Deciduous shrub	3 to 4 ft	Pink, white	Late spring	5 to 8	Light shade
Daphne cneorum Garlandflower, rose daphne	Evergreen ground cover	½ to 1 ft	Pink	Spring	5 to 7	Light shade
Daphne odora Winter daphne	Evergreen shrub	3 to 4 ft	Pink	Winter to early spring	8 to 10	Light shade
Davallia mariesii Squirrel's-foot fern, ball fern	Houseplant	6 to 10 in.			10 or indoors	Light shade
Delphinium elatum Delphinium	Hardy perennial	4 to 8 ft	Blue, pink, white, red, violet	Summer	2 to 8	Full sun
Dendrobium **orchids**	Houseplant	1 to 2½ ft	Lavender, white, yellow	Varies	10 or indoors	Light shade

CULTURE			
Soil	Water	Feeding	Special Characteristics
Rich soil; good drainage	Wet; don't let dry out	Heavy feeder	Sold as potted plant; single, double, fringed, crested flowers; heart-shaped leaves; needs slightly acid soil; container or houseplant.
Good drainage; organic matter	Medium water	Heavy feeder	Softer, finer texture than common Bermuda grass; shorter dormancy period; more water, fertilizer, and mowing needs than common Bermuda grass; many cultivars available.
Good drainage; organic matter	Medium water	Medium to heavy feeder	Easy to grow in most soils; likes heat; tolerates drought; wears very well; invasive; won't tolerate shade; takes abuse, but makes attractive lawn when given extra care; often browns in fall until spring.
Good drainage; organic matter	Medium water	Medium feeder	Easy to grow and not particular about water or temperature; usually grown as an annual.
Rich soil	Wet; don't let dry out	Heavy feeder	Dense ground cover in mild areas; common houseplant; shiny, leathery, light yellowish green fronds; good in containers and under camellias or other shrubs grown in similar conditions.
Good drainage; acid soil	Let dry out between waterings	Light feeder	Nearly leafless evergreen; trailing branches; very adaptable; best in dry, poor soils; tolerates drought and seacoast conditions, sandy soil; effective trailing over walls and down slopes; spreads 3 ft wide; prune if foliage becomes spindly.
Good drainage	Let dry out between waterings	Light feeder	Dense, vertical stems; foliage sparse or nonexistent; showy flowers; prefers infertile, poor soil; good specimen in shrub border, rock garden; intolerant of pruning when mature.
Good drainage; grows in poor soil	Let dry out between waterings	Light feeder	Nearly leafless evergreen; rampant, aggressive spreader; green stems provide winter interest.
Good drainage; organic matter	Medium water	Heavy feeder	Keep roots cool; lift roots in fall, store in sawdust; flowers vary from 1 to 8 in. wide; often grown as annual.
Good drainage	Medium water	Medium feeder	Larger than *D. cneorum;* extremely fragrant flowers open pink and fade to white; easiest daphne to grow; semievergreen in some zones.
Good drainage	Medium water	Medium feeder	Spreading, loose mass; finely textured foliage; very fragrant flowers; neutral soil; protect from sun and drying winds; mulch to keep roots cool and moist.
Good drainage	Let dry out between waterings	Medium feeder	Lustrous, dark green leaves; fragrant flowers; unpredictable; plant high to avoid crown rot; water infrequently during summer to increase blooming.
Good drainage	Medium water	Medium feeder	Wiry stems of small fronds with leaflets; brownish, furry, creeping rhizomes grow aboveground; likes filtered light, high humidity, cool temperatures; good in hanging pot.
Rich soil; good drainage; slightly alkaline soil	Medium water	Medium feeder	Difficult to grow; requires staking; best in cool climates.
Good drainage	Medium water	Medium feeder	Both evergreen and deciduous orchids; large flowers bloom in clusters along stem; needs very bright, indirect light and humidity; avoid roots standing in water.

NAME	HABIT		FLOWERS		ADAPTATION	
	Type	Height	Color	Time	Zones	Light
Deutzia gracilis Slender deutzia	Deciduous shrub	2 to 6 ft	White	Late spring	5 to 8	Full sun to light shade
Deutzia × magnifica Showy deutzia	Deciduous shrub	6 to 10 ft	White	Late spring to early summer	5 to 8	Full sun to light shade
Deutzia scabra Deutzia	Deciduous shrub	6 to 10 ft	White	Late spring to early summer	5 to 8	Full sun to light shade
Dianthus barbatus Sweet william	Half-hardy biennial	4 to 24 in.	White, pink, red, purple	Summer to fall		Full sun to light shade
Dianthus caryophyllus Carnation	Half-hardy perennial	1 to 3 ft	Pink, red, white	Late spring to early summer	7 to 10	Full sun
Dianthus chinensis China pink	Hardy annual	8 to 28 in.	White, pink, purple, red, lavender	Summer to fall		Full sun to light shade
Dianthus deltoides Maiden pink	Hardy perennial	8 to 12 in.	Pink, purple, white	Early summer	3 to 10	Full sun
Dianthus plumarius Cottage pink, Scotch pink	Hardy perennial	to 12 in.	Pink, red, white	Late spring to early summer	3 to 10	Full sun
Dicentra spectabilis Bleeding-heart	Hardy perennial	to 2½ ft	Pink, white	Late spring to early summer	2 to 8	Light shade
Dichondra micrantha (*D. repens*) Dichondra	Evergreen ground cover	to 3 in.			9, 10	Full sun to light shade
Dictamnus albus Gas plant	Hardy perennial	to 3 ft	White	Late spring to early summer	2 to 10	Full sun to light shade
Dieffenbachia species Dumb cane	Houseplant	to 6 ft			10 or indoors	Light shade
Diervilla sessilifolia Southern bush honeysuckle	Deciduous shrub	3 to 5 ft	Yellow	Early summer	5 to 8	Full sun to light shade
Digitalis purpurea Foxglove	Hardy biennial	2 to 5 ft	Purple, pink, white, red, yellow	Summer	4 to 9	Light shade
Dill *Anethum graveolens*	Tender annual herb	2 to 4 ft	Yellow	Summer to early fall		Full sun

	CULTURE		
Soil	**Water**	**Feeding**	**Special Characteristics**
Good drainage	Medium water	Medium feeder	Low, broad, mounded shrub; graceful, upright branches; dull green foliage; flowers on old wood, so prune immediately after flowering; cut out any winter dieback; showy only when in bloom.
Good drainage	Medium water	Medium feeder	A double-flowering hybrid; prune after flowering.
Good drainage	Medium water	Medium feeder	Dull green leaves with scallop-toothed edges; flowers white to pinkish; prune after flowering.
Good drainage; slightly alkaline soil	Medium water	Light feeder	Grown as an annual; sweet, fragrant flowers; most flowers are bicolored.
Good drainage; sandy soil	Let dry out between waterings	Light feeder	Fragrant flowers; usually short-lived.
Good drainage; slightly alkaline soil	Medium water	Light feeder	Leaves are grasslike and blue-gray; flowers are often bicolored.
Good drainage; sandy soil	Let dry out between waterings	Light feeder	Low growing and mat forming.
Good drainage; organic matter; sandy soil	Let dry out between waterings	Light feeder	Best in cool areas; water during drought; long-lived; flowers are bicolored.
Rich soil; good drainage; organic matter	Medium water	Heavy feeder	Tends to die down after blooming; will tolerate deep shade; keep plants out of drying winds.
Good drainage	Wet; don't let dry out	Medium feeder	Masses of dark green, cupped, horseshoe-shaped leaves; lawn substitute; moderate spreader; rarely needs mowing; tolerates only light foot traffic; start from seed or plugs.
Rich soil; good drainage; organic matter	Medium water	Medium feeder	Fragrant, lemon-scented foliage; long-lived; large, bushy, showy perennial.
Good drainage	Medium water	Medium feeder	Arching, oblong, pointed leaves; single trunk when young, multiple trunks when mature; give bright, indirect light; many cultivars available; leaves and stem toxic if ingested.
Good drainage	Medium water	Medium feeder	Native to eastern United States; good for erosion control on banks; spreads by underground stolons; good in rugged terrain where other plants will not survive; prune in early spring.
Good drainage; organic matter	Medium water	Medium feeder	Tolerates full sun and deep shade; self-sows abundantly; good as rear border plant; grown as a perennial.
Good drainage; acid soil	Wet; don't let dry out	Medium feeder	Culinary herb with light green, feathery foliage; greenish yellow flowers in umbels; self-sows readily; doesn't transplant well.

NAME	HABIT		FLOWERS		ADAPTATION	
	Type	Height	Color	Time	Zones	Light
Dimorphotheca sinuata Cape marigold	Half-hardy annual	6 to 15 in.	White, orange, yellow, pink	Summer to early fall		Full sun
Dizygotheca elegantissima False-aralia	Houseplant	10 to 12 ft			10 or indoors	Light shade
Dracaena deremensis 'Warneckii'	Houseplant	to 15 ft			10 or indoors	Light shade
Dracaena fragrans Corn plant	Houseplant	8 to 10 ft	White		10 or indoors	Light shade
Dracaena godseffiana Gold dust dracaena, spotted dracaena	Houseplant	to 10 ft			10 or indoors	Light shade
Dracaena marginata Red-margined dracaena	Houseplant	8 to 10 ft			10 or indoors	Light shade
Duchesnea indica Indian-strawberry, mock strawberry	Evergreen ground cover	to 4 in.	Yellow	Spring	4 to 10	Light shade
Dyssodia tenuiloba Dahlberg daisy, goldenfleece	Hardy annual	4 to 8 in.	Yellow	Spring to fall		Full sun
Echinacea purpurea Purple coneflower	Hardy perennial	3 to 5 ft	Purple	Summer to early fall	3 to 9	Full sun to light shade
Echinops exaltatus Globe thistle	Hardy perennial	3 to 6 ft	Blue	Summer	3 to 9	Full sun to light shade
Echinopsis species Sea urchin cactus	Houseplant	to 10 in.	Pink, red, white, yellow	Summer	10 or indoors	Full sun to half-day sun
Eggplant *Solanum melongena*	Tender annual vegetable	1½ to 3 ft				Full sun
Elaeagnus angustifolia Russian olive	Deciduous shrub or small tree	to 20 ft	Yellow	Early summer	2 to 9	Full sun
Elaeagnus pungens Silverberry	Evergreen shrub	6 to 15 ft	White	Fall	7 to 10	Full sun
Elaeagnus umbellata Autumn elaeagnus	Deciduous shrub	12 to 18 ft	White	Late spring	4 to 8	Full sun
Endive *Cichorium endiva*	Hardy annual vegetable	to 3 ft				Full sun to light shade

	CULTURE		
Soil	**Water**	**Feeding**	**Special Characteristics**
Good drainage; sandy soil	Let dry out between waterings	Light feeder	Best in dry areas; good winter color in warm climates.
Good drainage	Medium water	Medium feeder	Thin, dark green leaves, with lighter veins, divided into 9 segments with saw-toothed edges; slow growing; give bright, indirect light, older plants tolerate less light; very sensitive to water; avoid dry soil or wet soil; keep air moist.
Good drainage	Let dry out between waterings	Light feeder	Green leaves with white and gray streaks running lengthwise; leaves may reach 2 ft long, 2 in. wide; reliable foliage houseplant.
Good drainage	Let dry out between waterings	Light feeder	Single stem; tuft of arching, swordlike green leaves; cultivar 'Massangeana' is streaked with cream or yellow; occasionally yields sprays of fragrant white flowers; give bright, indirect light or filtered sun.
Good drainage	Medium water	Light feeder	Broad green leaves marbled with white and gold; keep soil moist, not soggy; give bright, indirect light or filtered sun.
Good drainage	Let dry out between waterings	Light feeder	Thin, red-edged leaves atop trunks that zigzag and curve; very bright light is best.
Good drainage; sandy soil	Medium water	Medium feeder	Dense, low, mat forming; spreads rapidly by runners; strawberrylike leaves and fruit.
Good drainage	Let dry out between waterings	Light feeder	Heat and drought tolerant; avoid overfertilizing; long blooming season; readily reseeds itself.
Good drainage; sandy soil	Medium water	Medium feeder	Drought and wind tolerant; shady conditions produce richer flower color.
Good drainage	Let dry out between waterings	Medium feeder	Flowers appear in balls; good for dried flower arrangements.
Good drainage; sandy soil	Let dry out between waterings	Medium feeder	Gray-green globular to oval stems; clusters of spines along ribbed stems; small growing; free flowering; keep moderately moist in the summer.
Good drainage; rich soil; organic matter	Medium water	Medium to heavy feeder	Susceptible to low-temperature injury; likes heat; good in containers; plants heavy with fruit may need support; pick fruit when young; good fruit has high gloss; cultivars available with different fruit color and size.
Good drainage	Medium water	Medium feeder	Fast-growing, shrubby tree; leaves willowlike, olive green above, silvery below; unusual, twisting trunk; attractive bark; thorny branches; yellow berries; tolerates cold and heat; messy fruit; can be used as hedge, screen, espalier.
Sandy soil	Medium water	Light feeder	Olive-colored foliage; thorny branches; edible red fruit; flowers inconspicuous but very fragrant; tolerates heat, drought, wind; prefers infertile soil; good hedge plant; cultivars available with variegated foliage.
Good drainage	Medium water	Medium feeder	Fast-growing, spreading shrub; young foliage is silvery; fragrant flowers; silvery fruit matures to red.
Good drainage; organic matter	Medium water	Medium feeder	Grown in same way as lettuce; best if grown for fall or winter harvest; has nutlike flavor; several cultivars available.

NAME	HABIT		FLOWERS		ADAPTATION	
	Type	Height	Color	Time	Zones	Light
Epimedium grandiflorum Bishop's-hat	Semievergreen ground cover	to 1 ft	Red, violet, white	Late spring to early summer	3 to 10	Light shade
Epipremnum aureum Pothos, devil's ivy	Houseplant	3 to 5 ft (trailing)			10 or indoors	Light shade
Episcia cupreata Flame violet	Houseplant	to 6 in.	Red	Summer	10 or indoors	Light shade
Eranthis cilicica Winter aconite	Hardy bulb	2 to 8 in.	Yellow	Early spring	4 to 9	Full sun to light shade
Eranthis hyemalis Winter aconite	Hardy bulb	2 to 8 in.	Yellow	Early spring	5 to 9	Full sun to light shade
Eremochloa ophiuroides Centipede grass					7 to 10	Full sun to light shade
Erica arborea Tree heath	Evergreen shrub or small tree	10 to 20 ft	White	Spring	9, 10	Full sun
Erica carnea Spring heath	Evergreen shrub	6 to 16 in.	Red	Winter to early summer	6 to 8	Full sun
Erica mediterranea Biscay heath	Evergreen shrub	4 to 7 ft			8 to 10	Full sun
Erica vagans Cornish heath	Evergreen shrub	2 to 3 ft	Pink	Summer to early fall	6 to 8	Full sun
Eriobotrya japonica Loquat	Evergreen tree	15 to 30 ft	White	Fall	8 to 10	Full sun
Erythronium species Fawn-lily	Hardy bulb	to 12 in.	White, yellow, purple	Spring to early summer	3 to 10	Light shade
Escallonia rubra Red escallonia	Evergreen shrub	6 to 15 ft	Red	Early summer to early fall	8 to 10	Light shade
Eschscholzia californica California poppy	Hardy annual	12 to 15 in.	Orange, yellow, red, white	Spring to early summer		Full sun to light shade
Eucalyptus cinerea Florist's eucalyptus	Evergreen tree	30 to 40 ft	White	Winter to spring	9, 10	Full sun to light shade

| | CULTURE | | |
Soil	Water	Feeding	Special Characteristics
Rich soil	Medium water	Heavy feeder	Long-lived; leathery, heart-shaped leaves turn reddish in fall; tolerates full sun if soil is rich, moist, and acidic; shallow, creeping roots; remove old leaves in spring.
Good drainage	Medium water	Light feeder	Climbing, trailing habit; heart-shaped green leaves splashed with white or cream; give bright, indirect light; keep warm and in humid location; pinch growth tips to encourage bushiness; avoid overfertilizing.
Good drainage; organic matter	Medium water	Medium feeder	Copper-colored leaves with silver veins; cascading stolons; good in hanging pot; small, tubular flowers; needs high humidity; keep moist; give bright light, no direct sun; pinch tips to encourage branching; leach plant with every watering.
Good drainage; organic matter	Medium water	Medium feeder	Green or bronze foliage; single, fragrant blossoms.
Good drainage; organic matter	Medium water	Medium feeder	Green or bronze foliage; single, fragrant flowers; good for naturalizing.
Good drainage; organic matter	Medium water	Light feeder	Adapts to poor soil; crowds out weeds; good, low-maintenance, general-purpose lawn; coarse textured; shallow rooted; tends to yellow from chlorosis; doesn't wear well.
Good drainage; sandy soil	Wet; don't let dry out	Light feeder	Awkward looking; fragrant flowers; needs infertile, acid soil; keep roots moist; shallow rooted.
Good drainage; sandy soil	Wet; don't let dry out	Light feeder	Dwarf, spreading form; prefers infertile, acid soil; keep roots moist; shallow rooted; prune yearly to keep attractive.
Good drainage; sandy soil	Wet; don't let dry out	Light feeder	Flowers insignificant; use as background foliage; give infertile, moist soil; prefers acid soil.
Good drainage; sandy soil	Wet; don't let dry out	Light feeder	Bushy shrub; needs infertile soil; keep roots moist; prefers acid soil; shallow rooted; shear after blooming.
Good drainage	Medium water	Medium feeder	Moderate growing; large, dark green, serrated leaves, rust-colored on underside; fragrant flowers, not showy; abundant orange-to-yellow fruit ripens late winter or spring; takes pruning as ground cover, espalier, or container plant; best in mild climate; tolerates alkaline soil.
Good drainage	Medium water	Medium feeder	Needs moisture all summer long; resents extreme heat; give sun in cool-summer areas; mulch in fall.
Good drainage	Medium water	Medium feeder	Fast growing; attractive, fragrant flowers produced year around in mild climates; dense, rounded, upright habit; dark green foliage; tolerates coastal conditions, mild drought; full sun in cooler areas; screen, windbreak, shrub border; pruning lessens windbreak effect.
Sandy soil; good drainage	Let dry out between waterings	Light feeder	Gray-green ferny foliage; tolerates drought and poor soils; does not transplant well—seed in place; reseeds freely.
Not particular	Medium water	Medium feeder	Moderate to fast growing; blue-gray foliage; attractive bark; tends to have multiple trunks, can be pruned to one; branches decorative; withstands wind; best in dry site or with fast drainage; small seed cups.

NAME	HABIT		FLOWERS		ADAPTATION	
	Type	Height	Color	Time	Zones	Light
Eucalyptus ficifolia Red-flowering gum	Evergreen tree	25 to 40 ft	Orange, pink, red, white	All year	9, 10	Full sun
Eucalyptus globulus Blue gum	Evergreen tree	75 to 100 ft	White	Winter	9, 10	Full sun
Eucalyptus gunnii Cider gum	Evergreen tree	40 to 70 ft	White	Spring to early summer	9, 10	Full sun
Eucalyptus polyanthemos Silver dollar eucalyptus	Evergreen tree	40 to 50 ft	White	Spring to summer	9, 10	Full sun
Eucalyptus rudis Desert gum	Evergreen tree	40 to 50 ft	White	Spring to summer	9, 10	Full sun
Eucalyptus sideroxylon Red ironbark	Evergreen tree	40 to 50 ft	Pink	Fall to spring	9, 10	Full sun
Eucalyptus viminalis Manna gum	Evergreen tree	to 100 ft	White	All year	9, 10	Full sun
Eucharis grandiflora Amazon lily	Tender evergreen bulb	to 1½ ft	White	Early spring	9, 10	Light shade
Eugenia uniflora Surinam cherry, pitanga	Evergreen shrub or small tree	6 to 25 ft	White	Late summer	10	Full sun
Euonymus alata Burning bush, winged euonymus	Deciduous shrub	to 10 ft			4 to 8	Full sun to deep shade
Euonymus fortunei Wintercreeper euonymus	Evergreen vine, ground cover	Climbs to 20 ft			5 to 8	Full sun to deep shade
Euonymus japonica Japanese euonymus	Evergreen shrub or small tree	10 to 15 ft			7 to 10	Full sun to light shade
Euphorbia corollata Flowering spurge	Hardy perennial	to 3 ft	White	Summer	4 to 9	Full sun
Euphorbia marginata Snow-on-the-mountain	Half-hardy annual	1½ to 2 ft	White	Summer to fall		Full sun to light shade
Euphorbia milii Crown-of-thorns	Evergreen shrub, houseplant	3 to 4 ft	Red, pink, orange, yellow	All year	10 or indoors	Light shade
Euphorbia myrsinites Myrtle euphorbia	Hardy evergreen perennial	3 to 6 in.	Yellow	Spring to early summer	4 to 9	Full sun

	CULTURE		
Soil	**Water**	**Feeding**	**Special Characteristics**
Not particular	Medium water	Medium feeder	Fast growing; dense foliage; dark green, large, and heavy leaves; striking blooms peak in July–August, most common color red; best on coast; frost tender; seed cups.
Not particular	Medium water	Medium feeder	Fast growing; common in California; very messy; branches break easily; too large for most gardens.
Not particular	Medium water	Medium feeder	Fast growing, upright; hardy; long, narrow, medium green leaves; good shade, windbreak, privacy screen; bell-shaped seedpods.
Good drainage	Medium water	Medium feeder	Fast growing; silvery gray foliage; attractive shape; good tree on seacoast or in desert; cylindrical seed cups.
Not particular	Medium water	Light feeder	Fast growing; gray-green foliage; rough, attractive bark; tolerates heat, wind, poor soil, coastal or desert conditions; seed capsules.
Good drainage	Medium water	Medium feeder	Moderate growing; gray-green foliage; attractive flowers; streets, parks, golf courses; goblet-shaped seed capsules.
Rich soil	Medium water	Medium feeder	Fast growing; rich green, weeping foliage; trunk whitish; striking silhouette; needs lots of room; tolerates poor soil; small seed capsules; flowers insignificant.
Rich soil	Medium water	Heavy feeder	Fragrant flowers; good container plant—blooms best when crowded; keep soil on dry side after blooming until renewed growth is seen.
Good drainage	Medium water	Medium feeder	Moderate growing; glossy green leaves darken in cold weather; fragrant flowers; edible fruit turns from green to crimson when ripe; effective as tall hedge; can be sheared.
Good drainage	Medium water	Medium feeder	Neat, vase-shaped habit; brilliant scarlet fall foliage; best fall color if grown in full sun; tolerates most soils except very wet ones; pruning causes uneven growth.
Good drainage	Medium water	Medium feeder	Variable in habit and size; tolerates all but wet soils; transplants easily; susceptible to numerous diseases and insects; some cultivars produce berries.
Good drainage	Medium water	Medium feeder	Low maintenance, tough; good for harsh conditions and poor soils but best in sunny, well-drained spot with good air circulation; susceptible to mildew, insects.
Grows in poor soil	Let dry out between waterings	Light feeder	Attractive fall foliage; flowers form in sprays; extremely tough and adaptable.
Grows in poor soil	Let dry out between waterings	Light feeder	Grows in any soil; drought tolerant; if broken, the gray-green leaves with white margins exude milky sap that may irritate the skin.
Good drainage	Medium water	Medium feeder	Succulent, woody plant; long, sharp thorns; leaves only at or near end of branches; give bright light, no full sun; can tolerate some drought; may bloom all year.
Grows in poor soil	Let dry out between waterings	Light feeder	Gray-green foliage; spreads invasively.

NAME	HABIT		FLOWERS		ADAPTATION	
	Type	Height	Color	Time	Zones	Light
Euphorbia pulcherrima Poinsettia	Deciduous shrub, houseplant	to 10 ft	Pink, red, white	Fall to winter	10 or indoors	Half-day sun
Fagus sylvatica European beech	Deciduous tree	70 to 80 ft			5 to 7	Full sun
Fatsia japonica Japanese aralia	Tender evergreen shrub, houseplant	to 15 ft			9, 10 or indoors	Half-day sun to full shade
Festuca arundinacea Tall fescue	Turfgrass	2 to 3 in.			3 to 9	Full sun to light shade
Festuca ovina **var.** *glauca* Blue fescue	Evergreen ground cover				3 to 10	Full sun
Festuca rubra Red fescue, creeping red fescue	Turfgrass	1 to 2 in.			4 to 8	Full sun to light shade
Festuca rubra **var.** *commutata* Chewing fescue	Turfgrass	1 to 2 in.			4 to 8	Full sun to light shade
Ficus benjamina Weeping fig	Houseplant	2 to 18 ft			10 or indoors	Half-day sun to light shade
Ficus elastica Rubber plant	Houseplant	2 to 10 ft			10 or indoors	Light shade
Ficus lyrata (*F. pandurata*) Fiddleleaf fig	Houseplant	5 to 10 ft			10 or indoors	Light shade
Ficus pumila Creeping fig	Evergreen vine, houseplant	Climbs to 30 ft			9, 10 or indoors	Half-day sun to light shade
Fig *Ficus carica*	Deciduous fruit tree	12 to 30 ft			7 to 10	Full sun
Filbert *Corylus maxima*	Deciduous nut tree	15 to 25 ft			4 to 8	Full sun
Fittonia verschaffeltii **var.** *argyroneura* Nerve plant, mosaic plant	Houseplant	6 to 8 in.			10 or indoors	Light shade

| | CULTURE | | |
Soil	Water	Feeding	Special Characteristics
Good drainage	Medium water	Medium feeder	Woody; "flowers" are bracts or modified leaves; give plenty of sun while blooming, protect from hot afternoon exposure; prefers slightly acid soil; allow soil to dry somewhat between waterings; must keep in total darkness 14 hours a day from Sept. 1 to Oct. 30 to get flowers.
Good drainage	Medium water	Medium feeder	Slow growing; tall, wide tree with dense foliage, smooth gray bark; attractive fall color; demands lots of room.
Good drainage	Medium water	Heavy feeder	Bold, green, lobed leaves, some variegated; fast growing; cool location with bright, indirect light; feed every 2 weeks during growing season; decrease water during winter; prune back in spring.
Good drainage; organic matter	Medium water	Medium feeder	Good, tough play lawn; green all year; some disease and insect resistance; coarse textured; tends to clump; good drought tolerance; wears best in spring and fall; takes heat; good cool-season grass for transition areas.
Good drainage	Medium water	Medium feeder	Attractive ornamental grass; hairlike leaves; grows in rounded bluish gray tufts; mounding habit; not practical lawn substitute; needs regular summer watering; clip back shaggy plants.
Good drainage; organic matter	Medium water	Light feeder	Fine texture; deep green color; grows well in shade or dry soils; tolerates acid soil; susceptible to summer diseases in hot climates, especially in moist, fertile soils; wears poorly; best in cool-summer areas.
Good drainage; organic matter	Let dry out between waterings	Light feeder	Will tolerate close mowing in cool-climate areas; very susceptible to summer diseases in hot climates, especially in moist, fertile soils; wears poorly; best in cool-summer climates.
Good drainage; rich soil	Medium water	Medium feeder	Arching, graceful branches; glossy, pointed leaves; give very bright, indirect light, frequent light feedings; keep evenly moist; avoid dry heat and sudden changes of environment; will tolerate direct sun if kept moist; prune out inner, shaded growth.
Good drainage; rich soil	Medium water	Medium feeder	Bold, dark green leaves; give bright light, frequent light feedings; avoid overfeeding; avoid dry heat and sudden changes of environment.
Good drainage; rich soil	Medium water	Medium feeder	Durable, deep green leaves shaped like a fiddle; give bright light, frequent light feedings; avoid dry heat and sudden changes in environment.
Good drainage; rich soil	Medium water	Medium feeder	Fast growing, trailing or climbing plant; small leaves; likes more moisture, shade, and richer soil than other ficus species.
Good drainage	Medium water	Light feeder	Low-branched, spreading, large-leafed, tropical-looking tree; bears 2 crops of fruit a year; requires little attention; drought resistant once established; can be left unpruned or cut back to control size; pruning back usually eliminates first crop; will sprout again if killed by frost; many varieties available.
Good drainage	Medium water	Medium feeder	Produces fall crop of roundish to oblong nuts; 2 varieties needed for cross-pollination; remove suckers.
Good drainage	Let dry out between waterings	Medium feeder	Semiupright to trailing growth; mosaic pattern of white veins on oval, green leaves; place in warm spot; keep air moist; good in hanging pot.

NAME	HABIT		FLOWERS		ADAPTATION	
	Type	Height	Color	Time	Zones	Light
Forsythia × intermedia Border forsythia	Deciduous shrub	8 to 10 ft	Yellow	Spring	5 to 9	Full sun
Fothergilla major Large fothergilla	Deciduous shrub	6 to 10 ft	White	Spring	4 to 8	Full sun
Fragaria chiloensis Wild strawberry, sand strawberry	Evergreen ground cover	to 6 in.	White	Spring	6 to 10	Full sun
Franklinia alatamaha Franklinia	Deciduous tree	20 to 25 ft	White	Late summer to early fall	5 to 8	Light shade
Fraxinus excelsior European ash	Deciduous tree	50 to 80 ft			4 to 7	Full sun
Fraxinus ornus Flowering ash	Deciduous tree	30 to 50 ft	White	Late spring	6 to 8	Full sun
Fraxinus pennsylvanica Green ash, red ash	Deciduous tree	30 to 50 ft			3 to 8	Full sun
Fraxinus velutina 'Modesto' Modesto ash	Deciduous tree	30 to 50 ft			8 to 10	Full sun
Freesia refracta Common freesia	Tender bulb	12 to 18 in.	White, yellow, red, lavender	Late fall to early spring	9, 10 or indoors	Full sun
Fritillaria imperialis Crown-imperial, fritillary	Hardy bulb	2½ to 4 ft	Yellow, orange, red	Spring	5 to 8	Full sun to light shade
Fuchsia × hybrida Common fuchsia	Semievergreen shrub	2 to 6 ft	Comes in all colors	Early summer to first frost	9, 10	Light shade
Fuchsia magellanica Hardy fuchsia	Semievergreen shrub	3 to 8 ft	Red	Early summer to first frost	6 to 10	Light shade
Gaillardia × grandiflora Blanket-flower	Hardy perennial	2 to 4 ft	Red, yellow	Early summer to early fall	2 to 10	Full sun
Gaillardia pulchella Blanket-flower	Half-hardy annual	10 to 18 in.	Yellow, red	Early summer to first frost		Full sun
Galanthus nivalis Common snowdrop	Hardy bulb	6 to 9 in.	White	Winter to early spring	3 to 9	Full sun to light shade
Garbanzo—*See* Chick pea						
Gardenia jasminoides Gardenia	Evergreen shrub	3 to 6 ft	White	Early summer to early fall	8 to 10	Light shade

	CULTURE		
Soil	**Water**	**Feeding**	**Special Characteristics**
Not particular	Wet; don't let dry out	Medium feeder	Fast growing; upright, vigorous, arching form; needs constant grooming; burst of early spring color; give lots of room to grow; remove one third of canes annually right after flowering or cut to the ground.
Organic matter; good drainage	Medium water	Medium feeder	Neat, rounded habit; profuse, honey-scented blooms; attractive fall foliage; acid soil; tolerates light shade and dry, rocky soils.
Good drainage; sandy soil	Medium water	Medium feeder	Parent of all commercial strawberries; dark green leaves turn reddish in winter; forms attractive, thick mat; tolerates seacoast conditions; mow lightly in spring; spreads by runners.
Rich soil	Medium water	Heavy feeder	Slow to moderate growing; open, upright shape; glossy green foliage turns orange-red in the fall; camellia-like flowers; acid soil; protect from wind; good lawn or patio tree.
Good drainage	Medium water	Medium feeder	Glossy, dark green, leathery leaves; good shade tree; susceptible to scales and borers.
Not particular	Medium water	Medium feeder	Fragrant flowers; green leaves turn yellow in fall; best for cool areas; tolerates wet soil, poor drainage; lawn and shade tree.
Not particular	Medium water	Medium feeder	Moderate growing; compact habit; easy to grow; tolerates drought, wet soil, severe cold.
Not particular	Medium water	Medium feeder	Upright branching habit; yellow fall color; weak wood; prone to anthracnose, mistletoe; good lawn and shade tree.
Good drainage	Medium water	Medium feeder	Very fragrant flowers; can be grown as a houseplant.
Good drainage; organic matter	Medium water	Medium feeder	Large, bell-shaped flowers with a musky scent; good container plant.
Rich soil; organic matter	Wet; don't let dry out	Heavy feeder	Evergreen in frost-free areas; trailing to upright habit; best in areas with cool summers; mulch well; protect from hot winds; pinch or prune back to encourage dense growth.
Rich soil; good drainage	Wet; don't let dry out	Heavy feeder	Dies to the ground each winter in cold climates; can reach 8 ft high in Deep South; profuse bloomer; flowers smaller than *F. × hybrida*.
Good drainage; sandy soil	Let dry out between waterings	Light feeder	Short-lived; requires annual division; tolerates heat and drought; avoid rich, moist soils; flowers are bicolored.
Good drainage; sandy soil	Let dry out between waterings	Light feeder	Tolerates drought, heat, and infertile soil.
Good drainage	Medium water	Medium feeder	Bell-shaped flowers; blue-green foliage; may bloom earlier in mild climates.
Good drainage; organic matter; acid soil	Medium water	Heavy feeder	Glossy leaves; very fragrant flowers; acid soil; needs hot summer to bloom well; good as specimen, in containers, hedges, low screen, espalier; takes full sun in foggy areas.

NAME	HABIT		FLOWERS		ADAPTATION	
	Type	Height	Color	Time	Zones	Light
Gardenia jasminoides **'Prostrata'** (*G. radicans*) Creeping gardenia	Evergreen ground cover	to 1 ft	White	Early summer	9, 10	Half-day sun to light shade
Garlic *Allium sativum*	Hardy perennial vegetable	2 to 3 ft			3 to 10	Full sun to light shade
Garlic chives, oriental garlic *Allium tuberosum*	Hardy perennial herb	12 to 18 in.	White	Summer	3 to 10	Full sun to light shade
Gaultheria procumbens Wintergreen, teaberry, checkerberry	Evergreen ground cover	3 to 6 in.	White	Late spring to early summer	3 to 8	Light shade
Gazania rigens Gazania, treasureflower	Half-hardy annual	6 to 15 in.	Red, orange, yellow, pink, bicolored	Summer to first frost		Full sun
Gelsemium sempervirens Carolina jasmine	Evergreen vine, ground cover	Climbs to 20 ft	Yellow	Early spring	9, 10	Full sun to half-day sun
Genista hispanica Spanish gorse, Spanish broom	Deciduous shrub	1 to 2 ft	Yellow	Early summer	6 to 9	Full sun
Genista tinctoria Common woadwaxen	Deciduous shrub	2 to 3 ft	Yellow	Early summer	4 to 7	Full sun
Geranium sanguineum Blood-red geranium	Hardy perennial	to 1½ ft	Magenta, white	Late spring to late summer	3 to 10	Full sun to light shade
Gerbera jamesonii Transvaal daisy	Tender perennial	12 to 18 in.	Red, orange, yellow, pink, white	Late spring to first frost	8 to 10	Full sun to light shade
Geum **hybrids** Avens	Half-hardy perennial	2 to 3½ ft	Red, orange, yellow	Late spring to late summer	5 to 10	Full sun
Ginkgo biloba Maidenhair tree, ginkgo tree	Deciduous tree	60 to 100 ft			4 to 10	Full sun
Gladiolus hybridus Garden gladiolus	Half-hardy bulb	to 6 ft	Comes in all colors except blue	Late summer to fall	8 to 10	Full sun
Gleditsia triacanthos **var.** *inermis* Thornless honeylocust	Deciduous tree	30 to 70 ft			4 to 9	Full sun
Gloriosa rothschildiana Glory lily, climbing lily	Tender bulb	4 to 6 ft	Red	Summer to early fall	9, 10	Full sun to light shade

	CULTURE		
Soil	Water	Feeding	Special Characteristics
Good drainage; organic matter; acid soil	Wet; don't let dry out	Medium feeder	Low, slow-growing, 2 to 3 ft wide form of common gardenia; glossy, dark green leaves, often streaked with white; fragrant flowers; small-scale ground cover or container plant.
Good drainage; rich soil	Medium water	Medium feeder	Grown for edible bulb; in all but coldest areas, plant in fall; in cold areas, plant in the spring; harvest garlic when tops fall over; elephant garlic is about 6 times larger than regular garlic, weighs up to a pound and has a mild flavor.
Good drainage; organic matter	Medium water	Medium feeder	Culinary herb with long, grasslike leaves; starlike blossoms produced on umbels; when snipping leaves, cut to the ground.
Good drainage; acid soil; organic matter	Wet; don't let dry out	Light feeder	Spreads to form low mat of foliage; best used in naturalistic planting; produces bright red berries.
Good drainage; sandy soil	Let dry out between waterings	Light feeder	Drought and wind tolerant; prefers hot summers; avoid heavy soils; grown as a perennial in mild climates.
Good drainage; organic matter	Medium water	Medium feeder	Shiny green, finely textured leaves; deciduous in cold climates; fragrant flowers; prune frequently to keep low; best used to cover large area; can be trained up trellis or fence.
Good drainage	Let dry out between waterings	Light feeder	Prefers dry, infertile soil; tolerates drought and seacoast conditions; spiny growth.
Good drainage	Let dry out between waterings	Light feeder	Small, neat, round habit; vertical, almost leafless, green stems; prefers dry, infertile soils; tolerates drought and coastal conditions well.
Good drainage	Medium water	Light feeder	Attractive fall foliage; mounded, spreading form; rich, moist soil promotes invasive growth; dwarf varieties available.
Good drainage; organic matter; acid soil	Medium water	Heavy feeder	Best in long, warm summers and high humidity; subject to crown rot; grown as an annual in all but the mildest climates.
Good drainage; organic matter	Medium water	Light feeder	Slow growing; avoid wet soil in winter; reliable in low temperatures if soil is dry; profuse bloomer.
Good drainage	Medium water	Medium feeder	Slow growing; bright green, fan-shaped leaves turn brilliant yellow in fall; very adaptable; tolerates smoke and air pollution; needs room; good park or large lawn tree.
Good drainage; organic matter	Medium water	Medium feeder	Will grow in colder zones if dug up and stored in winter.
Not particular	Medium water	Medium feeder	Moderate to fast growing; lacy appearance; foliage leafs out late in spring, drops early in fall; casts light shade; tolerates air pollution, highway salting, winds; prune some new growth to maintain upright branching.
Good drainage; organic matter	Medium water	Heavy feeder	Climbing plant that can be grown as a houseplant or container plant; provide trellis or support.

NAME	HABIT		FLOWERS		ADAPTATION	
	Type	Height	Color	Time	Zones	Light
Gomphrena globosa Globe amaranth	Tender annual	9 to 30 in.	Purple, lavender, white, pink, orange, yellow	Early summer to fall		Full sun
Gourds *Curcurbita* species	Tender annual vegetable	to 15 ft (trailing)	Yellow	Summer		Full sun
Grape *Vitis* species	Deciduous fruit vine	Climbs to 30 ft			4 to 10	Full sun
Grapefruit *Citrus paradisi*	Evergreen fruit tree	10 to 30 ft	White	Spring	9, 10	Full sun to half-day sun
Gynura aurantiaca Velvet plant	Houseplant	to 9 ft (trailing)			10 or indoors	Light shade
Gypsophila elegans Annual baby's breath	Hardy annual	8 to 24 in.	White, pink, red, lavender	Early summer to fall		Full sun
Gypsophila paniculata Baby's breath	Hardy perennial	to 3 ft	White, pink	Summer to early fall	3 to 10	Full sun
Halesia carolina Carolina silverbell	Deciduous tree	30 to 40 ft	White	Late spring	5 to 10	Full sun to light shade
Hamamelis × intermedia Hybrid witch hazel	Deciduous shrub	10 to 15 ft	Yellow	Winter to early spring	6 to 8	Full sun to light shade
Hamamelis japonica Japanese witch hazel	Deciduous shrub or small tree	10 to 30 ft	Yellow	Winter to early spring	5 to 9	Full sun to light shade
Hamamelis mollis Chinese witch hazel	Deciduous shrub or small tree	10 to 30 ft	Yellow	Winter to early spring	5 to 8	Full sun to light shade
Hamamelis vernalis Vernal witch hazel	Deciduous shrub	6 to 10 ft	Yellow, orange	Winter	5 to 9	Full sun to light shade
Hamamelis virginiana Common witch hazel	Deciduous shrub or small tree	to 20 ft	Yellow	Late fall to winter	4 to 9	Full sun to light shade
Hedera canariensis Algerian ivy	Evergreen vine, ground cover	to 20 ft (climbing and trailing)			6 to 10	Full sun to deep shade

	CULTURE		
Soil	**Water**	**Feeding**	**Special Characteristics**
Sandy soil; good drainage	Medium water	Light feeder	Easy to grow; tolerates extreme heat, drought, wind, and humidity; grown mainly for dried arrangements.
Good drainage; organic matter	Medium water	Medium feeder	Warm-season crop; require ample space to trail; can be trained on trellis; some bush varieties available; water deeply; much variation in size, shape, and color of cultivars.
Good drainage; organic matter	Medium water	Medium feeder	Ornamental and fruiting vine; European varieties are spur-pruned, American varieties need cane pruning; requires only nitrogen; provide a deep soil and good air circulation; subject to mildew; a large number of varieties, many adapted to specific regions.
Good drainage; organic matter	Medium water	Medium feeder	Best in hot areas, especially in the desert; in cool areas fruit is thick-skinned and pithy; plant trees high and avoid wetting the trunk and crown; self-fertile; fragrant flowers; prune only to remove dead or damaged branches and suckers.
Good drainage	Medium water	Medium feeder	Dark green, toothed leaves covered with purple hairs; give bright light; keep moist; flowers have unpleasant odor—remove buds; prune plant to keep compact.
Good drainage	Medium water	Light feeder	Best in chalky, alkaline soil, low in fertility; make successive plantings 2 weeks apart throughout spring for continual summer bloom.
Good drainage; slightly alkaline soil	Let dry out between waterings	Light feeder	Profuse bloomer; noninvasive; long-lived; soggy soil fatal; resents transplanting.
Organic matter; rich soil	Medium water	Medium feeder	Slow to moderate growing; leaves turn yellow in fall; brown fruit in winter; attractive flowers; best in cool soil with ample water; open growth, several stems; good shelter plant for azaleas and rhododendrons; can prune to single stem.
Rich soil	Wet; don't let dry out	Heavy feeder	Fragrant flowers; good fall color; needs deep soil.
Good drainage; organic matter	Medium water	Medium feeder	Flowers purplish near the base and slightly fragrant; red leaf color in the fall.
Good drainage; organic matter	Medium water	Medium feeder	Moderately slow growing; very fragrant flowers; dark green leaves are slightly rough above, felted below; attractive yellow foliage in the fall.
Rich soil	Wet; don't let dry out	Heavy feeder	Neater, smaller habit than *H. × intermedia;* pungently fragrant flowers; good fall color.
Rich soil	Wet; don't let dry out	Heavy feeder	Hardiest but largest and rangiest witch hazel; yellow fall color; fragrant flowers.
Good drainage	Medium water	Light feeder	Shiny green leaves with 3 to 5 lobes; roots itself as it spreads along the ground; tougher than English ivy (*H. helix*); requires more water and is more aggressive; mow ground cover every other year just prior to new growth.

NAME	HABIT		FLOWERS		ADAPTATION	
	Type	Height	Color	Time	Zones	Light
Hedera helix English ivy	Evergreen vine, ground cover, houseplant	to 20 ft (climbing and trailing)			5 to 10 or indoors	Half-day sun to deep shade
Helenium autumnale Sneezeweed	Hardy perennial	2½ to 6 ft	Red, yellow, orange, bicolored	Summer to first frost	3 to 10	Full sun
Helianthemum nummularium Sun-rose	Evergreen ground cover	6 to 8 in.	Pink, red, yellow	Summer	5 to 10	Full sun
Helianthus annuus Sunflower	Hardy annual	2 to 8 ft	Yellow	Summer		Full sun
Helichrysum bracteatum Strawflower, everlasting	Half-hardy annual	1½ to 3 ft	Red, yellow, orange, pink, white	Early summer to fall		Full sun
Heliotropium arborescens Heliotrope	Tender perennial	1 to 3 ft	Purple, pink, white	Late spring to early fall	7 to 10 or indoors	Full sun
Helleborus lividus var. *corsicus* Corsican hellebore	Half-hardy perennial	to 3 ft	Green	Spring	6 to 9	Light shade
Helleborus niger Christmas-rose	Hardy perennial	to 15 in.	White	Late winter to spring	3 to 9	Light shade
Hemerocallis hybrids Daylily	Hardy perennial	1½ to 4 ft	Warm colors, white, pink, violet, bicolored	Late spring to early fall	3 to 10	Full sun to light shade
Heuchera sanguinea Coralbells	Hardy perennial	1 to 2 ft	Pink, red, white	Summer	3 to 10	Full sun to light shade
Hibiscus rosa-sinensis Chinese hibiscus	Evergreen shrub	5 to 15 ft	Pink, red, yellow, white	Late summer to first frost	9, 10	Full sun
Hibiscus syriacus Shrub althea, rose-of-Sharon	Deciduous shrub	8 to 12 ft	Red, purple, violet, white	Late summer to first frost	6 to 9	Full sun
Hippeastrum species Amaryllis	Tender bulb, houseplant	1 to 2 ft	Pink, red, white	Winter to late spring	9, 10	Full sun to light shade
Horseradish *Armoracia rusticana*	Hardy perennial herb	1½ to 3 ft			4 to 10	Full sun
Hosta decorata Blunt-leaf plantain lily	Hardy perennial	to 2 ft	Violet	Summer	3 to 9	Light shade to deep shade

	CULTURE		
Soil	**Water**	**Feeding**	**Special Characteristics**
Good drainage	Medium water	Medium feeder	Good ivy for small spaces; not as invasive as and more attractive than *H. canariensis*; place in cool, bright spot; prune back in spring to encourage bushy growth; indoors give 3 to 4 hours direct sun during summer; many cultivars available.
Organic matter; tolerates clay soil	Wet; don't let dry out	Medium feeder	Profuse bloomer; tolerant of many soils; taller varieties need staking; divide annually or every other year to avoid overcrowding.
Good drainage	Let dry out between waterings	Light feeder	Branches root as they spread to form thick mat; adapted to dry summers; tolerates infertile soils; fire retardant; short-lived flowers; shear in spring.
Good drainage	Let dry out between waterings	Light feeder	Tolerant of heat and drought; tall varieties may need staking.
Good drainage; slightly alkaline soil	Medium water	Medium feeder	Best in areas of long, hot summers; plants may need support; popular for dried arrangements.
Good drainage; organic matter	Wet; don't let dry out	Heavy feeder	Some have a strong, sweet fragrance; dramatically dark foliage; will bloom through winter in mild climates; good container, greenhouse, or indoor plant; valued for vanilla-like fragrance of flowers; may grow as tall as 6 ft.
Good drainage; organic matter	Wet; don't let dry out	Medium feeder	Takes more sun and drought than other hellebores once established; protect from cold, drying winds in winter.
Good drainage; organic matter; acid soil	Wet; don't let dry out	Medium feeder	Moderately difficult to grow; resents disturbance.
Good drainage; organic matter	Medium water	Light feeder	Long-lived, noninvasive; some varieties fragrant; requires light shade in hot areas.
Good drainage; organic matter	Medium water	Light feeder	Some varieties have attractive fall and winter foliage; adaptable; divide every 3 or 4 years.
Good drainage	Medium water	Medium feeder	Medium growing; large, erect, round topped; tolerates coastal conditions; prefers hot summer; avoid wet weather; prune hard each spring to encourage blooming; best if grouped or massed in shrub border; leaves appear late in spring, drop early in fall.
Good drainage	Wet; don't let dry out	Medium feeder	Fast growing; needs sun and heat; protect from wind and frost; needs heat for good blooms; prune out one third of old wood each spring; feed monthly during growing season.
Good drainage; organic matter	Medium water	Medium feeder	Grown mainly as a houseplant; can be planted outdoors in warm climates.
Good drainage; organic matter	Wet; don't let dry out	Medium feeder	Culinary herb with long, narrow leaves; can become invasive; grown for thick taproots; harvested in fall.
Good drainage; organic matter	Medium water	Medium feeder	6-in. leaves rimmed with silvery white; compact.

NAME	HABIT		FLOWERS		ADAPTATION	
	Type	Height	Color	Time	Zones	Light
Hosta lancifolia Narrow-leaf plantain lily	Hardy perennial	to 2 ft	Lavender	Late summer	3 to 9	Light shade to deep shade
Hosta plantaginea Fragrant plantain lily	Hardy perennial	to 2 ft	White	Late summer to early fall	3 to 9	Light shade to deep shade
Hosta undulata Wavy-leaf plantain lily	Hardy perennial	1 to 2½ ft	Violet	Summer	3 to 9	Light shade to deep shade
Howea forsterana Kentia palm	Houseplant	5 to 10 ft			10 or indoors	Light shade
Hoya bella Waxflower, wax plant	Houseplant	4 to 10 ft (trailing)	White	Summer	10 or indoors	Half-day sun to light shade
Hyacinthus orientalis Common hyacinth	Hardy bulb	12 to 15 in.	Blue, white, purple	Spring	4 to 10	Full sun
Hydrangea macrophylla Bigleaf hydrangea	Deciduous shrub	4 to 8 ft	Blue, pink, white	Summer	7 to 10	Light shade
Hydrangea quercifolia Oakleaf hydrangea	Deciduous shrub	6 to 8 ft	White	Summer	6 to 9	Full sun to light shade
Hypericum calycinum Aaron's-beard, St. John's wort	Evergreen ground cover	to 12 in.	Yellow	Summer	6 to 10	Full sun
Hypericum × moseranum Goldflower, St. John's wort	Evergreen shrub	to 3 ft	Yellow	Summer	8 to 10	Full sun to light shade
Iberis amara Rocket candytuft	Half-hardy annual	12 to 18 in.	White	Early summer to first frost		Full sun
Iberis sempervirens Evergreen candytuft	Hardy perennial ground cover	½ to 1 ft	White	Spring	5 to 9	Full sun to light shade
Ilex aquifolium English holly	Evergreen tree	to 40 ft	White	Spring	7 to 9	Full sun to light shade
Ilex cornuta Chinese holly	Evergreen shrub or small tree	to 15 ft	White	Spring	7 to 9	Full sun to light shade
Ilex crenata Japanese holly	Evergreen shrub	5 to 10 ft	White	Spring	6 to 9	Full sun to light shade
Ilex decidua Possumhaw holly	Deciduous shrub or small tree	to 20 ft	White	Spring	5 to 9	Full sun to light shade

	CULTURE		
Soil	**Water**	**Feeding**	**Special Characteristics**
Good drainage; organic matter	Medium water	Medium feeder	Large quantity of flower stalks with profuse blossoms.
Good drainage; organic matter	Medium water	Light feeder	Large, fragrant flowers; heart-shaped leaves up to 10 in. long; 'Honeybells' and 'Royal Standard' commonly grown cultivars.
Good drainage; organic matter	Medium water	Medium feeder	Leaves striped with white and green, 6 to 8 in. long; more tolerant of full sun than other plantain lilies.
Good drainage; organic matter	Medium water	Medium feeder	Feather-shaped leaves arch outward from sturdy trunks; leaves scorch easily; water heavily and feed monthly during growing season, reduce in winter; protect from direct sun and dry air.
Good drainage	Medium water	Medium feeder	Shrubby plant, good for hanging baskets; waxy leaves; flowers tightly clustered, white with purple centers; allow soil to dry slightly between waterings; plants require less water and light during winter; best bloom if kept pot bound.
Rich soil	Medium water	Medium feeder	Fragrant flowers; many hybrids are available.
Rich soil; organic matter	Medium water	Heavy feeder	Neat foliage; rounded shape; large flowers; accepts seacoast conditions; sun on coast, shade inland; acid soil produces blue flowers, alkaline soil produces pink flowers; prune just after flowering.
Rich soil; good drainage	Wet; don't let dry out	Heavy feeder	Slow growing; upright, irregular shrub; coarse, clean foliage; lacy flowers; good fall color; needs slightly acid soil; tolerates heavy shade; mulch to keep roots cool; prune right after blooming; tends to sucker.
Good drainage	Medium water	Medium feeder	Semievergreen in colder climates; low-growing, spreading form; mow to ground every few years.
Good drainage	Medium water	Medium feeder	Low growing; one of few plants that will do well planted under eucalyptus trees.
Good drainage	Let dry out between waterings	Medium feeder	Tolerates drought, pollution, and heat; flowers are fragrant.
Good drainage	Medium water	Medium feeder	Mat forming; showy in bloom; dark green, finely textured foliage; do not overfertilize or will become loose and rangy; prune hard each year after flowering.
Rich soil; good drainage	Medium water	Medium feeder	Slow growing; variable leaf shape, color, and spininess; male plants will not have berries; protect from sun in hot, dry areas; many cultivars.
Rich soil; good drainage	Medium water	Medium feeder	Large, spiny, glossy, dark green leaves; large red berries on female plants; needs long warm season to set fruit.
Good drainage; acid soil	Medium water	Medium feeder	Neat, rounded shape; dark green, lustrous foliage; female plants have black berries; slow growing; tolerates some shade and pollution; prunes easily into hedge or border.
Rich soil; good drainage	Medium water	Medium feeder	Moderate growing; female plants have red berries retained well into winter.

NAME	HABIT		FLOWERS		ADAPTATION	
	Type	Height	Color	Time	Zones	Light
Ilex glabra Inkberry	Evergreen shrub	6 to 8 ft	White	Spring	3 to 9	Full sun to light shade
Ilex opaca American holly	Evergreen tree	45 to 50 ft	White	Spring	5 to 9	Full sun to light shade
Ilex verticillata Common winterberry	Deciduous shrub	6 to 9 ft	White	Spring	4 to 9	Full sun to light shade
Ilex vomitoria Yaupon holly	Evergreen shrub or small tree	15 to 20 ft	White	Spring	7 to 10	Full sun to light shade
Impatiens balsamina Balsam	Hardy annual	1 to 3 ft	Red, purple, pink, white	Early summer to fall		Full sun to light shade
Impatiens wallerana Impatiens, busy-lizzie	Half-hardy annual	6 to 18 in.	Red, orange, yellow, violet, white, pink, bicolored	Early summer to first frost		Light shade to deep shade
Ipomoea alba Moonflower vine	Half-hardy annual	to 15 ft (trailing)	White	Summer to first frost		Full sun
Ipomoea tricolor Morning glory vine	Half-hardy annual	8 to 10 ft (trailing)	Blue, purple, pink, red, white	Summer to first frost		Full sun
Iresine herbstii Beefsteak plant, bloodleaf	Houseplant	2 to 4 ft			10 or indoors	Half-day sun to light shade
Iris hybrids Iris	Hardy bulb	½ to 4 ft	Comes in all colors	Spring to early summer	3 to 10	Full sun
Iris cristata Crested iris	Hardy bulb	3 to 4 in.	Lavender	Early summer	5 to 10	Light shade
Iris danfordiae Danford iris	Hardy bulb	to 1 ft	Yellow	Early spring	4 to 10	Full sun
Iris × *germanica* var. *florentina* Orris, German iris	Hardy bulb	2 to 3 ft	White	Early spring to early summer	4 to 10	Full sun
Iris kaempferi Japanese iris	Hardy bulb	3 to 4 ft	White, blue, purple, pink, lavender	Summer	4 to 10	Full sun to light shade
Iris pseudacorus Water flag iris	Hardy bulb	3 to 3½ ft	Yellow	Summer	4 to 10	Full sun to light shade
Iris reticulata Netted iris	Hardy bulb	to 2 ft	Violet	Early spring	3 to 10	Full sun
Iris sibirica Siberian iris	Hardy perennial	1½ to 3 ft	Cool colors	Early summer	2 to 10	Full sun to light shade

	CULTURE		
Soil	**Water**	**Feeding**	**Special Characteristics**
Good drainage; acid soil	Wet; don't let dry out	Medium feeder	Very hardy; open spread, leggy; attractive dark green foliage; black berries on female plants; needs heavy pruning.
Rich soil; good drainage	Medium water	Medium feeder	Slow growing; pyramid shape; berries ranging in color from red and orange to yellow found on female plants.
Good drainage; organic matter	Wet; don't let dry out	Medium feeder	Abundant red berries on female plants; tolerates dry soil, prefers slightly acid soil; best planted in masses in border.
Rich soil; good drainage	Medium water	Medium feeder	Narrow, inch-long, dark green leaves; profuse red berries on female plants; tolerates alkaline soil; can be sheared into columnar form.
Organic matter; sandy soil	Medium water	Heavy feeder	Appreciates hot summers; in hottest areas give light shade; young plants subject to damping off.
Good drainage; sandy soil; organic matter	Wet; don't let dry out	Medium feeder	One of the best of the flowering shade plants.
Sandy soil; good drainage	Medium water	Light feeder	Twining habit; let climb or allow to sprawl; tolerates dry and infertile soils; blooms at night; fragrant flowers.
Good drainage; sandy soil	Medium water	Light feeder	Twining habit; grow on a fence or arbor or use as a ground cover; tolerant of dry soil; grows almost anywhere; also good container plant.
Good drainage	Medium water	Medium feeder	Heart-shaped leaves with light red veins; give bright light and humidity; can summer outdoors in protected location; pinch back to encourage branching.
Good drainage; organic matter	Medium water	Heavy feeder	Large and diverse group of plants; give light shade in hottest areas; never allow soil to remain soggy.
Good drainage	Medium water	Medium feeder	The rhizomes creep along soil surface and should not be covered with soil.
Good drainage	Medium water	Medium feeder	Water generously during active growth; short-lived; treat as an annual.
Good drainage	Medium water	Medium feeder	Swordlike leaves; large flowers with yellow beards, veined with blue; roots used in medicine and perfume.
Organic matter; acid soil	Wet; don't let dry out	Medium feeder	Plant thrives in boggy, rich soil; lime and alkaline soil fatal; feed with acid fertilizer.
Rich, acid soil; organic matter	Wet; don't let dry out	Medium feeder	Self-sows prolifically in boggy areas; needs acid soil.
Good drainage	Wet; don't let dry out	Medium feeder	Many hybrids available.
Rich, acid soil	Medium water	Medium feeder	Hardy, long-lived; tolerates wide range of soils.

NAME	HABIT		FLOWERS		ADAPTATION	
	Type	Height	Color	Time	Zones	Light
Jasminum mesnyi Primrose jasmine, Japanese jasmine	Evergreen shrub	to 10 ft	Yellow	Spring to summer	8 to 10	Full sun to light shade
Jasminum nudiflorum Winter jasmine	Deciduous shrub	10 to 15 ft	Yellow	Spring	6 to 9	Full sun to light shade
Juglans nigra Black walnut	Deciduous tree	50 to 150 ft			7 to 10	Full sun
Juniperus chinensis Chinese juniper	Needled evergreen trees, shrubs, and ground covers	6 in. to 50 ft			4 to 10	Full sun
Juniperus communis Common juniper	Needled evergreen shrub	5 to 10 ft			2 to 7	Full sun
Juniperus communis 'Saxatilis'	Needled evergreen ground cover	to 1 ft			5 to 10	Full sun
Juniperus conferta Shore juniper	Needled evergreen shrub, ground cover	1 to 2 ft			6 to 10	Full sun
Juniperus horizontalis Creeping juniper	Needled evergreen ground cover	to 1 ft			3 to 9	Full sun
Juniperus procumbens Japanese garden juniper	Needled evergreen ground cover	1 to 2 ft			5 to 10	Full sun
Juniperus scopulorum Rocky Mountain juniper	Needled evergreen tree	35 to 45 ft			4 to 9	Full sun to light shade
Juniperus virginiana Eastern red cedar	Needled evergreen tree	35 to 45 ft			3 to 9	Full sun to light shade
Kalanchoe blossfeldiana Flaming-katy	Houseplant	to 15 in.	Red, orange, pink, yellow	Winter to spring	10 or indoors	Light shade
Kale Brassica oleracea var. acephala	Hardy biennial vegetable	2 to 3 ft				Full sun to light shade
Kalmia latifolia Mountain laurel	Evergreen shrub	7 to 15 ft	Pink, white	Late spring to early summer	5 to 9	Full sun to light shade
Kerria japonica Japanese kerria	Deciduous shrub	3 to 6 ft	Yellow	Spring	5 to 9	Half-day sun to light shade

Soil	CULTURE		
	Water	Feeding	Special Characteristics
Good drainage	Medium water	Medium feeder	Vining or arching habit; dark green leaves; may flower during winter in mild climates; needs plenty of room; best if tied at desired height.
Good drainage	Medium water	Medium feeder	Viny shrub; graceful, weeping branches; glossy green leaves; may bloom during winter in mild climates; tie as *J. mesnyi* or allow to trail; prune to control growth.
Adaptive	Medium water	Medium feeder	Large-crowned shade tree; 1 to 1½ in., edible nuts in hard, thick shells; tree inhibits growth of many vegetables and flowers.
Sandy soil; good drainage	Let dry out between waterings	Light feeder	Very diverse species; prefers alkaline soils; low maintenance.
Good drainage; sandy soil	Let dry out between waterings	Light feeder	Spiny blue-green or gray scaly leaves that turn yellowish or brownish green in winter; adapts to poorest, driest soils; very susceptible to blight; spreads 8 to 12 ft.
Good drainage; sandy soil	Medium water	Light feeder	Prostrate form with upward-spreading branchlets; gray-green foliage; prickly clusters of tiny scaly leaves; tolerates some shade but becomes woody, loses color.
Sandy soil; good drainage	Let dry out between waterings	Light feeder	Intense bluish green foliage; prostrate growth; spreads slowly 6 to 8 ft wide; forms attractive, dense mat; tolerates seacoast conditions; good ground cover in coastal areas; will not tolerate wet, heavy soil.
Good drainage; sandy soil	Let dry out between waterings	Light feeder	Low, spreading ground cover; turns grayish purple in winter; susceptible to blight.
Good drainage; sandy soil	Let dry out between waterings	Light feeder	Prostrate form, spreading slowly to 10 to 15 ft wide; susceptible to blight; *J. procumbens* 'Nana' is dwarf form that grows 6 in. high.
Good drainage	Medium water	Medium feeder	Slow growing; broad, pyramid form; brownish red bark; blue-gray scaly leaves; best juniper for areas of heat, drought; tall hedge, screen, windbreak; many cultivars available.
Good drainage	Medium water	Medium feeder	Medium growing; pyramid shape; bright green scaly leaves turn bronze in cold weather; attractive blue cones in winter; adaptive to soils and climates; avoid hot, dry winds; tall hedge, screen, windbreak.
Good drainage; sandy soil	Let dry out between waterings	Medium feeder	Shiny green, oval, smooth-edged or scalloped leaves tinged with red; likes filtered sun or bright, indirect light in warm environment; after blooming, prune top.
Good drainage; organic matter	Medium water	Heavy feeder	Member of cabbage family; doesn't tolerate heat as well as collards; grows best in cool of fall; flavor improved by frost; 'Dwarf Blue Curled' and 'Vates' are the most widely planted varieties; requires 55 days to maturity.
Good drainage; organic matter; acid soil	Medium water	Medium feeder	Slow growing; dense, rounded, and neat when young, becoming gnarled and picturesque in old age; shade in hot summer areas.
Good drainage; grows in poor soil	Medium water	Medium feeder	Slow growing; tough, carefree shrub for shady places; fertile soil decreases flowering and encourages rank, weedy growth; prune right after flowering.

NAME	HABIT		FLOWERS		ADAPTATION	
	Type	Height	Color	Time	Zones	Light
Kniphofia uvaria Torch lily, red-hot-poker	Hardy perennial	2 to 4 ft	Red	Late summer to early fall	7 to 10	Full sun
Koelreuteria paniculata Goldenrain tree, varnish tree	Deciduous tree	25 to 35 ft	Yellow	Summer	5 to 9	Full sun
Kohlrabi *Brassica oleracea* var. *caulorapa*	Half-hardy biennial vegetable	2 to 3 ft				Full sun to half-day sun
Kolkwitzia amabilis Beautybush	Deciduous shrub	6 to 10 ft	Pink	Late spring	5 to 8	Full sun
Kumquat *Fortunella* species	Evergreen fruit tree	5 to 15 ft	White	Spring	9, 10	Full sun to half-day sun
Laburnum × *watereri* 'Vossii' Goldenchain tree	Deciduous tree	20 to 30 ft	Yellow	Late spring	5 to 7	Full sun to light shade
Lagerstroemia fauriei Japanese crape myrtle	Deciduous tree	12 to 20 ft	White	Summer to early fall	7 to 10	Full sun
Lagerstroemia indica Crape myrtle	Deciduous shrub or small tree	10 to 30 ft	Lavender, pink, red, white	Summer to early fall	7 to 10	Full sun
Lantana montevidensis Trailing lantana	Tender perennial ground cover	1 to 2 ft	Lavender	All year	9, 10	Full sun to half-day sun
Larix kaempferi Japanese larch	Needled deciduous tree	50 to 60 ft			4 to 7	Full sun
Lathyrus odoratus Sweet pea	Hardy annual	2 to 6 ft	Red, purple, pink, white, bicolored	Spring to early summer		Full sun to half-day sun
Laurus nobilis Sweet bay, laurel bay, Grecian laurel	Evergreen shrub or small tree	12 to 30 ft	Yellow	Early summer	8 to 10	Full sun to light shade
Lavandula angustifolia English lavender	Evergreen shrub	1½ to 4 ft	Lavender, purple	Early summer to first frost	5 to 10	Full sun
Leek *Allium ampeloprasum*	Hardy perennial vegetable	to 3 ft			4 to 10	Full sun to half-day sun

Soil	CULTURE		
	Water	Feeding	Special Characteristics
Good drainage	Medium water	Light feeder	Gray-green foliage forms mound 12 to 30 in. high; brightly colored flower spike rises above; long-lived plant; avoid windy spots.
Not particular	Medium water	Medium feeder	Moderate growing; spreading, open branches, flat top; soft, medium-green leaves; profuse summer bloomer; papery fruit capsules resembling Japanese lanterns appear in late summer and fall; deep rooted; tolerates wind, drought, alkaline soil, cold.
Good drainage; organic matter	Medium water	Heavy feeder	Member of cabbage family; cool-weather vegetable; plant in early spring so growth is almost complete before full heat of summer; harvest when 2 to 3 in. in diameter, otherwise becomes tough; several cultivars available.
Good drainage	Medium water	Medium feeder	Fast growing; upright, arching form; can become leggy; needs plenty of room; limited value when not in bloom; profuse bloomer; prune out older stems yearly after flowering; renew overgrown shrubs by cutting to ground.
Good drainage; organic matter	Medium water	Medium feeder	Related to citrus; tiny, round to oval orange fruit; sour flesh and sweet rind; foliage is attractive; fruit used in preserves or eaten fresh, skin and all.
Good drainage	Medium water	Medium feeder	Moderate growing; dense, upright, vase-shaped crown; grown for hanging flower clusters; leaves, fruit, and flowers poisonous; provides some shade in hottest areas; best in mild climate.
Good drainage	Medium water	Medium feeder	Slow growing; attractive bark; water infrequently but deeply; resists powdery mildew; prune to induce new growth, flowers.
Good drainage	Medium water	Medium feeder	Medium growing; vase shaped when multitrunked, round headed when trained to single trunk; profuse blooms; attractive bark; best in hot, dry climate since subject to powdery mildew; prune lightly to induce new growth and blooms.
Not particular	Let dry out between waterings	Light feeder	Fast growing; vinelike stems, 3 to 4 ft long, root as they spread; dark green, oval leaves; tolerates drought, poor soil; cut out dead patches in early spring; good for large-scale planting.
Not particular	Medium water	Medium feeder	Fast growing; blue-green, feathery foliage; good yellow fall color; attractive cones hang on in winter; not for warm winter climates; can be dwarfed in container.
Organic matter; slightly alkaline soil	Wet; don't let dry out	Heavy feeder	Pleasant fragrance on some varieties; best in cool seasons; subject to powdery mildew.
Good drainage	Medium water	Medium feeder	Slow growing; compact, often multistemmed; aromatic, dark green leaves used in cooking; small flowers; dark purple berries; little water once established; background shrub, small tree, container plant; easy to shape.
Good drainage; sandy soil	Medium water	Medium feeder	Bright green to gray foliage; fragrant foliage and flowers; blooms on spikes.
Rich soil; good drainage	Wet; don't let dry out	Medium feeder	Culinary plant with long, flat leaves and round, thick stems; used as a vegetable and sometimes as an herb; does not form bulbs; needs 140 days to grow from seed, 80 days from transplants; sow seeds in late winter; harvest in fall of first year.

NAME	HABIT		FLOWERS		ADAPTATION	
	Type	Height	Color	Time	Zones	Light
Lemon *Citrus limon*	Evergreen fruit tree	4 to 25 ft	White	Spring	9, 10	Full sun to half-day sun
Lemon balm *Melissa officinalis*	Hardy perennial herb	2 to 3 ft			4 to 10	Full sun to light shade
Leptospermum laevigatum Tea tree	Evergreen shrub or small tree	15 to 30 ft	White, pink, red	Spring	9, 10	Full sun
Lettuce *Lactuca sativa*	Hardy annual vegetable	to 2 ft				Full sun to light shade
Leucojum aestivum Summer snowflake	Hardy bulb	to 1½ ft	White	Late spring	4 to 10	Full sun to light shade
Leucojum vernum Spring snowflake	Hardy bulb	to 1 ft	White	Spring	4 to 10	Full sun to light shade
Leucothoe fontanesiana Drooping leucothoe	Evergreen shrub	3 to 5 ft	White	Spring	5 to 7	Half-day sun to light shade
Ligustrum amurense Amur privet	Deciduous shrub	12 to 15 ft	White	Early summer	4 to 7	Full sun to light shade
Ligustrum japonicum Japanese privet	Evergreen shrub	6 to 12 ft	White	Early summer	7 to 10	Full sun to light shade
Ligustrum lucidum Glossy privet	Evergreen tree	35 to 40 ft	White	Summer	8 to 10	Full sun to light shade
Ligustrum ovalifolium California privet	Semievergreen shrub	to 15 ft	White	Early summer	6 to 10	Full sun to light shade
Lilium candidum Madonna lily	Hardy bulb	to 3½ ft	White	Summer	3 to 10	Full sun to light shade
Lilium speciosum Speciosum lily	Hardy bulb	to 3 ft	Red, white	Late summer to early fall	3 to 10	Full sun to light shade
Lime *Citrus aurantifolia*	Evergreen fruit tree	7 to 15 ft	White	Spring	10	Full sun to half-day sun
Limonium sinuatum Statice, notchleaf sea lavender	Half-hardy biennial	1 to 2½ ft	Rose, blue, lavender	Early summer to first frost		Full sun

	CULTURE		
Soil	**Water**	**Feeding**	**Special Characteristics**
Good drainage; organic matter	Medium water	Medium feeder	Does not tolerate excessive heat or cold; protect from frost; grow in southern coastal areas or mildest northern areas; fragrant flowers may appear again in summer; prune only dead or damaged wood and suckers; plant high; protect from hot, dry winds; several cultivars available.
Sandy soil	Medium water	Medium feeder	Culinary and medicinal herb has dark green, heart-shaped leaves with scalloped edges; inconspicuous flowers; lemon-scented foliage.
Good drainage	Medium water	Medium feeder	Soft, casual branching habit twisting to form good canopy; foliage gray-green; doesn't need much water; good as single specimen or grouped to form thick screen.
Good drainage; organic matter	Wet; don't let dry out	Heavy feeder	Cool-season vegetable, tolerates cold better than heat; keep moist; may be started in cold frame before outdoor sowing is possible; thin plants to avoid crowding; major lettuce groups include crisphead (iceberg type), butterhead, leaf lettuces, romaine, and celtuce; much variation within each group.
Good drainage	Medium water	Medium feeder	Slightly larger than *L. vernum*; 4 to 8 bell-shaped flowers per stem.
Good drainage	Medium water	Medium feeder	Single, bell-shaped flowers; white with green tips.
Good drainage; organic matter; acid soil	Medium water	Medium feeder	Graceful, fountainlike form; fragrant flowers; foliage is bright green to bronze in spring and purplish in winter; needs moist, acid soil; tolerates deep shade; protect from drying winds, drought; good with azaleas, rhododendrons, and other acid-loving plants.
Good drainage	Medium water	Medium feeder	Hardy; clean, medium- to fine-textured foliage; good for hedge.
Good drainage	Wet; don't let dry out	Medium feeder	Dense, compact habit; lustrous leaves; fairly fast growing; protect from hot sun; container, topiary, hedge, or screen plant.
Not particular	Medium water	Medium feeder	Fast growing; dense, often multitrunked; glossy, deep green foliage; berrylike, blue-black fruit; tolerates salt winds and many soils; shade tree, street tree, screen, container plant, or sheared hedge.
Good drainage	Medium water	Medium feeder	Evergreen in mildest climates; glossy leaves; popular hedge; can be sheared to any height.
Good drainage	Medium water	Medium feeder	Adding lime to soil aids growth; sometimes difficult to establish.
Good drainage	Medium water	Medium feeder	One of the last lilies to bloom; fragrant flowers.
Good drainage; organic matter	Medium water	Medium feeder	Most tender of all citrus; needs mildest winters and high heat; bears fruit periodically all year with heaviest ripening in the summer and fall; very thorny and thick headed, prune to remove dead or damaged wood, suckers, and old fruiting wood; plant high; most common cultivars are 'Bears' and 'Mexican'.
Good drainage; sandy soil	Let dry out between waterings	Light feeder	Tolerates seacoast conditions, heat, and drought; irregular blooming habit; good for dried arrangements.

NAME	HABIT		FLOWERS		ADAPTATION	
	Type	Height	Color	Time	Zones	Light
Liquidambar formosana Chinese sweet gum	Deciduous tree	40 to 60 ft			6 to 9	Full sun
Liquidambar styraciflua American sweet gum	Deciduous tree	60 to 75 ft			6 to 9	Full sun
Liriodendron tulipifera Tulip tree, yellow poplar, tulip poplar	Deciduous tree	60 to 70 ft	Yellow	Late spring to early summer	4 to 9	Full sun
Liriope muscari Bigleaf lilyturf	Evergreen ground cover	to 2 ft	Violet	Summer to early fall	7 to 10	Light shade
Liriope spicata Creeping lilyturf	Evergreen ground cover	to 1 ft	Lavender	Summer to early fall	5 to 10	Light shade
Lobelia cardinalis Cardinal flower	Hardy perennial	3 to 4 ft	Red	Summer to early fall	2 to 9	Light shade
Lobelia erinus Edging lobelia	Half-hardy annual	4 to 8 in.	Blue, violet	Late spring to early fall		Full sun to light shade
Lobularia maritima Sweet alyssum	Hardy annual	4 to 8 in.	Lavender, white, pink	Spring to first frost		Full sun to light shade
Lolium multiflorum Annual rye grass, common rye grass, Italian rye grass	Turfgrass	1 to 2½ in.			6 to 8	Full sun to light shade
Lolium perenne Turf-type perennial rye grass	Turfgrass	1 to 2 in.			4 to 9	Full sun to light shade
Lonicera fragrantissima Winter honeysuckle	Deciduous shrub	6 to 10 ft	White	Spring	5 to 10	Full sun
Lonicera japonica 'Halliana' Hall's Japanese honeysuckle	Deciduous vine, ground cover	to 15 ft (climbing or trailing)	White	Summer	5 to 10	Full sun to light shade
Lonicera maackii Amur honeysuckle	Deciduous shrub	to 15 ft	White	Early summer	3 to 8	Full sun
Lonicera tatarica Tartarian honeysuckle	Deciduous shrub	to 12 ft	Pink, red, white	Late spring	3 to 8	Full sun
Lotus berthelotii Parrot's-beak	Evergreen ground cover	3 to 4 in.	Red	Late spring to summer	10	Full sun

	CULTURE		
Soil	**Water**	**Feeding**	**Special Characteristics**
Good drainage; rich soil	Medium water	Medium feeder	Moderate growing; maplelike leaves; very good fall color; flowers inconspicuous; prickly fruit in the fall; upright growth, spreading with age; good skyline, street, lawn, or garden tree; effective tall screen; prune only to shape.
Rich soil	Medium water	Medium feeder	Slow to moderate growing; star-shaped leaves; rich, fall colors; prickly fruit in the fall; good skyline, garden, street tree; tall screen, grove.
Rich soil; good drainage	Medium water	Heavy feeder	Fast growing; unusually shaped bright green leaves turn yellow in fall; tall, pyramid shape; needs lots of room—open areas, parks, golf courses, large lawn; good skyline tree; avoid drought areas.
Not particular	Let dry out between waterings	Light feeder	Coarse, clumping, dark green grasslike leaves; 4 to 8 in. long spikelets of flowers; blue-black berries in the fall; clip off any yellowed leaves.
Not particular	Let dry out between waterings	Light feeder	Moderate growing; coarse, clumping, dark green grasslike leaves; spreads by underground stems; forms denser mat than *L. muscari*; cut out any yellowed leaves.
Rich soil; good drainage; organic matter	Wet; don't let dry out	Medium feeder	Short-lived; tolerant of full sun if kept moist; mulch well.
Sandy soil; organic matter	Wet; don't let dry out	Medium feeder	Doesn't withstand heat well; plant in partial shade in hot-summer areas; long-lasting color.
Good drainage	Medium water	Light feeder	Tolerant of drought and heat; slightly fragrant flowers; self-sows freely.
Good drainage; organic matter	Wet; don't let dry out	Light to medium feeder	Aggressive; fast germinating, quick to establish; poor tolerance to heat and cold; doesn't mow cleanly.
Good drainage; organic matter	Medium water	Medium feeder	Fast germination and establishment; improved heat and cold resistance; tough play lawn; suffers from winterkill in coldest climates; cleaner mowing than annual rye grass; impairs establishment of other grasses if more than 25% of a seed mix.
Good drainage	Medium water	Medium feeder	Arching, somewhat stiff growth; very fragrant flowers; red fruit; prune to shape; can be used as hedge or background plant.
Not particular	Medium water	Light feeder	Evergreen in mild climates; twining, climbing growth habit with support; can also be allowed to sprawl; soft, downy, green leaves; fragrant flowers; trumpet-shaped blooms turn yellow with age; drought tolerant; invasive.
Good drainage	Medium water	Medium feeder	One of the hardiest honeysuckles; tall and spreading growth; white flowers age to yellow; red fruit follows.
Good drainage	Medium water	Medium feeder	Bluish green, dense foliage; upright, arching form; fragrant flowers; showy red berries; can become leggy; prune after flowering; renew overgrown plants by pruning to the ground.
Good drainage	Medium water	Medium feeder	Low-growing, trailing, flat branches; clusters of soft, needlelike, silvery green leaves; vinelike gray-brown branches; profuse blooms shaped like parrot's beak; good bank cover; give moderate to light waterings.

NAME	HABIT		FLOWERS		ADAPTATION	
	Type	Height	Color	Time	Zones	Light
Lupinus, **Russell hybrids** Russell lupines	Hardy perennial	4 to 5 ft	Red, orange, yellow, blue, pink, purple, white	Early summer	3 to 9	Full sun to light shade
Lychnis chalcedonica Maltese-cross	Hardy perennial	2 to 3 ft	Red	Summer	3 to 10	Full sun
Lycoris africana Yellow spider	Half-hardy bulb	to 1½ ft	Yellow	Late summer	7 to 10	Full sun to light shade
Lysimachia nummularia Moneywort	Hardy perennial	1 to 2 ft	Yellow	Summer	3 to 10	Light shade to deep shade
Lythrum salicaria Purple loosestrife	Hardy perennial	3 to 5 ft	Pink, purple	Summer to early fall	3 to 10	Full sun to light shade
Maclura pomifera Osage orange	Deciduous tree	to 60 ft			4 to 10	Full sun
Magnolia acuminata Cucumber tree	Deciduous tree	50 to 80 ft	Yellow	Late spring to summer	4 to 8	Full sun
Magnolia grandiflora Southern magnolia	Evergreen tree	60 to 75 ft	White	Early summer to fall	6 to 9	Full sun
Magnolia quinquepeta Lily magnolia	Deciduous shrub	8 to 12 ft	Purple	Spring	6 to 8	Full sun to light shade
Magnolia × soulangiana Saucer magnolia	Deciduous shrub or small tree	15 to 25 ft	Pink, purple, white	Spring	5 to 9	Full sun to light shade
Magnolia stellata Star magnolia	Deciduous shrub or small tree	10 to 20 ft	White	Winter to early spring	4 to 9	Full sun to light shade
Magnolia virginiana Sweet bay magnolia	Semievergreen shrub or small tree	10 to 20 ft	White	Early summer to early fall	5 to 9	Full sun to light shade
Mahonia aquifolium Oregon grape	Evergreen shrub	3 to 9 ft	Yellow	Spring	5 to 9	Light shade
Mahonia bealei Leatherleaf mahonia	Evergreen shrub	10 to 12 ft	Yellow	Spring	6 to 10	Light shade
Mahonia repens Creeping mahonia	Evergreen ground cover	1 to 2 ft	Yellow	Spring	6 to 10	Full sun to light shade

	CULTURE		
Soil	**Water**	**Feeding**	**Special Characteristics**
Good drainage	Medium water	Light feeder	Adapted only to cool-summer, humid climates; mulch to keep roots cool; often short-lived.
Good drainage	Medium water	Light feeder	Can become invasive; generally short-lived.
Good drainage	Medium water	Medium feeder	Good in containers—best when crowded; leaves appear in spring and die back in summer before flowers bloom.
Rich soil; organic matter	Wet; don't let dry out	Medium feeder	Well adapted to boggy conditions; can be invasive.
Rich soil	Medium water	Light feeder	Reseeds heavily in wet areas; long-lived.
Not particular	Let dry out between waterings	Light feeder	Fast-growing, thorny tree; usually 20 to 40 ft high under cultivation; open, spreading habit; medium green leaves; inedible, bumpy, yellow-green fruit on female plants if male plant also present; tolerates heat, cold, wind, drought, poor soil; can be used as a hedge or a tree; needs water until established.
Good drainage; rich soil; organic matter	Medium water	Heavy feeder	Fast growing; glossy green leaves; dense shade; needs room; cold hardy; intolerant of hot, dry winds.
Good drainage; organic matter; rich soil	Medium water	Heavy feeder	Moderate growing; lustrous, heavy-textured leaves; large, fragrant flowers; appreciates heat; avoid foot traffic around base; street, lawn, or wall tree; also good for large container or espalier; 'St. Mary's' stays smaller.
Good drainage; rich soil	Medium water	Heavy feeder	Slow growing; showy, fragrant flowers purple on the outside, white inside; plant in protected location; specimen, in groups, or in shrub border.
Good drainage; rich soil; organic matter	Medium water	Heavy feeder	Moderate growing; showy fragrant flowers; rather coarse, green foliage; lawn, garden specimen, or corner.
Good drainage; rich soil; organic matter	Medium water	Heavy feeder	Moderate growing; fragrant, straplike petals; flowers can be damaged by frost; good specimen tree.
Good drainage; rich soil; organic matter	Medium water	Heavy feeder	Evergreen in the South, deciduous in colder areas; extremely fragrant flowers; leaves glossy above, whitish beneath; similar to *M. grandiflora*, except smaller.
Organic matter; acid soil	Wet; don't let dry out	Medium feeder	Open, loose form; irregular, spreading habit; spiny, hollylike leaves, showy flowers; protect from hot sun and winds; best in shrub border; prune after flowering to maintain 3 ft height.
Rich soil	Wet; don't let dry out	Heavy feeder	Vertical form; good structural interest; showy flowers; blue, grapelike fruit; will not tolerate drought, hot sun, or wind; difficult to prune.
Rich soil	Medium water	Medium feeder	Bluish green, spiny, hollylike leaves; flowers in clusters; dark purple, grapelike berries in the fall; spreads rapidly by underground stems; best in light shade.

NAME	HABIT		FLOWERS		ADAPTATION	
	Type	Height	Color	Time	Zones	Light
Malus species Crab apple	Deciduous tree	10 to 25 ft	Pink, red, white	Spring	3 to 10	Full sun
Malus baccata Siberian crab apple	Deciduous tree	15 to 30 ft	White	Spring	2 to 8	Full sun
Malus floribunda Japanese flowering crab apple	Deciduous tree	15 to 25 ft	White	Spring	4 to 8	Full sun
Malus sargentii Sargent crab apple	Deciduous tree	to 8 ft	White	Late spring	4 to 8	Full sun
Mandarin orange *Citrus reticulata*	Evergreen fruit tree	6 to 20 ft	White	Spring	9, 10	Full sun to half-day sun
Maranta leuconeura Prayer plant	Houseplant	to 8 in.			10 or indoors	Light shade
Matthiola incana Stock	Hardy biennial	12 to 30 in.	White, pink, lavender, red, purple	Spring to early fall		Full sun to half-day sun
Maytenus boaria Mayten tree	Evergreen tree	30 to 40 ft			8 to 10	Full sun to light shade
Melia azedarach Chinaberry	Deciduous tree	30 to 40 ft	Lavender	Early summer	7 to 10	Full sun
Mentha requienii Corsican mint	Evergreen ground cover	1 to 3 in.	Lavender	Summer	7 to 10	Full sun to light shade
Mertensia virginica Virginia bluebells	Hardy perennial	12 to 24 in.	Blue	Spring	3 to 8	Deep shade
Metasequoia glyptostroboides Dawn redwood	Needled deciduous tree	80 to 100 ft			5 to 9	Full sun to light shade
Mimulus × hybridus 'Grandiflorus' Monkeyflower	Half-hardy annual	6 to 8 in.	Yellow, red, bicolored	Early summer to early fall		Light shade

	CULTURE		
Soil	**Water**	**Feeding**	**Special Characteristics**
Good drainage; organic matter	Medium water	Medium feeder	Very decorative fruit tree; many cultivars available with variations in flower, fruit, and foliage size and color; much variation in zone tolerance; leaf color varies from green to bronze or red, some variegated; edible fruit used in jellies; self-fertile; produces abundant fruit on long-lived spurs; can be grafted; subject to same diseases as apples; scab often a problem; choose resistant varieties.
Good drainage	Medium water	Medium feeder	Vase shaped; fragrant flowers; requires winter chilling; lawn, along fences, driveway, walk; prune only to establish framework.
Good drainage	Medium water	Medium feeder	Arching spread; red buds turn pinkish white when open; reddish yellow fruit; profuse bloomer; requires winter chill; prune only to establish framework; lawn, driveway, fence, walkway.
Good drainage	Medium water	Medium feeder	Slow growing; dwarf, spreading; very disease resistant; fragrant flowers, red in bud; masses of dark red fruit; needs winter chill.
Good drainage; organic matter	Medium water	Medium feeder	Needs high heat or fruit will be sour; small, loose-skinned fruit sometimes called tangerine or satsuma; prune only to remove dead, diseased, or sucker growth; plant high; protect from frosts; several cultivars available.
Organic matter	Medium water	Medium feeder	Green leaves marked with bronze; in daytime foliage lies flat, at night it turns upward; give warm, humid environment; give bright, indirect light.
Good drainage; organic matter	Medium water	Heavy feeder	Pleasant fragrance; grows best in cool, moist weather; often grown as an annual; does not flower well in dry heat; will bloom through winter in mild climates.
Good drainage	Medium water	Medium feeder	Slow growing; graceful, weeping habit; tolerates heat, salinity, seaside conditions; lawn, patio, raised bed, driveway; remove any unwanted side growth.
Not particular	Let dry out between waterings	Light feeder	Fast growing; spreading, umbrellalike crown; poisonous yellow berries; tolerates hot, dry climates; grows where most trees won't.
Good drainage; rich soil	Medium water	Medium feeder	Low-growing, vigorous spreader; forms soft, green carpet; fragrant foliage; self-sows; may die down in freezing temperatures, but will reappear in the spring; good ground cover for small spaces, between stepping-stones.
Organic matter	Medium water	Medium feeder	Noninvasive; dies down in summer; prefers cool, moist soil; does best in cool-summer climates.
Good drainage; organic matter	Medium water	Medium feeder	Fast growing; light green foliage; horizontal, pendulous branches; small cones; needles turn orange-brown to rust in fall; bark reddish brown; avoid hot, dry winds or salt winds; keep moist; protect from hot sunlight in enclosed areas; best in groves; young tree grows well in a container.
Good drainage; organic matter	Wet; don't let dry out	Heavy feeder	Long bloom season; will adjust to boggy situations or occasional flooding.

| NAME | HABIT | | FLOWERS | | ADAPTATION | |
	Type	Height	Color	Time	Zones	Light
Mirabilis jalapa Four-o'clock, beauty-of-the-night, marvel-of-Peru	Tender perennial	1½ to 3 ft	White, yellow, red, pink, bicolored	Early summer to early fall	8 to 10	Full sun to light shade
Moluccella laevis Bells-of-Ireland	Hardy annual	2 to 3 ft	Green	Early summer to first frost		Full sun to light shade
Monarda didyma Bergamot, beebalm, Oswego tea	Hardy perennial herb	to 3 ft	Red	Summer	4 to 10	Full sun to light shade
Monstera deliciosa Monstera, split-leaf philodendron	Houseplant	to 6 ft			10 or indoors	Light shade
Moraea iridoides (*Dietes vegeta*) Butterfly-iris, fortnight-lily	Half-hardy evergreen bulb	to 4 ft	White	Late spring	8 to 10	Full sun
Morus alba White mulberry, fruitless mulberry	Deciduous tree	30 to 50 ft			4 to 10	Full sun
Muscari botryoides Common grape hyacinth, Italian grape hyacinth	Hardy bulb	6 to 12 in.	Blue	Spring to late spring	3 to 10	Full sun to light shade
Muskmelon *Cucumis melo*	Tender annual vegetable	6 to 12 ft				Full sun
Mustard, Indian-mustard, mustard greens *Brassica juncea*	Hardy annual vegetable	to 1½ ft				Full sun to light shade
Myosotis sylvatica Forget-me-not	Half-hardy biennial	6 to 12 in.	Blue, pink, white	Early spring to summer		Light shade
Myrica pensylvanica Northern bayberry	Deciduous shrub	5 to 12 ft			2 to 7	Full sun to light shade
Myrtus communis Myrtle	Evergreen shrub	5 to 15 ft	White	Summer	9, 10	Full sun to light shade
Nandina domestica Heavenly-bamboo	Evergreen shrub	6 to 8 ft	White	Early summer	7 to 10	Full sun to light shade

	CULTURE		
Soil	**Water**	**Feeding**	**Special Characteristics**
Good drainage	Wet; don't let dry out	Heavy feeder	Fragrant; blooms afternoons and evenings; tolerates humidity, drought, heat, and air pollution; treated as an annual in colder climates; roots may be dug up in fall and stored in winter for spring replanting.
Good drainage	Medium water	Heavy feeder	Needs staking; good for dried arrangements; appreciates long, mild summers.
Organic matter	Wet; don't let dry out	Medium feeder	Herb with oval, pointed leaves; aromatic foliage; flowers attract hummingbirds; prefers slightly acid soil; prune in the fall.
Good drainage	Let dry out between waterings	Medium feeder	Large, perforated and deeply cut leaves; climbing, vining habit; aerial roots; give bright, indirect light; tolerates shade; can cut top of plant back to limit growth.
Good drainage	Let dry out between waterings	Medium feeder	White flowers spotted with brownish yellow and purplish blue; can be planted outdoors in warm, practically frost-free areas.
Not particular	Medium water	Medium feeder	Bright green, irregularly lobed leaves; available as either a fruiting or fruitless tree; fruiting types produce white, pinkish or blackish purple fruits; can be very messy; fruitless better as ornamental; fast growing in hot climates; tolerates some drought; tolerates alkaline soils; good shade tree.
Good drainage	Medium water	Medium feeder	Fragrant flowers; good in containers; cultivar 'Album' has white flowers.
Good drainage; organic matter	Medium water	Medium feeder	Warm-season vegetable; requires ample space; requires plenty of water during vine stage but less during fruit ripening period; in short-season or cool-summer climates, grow extra-early varieties or start seeds indoors 3 to 4 weeks before outdoor planting; many cultivars available with variation in size, shape, flavor, and maturation dates.
Rich soil	Medium water	Heavy feeder	Cool-weather, short-day crop; bolts to seed very early; plant as soon as soil can be worked.
Rich soil; good drainage	Wet; don't let dry out	Heavy feeder	Best in regions with long, cool spring; often grown as an annual; performs well in wet soil; self-sows freely; tolerates full sun in cool regions.
Sandy soil; tolerates clay soil	Medium water	Light feeder	Dense form; clean, lustrous green foliage; grayish white, waxy berries on female plants; all plant parts aromatic; tolerates seacoast conditions, infertile and dry soils; good for large-scale massing; prune old, leggy plants to ground level.
Good drainage	Medium water	Medium feeder	Glossy, bright green foliage; round, bushy shrub; fragrant foliage; black berries; unpruned, can reach 15 ft tall; informal hedge, screen, mass, sheared as formal hedge; tolerates heat and drought.
Not particular	Medium water	Medium feeder	Vertical form; delicate, wispy foliage; bright red berries; good fall color; protect from hot sun; tolerates drought once established; semideciduous in colder climates; prune out old, leggy canes.

NAME	HABIT		FLOWERS		ADAPTATION	
	Type	Height	Color	Time	Zones	Light
Narcissus **hybrids** Daffodils	Half-hardy to hardy bulbs	4 to 18 in.	Yellow, orange, white, bicolored	Early spring to late summer	4 to 10	Full sun to partial shade
Narcissus bulbocodium Petticoat daffodil	Half-hardy bulb	6 to 15 in.	Yellow	Early spring	7 to 10	Full sun to light shade
Narcissus jonquilla Jonquil	Hardy bulb	12 to 18 in.	White, yellow	Spring	5 to 10	Full sun to light shade
Narcissus tazetta Polyanthus narcissus	Half-hardy bulb	12 to 18 in.	White, yellow	Spring	8 to 10	Full sun to light shade
Nectarine *Prunus persica* var. *nucipersica*	Deciduous fruit tree	10 to 20 ft	Pink	Spring	5 to 9	Full sun
Nemophila menziesii Baby-blue-eyes	Half-hardy annual	6 to 12 in.	Blue	Early summer to first frost		Full sun to light shade
Nephrolepis exaltata Sword fern, Boston fern	Houseplant	2 to 4 ft			10 or indoors	Light shade
Nerium oleander Oleander	Evergreen shrub	8 to 12 ft	Pink, red, white, yellow	Late spring to fall	8 to 10	Full sun
Nicotiana alata Flowering tobacco, nicotiana	Tender perennial	12 to 36 in.	White, red, pink, green, yellow	Early summer to first frost		Full sun to light shade
Nierembergia hippomanica Cupflower	Tender perennial	6 to 12 in.	Purple, blue-violet	Early summer to early fall	9, 10	Full sun to light shade
Nigella damascena Love-in-a-mist	Hardy annual	12 to 30 in.	Blue, pink, white	Early summer to early fall		Full sun
Nyssa sylvatica Black tupelo, blackgum, sourgum, pepperidge	Deciduous tree	30 to 50 ft			4 to 9	Full sun
Okra, gumbo *Abelmoschus esculentus*	Tender annual vegetable	3 to 7 ft	Yellow	Summer		Full sun
Olea europaea Olive	Evergreen tree	20 to 30 ft			9, 10	Full sun
Onion *Allium cepa*	Hardy biennial vegetable	to 4 ft				Full sun

| | CULTURE | | |
Soil	Water	Feeding	Special Characteristics
Good drainage	Medium water	Medium feeder	Colorful flowers; available in hundreds of varieties; good for naturalizing; allow foliage to yellow before cutting back.
Good drainage	Medium water	Medium feeder	Small flowers; good in containers; allow foliage to yellow before cutting back.
Good drainage	Medium water	Medium feeder	Flowers fragrant; good in containers; allow foliage to yellow before cutting back.
Good drainage	Medium water	Medium feeder	Fragrant flowers; often used for indoor forcing; good in containers; allow foliage to yellow before cutting back.
Good drainage; organic matter	Medium water	Medium to heavy feeder	Nectarines differ from peaches only in having a smooth skin and a slightly different flavor; require same care as peaches but more susceptible to brown rot; many early, midseason, and late varieties available.
Sandy soil; good drainage	Medium water	Light feeder	Self-sows freely; easy to grow; water freely if grown in full sun.
Good drainage	Medium water	Medium feeder	Long, swordlike fronds; give bright light, no direct sun; provide some humidity, keep moist, common cultivars include 'Bostoniensis' (Boston fern), 'Fluffy Ruffles', and 'Whitemanii'.
Not particular	Let dry out between waterings	Light feeder	Broad, rounded, bulky form; coarse foliage; attractive flowers; tolerates heat, drought, salt; all parts poisonous; excellent in desert gardens.
Good drainage; organic matter	Wet; don't let dry out	Heavy feeder	Flowers open late in the day, release fragrance in the evening; daylight varieties available; flowers fade in full sun in dry climates; usually grown as an annual.
Good drainage; organic matter; sandy soil	Medium water	Medium feeder	Provide shade in areas with hot summers; usually grown as an annual.
Good drainage; sandy soil	Let dry out between waterings	Heavy feeder	Attractive seedpods; short flowering period; may need staking; make successive plantings.
Not particular	Medium water	Medium feeder	Moderate growing; dense, glossy, dark green foliage; outstanding fall color (coppery red); dramatic winter silhouette; tolerates poor drainage, any soil, occasional drought.
Good drainage; organic matter	Medium water	Medium feeder	Warm-season vegetable grown for edible pods; several cultivars available; dwarfs grow to 3 ft, tall growers to 7 ft.
Good drainage	Let dry out between waterings	Medium feeder	Fast growing when young, slows down with age; gray-green, willowlike leaves; attractive, gnarled trunk; edible fruit; easy to transplant any age; tolerates shallow, alkaline, stony soil, little fertilizer; thrives in areas with hot, dry summers; withstands heavy pruning; 'Swan Hill' is fruitless.
Good drainage	Medium water	Heavy feeder	Culinary plant with bulbous root; long, green leaves; treated as biennial or long-season annual.

NAME	HABIT		FLOWERS		ADAPTATION	
	Type	Height	Color	Time	Zones	Light
Ophiopogon jaburan Jaburan lilyturf, white lilyturf	Evergreen ground cover	to 2 ft	White	Summer to early fall	7 to 10	Full sun to light shade
Ophiopogon japonicus Mondo grass	Evergreen ground cover	8 to 12 in.	Purple	Summer	7 to 10	Full sun to light shade
Orange *Citrus sinensis*	Evergreen fruit tree	10 to 30 ft	White	Spring	9, 10	Full sun to half-day sun
Oregano *Origanum vulgare*	Hardy perennial herb	to 2½ ft			5 to 10	Full sun
Ornithogalum arabicum Arabian star-of-Bethlehem	Half-hardy bulb	to 24 in.	White	Late spring to early summer	8 to 10	Full sun
Ornithogalum umbellatum Star-of-Bethlehem	Hardy bulb	to 12 in.	White	Spring to early summer	5 to 10	Full sun
Osmanthus americanus Devilwood osmanthus, American olive	Evergreen shrub or small tree	to 45 ft	White	Early spring	7 to 9	Full sun
Osmanthus fragrans Sweet olive	Evergreen shrub or small tree	10 to 30 ft	White	Early spring to late fall	8 to 10	Light shade
Osmanthus heterophyllus Holly olive	Evergreen shrub	6 to 20 ft	White	Fall	7 to 9	Light shade
Osteospermum fruiticosum African daisy or trailing African daisy	Evergreen ground cover	6 to 12 in.	White and purple	Inter-mittently all year	8 to 10	Full sun
Ostrya virginiana American hophornbeam	Deciduous tree	30 to 35 ft			4 to 9	Full sun
Oxalis bowiei Bowie oxalis	Half-hardy bulb, houseplant	6 to 12 in.	Pink, purple	Summer	8 to 10 or indoors	Full sun to light shade
Oxydendrum arboreum Sourwood	Deciduous tree	30 to 40 ft	White	Summer	6 to 9	Full sun
Pachysandra terminalis Japanese spurge	Evergreen ground cover	6 to 8 in.	White	Late spring	4 to 10	Light shade to deep shade
Paeonia hybrids Herbaceous peony	Hardy perennial	2 to 4 ft	Pink, red, white, yellow	Late spring to early summer	5 to 8	Full sun to light shade

| Soil | CULTURE | | |
	Water	Feeding	Special Characteristics
Good drainage	Medium water	Light feeder	Dense clumps of coarse, dark green leaves; green stems; give sun on coast, shade elsewhere; cultivar 'Variegatus' is low growing with white, striated flowers.
Good drainage	Medium water	Light feeder	Dense clumps of coarse, dark green leaves; coarse foliage; small flowers; pea-sized blue fruit; spreads by means of fleshy, subsurface stems; slow growing until established; give sun in coastal areas, shade elsewhere.
Good drainage; organic matter	Medium water	Medium feeder	Very attractive tree; fragrant blooms; prune only to remove dead, diseased, or sucker growth; plant high; some of the most popular varieties are 'Valencia', a juice orange, and 'Washington', a navel orange.
Good drainage	Medium water	Medium feeder	Culinary herb with oval leaves, dark green in color; shrubby growth; pale pinkish white blossoms; aromatic foliage; good container plant.
Good drainage	Medium water	Medium feeder	Fragrant flowers; good in containers.
Good drainage	Medium water	Medium feeder	Blooms close at night; good in containers.
Good drainage	Medium water	Medium feeder	Fragrant flowers, olivelike fruit in the fall; slow to moderate growth; leaves are glossy green above, yellowish below; best planted in garden where watered and fertilized regularly.
Tolerates clay soil	Medium water	Light feeder	Compact, neat form; glossy foliage; fragrant flowers heaviest in spring and summer; very adaptable and easy to grow; prune any time of year; can be trained as a tree or espalier.
Tolerates clay soil	Medium water	Light feeder	Lustrous, spiny, dark green leaves; fragrant flowers; very shade tolerant; good hedge; dwarf cultivars available.
Good drainage	Medium water	Medium feeder	Rapidly spreading; good cover for banks and sunny areas; drought tolerant once established; showy flowers with deep purple center, rays fading to white.
Not particular	Medium water	Medium feeder	Slow growing; small, graceful tree; attractive bark; medium green foliage turns yellow in fall; tolerates wide range of soil; somewhat difficult to transplant.
Good drainage	Medium water	Medium feeder	Cloverlike foliage.
Rich, acid soil	Medium water	Medium feeder	Slow growing; pyramid form; light, feathery appearance; young leaves unfold bronze, turn green; brilliant scarlet fall color; large sprays of fragrant flowers; needs acid soil, no competition; good terrace or patio tree.
Rich, acid soil	Wet; don't let dry out	Medium feeder	Veined, dark green, oval leaves toothed near the ends; spreads rapidly by underground runners; forms a dense cover of uniform height; the cultivar 'Green Carpet' is darker green and has more flowers.
Rich soil; good drainage; organic matter	Medium water	Medium feeder	Long-lived; huge, often fragrant flowers; requires winter-chilling period to bloom well; needs good air circulation around plants; never allow fresh manure or fast-acting nitrogen to come in direct contact with roots.

NAME	HABIT		FLOWERS		ADAPTATION	
	Type	Height	Color	Time	Zones	Light
Paeonia suffruticosa Tree peony	Deciduous shrub	4 to 6 ft	Red, purple, violet, orange, yellow	Late spring to early summer	5 to 7	Full sun to light shade
Papaver nudicaule Iceland poppy	Tender perennial	2 to 3 ft	Red, purple, white, pink, orange	Spring to summer	1 to 8	Full sun
Papaver orientale Oriental poppy	Hardy perennial	2 to 4 ft	Orange, pink, red, white	Early summer	2 to 9	Full sun to light shade
Papaver rhoeas Shirley poppy, field poppy	Hardy annual	1 to 2 ft	Red, purple, white, pink, orange	Spring to summer		Full sun
Parsley *Petroselinum crispum*	Tender biennial herb	10 to 15 in.			3 to 10	Full sun to light shade
Parsnip *Pastinaca sativa*	Half-hardy biennial vegetable	1½ ft				Full sun to light shade
Parthenocissus quinquefolia Virginia creeper, woodbine	Deciduous vine, ground cover	Climbs to 50 ft			4 to 10	Full sun to light shade
Paspalum notatum Bahia grass	Turfgrass	1½ to 3 in.			8 to 10	Full sun to light shade
Paulownia tomentosa Empress tree, royal paulownia	Deciduous tree	40 to 60 ft	Violet	Spring	5 to 9	Full sun
Paxistima myrsinites Oregon boxwood	Evergreen ground cover	2 to 4 ft			6 to 10	Full sun
Pea, garden pea, English pea *Pisum sativum*	Half-hardy annual vegetable	Climbs to 6 ft				Full sun to half-day sun
Peach *Prunus persica*	Deciduous fruit tree	10 to 20 ft	Pink	Spring	5 to 9	Full sun
Peach and nectarine, genetic dwarf *Prunus persica*	Dwarf fruit trees	to 5 ft	Pink	Spring	6 to 9	Full sun

	CULTURE		
Soil	**Water**	**Feeding**	**Special Characteristics**
Rich soil; organic matter	Wet; don't let dry out	Heavy feeder	Open, leggy form; attractive, large flowers; blossoms short-lived; leaves are deeply lobed.
Sandy soil; good drainage; organic matter	Medium water	Heavy feeder	Short-lived perennial often grown as an annual; in mild climates, blooms in winter and early spring from plants set out in fall.
Good drainage	Medium water	Light feeder	Foliage dies down in summer; best in regions of cool summers; short-lived in warm climates; mulch in summer to keep roots cool; brief flowering period.
Sandy soil; good drainage; organic matter	Medium water	Heavy feeder	Short bloom season; prefers cool-summer climates.
Rich soil	Wet; don't let dry out	Medium feeder	Tender herb, usually grown as annual; dark green, deeply curled leaves; slow to start; protect from frost; all parts edible.
Good drainage; organic matter	Medium water	Medium feeder	Grown as an annual; needs loose soil; requires 100 to 120 days from seed; roots can be left in ground all winter to develop sweet, nutlike flavor, or dig up in the late fall and store in moist sand.
Rich soil	Wet; don't let dry out	Heavy feeder	Rambling vine; fast growing; leaves divided into heavily veined leaflets; blue fruit; foliage turns red in fall; covers large area quickly and densely; controls erosion on slopes.
Good drainage; organic matter	Medium water	Medium feeder	Fast growing; needs frequent mowing; forms coarse, open lawn; drought tolerant; extensive root system valued for erosion control; tolerates infertile, sandy soils; wears well.
Rich soil; good drainage	Medium water	Medium feeder	Fast growing; dense foliage; wide, rounded head; vanilla-scented flowers; tolerates city pollution; needs mild climate to flower well; give plenty of space.
Good drainage; acid soil	Medium water	Medium feeder	Low maintenance; tolerates some shade; branches root as they spread.
Good drainage; organic matter	Medium water	Medium feeder	Cool-season crop; grown in early spring to midsummer in cooler areas and in fall, winter, and very early spring where warmer; available as low growers or climbing vines.
Good drainage; organic matter	Medium water	Medium to heavy feeder	Cannot tolerate extreme winter cold or late frost; best if pruned heavily each year to maintain size and encourage new growth along branches; thin fruit to 6 in. apart when they are thumbnail size; most varieties self-fertile; requires winter chill—pick varieties to suit climate; peach leaf curl can be a problem; many early, midseason, and late varieties.
Good drainage; organic matter	Medium water	Medium to heavy feeder	Form dense bushes with long leaves; showy, usually semidouble flowers; not winter hardy; normal-sized fruit; can be grown in containers; require minimal pruning, although fruit must be thinned; fruit not as good as standard varieties; more susceptible to mites; most require winter chill.

NAME	HABIT		FLOWERS		ADAPTATION	
	Type	Height	Color	Time	Zones	Light
Peanut *Arachis hypogaea*	Tender annual vegetable	12 to 18 in.				Full sun to half-day sun
Pear *Pyrus communis*	Deciduous fruit tree	15 to 25 ft	White	Early spring	5 to 9	Full sun
Pecan *Carya illinoinensis*	Deciduous nut tree	to 75 ft			6 to 9	Full sun
***Pelargonium* species** Scented geraniums	Tender perennial	2 to 4 ft	Pink, white	Summer	9, 10	Full sun
Pelargonium domesticum Pelargonium, Martha Washington geranium	Tender perennial	to 3 ft	White, pink, red, lavender, purple	Spring and summer	9, 10	Full to light shade
Pelargonium × hortorum Geranium	Tender perennial	12 to 24 in.	Red, pink, orange, white	Late spring to first frost	9, 10	Full sun
Pelargonium peltatum Ivy geranium	Tender evergreen perennial, ground cover	1 to 3 ft (trailing)	White, pink, rose, red, lavender	Late winter to early fall	9, 10	Full sun
Pellaea rotundifolia Button fern	Tender perennial, houseplant	12 to 18 in.			10 or indoors	Light shade
Pennisetum alopecuroides Fountain grass	Hardy perennial	2 to 3½ ft	Tan	Late summer to fall	6 to 10	Full sun
***Peperomia* species** Peperomia	Tender perennial, houseplant	4 to 6 in.	White		10 or indoors	Light shade
Pepper *Capsicum* species	Tender perennial vegetable	2 to 4 ft			10	Full sun
Peppergrass, garden cress *Lepidium sativium*	Hardy annual vegetable	to 2 ft				Full sun to half-day sun
Peppermint *Mentha × piperita*	Hardy perennial herb	1 to 2 ft	Purple	Summer to early fall	4 to 10	Full sun to light shade
Persimmon, American *Diospyros virginiana*	Deciduous fruit tree	30 to 50 ft			5 to 9	Full sun
Persimmon, oriental *Diospyros kaki*	Deciduous fruit tree	20 to 30 ft			7 to 10	Full sun

| | CULTURE | | |
Soil	Water	Feeding	Special Characteristics
Good drainage; sandy soil	Medium water	Medium feeder	Legume grown for underground pods; requires long, warm growing season; 110 to 120 days; needs generous supply of lime in top 3 to 4 in. of soil where pods form; give adequate water up until 2 weeks before harvest, then cut back; Virginia peanuts—2 seeds per pod, Spanish peanuts—2 to 6 seeds per pod.
Good drainage; organic matter	Medium water	Medium feeder	Long-lived, pyramidal tree with strongly vertical branching habit; requires little pruning; tolerates damp, heavy soils better than most other fruit trees; bears fruit on long-lived spurs; requires pollinator; dwarf varieties available; easy to train, espalier; fire blight can be a problem; many varieties.
Good drainage	Medium water	Medium feeder	Moderate growing; food tree; needs deep soil; susceptible to scab.
Good drainage; sandy soil	Let dry out between waterings	Medium feeder	Shrubby form; wide variety of fragrances; foliage varies from small, delicate leaves to large, rounded leaves; cultivars with variegated foliage.
Good drainage	Medium water	Light feeder	Large showy flowers with brilliant blotches and markings of darker colors; in warm weather, water deeply once a week; susceptible to aphids and whiteflies.
Acid soil; good drainage	Let dry out between waterings	Medium feeder	Long blooming season; attractive foliage; newer hybrids are more heat tolerant; often grown as an annual.
Good drainage	Medium water	Light feeder	Trailing plant with 2 upper petals blotched or striped; many varieties with profuse blooming.
Good drainage	Medium water	Medium feeder	Round, leathery leaflets; give filtered light.
Rich soil	Let dry out between waterings	Medium feeder	Yellow foliage in fall; tolerates drought; dormant in winter.
Good drainage	Let dry out between waterings	Medium feeder	Slow growing; *P. argyreia* (watermelon peperomia) and *P. caperata* (emerald-ripple) are commonly grown species; wide variety of leaf shapes, textures, and colors.
Good drainage; organic matter	Wet; don't let dry out	Medium feeder	Grown as an annual in colder zones; prefers hot-weather climates to set fruit properly; grow from seed or transplants; protect from any late frost; main groups are sweet peppers and hot peppers.
Good drainage; organic matter	Medium water	Medium feeder	Cool-season plant; fast growing; similar in appearance to parsley; best grown in short days of early spring or fall; seeds need light to germinate.
Rich soil	Wet; don't let dry out	Medium feeder	Fast-growing culinary and medicinal herb; aromatic leaves; can become invasive.
Good drainage	Medium water	Medium feeder	Moderate growing; fruits ripen after frost; more widely adapted than *D. kaki*; tolerates wide range of soils and climates.
Good drainage; rich soil	Medium water	Medium feeder	Large, glossy foliage with good fall color; heavy crop of orange-red fruit in the fall, hangs on until winter; good fruit tree for ornamental use; prune only to remove dead wood or shape tree; will set fruit without pollination; several varieties available.

NAME	HABIT		FLOWERS		ADAPTATION	
	Type	Height	Color	Time	Zones	Light
Petunia × hybrida Petunia	Tender perennial	10 to 18 in.	Violet, pink, red, purple, yellow, white, bicolored	Late spring to first frost	9, 10	Full sun
Phellodendron amurense Amur corktree	Deciduous tree	30 to 50 ft			4 to 8	Light shade
Philadelphus coronarius Mock orange	Deciduous shrub	10 to 12 ft	White	Late spring	5 to 8	Full sun to light shade
Philodendron bipinnatifidum Twice-cut philodendron, fiddleleaf philodendron	Houseplant	6 to 8 ft			10 or indoors	Light shade
Philodendron scandens Heartleaf philodendron	Houseplant	2 to 5 ft			10 or indoors	Light shade
Phlox drummondii Annual phlox	Half-hardy annual	6 to 20 in.	White, pink, red, bicolored	Late spring to first frost		Full sun
Phlox paniculata Summer phlox, garden phlox	Hardy perennial	2 to 4 ft	Red, pink, purple, lavender, white	Summer to early fall	4 to 10	Full sun to half-day sun
Phlox subulata Moss pink	Hardy evergreen perennial, ground cover	to 6 in.	Lavender, pink, red, white	Spring	3 to 10	Full sun
Phoenix roebelenii Pygmy date palm	Evergreen shrub, houseplant	to 4 ft			9, 10 or indoors	Light shade
Photinia × fraseri Fraser photinia	Evergreen shrub	10 to 15 ft	White	Spring	7 to 10	Full sun
Photinia serrulata Chinese photinia	Evergreen shrub or small tree	20 to 30 ft	White	Spring	7 to 10	Full sun
Phyla nodiflora Lippia	Evergreen ground cover	2 to 6 in.	Lavender	Spring to summer	9, 10	Full sun to light shade
Picea abies Norway spruce	Needled evergreen tree	to 100 ft			3 to 8	Full sun
Picea glauca White spruce	Needled deciduous tree	40 to 60 ft			2 to 6	Full sun

Soil	CULTURE		
	Water	Feeding	Special Characteristics
Good drainage; sandy soil	Medium water	Heavy feeder	Pinch young plants to promote blooming; dependable and versatile; young seedlings can withstand hot sun; grown as an annual in all but the mildest climates.
Rich soil; good drainage	Medium water	Heavy feeder	Moderate growing; large, glossy, dark green leaves; attractive, corky bark, gray-black in color; shallow roots—avoid streets or lawns; good shade tree; black fruit; flowers inconspicuous; tolerates drought once established.
Not particular	Medium water	Medium feeder	Coarse, leggy, irregular form; very fragrant flowers; easy to grow; prune annually right after flowering.
Good drainage	Medium water	Medium feeder	Deeply cut, star-shaped, large leaves.
Good drainage	Medium water	Light feeder	Vigorous climbing habit; long, glossy, deep green leaves; give bright, indirect light; a subspecies, *P. scandens oxycardium,* is the commonly grown florist's philodendron.
Good drainage; sandy soil; organic matter	Medium water	Heavy feeder	Tolerates heat, but flowers will decline; avoid watering late in the day.
Rich soil; good drainage; organic matter	Wet; don't let dry out	Heavy feeder	Requires staking; provides massive color display; many cultivars available.
Sandy soil	Medium water	Medium feeder	Mat forming; profuse bloomer.
Good drainage; organic matter	Medium water	Medium feeder	Delicate, dwarf form; straight, symmetrical shape; branching, narrow-leaf fronds with pendulous habit; give bright, indirect light; water heavily and feed monthly during growing season, reduce during winter; protect from dry air.
Good drainage; organic matter	Medium water	Medium feeder	Moderate growing; rounded form; bronzy red new growth in spring; red berries easy to restrain; can prune as screen, hedge, espalier, or train as single-stemmed small tree; susceptible to fire blight.
Good drainage	Medium water	Medium feeder	Large, coarsely textured leaves; profuse flowers; red berries; can prune as a screen.
Good drainage	Medium water	Medium feeder	Green foliage forms dense mat; spreads by surface runners; good lawn substitute; flowers tiny, spotted with yellow; best in sun; mow flowers off for use as a lawn; drought and heat tolerant; in full sun, growth is more compact.
Not particular	Medium water	Medium feeder	Fast growing; pyramidal form; branchlets become pendulous as tree ages; prefers cool, moist area; avoid low fertility; prune to shape only; good windbreak, tall screen, specimen; attractive cones; hot weather weakens tree.
Not particular	Medium water	Medium feeder	Moderate growing; conical shape with drooping branchlets; blue-green foliage; best in cold climates.

NAME	HABIT		FLOWERS		ADAPTATION	
	Type	Height	Color	Time	Zones	Light
Picea glauca 'Conica' Dwarf Alberta spruce	Needled evergreen shrub	6 to 8 ft			2 to 6	Full sun
Picea pungens Colorado spruce	Needled evergreen tree	80 to 100 ft			3 to 7	Full sun
Pieris forrestii Chinese pieris	Evergreen shrub	6 to 10 ft	White	Spring	8 to 10	Light shade
Pieris japonica Japanese pieris	Evergreen shrub	9 to 12 ft	Pink, white	Early spring	6 to 8	Light shade
Pilea cadierei Aluminum-plant	Houseplant	to 12 in.			10 or indoors	Light shade
Pilea nummulariifolia Creeping-charlie	Houseplant	3 to 5 ft			10 or indoors	Light shade
Pinus canariensis Canary Island pine	Needled evergreen tree	60 to 80 ft			8 to 10	Full sun
Pinus densiflora Japanese red pine	Needled evergreen tree	50 to 60 ft			4 to 7	Full sun
Pinus glabra Spruce pine	Needled evergreen tree	to 100 ft			8, 9	Full sun
Pinus mugo var. *mugo* Dwarf mugo pine	Needled evergreen shrub	2 to 4 ft			2 to 7	Full sun to light shade
Pinus nigra Austrian pine	Needled evergreen tree	60 to 80 ft			4 to 8	Full sun
Pinus palustris Longleaf pine	Needled evergreen tree	50 to 80 ft			8, 9	Full sun
Pinus parviflora Japanese white pine	Needled evergreen tree	25 to 50 ft			5 to 7	Full sun
Pinus radiata Monterey pine	Needled evergreen tree	60 to 100 ft			8 to 10	Full sun
Pinus resinosa Red pine, Norway pine	Needled evergreen tree	50 to 90 ft			3 to 7	Full sun

	CULTURE		
Soil	**Water**	**Feeding**	**Special Characteristics**
Good drainage	Medium water	Medium feeder	Very slow growing; stiff conical form; finely textured, light green needles; best in cold climates.
Not particular	Medium water	Medium feeder	Growth slows as tree ages; stiff branches; forms narrow pyramidal shape; needles vary from dark green to blue green to steel blue; tends to lose its lower branches as it matures.
Good drainage; acid soil	Medium water	Medium feeder	Denser, wider habit than *P. japonica*; new foliage is showy scarlet; fragrant flowers.
Good drainage; acid soil	Wet; don't let dry out	Medium feeder	Slow growing; upright, irregular outline; attractive, dark green foliage; new spring growth is bronzy red; needs protection from wind and sun.
Good drainage	Let dry out between waterings	Medium feeder	Fleshy stems, silver-splashed leaves; give bright, indirect light; avoid cold drafts.
Good drainage	Medium water	Heavy feeder	Fast growing; small, round, slightly hairy leaves; creeping habit; give bright, indirect light; pinch back.
Good drainage	Medium water	Light feeder	Fast growing; upright, pyramidal shape; needles in bundles of 3, 9 to 12 in. long; cones 4 to 9 in.; foliage of young tree blue-green, darkens with age; drought tolerant; good shade tree.
Good drainage	Medium water	Light feeder	Fast growing; open, loose habit; branches horizontal; usually 2 or more trunks; needles bright blue-green or yellow-green, bundles of 2, 2½ to 5 in. long; cones 2 in.; attractive reddish orange bark; avoid cold winds.
Good drainage	Medium water	Light feeder	Low-branching tree; drooping branches; grows naturally in damp, coastal woods; when young use as screen; good specimen tree.
Rich soil	Let dry out between waterings	Medium feeder	May grow to 10 ft high; can be pruned annually by removing two thirds of each young candle in spring; best in groupings or massed.
Good drainage	Medium water	Light feeder	Moderate growing; dense growth; needles 2 in a bundle, sharp, stiff, 4 to 8 in. long; cones 3 in.; tolerates city conditions; withstands winter cold and wind.
Good drainage; sandy soil	Medium water	Light feeder	Needles in bundles of 3, 8 to 15 in. long; cones 6 to 12 in. long; sparse branches; tree "grasslike" when young; grows poorly in heavy soil.
Good drainage	Medium water	Light feeder	Slow growing; hardy; needles in bundles of 5, 1½ in. long; cones 2 to 3 in., remain on tree 6 to 7 years; needs ample room; specimen tree; cultivar 'Glauca' has silver blue needles.
Good drainage	Medium water	Light feeder	Fast growing; needles bright green, 2 to 3 in a bundle, 3 to 7 in. long; cones 3 to 5 in., stay on tree many years; develops roundish, flattish crown with age, often contorted by wind; thrives in cool, coastal climate; susceptible to smog damage; prune to maintain denseness; windbreak, screen, large hedge.
Good drainage	Medium water	Light feeder	Medium growing; very dense crown; slightly drooping branches; long, flexible, 4 to 6 in. dark green needles in bundles of 2; 4 to 7 in. long cones; reddish brown bark tolerates cold; grows well in poor soils.

NAME	HABIT		FLOWERS		ADAPTATION	
	Type	Height	Color	Time	Zones	Light
Pinus strobus White pine	Needled evergreen tree	50 to 80 ft			3 to 8	Full sun
Pinus sylvestris Scotch pine, Scots pine	Needled evergreen tree	30 to 60 ft			3 to 8	Full sun
Pinus taeda Loblolly pine	Needled evergreen tree	60 to 80 ft			7 to 9	Full sun
Pinus thunbergiana Japanese black pine	Needled evergreen tree	20 to 40 ft			5 to 9	Full sun
Pistacia chinensis Chinese pistache	Deciduous tree	50 to 60 ft			6 to 10	Full sun
Pittosporum tobira Tobira, Japanese pittosporum	Evergreen shrub	6 to 15 ft	White	Spring	8 to 10	Full sun to light shade
Pittosporum undulatum Victorian box	Evergreen tree	20 to 40 ft	White	Spring	9, 10	Full sun to light shade
Platanus × acerifolia London plane tree	Deciduous tree	70 to 100 ft			5 to 9	Full sun
Platycerium bifurcatum Staghorn fern	Houseplant	2 to 3 ft			10 or indoors	Light shade
Platycodon grandiflorus Balloonflower	Hardy perennial	2 to 3 ft	Blue, pink, white	Summer to early fall	3 to 10	Full sun to light shade
Plectranthus australis Swedish ivy	Evergreen ground cover, houseplant	3 to 10 ft (trailing)	White	Summer	10 or indoors	Light shade
Plum, European *Prunus domestica*	Deciduous fruit tree	15 to 20 ft	White	Late spring	5 to 8	Full sun
Plum, Japanese *Prunus salicina*	Deciduous fruit tree	15 to 20 ft	White	Early spring	5 to 9	Full sun
Poa pratensis Common Kentucky blue grass	Turfgrass	1½ to 2 in.			3 to 7	Full sun to light shade

	CULTURE		
Soil	Water	Feeding	Special Characteristics
Good drainage	Medium water	Light feeder	Slow growing when young; needles in bundles of 5, 3 to 5 in. long; best in sandy loam or silty soils; needs regular watering.
Good drainage	Medium water	Light feeder	Twisted, blue-green needles in bundles of 2, 1½ to 3 in. long; cones 2 in.; bark of young tree reddish brown, maturing to graying red-brown; drooping branches, picturesque when mature; popular Christmas and specimen tree.
Tolerates clay soil	Medium water	Light feeder	Needles in bundles of 3, 6 to 8 in. long; grow in open area as shade tree; does poorly in sandy, well-drained soil.
Good drainage	Medium water	Light feeder	Fast growing; needles bright green, stiff, in bundles of 2, 3 to 4 in. long; cones 2 to 3 in. long; large, white terminal buds; broad, spreading branches; good seacoast evergreen; can be sheared to Christmas-tree shape, bonsai, container, specimen.
Not particular	Medium water	Medium feeder	Moderate growing; best in summer heat; bright green leaves up to 12 in. long, brilliant shades of yellow, orange, red in fall; good lawn or street tree; female tree produces berries if male tree nearby; may need extra pruning when young to develop good shape.
Good drainage	Medium water	Medium feeder	Dark green, clean, leathery foliage; fragrant flowers; tolerates deep shade, mild drought; doesn't take heavy pruning; pinch back only.
Good drainage	Medium water	Medium feeder	Slow to moderate growing; fragrant flowers; leaves waxy, medium to dark green, wavy edged; lawn, street tree, container, pruned as screen; sticky fruit can be messy.
Not particular	Medium water	Medium feeder	Fast growing; open, spreading crown; maplelike, green leaves; brown, ball-shaped fruit; attractive green and white flaking bark; tolerates drought, poor soil, city conditions.
Organic matter	Medium water	Medium feeder	Broad, lancelike fronds divide in the middle, and ends look like stag antlers; best grown attached to bark or wood; air plant; keep moist; can summer outside on shaded patio.
Good drainage; sandy soil	Medium water	Medium feeder	Long-lived; tolerates many soils, but will not take wet soils in winter; will flower in hot, dry locations; tall plants may require staking.
Good drainage	Wet; don't let dry out	Heavy feeder	Waxy, leathery, bright green leaves; keep soil moist, not soggy; give bright, indirect light.
Good drainage; organic matter	Medium water	Medium feeder	Blooms later than Japanese plum, better adapted to areas of late frost, rainy spring weather; fruit ranges in color from green and yellow to almost black; requires moderately high chilling; needs less pruning and thinning than Japanese varieties; most varieties are self-pollinating; makes good prunes when dried.
Good drainage; organic matter	Medium water	Medium feeder	Larger fruit than European varieties; range in color from green to yellow.
Good drainage; organic matter	Wet; don't let dry out	Heavy feeder	The most popular cool-season lawn grass; not a good grass for the Southeast, but will grow in some warm areas of West Coast if given proper care; suffers in summer heat; poor wearability in summer, good in spring and fall; makes a dense, dark green, medium-textured lawn; many improved varieties available.

NAME	HABIT		FLOWERS		ADAPTATION	
	Type	Height	Color	Time	Zones	Light
Podocarpus macrophyllus Yew pine	Evergreen tree	25 to 35 ft			8 to 10	Full sun to light shade
Polianthes tuberosa Tuberose	Tender bulb	to 3 ft	White	Late summer to early fall	9, 10	Light shade
Polygonatum commutatum Great Solomon's-seal	Hardy perennial	3 to 5 ft	White	Late spring to early summer	4 to 10	Light shade to deep shade
Polygonum capitatum Pink clover blossom	Evergreen ground cover	5 to 8 in.	Pink	All year	9, 10	Full sun
Polypodium aureum Rabbit's-foot fern, golden polypody fern	Houseplant	to 3 ft			10 or indoors	Light shade
Polystichum munitum Western sword fern	Evergreen ground cover	2 to 3½ ft			4 to 10	Deep shade
Pomegranate *Punica granatum*	Deciduous fruit tree	12 to 15 ft	Red, white, orange, yellow	Summer	7 to 10	Full sun
Populus alba White poplar	Deciduous tree	40 to 70 ft			4 to 9	Full sun
Populus deltoides Eastern poplar, cottonwood	Deciduous tree	75 to 100 ft			2 to 10	Full sun
Populus nigra 'Italica' Lombardy poplar	Deciduous tree	70 to 90 ft			2 to 9	Full sun
Portulaca grandiflora Rose moss	Tender annual	4 to 8 in.	Red, yellow, white, pink, purple	Late spring to first frost		Full sun
Potato Solanum tuberosum	Tender perennial vegetable	to 2 ft				Full sun
Potentilla cinerea Alpine cinquefoil	Evergreen ground cover	to 4 in.	Yellow	Spring to summer	3 to 10	Full sun to light shade
Potentilla fruticosa Bush cinquefoil	Deciduous shrub, ground cover	1 to 4 ft	Red, orange, yellow	Early summer to first frost	2 to 7	Full sun to light shade

| Soil | CULTURE | | |
	Water	Feeding	Special Characteristics
Good drainage	Medium water	Medium feeder	Slow growing; erect, columnar form; long, narrow, stiff leaves on lightly drooping branches; best in protected location; good container plant; easy to prune as espalier, hedge, topiary, screen, street, or lawn tree.
Good drainage	Medium water	Medium feeder	Strong, sweet fragrance; long growing season; often grown as annual because it may not bloom second year; needs warmth.
Organic matter	Medium water	Medium feeder	Attractive foliage; will tolerate dry soil, but best in cool, moist soil; long-lived; noninvasive.
Good drainage	Let dry out between waterings	Light feeder	Wiry, trailing, reddish stems; elliptical dark green to pinkish leaves; flowers bloom most of the year; mounding, spreading form; invasive.
Good drainage; organic matter	Medium water	Medium feeder	Low growing; rusty brown, creeping rhizomes; wiry stems; straplike leaves; many deeply cut, ruffled leaflets; fronds grow 2 to 5 ft long, blue-green above and whitish below; good in hanging basket; give filtered light.
Organic matter	Wet; don't let dry out	Medium feeder	Hardy fern; leathery, sword-shaped fronds.
Good drainage	Medium water	Medium feeder	Dense twiggy mass of arching foliage; showy flowers; edible fruit; yellow fall color; tolerates heat, drought, alkaline soils; water regularly and deeply for best fruit.
Not particular	Medium water	Medium feeder	Fast growing; tall and wide spreading, hardy; foliage dark green above and silvery white below, shaped like small maple leaf; tolerates seacoast conditions, poor sandy soil; persistent sprouting from root system; the cultivar 'Pyramidalis' is a good screen, doesn't root-sprout, and has a columnar form.
Not particular	Medium water	Medium feeder	Very fast growing; soft, white wood; drooping catkins appear on leaves in spring; fruit is a small cap that produces "cottony" discharge; easy to cultivate; tolerates most soils; very invasive roots.
Not particular	Medium water	Medium feeder	Fast growing; columnar with upward-reaching branches; foliage bright green, triangular, yellow in fall; suckers; roots invasive; good as tall screen, windbreak, accent; susceptible to stem canker; cultivar *P. nigra* 'Thevestina' has white bark, broader shape, and is more resistant to canker.
Good drainage; sandy soil	Let dry out between waterings	Light feeder	Heat and drought tolerant; flowers close during day and in cloudy weather; reseeds readily.
Good drainage; organic matter	Medium water	Medium feeder	Grown as an annual; needs frost-free growing season; ideal climate has cool summer; needs loose, slightly acid soil, high in potash; mulch heavily; many early, midseason, and late varieties available.
Good drainage	Medium water	Medium feeder	Fast growing; spreads by surface runners; grows in tufts; 5 wedge-shaped, bright green, coarsely toothed leaflets; popular in the Pacific Northwest.
Not particular	Medium water	Medium feeder	Dense, upright, rounded form; finely textured, bright green foliage; tolerates any soil, extreme cold, and drought; flowers best in full sun; many cultivars available.

NAME	HABIT		FLOWERS		ADAPTATION	
	Type	Height	Color	Time	Zones	Light
Potentilla tabernaemontanii Spring cinquefoil	Evergreen ground cover	3 to 6 in.	Yellow	Spring to summer	6 to 10	Full sun to light shade
Primula japonica Japanese primrose	Half-hardy perennial	to 30 in.	Pink, purple, white	Late spring to early summer	5 to 10	Light shade
Primula × polyantha Polyantha primrose	Hardy perennial	to 12 in.	All colors	Winter to spring	5 to 10	Light shade
Primula vulgaris English primrose	Half-hardy perennial	½ to 3 ft	All colors	Winter to late spring	5 to 10	Light shade
Prunus caroliniana Cherry-laurel	Evergreen shrub or small tree	18 to 40 ft	White	Winter to spring	7 to 10	Full sun
Prunus cerasifera Cherry plum	Deciduous tree	to 25 ft	White	Winter to early spring	4 to 8	Full sun
Prunus glandulosa Dwarf flowering almond	Deciduous shrub	4 to 5 ft	White, pink	Late spring	5 to 8	Full sun to light shade
Prunus ilicifolia Hollyleaf cherry	Evergreen shrub or small tree	12 to 30 ft	White	Early spring	9, 10	Full sun to light shade
Prunus laurocerasus English laurel	Evergreen shrub or small tree	15 to 30 ft	White	Spring	7 to 10	Light shade
Prunus sargentii Sargent cherry	Deciduous tree	to 50 ft	Pink	Spring	5 to 8	Full sun
Prunus serrulata Japanese flowering cherry	Deciduous tree	20 to 25 ft	White	Spring	6 to 9	Full sun
Prunus tomentosa Nanking cherry, Manchu cherry	Deciduous shrub	6 to 8 ft	White	Spring	2 to 8	Full sun to light shade
Prunus triloba Flowering almond	Deciduous shrub	8 to 10 ft	Pink	Spring	6 to 9	Full sun to light shade
Prunus virginiana Common chokecherry	Deciduous shrub or small tree	15 to 30 ft	White	Spring	2 to 7	Full sun
Prunus yedoensis Yoshino flowering cherry	Deciduous tree	to 40 ft	White, pink	Spring	6 to 8	Full sun
Pseudotsuga menziesii Douglas fir	Needled evergreen tree	40 to 80 ft			5 to 7	Full sun to light shade

	CULTURE		
Soil	Water	Feeding	Special Characteristics
Good drainage	Medium water	Medium feeder	Fast growing; spreads by surface runners; 5 wedge-shaped, bright green, coarsely toothed leaflets; 4-petaled flowers borne singly but in profusion.
Rich, acid soil; organic matter.	Wet; don't let dry out	Heavy feeder	Boggy conditions are best.
Rich soil; good drainage; organic matter	Wet; don't let dry out	Medium feeder	Large, bold blooms; frequent division needed, otherwise plants are short-lived.
Rich soil; good drainage; organic matter	Wet; don't let dry out	Heavy feeder	Best in mild, humid climates without extreme temperature changes; protect from hot afternoon sun.
Good drainage	Medium water	Medium feeder	Often forms dense thicket; dense foliage, glossy green leaves; black fruit; best in coastal areas; drought tolerant once mature.
Good drainage	Medium water	Medium feeder	Leaves dark green; fruit yellow or reddish, quite sweet; used as rootstock for various stone fruits; the cultivar 'Atropurpurea' has purple leaves.
Good drainage	Medium water	Medium feeder	Upright, awkward growth; unappealing when not in flower.
Good drainage	Medium water	Medium feeder	Moderate growing; dark green, hollylike leaves; new growth lighter green; edible fruit; small tree, clipped hedge, or tall screen.
Good drainage	Medium water	Medium feeder	Fast growing; large, dark green leaves; common as hedge, screen, or background plant; prune selectively—shearing mutilates large leaves; dwarf cultivars available.
Good drainage	Medium water	Medium feeder	Moderate growing; hardy; attractive bark; orange-red fall color.
Good drainage	Medium water	Medium feeder	Fragrant, double white flowers; over 120 cultivars—'Amano-gawa' is 20 ft tall, narrow, upright, and has pink flowers; 'Kwanzan' is 12 to 18 ft tall, wide spreading, and has double, deep pink flowers.
Good drainage	Medium water	Medium feeder	Picturesque, open form; attractive bark; fragrant flowers; edible fruit; can be sheared into an attractive, dense hedge although fruit is sacrificed.
Good drainage	Medium water	Medium feeder	Large, treelike shrub; profuse bloomer.
Good drainage	Medium water	Medium feeder	Dark purple fruit; the cultivar 'Shubert' has leaves that remain red all summer.
Good drainage	Medium water	Medium feeder	Fast growing; curving branches; open form; pinkish white flowers; one of the best flowering cherry varieties.
Good drainage	Medium water	Medium feeder	Fast growing; pyramid shape; as tall as 300 ft in forests; soft, flat, bluish green needles arranged spirally on stems; fragrant foliage; reddish brown cones hang down; takes some wind; can be grown as clipped hedge if topped and trimmed.

NAME	HABIT		FLOWERS		ADAPTATION	
	Type	Height	Color	Time	Zones	Light
Pumpkin *Cucurbita* species	Tender annual vegetable	8 to 12 ft		Summer		Full sun
Pyracantha coccinea Scarlet firethorn	Evergreen shrub	8 to 10 ft	White	Spring	6 to 9	Full sun
***Pyracantha koidzumii* 'Santa Cruz'** Firethorn	Evergreen ground cover	2 to 4 ft	White	Spring	8 to 10	Full sun
Pyrus calleryana Callery pear	Deciduous tree	25 to 50 ft	White	Spring	5 to 9	Full sun
Pyrus kawakamii Evergreen pear	Evergreen shrub or small tree	to 30 ft	White	Winter to early spring	8 to 10	Full sun
Quercus agrifolia Coast live oak	Evergreen tree	20 to 70 ft			9, 10	Full sun
Quercus alba White oak	Deciduous tree	60 to 80 ft			4 to 9	Full sun
Quercus bicolor Swamp white oak	Deciduous tree	60 to 70 ft			4 to 8	Full sun
Quercus coccinea Scarlet oak	Deciduous tree	50 to 80 ft			3 to 8	Full sun
Quercus macrocarpa Bur oak	Deciduous tree	60 to 80 ft			3 to 8	Full sun
Quercus nigra Water oak, possum oak	Deciduous tree	50 to 80 ft			6 to 8	Full sun
Quercus palustris Pin oak	Deciduous tree	60 to 80 ft			5 to 9	Full sun
Quercus phellos Willow oak	Deciduous tree	50 to 80 ft			6 to 9	Full sun to light shade
Quercus robur English oak	Deciduous tree	40 to 60 ft			5 to 8	Full sun
Quercus rubra Red oak	Deciduous tree	60 to 80 ft			5 to 8	Full sun

	CULTURE		
Soil	**Water**	**Feeding**	**Special Characteristics**
Good drainage; organic matter	Medium water	Medium feeder	Warm-season crop; requires ample space to trail; can be trained on trellis; some bush varieties available; water deeply; many cultivars available.
Good drainage	Medium water	Light feeder	Variable forms; showy spring flowers; attractive red berries; thorns; semievergreen in northern climates; hard to prune; give ample space; many cultivars available.
Not particular	Let dry out between waterings	Light feeder	Dark green, oval leaves serrated at the tips; masses of short-lived flowers; clusters of red berries in the fall; prostrate, rapidly spreading growth habit.
Good drainage	Medium water	Medium feeder	Moderate growing; profuse bloomer; crimson-red fall color; shiny, dark green leaves with serrated edges; very adaptable; messy, inedible fruit; fire-blight resistant; several important cultivars available; 'Bradford' is fruitless.
Not particular	Medium water	Medium feeder	Moderate growing; grows naturally as spreading shrub, train as single- or multitrunked tree; shiny green, wavy-edged leaves; good espalier, container, patio, street tree; aphids and fire blight a problem.
Rich soil	Let dry out between waterings	Medium feeder	Rounded, wide-spreading canopy; smooth gray bark; shiny, hollylike leaves; good shade tree; no watering after tree is established.
Good drainage	Medium water	Medium feeder	Slow growing; pyramid shape when young, becomes dense and broad as it matures; bright green, deeply lobed leaves turn red in fall; gray bark; rugged framework.
Rich soil	Medium water	Medium feeder	Slow growing; broad, open crown; similar to Q. alba, but with coarser leaves; does well in moist to wet soils; native to eastern and central North America.
Rich soil	Medium water	Medium feeder	Fast growing; high, light, open branching; bright green, deeply cut leaves; bright scarlet fall color; good street or lawn tree; roots grow deep.
Good drainage	Medium water	Medium feeder	Leaves glossy green above, whitish below; rugged appearance.
Rich soil	Wet; don't let dry out	Medium feeder	Conical to round top; mostly deciduous, but evergreen in some regions; small, lobed, or entire leaves; easily transplanted; takes moist to wet conditions.
Good drainage	Medium water	Medium feeder	Moderate to fast growing; slender when young, more open and round headed as matures; reddish brown bark; lower branches droop; glossy, deep green leaves, deeply cut into lobes; leaves turn brown in fall and can hang on all winter; stake young trees.
Good drainage	Medium water	Medium feeder	Fast growing; pyramidal when young, opening with age; graceful appearance; bright green, willow-like leaves; yellowish fall color.
Good drainage	Medium water	Medium feeder	Wide head and fairly short trunk; fairly fast growth; leaves hold late in fall; little fall color.
Rich soil	Medium water	Medium feeder	Fast growing; broad, round-topped crown; new leaves are red in spring, turning green; foliage sharp-pointed lobes; stake young plants; deep roots; attractive fall color; big lawns, parks, broad avenues.

NAME	HABIT		FLOWERS		ADAPTATION	
	Type	Height	Color	Time	Zones	Light
Quercus virginiana Southern live oak, live oak	Evergreen tree	to 60 ft			8 to 10	Full sun
Radish *Raphanus sativus*	Half-hardy annual vegetable	4 to 12 in.				Full sun to light shade
Ranunculus asiaticus Persian buttercup, turban buttercup	Half-hardy bulb	18 to 30 in.	Red, pink white, orange, yellow	Late spring to early summer	8 to 10	Full sun
Raphiolepis indica India hawthorn	Evergreen shrub	3 to 5 ft	White, pink	Winter to spring	8 to 10	Full sun
Raspberry (red, black, purple) *Rubus* species	Cane berry	6 to 9 ft	White	Late spring to summer	3 to 9	Full sun
Rhamnus alaternus Italian buckthorn	Evergreen shrub or small tree	12 to 20 ft			7 to 9	Full sun to light shade
Rhamnus frangula Alder buckthorn	Deciduous shrub or small tree	10 to 18 ft	White	Spring to summer	2 to 8	Full sun to light shade
Rhapis excelsa Bamboo palm	Shrub, houseplant	5 to 10 ft			10 or indoors	Light shade
Rhododendron arborescens Sweet azalea	Deciduous shrub	8 to 20 ft	White	Summer	4 to 7	Light shade
Rhododendron impeditum Cloudland rhododendron	Evergreen shrub	to 18 in.	Lavender	Spring	5 to 7	Light shade
Rhododendron kaempferi Torch azalea	Deciduous shrub	4 to 8 ft	Red, pink, white, orange, yellow	Late spring to early summer	6 to 8	Light shade
Rhododendron × kosteranum Mollis hybrid azaleas	Deciduous shrub	3 to 8 ft	Red, white, yellow	Late spring	5 to 7	Full sun to light shade
Rhododendron vaseyi Pinkshell azalea	Deciduous shrub	5 to 10 ft	Pink	Late spring	5 to 8	Light shade
Rhododendron viscosum Swamp azalea	Deciduous shrub	3 to 8 ft	Pink, white	Summer	4 to 9	Light shade
Rhododendron Belgium Indica hybrid azaleas	Evergreen shrub	3 to 10 ft	Pink, red, violet, white	Fall to spring	9, 10	Light shade
Rhododendron Gable hybrid azaleas	Evergreen shrub	2 to 4 ft	Pink, red, purple	Late spring	6 to 8	Light shade
Rhododendron Knap Hill-Exbury hybrid azaleas	Deciduous shrub	4 to 8 ft	Red, pink, white, orange, yellow	Late spring to early summer	6 to 8	Light shade

	CULTURE		
Soil	**Water**	**Feeding**	**Special Characteristics**
Rich soil	Medium water	Medium feeder	Deciduous in northern limits of its habitat; moderate- to fast-growing tree; broad, spreading habit; massive trunk and branches; smooth edged, shiny dark green leaves above, whitish below; thrives on ample water; very attractive oak.
Good drainage; organic matter	Medium water	Medium feeder	Very fast growing; divided into 2 groups—summer and winter radishes.
Good drainage	Medium water	Medium feeder	Best in areas of cool nights and sunny, but not hot, days; plant after danger of frost in the spring in zones colder than 8.
Good drainage	Medium water	Medium feeder	Neat, dense, restrained habit; leathery foliage; may repeat blooming in fall; tolerates partial shade, mild drought.
Good drainage; organic matter	Medium water	Medium feeder	Berries form on year-old canes; remove canes that have fruited; everbearing varieties bear on ends of new canes; remove ends after fruiting.
Not particular	Medium water	Medium feeder	Fast growing; dense growth; tall shrub or multistem tree; can be pruned to single stem, sheared, or shaped; bright green, oval, shiny leaves; flowers inconspicuous; tiny black fruit; tolerates drought, wind, heat; fast screen or clipped hedge.
Good drainage	Medium water	Medium feeder	Dense habit and rapid growth; lustrous, dark green leaves; fruit turns from green to red to black, appears while plant is still flowering; can be trained as hedge.
Good drainage; organic matter	Medium water	Medium feeder	6 to 12 in. wide fans composed of 4 to 10 thick, shiny leaves; hairy main trunk; thin, arching stems; give bright, indirect light; excellent container palm; outdoor specimen and hedge in warmest climates.
Good drainage; organic matter; acid soil	Medium water	Medium feeder	Fragrant flowers; attractive fall foliage.
Good drainage; organic matter; acid soil	Medium water	Medium feeder	Dense, tiny, gray-green foliage; attractive in sheltered spot of rock garden; more sensitive than most rhododendrons to hot, dry summers.
Good drainage; organic matter; acid soil	Medium water	Medium feeder	Semievergreen in southern limits of habitat; good fall foliage color; profuse bloomer; large flowers; relatively intolerant of hot summers.
Good drainage; organic matter; acid soil	Medium water	Medium feeder	Restrained, rounded form; grows well in full sun.
Good drainage; organic matter; acid soil	Medium water	Medium feeder	Graceful shape, irregular habit; attractive fall foliage color.
Organic matter; acid soil	Wet; don't let dry out	Medium feeder	Loose, open habit; fragrant flowers; thrives in damp, soggy soils.
Good drainage; organic matter; acid soil	Medium water	Medium feeder	More tender than Southern Indica hybrids.
Good drainage; organic matter; acid soil	Medium water	Medium feeder	Foliage tends to redden in northern climates and in the fall.
Good drainage; organic matter; acid soil	Medium water	Medium feeder	Medium-green foliage turns bright yellow, orange, or red in fall; profusion of large flowers; some cultivars hardy to zone 4.

NAME	HABIT		FLOWERS		ADAPTATION	
	Type	Height	Color	Time	Zones	Light
Rhododendron Southern Indica hybrid azaleas	Evergreen shrub	4 to 15 ft	Pink, red, violet, white	Spring	9, 10	Light shade
Rhoeo spathacea (*R. discolor*) Moses-in-the-cradle	Evergreen perennial, houseplant	12 to 18 in.	White		10 or indoors	Light shade
Rhoicissus capensis Oakleaf ivy, evergreen grape	Evergreen vine, ground cover, houseplant	10 to 15 ft			10 or indoors	Light shade
Rhubarb *Rheum rhabarbarum*	Hardy perennial vegetable	2 to 3 ft			3 to 10	Full sun to light shade
Rhus copallina Flameleaf sumac, shining sumac	Deciduous shrub	8 to 15 ft			5 to 9	Full sun
Rhus glabra Smooth sumac	Deciduous shrub or small tree	10 to 20 ft			3 to 7	Full sun to light shade
Rhus lancea African sumac	Evergreen tree	to 25 ft			8 to 10	Full sun
Robinia pseudoacacia Black locust	Deciduous tree	40 to 75 ft	White	Late spring to early summer	4 to 9	Full sun
Rosa banksiae Bank's rose, Lady Bank's rose	Evergreen vine	to 25 ft	White, yellow	Late spring to summer	7 to 10	Full sun to half-day sun
Rosa foetida Austrian briar	Deciduous shrub	3 to 5 ft	Yellow	Late spring to early summer	4 to 10	Full sun to half-day sun
Rosa hugonis Father Hugo rose	Deciduous shrub	to 8 ft	Yellow	Late spring	7 to 10	Full sun to half-day sun
Rosa multiflora Japanese rose	Deciduous shrub	8 to 10 ft	White	Early summer	5 to 10	Full sun to half-day sun
Rosa odorata Tea rose	Semievergreen shrub	15 ft	Pink	Summer	7 to 10	Full sun to half-day sun

| | CULTURE | | |
Soil	Water	Feeding	Special Characteristics
Good drainage; organic matter; acid soil	Medium water	Medium feeder	Tolerates more sun and grows more vigorously than Belgium Indica hybrids.
Good drainage	Medium water	Medium feeder	Sword-shaped leaves, rather erect, dark green with purple undersides; small flowers held tightly in boat-shaped bracts down among the leaves; plant tolerates adverse conditions.
Good drainage	Let dry out between waterings	Light feeder	Vigorous trailing vine with grapelike tendrils; lobed leaves shaped like oak leaves; tolerates deep shade indoors; foliage takes full sun outdoors if roots are kept moist and shaded.
Good drainage; organic matter	Medium water	Heavy feeder	Grown for edible leafstalks; leaves are poisonous; needs at least 2 months of temperatures near freezing and a long, cool spring; give ample space; begin harvesting in second year; start from root divisions.
Good drainage	Medium water	Medium feeder	Open, picturesque form; large, compound leaves; attractive fall color; can reach 30 ft high.
Good drainage	Medium water	Medium feeder	Needs room; deep green leaves turn scarlet in fall; red fruit in fall and winter; berries used to make dye; common plant in eastern United States.
Good drainage	Medium water	Light feeder	Slow growing; open, spreading, graceful, weeping habit; small fruit on female tree; tolerates drought and high heat—good desert tree; dark red, rough bark; can prune as hedge, screen, single-trunked tree.
Not particular	Medium water	Light feeder	Fast growing; sparse, open branches; often multistemmed; umbrellalike form; fragrant flowers; beanlike pods; thorny branches; deeply furrowed brown bark; tolerates heat, drought, neglect; invasive, suckering roots; train as young tree.
Good drainage	Medium water	Medium feeder	Trailing, climbing growth habit; good for covering arbors, fences; will trail along ground; 'Alba Plena' has double white, fragrant flowers; 'Lutea' produces double yellow scentless flowers; disease resistant.
Good drainage; organic matter	Medium water	Medium feeder	Slender, erect, or branching stems; leaves smooth or slightly hairy; single flowers with strange odor; best in full sun, warm soil; the variety 'Bicolor' has single flowers that are coppery red inside and yellow outside; 'Persiana' has double yellow flowers; prune to remove weak and dead wood.
Good drainage; organic matter	Medium water	Medium feeder	Dense growth; arching stems; attractive gray-green foliage; profuse, faintly scented, single flowers; use in borders, screens, or trained on trellis; prune oldest wood to ground each year; water deeply.
Good drainage	Medium water	Medium feeder	Pink-flowered varieties also available; spiny and smooth forms available; dense, arching growth habit; best for large areas; rapid and often invasive grower.
Good drainage	Medium water	Medium feeder	Partly climbing habit; pink flowers are double, very fragrant.

NAME	HABIT		FLOWERS		ADAPTATION	
	Type	Height	Color	Time	Zones	Light
Rosa rugosa Ramanas rose, sea tomato	Deciduous shrub	3 to 8 ft	Pink, red, white, yellow, purple	Summer	3 to 10	Full sun to half-day sun
Rosa virginiana Virginia rose	Deciduous shrub	to 6 ft	Pink	Summer	4 to 10	Full sun to half-day sun
Rosa Climbing roses	Deciduous shrub	6 to 20 ft	Red, yellow, orange, lavender, pink, white	Late spring to fall	3 to 10	Full sun to half-day sun
Rosa Floribunda hybrids	Deciduous shrub	2 to 5 ft	Red, lavender, pink, white, orange, yellow	Early summer to first frost	4 to 10	Full sun to half-day sun
Rosa Grandiflora hybrids	Deciduous shrub	6 to 10 ft	Red, lavender, pink, white, orange, yellow	Late spring to fall	4 to 10	Full sun
Rosa Hybrid teas	Deciduous shrub	2 to 6 ft	Red, lavender, pink, white, orange, yellow	Spring to fall	3 to 10	Full sun to half-day sun
Rosa Miniature roses	Semievergreen shrub	6 in. to 3 ft	Pink, red, yellow, orange, white	Late spring to fall	8 to 10	Full sun to light shade
Rosa Polyantha roses	Deciduous shrub	18 to 24 in.	Pink, yellow, white	Late spring to fall	3 to 10	Full sun to half-day sun
Rudbeckia fulgida Black-eyed-susan	Hardy perennial	1 to 2½ ft	Yellow	Summer to early fall	3 to 10	Full sun
Rudbeckia hirta var. *pulcherrima* Gloriosa daisy, brown-eyed-susan	Half-hardy perennial	2 to 3 ft	Yellow, orange, bicolored	Early summer to fall	4 to 10	Full sun
Rutabaga *Brassica napus*	Half-hardy biennial vegetable	1 to 2 ft				Full sun to light shade
Sage *Salvia officinalis*	Hardy perennial herb	to 2 ft	Blue, white, pink	Summer	4 to 10	Full sun
Sagina subulata Irish moss	Evergreen ground cover	3 to 4 in.	White	Summer	5 to 10	Full sun to light shade

	CULTURE		
Soil	**Water**	**Feeding**	**Special Characteristics**
Good drainage; organic matter	Medium water	Medium feeder	Vigorous, extremely hardy shrub; single and double flowers; cinnamon fragrance; bright red hips; attractive foliage; tolerates hard freezes, wind, drought, seacoast conditions; water deeply.
Good drainage	Medium water	Medium feeder	Single blooms 2 to 3 in. wide; sweet fragrance; attractive fall color; bright red twigs in winter; easily kept to 3 ft by pruning.
Good drainage; organic matter	Medium water	Medium to heavy feeder	Long, pliable canes; produce blooms identical to parents; need good air circulation; tie to a support; after blooming, cut back flower clusters; protect in cold-winter areas.
Good drainage; organic matter	Medium water	Medium to heavy feeder	Flowers borne in clusters; profuse bloomers; disease resistant, hardy, low growing; best landscape roses—borders, informal hedges, containers; water deeply; provide winter protection in cold-winter areas.
Good drainage; organic matter	Medium water	Medium to heavy feeder	Roses developed between cross of floribundas and hybrid teas; flowers borne in clusters; bloom continually; strong, hardy plants; protect in areas where winter temperatures consistently drop below 20° F; water deeply.
Organic matter; good drainage	Medium water	Medium to heavy feeder	Flowers borne singly on long stems or in clusters; wide range of colors, many bicolored; most fragrant; continual bloomers; water deeply; provide winter protection where winter temperatures persist below 20° F.
Good drainage; organic matter	Medium water	Medium feeder	Can be grown indoors or outside, in containers or in the ground; hardier than hybrid teas; shallow rooted; require constant watering; prune according to use; most are everblooming.
Good drainage; organic matter	Medium water	Medium to heavy feeder	Small flowers borne in large clusters; low growing; continual blooming; use in bedding, low hedges, and front border plantings; good in containers; water deeply.
Good drainage	Let dry out between waterings	Light feeder	Long-lived; profuse bloomer; restrained growth; water during dry periods.
Good drainage; organic matter	Medium water	Medium feeder	Tolerates poor, dry soil; appreciates hot summers; tall varieties may need staking; usually grown as an annual.
Good drainage; organic matter	Medium water	Medium feeder	Edible, yellow roots; matures late in year; stores well in the ground.
Good drainage; grows well in poor soil	Let dry out between waterings	Light feeder	Culinary herb with long, oval, gray-green, coarsely textured, fragrant leaves; cultivars with yellow or red leaf margins are available.
Good drainage; rich soil	Wet; don't let dry out	Heavy feeder	Dense rounded tufts of tiny, awl-shaped, deep green leaves; spreads by creeping stems.

NAME	HABIT		FLOWERS		ADAPTATION	
	Type	Height	Color	Time	Zones	Light
***Saintpaulia* species** African violet	Houseplant	3 to 6 in.	Pink, red, violet, purple, white	All year	10 or indoors	Light shade
Salix babylonica Weeping willow	Deciduous tree	30 to 50 ft			5 to 9	Full sun
Salix discolor Pussy willow	Deciduous shrub	to 20 ft	Gray	Early spring	4 to 8	Full sun to light shade
Salpiglossis sinuata Painted-tongue	Half-hardy annual	2 to 3 ft	Purple, red, yellow, blue, pink	Summer to first frost		Full sun
Salvia splendens Scarlet sage	Tender annual	6 to 36 in.	Red, pink, purple, white	Early summer to first frost		Full sun to light shade
Salvia × superba Perennial salvia	Hardy perennial	2 to 3 ft	Purple	Summer	5 to 10	Full sun
Sansevieria trifasciata Sansevieria, snake plant, mother-in-law's-tongue	Evergreen perennial, houseplant	1 to 4 ft			10 or indoors	Light shade
Sarcococca hookerana* var. *humilis Small Himalayan sarcococca	Evergreen ground cover	to 2 ft	White	Spring	5 to 10	Light shade to deep shade
Sassafras albidum Common sassafras	Deciduous tree	30 to 50 ft			5 to 8	Full sun
Scabiosa caucasica Pincushion-flower	Hardy perennial	to 2½ ft	Blue, pink, purple, lavender, white	Early summer to early fall	2 to 10	Full sun
Schizanthus × wisetonensis Butterfly flower, poor-man's-orchid	Half-hardy annual	12 to 24 in.	Pink, yellow, violet, red, bicolored	Late summer to first frost		Full sun to light shade
Schlumbergera bridgesii Christmas cactus, Easter cactus	Houseplant	to 18 in.	Red	Winter	10 or indoors	Light shade
Scilla siberica Siberian squill	Hardy bulb	3 to 6 in.	Blue	Early spring	3 to 8	Full sun to light shade
Sedum acre Mossy stonecrop, gold-moss stonecrop	Evergreen ground cover	to 2 in.	Yellow	Late spring to early summer	4 to 10	Full sun to half-day sun

| | CULTURE | | |
Soil	Water	Feeding	Special Characteristics
Organic matter	Medium water	Medium feeder	Rosettes of velvety leaves; clusters of flowers; needs plenty of bright, indirect light; protect from hot summer sun; heavy feeder during flowering; many cultivars available, including miniatures.
Not particular	Wet; don't let dry out	Heavy feeder	Fast growing; heavy, rounded head; branchlets drooping to ground; long, medium olive green leaves turn yellow in fall; needs room to grow; may need training to develop single trunk; aggressive roots; good screen, interesting winter silhouette.
Not particular	Wet; don't let dry out	Medium feeder	Attractive, fuzzy gray catkins; fast growing; forms mass of upright stems; messy and unruly.
Good drainage; organic matter; sandy soil	Medium water	Medium feeder	Prefers cool summers; don't overfertilize—sensitive to nitrogen; may need staking.
Good drainage; organic matter; rich soil	Medium water	Heavy feeder	Tolerant of mild drought and intense heat.
Good drainage; grows well in poor soil	Let dry out between waterings	Light feeder	Flowers densely whorled on spikes; attractive gray-green foliage; leaves aromatic when crushed.
Good drainage	Let dry out between waterings	Light feeder	Lance-shaped, dark green leaves with yellow-striped margins and horizontal bands of gray-green; rosette form; give bright, indirect light, warm location; tolerates poor growing conditions.
Organic matter; acid soil	Medium water	Medium feeder	Spreads by underground runners; glossy, dark green foliage; fragrant flowers; black berries; protect from wind; pinch tips to encourage horizontal branching.
Sandy soil; good drainage	Medium water	Medium feeder	Moderate growing; various-shaped leaves turn yellow to red in fall; flowers on female trees followed by dark blue berries on bright red stalks; won't tolerate alkaline soil; hard to transplant; won't take long, hot-summer drought; roots made into tea.
Good drainage; sandy soil; slightly alkaline soil	Medium water	Medium feeder	Long bloom season; avoid summer drought and winter sogginess; amend soil with organic matter.
Rich soil; good drainage; organic matter	Medium water	Medium feeder	Late bloomer; not adapted to intense heat; limited to cool-summer regions.
Rich soil	Medium water	Heavy feeder	Bright green arching branches; smooth, scalloped joints; drooping habit; multitrumpeted flowers; prefers bright, reflected light; can summer outdoors in partial shade; must have high light, cool nights, and short days in the fall to flower; cut down on fertilizer during winter.
Good drainage; organic matter	Wet; don't let dry out	Medium feeder	Good for naturalizing; needs cold winters.
Not particular	Let dry out between waterings	Light feeder	Vigorous plant; tiny leaves less than ¼ in. long; stays green through coldest winters.

NAME	HABIT		FLOWERS		ADAPTATION	
	Type	Height	Color	Time	Zones	Light
Sedum morganianum Donkey's-tail, burro's-tail	Houseplant	3 to 4 ft	Pink	Spring	10 or indoors	Light shade
Sedum spectabile **and hybrids** Showy stonecrop, showy sedum	Hardy perennial	to 2 ft	Pink, white	Late summer to early fall	3 to 10	Full sun to light shade
Sempervivum tectorum Hen-and-chicks, houseleek	Hardy perennial	6 to 12 in.	Pink	Summer	4 to 10	Full sun
Senecio cineraria Dusty-miller	Tender perennial	to 2½ ft	Yellow	Early summer to early fall	8 to 10	Full sun to light shade
Senecio rowleyanus String-of-beads	Houseplant	2 to 6 ft (trailing)			10 or indoors	Light shade
Sequoiadendron giganteum Giant redwood, big tree	Needled evergreen tree	40 to 100 ft			7 to 10	Full sun
Sequoia sempervirens Coast redwood	Needled evergreen tree	50 to 90 ft			7 to 10	Full sun to light shade
Shallot *Allium cepa* var. *aggregatum*	Biennial vegetable	1 to 1½ ft	White	Late summer to early fall	3 to 10	Full sun to light shade
Sinningia speciosa Common gloxinia	Tender bulb	6 to 10 in.	Blue, red, white, purple	All year	10 or indoors	Light shade
Skimmia japonica Japanese skimmia	Evergreen shrub	4 to 5 ft	White	Spring	8, 9	Light shade
Soleirolia soleirolii Baby's tears	Evergreen ground cover, houseplant	to 3 in.			10 or indoors	Light shade
Solidago **hybrids** Goldenrod	Hardy perennial	18 to 40 in.	Yellow	Late summer to early fall	3 to 10	Full sun
Sophora japonica Japanese pagoda tree	Deciduous tree	50 to 75 ft	White	Summer to early fall	5 to 8	Full sun to light shade
Sorbus alnifolia Korean mountain ash	Deciduous tree	40 to 50 ft	White	Late spring	4 to 7	Full sun

| | CULTURE | | |
Soil	Water	Feeding	Special Characteristics
Good drainage; sandy soil	Let dry out between waterings	Medium feeder	Trailing habit; light gray to blue-green leaves ½ to 1 in. long, oval and plump; leaves cluster creating a braided or ropelike effect; ideally for hanging containers.
Grows in poor soil	Wet; don't let dry out	Light feeder	Blossoms of some cultivars turn bronze as they mature; leaves thick and fleshy; mounding growth; long-lived; noninvasive; will tolerate boggy soils; needs light shade in hot climates.
Good drainage	Let dry out between waterings	Light feeder	Succulent growth; thick leaves form rosette; mother plant dies when flowers appear, young plants take over.
Good drainage; organic matter	Let dry out between waterings	Light feeder	Grown for attractive silver gray foliage; usually grown as an annual; tolerates drought and poor soil; remove flower buds.
Good drainage; sandy soil	Let dry out between waterings	Light feeder	Hanging stems bearing ½ in. spherical leaves with pointed tips and a single translucent band across them; look like green beads; flowers fragrant; used in hanging baskets.
Rich soil	Medium water	Medium feeder	Moderate growing; pyramid form; dense, stiff foliage; gray-green needles; reddish brown bark and cones; water deeply but infrequently; needs lots of room; can reach 325 ft in forests.
Rich soil	Wet; don't let dry out	Medium feeder	Narrow, pyramid form; best adapted to fog belt of northern California and Oregon; fast growing; reddish brown bark; flat, pointed, narrow needles medium green on top, grayish underneath; small, round cones; near or on lawn, in grove; topped once a year as hedge; can reach 350 ft in forests.
Good drainage; organic matter	Medium water	Medium to light feeder	Grown as an annual; multiplier type of onion, dividing into clump of smaller bulbs; most set no seeds; lift clusters of bulbs at end of each growing season and replant smaller ones in the fall; harvest when tops die down in summer.
Rich soil; good drainage	Medium water	Medium feeder	Houseplant or greenhouse; may bloom any time of year but requires 2 to 3 month rest period between flowerings; give bright light, but not direct sun.
Good drainage	Medium water	Medium feeder	Grown for fragrant flowers and attractive fruit; roundish growth habit; requires both male and female plants to get the bright red berries; can be grown farther north in sheltered areas along the coast.
Good drainage	Wet; don't let dry out	Medium feeder	Compact, creeping form; tiny, delicate leaves on thin, trailing stems; give moist, greenhouse conditions, bright, indirect light; good in terrariums; tolerates deep shade outdoors.
Good drainage	Medium water	Light feeder	Striking flower color; profuse blooms; long-lived; avoid either very wet or dry soil.
Not particular	Medium water	Medium feeder	Slow to moderate growing; blooms at 8 to 10 years old; dark green, divided leaves; yellow fall color; seedpods 2 to 3½ in. long; streets, gardens, parks, lawns.
Good drainage	Medium water	Medium feeder	Moderate growing; dense, oval form; shiny green leaves; bright red berries in fall; brilliant, attractive fall foliage; the cultivar 'Redbird' has dark green leaves and is an abundant fruiter.

NAME	HABIT		FLOWERS		ADAPTATION	
	Type	Height	Color	Time	Zones	Light
Sorbus aucuparia European mountain ash	Deciduous tree	to 60 ft	White	Late spring	2 to 7	Full sun to light shade
Sorrel, French sorrel *Rumex scutatus*	Hardy perennial herb	to 3 ft			3 to 10	Full sun
Spathiphyllum **species** Peace lily, spatheflower	Evergreen perennial, houseplant	1 to 3 ft	White	Spring to fall	10 or indoors	Light shade
Spearmint *Mentha spicata*	Hardy perennial herb	1 to 2 ft			4 to 10	Full sun to light shade
Spinach *Spinacia oleracea*	Half-hardy annual vegetable	to 2 ft				Full sun to half-day sun
Spiraea japonica Japanese spirea	Deciduous shrub	4 to 5 ft	Pink	Summer	5 to 8	Full sun
Spiraea × vanhouttei Vanhoutte spirea	Deciduous shrub	to 6 ft	White	Spring	5 to 9	Full sun
Squash *Curcurbita* species	Tender annual vegetable	4 to 12 ft				Full sun
Stachys byzantina Lamb's-ears, wooly betony	Hardy perennial	6 to 12 in.	Purple	Summer to early fall	4 to 10	Full sun
Stenotaphrum secundatum St. Augustine grass	Turfgrass	1 to 2½ in.			7 to 8	Full sun to light shade
Stokesia laevis Stoke's aster	Hardy perennial	12 to 18 in.	Blue	Summer	6 to 10	Full sun
Strawberry *Fragaria × ananassa*	Hardy perennial berry	6 in. to 1 ft	White	Spring to fall	3 to 10	Full sun
Streptocarpus **species** Cape primrose	Evergreen perennial, houseplant	1 to 2 ft	Blue, red, pink, violet, white	Late winter to spring	10 or indoors	Light shade
Styrax japonicus Japanese snowbell	Deciduous tree	to 30 ft	White	Early summer	5 to 8	Full sun to light shade
Summer savory *Satureja hortensis*	Hardy annual herb	to 18 in.	Lavender, white	Summer		Full sun

	CULTURE		
Soil	**Water**	**Feeding**	**Special Characteristics**
Good drainage	Medium water	Medium feeder	Fairly rapid growth to 25 to 30 ft; narrow, upright form, rounding with age; leaves divided, dull green above, gray-green beneath; red berries late summer–early fall; susceptible to fire blight.
Rich soil	Medium water	Medium feeder	Culinary herb with narrow, dark leaves; reddish green spikes of flowers; leaves slightly arrow-shaped.
Good drainage	Wet; don't let dry out	Medium feeder	White bract encloses true flowers; spoon-shaped leaves; can grow in dark location but will not flower; attractive foliage plant when not in bloom; heavy feeder in high summer heat.
Rich soil	Wet; don't let dry out	Medium feeder	Culinary and medicinal herb with crinkly, pointed leaves; reddish square stems; spreading invasive habit; aromatic leaves.
Good drainage; organic matter	Medium water	Medium feeder	Cool-weather crop; tends to bolt; use bolt-resistant varieties for spring planting; can be grown through winter in mild areas—tolerates temperatures into low 30s (F); many cultivars available.
Good drainage	Medium water	Medium feeder	Prune late winter–early spring; flowers range from pale to deep pink and sometimes white.
Good drainage	Medium water	Medium feeder	Fast growing; arching, fountainlike form; needs lots of room; prune directly after bloom; borders, massing.
Good drainage; organic matter	Medium water	Medium feeder	Warm-season crop; requires ample space to trail and vine; can be trained on trellis; some bush varieties available; water deeply; major squash groups include summer and winter varieties; many cultivars of varying shapes, sizes, and colors are available.
Good drainage	Let dry out between waterings	Light feeder	Silvery white, wooly foliage; prone to rot in muggy, humid climates; divide regularly.
Good drainage; organic matter	Medium water	Medium feeder	Easy to grow; robust; good shade grass; tolerates a salty soil; needs frequent waterings; very susceptible to several diseases during prolonged rain; tends to thatch badly; wears poorly; likes neutral to lime soil.
Good drainage	Medium water	Light feeder	Most effective in mixed border; not particular about soil; but intolerant of wet soil in winter.
Good drainage; rich soil; organic matter	Medium water	Medium feeder	Plant grown for its edible red berries; planting time depends on climate; may be grown in rows, hills, or containers; plant with crown above soil; mulch well; water frequently; protect from hard winter frosts by mulching with straw; many varieties available adapted to different regions.
Good drainage	Wet; don't let dry out	Medium feeder	Stemless, fleshy leaves; trumpetlike flowers; prefers cool environment, humidity; keep moist; provide very bright, indirect light.
Rich soil; good drainage	Medium water	Medium feeder	Slow to moderate growing; horizontal branching; spreading, flat-topped tree; attractive bark; neat, bushy form; profuse bloomer; train to control shrubbiness; lawn, patio tree.
Good drainage; rich soil	Medium water	Medium feeder	Culinary herb with small, narrow, dark green leaves; reddish stems; becomes slightly woody when plant flowers.

NAME	HABIT		FLOWERS		ADAPTATION	
	Type	Height	Color	Time	Zones	Light
Sweet marjoram *Origanum majorana*	Tender perennial herb	1 to 2 ft			4 to 10	Full sun
Sweet potato *Ipomoea batatas*	Tender perennial vegetable	to 2 ft				Full sun
Syngonium podophyllum Arrowhead vine	Houseplant	2 to 5 ft (trailing)			10 or indoors	Light shade
Syringa × chinensis Chinese lilac	Deciduous shrub	8 to 15 ft	Lavender, purple	Late spring	4 to 7	Full sun to light shade
Syringa oblata Korean lilac	Deciduous shrub	to 12 ft	Lavender	Late spring	4 to 7	Full sun to light shade
Syringa × persica Persian lilac	Deciduous shrub	4 to 8 ft	Lavender	Late spring	5 to 9	Full sun to light shade
Syringa reticulata Japanese tree lilac	Deciduous shrub or small tree	to 30 ft	White	Early summer	4 to 8	Full sun to light shade
Syringa villosa Late lilac	Deciduous shrub	9 to 10 ft	Lavender, pinkish white	Early summer	3 to 7	Full sun to light shade
Syringa vulgaris Common lilac	Deciduous shrub	8 to 15 ft	Lavender	Late spring	3 to 7	Full sun to light shade
Tagetes erecta African marigold	Half-hardy annual	6 to 36 in.	Yellow, orange	Early summer to first frost		Full sun
Tagetes erecta × patula Triploid marigolds, 3-N marigolds	Tender annual	12 to 20 in.	Yellow, orange	Early summer to first frost		Full sun
Tagetes patula French marigold	Half-hardy annual	6 to 18 in.	Yellow, orange, bicolored	Early summer to first frost		Full sun
Tamarix hispida Kashgar tamarisk	Deciduous shrub	to 15 ft	Pink	Late summer to early fall	5 to 8	Full sun
Tamarix ramosissima Five-stamen tamarisk	Deciduous shrub	10 to 15 ft	Pink	Summer to early fall	2 to 8	Full sun
Tanacetum vulgare Tansy	Hardy perennial herb	to 3 ft	Yellow	Summer	4 to 10	Full sun

| | CULTURE | | |
Soil	Water	Feeding	Special Characteristics
Good drainage; slightly alkaline soil	Medium water	Medium feeder	Culinary herb with small, oval leaves light green on top, gray-green underneath; often grown as an annual.
Good drainage; organic matter	Medium water	Medium feeder	Grown as an annual; requires ample summer heat; feed with low-nitrogen fertilizer; rarely flowers in United States; flavor improves with storage after harvesting; very frost tender; trailing vine.
Good drainage	Medium water	Medium feeder	Climbing or trailing plant; young leaves 3 in. long, arrow shaped, borne at end of erect stalks; dark green with silvery white variegation; as plant matures, leaves become lobed, stems begin to climb, leaf fans into leaflets, turning solid green; give moist, warm environment; bright, indirect light.
Good drainage; slightly alkaline soil	Medium water	Medium feeder	Although can grow taller, usually reaches about 6 ft high; more graceful habit and finer-textured foliage than common lilac; blooms profusely; give light shade in hottest areas; fragrant flowers.
Good drainage; slightly alkaline soil	Medium water	Medium feeder	One of earliest-blooming lilacs; only lilac with fall color; fragrant flowers; heavy bloomer; give light shade in hottest areas.
Good drainage; slightly alkaline soil	Medium water	Medium feeder	Small leaves; heavy profusion of fragrant flowers; give light shade in hottest areas.
Good drainage; slightly alkaline soil	Medium water	Medium feeder	Moderate growing; dense foliage; interesting bark; heavy-scented flowers; open, upright, spreading branches with round outline; very drought resistant; small shade or street tree.
Good drainage; slightly alkaline soil	Medium water	Medium feeder	One of hardiest lilacs; dense, upright growth; profuse bloomer; fragrant flowers; give light shade in hottest areas.
Good drainage; slightly alkaline soil	Medium water	Medium feeder	Upright, irregular growth; gray to dark green or bluish green leaves; fragrant flowers; long-lived; rejuvenate old plants by cutting to ground; very susceptible to mildew; light shade in hottest areas; many cultivars available.
Good drainage; rich soil	Medium water	Medium feeder	Self-sows profusely; tolerates moderately dry soil; don't overfertilize; taller varieties need staking.
Good drainage; rich soil	Medium water	Medium feeder	Tolerates moderately dry soil; don't overfertilize.
Good drainage; rich soil	Medium water	Medium feeder	Self-sows profusely; tolerates moderately dry soil; don't overfertilize.
Sandy soil	Medium water	Light feeder	Slender, wispy form; needlelike foliage; tolerates seacoast conditions, drought, harsh winds; periodic watering; leggy and rangy in fertile soil; prune early spring while dormant.
Sandy soil	Medium water	Light feeder	Large, leggy habit; hardy; invasive roots; tolerates seacoast conditions, drought, winds; prune hard in fall.
Not particular	Medium water	Medium feeder	Large, bright green medicinal herb; fernlike leaves; buttonlike flowers; fragrant foliage; easy to grow, can become invasive.

NAME	HABIT		FLOWERS		ADAPTATION	
	Type	Height	Color	Time	Zones	Light
Tangelo *Citrus × tangelo*	Evergreen fruit tree	10 to 30 ft	White	Spring	10	Full sun
Tarragon *Artemisia dracunculus*	Hardy perennial herb	2 to 3 ft			5 to 10	Full sun
Taxodium distichum Bald cypress	Needled deciduous tree	70 to 80 ft			5 to 10	Full sun
Taxus baccata English yew	Needled evergreen tree	25 to 40 ft			6 to 7	Full sun
Taxus cuspidata Japanese yew	Needled evergreen tree	40 to 50 ft			5 to 7	Full sun
Taxus × media Anglojap yew	Needled evergreen tree	to 40 ft			5 to 7	Full sun
Thalictrum aquilegifolium Columbine meadowrue	Hardy perennial	to 3 ft	Pink, white	Late spring to early summer	5 to 10	Light shade
Thuja occidentalis American arborvitae, northern white cedar	Needled evergreen tree	40 to 50 ft			3 to 8	Full sun
Thuja plicata Western red cedar, canoe cedar, giant arborvitae	Needled evergreen tree	50 to 70 ft			5 to 7	Full sun
Thunbergia alata Black-eyed-susan vine, clock vine	Half-hardy annual	Climbs to 6 ft	Orange, yellow, white	Early summer to early fall		Full sun to light shade
Thyme *Thymus vulgaris*	Hardy perennial herb	to 12 in.	Pink, white	Late spring to summer	4 to 10	Full sun
Thymus praecox* var. *articus Creeping thyme	Hardy perennial ground cover	2 to 6 in.	Pink	Late spring to early fall	4 to 10	Full sun
Tigridia pavonia Tigerflower, shellflower	Half-hardy bulb	to 1½ ft	Red, orange, yellow, pink, white	Summer	7 to 10	Full sun
Tilia americana American linden, basswood	Deciduous tree	40 to 60 ft	Yellow	Summer	2 to 9	Full sun
Tilia cordata Littleleaf linden	Deciduous tree	60 to 70 ft	Yellow	Summer	4 to 7	Full sun
Tilia × europaea European linden	Deciduous tree	to 120 ft	Yellow	Summer	3 to 9	Full sun

| Soil | CULTURE | | |
	Water	Feeding	Special Characteristics
Good drainage; organic matter	Medium water	Medium feeder	A cross between a mandarin and a grapefruit; loose skin; sugar content of a mandarin; requires cross-pollination from other citrus, such as the 'Valencia' orange; prune to remove only dead, diseased, or sucker growth; plant high.
Good drainage; sandy soil	Let dry out between waterings	Medium feeder	Culinary herb; does not produce seeds; propagate by division.
Not particular	Medium water	Medium feeder	Moderate to fast growing; deciduous conifer with tiny leaves; tolerates both drought and poor drainage; survives swampy conditions.
Good drainage	Medium water	Medium feeder	Dark green foliage; can be pruned into formal shapes, hedges.
Good drainage	Medium water	Medium feeder	Can prune into formal shapes, hedges.
Good drainage	Medium water	Medium feeder	Hybrid with wide variety of cultivars; can be pruned into formal shapes, hedges.
Rich soil; organic matter	Wet; don't let dry out	Medium feeder	Grayish green foliage; leaves are smaller than columbine, but similar.
Good drainage	Medium water	Medium feeder	Slow to moderate growing; bright green to yellow-green foliage; flat sprays of needles on branches with upsweeping tips; effective hedge or tall screen; tolerates wet soil, but tends to yellow or brown in open, wet, windy areas.
Not particular	Medium water	Medium feeder	Slow growing; pyramid form; bright green to dark green, lacy foliage; slender branches; tolerates wet soils; good skyline tree in large, open area; can be sheared as large hedge or screen.
Good drainage; organic matter; rich soil	Wet; don't let dry out	Medium feeder	Best in cool-summer regions; grows rapidly; needs support.
Good drainage	Medium water	Medium feeder	Culinary herb with a shrubby form; opposite leaves, tiny woodlike stems; needs light soil; cultivar 'Argenteus' has small leaves with silver variegation.
Good drainage	Medium water	Medium feeder	Low-growing herb; delicate appearance; fragrant foliage; good ground cover.
Good drainage	Wet; don't let dry out	Medium feeder	Flowers last only 1 day but are quickly followed by others; dig up and store after foliage yellows in zones colder than 7.
Rich soil	Medium water	Medium feeder	Moderate-growing tree; straight trunk; dense crown; dull, dark green foliage; somewhat heart-shaped leaves; fragrant, yellowish flowers; keep moist; stake young trees; good street tree.
Rich soil	Medium water	Medium feeder	Moderate to fast growing; symmetrical habit; dark green, heart-shaped leaves; very fragrant flowers; best in moist soils; tolerates heat, drought, city conditions; lawn or street tree.
Rich soil	Medium water	Medium feeder	Moderate-growing tree; fragrant flowers; suckers badly; linden most susceptible to aphids; stake and shape young trees.

NAME	HABIT		FLOWERS		ADAPTATION	
	Type	Height	Color	Time	Zones	Light
Tilia platyphyllos Bigleaf linden	Deciduous tree	60 to 80 ft	Yellow	Summer	4 to 9	Full sun
Tithonia rotundifolia Mexican sunflower	Half-hardy annual	4 to 6 ft	Red, orange	Summer to early fall		Full sun
Tolmiea menziesii Piggyback plant, mother-of-thousands	Houseplant	to 2 ft			10 or indoors	Light shade
Tomato *Lycopersicon lycopersicum*	Tender perennial vegetable	to 6 ft			9, 10	Full sun
Torenia fournieri Wishbone flower	Tender annual	8 to 12 in.	Blue and yellow	Early summer to early fall		Light shade to deep shade
Trachelospermum asiaticum Asiatic jasmine	Evergreen vine, ground cover	to 15 ft	Yellow	Early spring to summer	9, 10	Light shade
Trachelospermum jasminoides Starjasmine	Evergreen vine, ground cover	to 20 ft	White	Early spring to summer	9, 10	Light shade
Tradescantia **species** Wandering-Jew, inch plant	Tender perennial, houseplant	3 to 10 ft			10 or indoors	Half-day sun to light shade
Tradescantia virginiana Spiderwort	Hardy perennial	18 to 36 in.	Blue, pink, purple, red, white	Early summer to early fall	4 to 10	Full sun to deep shade
Trollius europaeus **and hybrids** Common globeflower	Hardy perennial	1 to 3 ft	Yellow, orange	Spring	3 to 10	Light shade
Tropaeolum majus Nasturtium	Hardy annual	1 to 10 ft	Red, white, orange, yellow, bicolored	Early summer to early fall		Full sun
Tsuga canadensis Canadian or eastern hemlock	Needled evergreen tree	40 to 70 ft			4 to 8	Full sun to light shade
Tsuga canadensis 'Pendula' Sargent's weeping hemlock	Needled evergreen shrub	5 to 10 ft			4 to 8	Light shade
Tsuga caroliniana Carolina hemlock	Needled evergreen tree	50 to 70 ft			5 to 7	Full sun to light shade
Tulipa **hybrids** Tulip hybrids	Hardy bulbs	6 to 30 in.	Variety of colors	Spring and fall	3 to 10	Full sun to light shade

	CULTURE		
Soil	**Water**	**Feeding**	**Special Characteristics**
Rich soil	Medium water	Medium feeder	Moderate-growing tree; largest leaves of any linden; fragrant yellow-white flowers; young trees need staking, shaping.
Good drainage	Let dry out between waterings	Light feeder	Tolerates drought and heat; may require staking; use as background border; open, coarse habit.
Good drainage	Wet; don't let dry out	Medium feeder	Hairy, bright green leaves; plantlets form at junction of leaf and stem; give bright, indirect light and cool, well-ventilated spot; avoid hot, dry air; prune to shape.
Good drainage; organic matter	Medium water	Medium feeder	Grown as annual; requires warm weather; frost tender; sensitive to low night temperatures; give uniform moisture; grown from seed or transplant; many varieties available.
Good drainage; organic matter	Wet; don't let dry out	Heavy feeder	Appreciates high humidity; interesting flower shape; bicolored blooms.
Rich soil	Medium water	Medium feeder	Twining rambler; somewhat broader leaves than starjasmine; fragrant flowers; slow growing, woody with age.
Rich soil	Medium water	Medium feeder	Twining rambler; long, woody stems; oval, deep-green leaves; small, fragrant, starlike flowers; slow growing.
Good drainage	Medium water	Medium feeder	Trailing foliage; leaves alternate along thick, succulent stems; give bright light with some direct sun; fast growing, easy to care for; many colorful cultivars available.
Rich soil	Wet; don't let dry out	Medium feeder	Foliage grasslike; long-lived; can become invasive.
Rich soil; organic matter	Wet; don't let dry out	Medium feeder	Excellent choice for moist, heavy soils or around a pool; grow in bushy, rounded masses; long-lived; restrained; tolerates full sun if kept moist; tolerates deeper shade; avoid boggy soil.
Good drainage; sandy soil	Medium water	Light feeder	Available in climbing and dwarf varieties; avoid high-nitrogen fertilizer; best in regions of dry, cool summers; tolerates drought; leaves and flowers edible; aphids may be a problem.
Good drainage; rich, acid soil	Medium water	Medium feeder	Moderate growing; graceful pyramidal shape; horizontal branches; dense, flat, deep green sprays of needles; thrives in deep, moist loam; resents dry winds, drought, prolonged heat; can be sheared and trained as thick hedge.
Good drainage; rich, acid soil	Wet; don't let dry out	Medium feeder	Graceful, pendulous habit; refined foliage; tolerates full sun; protect from wind, drought, waterlogged soil, hot summer temperatures; good in container, specimen plant.
Good drainage; rich, acid soil	Medium water	Medium feeder	Moderate growing; pyramidal; not as hardy as *T. canadensis*; needs acid soil; more tolerant of city conditions; slightly pendulous branches give soft appearance.
Good drainage	Medium water	Medium feeder	Thousands of hybrids providing abundant choice of height, form, flower color, and blooming date; fall flowering possible from forced bulbs; do not naturalize well.

NAME	HABIT		FLOWERS		ADAPTATION	
	Type	Height	Color	Time	Zones	Light
Tulipa fosterana Foster tulip	Hardy bulb	8 to 20 in.	Red	Spring	5 to 10	Full sun to light shade
Tulipa greigii Greig tulip	Hardy bulb	8 to 12 in.	Red	Spring	5 to 10	Full sun to light shade
Tulipa kaufmanniana Waterlily tulip	Hardy bulb	4 to 8 in.	White, yellow	Spring	5 to 10	Full sun to light shade
Turnip *Brassica rapa*	Half-hardy biennial vegetable	1 to 2 ft				Full sun to light shade
Ulmus americana American elm	Deciduous tree	60 to 80 ft			3 to 9	Full sun
Ulmus parvifolia Chinese elm	Deciduous tree	40 to 60 ft			5 to 9	Full sun
Ulmus pumila Siberian elm	Deciduous tree	30 to 50 ft			4 to 9	Full sun
Verbena × *hybrida* Garden verbena	Half-hardy perennial	6 to 8 in.	Comes in all colors	Early summer to fall	7 to 10	Full sun
Verbena peruviana Peruvian verbena, trailing verbena	Evergreen ground cover	4 to 6 in.	Red	Spring to fall	10	Full sun
Veronica **hybrids** Speedwell	Hardy perennial	2 to 2½ ft	Blue, pink, white, purple	Summer	4 to 10	Full sun
Veronica spicata Spike speedwell	Hardy perennial	to 18 in.	Blue	Summer	4 to 10	Full sun
Viburnum × *burkwoodii* Burkwood viburnum	Evergreen shrub	8 to 10 ft	White	Spring	4 to 8	Full sun to light shade
Viburnum carlesii Korean-spice viburnum	Deciduous shrub	4 to 8 ft	White	Spring	5 to 8	Full sun to light shade
Viburnum farreri (*V. fragrans*) Fragrant viburnum	Deciduous shrub	8 to 12 ft	Pink, white	Winter to early spring	5 to 10	Full sun to light shade
Viburnum macrocephalum Chinese snowball viburnum	Semievergreen shrub	6 to 12 ft	White	Late spring to early summer	7 to 10	Full sun to light shade
Viburnum opulus European cranberry bush	Deciduous shrub	8 to 12 ft	White	Late spring	4 to 8	Full sun to light shade
Vinca major Periwinkle	Evergreen ground cover	to 2 ft	Blue	Spring	6 to 10	Light shade

	CULTURE		
Soil	**Water**	**Feeding**	**Special Characteristics**
Good drainage	Medium water	Medium feeder	Early flowering; 4-in. blossoms.
Good drainage	Medium water	Medium feeder	Early flowering; long-lasting 6-in. blooms; leaves usually streaked with brown.
Good drainage	Medium water	Medium feeder	Very early bloom; large, ornamental flowers.
Good drainage; organic matter	Medium water	Medium feeder	Grown as an annual; cool-weather vegetable; fast maturing; grow in spring in northern areas; grow in fall and winter in warmer areas; different cultivars available.
Adaptive	Medium water	Medium feeder	Fast growing; stately, oval canopy; dark green, toothed leaves; not recommended for planting due to Dutch elm disease.
Not particular	Medium water	Medium feeder	Fast growing; open canopy; subtle red fruit in fall; yellow to purple leaves in fall; loses outer bark with age to reveal pale yellow inner bark; tolerates alkaline, poor, compact soil; tolerates heat, drought; semievergreen in mild climates.
Adaptive	Medium water	Medium feeder	Hardy in extreme cold and heat; weak crotches; shallow roots; sometimes grown in shelterbelt; seldom useful as a single tree.
Good drainage; rich soil	Medium water	Heavy feeder	Short-lived perennial usually grown as an annual; heat tolerant; prone to mildew in heavy, wet soil; will not flower well in shade; moderately tolerant of drought.
Good drainage	Medium water	Light feeder	Fast growing; forms flat mat of green foliage; small leaves closely spaced along stems; good flower color, long bloom season; grown as annual in cold-winter areas; thrives in hot, sunny locations; drought tolerant once established; cut back severely in fall; tolerates seacoast conditions; many cultivars available.
Good drainage	Medium water	Medium feeder	Showy flower spikes; long-lived; tolerates light shade.
Good drainage	Medium water	Medium feeder	Many branches; densely produced flower spikes.
Not particular	Medium water	Medium feeder	Upright habit; fragrant flowers; buds are pink; semievergreen or deciduous in cool climates in the North; can prune to shape.
Not particular	Medium water	Medium feeder	Rounded, dense form; fragrant flowers; can prune to shape; tolerates both alkaline and acid soils.
Good drainage	Wet; don't let dry out	Medium feeder	Fragrant, very early flower clusters; tolerates both acid and alkaline soil and heavy soils; prune to shape.
Not particular	Medium water	Medium feeder	Dense, rounded shrub; large flower clusters; tolerates acid and alkaline soils.
Not particular	Medium water	Medium feeder	Large, spreading shrub; delicate flowers; bright red, berrylike fruit in fall; good fall foliage color; susceptible to aphids; prune to shape; tolerates acid and alkaline soils.
Good drainage; organic matter	Medium water	Medium feeder	Glossy, dark green leaves; trailing, rooting stems; spreads rapidly; very invasive; tolerates deeper shade.

NAME	HABIT		FLOWERS		ADAPTATION	
	Type	Height	Color	Time	Zones	Light
Vinca minor Periwinkle	Evergreen ground cover	to 6 in.	Blue	Spring	4 to 10	Light shade
Viola odorata Sweet violet	Hardy perennial ground cover	to 8 in.	Pink, violet, white	Spring	6 to 10	Light shade
Viola tricolor Johnny-jump-up	Hardy perennial	6 to 12 in.	Purple, yellow, white	Spring to early fall	4 to 10	Full sun to light shade
Viola × wittrockiana Pansy, viola	Tender perennial	4 to 9 in.	White, purple, red, orange, yellow	Late spring to summer	5 to 10	Full sun to light shade
Walnut, English *Juglans regia*	Deciduous nut tree	40 to 60 ft			5 to 10	Full sun
Watermelon *Citrullus lanatus*	Tender annual vegetable	6 to 10 ft				Full sun
Weigela florida Old-fashioned weigela	Deciduous shrub	4 to 10 ft	Pink	Late spring to early summer	5 to 8	Full sun
Xylosma congestum Shiny xylosma	Evergreen shrub or small tree	8 to 15 ft			8 to 10	Full sun to light shade
Zantedeschia aethiopica Common calla lily	Tender bulb	to 3 ft	White	Spring to summer	9, 10	Light shade
Zantedeschia elliottiana Golden calla	Tender bulb	18 to 24 in.	Yellow	Summer	9, 10	Light shade
Zelkova serrata Japanese zelkova	Deciduous tree	50 to 60 ft			5 to 8	Full sun
Zephyranthes candida Autumn zephyr-lily	Half-hardy bulb	to 8 in.	White	Late summer to early fall	8 to 10 or indoors	Full sun
Zinnia elegans Common zinnia	Half-hardy annual	6 to 40 in.	All colors except blue	Early summer to fall		Full sun
Zoysia **species** Zoysia grass	Turfgrass	½ to 1 in.			8 to 10	Full sun to light shade
Zoysia tenuifolia Korean grass, Mascarene grass	Ornamental grass	3 to 5 in.			9, 10	Full sun to light shade

	CULTURE		
Soil	**Water**	**Feeding**	**Special Characteristics**
Good drainage; organic matter	Medium water	Medium feeder	Hardier than *V. major*; tolerates deeper shade; trailing stems; glossy green leaves; one of the best ground covers; several cultivars available.
Rich soil	Wet; don't let dry out	Heavy feeder	Spreading, low-growing plant; heart-shaped leaves with crinkled edges; small, extremely fragrant flowers; cultivars have variations in flower color and shape.
Rich soil	Wet; don't let dry out	Medium feeder	Short-lived perennial grown as annual; low, tufted growth; good bloomer; give partial shade in warmer areas; self-sows invasively.
Good drainage; organic matter; rich soil	Wet; don't let dry out	Heavy feeder	Does not tolerate heat; best in cool-summer regions; highly cold resistant; usually grown as an annual.
Good drainage	Medium water	Medium feeder	Silver gray bark; dense foliage; fast growing; bears nuts in summer; requires large area; can be very messy; tends to be out of leaf for long period of time; give deep irrigation; prune in summer or fall.
Good drainage; organic matter	Medium water	Medium feeder	Requires more summer heat than muskmelons; give ample water during vining period; needs lots of room.
Good drainage	Medium water	Medium feeder	Coarse, rangy form; profuse bloomer; adaptable to soil and shade; requires heavy pruning; best in borders, masses, groupings where awkward form is hidden when not in bloom; many cultivars available.
Not particular	Medium water	Medium feeder	Slow-growing, round, loose form; shiny, yellow-green foliage; tolerates any soil; responds well to pruning, can train as espalier or small tree; tolerates heat, drought.
Not particular	Wet; don't let dry out	Medium feeder	Blooms almost continually in mild climates; can tolerate full sun on the coast; good houseplant; grows in boggy situations; nearly evergreen in mild areas.
Good drainage	Wet; don't let dry out	Medium feeder	Attractive leaves, spotted with silvery white; needs plenty of moisture during growing season; good houseplant.
Good drainage	Medium water	Medium feeder	Moderate to fast growing; eventually vase shaped; attractive fall foliage; gray bark, mottles with age; water deeply to encourage deep roots; head back and thin when young to promote strong framework.
Good drainage	Medium water	Medium feeder	Leaves evergreen in mild climates; rushlike foliage; flowers tinged with pink; good houseplant.
Good drainage; organic matter	Medium water	Medium feeder	Best in hot, dry climates with long summers; never water late in day; avoid cool locations and damp air; prone to powdery mildew at end of summer.
Good drainage; organic matter	Medium water	Medium feeder	Forms dense, fine-textured lawn; resistant to weeds; tolerates heat and drought; relatively free of diseases and insects; very slow to establish; won't thrive in cool or short summers; tough to mow if left too long; tends to build thatch; wears well.
Good drainage	Medium water	Medium feeder	A true grass; tufting, mounding habit; don't mow; velvety turf; fine, dense, dark green leaves; evergreen where temperatures above freezing; turns brown at first frost, but recovers; slow spreading; drought resistant; takes light traffic.

INDEX

U.S. Measure and Metric Measure Conversion Chart

	Symbol	When you know:	Multiply by:	To find:	Rounded Measures for Quick Reference		
		Formulas for Exact Measures					
Mass	oz	ounces	28.35	grams	1 oz		= 30 g
(Weight)	lb	pounds	0.45	kilograms	4 oz		= 115 g
	g	grams	0.035	ounces	8 oz		= 225 g
	kg	kilograms	2.2	pounds	16 oz	= 1 lb	= 450 g
					32 oz	= 2 lb	= 900 g
					36 oz	= 2¼ lb	= 1000g (1 kg)
Volume	pt	pints	0.47	liters	1 c	= 8 oz	= 250 ml
	qt	quarts	0.95	liters	2 c (1 pt)	= 16 oz	= 500 ml
	gal	gallons	3.785	liters	4 c (1 qt)	= 32 oz	= 1 liter
	ml	milliliters	0.034	fluid ounces	4 qt (1 gal)	= 128 oz	= 3¾ liter
Length	in.	inches	2.54	centimeters	⅜ in.	= 1 cm	
	ft	feet	30.48	centimeters	1 in.	= 2.5 cm	
	yd	yards	0.9144	meters	2 in.	= 5 cm	
	mi	miles	1.609	kilometers	2½ in.	= 6.5 cm	
	km	kilometers	0.621	miles	12 in. (1 ft)	= 30 cm	
	m	meters	1.094	yards	1 yd	= 90 cm	
	cm	centimeters	0.39	inches	100 ft	= 30 m	
					1 mi	= 1.6 km	
Temperature	°F	Fahrenheit	⅚ (after subtracting 32)	Celsius	32°F	= 0°C	
	°C	Celsius	⅚ (then add 32)	Fahrenheit	212°F	= 100°C	
Area	in.²	square inches	6.452	square centimeters	1 in.²	= 6.5 cm²	
	ft²	square feet	929.0	square centimeters	1 ft²	= 930 cm²	
	yd²	square yards	8361.0	square centimeters	1 yd²	= 8360 cm²	
	a.	acres	0.4047	hectares	1 a.	= 4050 m²